SYSTEMATIC THEOLOGY

Πᾶσα γραφὴ θεόπνευστος καὶ ὠφέλιμος πρὸς διδασκαλίαν —St PAUL

The whole drift of the Scripture of God, what is it but to teach Theology ?   Theology, what is it but the Science of things divine ?   What Science can be attained unto without the help of natural Discourse and Reason ?—HOOKER

BY

JOHN MILEY, D.D., LL D.

Professor of Systematic Theology in Drew Theological Seminary, Madison, New Jersey

VOLUME I

NEW YORK: HUNT & EATON
CINCINNATI: CRANSTON & STOWE
1892

TABLE OF CONTENTS.

INTRODUCTION.

PART I.—THEISM.

CHAPTER I.

PRELIMINARY QUESTIONS.

PART II.—THEOLOGY.

CHAPTER III.

GOD IN ATTRIBUTES

CHAPTER IV.

DIVINE PREDICABLES NOT DISTINCTIVELY ATTRIBUTES.

CHAPTER VIII.

TRUTH OF THE TRINITY.

CHAPTER IX.

GOD IN CREATION.

CHAPTER X.

GOD IN PROVIDENCE.

PART III.—ANTHROPOLOGY.

CHAPTER I

PRELIMINARY QUESTIONS.

CHAPTER II.

PRIMITIVE MAN.

CHAPTER III.

QUESTION OF PRIMITIVE HOLINESS.

CONTENTS. xiii

CHAPTER VI.

DOCTRINE OF NATIVE DEPRAVITY.

CHAPTER VII.

PROOFS OF NATIVE DEPRAVITY.

CHAPTER VIII.

ORIGIN OF DEPRAVITY.

CHAPTER IX.

REALISTIC MODE OF ADAMIC SIN.

CHAPTER X.

REPRESENTATIVE MODE OF ADAMIC GUILT.

CHAPTER XI.

GENETIC LAW OF NATIVE DEPRAVITY.

CHAPTER XII.

DOCTRINE OF NATIVE DEMERIT.

INTRODUCTION.

THEOLOGY holds a chief place in human thinking. In a purely intellectual view no questions have greater interest for scientific and philosophic thought. Besides, our moral and religious sensibilities, the profoundest of our nature, contribute an intensity of interest peculiar to theological study. This does not mean that religious feeling is the norm or ruling principle of theology. This study has its intellectual cast, just as questions of science and philosophy. Any peculiarities of theology relate mostly to the character of its subjects and the sources of its facts. The study of these facts, the processes of induction, and the doctrinal generalizations are in the same intellectual mode which we observe in other spheres of truth. The Scriptures are rich in doctrinal material, but in elementary form; and it is only through a scientific mode of treatment that these elements can be wrought into a theology in any proper sense of the term. "The whole drift of the Scripture of God, what is it but only to teach theology? Theology, what is it but the science of things divine? What science can be attained unto without the help of natural discourse and reason?" [1]

Before entering upon the formal treatment of any great subject the way should be prepared, and the subject itself be PREPARATORY set in as clear a light as practicable. This is specially REQUISITES urgent in the case of systematic theology. The Introduction is for this end, and its attainment requires several things. The several forms of theology must be distinguished and defined. We shall thus reach a clearer view of systematic theology. The true sources of theology must be determined and mistaken sources set aside. As the doctrinal value of the Scriptures hinges upon the question of their divine original, the proofs of such an original must be fully recognized.[2] Attention must be given to the grounds of certitude in doctrinal truths and to the consistency of faith with the requisite certitude, that we may secure a scientific construction of the-

---

[1] Hooker: *Ecclesiastical Polity*, book iii, sec. 8

[2] The doctrine of inspiration will be treated in an appendix to the second volume.

2

ology.   Finally, the method of systemization must be considered
in order to determine what doctrines should be included in the system and in what order they should be treated.

I. THEOLOGY.

1. *Sense and Use of the Ground-term.*—The term theology is
formed from the Greek words θεός and λόγος, and means primarily
a discourse concerning God, or a doctrine of God.   It was in use
anterior to Christianity, and in literature entirely apart from the
divine revelation.   Aristotle wrote of theology as one of the sciences,
and as the highest of all, because it treated of the highest of all
beings.   The Greeks gave the name of theologian—θεολόγος—severally to such poets as Hesiod and Orpheus, because they sang of the
gods and the origin of things, though with only poetic inspiration.

We are more concerned with the use of this term in the expres-
THEOLOGY IN sion of Christian thought.   In this use the primary
CHRISTIAN sense has been greatly broadened, so that it often means
THOUGHT. the sum of Christian doctrine.   This appears in what
may be accepted as its proper definitions.   "God is the source and
the subject and the end of theology.   The stricter and earlier use
of the word limited it to the doctrine of the triune God and his
attributes.   But in modern usage it includes the whole compass of
the science of religion, or the relations of all things to God."[1]   "Theology, therefore, is the exhibition of the facts of Scripture in their
proper order and relation with the principles or general truths involved in the facts themselves, and which pervade and harmonize
the whole."[2]   These definitions reach far toward a definition of
systematic theology, and yet do not transcend the meaning of the
term theology in its present use.   As the ground-term it may consistently be used in so broad a sense.   There is still a place for the
distinct form of systematic theology.

2. *Theology with Differentiating Terms.*—Under this head we
may state briefly and in a definitive manner, the different forms or
distinctions of theology.

Natural theology has its special distinction from revealed the-
NATURAL THE- ology.   This points directly to a distinction of sources.
OLOGY. The light of nature is the source of the one, and revelation
the source of the other.   This distinction means the limitations of
the natural compared with the revealed.   Many of the deeper
truths of Christianity could never be discovered simply in the light
of nature.   No truths of theology are so clearly given therein as in

[1] Pope : *Christian Theology*, vol. i, p. 3.
[2] Hodge : *Systematic Theology*, vol. i, p. 19.

the Scriptures. Yet the existence of God and our moral responsibility to him, and the duties of obedience and worship, are manifest in the light of nature. We must find in nature the proof of God's existence before we are prepared for the question of a revelation from him. In view of these facts we may properly retain the formula of natural theology. Revealed theology, simply as such, needs no further statement at this point.

Exegetical theology is a formula in use, particularly in the terminology of theological seminaries. It has no direct EXEGETICAL doctrinal meaning, its specific office being simply the THEOLOGY interpretation of the Scriptures ; but it is properly named here because of the valuable service which biblical exegesis renders in preparing the material with which the theologian must construct his doctrines. This will be pointed out in another place.

Biblical theology is closely related to exegetical, but advances to a doctrinal position. The Scriptures furnish the material with which it works, and which it casts into doctrinal forms. Biblical theology has nothing to do with the confessions or formulas of faith which appear in the history of doctrines. In dealing with such creeds it departs from its own proper sphere and enters that of dogmatic theology. While limited to the Scriptures it need not cover the whole, and rarely does. Sometimes the Old Testament is the subject,[1] and sometimes the New.[2] Often the chosen part is only a small fraction of the Scriptures.[3] With such limitation the term biblical can properly mean only the form of theology.

Dogmatic theology has its proper distinction from both biblical and systematic, though often used in the same sense as DOGMATIC the latter. It is not limited to the Scriptures, like the THEOLOGY. biblical, nor has it by any requirement the comprehensiveness of the systematic. Dogmatic theology deals largely with the same material as historical theology, but in a different mode. Its work is with creeds or symbols of faith, not, however, in a mere presentation of their contents or history of their formation, but rather in a discussion of the doctrines which they embody. It may be in its mode either affirmative or controversial. Mostly, dogmatic theology devotes itself to the creed of a particular school. There is no necessary inclusion of all the doctrinal symbols of such school. Dogmatic theology may be just as free from dogmatism in any philosophic sense of the term, and just as scientific in its principles and method, as systematic theology. Its distinctive character

[1] Oehler : *Theology of the Old Testament.*
[2] Schmid : *Biblical Theology of the New Testament.*
[3] Crooks and Hurst : *Theological Encyclopædia and Methodology*, pp. 291–298.

is in its close connection with doctrinal symbols and the permissible limitation of its subjects.

Historical theology is often used in a sense to include ecclesi-
HISTORICAL astical history, but the doctrines of the Church are its
THEOLOGY. specific subject. In its subject, therefore, it is closely related to dogmatic theology, but still has its own distinctive character. This will appear in the statement of its definitive facts. It is the office of historical theology to trace the history of doctrines from their incipiency in individual opinion down to their full development and formation. The truth of a doctrine is no condition of its proper place in this history. Athanasianism and Arianism, Augustinianism and Pelagianism, Protestantism and Romanism, Arminianism and Calvinism, are alike entitled to candid treatment. Such treatment fulfills the office of historical theology. When the historian of doctrines enters into their formal discussion, supporting some and controverting others, he so far departs from his own proper function and enters the sphere of dogmatic theology.

In logical order, practical theology follows the systematic; yet
PRACTICAL for the present we find it convenient to reverse this
THEOLOGY order. Theology in its strictly doctrinal sense is viewed as completed when we reach practical theology; so that the latter has no proper doctrinal content. Yet it is so related to the practical ends of theology as to be fairly entitled to the use of the ground-term. Practical theology is concerned with the methods for the effective application of doctrinal truths to their practical ends. "It thus possesses a claim to scientific character. For while all theology aims, in its character as a positive science, to affect the life of human beings, it is yet incomplete without that department which is most directly engaged in carrying that positive aim into effect. It is, accordingly, with entire justice that practical theology has been termed by Schleiermacher 'the crown of the tree.'"[1] The truth should be specially emphasized, that the practical forces of Christianity, whether for the Christian life or the evangelizing work of the Church, are embodied in the doctrines of Christian theology. This is the requirement for the methods of practical theology whereby these forces may be most effectively applied to the Christian life and the work of the Church.

3. *Definitive Facts of Systematic Theology.*—In stating the other forms of theology the distinctive character of the systematic also appeared; but for clearness of view we require additional statements.

[1] Crooks and Hurst: *Theological Encyclopædia and Methodology,* p. 473.

The special subjects of systematic theology are the doctrines of Christianity. It is not meant that the doctrines so designated have their only source in the New Testament. All the doctrines of religion which have a ground of truth in either nature or the Old Testament also belong to this form of theology. But as the doctrines from such sources have their recognition and fuller unfolding in the New Testament we may properly designate all as the doctrines of Christianity. The sense of the term doctrine is not hidden. Any principle or law reached and verified through a proper induction is a doctrine, whether in science, philosophy, or theology. Thus there are doctrines of physics, chemistry, geology, ethics, metaphysics. So in theology: certain truths reached and verified through a proper induction are doctrines in the truest sense of the term. We may instance the personality of God, the divine Trinity, the person of Christ, the atonement, justification by faith. Systematic theology deals with such truths, and for completeness it must include the sum of Christian doctrines.

The doctrines severally must be constructed in a scientific manner. A system of theology is a combination of doctrines in scientific accord. But the several doctrines are no more at hand in proper form than the system itself. Hence the requirement for the construction of the doctrines severally. This is possible only through a scientific process. Through a careful study of the facts of geology the doctrines of the science are reached and verified, while in turn they illuminate the facts. Through a careful study and profound analysis of the relative facts the great doctrine of gravitation was reached and verified. The multiform facts are thus united and interpreted and set in a light of new interest. So must systematic theology study the elements of doctrinal truth, whether furnished in the book of nature or the book of revelation, and in a scientific mode combine them in doctrines. Very many facts point to a divine Providence, moral responsibility, human sinfulness, atonement in Christ; but only through a like scientific use of the facts can we reach the great doctrines which underlie these formulas. The method is exemplified in the construction of a doctrine of the Trinity by the Council of Nice and a doctrine of the person of Christ by the Council of Chalcedon. Such symbols, however, give merely the forms of doctrinal expression, not the processes of doctrinal construction. Systematic theology is concerned with the whole work of construction.

The doctrines, separately constructed, must be combined in a

(margin note: DOCTRINES THE SUBJECT)

(margin note: TREATMENT OF EACH DOCTRINE.)

system. Only thus can we reach a systematic theology. The same

principle which rules the construction of the doctrines severally must rule their systemization. As all the elements combined in a doctrine must be in scientific accord, so all the doctrines combined in a system must be in like agreement. As discordant elements cannot constitute a doctrine, so discordant doctrines cannot constitute a system. Hence the requirement of consistency in all the doctrines combined in the system must be faithfully observed. As this imperative law of systemization is manifest on its statement, and also must often appear in future discussions, it here requires no formal illustration.

The three facts presented under the present head characterize systematic theology and differentiate it from the other forms previously stated. Its specific subjects are the doctrines and the sum of the doctrines. It must construct the doctrines severally in a scientific form. In this construction there must be a constant view to the ruling principles of the system, else the doctrines may lack the necessary consistency. Finally, the doctrines must be combined in a system under the imperative law of a complete scientific agreement. There is no specific function of interpretation, as in exegetical theology; no restriction to a purely scriptural ground, as in biblical theology, and which may limit its treatment to a mere fraction of the Scriptures; no dealing chiefly with ecclesiastic symbols of faith and without any requirement of a system, as in dogmatic theology; no simply historic office in tracing the development and formation of doctrines and giving their contents, as in historical theology. Systematic theology is broader and deeper. It must include all the doctrines which properly belong to a system, and may freely command all the resources of doctrinal truth.

4. *Relation of Systematic to Other Forms of Theology.*—The different forms of theology are not severally isolated. Otherwise there could be no proper methodology in the curriculum of theological study. They are so related as readily to take their places in a logical order. There is a close relation of systematic theology to the other forms. particularly in the fact that mostly they furnish the material, and much of it well prepared, for its use in the construction of doctrines.

This appears in the case of exegetical theology. The doctrines

are grounded in the Scriptures and, to be true, must be true to the sense of the Scriptures. The doctrinal sense lies chiefly in the appropriate texts, what we call the proof-texts. It is the office of exegesis to give this sense. In this view the texts are for doctrine what facts are for science. Hence exegesis fulfills in the former the office of observation and experiment in the latter. The intimate relation between exegetical and systematic theology and the valuable service which the former renders the latter are thus clearly seen. Systematic theology, however, still has its own office to fulfill. As the generalizations of science are a distinct work from the finding of the facts, so the construction of doctrines is a distinct work from the interpretation of texts. Biblical theology is subsidiary to systematic in a manner kindred to the exegetical.

There is also an intimate relation to historical theology. In this view we may include the dogmatic with the historical, RELATION TO as both deal so largely with the same material. The HISTORICAL two give us the history of doctrinal opinion and the re- THEOLOGY. sults of doctrinal construction. The doctrines so constructed are not authoritative for systematic theology, but may render valuable service in the prosecution of its own work. This may be the case even when the method is wrong and the results erroneous. It has been so in relation to various sciences. Alchemy prepared the way for chemistry, and with all its vagaries performed a valuable service. Astrology prepared the way for astronomy, and the gathered facts were of great service in the transition from the false theory to the true. The method of Linnæus in botany is no longer accepted, but the work which he wrought is of value to this day. No wise worker in these spheres of science has overlooked this preparatory work or failed to appropriate its fruits. So may the systematic theologian find help in dogmatic and historical theology. This history discloses many errors in theology, and many errors appear in dogmatic symbols; but the true can be set over against the false and be seen the more clearly in the contrast. Besides, in many instances the truth of doctrine has been reached and well formulated. The history of doctrines may thus help the work of systematic theology.

II. SOURCES OF THEOLOGY.

On this question, as on many others, opposing theories have been pushed to extremes beyond the truth in either. When it is said that both nature and revelation are sources of theology there is truth in both views; but when it is said, on the one hand, that nature is the only and entirely sufficient source, and, on the other, that revelation is the only source, neither position is true. These are the opposite extremes of error. The one theory maintains ERRONEOUS that whatever we need to know of God and his will and VIEWS. of our own duty and destiny may be discovered in the light of nature; the other, that nature makes no revelation of God and duty, and, at most, can only respond to the disclosures of a divine revelation. The former position is naturally assumed by infidels who yet hold the existence of God and the moral and religious constitution of man. It is necessary for them to exalt the light of nature. Christianity early encountered this position of infidelity. Notably was it the position of the leading deists of England in the seventeenth and eighteenth centuries. Christian apologists have not been entirely free from the opposite tendency. Some have seemed reluctant to concede any resource of religious truth in the light of nature, lest they might jeopard the strongest ground of defense against the assaults upon the Christian faith. There was very little of this tendency with the great champions of revelation against the English deists. Near the close of this great debate, however, and especially at a later period, the position was assumed which logically excludes all grounds of a natural theology. Such is really the position of Watson.[1] No doubt the philosophy of Locke contributed much to this tendency, though he himself wrote on Christianity with an apologetic aim and fully admitted a light of nature, but controverted its sufficiency.[2]

On the broadest division there are two sources of theology—nature and revelation. They are very far from any equality; TWO SOURCES OF THEOLOGY. in fullness, clearness, and authority fairly comparable only by contrast. Some great truths of Christian theology are peculiar to revelation. Yet the first question of all religion, the existence of God, must be taken first to nature. The best Christian thinkers agree in these two sources. For the present we are merely stating them. The question of secondary sources will follow their more direct treatment.

1. *Nature a Source of Theology.*—By nature we here mean all things and events other than the divine revelation as distinctively such and which may, in any mode or degree, manifest God or his will or any other truth which is properly theological in its content. Whether such truth is an intuition of the primary reason, or a conclusion of the logical reason, or a product of the moral and religious consciousness, it is a truth through the light of nature. For the present we omit the Christian consciousness as a specific form of the religious consciousness, because it has been placed in such relation to this question as to require a separate consideration. There is a sense in which all knowledge is from God. He is the Author of our faculties and their correlations to objective truths which render knowledge possible. As between

---

[1] *Theological Institutes,* vol. i, chaps. iii–viii.
[2] *The Reasonableness of Christianity,* Works, vol. vii.

nature and revelation there is still the profound difference in the modes of knowledge : in the one case its acquisition in the use of human faculties ; in the other its imme- DISTINCTION OF NATURE AND REVE- LATION. diate communication by the divine agency. Our intu- itions of truth are no exception. In this case the mode of acquisition is as purely human and as really different from its immediate divine communication as in the acquisition of knowledge in the use of the logical faculties. In the one case the discovery of truth is mediated by the use of our own faculties ; in the other it is immediately given by the supernatural agency of God. It is important thus sharply to discriminate these two modes of truth, for only thus can we properly distinguish nature and revelation as sources of theology.

These statements may suffice for the present, for we are not yet studying the theology of nature, but simply defining and discriminating nature as a source of theology. How far this source may be valid and available for a knowledge of God and of our relations to him is for future inquiry. Without any incongruity of method we might here consider the religious ideas everywhere disclosed in human history—ideas of God or of some supernatural Being, whose providence is ever over mankind and whom men should worship and obey ; ideas of moral obligation and responsibility, of future existence and retribution. And, further, we might consider the evidence that these ideas are traceable to the light of nature and rationally traceable to no other source. With these facts established, and with the manifest theological content of these ideas, we should have the truth of a theology in the light of nature. But as these questions must arise with the question of theism it is better to defer them.

It is proper here to point out that the Scriptures fully recognize the works of nature and the moral constitution of man as manifestations of God and various forms of religious truth. This is so clearly the case that it may well be thought singular that any who accept their supreme authority, and, particularly, that assume to find in a supernatural revelation the only true original of theological truth, should either overlook this recognition as a fact or its conclusive significance for a natural theology.

Nature in its manifold forms is a manifestation of the perfections, providence, and will of God. "The heavens declare the glory of God ; and the firmament showeth his handi- A LIGHT OF NATURE. work"[1] The orderly forms of the heavens, their magnitude and magnificence, are a manifestation of the wisdom and power of God,

[1] Psa. xix, 1.

a mirror in which his glory shines. The manifestation is unto all people. " Lift up your eyes on high, and behold who hath created these *things,* that bringeth out their host by number . he calleth them all by names by the greatness of his might, for that *he is* strong in power ; not one faileth."[1] This is God's appeal to men, that in the heavens they would behold his power and wisdom and providence It would be useless to look upon the heavens for any such purpose if they are not a manifestation of these perfections in God. In the view of Paul facts of nature witnessed for God unto men in the darkness of heathenism : " Nevertheless he left not himself without witness, in that he did good, and gave us rain from heaven, and fruitful seasons, filling our hearts with food and gladness."[2] These facts could be witnesses of God unto men only as manifestations of his being and providence. The great words of Paul uttered on Mars' Hill are replete with the same ideas.[3] His words in vindication of the divine judgments upon the wicked heathen are specially noteworthy . " Because that which may be known of God is manifest in them ; for God hath showed it unto them. For the invisible things of him from the creation of the world are clearly seen, being understood by the things that are made, *even* his eternal power and Godhead ; so that they are without excuse."[4] Words could not well be more to the point.

The Scriptures assert a common moral responsibility under the A LIGHT OF THE MORAL REASON. light of nature This fact is the more decisive of the sense of Scripture on the present question, because the responsibility asserted is not such as might arise under atheism or pantheism, but such as requires the idea of God as a moral ruler. This is clearly seen in the appropriate texts: " For the wrath of God is revealed from heaven against all ungodliness and unrighteousness of men, who hold the truth in unrighteousness. . . Because that, when they knew God, they glorified *him* not as God, neither were thankful ; but became vain in their imaginations, and their foolish heart was darkened."[5] The application is to the heathen under the light of nature, just as to men under a formally revealed law. This is clear from the whole connection, and particularly from the omitted verses—19, 20. It is thus the sense of the apostle that under the light of nature men may so know God and his will as to be morally responsible to him. It is upon this ground that divine retribution is visited upon the Gentiles as upon the Jews, whose lives are in common given to wickedness.[6] Gentiles without the law may yet by nature fulfill

---

[1] Isa xl, 26   [2] Acts xiv, 17.   [3] Acts xvii, 24–29.
[4] Rom. i, 19, 20.   [5] Rom i, 18, 21.   [6] Rom ii, 1–11.

its moral duties. In this they are a law unto themselves, and show the work of the law written in their hearts. The conscience of such is active in either self-approval or self-condemnation, and equally in the moral judgment of others.[1] All this means a moral responsibility under the light of nature—such a responsibility as can arise only with the idea of God as moral ruler. Thus in two modes—by an appeal to the works of nature as a manifestation of God and his will and providence, and by the fact of moral responsibility under the law of nature—the Scriptures fully recognize the light of nature as a source of theology. It is yet the sense of the Scriptures that there is a profound moral need of higher forms of religious truth which the light of nature cannot disclose.

2. *Revelation the Source of Theology.*—We here need a definitive sense of revelation, though not an exact distinction be- SENSE OF REV-tween revelation and inspiration. Religious truth com- ELATION municated through a supernatural agency of God is a revelation. In this view the supernatural divine agency is the defining fact of revelation, and will fully answer for the present requirement. The mode of this agency in the communication of religious truth, except that it must be supernatural, is indifferent to its definitive function. Whether the communication is by sign, or word, or immediate inspiration, the agency is equally supernatural and the communication equally a divine revelation. This supernatural agency as the defining fact of revelation thoroughly distinguishes it from nature as a source of theology.

It follows that revelation has no necessary biblical limitation. Relative facts neither require such a limitation nor NO NECESSARY justify its assumption. In all generations sincere and BIBLICAL LIMI-devout souls have been seeking for God and truth. In TATION a profound sense of need and out of the thick darkness they have cried to Heaven for light and help. Who shall say that no such prayer has ever been answered? According to the defining fact of revelation, as above stated, any religious truth divinely given in such answer, though not verified to the recipient as from God, is yet a revelation. And to this source we would trace the higher religious truths reached by heathen minds, rather than to unaided reason and the light of nature, or to tradition. Yet, the highest truths even so reached fall infinitely below the moral and religious needs of mankind, and equally below the truths given in the Scriptures. Besides, they lack the seal of a divine original, and, therefore, the certainty and authority necessary to their truest religious value. While, therefore, we cannot question the divine communi-

[1] Rom. ii, 14, 15.

cation of some religious truth to devout minds, yet in a stricter sense, as in the common theological view, revelation and the Scriptures are one.

The Holy Scriptures are one source, and by all pre-eminence *the* source, of theology. Whether a divine revelation or not, or whatever their source, they contain the highest religious truths ever attained by mankind. Let a comparison be made with all that poets have sung and philosophers uttered, with all that is contained in the sacred books of other forms of religion, and the theology of the Scriptures will stand only in the clearer light of peerless excellence. If tested by the purest moral and religious intuitions, or by the sharpest inquisition of the logical reason, or by the profoundest sense of religious need, or by the satisfaction which its truths bring to the soul, or by its sublime power in the spiritual life, the theology of the Scriptures rises infinitely above all other theologies of the world. That they are a direct revelation from God, with the seal of a divine original clearly set upon them, gives to their theology a certainty and sufficiency, a grace and value, specially divine.

3. *Mistaken Sources.*—Under this head we may point out three mistaken sources of theology, severally designated as the confessional, the traditional, and the mystical.

A confessional source is omitted by many, but finds a place in the analysis and classification of some.[1] It should be noted that where creeds or confessions of faith are classed as a source of theology they are accounted such only in a secondary sense. This qualified sense, however, goes beyond the truth, or, if kept within the truth, loses all proper meaning of a source of theology. In the treatment of historical theology we stated the value of creeds and confessions to systematic theology. They embody the results of much preparatory work, and furnish much valuable material; but they have no authoritative quality, and therefore cannot be reckoned a source of theology. They are true or false in doctrine just as they are true or false to the Scriptures; and this fact of subordination denies to them all proper place among the sources of theology. Van Oosterzee's own explanatory statement really accords with this view: "The confessional writings of the Church (fons secundarius) cannot possibly be placed on a line with Holy Scripture, but must, on the contrary, be tested by, and if necessary altered according to, this latter. They contain no law for, but are expressions of, the

Marginal notes: THE SUPREME SOURCE. / CONFESSIONAL SOURCE.

[1] Van Oosterzee. *Christian Dogmatics*, vol. i, pp 18–21; Smith. *Introduction to Christian Theology*, p 61

belief which the Christian Church since the earliest times has constantly confessed." Dr. Smith reaches the same view. "Confessions are the voice of the Church, to which Christ promised his Spirit. But neither experience nor confessions can create new doctrines." This limitation denies to confessions any place among the proper sources of theology. It is better not to place among these sources any thing which does not possess the quality of a true source.

In Romanism tradition is held to be co-ordinate with the Scriptures in matters of faith and morals. This is the doctrine decreed by the Council of Trent. "The sacred and holy, œcumenical, and general Synod of Trent, . . . following the example of the orthodox fathers, receives and venerates with an equal affection of piety and reverence all the books both of the Old and of the New Testament—seeing that one God is the author of both —as also the sacred traditions, as well those pertaining to faith as to morals, as having been dictated, either by Christ's own word of mouth or by the Holy Ghost, and preserved in the Catholic Church by a continuous succession."[1]

TRADITIONAL SOURCE

Tradition—παράδοσις—properly means any instruction delivered from one to another, whether orally or in writing. Within a proper limitation of time and under favorable conditions even oral tradition may be of value. It was so in apostolic times and even later. So Paul exhorted the Christians of Thessalonica to observe the traditions received from him, whether by word or epistle, and to withdraw from any who refused this observance.[2] The earlier fathers appealed to apostolic traditions, and might do so with safety and profit. They were still near the apostles, whose sacredly treasured words might be securely transmitted through the succession of Christian teachers. But the time-limit of this law was soon passed, and the favoring conditions gave place to perverting influences ; so that no ground is conceded to the Romish doctrine of tradition, which makes it co-ordinate with the Scriptures and asserts its perpetuity through the papacy. "In coming to a decision on this question every thing depends upon making the proper distinctions with regard to *time*. In the first period of Christianity the authority of the apostles was so great that all their doctrines and ordinances were strictly and punctually observed by the churches which they had planted. And the doctrine and discipline which prevailed in these apostolic churches were, at that time, justly considered by others to be purely such as the apostles them-

---

[1] Schaff. *Creeds of Christendom*, vol. ii, pp. 79, 80.
[2] 2 Thess. ii, 15 ; iii, 6.

selves had taught and established. This was the more common, as the books of the New Testament had not, as yet, come into general use among Christians. Nor was it, in that early period, attended with any special liability to mistake . . . But in later periods of the Church the circumstances were far different. After the commencement of the third century, when the first teachers of the apostolic churches and their immediate successors had passed away and another race came on, other doctrines and forms were gradually introduced, which differed in many respects from apostolical simplicity. And now these innovators appealed more frequently than had ever been done before to apostolical tradition, in order to give currency to their own opinions and regulations. Many at this time did not hesitate, as we find, to plead apostolical traditions for many things at variance not only with other traditions, but with the very writings of the apostles, which they had in their hands. From this time forward tradition became naturally more and more uncertain and suspicious."[1]

TRADITION IN-TRUSTED TO INSPIRATION Romanism could not trust these traditions to the ordinary mode of transmission. All trustworthiness would long ago have been lost. As any special rumor, often repeated from one to another, loses its original character and certainty, so the apostolic traditions, if transmitted simply by repetition through all Christian centuries, could no longer be trustworthy or possess any authority in either doctrines or morals. To meet this exigency Romanism assumes for itself an abiding inspiration—such an inspiration as rendered the apostles infallible teachers and perpetuates its own infallibility. Tradition is thus guarded and guaranteed.[2] This abiding inspiration is now held to center in the papacy. "As Peter held the primacy in the circle of apostles, so the pope holds it in the circle of bishops. In the doctrine of the primacy the system of Catholicism reaches its climax. From the Roman chair the apostle is still speaking on whom, according to the will of the Lord, his Church was to be built; here the Church has an infallible testimony of the truth elevated above all doubt; for, as the central organ of inspiration, the pope has unlimited authority and power to ward off all heresy. In so far as he speaks *ex cathedra* his consciousness is a divine-human consciousness, and he is so far *vicarius Christi*. As Peter once said to the Redeemer, 'Lord, to whom shall we go? Thou hast the words of eternal life,' so all Christendom turns in the same way—not to Christ, but to the successor of Peter."[3] Such extravagances

---

[1] Knapp. *Christian Theology*, p 39

[2] Martensen: *Christian Dogmatics*, p. 28.   [3] *Ibid.*, p. 29.

come along with the inspiration which Romanism assumes as the guarantee of its doctrine of tradition.

The doctrine is open to destructive criticism. There is no promise of any such inspiration of the ministry that CRITICISM OF should succeed the apostles. There is no evidence of THE ROMISH any such inspiration in the line of the papacy, but con- THEORY clusive evidence of the contrary. The disproof is in the many errors of Romanism. If endowed with apostolic inspiration it could not lapse into error. This is its own doctrine. Yet its errors are many. There is the apostasy from the Nicene creed into the Arian heresy. There is the full and hearty acceptance of the Augustinian theology, and then there are very serious departures from it. Whether this system is true or false Romanism must have been in error either in the first case or in the second. The worship of Mary, transubstantiation, the sacrifice of the mass, the priesthood of the ministry, the saving efficacy of the sacraments, purgatory—all these are errors of doctrine and practice in Romanism, and the disproof of its apostolic inspiration.[1]

The doctrine means the incompleteness and obscurity of the Scriptures. If tradition is their necessary complement they must be incomplete and insufficient for the requirements of faith and duty. Such a view degrades them and openly contradicts the divine testimony to their sufficiency. The Scriptures are "profitable for doctrine, for reproof, for correction, for instruction in righteousness; that the man of God may be perfect, thoroughly furnished unto all good works."[2] What need we more? And these are among the last words of Paul. The doctrine of tradition, more than all else, leads to a denial of the Scriptures to the people. The law of this consequence is easily disclosed. If the papacy is endowed with an infallible inspiration in order to determine and interpret the apostolic traditions it must be the sole interpreter of the Scriptures. The one fact follows from the other. There can be no right of private interpretation in the presence of infallibility. The people must have no judgment as to the sense of the Scriptures. Therefore the people should not have the Scriptures. This simply completes, in a practical way, the denial of the right of private judgment. There must be an absolute subjection of the people to this hierarchy. It is hard to think of any high manliness or real fitness for civil liberty under such ecclesiastical abjectness. The detriment to the spiritual life must be great. Religion can no longer be viewed as a living union with Christ, but must be viewed as an outward conformity to the requirements of the Church. The

[1] Hodge Systematic Theology, vol. 1, pp. 144–149. [2] 2 Tim iii, 16, 17.

doctrine of infallibility "must react upon the community in this way, that the subject may now the more easily think to determine his obedience to God by his obedience to the Church, its dogmas, and its morality, and to possess in that way true Christianity. This has happened, if in different forms, in both the Greek and Romish communions."[1] The dismission of this mistaken source from the position it has so long held would greatly serve the interests of theology and the Christian life.[2]

We named mysticism as a third mistaken source of theology. It MYSTICAL SOURCE. would be more accurate to speak of the source which mysticism assumes than of itself as such a source. Mysticism is the doctrine of an immediate insight into truth. This deeper principle is readily carried into the sphere of religion, which, indeed, is its special sphere. It is a philosophy in which the mind seeks repose from the unrest of skepticism. In the view of Cousin the movement of philosophic thought is through sensationalism and idealism into skepticism.[3] Morell follows him in this view.[4] It was no difficult task for Hume and Berkeley to deduce idealism from sensationalism. Nor was it more difficult for Hume to resolve idealism into skepticism. But there can be no mental rest in skepticism. Another philosophy is an imperative requirement. The next movement is into mysticism. Here truth will stand in the open vision, especially in the sphere of religion. The immediate insight into truth is through some form of divine illumination.

Mysticism appears in different forms, and its definitions vary accordingly. VARIOUS FORMS OF MYSTICISM. "Whether in the Vedas, in the Platonists, or in the Hegelians, mysticism is nothing more nor less than ascribing objective existence to the subjective creations of our own faculties, to ideas or feelings of the mind; and believing that by watching and contemplating these ideas of its own making it can read in them what takes place in the world without."[5] This may accurately give the principle of mysticism and all the actual mental facts, but does not give all the assumed facts in its higher religious forms. In these the mind is divinely illuminated and lifted above its natural powers, and truth and God are immediately seen. "Mysticism in philosophy is the belief that God may be

---

[1] Dorner: *Christian Doctrine*, vol. i, p. 83.

[2] Goode: *Divine Rule of Faith and Practice*; Elliott: *On Romanism*, vol. i, chaps. ii–vi.

[3] *History of Modern Philosophy*, vol. i, pp. 343–364.

[4] *Modern Philosophy*, Introduction, sec. v.

[5] Mill: *Logic*, book v, chap. iii, sec. iv.

known face to face, without any thing intermediate. It is a yielding to the sentiment awakened by the idea of the infinite, and a running up of all knowledge and all duty to the contemplation and love of him."[1] "Mysticism despairs of the regular processes of science; it believes that we may attain directly, without the aid of the senses, and without the aid of reason, by an immediate intuition, the real and absolute principle of all truth, God."[2] "Mysticism, whether in religion or philosophy, is that form of error which mistakes for a divine manifestation the operation of a merely human faculty."[3]

There are elements of truth in mysticism, while its errors are mostly by exaggeration. The sensibilities, particularly ELEMENTS OF the moral and religious, have a value for knowledge not TRUTH usually accorded them; but when they are exalted above reason and revelation truth is lost in the exaggeration. This is specially true of Christian mysticism. There is a communion of the soul with God, and an activity of religious feeling which is the very life of that communion. There is a divine illumination which lifts the soul into a higher capacity for knowing God and truth; but there is no new revelation. Mysticism has rendered good service in emphasizing the interior spiritual life and the communion of the soul with God in a conscious experience, but has added nothing to the Scriptures in the form of wholesome doctrine. There is no higher privilege of the interior spiritual life than the Scriptures clearly open. Here is the fellowship with the Father, and with his Son Jesus Christ,[4] the love and indwelling of the Father and the Son,[5] the work of the Spirit which gives strength to the inner man, the indwelling of Christ by faith, the rooting and grounding of the soul in love, the knowing the love of Christ which passeth knowledge, the being filled with all the fullness of God.[6] No healthful doctrine of the divine communion transcends these privileges. But there is here no promise of a vision of God which shall supersede the Scriptures or bring higher truth to the soul. There are promises of divine inspiration as the mode of higher revelations of truth, but definitely and exclusively to the chosen mediums of such inspiration and revelation. This, however, is a work of the Spirit entirely apart from his offices in the personal Christian life, and, while vital to a divine revelation, means nothing for a state of personal attainment in the Christian life which shall be the source of doctrinal truth.

[1] Krauth-Fleming· Vocabulary, Mysticism.
[2] Cousin : History of Modern Philosophy, vol. ii, p. 114.
[3] Vaughan · Hours with the Mystics, vol. i, p. 22.
[4] 1 John i, 3.   [5] John xiv, 21, 23.   [6] Eph. iii, 16–19.
3

While we find some good in mysticism we do not find it clear of FLEMENTS OF evil. It is not questioned that mysticism furnishes EVIL examples of a pure and elevated Christian life. We may instance Tauler, Gerson, Boehm, Fénelon, Madame Guyon, Thomas à Kempis. The Friends have furnished many such examples. Still, the deeper principles of mysticism easily run into excesses which are not clear of evil. With the assumption of a spiritual state above the usefulness of reason and revelation, a state in which the soul is so lost in God as to be wholly subject to his supernatural guidance, religious feeling may readily be kindled to intensity, when the prudence and wisdom which should ever rule the Christian life must sink beneath a rashness and arrogance of spirit which easily run into evil excesses. The tendency is, on the one hand, to a reckless fanaticism; on the other, to a quietism, a state of absorbing contemplation or religious reverie, quite apart from the practical duties of the Christian life. In the extremer forms of mysticism, and forms not unnatural to its deeper principles, it has sometimes run into the impious heresy of antinomianism. Mysticism is in no true sense a source of theology.[1]

4. *Concerning the Christian Consciousness.*—The question is whether the Christian consciousness is in any proper sense a source of theology. Those who assume the affirmative differ widely respecting the measure in which it is such a source. Some claim so little as scarcely to reach the idea of a source of theology, while others make religious feeling the norm and source of the whole system of doctrines.

In the moderate view it is held that certain facts of Christian THE MODERATE experience witness to the truth of certain correlate VIEW. tenets of doctrine. For instance, it is claimed that in Christian experience there is the consciousness of a sinful nature which deserves penal retribution, and, therefore, that the doctrine of such a form of native sinfulness is true. Such an argument often appears in the interest of the Augustinian anthropology. But no source of theology is thus reached. Such a form of sinfulness, even if a reality, could not directly become a fact of consciousness. The philosophy of consciousness so decides. There might still be the moral conviction that inherited depravity is of the very nature of sin, but only after the doctrine of such a form of sin is placed in one's creed. In this case the moral conviction would simply be the response of the conscience to the moral judgment embodied in the

---

[1] Jouffroy: *Introduction to Ethics,* vol i, lect. v; Cousin. *The True, the Beautiful, and the Good,* lect v; Morell: *Modern Philosophy,* part ii, chap. vii, Vaughan: *Hours with the Mystics.*

creed. But a doctrine which must precede a particular form of consciousness as its necessary condition cannot even find its proof, much less its source, in such a consciousness. What is true in this case is equally true in all like cases.

We are more concerned with the stronger view of the religious consciousness as related to theology. This view is of HIGHER FORM comparatively recent development, and has its chief OF THE DOC-representation in Schleiermacher. "It is only in the TRINE.

present century, and chiefly through the influence of Schleiermacher, that the Christian consciousness began to be considered a source of dogmatics. He started with his investigation from man's feeling of his unlimited dependence. Dogma is for him the development of the utterances of the pious self-consciousness, as this is found in every Christian, and is still more determined by the opposition between sin and grace. In other words, it is the scientific expression of the pious feeling which the believer, upon close self-examination, perceives in his heart. Thus this consciousness is here the gold-mine from which the dogmas must be dug out, in order to 'found' them afterward, as far as possible, in Holy Scripture. In the individual it is the result of the spirit of the community, as this is a revelation of the Spirit of Christ. Of this 'Gemeingeist' Schleiermacher allows, it is true, that it must continually develop and strengthen itself by the words of Scripture, but not that it must find in the latter its infallible correcting rule. For him the highest principle of Christian knowledge is thus something entirely subjective, and the autonomy of his self-consciousness is the basis of his entire system."[1] This citation is valuable, not only in its historic aspect, but specially as a statement of the stronger view of the Christian consciousness as a source of theology.

There is a Christian consciousness. This is not a mere speculation, but a fact of experience. The conditions of this LAW OF THE consciousness are obvious. It is clearly impossible CHRISTIAN without the central truths of Christianity. No soul CONSCIOUSNESS ever reached it, or ever can reach it, through reason or the light of nature. It is impossible under any other form of religion. In every state of consciousness respecting any objective truth or reality, such truth or reality must be mentally apprehended before there can be any such response of the sensibilities as shall constitute the state of consciousness. This law conditions the active state of the sensibilities; and it is only in their active state that they can have any place in consciousness. In any such state of

[1] Van Oosterzee: *Christian Dogmatics*, vol. i, pp. 22, 23.

love, hatred, resentment, hope, fear, sympathy, or reverence the
proper object must be present to thought as in perception or in
some form of mental representation. This is the invariable and
necessary order of the facts · first, the mental apprehension of objective truths or realities; and, second, the response of the sensibilities in active forms of feeling, according to the character of
their respective objects as mentally viewed. The religious sensibilities are subject to the same laws.

We may view the religious consciousness as far broader than the
VARIATIONS OF
THE RELIGIOUS
CONSCIOUS-
NESS. Christian. In this view the latter is a specific type of
the former. There are, indeed, many specific types, as
may readily be seen in the religions of the world. There
are variations of the religious consciousness, according
to the variations of these religions. We may instance Confucianism,
Brahmanism, Buddhism, Zoroastrianism, Mohammedanism, Judaism ; each has its own appropriate form of the religious consciousness. The Christian consciousness differs widely from each of the
others. There are also differences in the Christian consciousness,
as between Romanism and Protestantism, Trinitarianism and Unitarianism, Calvinism and Arminianism. The question is to account
for such differences. The real point is that they cannot be accounted for on any theory which makes religious feeling the source
of theology, and, further, that the true account disproves such a
source.

The theory which makes religious feeling the source of theology
places the feeling before the ideas or truths which constitute the
theology. In this order of the facts, instead of the doctrines determining the cast of the feeling, the feeling determines the form and
content of the doctrines. If this be the case religious feeling must
be purely spontaneous to our nature, neither evoked nor modified
by any religious ideas or doctrinal views. It is itself the norm and
ruling principle of religion. Why then should it so vary in the
forms of its development ? The theory can make no answer to this
question. It allows nothing back of this feeling which can determine these variations. Their explanation must come from the op-
LAW OF THESE
VARIATIONS. posite position. The religious consciousness varies in
the different forms of religion because they differ in the
tenets of doctrine. There are different views of God and man, of
duty and destiny. These views act upon the feelings and determine the cast of the religious consciousness. A thorough analysis
of these religions will find in each a form of consciousness in accord
with its doctrines. The doctrinal view of God is specially a determining force in the religious consciousness. So far from this con-

sciousness determining the view of God just the contrary is the truth : the view of God determines the cast of the consciousness.[1] The Christian consciousness is peculiar to Christianity and impossible to any other form of religion, because many of its doctrines, particularly in the fullness of their unfolding, are peculiar to itself. Only in this manner can we explain the variations of the Christian consciousness as previously noted. Romanism and Protestantism, Trinitarianism and Unitarianism, Calvinism and Arminianism, differ in ruling doctrines, doctrines to which the religious feelings respond, and from the influence of which they receive their own cast. This is the law of variations in the Christian consciousness.

In view of the facts above given the conditions of the Christian consciousness are manifest. There is no possibility of the feelings which constitute this consciousness without the central truths of Christianity. These truths must not only be in the mental apprehension, but must also be accepted in faith. Only thus can they have power in the religious consciousness. When so apprehended and believed, they have such power because they are thus seen to be truths of profound interest. Now the religious nature responds to them in appropriate forms of feeling. This is the law of the Christian consciousness in the general view, and of its variations in different schools of theology. To assume the religious feelings as first in order, and then to find in them the central truths REVERSION OF of theology, is to reverse the logical and necessary order THE TRUE OR-of the facts. Clearly a knowledge of the central truths DER of Christianity conditions the Christian consciousness and must be first in order. It may still be true, and indeed is true, that we more fully grasp these truths of doctrine through the response of the religious sensibilities, but this simply concerns our capacity for the clearest knowledge, and has nothing to do with the fixed order of the facts in the Christian consciousness.

As the Christian consciousness is thus conditioned by the possession of the central truths of Christian theology, it is impossible to deduce these truths from that consciousness. Back of these truths there is no Christian consciousness to begin with. The theory under review tacitly admits this by beginning, back of this specific form of consciousness, simply with religious feeling, the feeling of absolute dependence upon God. But there is no source of Christian theology in such a feeling. It has no content from which may be deduced the doctrine of the Trinity, the Christian doctrine of sin, the atonement in Christ, justification by faith, or regeneration and

[1] Walker : *Philosophy of the Plan of Salvation.* Miley . " The Idea of God as a Law of Religious Development," *Methodist Quarterly Review,* January, 1865.

a new spiritual life through the agency of the Holy Spirit. There is apologetic value in the Christian consciousness, but no source of Christian theology. "To the Christian truth, in accordance with the Gospel believed and confessed by the Church, the Christian consciousness gives a witness, with reason estimated highly. Only when objective truth finds a point of contact in the subjective consciousness does it become the spiritual property of mankind, and can it be thus properly understood and valued. So far, and so far only, does the Christian consciousness deserve a place among the sources of dogmatics. But since the doctrine of salvation can be derived neither from reason, nor from feeling, nor from conscience, and the internal consciousness only attests and confirms the truth, after having learned it from Scripture, this last must always be valued as the principal source."[1]

III. Scientific Basis of Theology.

1. *Certitude a Requirement of Science.*—"Science is knowledge evident and certain in itself, or by the principles from which it is deduced, or with which it is certainly connected."[2] Any proper definition of science will carry with it the sense of certitude. This certitude has special respect to the facts in which a science is grounded, or to the principles upon which it is constructed. There is a distinction of sciences, as intimated in the previous sentence. It is the distinction between the experimental, or inductive, and the exact, or deductive, as the mathematical. The latter are constructed upon principles. These principles are axiomatic and, therefore, certain in their own light. If these principles are taken into exact and clear thought, and all the deductions are legitimate, certitude goes with the scientific construction. The facts in which the empirical sciences are grounded are very different from such principles. They are facts to be studied by observation and the tests of experiment. They must be surely and accurately known before they can be wrought into a science. But a mere knowledge of facts, however exact and full, is not in itself a science. There must still be a generalization in some principle or law which interprets the facts, and which they fully verify. Such is the method in this class of sciences. It is no absolute guarantee against mistakes in respect to either the facts or the generalization, but must be observed for any scientific attainment. The history of science records many mistakes, and mistakes still occur; so that some things called science

---

[1] Van Oosterzee: *Christian Dogmatics*, vol. i, p. 22. We highly commend the treatment of this question by the author just cited.
[2] Krauth-Fleming: *Vocabulary*, "Science."

are falsely so called. In such cases the boasted certitude is bald assumption.

If theology is to receive a scientific construction, it must possess the requisite grounds of certitude. This does not mean NECESSARY IN that its grounds must be precisely the same as in the THEOLOGY. abstract sciences, or in the experimental sciences, but must mean a measure of certitude sufficient for the scientific construction. Without such a ground there can be no attainment of science in theology. "Besides, certainty upon Christian grounds has no wish to withdraw from those universal rules and laws, according to which a legitimate certainty is formed; were it otherwise, Christian theology could be no longer represented as a branch in the series of human sciences."[1] The several doctrines might be legitimate to the accepted facts or grounds on which they are constructed, and also in such accord with each other as to meet the logical requirements for systemization, but without the requisite certainty in the grounds there could still be no true science of theology.

2. *Unwarranted Limitation to Empirical Facts.*—Science is often so defined as to deny to theology all rightful claim to a scientific position. The definition limits science to purely empirical facts, on the assumption that only such facts have the certitude requisite to scientific treatment. "Students of the physical sci- NARROW AIM ences have accustomed themselves of late to limit the OF SCIENTISTS. word science exclusively to empirical science, and even, in some cases, to the empirical grade of physical science. Thus Professor Simon Newcomb, in his address before the American Scientific Association in 1878, said: 'Science concerns itself only with phenomena and the relations which connect them, and does not take account of any question which does not in some way admit of being brought to the test of observation.' This, he says, is 'fundamental in the history of modern science.' Even so considerate and philosophical a writer as Janet says: 'Doubtless philosophical thought mingles always more or less with science, especially in the sphere of organized being; but science rightly strives to disengage itself more and more from it, and to reduce the problem to relations capable of being determined by experience.'[2] This is a legitimate characteristic and aim of empirical science, but it has no right to appropriate to itself exclusively the name of science and to distinguish itself from philosophy and theology. This abuse of the word is, however, becoming common. The three grades are habitually designated as science, philosophy, and theology, implying that the two latter are not science. There is a mighty power in words, and

[1] Dorner: *Christian Doctrine*, vol. i, p. 59.   [2] *Final Causes*, p. 117.

it is an unworthy artifice for the students of physical science to appropriate to their own branch of study the name science, and to themselves the name scientists. They can justify this only by reverting to the complete positivism of Comte and avowing and maintaining that knowledge is limited to the observations made by the senses." [1]

The limitation of science to facts of observation or experience TRUTH BROAD- must be made upon the assumption that only such facts ER THAN EX- can be sufficiently known for scientific treatment. But PERIENCE. sense-experience is not the limitation of thought, and thought must transcend it in order to any attainment of science. Perception transcends experience. Experience is through sensation; perception through the cognitive activity of thought. Phenomenalism is the utmost attainment of mere empiricism. All science lies beyond this limit. The relations of phenomena necessary to science are not given in sensation. Much less are the laws or principles which underlie and interpret phenomena so given. These principles can be reached only through the activities of rational thought. No scientific classification is possible without the processes of abstraction and generalization. These processes are the office of the discursive or logical faculty, not of the presentative faculty as concerned with empirical facts. The sensationalism which underlies and determines this narrow sense of science is mere phenomenalism, mere positivism, which knows nothing of substance, cause, or law. The legitimate result is an utter skepticism, and an exclusion of all the certitude of truth necessary to science.

Empirical knowledge, or knowledge acquired by observation or ALL EXPERI- experience, is purely individual. This fact has not ENCE PURELY been properly emphasized, especially in its relation to INDIVIDUAL. this narrow limitation of science to facts empirically known. Its consequence is that every scientist is limited to the facts of his own individual observation or testing. No facts can be taken on testimony, however competent the witnesses. Testimony addresses itself to faith, not to a testing experience. This result is determined by the laws of mind, not by the nature of the facts concerned in the testimony. Hence empirical facts are no exception. If presented only on testimony they can be received only in faith. This narrow sense of science, with its fixed empirical limitations, has no place for faith, and must exclude it as openly contradictory to its own principles. Moreover, its admission would be a fatal concession to theology, in which faith has so important a

[1] Harris: *Philosophical Basis of Theism*, pp. 300, 301.

function. Hence we emphasize this fact, that on the truth of any principle which determines the limitation of science to facts of observation or experience all empirical knowledge available for science is strictly individual. As the observation or experience of no one can become the observation or experience of another, so the empirically acquired knowledge of no one can be of any scientific use to another. The scientific work of each must proceed only with his own empirical acquirement and within its determining limitation.

Now, with these narrow limits let any one attempt the construction of a science—whether of cosmogony, geology, biology, or astronomy, it matters not. Is any one possible under the limitation to empirical facts as actually known in observation or experience? Especially is any one possible with the inevitable limitation to a mere individual observation or experience? Are the facts necessary to the verification of the nebular cosmogony empirically known to any single mind? Are the facts necessary to a science of geology, or to a science of biology, so known? There is no true science of astronomy without the great law of gravitation. This law, however, is no empirical truth, but a rational deduction from certain observed facts. The law of its attractive force expressed in the formula, directly as the mass and inversely as the square of the distance, is reached only in rational thought which transcends experience. Yet astronomy, with all the confidence of scientific certainty, asserts the reign of gravitation, according to this law of its energy, over the physical universe, and therefore over measureless portions which lie infinitely beyond the observed facts from which it is inferred, and equally beyond the possible tests of experience.

And what shall be done with mathematics on this empirical limitation of science? Mathematics is not an empirical science. The axiomatic principles on which it builds are open only to the intuition of thought, not to the sight of the eye or the touch of the finger. They are subject to no tests. That parallel lines cannot inclose a space, and that all the radii of a circle are equal, are absolute truths for thought, but truths which can never be empirically verified. What, then, can these empirical limitationists do with mathematics? Perhaps nothing better than to go with Comte and give it a mere phenomenal character. But in doing this they should not forget that the phenomenal is purely for sense-perception, while mathematics is purely for thought, and therefore without any phenomenal quality. The only other alternative is to deny to mathematics any place in the category of the sciences. Either result utterly discredits this narrow empiricism.

[marginal note: SERIOUS TROUBLE FOR EMPIRICISTS.]

Certain positions are thus surely gained. One is that the lim-
NO EMPIRICAL   itations of science to facts of sense-experience renders
LIMITATIONS   science impossible. This limitation assumes that only
OF SCIENCE.   such facts are sufficiently known or certain for scientific use. But this assumption is inevitably grounded in sensationalism, which logically results in skepticism, and therefore excludes
the certitude necessary to science. Hence, as we have seen, thought
must transcend all sense-experience and be valid in its own light
in order to any scientific attainment. Another is that empirical
grounds are wholly unnecessary to the most exact and certain forms
of science, as appears above question in the instance of mathematics. It follows that theology must not be denied, and cannot
logically be denied, a scientific position simply because it is not
grounded in empirical facts in the manner of the physical sciences.
Science has no such limitation.[1]

3. *Grounds of Certitude in Theology.* — Here two questions
arise : What are the grounds of theology ? and, Do these grounds
possess the certitude requisite to a science of theology ? However,
it is not important to the present treatment to hold the two in entire separation. Nor do we need a full discussion of all the matters
concerned in these questions. This would be quite impracticable
and out of the order of a proper method. Such a discussion would
involve the whole question of theism, which properly forms a distinct part of theology. It would also include the whole question
of Christian apologetics, which is no necessary part of systematic
theology.

The first truth of theology is the existence of God. Without
CERTAINTY OF   this truth there is no theology in any proper sense of
THEISM.   the term, and therefore no place for a science of theology. As we have previously seen, in the broadened sense of theology many other truths are included than those relating directly to
God, but his existence is ever the ground-truth, and these other
truths receive their theological cast from their relation to him.
The proofs of the existence of God will be considered in the proper
place. In the light of reason they are conclusive and give certainty to this ground-truth of theology. In the light of reason, as
reason interprets nature and man, the existence of God is a more
certain truth than the existence of a physical universe as studied in
the light of sensationalism—that favorite philosophy with the empirical scientists who deny to theology the position of a science.
More philosophic thinkers have questioned the truth of the latter
than the truth of the former. The existence of God is a more

[1] Bowne. *Philosophy of Theism*, p. 102.

certain truth than the great law of gravitation which underlies the science of astronomy. With the existence of God, the harmony of the heavens can be explained without the law of gravitation. Without his existence, neither this harmony nor the manifold adjustments of nature can be explained.

There is a theological anthropology which deals with the religious nature of man and its manifestations in human history. Man is a religious being. He is such by the constitution of his nature. This is rarely questioned by philosophic thinkers. The purpose of infidelity to eliminate religion from human life is a thing of the past. Real thinkers of the present have no such aim nor any thought of its possibility. Naturalistic evolutionists must admit, and do admit, that nothing in the constitution of man is more thoroughly organic than his religious nature. With no other characteristic is human history more thoroughly replete. "An unbiased consideration of its general aspects forces us to conclude that religion, every-where present as a weft running through the warp of human history, expresses some eternal fact."[1] "No atheistic reasoning can, I hold, dislodge religion from the heart of man." "The facts of religious feeling are to me as certain as the facts of physics."[2] The facts of religious feeling are facts of consciousness, just as any other facts of consciousness in our mental life, and therefore just as certain as any others But the facts of consciousness are even more certain than the facts of physics or the properties of matter.

THEOLOGICAL ANTHROPOLOGY.

The facts of our religious nature, thus clear and certain in the consciousness and ever manifest in human history, must be open to scientific treatment. The certitude requisite to such treatment is above question, and fully conceded. As no facts of our mental life and no facts of physics are either more certain or more distinct and definite than the religious, we must either concede a scientific position to the latter or deny it to the former. This is the imperative requirement of consistency. Hence, any objection to a scientific treatment of the facts of man's religious nature must be made, not against such treatment itself, but against its theological significance. Empirical scientists announce the purpose and expectation of extending the laws of physical nature over the realms of life and mind.[3] On this assumption all phenomena, vital, mental, religious, just as the material, must proceed according to physical laws and as the

FACTS FOR THEOLOGICAL SCIENCE.

[1] Spencer First Principles, p 20.
[2] Tyndall: Prefaces to the Belfast Address
[3] Huxley: Lay Sermons, p. 138; Tyndall: Belfast Address, p 55.

effect of mechanical forces. The result must be accepted as the true science of mind, even in its highest rational and religious facts. If this aim is ever achieved the rational and religious facts of mind must yield to an empirical testing, just as the facts of physical nature. They never can be so tested. They are facts for philosophic treatment, and philosophy will never yield them to the physical realm, but ever assert for them a distinct and higher ground in spiritual mind. The failure of empirical science to bring these moral and religious facts into the order of physical phenomena neither affects their reality nor changes their distinct and definite form as facts of consciousness and historic manifestation. As such facts, they are open to scientific treatment in the light of philosophy, and have a profound significance for theology. In its anthropological sphere theology deals, not with fancies, but with what is most real and definite in the constitution and history of man.

As the Scriptures are the chief source of theology they must be CERTITUDE IN grounded in truth in order to the certitude which a THE SCRIPT- science of theology requires. The issue is not shunned URES at this point. It is not shunned in the instance of theologians who proceed to the scientific treatment of doctrines without an introductory verification of the Scriptures. In such case they proceed on the warranted ground that already this verification has been frequently and fully achieved. This is a thoroughly legitimate method, and a very common one in many branches of science. One man furnishes facts, or what he reports to be facts, as found in his own observation or testing; another accepts them as such and proceeds to generalize them in some principle or law of science. If there is no error respecting either the facts or the generalization, the result is just as valid as if one person performed the whole work. When one deals with such facts at second hand the only requirement is that they be so accredited as to possess the certitude requisite to their scientific use. This method is equally valid for the theologian. Still, he does not proceed simply upon the testimony of others, however competent, that they have thoroughly examined the evidences in the case and found them conclusive of a divine original of the Scriptures; he examines for himself, and to himself proves their divine verity before proceeding to the scientific treatment of their doctrinal contents. With the omission of this discussion from any actual place in his theology, his method is still far more exact and thorough than in many instances of scientists in secular branches, who hastily accept facts at second hand and proceed without any proper warrant of the certitude requisite to their scientific use. Further information has often brought confusion to the hasty generalizations thus reached. If the Scriptures are a divine revelation it follows, of course, that their doctrinal contents possess all the certitude requisite to a science of theology. However, in view of the facts above given we may pass this whole question with a very summary statement, especially as some points must recur with the treatment of faith in relation to a science of theology.

On the ground of theism a divine revelation is possible. The only reason for asserting so manifest a truth is that it POSSIBILITY OF has been disputed. The question may be appealed to A REVELATION. reported facts of Scripture without the assumption of their truth, which, indeed, is not directly concerned in the present issue. This is claimed as manifestly true, that on the ground of theism God's intercourse with men as related in the Scriptures is certainly possible. He could commune with Moses in all the modes related, and communicate to him all the truth claimed to have been so given. So, by word and dream and vision and inspiration, he could give truth to the prophets and identify it as from himself. They could thus be the medium of divine revelations and the unerring prophets of a far-reaching future. On the same ground the divine incarnation is entirely possible; and the Son so present with men could reveal the Father and communicate the great truths of religion which lie in the gospels. All the reported instances of his intercourse with his disciples and his religious instructions to them are possible. The promised mission of the Spirit as a revealer of religious truth in the minds of its chosen messengers is possible. The same Spirit, in the fulfillment of this mission, could secure through them the proper utterance and record of the truths so revealed. The conclusion is the possibility of a divine revelation.

Sometimes the objection to the possibility of a divine revelation takes a specially subtle form. It proceeds on the as- A SUBTLE OB-sumption that our purely subjective ideas are the full JECTION measure of our spiritual cognitions. Hence no communication from without can transcend these subjective limitations. Nothing, therefore, in the form of religious truth can be added by revelation to what we already know. The fallacy of this objection lies in the tacit assumption that our subjective state is without any possible improvement whereby we may grasp higher forms of truth given by instruction. A little testing will expose this fallacy. No such law of subjective limitation renders fruitless instruction in science or art. No such law rules the sphere of ethics or bars all improvement of moral ideas through instruction. The moral and religious instructions of the mother are not rendered powerless by any fixed limitation imposed by the subjective ideas of her child. In instances without number heathen minds have been raised to higher ideas of God and truth through Christian instruction. No such law precludes the possibility of a divine revelation. God is not bound by the limitations of our purely subjective ideas. He can communicate truth which shall marvelously clear these ideas, and, with an ever-growing power of spiritual perception, ever give us more truth and light.

On the ground of theism a divine revelation is rationally probable. PROBABILITY OF A REVELATION. This proposition looks only to an antecedent probability. Hence it must not be maintained by any rational claim of the Scriptures to a divine original, but find its support in considerations quite apart from such claim. A few may be briefly stated:

God is benevolently concerned for our well-being. As infinitely wise and good, as our Creator and Father, he must care for our moral and spiritual good.

We are the subjects of a moral government of God's own ordination and administration. The truth of this position is affirmed by the suffrage of mankind, though not always with the conception of its highest theistic ideas. The human soul, with rarest exceptions, asserts its own sense of moral responsibility to a divine Ruler. This common affirmation must be accepted as the expression of a profound reality. On the ground of theism its truth cannot be questioned.

The highest moral and religious truth is profoundly important. As our secular interests render an accurate and full knowledge of nature and of the arts and sciences which concern our present well-being very desirable, so that truth which is necessary to our moral and spiritual good must be intensely desirable. This desirableness rises with the infinite measure of the interests which such truth concerns.

The highest certainty of religious truth is profoundly desirable. Doubtful truths do not meet the conscious needs of the soul. We need truth as truth is with God, and as revealing his mind and will. His mind is the only sufficient source of spiritual truth, and it must deeply concern us to know the behests of his will. Hence the desirableness of truth known to have come from God. The heart of humanity craves such truth. The history of mankind reveals this craving.

We can have no such religious truth as the world needs and craves, truth in the highest form and certainty, except as a divine revelation. The case may be appealed to the history of the race, and in view of the profoundest questions of religious interest and concern. Apart from the Scriptures, or on a denial of their divine original, we have no such full and certain knowledge as we need respecting either God or ourselves, or his will and the duties of love and obedience that we should render him, or the means of relief from the burden of sin which all hearts bear, or the graces of the purest, best life. The best minds of the race have deeply felt these wants and avowed the conviction that such truth and light could come to man only as a revelation from heaven.

A divine revelation is, therefore, a rational probability. The facts just considered so affirm. On the one hand we have the character of God and his relations to us; on the other, our own profound need of religious truth— THE FACTS SHOW THE PROBABILITY. truth of such fullness and certainty that its only possible mode of attainment is in a divine revelation. It is therefore rationally probable that God shall in some mode above the light of nature or the resources of human reason reveal himself to men. He has placed the sun in the heavens as a light for the natural world; and has he no divine light for the moral world? Must each soul be its own and only prophet? Shall no one sent from God speak to us? Shall the heavenly Father, veiled from the eye of his children, be forever silent to their ear? Shall he never speak to the world so long waiting and listening for his voice?

A revelation is possible only through a supernatural agency of God. Any manifestation of religious truth in the works of nature or the moral constitution of man may be called a revelation, but only in a popular sense. In REVELATION A SUPERNATURAL COMMUNICATION. such case there is no direct communication of truth from God, but only the discovery of truth by human faculties. If we even assume a divine illumination of human minds, the result would be simply a clearing of their spiritual vision, but no other disclosure of truth than in the works of God. The true idea of a divine revelation carries with it the sense of a direct communication of truth through the agency of God. That agency must be supernatural, whatever the modes in which it works. There are doctrinal contents of Christianity which have no manifestation in nature, and therefore could never be discovered or known as truths, except as attested communications from God. We may instance the doctrine of the Trinity, the doctrine of sin in its more distinctive facts, the divine incarnation, the personality of Christ, the atonement in Christ, justification by faith, the mission and work of the Holy Spirit. As these central and essential truths of

Christianity can be known as truths only as attested communications through a supernatural agency of God, we must accept and maintain such an agency in the original of the Scriptures, wherein we find these truths; for only thus can we secure the certitude requisite to a science of theology which has its chief source in the Scriptures.

On the ground of theism such a supernatural agency has no
THE SUPER- serious perplexity for rational thought; indeed, it is
NATURAL open and clear as compared with any account of mate-
AGENCY WITH- rial and mental phenomena on the ground of purely
OUT PERPLEX-
ITY. mechanical forces. There are greater perplexities in
the science of physics than in the theory of a supernatural agency of God in a revelation of religious truths. Who can explain the forces of chemical affinity, or the strength of cohesion as exemplified in the steel cables which support the Brooklyn Bridge? The reciprocal attraction of the earth and the sun across the vast space which separates them seems very simple in idea, but it has no rationale in human thought. The perplexity ever deepens as we extend the reign of this law over the physical universe. There is no seeming possibility of any such mechanical force. This is the real point of perplexity. No such perplexity besets the theory of a supernatural agency of God in a revelation of religious truth. Such an agency is not only free from valid objections, but has the support of weighty reasons. All the facts which render a divine revelation rationally probable render equally probable a supernatural agency as the necessary mode of its communication.

A divine revelation must be supernaturally attested. There is
SUPERNATU- here a profound distinction between its primary recipi-
RAL ATTESTA- ents and the many to whom they publish it. To the
TION NECES-
SARY. former it may be verified as a revelation in the mode of
its communication; but this will not answer for the many who receive it on their testimony. Its chosen messengers must be accredited in a manner assuring to the people that they are messengers of truth from God. Miracles are the best, and rationally the most probable, means to this end. Prophecy is just as supernatural, and its fulfillment just as conclusive of a divine commission, but often there must be long waiting before the fulfillment completes this credential. Prophecy has great apologetic value, especially for the generations succeeding the founding of Christianity, but this necessary delay prevents the prompt and direct attestation furnished by miracles. A revelation may have the support of many forms of evidence, as the Scriptures have, while it is still true that miracles are the most appropriate credential of its messengers.

There is no credulity in the ready belief that the religious teacher who works miracles in the name of God is his messenger of truth to men.[1] The reason for this faith was never clearer or surer than now. Just as science establishes the uniformity of the laws of nature, so does a supernatural event absolutely evince the immediate agency of God as its cause. Hence the religious teacher by whom he works miracles must be his messenger of truth to men.

On the ground of theism there is no antecedent presumption against miracles, but, rather, a strong presumption in their favor. We have previously pointed out the antecedent rational probability of a divine revelation. NO PRESUMP-TION AGAINST MIRACLES There is a like probability of miracles as the appropriate and really necessary attestation of such a revelation. Unwise definitions have needlessly furnished occasion for objections to such a mode of attestation. While nothing of the necessary content of a miracle should be omitted from its definition, nothing unnecessary should be included. A miracle does not mean any abrogation or suspension of the laws of nature. Yet such ideas have often been put into its definitions, which have thus furnished the special ground of objection. A miracle is a supernatural event wrought by the immediate agency of God, to accredit some messenger as divinely commissioned or some truth as divinely given. The divine energizing touches the law of nature simply at the point of the miracle, and in a manner to produce it, but no more abrogates or suspends such law, as a law of nature, than the casting a stone into the air annuls the law of gravitation. The raising of Lazarus leaves undisturbed the laws of nature which reign over the vast realms of the living and the dead. The agency of God in a miracle, while thoroughly supernatural, is just as orderly with respect to the laws of nature as the agency of man in the use of any chemical or mechanical force. Hence all such objections are utterly void.[2]

The facts thus maintained have apologetic value, not, however, as direct proofs of a divine revelation, but specially as obviating leading objections and clearing the way for the OBJECTIONS OBVIATED full force of the evidences of such a revelation. We have not the more difficult task of facing any strong presumption against either its possibility or probability. On the ground of theism, a divine

---

[1] John iii, 2.

[2] Butler. *Analogy*, part ii, chap. ii, Mozley · *Miracles*, lect. 1, Bushnell · *Nature and the Supernatural*, chap. xi; Paley: *Evidences of Christianity*, "Preparatory Considerations," Mansell. *Aids to Faith*, essay 1: Christlieb. *Modern Doubt and Christian Belief*, lect. v; Foster · *The Supernatural Book*, "Argument from Miracles."

4

revelation is clearly possible and strongly probable, while a super-natural agency of God as the necessary mode of its communication fully shares the probability. Further, there is not only no anteced-ent presumption against miracles, but as the best means of attest-ing a divine revelation they are rationally probable. Thus the evidences of such a revelation do not encounter any balancing, or nearly balancing, disproof, so that they really prove nothing, or, at best, leave the question in uncertainty : they come to the proof of what is antecedently probable, and their whole weight is available for this end. The certitude requisite to a science of theology is thus attainable.

The Holy Scriptures are a divine revelation of religious truth. EFFECTIVE WORK OF APOLOGETICS. On this question Christian apologetics has shunned no issue with infidelity. Against the many forms of at-tack the defense has been prompt and effective. The victory is with the defenders of the Christian faith. Beyond this defensive service the evidences for the truth and divine original of the Scriptures have been presented in their fullness and logical conclusiveness. The authenticity of the Scriptures is an established truth. The fulfillment of the prophecies and the reality of the miracles infallibly accredit the sacred writers as messengers of truth from God. The complete harmony of the sacred books, occupying, as they do, so many centuries in their composition, and the peculiar character of their doctrinal, moral, and religious contents unite in the same attestation. The founding and triumphant propagation of Christianity as open facts of history, together with its marvelous power in the moral and religious life of mankind, for any rational account absolutely require the divine mission of the Christ. The unique character of our Lord as portrayed in the New Testament is itself conclusive of the divine origin of Christianity. Only with a pattern from the holy mount of God could the human mind rise to the conception of such a character. In all the creative thought of the world there is no approach toward such a conception. The simple artists of the New Testament who wrought this portrait must have had the divine original before them.[1]

---

[1] On the truth of Christianity, with the truth of the Scriptures—Paley · The Evidences of Christianity ; Mair · Studies in Christian Evidences ; Wilson : Evi-dences of Christianity ; Fisher . Supernatural Origin of Christianity ; Keith . Demonstration of the Truth of Christianity ; Bishop Thomson . Evidences of Revelation ; Hopkins · Evidences of Christianity ; Rawlinson . Historical Evi-dences of the Truth of the Scripture Records ; Chalmers : Evidences of Christian-ity ; Rogers : Superhuman Origin of the Bible ; Alexander : Evidences of Chris-tianity ; Christlieb . Modern Doubt and Christian Belief ; Aids to Faith—Replies to " Essays and Reviews ;" Bishop McIlvaine : Evidences of Christian-

Christ openly submitted the truth of his doctrine to the test of experience, not the same in form or mode as that on which empirical science builds, but an experience just as real and that just as really grasps the truth. "My doctrine is not mine, but his that sent me. If any man will do his will, he shall know of the doctrine, whether it be of God, or *whether* I speak of myself."[1] The same principle is given in these words: "He that believeth on the Son of God hath the witness in himself."[2] These texts mean that through experience we may come to know the doctrine of Christ as the very truth of God, and to know Christ as the Messiah and Saviour. There is another mode of experience through which we reach the truth of Christianity. "The Spirit itself beareth witness with our spirit, that we are the children of God." "And because ye are sons, God hath sent forth the Spirit of his Son into your hearts, crying, Abba, Father."[3] Here is the consciousness of a gracious sonship, a consciousness wrought by the Holy Spirit. This is its distinction of mode, but it is none the less a fact of consciousness, and, therefore, a veritable fact of experience. In this experience we grasp the central facts of Christianity, and the truth of Christianity itself.

The certitude requisite to a science of theology is thus reached. The result is not affected by any peculiarity of the experience, as compared with that which underlies the physical sciences. The method is the same in both, and as valid in the former as in the latter. Some truths we grasp by intuition. "There are other truths that come to verification in consciousness by a process, or by practical experiment; such are more commonly called truths of experience—that is, we prove them by applying experimental tests and by realizing promised results. Such are truths of the following and similar kind Christ promises to realize in us certain experiences if we will comply with certain conditions. It is the common law of experimental science. When

ity; *Faith and Free Thought, Lectures;* Bishop Foster: *The Supernatural Book*:

Argument from the character of Christ—Ullman: *The Sinlessness of Jesus;* Barnes: *The Evidences of Christianity,* lect. viii; Bayne: *The Testimony of Christ to Christianity;* Young: *The Christ of History;* Hopkins: *Evidences of Christianity,* lect viii; Mozley: *Lectures and Other Theological Papers,* pp. 116–135, Fisher: *Supernatural Origin of Christianity,* essay xii, Schaff: *The Person of Christ,* Bushnell *Nature and the Supernatural,* chap. x; Hardwicke: *Christ and Other Masters;* Lacordaire: *Jesus Christ;* Luthardt: *Fundamental Truths of Christianity,* lect x, Rowe: Lect ii, *Bampton Lectures,* 1877.

[1] John vii, 16, 17.   [2] 1 John v, 10.   [3] Rom. viii, 16; Gal. iv, 6.

we find at the end of an experiment a result, we demonstrate in experience a truth. Henceforth we know it to be a truth, because we have made it matter of experience, not because of any external testimony to it. Such is precisely the test which Christ proposes; if we do certain things we shall come to certain knowledges; if we come to him we shall find rest; if we do his will we shall know of the doctrine; if we believe we shall be saved; old things will pass away, and all things will become new; we will become new creatures; a new life will come to us, and will evidence itself in our consciousness, and in the total change of our whole character, external and internal; for sorrow we shall have joy; for a sense of guilt we will receive a sense of pardon; for a love of sin we will have given to us a hungering and thirsting after righteousness; from feeling that we are aliens and strangers we shall come to know that we are the children of God—the Abba, Father, will be put upon our tongues and in our hearts."[1]

The Christian centuries furnish innumerable instances of such INSTANCES OF THIS EXPERI-ENCE experience. They are found among the most diverse races, and among the most gifted and cultured, as among the uncultured and lowly. They are competent witnesses to the reality of this experience. They know the facts of the experience as revealed in their own consciousness, and their testimony has often been given at a cost which allows no question of their integrity. The certainty of Christian truth is thus reached through experience. Further, there is here a unity of experience which verifies the truth and divinity of Christianity. This experience is one through all the Christian centuries and in all the diversities of condition. There must, therefore, be reality and divinity in the Christianity out of which it springs. The physical sciences would be impossible without a uniformity of experience. There must be a unity of experience. The objective facts must be the same for all. There could be no such unity without the reality of the objective facts of experience. This principle is just as valid in Christianity as in the physical sciences. If these sciences deal with realities, so does Christian theology deal with realities. The truth of Christianity is thus realized in Christian experience, and in the most thorough manner. "The nerve of the matter does not lie here—that both exist side by side, the outward and objective testimony and the personal and subjective spirit; it lies here—that both the genuinely objective and the subjective are brought into one, and thus into *a bond of unity,* by virtue of which our certainty knows itself to be grounded in objective Christian truth that makes itself

[1] Bishop Foster: *The Supernatural Book,* p. 318

evident and authoritative to the spirit."[1]   We thus have the certitude requisite to a science of theology.

4. *Consistency of Faith with Scientific Certitude.*—Theology is denied a scientific position on the assumption that it deals with matters of faith, not with matters of fact. This assumption goes beyond the truth. We have just seen that the vital facts of theology are grasped in experience as really as the facts of empirical science. Yet we admit an important office of faith in theology. It is in the mode of faith that we apprehend various truths of theology. If a scientific position is therefore denied to theology it must be on the assumption that such faith rests on mere authority, and is wholly without rational ground. Again, the assumption is false to the facts. The evidences which verify the Scriptures as a divine revelation constitute a rational ground of faith. That gratuitous assumption wholly ignores the Christian apologetics which sets forth this ground.

Faith is not a blind acceptance of any alleged fact or principle, but its acceptance on rational ground. Such ground RATIONAL lies in the sufficient evidence of its truth. All faith GROUND OF that is properly such has respect to evidence as its ra- FAITH tional warrant. It follows that faith in its proper sense is a thoroughly rational state or act of the mind. There is no exception. Faith sometimes takes the form of trust. In a profound sense of need the soul trusts in God for his gracious help. The rational ground of this trust lies in the evidences of his goodness. The case is not other even when in seasons of deepest trial there is no outer light upon the ways of God. The evidences of his wisdom and love still furnish a thoroughly rational ground of trust. It was so with Abraham in the offering up of his son,[2] with Job when seemingly God was against him;[3] with Paul, who in the deepest trials still knew whom he believed, and in whom therefore he still rested with an unwavering trust.[4] There are mysteries of doctrine in theology. We may instance the Trinity and the person of Christ. We have no power to comprehend these doctrines; and yet we accept them in faith. It will readily be asked, How can such a faith be rational? Science is as really concerned in this question as theology. There are many mysteries of nature within the assumed attainments of science.[5] That every atom of matter attracts every other atom of the universe, even to the remotest world, is as profound a mystery for rational thought as either the Trinity or

[1] Dorner *Christian Doctrine*, vol. i, p. 154

[2] Heb. xi, 17–19.   [3] Job xiii, 15   [4] 2 Tim. i, 12

[5] Bowne : *Philosophy of Theism*, pp 17, 18.

the person of Christ. But the question utterly mistakes the nature
and grounds of faith. In no case is the rational comprehension of any alleged fact or principle the ground of faith in its
truth. Such ground lies wholly in the evidence of its truth.
When the evidence is adequate the faith is rational. Nor is the
mystery of a doctrine in any sense opposed to the rationality of
faith in its truth when the evidence is adequate. Such is our faith
in the doctrines of the Trinity and the person of Christ. These
doctrines are in the Scriptures; and the Scriptures bear the seal of
a divine original. They are a revelation of truth from God. The
proof is conclusive. God's revelation of truth is truth itself, and
the most certain truth. The principle is valid for all the doctrinal
contents of the Scriptures. Thus when we reach the true grounds
of faith we still find the certitude requisite to a science of theology.

The empirical sciences cannot exclude the principle of faith.

NO SCIENCE
POSSIBLE
WITHOUT
FAITH.
Such exclusion would reduce them to the narrowest
limits, if not render them wholly impossible. We
previously pointed out that all empirical knowledge of
facts is purely personal. No one can share the experiences of another. Hence the scientist, in whatever sphere of nature, must either limit himself to facts of his own observation or
appropriate the observations of others. In the former case the attainable facts are insufficient for the construction of any science.
This exigency constrains the use of reported observations. This
use is very common in the treatment of the sciences. It appears
in astronomy, in geology, in archæology, in chemistry, in botany,
in physiology, in natural history, in any and all of the sciences.
The only ground of certainty in the facts so used is the testimony
of such as report them. But testimony furnishes no empirical
knowledge; it furnishes the ground of faith, and of faith only.
Thus it is that the empirical sciences largely build on faith, and
must so build. Theology has the same right, and is equally sure
of its facts. We have philosophies of history, which, if properly
such, must contain all that a science of history could mean. No
man can be personally cognizant of facts sufficient in number for
such a philosophy or science. Faith in facts as given on testimony
must underlie all such work.[1] If this mode is valid for science it
must be valid for theology.

There is another fact which concerns this question. It is not
only true that one's experience is purely personal to himself, but
equally true that his experience is purely of individual things. In
all the realm of nature no one has, or can have, empirical knowl-

[1] Tatham: *Chart and Scale of Truth*, vol. i, pp. 204-208.

edge of any thing beyond the few facts of his own observation or testing. Families, species, genera, as known in science or logic, are no empirical cognitions, but creations of thought which must transcend experience. Yet they are necessary ideas of science. By a proper testing one finds the qualities of a specimen of metal or mineral, or of a particular plant or animal, and proceeds to a scientific classification of all like instances as possessing the same qualities. However, the principle on which he proceeds is just the reverse of the Aristotelian, that what is true of the class is true of each individual; it is that what is true of one or a few is true of all like instances. But how does he know that the many untested cases are so like the tested few as to meet the requirements of a scientific classification? It will not suffice that in appearance they are the same. The appearance is merely superficial, and may fail to give the interior facts. The qualities of the few tested cases were not given in the appearance, but found by a deep and thorough searching. There is no such testing or empirical knowledge, except in a very few instances of the great multitude assumed to be covered by the science. Thus it is that in every sphere of nature science is made to cover a vast aggregate of individuals which were never properly tested. How can empirical science justify itself in such cases? Only on the assumption of some principle that guarantees the uniformity of nature, or that determines the intrinsic identity of things superficially alike. Such science could not else proceed beyond the few facts empirically known, and therefore would be an impossibility. We are not here concerned to dispute the legitimacy of this method of science; but we may with propriety point out and emphasize its wide departure from that narrow empiricism on the ground of which the claim of theology to a scientific position is denied. The ground of this denial is thus entirely surrendered. Science itself has too much to do with matters of faith to dispute the scientific claim of theology because it has to do with such matters. There is no inconsistency of faith with scientific certitude.[1]

5. *The Function of Reason in Theology.*—The errors of rationalism must not discredit the offices of our rational intelligence in questions of religion and theology. A system of Christian doctrines is no more possible without rational thought than the construction of any science within the realm of nature. There is in the two cases the same intellectual requirement in dealing with the material out of which the science is wrought.

[1] Herbert: *Modern Realism*, pp 357-367

The idea of religion as a faith and practice is the idea of a person rationally endowed and acting in the deepest form of his rational agency. It is true that a religious life is impossible without the activity of the moral and religious sensibilities—just as there cannot be for us either society, or friendship, or country, or home, or a world of beauty without the appropriate feeling. But mere feeling will not answer for any of these profoundly interesting states. There must be the activity of thought as the condition and illumination of such feeling. So it is in religion: God and duty must come into thought before the heart can respond in the proper religious feeling, or the life be given to him in true obedience and worship. The religious sensibilities are natively as strong under the lowest forms of idolatry as under the highest forms of Christian theism, and should yield as lofty a service, if religion were purely a matter of feeling. The religious life and worship take their vastly higher forms under Christian theism through higher mental conceptions of God and duty. There is thus manifest a profound office of our rational intelligence in religion.

REASON NECESSARY TO RELIGION.

There is not a question of either natural or revealed religion that is not open to rational consideration. Even the truths of Scripture which transcend our power of comprehension must in some measure be apprehended in their doctrinal contents in order to their acceptance in a proper faith.

ALL QUESTIONS OF RELIGION OPEN TO RATIONAL CONSIDERATION.

If we should even assume that the existence of God is an intuitive truth, or an immediate datum of the moral and religious consciousness, we must still admit that the question is open to the treatment of the logical reason. We have seen that the Scriptures fully recognize in the works of nature the proofs of the divine existence. These proofs address themselves to our logical reason, and can serve their purpose only as apprehended in our rational intelligence. When so apprehended and accepted as rationally conclusive, theism is a rational faith. Such has ever been the position of the most eminent Christian theists. They have appealed the question of the divine existence to the rational proofs furnished in the realm of nature and in the constitution and consciousness of man. Thus they have found the sure ground of their own faith and successfully repelled the assaults of atheism. The many treatises in the maintenance of theism fully recognize the profound function of our logical reason in this ground-truth of religion.

THEISM IS A RATIONAL FAITH.

The idea of a divine revelation is the idea of a capacity in us for its reception. A divine revelation is, in the nature of it, a divine communication of truth, and especially of moral and religious truth. There can be no communication of such truth where there is no capacity for its apprehension and reception. Without such capacity the terms of such a revelation would be meaningless. There can be no such capacity without our rational intelligence. We admit the value of our moral and religious sensibilities in our spiritual cognitions; not, however, as in themselves cognitive, but as subsidiary to the cognitive power of our rational faculties. Many of the facts and truths of revelation, as given in the Scriptures, are cognizable only in our logical reason. Hence the idea of a divine revelation assumes an important office of our reason in theology.

REASON CONDITIONS A REVELATION.

Are the Scriptures a revelation of truth from God? An affirmative answer must rest on rational grounds of evidence. This means that the whole question of evidence is open to rational treatment. The divine origin of the Scriptures is a question of fact. Such an origin can be rationally accepted in faith only on the ground of verifying evidence. All such evidence addresses itself to the logical reason. In experience we may reach an immediate knowledge of certain verities of religion; but all such experience is purely personal, and if it is to possess any apologetic value beyond this personal limitation, or in the mind of others, it must be treated as logical evidence of the truths alleged to be so found. Even the subjects of this experience may severally take it up into the rational intelligence and treat it as logical proof of the truths assumed to be immediately reached in experience. Beyond such experience the whole question of a divine revelation in the Scriptures is a question of rational proofs. By rational proofs we mean such facts of evidence as satisfy our logical reason. A question of fact is a question of fact, in whatever sphere it may arise. In this view the question of a divine original of the Scriptures is not different from other questions of fact within the realms of history and science. The proofs may lie in peculiar or widely different facts, but they are not other for rational thought or the logical reason. Christ openly appealed to the proofs of his Messiahship, and demanded faith on the ground of their evidence. The apostles furnished the credentials of their divine commission as the teachers of religious truth. The Scriptures demand no faith except on the ground of evidence rationally sufficient. The Church has ever recognized this function of reason respecting the divine origin of the Scriptures. Every Christian apologist, from the earliest to the latest,

APOLOGETICS AN APPEAL TO REASON

has appealed this question to our rational intelligence, on the assumption of proofs appropriate and sufficient as the ground of a rational faith in its truth. Such is the office of reason respecting the truth of a divine revelation.

Our position may seem to concede the logical legitimacy of the "higher criticism," with its destructive tendencies. If the Scriptures ground their claim to a divine original in rational proofs, have not all seemingly opposing facts a right to rational consideration as bearing upon that great question? Yes; and if such facts should ever be found decisively stronger than the proofs the divine origin of the Scriptures could no longer be held in a rational faith. The rights of logic must be conceded; and Christian apologetics has too long appealed this question to our logical reason now to forbid a consideration of seemingly adverse facts in a manner logically legitimate to its own principles and method. This is conceded in the manner of meeting the issues of the "higher criticism." Here are such questions as the Mosaic authorship of the Pentateuch, the unitary authorship of Isaiah, the genuineness and prophetic character of the Book of Daniel—questions which deeply concern the evidences of the divine original of the Scriptures. How are the destructionists met on these and similar issues? Not by denying their logical right to raise such questions, but by controverting the facts which they allege and disproving the conclusions which they reach. In these matters logic suffers many wrongs at their hand. Nor can any legitimacy of the questions raised free much of the "higher criticism" from the charge of an obtrusive and destructive rationalism.

What are the contents of the Scriptures? What are the facts which they record, with their meaning? What are their ethical and doctrinal teachings? All these questions are open to the investigation of the logical reason—just as the contents of other books. It is not meant that the spiritual mood of the student is indifferent to these questions. It may be such as to blind the mental eye, or such as to give it clearness of vision. Such is the case on many questions of the present life. What in one's view is proper and right in another's is wrong and base. What to one is lofty patriotism is to another the outrage of rebellion or lawless and vindictive war. What one views as saintly heroism another views as cunning hypocrisy or a wild fanaticism. So much have our subjective states to do with our judgments. But we are responsible for these states, and therefore for the judgments which they so much influence. A proper adjustment of our mental state to any subject

Marginal notes: RIGHT AND WRONG OF THE "HIGHER CRITICISM."

CONTENTS OF THE SCRIPTURES A RATIONAL INQUIRY

in which the sensibilities are concerned is necessary to the clearer and truer view of it. Such state, however, is not the organ of knowledge, but a preparation for the truer judgment. Sobriety is proper for all questions. Devoutness is the only proper mood for the study of the questions of religion, and therefore for the study of the contents of the Scriptures Such a mental mood is our duty in the study of the Scriptures, not that it is in itself cognizant of their contents, nor that it determines the judgment, but simply that it clears the vision of our reason and so prepares it for the discovery of the truth. With such a mental mood it is the function of our reason to ascertain the religious and doctrinal contents of the Scriptures.

A high function of the logical reason in systematic theology can hardly be questioned. A system of theology is a scientific construction of doctrines. The method is determined by the laws of logic. These laws rule all scientific work Any violation of their order is a departure from the scientific method. They are the same for theology as for the sciences in the realm of nature. The method of every science is a rational method. Science is a construction in rational thought. A system of theology is such a science. The construction of such a system is the function of reason in theology. *OFFICE OF REASON IN SYSTEMATIC THEOLOGY.*

A glance at the errors of rationalism will clearly show that there is not an item of such error in the doctrine of reason above maintained. We speak of errors of rationalism with respect to its distinctions of form rather than in view of fundamental distinctions. While varying in the matters specially emphasized, it is one in determining principle. Human reason is above all necessity and authority of a divine revelation : this is rationalism. *THE FUNCTION OF REASON IN RELIGION FREE FROM RATIONALISM*

The English deism of the seventeenth and eighteenth centuries was thoroughly rationalistic in its ground It denied all necessity for a supernatural revelation and exalted reason to a position of entire sufficiency for all the moral and religious needs of man. Whatever he needs to know respecting God and duty and a future destiny may be discovered in the light of nature. The law of nature is the cardinal idea. In consequence of this fact this form of rationalism was often called naturalism ; and, further, it was so called in distinction from the supernaturalism which underlies the Scriptures as a divine revelation. The rationalistic principles, as above stated, are the principles of the notable book of Lord Herbert which initiated this great deistic movement.[1] There is no concession that only obscure views *RATIONALISM OF THE ENGLISH DEISM.*

[1] *De Veritate, prout Distinguitur a Revelatione.*

of morality and religion are attainable by the light of reason. The position is rather that on these great questions reason is quite equal, or even superior, to the Scriptures. Many followed Herbert in the maintenance of like views : Blount,[1] Toland,[2] Collins,[3] Tyndall,[4] and others whose names are here omitted. The titles of their works clearly evince their rationalistic ground. Some of them mean an assumption to account for the Scriptures and for Christianity on purely natural grounds. The law of nature and the sufficiency of the law of nature are the ruling ideas. There is a law of nature in the sense of a light of nature on the questions of morality and religion. Nor was this idea at all original with these deists. It is in the Scriptures, in the earlier Christian literature, and so continued through the Christian centuries. About the time of Herbert, and without reference to the deistic movement which he initiated, eminent Christian writers maintained this law. We may instance Grotius[5] and Hooker.[6] These eminent authors, however, were profoundly loyal to the Scriptures as a revelation of truth from God, and the only sufficient source of truth on the great questions of morality and religion. Thus the rationalistic errors of this deism were wholly avoided. It is in this manner that the functions of reason in questions of religion, which we previously set forth, are entirely free from these errors.

Christian apologists were promptly on hand for the defense of the Scriptures as an actual and necessary revelation of truth from God, and so continued on hand through this long contention. It was a hundred-years' war. These champions of Christianity are far too numerous for individual mention. We may instance a few with their works : Cumberland,[7] Parker,[8] Wilkins,[9] Locke,[10] Lardner,[11] More,[12] Cudworth,[13] Howe,[14] Butler.[15] Varying phases of the persistent deism called for variations in the defensive and aggressive work of the Christian apologists. These variations in some measure appear in the titles of their works. While some maintained a high doctrine of reason in questions of religion, others, especially

[1] *Oracles of Reason.*

[2] *Christianity Not a Mystery.*

[3] *Grounds and Reasons of the Christian Religion.*

[4] *Christianity as Old as the Creation.*

[5] *Rights of Peace and War.*

[6] *Ecclesiastical Polity,* book i.

[7] *De Legibus Naturæ Disquisitio Philosophica.*

[8] *Demonstration of the Law of Nature and of the Christian Religion.*

[9] *The Principles and Duties of Natural Religion.*

[10] *Reasonableness of Christianity.*

[11] *Vindication of the Miracles of Our Lord.*

[12] *Dialogues ; Mystery of Godliness.*

[13] *Intellectual System.*

[14] *Living Temple,* part i.

[15] *Analogy.*

some of the later apologists, assumed a ground far too low ; but all agreed, and those of the higher doctrine as really as those of the lower, in the necessity and value of the Scriptures as a revelation of truth from God. All were thus wholly free from the errors of rationalism.[1]

The German rationalism is less definite and uniform than that of the English deism, but not less real. The same su- GERMAN RA-premacy of reason is maintained. An inspiration of TIONALISM the Scriptures is often admitted, and also that it gives to the Scriptures value for religion. But it is not such an inspiration as answers to the truth of the doctrine; nor such as can give authority to the Scriptures in matters of faith and practice. As some minds are specially gifted in the sphere of philosophy, or statesmanship, or mechanics, or art, so some minds are specially gifted in the sphere of religion. But this is from an original endowment, not from any immediate divine inspiration. There is no true inspiration, and therefore no divine authority of the Scriptures. Their contents are subject to the determining test of human reason. Whatever will not answer to this test must be rejected. What remains cannot be conceded any divine authority, but must take its place in the plane of human reason. Any value it may possess for religion must arise, not from a divine original, but from the approval of our reason. The profoundest truths of Christianity must be open to philosophic treatment and determination. Reason must comprehend the divine Trinity and the personality of the Christ, if these doctrines are to be accepted as truths of religion. The consequence must be either their outright rejection or their utter perversion through a false interpretation. This unqualified subjection of the Scriptures, with all their doctrinal contents, to the determination of human reason is the essence of the German rationalism on the questions of religion. These statements are fully justified by the best definitions of rationalism, such as may be found in the works of Wegscheider, Staudlin, Hahn, Rose, Bretschneider, McCaul, Saintes, and Lecky. These definitions are given at length in the excellent work of Bishop Hurst.[2] The substance is in this brief definition: " Rationalism, in religion, as opposed to supernaturalism, means the adoption of reason as our sufficient and only guide, exclusive of tradition and revelation."[3]

Such rationalism leads on to the perversion or elimination of all the vital truths of Christian theology, not because they are in any proper sense opposed to human reason, but because they have their

[1] Gillett. *The Moral System*, Introduction.
[2] *History of Rationalism*, Introduction   [3] Krauth-Fleming. *Vocabulary*.

only source and sufficient ground in the Scriptures. If truths at
all, they are divinely revealed truths. The ground of
their truth lies in the evidences which verify the
Scriptures as a divine revelation. To accept them
simply on such ground is contrary to the ruling principles of rationalism. Their rejection is the legitimate consequence. That
such consequence followed the prevalence of rationalism in Germany is simply the truth of history.[1] The inspiration of the
Scriptures, the Adamic fall and corruption of the race, the redemption and salvation in the vicarious sacrifice of Christ, justification
by faith, spiritual regeneration, a new life in the Holy Spirit—these
vital truths could not remain under the dominance of rationalism. .
Their rejection is simply the consequence of their inconsistency
with the determining principles of rationalism, and not that they
are in any true sense opposed to our rational intelligence. There
is nothing unreasonable in the doctrine of a divine revelation of
truths of religion above our own power of discovery; nothing unreasonable in the vital truths so given in the Scriptures. Even the
truths which surpass our power of comprehension do not contradict our reason. That any revealed truth should contradict our
reason would itself contradict all the ruling ideas of a divine revelation. There are rights of reason in questions of religion which
such a revelation may not violate, and which, indeed, would thereby render itself impossible. "We must have rational grounds for
the acceptance of a supernatural revelation. It must verify its
right to teach authoritatively. Reason must be competent to judge,
if not of the content, at least of the credentials, of revelation. But
an authority proving by reason its right to teach irrationally is an
impossible conception."[2] But truths of Scripture which, as the
divine Trinity and the personality of the Christ, transcend our
power of comprehension are not on that account in any contradiction to our reason, nor in any proper sense irrational. The
infinity of space is not an irrational idea. Indeed, it is a necessary
truth of our reason; and yet it is quite as incomprehensible as
either the divine Trinity or the personality of the Christ. But
the determining principles of rationalism, which hold the subjection of all questions of religion to a philosophic rationale, must reject these great and vital truths of Christianity.

The high function of reason in questions of religion and theology,
as previously maintained, is entirely free from all these errors of
rationalism. It is thoroughly loyal to the Scriptures as a super-

[1] Hurst : *History of Rationalism*, chap. viii.
[2] Caird · *Philosophy of Religion*, pp. 69, 70.

natural revelation of truth from God, and submissive to their authority in questions of faith and practice. It heartily accepts the vital truths of Christianity on the ground of their divine original. This is no blind submission of TRUE LOYALTY TO THE SCRIPTURES. our reason to mere authority. The word of God contains within itself the highest reason of its truth. Nothing is accepted with higher reason of its truth than that which God has spoken. The Scriptures ground their claim upon our acceptance in the sufficient proofs that they are the word of God. In this they duly respect our rational intelligence. Evangelical theology ever renews this tribute. It is useless to object that the authority conceded to the Scriptures in questions of religion would require the belief of things most irrational, or even contradictory to our reason, if divinely revealed. The objection is ruled out as utterly irrelevant and groundless. Such a divine revelation is unthinkable.[1]

IV. SYSTEMIZATION A RIGHT OF THEOLOGY.

Whatever is open to scientific treatment may rightfully, and with the warrant of reason, be so treated. There is no exception. On this common ground geology, physiology, and entomology rightfully take their place with astronomy, psychology, and anthropology in the list of the sciences. The denial of such right to theology would bar the entrance of science into the sphere which infinitely transcends every other in the richness of its material and the value of its truths.

1. *Theology Open to Scientific Treatment.*—In treating the scientific basis of theology we found in the facts all the certitude requisite to the construction of a science. The point here is that, beyond the requisite certitude, these facts are open to scientific construction. Out of the facts respecting God, as manifest in nature and revealed in Scripture, we may construct a doctrine of God. So out of the facts of Scripture we may construct a doctrine of the Trinity, and a doctrine of the person of Christ. Thus we may proceed, as theologians have often exemplified, with all the great truths of Christian theology respecting sin, atonement, justification, regeneration, and the rest. Then doctrine agrees with doctrine. The doctrines of sin, justification, and regeneration are in full scientific accord. The Christology of the Scriptures is neces-

[1] Rose: *The State of Protestantism in Germany;* McCaul: *Thoughts on Rationalism;* Saintes: *Histoire du Rationalisme,* Lecky: *History of the Rise and Influence of the Spirit of Rationalism in Europe;* Mansel: *Limits of Religious Thought;* Hurst: *History of Rationalism;* Fisher: *Faith and Rationalism;* Hagenbach: *German Rationalism in its Rise, Progress, and Decline.*

sary to their soteriology. The doctrine of soteriology through the atonement in Christ and the agency of the Holy Spirit requires the doctrine of the Trinity. Doctrines so related clearly admit of systemization.

2. *Objections to the Systemization.*—In view of the many divergences from a thoroughly evangelical theology, objections to systematic theology, and indeed to all doctrinal theology, should cause no surprise. Evangelical Christianity centers in the vital doctrines of Christian theology. Hence any departure from evangelical Christianity means opposition to its vital doctrines. Even some in evangelical association largely discount, or even decry, all doctrinal theology. This cannot be other than detrimental to the vital interests of Christianity.

One objection may be put in this form: Religion is a life, not a doctrine. This objection emphasizes the subjective form of religion. True religion is a right state of feeling and a practice springing out of such feeling. Religion is of the heart, not of the head. If the heart is right the religion is right, whatever be the doctrine. The meaning of the objection is that the cardinal doctrines of the Gospel may hinder a right state of religious feeling, but cannot be helpful to such a state. This view must be in favor with all forms of theological rationalism, and the more as the departure is the farther from a true evangelical ground.

DOCTRINE NEC-
ESSARY TO RE-
LIGION.

The truth in this case is that religion is both a life and a doctrine. Religion has its subjective form in an active state of the moral and religious sensibilities. We cannot else be religious But doctrines have a necessary part in their conditioning relation to such a state of feeling. The truth of this statement is the truth of a vital connection of doctrines with the religious life. The contrary view is philosophically shallow and false to the facts of Christian history. A religious movement, with power to lift up souls into a true spiritual life, must have its inception and progress in a clear and earnest presentation of the vital doctrines of religion. The order of facts in every such movement in the history of Christianity has been, first a reformation of doctrine, and then through the truer doctrine a higher and better moral and spiritual life Let the Lutheran reformation and the Wesleyan movement be instanced in illustration. Such has ever been, and must forever be, the chronological order of these facts, because it is the logical order. When souls move up from a sinful life or a dead formalism into a true spiritual life they must have the necessary reasons and motives for such action. The religious feelings must be quickened into practical activity. This is the necessity for doctrinal truth. Religious feelings without definite practical truths to which they respond can have little beneficial result in the moral and spiritual life, because the necessary reasons and motives for such a life are not present to the mind. When such reasons and motives are presented they must be embodied in the vital doctrines of the Gospel. Why should we repent of sin? Why believe in Christ for salvation? Why be born of the Spirit? Why be consecrated to God in a life of holy obedience and love? The true answers to these profound questions of the religious life must give the essential doctrines of Christian theology. If we should repent of sin, God must be our moral Ruler, and we his subjects, with responsible moral freedom. If we should believe in Christ for salvation, he must be the divine Son of God, incarnate in our nature, and his blood an atonement for our sins. If we must be born of the Spirit, we are a fallen race, with native depravity, and the Spirit a divine personal agent in the work of our salvation. If we should be consecrated to God in a life of holy obedience and love, it must be for reasons of duty and motives of spiritual well-being which are complete only in the distinctive doctrines of Christianity. These doctrines are not mere intellectual principles or dry abstractions, but living truths which embody all the practical forces of Christianity. The spiritual life takes a higher form under evangelical Christianity than is possible under any other form, whether ritualistic or rationalistic, because therein the great doctrines of the Gospel are apprehended in a living faith and act with their transcendent practical force upon all that enters into this life. It is surely true that any theory which discounts the value of doctrines in the Christian life is philosophically shallow.[1]

It is objected to the systemization of theology that it is valueless. In the logical order of the facts the formation of the doctrines severally must precede their construction in a system. Hence it is objected that the systemization SYSTEMIZA-TION NOT VAL-UELESS. can add nothing of value to these doctrines. It might here suffice to answer that if nothing is thus added neither is any thing abstracted; so that these doctrines suffer no detriment by their systemization. Hence the objection can have no special pertinence as against the systemization of theology, and really means opposition to all doctrinal theology. If, however, we have the doctrines, and must have the doctrines if we would have the life of Christianity, there can be no valid objection against their systemization. That systemization adds nothing of value

[1] Caird : *Philosophy of Religion*, pp 165-175.

is just the contrary of the truth. This question, however, has a
more appropriate place.

One more objection we may notice.   Doctrinal theology, and
not the especially systematic theology, engenders bigotry. Nei-
source of ther by necessity nor even by any natural tendency is a
bigotry system of theology which embodies the cardinal truths
of Christianity the source of bigotry. When these doctrines are
embraced in a living faith there must be a profound sense of their
importance, and they may be, and should be, held with tenacity
and maintained with earnestness.   This is but a proper and dutiful
contention for the faith once delivered to the saints.[1] Such contention, however, is not bigotry.   It is no blind zeal for things indifferent or of little moment, but a living attachment to the vital
truths of Christianity for the weightiest reasons.   In the forms of
rationalism from which our Lord is almost entirely dismissed little
Christian truth remains which any one should hold tenaciously or
for which he should contend earnestly ; but there is a bigotry of
negation, and the self-styled liberalist is often most illiberal.   As it
respects bigotry or the spirit of a true magnanimity, evangelical
theology has no concession to make to a vaunting liberalism.

3. *Reasons for the Systemization.*—There are many reasons.   A
few may be briefly stated.

A scientific treatment or systemization of theology is a mental
a mental re- requirement.   As by a mental tendency we are im-
quirement pelled to a study of the qualities of things, so by a
tendency equally strong we are led to a study of their relations.
This is inevitable in all profounder study.   These relations are as
real and interesting for thought as the things in their several individualities.   The most thorough study of the facts of geology,
natural history, astronomy, psychology, or ethics can neither satisfy nor limit the researches of thought.   A law of the mind com-
pels a comparison and classification of those facts in the order of
their relations, and a generalization in the laws which unite and
interpret them.   There is the same mental requirement in the study
of theology.

The results justify the systemization.   The beneficial results in
beneficial science and philosophy are manifest.   It is only
results through the inception of scientific thought, in however
crude a form, that things begin to pass out of their isolated individualities into classes.   In the extent of this result the knowledge of one is the knowledge of many.   As classifications are broadened and grounded in deeper principles knowledge advances.   The

[1] Jude 3.

more comprehensive the generalizations the fuller is the knowledge. This is the only method of advancement from the merest rudiments of knowledge up to the highest attainments of science and philosophy. Theology must not be denied this method through which other spheres of study have profited so much. It has the same right as others. It is only through a scientific treatment of doctrines that the highest attainments in theology are possible. The scientific method is thus of value in theology, just as in other spheres of knowledge. The great doctrines of religion are most intimately related and must be in scientific accord. Their scientific agreement can be found only as they are brought into systematic relations. Each doctrine is the clearer as it is seen in the light of its harmony with other doctrines. With such relations of these doctrines, it is only through their systemization that we can reach the highest knowledge of theological truth.

V. METHOD OF SYSTEMIZATION.

There is nothing in theology determinative of a oneness of method in the systemization of its doctrines. Hence variations of method naturally arise from different casts of mind. Some regard one truth as the more central and determining, while in the view of others, not less scientific or exact, some other truth should hold the ruling place. Such truth, whatever it may be, determines the method of systemization.

1. *Various Methods in Use.*—We have no occasion for even the naming of all these methods, much less for their review. STATEMENT OF Seven are given in the following very compact state- METHODS. ment : "(*a*) The analytic method of Calixtus begins with the assumed end of all things, blessedness, and then passes to the means by which it is secured. (*b*) The trinitarian method of Leydecker and Martensen regards Christian doctrine as a manifestation successively of the Father, Son, and Holy Spirit. (*c*) The federal method of Cocceius, Witsius, and Boston treats theology under the two covenants. (*d*) The anthropological method of Chalmers and Rothe. The former begins with the disease of man and passes to the remedy ; the latter divides his dogmatic into the consciousness of sin and the consciousness of redemption. (*e*) The Christological method of Hase, Thomasius, and Andrew Fuller treats of God, man, and sin as presuppositions of the person and work of Christ. Mention may also be made of (*f*) The historical method, followed by Ursinus, and adopted in Jonathan Edwards's *History of Redemption* ; and (*g*) The allegorical method of Dannhauer, in which man is described as a wanderer, life as a road, the Holy Spirit as a light, the Church as a candlestick, God as the end, and

heaven as the home." ¹   Only representative names are given with
these several methods.   Other names might be added and other
methods given.   Some would vary the above analysis and classification.   While Edwards treats redemption in the order of its biblical history, his theological method is clearly Christological.   That
of Dannhauer is just as clearly anthropological.

The aim of such methods is a unity of systematic theology which
UNITY OF DOC- is really unattainable.   There is no one principle, as
TRINES THE mostly these methods assume, in which all the doctrines
AIM. unite—no one doctrine out of which all the others may
be developed.   This may readily be shown.   In one theory blessedness is the assumed end of all things.   How can we reach this view ?
Only through the idea of God.   Hence this idea is first in order,
and the deeper truth   Further, neither the doctrine of sin nor the
doctrine of redemption can be deduced from the notion of blessedness
as the end of existence.   The anthropological method is quite as
fruitless   There is no attainment of a Christian doctrine of sin
without a Christian doctrine of God.   Hence the latter cannot be
deduced from the former.   Nor can the Christian doctrine of atonement be deduced simply from the fact of sin   No deeper unity is
THE CHRISTO- reached through the Christological method.   To the
CENTRIC names above given with this method we may add that
METHOD of Henry B. Smith as one of the latest to adopt it.
With this Christological center his leading divisions are : 1. The
antecedents of redemption ; 2. The Redeemer and his work ; 3. The
consequents of redemption ²   Antecedents and consequents are
very different terms, and mean very different relations to Christ :
the former, a relation simply in the order of time, the latter a
relation in the order of effects, or at least in the order of logic.
With this wide difference between the two classes of truths in
their relation to Christ, the unity of systematic theology thus
attempted is surely not attained.   In the subdivisions the fruit-
lessness of the method, as it respects this unity, is manifest.
There is nothing peculiar to this method, but all proceeds in the
usual natural or logical order of the doctrinal topics.   There is a
profound sense in which the doctrine of Christ is the central
truth of Christian theology ; but it is still true that other doctrines,
such as the doctrine of God and the doctrine of the Trinity, must
precede this doctrine, because we cannot else reach a true doctrine
of the person and work of Christ.   Hence the system of doctrines
cannot be developed from a purely Christological source.   This is

¹ Strong · *Systematic Theology*, p 27
² *Introduction to Christian Theology*, p. 225.

really admitted by Nitzsch, though his own method is substantially the Christological : "It cannot, therefore, be doubted that the idea of a Redeemer, or the dogma of Christ, is the primary, fundamental, and inclusive dogma of Christian doctrine, as such ; only the series of Christian dogmas cannot be developed in one and the same direction from the doctrine of the Redeemer ; for the mere progressive development of the dogma of Christ looks back, in all its elements, upon other truths which, indeed, though not independent of Christ, of his being and state, still, at the same time, are acknowledged as suppositions of his personal being and work by means of a regressive development." [1] We have thus glanced at some of these methods to show their insufficiency for the deeper unity of systematic theology at which they aim. What is thus true of some is true of all.

2. *True Method in the Logical Order.*—The method of treatment should conform to the nature of the subject. The deductive method is applicable to mathematics, but not to chemistry or psychology. Nor is it applicable to Christian theology, and for the reason already pointed out—that there is no one principle or doctrine from which the others may be deduced. In theology the work of systemization is constructive, and must proceed in a synthetic mode. In a true systemization each doctrine must be scientifically constructed, and the several doctrines must be brought into complete scientific accordance. No higher unity of systematic theology is attainable. The synthetic method will fully answer for this attainment.

By the logical order of doctrines we here mean the order in which they arise for thought, and for the most intel- SENSE OF LOGligible treatment. In this view the logical order is ICAL ORDER. little different from the natural order. Each truth, except the first, must take its place in such relation to preceding truths as shall set it in the clearest light. God is the ground-truth in religion, and therefore the first in order. Every other truth, if it would be the more clearly seen, must be viewed in the light of this first truth. For a like reason anthropology must precede Christology, and Christology must precede soteriology. This is what we here mean by the logical order.

3. *Subjects as Given in the Logical Order.*—Only a very summary statement is here required.

Theism : The existence of a personal God, Creator, Preserver, and Ruler of all things.

Theology : The attributes of God ; the Trinity ; creation and providence—in the fuller light of revelation.

_____
[1] *System of Christian Doctrine*, p. 124.

Anthropology: The origin of man; his primitive state and apostasy; the consequent state of the race.

Christology: The incarnation of the Son; the person of the Christ.

Soteriology: The atonement in Christ; the salvation in Christ.

Ecclesiology. The Church; the ministry; the sacraments; means of grace.

Eschatology: The intermediate state; the second advent; the resurrection; the judgment; the final destinies.

Apologetics is not of the nature of a Christian doctrine, and may properly be omitted from the system, as it often is. Any sufficient reason for its inclusion might properly require a treatment of all questions of canonicity, textual integrity, higher criticism, genuineness, and authenticity which in anywise concern the truth of a divine original of the Scriptures Apologetics would thus become a disproportionate magnitude in a system of doctrines.

Neither is ethics, especially theoretical or philosophical ethics, of the nature of a Christian doctrine. It is true that the grounds and motives of Christian duty lie in Christian doctrine. The requirements of such duty should not be omitted, nor can they, in any proper treatment of soteriology. But it is not a requirement of systematic theology that ethics should form a distinct part.[1]

---

[1] On the method of systematic theology—Nitzsch · *System of Christian Doctrine*, Introduction, iv; Crooks and Hurst *Theological Encyclopædia and Methodology*, pp. 420-424; Shedd · *Dogmatic Theology*, vol. i, chap. i; Dorner : *System of Christian Doctrine*, vol. i, pp. 168-184; Van Oosterzee · *Christian Dogmatics*, Introduction; Räbiger : *Theological Encyclopædia*, vol. ii, Third Division.

PART I.

THEISM.

THEISM.

CHAPTER I.

PRELIMINARY QUESTIONS.

I. The Sense of Theism.

1. *Doctrinal Content of the Term.*—Theism means the existence of a personal God, Creator, Preserver, and Ruler of all things. Deism equally means the personality of God and also his creative work, but denies his providence in the sense of theism. These terms were formerly used in much the same sense, but since early in the last century deism has mostly been used in a sense opposed to the Scriptures as a divine revelation, and to a divine providence. Such is now its distinction from theism. Pantheism differs from theism in the denial of the divine personality. With this denial, pantheism can mean no proper work of creation or providence. The philosophic agnosticism which posits the Infinite as the ground of finite existences, but denies its personality, is in this denial quite at one with pantheism. The distinction of theism from these several opposing terms sets its own meaning in the clearer light. Creation and providence are here presented simply in their relation to the doctrinal content of theism. The methods of the divine agency therein require separate treatment. Nor could this treatment proceed with advantage simply in the light of reason; it requires the fuller light of revelation.

2. *Historic View of the Idea of God.*—Religion is as wide-spread as the human family and pervades the history of the race. But religion carries with it some form of the idea of God or of some order of supernatural existence. There is no place for religion without this idea. This is so thoroughly true that the attempts to found a religion without the notion of some being above us have no claim to recognition in a history of religion. But while religion DIVERSE IDEAS so widely prevails it presents great varieties of form, es- OF GOD pecially in the idea of God, or of what takes the supreme place in the religious consciousness. Such differences appear in what are

called the ethnic. religions, the religions of different races. Of these
James Freeman Clarke enumerates ten.[1] Some make the number
greater, others less. However, the exact number does not concern
our present point In the instances of Confucianism, Brahmanism,
and Buddhism there are wide variations in the conception of God,
and equally so in the other ethnic religions. As we look into details
these variations are still more manifest. In view of the objects
worshiped, the rites and ceremonies of the worship, the sentiments
uttered in prayer and praise, we must recognize very wide differences
of theistic conception. The case is not really other, because so
many of these ideas are void of any adequate truth of theism.
They are still ideas of what is divine to the worshiper and have their
SOMETHING place in the religious consciousness. We can hardly
MORE THAN think that in the low forms of idolatry there is nothing
THE IDOL more present to religious thought and feeling than the
idol. "Even the stock or stone, the rudest fetich before which
the savage bows, is, at least to him, something more than a stock
or stone ; and the feeling of fear or awe or abject dependence with
which he regards it is the reflex of a dim, confused conception of
an invisible and spiritual power, of which the material object has
become representative."[2]

3. *Account of Perverted Forms of the Idea.*—These perverted
forms arise, in part, from speculations which disregard the imperative laws of rational thinking, and, in part—mostly, indeed—from
vicious repugnances to the true idea. When God is conceived
under the form of pantheism, or as the Absolute in a sense which
precludes all predication and specially denies to him all personal
attributes, the idea is the result of such speculation as we have just
now characterized, or a creation of the imagination. In either form
the idea is just as impotent for any rationale of the cosmos as the
baldest materialism. Neither has any warrant in rational thought.
ORIGIN OF When God is conceived under the forms of idolatry the
IDOLATRY. conception is from a reaction of the soul against the
original idea. The reaction is from a repugnance of the sensibilities to the true idea, not from any discernment of rational thought.
This is the account which Paul gives of the source and prevalence
of idolatry.[3] His account applies broadly to the heathen world.
"When they knew God, they glorified him not as God, neither
were thankful ; but became vain in their imaginations, and their

---

[1] *Ten Great Religions.*

[2] Caird : *The Philosophy of Religion,* p 177. See also, Flint : *Antitheistic Theories,* p. 521 ; Muller : *Origin of Religion,* p. 101.

[3] Rom. i, 21–25, 28.

foolish heart was darkened." Thus closing their eyes to the light of nature in which God was manifest, they "changed the glory of the uncorruptible God into an image made like to corruptible man, and to birds, and four-footed beasts, and creeping things." It was because "they did not like to retain God in their knowledge."

4. *Definitive Idea of God.*—A definition of God that shall be true to the truth of his being and character is a difficult at- DIFFICULTY OF tainment. This must be apparent whether we study DEFINING GOD definitions as given, or the subject of definition. God is for human thought an incomprehensible Being, existing in absolute soleness, apart from all the categories of genus and species. Hence the difficulty of definition. The true idea cannot be generalized in any abstract or single principle. As the Absolute or Unconditioned, God is simply differentiated from the dependent or related ; as the Infinite, from the finite. The essential truths of a definition are not given in any of these terms.' As the Unknowable, the agnostic formula is purely negative and without definitive content. Absolute will cannot give the content of a true idea of God. In order to the true idea, will must be joined with intellect and sensibility in the constitution of personality. Some of the divine titles have the form of a definition, but are not such in fact. God is often named the Almighty,[1] but this expresses simply his omnipotence, which is only one of his perfections. Another title is Jehovah,[2] which signifies the eternal, immutable being of God ; but while the meaning is profound the plenitude of his being is not expressed. "God is love."[3] There is profound truth here also ; but the words express only what is viewed as supreme in God.

The citation of a few definitions may be useful. "The first ground of all being ; the divine spirit which, unmoved INSTANCES OF itself, moves all ; absolute, efficient principle ; abso- DEFINITION. lute notion ; absolute end."—*Aristotle.* This definition conforms somewhat to the author's four forms of cause. It contains more truth of a definition than some given by professedly Christian philosophers. "The moral order of the universe, actually operative in life."—*Fichte.* Lotze clearly points out the deficiencies of this definition.[4] It gives us an abstract world-order without the divine Orderer. "The absolute Spirit ; the pure, essential Being that makes himself object to himself : absolute holiness ; absolute power, wisdom, goodness, justice."—*Hegel.* "A Being who, by his understanding and will, is the Cause (and by consequence the Author) of nature ; a Being who has all rights and no duties ; the supreme

---

[1] Particularly in the book of Job.   [2] Exod vi, 3.
[3] 1 John iv, 16.   [4] *Microcosmus,* vol. ii, pp. 673, 674.

perfection in substance; the all-obligating Being; Author of a universe under moral law; the moral Author of the world; an Intelligence infinite in every respect."—*Kant.* "*God* is derived incontestably from *good* and means the Good itself in the perfect sense, the absolute Good, the primal Good, on which all other good depends—as it were, the Fountain of good. Hence God has been styled the Being of beings (*ens entium*), the supreme Being (*ens summum*), the most perfect Being (*ens perfectissimum s. realissimum*)."—*Krug.* "The absolute, universal Substance; the real Cause of all and every existence; the alone, actual, and unconditioned Being, not only Cause of all being, but itself all being, of which every special existence is only a modification."—*Spinoza.* This is a pantheistic definition. "The *ens a se,* Spirit independent, in which is embraced the sufficient reason of the existence of things contingent—that is, the universe."—*Wolf.* These citations are found in the useful work of Krauth-Fleming.[1] Some of them con- DEFICIENT tain much truth, particularly Hegel's and Kant's. The DEFINITIONS serious deficiency is in the omission of any formal assertion of the divine personality as the central reality of a true definition. On the other hand, too much account is made of the divine agency in creation and providence. This agency is very properly included in a definition of theism, particularly in its distinction from deism and pantheism, but is not necessary to a definition of God himself.

We may add a few other definitions "God is the infinite and personal Being of the good, by and for whom the finite hath existence and consciousness; and it is precisely this threefold definition —God is spirit, is love, is Lord—this infinite personal Good, which answers to the most simple truths of Christianity."[2] Martensen gives the elements of a definition substantially the same.[3] "God is a Spirit, infinite, eternal, and unchangeable, in his being, wisdom, power, holiness, justice, goodness, and truth."[4] Dr. Hodge thinks this probably the best definition ever penned by man. PERSONALITY Personality is the deepest truth in the conception of THE DEEPEST God and should not be omitted from the definition. TRUTH With this should be combined the perfection of his personal attributes. All the necessary truths of a definition would thus be secured. Hence we define thus: *God is an eternal personal Being, of absolute knowledge, power, and goodness.*[5]

[1] *Vocabulary of the Philosophical Sciences,* pp. 683, 684.
[2] Nitzsch: *Christian Doctrine,* p. 141.   [3] *Christian Dogmatics,* p. 73.
[4] *Westminster Confession, Shorter Catechism*
[5] We give a few references, in some of which, however, we find elaborate characterizations of God, rather than compact definitions. Watson *Theolog-*

II. Origin of the Idea of God.

1. *Possible Sources of the Idea.*—We here mean, not any mere notion of God without respect to its truth, or as it might exist in the thought of an atheist, but the idea as a conviction of the divine existence. How may the mind come into the possession of this idea?

There are faculties of mind which determine the modes of our ideas. Some we obtain through sense-perception. MENTAL MODES Sense-experience underlies all such perception. We OF IDEAS cannot in this mode reach the idea of God. Many of our ideas are obtained through the logical reason. They are warranted inferences from verified facts or deductions from self-evident principles. Through the same faculty we receive many ideas, with a conviction of their truth, on the ground of human testimony. There are also intuitive truths, immediate cognitions of the primary reason. The conviction of truth in these ideas comes with their intuitive cognition. Through what mode may the idea of God be obtained? Not through sense-perception, as previously stated. Beyond this it is not necessarily limited to any one mental mode: not to the intuitive faculty, because it may be a product of the logical reason or a communication of revelation—to the logical reason; nor to this mode, because it may be an immediate truth of the primary reason.

If the existence of God is an immediate cognition of the reason, will it admit the support and affirmation of logical proof? LOGICAL REA-We have assumed that it will. Yet we fully recognize SON AS RE-the profound distinction in the several modes of our LATED TO IN-ideas. The logical and intuitive faculties have their TUITION respective functions, and neither can fulfill those of the other. Further, intuitive truths are regarded as self-evident, and as above logical proof. Yet many theists, learned in psychology and skilled in logic, while holding the existence of God to be an intuitive truth, none the less maintain this truth by logical proofs. We may mistake the intuitive content of a primary truth and assume that to be intuitive which is not really so. Many a child learns that two and three are five before the intuitive faculty begins its activity, particularly in this sphere. The knowledge so acquired is not intuitive. Yet that two and three are five is an intuitive truth. But wherein? Not

ical Institutes, vol. i, pp. 263–269; Knapp: *Christian Theology*, pp. 85, 86, Cocker: *Theistic Conception of the World*, pp. 27–37; Martineau. *Essays, Philosophical and Theological*, vol. ii, pp. 187–189; Christlieb: *Modern Doubt and Christian Belief*, pp. 219–225, Shedd. *Dogmatic Theology*, vol. i, pp. 151–194; Lotze: *Microcosmus*, vol. ii, pp. 659–688.

in the simple knowledge which a child acquires, but in the necessity of this truth which the reason affirms, in the cognition that it is, and must be, a truth in all worlds and for all minds. That things equal to the same thing, or weights equal to the same weight, are equal to one another is an axiomatic truth; but it is its necessary truth that is an intuitive cognition, while a practical knowledge of the simple fact of equality may be acquired in an experimental mode. The point made is that some truths, while intuitional in some of their content, may yet be acquired in an experimental or logical mode. \ So, while the existence of God may be an immediate datum of the moral and religious consciousness, it may also be a legitimate subject for logical proofs. It is a truth in the affirmation of which the intuitive reason and the logical reason combine. Hence in holding the existence of God to be an immediate cognition of the mind we are not dismissing it from the sphere of logical proofs.

2. *An Intuition of the Moral Reason.*—The idea of God as a sense or conviction of his existence is a product of the intuitive faculty. There is an intuitive faculty of the mind—the faculty of immediate insight into truth. Thorough analysis as surely finds such a faculty as it finds the other well-known faculties—such as the presentative, the representative, and the logical. To surrender these distinctions of faculty is to abandon psychology. To hold the others on the ground of such distinctions is to admit an intuitive faculty. It is just as distinct and definite in its function as the others, and just as different from them as they are from each other. There is nothing surer in psychology than the intuitive faculty. Of all mental philosophies the intuitional is the surest of its ground. The truths immediately grasped by the primary reason or the intuitive faculty are such as the axioms of geometry, space, time, being, causation, moral duty, and responsibility.

THERE IS AN INTUITIVE FACULTY.

The reality of an intuitive faculty means neither its independence of the mental state nor its equality in all minds. It may run through a vast scale of strength, just as the other faculties as they exist in different minds. It is conditioned by the mental development, and may be greatly influenced by the state of the sensibilities. Some of our intuitions, such as time and space, and the axioms of geometry, are purely from the intellect, and, therefore, quite free from such influence; but it is very different in the case of moral duty and responsibility, not less intuitional in their character. There may be a repugnance of the sensibilities so intense as to blind the mind to the reality of these truths. Even the more purely intellectual

INTUITION CONDITIONED BY THE MENTAL STATE

intuitions, such as causation itself, may be formally denied, simply because of their contrariety to the accepted system of philosophy, as in the instance of Hume and Mill. There is no place for the primary reason in the sensationalism which they espoused, and hence their denial of its reality. Such are the possible repressions or denials of the intuitive faculty, simply because it is a mental faculty and in such close relation with the others. Like the others, it must have proper opportunity for the fulfillment of its own functions. The trained mind has a much clearer insight into axiomatic truths than the rustic mind. The æsthetic intuitions of the cultured and refined greatly excel those of the crude mind whose life is little above the animal plane. The moral and religious intuitions of Paul infinitely transcended those of the self-debased and brutalized Nero. So much is the intuitive faculty subject to the mental state. It is none the less a reality in the constitution of the mind, with its own functions in our mental economy.

It is not only true that the intuitive faculty may thus be affected by our mental state, but also true that our moral intuitions are conditioned by the presence and activity of the appropriate moral feeling. Pure intellect may have immediate insight into axiomatic truths, but not MORAL INTUITION CONDITIONED BY THE SENSIBILITIES. into truths within the æsthetic and moral spheres. Here the appropriate sensibility is the necessary condition. This does not mean that any of our sensibilities have in themselves cognitive power, but that they are necessary to some forms of cognition. "It would be absurd to say that the moral affections have any place in a question of natural history, or chemistry, or mechanics, or any department of science; because the moral affections have nothing to do with the faculties or perceptions which are concerned with that subject-matter; but in questions relating to religion the moral affections have a great deal to do with the actual perception and discernment by which we see and measure the facts which influence our decision." [1] In like manner Hopkins distinguishes between pure reason and the moral reason, meaning by the former the faculty of immediate insight into truths which concern the intellect only, and by the latter the faculty of immediate insight into moral truths, particularly the ground of moral obligation. This insight he holds to be conditioned on a sensibility. [2] It is not meant that the moral reason is any less intuitive or rational than the pure reason, but only that, as related to a different class of truths, the

[1] Mozley : *Lectures and Other Theological Papers*, p. 8.
[2] *The Law of Love*, p. 40.

moral sensibilities are necessary to its insight. That the sensibilities which condition such insight must be in a proper state or tone in order to furnish the proper condition is clear to rational thought. That they may be, and often are, out of such state or tone is a fact above question. Hence neither errors of moral judgment nor even the denial, at times, of moral duty and responsibility makes any thing against the reality of a faculty of moral intuition. These facts will be of service in our further discussion.

The idea of God is an intuition of the moral reason. We previously pointed out the only difference between pure reason and moral reason—that the latter is conditioned upon the appropriate sensibilities. There must be an activity of the moral or religious sensibilities, not as in themselves cognitive, but as necessary to the capacity of the mind for this intuition. The idea of God has the determining criteria of an intuition in its universality and necessity. Of course both are denied, but without the warrant of either facts or reason.

IDEA OF GOD AN INTUITION OF THE MORAL REASON

In disproof of its universality instances of atheism are alleged. We have no dialectic interest in disputing the fact of real instances of speculative atheism, though not a few theists deny it. If there really are such, they can easily be accounted for on the ground of facts previously explained. We have seen that sensationalism is possible as a philosophy, though it leads to a denial of all intuitional truths, causation itself, and the axiomatic truths of mathematics. We have seen that through a perversity of the feelings the mind may be so blinded as not to see the most certain moral truths, or so prejudiced as openly to deny them. We have further seen that, while the moral and religious sensibilities are necessary to the intuition of moral and religious truth, they may be in a state of aversion or antagonism which refuses the proper condition for such intuition. It was shown that these facts do not in the least affect the reality of our intuitions. So neither the possibility nor the actuality of instances of speculative atheism can in the least discredit the truth that the idea of God is an intuition of the moral reason. When atheism puts itself forward as the contradiction of this truth it must be reminded that on the same principle it must deny all intuitive truths, for all have suffered a like contradiction. Indeed, atheism must deny all. No philosophy which renders atheism possible can admit the reality of our rational and moral intuitions. Theism is entirely satisfied with the issue at this point. It is grounded in the intuitional philosophy, while atheism is grounded in sensationalism, which must deny all intuitions of the reason. The truth is with theism.

ATHEISM NO DISPROOF OF ITS UNIVERSALITY

The criteria of an intuition are denied to the idea of God on the assumption that there are heathen tribes without this idea. Whether there are such instances is a question of fact. Whether their actuality would disprove the intuitive character of this idea is a question of logic.

The absence of this idea from minds in the lower grades of heathenism could not disprove its intuitional character.[1] ATHEISTIC HEATHENISM NO DISPROOF The reality of intuitional ideas does not mean their existence in infant minds, or even in the incipiency of youthful intelligence. In such states there is not yet the mental development necessary to the cognition of intuitive truths. This might be the case with the lowest heathen respecting the idea of God. That such minds know nothing of axiomatic truths, or of the principle of causation, or know not that five and five must be ten for all minds comprehending the terms, means nothing against the intuitional character of such truths.[2] So if such heathen should be found without any religious sentiment or any idea of God it would simply mean a lack of sufficient mental and moral development for the origin of such sentiment or idea.

Respecting the question of fact, the proof is against the existence of any such heathen. The profoundest students of NO ATHEISTIC HEATHENISM man's deeper nature are reaching the one conclusion, that he is constitutionally religious. If this is the fact, as surely it is, only the strongest historic proof could verify the existence of any tribe wholly without a religion. There is no such proof. The many reports of such tribes have been discredited. Some of these reports may have been colored by prejudice. This would be quite natural to minds in anywise skeptical or antitheistic. Not all prejudice is with theistic minds. That some have been without qualification for a proper judgment, or hasty in their conclusion, seems clear. It is not the adventurer, or sight-seer, or explorer, or even the student of some science of nature that has the proper qualification. There might be rare exceptions in the last instance. There is wanting the necessary knowledge of mind, the clear insight into the deeper nature of man. There is no other question on which the savage mind is so reserved or so difficult of access. "Many savages shrink from questions on religious topics, partly, it may be, from some superstitious fear, partly, it may be, from their helplessness in putting their own unfinished thoughts and sentiments into definite language."[3] This view is verified by facts.

[1] Morell: *Philosophy of Religion*, p. 294.

[2] McCosh *Intuitions of the Mind*, pp 48, 49.

[3] Müller. *Origin and Growth of Religion*, p. 91. See Flint. *Antitheistic Theories*, p. 256, and Quatrefages: *The Human Species*, p. 474.

Müller gives an instance in which some good Benedictine missionaries labored three years among native Australians without discovering any adoration of a deity, whether true or false. Yet they afterward discovered that these "natives believed in an omnipotent Being, who created the world. Suppose they had left their station before having made this discovery, who would have dared to contradict their statements?" With such a case before us we see how easy it is for men without the proper qualification, with a sojourn of only a few days, with no other intercourse than through an interpreter, to bring away false reports of atheistic tribes.

Sir John Lubbock formally discusses this question, maintaining FLINT'S RE- the position that among savages there are not a few VIEW OF LUB- atheistic tribes—people without any religion or any BOCK idea of a deity.[1] He surveys a very wide field and cites many authors. Professor Flint places him at the head of writers on that side of the question: "Sir John Lubbock is, so far as I am aware, entitled to the credit of having bestowed most care on the argument. He has certainly written with more knowledge and in a more scientific spirit than Buchner, Pouchet, O. Schmidt, or Moritz Wagner. He has brought together a much larger number of apparent facts than any one else on the same side has done."[2] It is with this author that Professor Flint joins issue, and follows him, "paragraph by paragraph."[3] It is made clear that in some instances Lubbock mistook the full meaning of some of the authors whom he cited; that other authors were themselves in error. Many authorities are cited which disprove their statements. The review is thorough and the refutation complete.

Other profound students of this question reach the conclusion FURTHER that the idea of God or of some supernatural being or TESTIMONY beings is universal. "Little by little the light has appeared, and the result has been that Australians, Melanesians, Bosjesmans, Hottentots, Kaffirs, and Bechuanas have, in their turn, been withdrawn from the list of atheist nations and recognized as *religious.*"[4] It should be noted that the peoples here named are among the lowest of the race. "Obliged, in my course of instruction, to review all human races, I have sought atheism in the lowest as well as in the highest. I have nowhere met with it, except in individuals, or in more or less limited schools, such as those which existed in Europe in the last century, or which may still be seen in the present day."[5] In connection with these citations there is a thorough discussion of this question, and one thoroughly

---

[1] *Prehistoric Times,* chap. xv.　　　[2] *Antitheistic Theories,* p. 259.
[3] *Ibid.,* lect. vii.　[4] Quatrefages: *The Human Species,* p. 475.　[5] *Ibid.,* p. 482.

conclusive of the author's position. "We may safely say that, in
spite of all researches, no human beings have been found anywhere
who do not possess something which to them is religion ; or, to put
it in the most general form, a belief in something beyond what
they can see with their eyes."[1] We thus have the authority of
two most thorough students of this question, and to whose judgment must be conceded the utmost impartiality.   In support
of his own position, Muller cites Professor Tiele: "The statement that there are nations or tribes which possess no religion
rests either on inaccurate observations or on a confusion of ideas.
No tribe or nation has yet been met with destitute of belief in
any higher beings, and travelers who asserted their existence have
been afterwards refuted by facts.   It is legitimate, therefore, to
call religion, in its most general sense, a universal phenomenon of
humanity."[2]

Religion even in its lowest form means the idea of some supernatural being or beings.   No fetich devotee can invest RELIGION
a divinity in a brook or tree or stone without the pre- MEANS A THE-
vious idea of its existence.   The same is true up ISTIC IDEA
through all grades of idolatry.   There are higher ideas of divinity
than the idol would suggest.   Idolatry is born of religious degeneration; its lowest forms, of successive degenerations.   It would
please evolutionists to find in fetichism a primitive religion, but
the facts of religious history forbid it.   These facts point to a
primitive monotheism.   The doctrine of St. Paul is A PRIMITIVE
fully vindicated, that idolatry is born of religious de- MONOTHEISM.
generation from a knowledge of the true God.   The most ancient
ethnic religions, however idolatrous in their later history, were
originally monotheistic.   Such was the Egyptian.   Renouf, after
maintaining this view, proceeds thus: "There are many very
eminent scholars who, with full knowledge of all that can be said
to the contrary, maintain that the Egyptian religion is essentially
monotheistic, and that the multiplicity of gods is only due to the
personification of 'the attributes, characters, and offices of the supreme God.'   No scholar is better entitled to be heard on this subject than the late M. Emmanuel Rougé, whose matured judgment
is as follows: 'No one has called in question the fundamental
meaning of the principal passages by the help of which we are able
to establish what ancient Egypt has taught concerning God, the
world, and man.   I said *God*, not *the gods*.   The first characteristic

[1] Muller . *Origin of Religion*, p. 76.
[2] *Outlines of the History of Religion*, p. 6.   Tiele also is a high authority on
this question.

of the religion is the Unity [of God] most energetically expressed:
God, One, Sole and Only: no others with Him.   He is the Only
Being—living in truth.   Thou art One, and millions of beings
proceed from thee.   He has made every thing, and he alone has not
been made.   The clearest, the simplest, the most precise conception.' " [1]   James Legge, professor of the Chinese language and literature in the University of Oxford, maintains the monotheism of
the primitive religion of the Chinese.[2]   Monotheism is found in the
religion of the very ancient Aryans, the genetic source of the Hindus
and Persian, Greek and Roman, Teuton and Celt.   In the name
Heaven-Father, under which that ancient people knew and worshiped God, Muller finds a bud which bloomed into perfection in
the Lord's Prayer.   "Thousands of years have passed since the
Aryan nations separated to travel to the north and south, the west
and the east ; they have each formed their languages, . . . but
when they search for a name for what is most exalted and yet most
dear to every one of us, when they wish to express both awe and
love, the infinite and the finite, they can but do what their old fathers did when, gazing up to the eternal sky, and feeling the presence of a Being as far as far, and as near as near can be; they can
but combine the self-same words and utter once more the primeval
Aryan prayer, Heaven-Father, in that form which will endure forever, ' Our Father which art in heaven.' " [3]   A few references may
be given.[4]

   The idea of a divine existence is a necessary intuition of the
A NECESSARY   mind.   By a necessary intuition we mean one that
IDEA.   springs immediately from the constitution of the mind,
and that, under the proper conditions, must so spring.   As there
is thus a necessary intuition of axiomatic, æsthetic, and moral
truths, so is there a necessary intuition of a divine existence.   Instances of speculative atheism cannot disprove this fact.   Nor could
the discovery of atheistic tribes of heathen disprove it.   We previously explained the consistency of such facts with the universality of the idea of God; and in the same manner their consistency
with its necessity is fully explained   That explanation need not
here be repeated.

   The universality of the idea of God means its necessity, or that,
under the proper conditions, it is spontaneous to the moral and
religious constitution of the mind.   There is no other sufficient

[1] Renouf · *The Religion of Ancient Egypt.* pp. 92, 93.
   [2] *The Religions of China*, pp. 8–11   [3] Muller : *Science of Religion*, p. 72.
   [4] Maurice : *Religions of the World*, lects. ii–iv , Wordsworth . *The One Religion*, pp. 82–86 , Rawlinson : *Religions of the Ancient World*, pp. 29–31.

account of its universality. The account has often been attempted on the ground of tradition. This has been a favorite ONLY ACCOUNT method with some Christian apologists who maintain OF ITS UNI-the necessity of a divine revelation against that form of VERSALITY infidelity which holds the sufficiency of the light of nature for all the moral and religious needs of man.[1] As tradition is presented simply as the mode of perpetuating the idea of God, this method of accounting for its universality must assume a primitive revelation of the idea. Of course no antitheistic theory could admit such an original. Christian theists do not question the fact of such a primitive revelation, but may with reason dispute the sufficiency of tradition for its perpetuation through all generations. It is true that some traditions, even without any element of profound permanent interest, have lived through all the centuries of human history, as, for instance, some incidents of the fall of man and the Noachian flood; but it cannot hence be inferred that the idea of God could be thus perpetuated. There is a wide difference in the two cases. The difference lies in this, that the idea of God has ever encountered a strong antagonism in the human sensibilities. We have seen that on this ground St. Paul accounts for the religious degeneration from the knowledge and worship of the true God into idolatry, and that the history of religion confirms this account. Mere tradition could not have perpetuated the primitive revelation against such a force. Were not the idea of God native to the human mind this antagonism of the sensibilities, strengthened and intensified by vicious habits, would long ago have led most races to its utter abandonment. It is this innateness of the idea that has perpetuated it in human thought and feeling.[2]

Some would account for the universality of this idea through the manifestation of God in the works of nature. In this view there is doubtless reference to the well-known words of Paul.[3] There is a further teaching of Paul on this question.[4] The two passages are not in any contrariety, but clearly mean different modes of the idea of God and duty. The law written in the heart means an intuition of God and duty in the moral reason. This is so different from the manifestation of God in the outward works of nature that it cannot take the same place with that manifestation in the service of those who in that mode would account for

---

[1] We may instance Ellis: *Knowledge of Divine Things from Revelation, Not from Reason or Nature;* Leland *Necessity of Revelation;* Watson: *Theological Institutes,* part 1, chaps. iii–vi.

[2] Flint: *Theism,* pp 23, 338; Cooker: *Christianity and Greek Philosophy,* pp 86–96   [3] Rom. i, 19, 20   [4] Rom. ii, 14, 15.

the universal idea of a God. With this distinction between the moral reason and the works of nature as a manifestation of God, these works address themselves to the logical reason, and the conclusion of his existence can be reached only through a logical process. But the idea of God does not wait for our reasoning processes. It springs into life before the logical faculty gets to work, especially upon so high a theme. Exemplifications are without number. The heathen world is full of them If the logical process is disclaimed the theory is surrendered, and beholding the works of nature becomes the mere occasion of the idea of God, while the idea itself is native to the moral and religious constitution of the mind. It remains true that the universality of the idea means its necessity. The idea therefore answers to the essential criteria of an intuition in its universality and necessity.

THE IDEA HAS THE CRITERIA OF AN INTUITION

Neither a primitive revelation, nor the logical reason, nor both together could account for the persistence and universality of the idea of a God without a moral and religious nature in man to which the idea is native. "A revelation takes for granted that he to whom it is made has some knowledge of God, though it may enlarge and purify that knowledge."[1] The voice of God must first be uttered within the soul. "But this voice of the divine ego does not first come to the consciousness of the individual ego, *from without;* rather does every external revelation presuppose already this inner one; there must echo out from within man something kindred to the outer revelation, in order to its being recognized and accepted as divine."[2] We are not here contradicting a previous position, that the idea of God might have its origin in either revelation or the logical reason. With the truth of that position, from which we do not depart, it would still be true that only with the intuitive source of the idea could it hold possession of the soul with such persistence and universality. It is true that in the history of the race we mostly find the theistic conception far below the truth of theism; but we have given the reasons for this fact without finding in them any contradiction to its intuitional character When we consider how early this idea rises in the mind; how persistently it holds its place through all conditions of the race; how it cleaves to humanity through all perversions and repugnances, we must think it an intuition of the moral reason.[3]

[1] H B Smith. *Faith and Philosophy,* p. 18
[2] Wuttke. *Christian Ethics,* vol. ii, p. 103.
[3] Mansel. *Limits of Religious Thought.* p. 115, Muller : *Science of Religion,* p. 12; Raymond *Systematic Theology,* vol. i, pp. 247-262 ; Fisher, *Supernat-*

3. *Objective Truth of the Idea.*—Our intuitions must give us objective truth. This may be denied, but only with TRUTH OF OUR the implication of agnosticism or utter skepticism. No INTUITIONS. mental faculty can be more trustworthy than the intuitive. If our intuitions are not truths, no results of our mental processes can be trusted. Our perceptions can have no warrant of truthfulness. Perception itself is as purely a mental work as any act of intuition. The sense-experiences which precede and condition our perceptions can be no guarantee against errors of result. If the mind cannot be trusted in its intuitions, why should it be trusted in the interpretation of the sense-experiences which mediate its perceptions? Mistakes have been made in all spheres where results are reached through a mental process, while no intuition has ever been found in error. Whatever material experience may furnish the scientist, and however necessary or useful it may be, yet the construction of a science is itself a purely mental work. All logical processes are purely mental. Mistakes are made in both experience and logic, yet we trust our faculties in both. Much more should we trust our intuitions. The more closely our mental processes are related to intuitive principles the more certainly are the results true. Hence, to deny the truthfulness of our intuitions is to discredit all our mental faculties, with agnosticism or utter skepticism as the result.

If theism must be exchanged for atheism, all rational intelligence must be added to the sacrifice. Atheism can demand THEISM UNDER-nothing less. If our faculties are wholly untrustworthy, LIES REASON-or if all mental facts belong to the order of material causalities, as atheism must assume, mind as a rational agency can have no place or part in the system. It is in this view that some Christian philosophers hold theism to be the necessary and only sufficient ground of rational intelligence. "We analyze the several processes of knowledge into their underlying assumptions, and we find that the assumption which underlies them all is a self-existent intelligence, who not only can be known by man, but must be known by man in order that man may know any thing besides."[1] "The processes of reflective thought essentially imply that the universe is grounded in and is the manifestation of reason. They thus rest on the assumption that a personal God exists."[2] "We conclude, then,

ural *Origin of Christianity*, pp. 563–575; Temple: *Religion and Science*, lect. ii; Van Oosterzee: *Christian Dogmatics*, vol i, p. 239; Calderwood: *Philosophy of the Infinite*, p. 46

[1] Porter: *The Human Intellect*, p. 662.

[2] Harris: *Philosophical Basis of Theism*, p. 81.

from the total argument, that if the trustworthiness of reason is to be maintained it can be only on a theistic basis; and since this trustworthiness is the presupposition of all science and philosophy, we must say that God, as free and intelligent, is the postulate of both science and philosophy. If these are possible, it can be only on a theistic basis."[1] If knowledge is possible there must be a rational order of things in correlation with rational mind. On the ground of atheism there can be no such order, and no such mind. Science and philosophy are no longer possible, rational intelligence no longer a characteristic of mind. Yet, after all grounds of knowledge are denied, atheism proceeds to give us a rational account of the cosmos from the initial movement in the primordial fire-mist up to the culmination in man. Down with reason in order to a riddance of God; up with reason to an independence of any rational ground of the universe. This is the demand. "Poor atheism . . . first puts out its eyes by its primal unfaith in the truth of our nature and of the system of things, and then proceeds to make a great many flourishes about 'reason,' 'science,' 'progress,' and the like, in melancholy ignorance of the fact that it has made all these impossible. If consistent thinking were still possible one could not help feeling affronted by a theory which violates the conditions of all thinking and theorizing. It is an outlaw by its own act, yet insolently demands the protection of the laws it seeks to overthrow. Supposing logical thought possible, there seems to be no escape from regarding atheism as a pathological compound of ignorance and insolence. On the one hand, there is a complete ignorance of all the implications of valid knowing, and on the other a ludicrous identification of itself with science."[2]

If atheism is true, then man is out of harmony with truth, and

MIND IN HAR-MONY WITH TRUTH.

is by his own mental constitution determined to error. The error to which he is thus determined is no trivial idea, but one that has wrought more deeply and thoroughly into human thought and feeling than any other. Such is the idea of God. Singular it is that the forces of material nature should ever originate such an idea, and singular that they should make man the victim of such a delusion and in such discord with reality, while at the same time evolving the harmonies of the universe. Man is not so formed. His mental faculties are trustworthy, and he is capable of knowledge. The intuitions of his reason are absolute truths. The intuition of God in the moral reason of the race is the truth of his existence.

[1] Bowne: *Philosophy of Theism*, pp. 116, 117.   [2] *Ibid.*, p. 265.

CHAPTER II.

PROOFS OF THEISM.

ARGUMENTS in proof of theism are of two kinds · the ontological or *a priori*, and the *a posteriori* Of the former CLASSIFICA-kind there is really only one argument, though it is TION OF ARGU-constructed in different forms. Its principle or ground MENTS is a conception of God which is assumed to conclude his existence. The *a posteriori* arguments are variously named and classed. We shall treat them under the terms cosmological, teleological, and anthropological, and in the order as thus named These arguments are inductive in logical form, and proceed from phenomena to ground, from particulars to principle or law, from effects to cause. The cosmological is grounded in the principle of causation, and proceeds with the dependence of the cosmos as the requirement of a personal cause The teleological takes the position of final cause, and proceeds with the evidences of rational purpose in the adjustments of the cosmos. The anthropological, partly cosmological and partly teleological in method, proceeds with facts in the constitution and history of man which evince and require, not only intelligence and will, but also a moral nature in the Author of his existence. These arguments are simple in form, and were in use in this discussion long before the Christian era They are open to almost limitless elaboration, but may be presented in brief form. This shall be the manner of our own treatment.

I. THE ONTOLOGICAL ARGUMENT.

1. *Logical Ground of the Argument.* — This argument is grounded in some primary conception of God, or in some *a priori* truths, which are assumed to embody the proof of his existence. These primary conceptions vary in different constructions of the argument; but the variations need not here be stated, as they must appear in the progress of the discussion We have no occasion to notice the slighter shades of variation. It will suffice that we present the argument in a few leading forms of its construction.

2. *Different Constructions of the Argument.*—The original of this argument is conceded to Anselm. His own construction of

it is substantially in this form : We have the idea of the most perfect Being, a Being than whom a greater or more perfect cannot be conceived. This idea includes, and must
include, actual existence, because actual existence is of
the necessary content of the idea of the most perfect. An ideal
being, however perfect in conception, cannot answer to the idea of
the most perfect. Hence we must admit the actual existence, for
only with this content can we have the idea of the most perfect
Being. This most perfect Being is God. Therefore God must
exist.[1]

THE ANSELMIC CONSTRUC-TION.

Of course this argument could not pass unquestioned. Gaunilon,
a monk of Marmoutier, was promptly forward with a logical criticism.[2] Many have followed him. One point of criticism is obvious.
We readily form the idea of purely imaginary beings. Hence actual existence cannot be deduced from any such idea. Anselm re-
plied, and his reply has often been repeated, that the objection is
valid with respect to imperfect or finite beings, because in their
case actual existence is not of the necessary content of the idea,
but that it is groundless as against the idea of the most perfect Being,
because in this case actual existence is of the necessary content of
the idea. This idea is not an intuitive conception. Proper analysis discloses the process of its construction. There is put into it
whatever is regarded as necessary to constitute it the conception of
the most perfect Being. For this reason the actual existence of the
Being conceived must be put into the content of the idea. It is
easy to add necessary existence to the actual existence of such a
Being. But the possession of an idea merely through such a process of logical construction cannot conclude the truth of the divine
existence.[3]

The argument as constructed by Des Cartes is thus summarily
stated : "I find in me the notion of God, which I cannot
have formed by my own power, since it involves a higher
degree of reality than belongs to me. It must have for its Author
God himself, who stamped it upon my mind, just as the architect
impresses his stamp on his work. God's existence follows also from
the very idea of God, since the essence of God involves existence—
eternal and necessary existence."[4] The last sentence, so far as it
constitutes a distinct argument, drops into the Anselmic form, and

CONSTRUCTION BY DES CARTES.

---

[1] Anselm: *Proslogion*, translated, with Gaunilon's criticism and Anselm's
reply, in *Bibliotheca Sacra*, July and October, 1851.

[2] *Liber pro Insipienti.*

[3] Ueberweg: *History of Philosophy*, vol. i, pp. 378, 383–386.

[4] *Ibid.*, vol. ii, pp. 41, 42.

hence requires no separate consideration. To the argument, as put in the former part of the citation, it is objected—just as against the Anselmic—that we have ideas of purely imaginary beings, and hence that objective reality is no implication or consequence of our mental conception. The objection is admitted so far as it relates to ideas of finite existences, and for the reason that the mind itself can originate such ideas; but it is declared groundless respecting the idea of God, for the origin of which he only is sufficient cause.

It can hardly escape notice that this argument is inductive rather than ontological, and really the same in its principles and method as the cosmological argument. Nor is it conclusive. The assumption that the idea of God cannot originate in the human mind is neither self-evident nor provable. The conclusion of God's existence as its only sufficient cause can have no more certainty than that primary assumption.[1]

Dr. Samuel Clarke attempted a demonstration of the existence of God mostly on *a priori* principles, and so far con- CLARKE'S CON-structed an ontological argument.[2] A brief statement STRUCTION. of his leading principles will suffice: 1. Something has existed from eternity. As something now is, something always was; for, otherwise, present things must have been produced from nothing, which is absolutely impossible. 2. There has existed from eternity some one unchangeable and independent Being; for, otherwise, there must have been an eternal succession of changeable and dependent beings, which is contradictory and absurd. 3. The unchangeable and independent eternal Being must be self-existent, or exist necessarily. This necessity must be absolute, as originally in the nature of the thing itself, and not simply from the demand of thought. From these principles further deductions are made respecting the perfections of the one eternal Being. The further attempt to prove the necessary existence of an eternal and infinite Being from the nature of space and time does not add to the strength of the argument. It may readily be granted that infinite space and infinite duration are necessities of thought and realities in fact; but they are not such realities as require a ground in essential or infinite being. They are neither attributes nor modes of such being, and would in themselves be the very same were there no essential being, or no mind to conceive them.

Kant's construction of this argument is not unlike that of Clarke. Necessary existence is the only ground of possible existence; there-

---

[1] Saisset: *Modern Pantheism*, vol. i, pp 27–64.

[2] *Demonstration of the Being and Attributes of God*, in the Boyle Lectures, vol ii

fore some being must necessarily exist. The necessary Being is

KANT'S CONSTRUCTION single; is simple; is immutable and eternal; is the supreme reality; is a Spirit; is God.[1] These several points are briefly but vigorously maintained.

We have presented only a few of the many forms in which this argument has been constructed. The chief aim has been to give a little insight into its principles and method. Its prominence in theistic discussion is such that it could not with propriety be omit-ESTIMATES OF ITS VALUE. ted. Estimates of its value as a proof of theism greatly differ. With some, now the very few, it is the strongest proof, while with others it is logically valueless. Among recent authors, Dr. Shedd occupies in its treatment two thirds of the pages given to the proofs of theism, while Bishop Foster dismisses it with little more notice than to remark that he never caught the argument.

II. THE COSMOLOGICAL ARGUMENT.

This argument requires the truth of three things: the principle REQUIREMENTS OF THE ARGUMENT. of causation; the dependence of the cosmos; the inadequacy of the forces of nature to its formation. Only with the truth of each can the argument furnish any proof of theism. With the truth of each the proof is conclusive.

1. *Validity of the Law of Causation.*—It is the doctrine or law of causation that every phenomenon or event must have a cause. Mere antecedence, however uniform, will not answer for the idea of cause. There must be a causal efficience in the antecedence; an antecedence with which the phenomenon or event must result, and without which it cannot result. Such is the idea of causation in which the cosmological argument is grounded. Certain postulates of the principle will be subsequently stated in order to set it in the clearest light.

The principle of causation is a truth of the reason; a self-evident CAUSATION A TRUTH OF THE REASON. truth; a truth which one may speculatively deny, but the contrary of which he cannot rationally think. The principle is practically true for all men; true in mechanics, in chemistry, in the laws of geology, in the science of astronomy, in the conservation of energy. As a self-evident or necessary truth, it needs no proof; it needs only to be set in the clear light.

"Now, that our belief in efficient causation *is* necessary can be made plain. Let any one suppose an absolute void, where nothing exists. He, in this case, not only cannot think of any thing begin-

---

[1] *Grounds of Proof for the Existence of God*: Richardson's translation.

[2] For full historic information respecting this argument: Flint: *Theism*, lect. ix, with notes.

ning to be, but he knows that no existence could come into being. He affirms this—every man in the right use of reason affirms it—with the same necessity with which he affirms the impossibility that a thing should be, and not be, contemporaneously. The opposite, in both cases, is not only untrue, but inconceivable—contradictory to reason. Such is the foundation of the principle, *ex nihilo nihil fit.* But if a phenomenon is wholly disconnected from its antecedents, if there be no shadow of a causal nexus between it and them, we may think them away, and then we have left to us a perfectly isolated event, with nothing before it. In other words, it is just as impossible to think of a phenomenon which stands in no causal connection with any thing before it as it is to think of an event, or even of a universe, in the act of springing into being out of nothing. Futile is the attempt to empty the mind of the principle of efficient causation; and were it successful, its triumph would involve the overthrow of all assured knowledge, because it would be secured at the cost of discrediting our native and necessary convictions." [1] The special point of value in this citation is in setting the idea of an event in the clear light of absolute isolation from cause. No man who is true to rational thought can think the possibility of such an event. That he cannot is because the idea of efficient causation is a necessary idea. No axiom of geometry asserts for itself a profounder necessity of thought.

Hume vainly attempted to explain the idea of causation as arising from the observation of invariable sequence in the processes of nature. [2] This would give its genesis in experience, and deprive it of all intuitive character. HUME'S DOCTRINE OF CAUSE. The interpretation contradicts the original necessity. If the idea had no deeper origin, thinkers could easily free their minds from the conviction of its necessary truth. This they cannot do. Nor has invariability of succession any thing to do with the origin of the idea. Back of all observation of the uniformity of events, and on occasion of any individual fact, there is present to thought the necessary principle that every event must have a cause. Uniformity of succession may condition the knowledge of a particular cause, but cannot condition the idea of efficient cause. This arises immediately and necessarily on the observation of the most isolated event. "The discovery of the connection of determinate causes and determinate effects is merely contingent and individual—merely the datum of experience; but the principle that every

[1] Fisher. *Supernatural Origin of Christianity,* pp. 543, 544

[2] *Inquiry Concerning the Human Understanding,* sec. vii; *A Treatise of Human Nature,* book i, sec. xiv.

event should have its causes is necessary and universal, and is imposed on us as a condition of our human intelligence itself."[1]

BROWN'S DOCTRINE OF CAUSE

Brown professedly finds a deeper origin of the idea of cause than that given by Hume, but equally eliminates from his doctrine all necessity of the idea.[2] Beyond any observed uniformity of succession, there is the broader idea that under the same conditions the past has been, and the future will be, as the present. But so long as the principle of causation is omitted nothing of real value is added to the doctrine of Hume. Nor is there, apart from the omitted principle of causation, any ground for this hypothetic extension of the idea of invariable sequence.[3]

ADEQUACY OF CAUSE

The idea of cause is not completed without the element of adequacy. The notion of efficiency must rise into the notion of sufficiency. Any deficiency of cause would leave the whole surplus of result as utterly unaccounted for as if there were no cause. Hence the necessity of thought for efficient causation equally requires an adequate cause—a cause which shall account for the entire effect. This principle has important implications. Could the eternity of matter and the eternal activity of its forces be proved beyond question, and could the nebular cosmogony, as it respects the formation of material orbs, be equally proved, these facts would fall infinitely short of a sufficient account in causation for life in its manifold forms, or for mind with its large rational and moral endowments.

ORIGINAL CAUSE

The idea of causation is complete only with the idea of an original cause. Mostly, the term ultimate is here used for the expression of the idea, but we prefer the term original. There is no cause which satisfies the idea of causation in a concatenation of causes, or in a series of natural events. However long the series, each event is as much an effect as a cause. However long the chain, the first link is as really an effect as any intermediate or even the last link, and equally requires a cause. But a beginning can have no cause under a law of mediate causation. There is still the necessity for an original, self-efficient cause ; a cause having forward relation to effects, but no backward relation to cause. *The cause* which satisfies our necessary idea must stand back of all events in the chain of mediate causes, and in absolute independence of them. "When we speak of a cause then, and of the idea of a cause which we have in our minds, the question to be decided is, Does this idea

---

[1] Hamilton : *Metaphysics*, p. 534

[2] *Inquiry into the Relation of Cause and Effect.*

[3] Mill's doctrine substantially that of Hume and Brown : *Logic*, book iii, chaps. xxi, xxii.

demand finality, or is it satisfied by an infinite chain and series of causes? We assert, then, that this idea demands finality; and adopting the maxim, '*Causa causæ, causa causati*,' we say that if a cause goes back to a further cause, then the first of these two causes is not a true and real cause, and does not satisfy the idea of a cause in our minds; and so on through ever so long a chain, until we come to a cause which has no further cause to which it goes back. That is our interpretation of the idea of cause, and we say that any other interpretation of the idea is a false one, and sets up a counterfeit cause instead of a real and true one. Let us examine what we do in our minds, in conceiving the idea of cause. First we go back for a cause; the natural want and ὄρεξις is a retrogressive *motion* of the mind. But just as the first part of the idea of cause is motion, so the last is a rest; and both of these are equally necessary to the idea of cause. And unless both of these are fulfilled in the ultimate position of our minds, we have not the proper idea of causation represented in our minds; but a law of thought is violated, that law which we obey in submitting to the relation of cause at all." [1]

Eternity of being is an inevitable implication of the principle of causation If being is a reality, being must have been eternal. Nothing can be no cause. Hence an antecedent nothingness would mean the origin of being and of the universe from nothing. This is impossible in fact, and impossible in thought. Being must have been eternal. "The idea of causation applied to this universe, then, as has been said, takes us up to an Eternal, Original, Self-existing Being. For 'how much thought soever,' says Clarke, 'it may require to demonstrate the other attributes of such a Being, . . . yet as to its existence, that there is somewhat eternal, infinite, and self-existing, which must be the cause and original of all other things—this is one of the first and most natural conclusions that any man who thinks at all can form in his mind. . . . All things cannot possibly have arisen out of nothing, nor can they have depended on one another in an endless succession. . . . We are certain therefore of the being of a Supreme Independent Cause; . . . that there is something in the universe, actually existing without, the supposition of whose not-existing plainly implies a contradiction.' Kant agrees with Clarke up to this point in the argument. He coincides with him in the necessity of an ultimate or a First Cause, as distinguished from an infinite chain of causes. 'The reason,' he says, 'is forced to seek somewhere its resting point in the *regressus* of the conditional. . . . If

CAUSATION IMPLIES ETERNITY OF BEING.

---

[1] Mozley: *Faith and Free Thought*, p. 20.

something, whatever it may be, exists, it must then be admitted
that something exists necessarily. For the contingent exists only
under the condition of another thing, as its cause, up to a cause
which exists not contingently, and, precisely on this account, without condition, necessarily. This is the argument whereon reason
founds its progression to the original Being. . . . I can never complete the regression to the conditions of the existing, without admitting a necessary being. . . . This argument, though certainly
it is transcendental, since it rests upon the internal insufficiency
of the contingent, is still so simple and natural that it is adapted
to the commonest intelligence.' " [1]

These are the necessary ideas of causation : efficiency, adequacy,
originality ; and these ideas require for the satisfaction of thought
an eternal being as the ground of dependent existences. [2]

2. *Dependence of the Cosmos.*—At an earlier day contingency
was mostly used instead of dependence for the expression of the
same idea. Leibnitz proceeded *a contingentia mundi* to the proof
of the divine existence. We use the word dependence as now
TEMPORAL ORI- preferable. The question of dependence is mainly the
GIN OF THE question of a temporal origin of the cosmos. Whatever
COSMOS. begins or becomes is dependent upon a sufficient cause
for its existence. This truth is determined by the principle of
causation. Science verifies the dependence of the cosmos. A summary statement of facts will show this.

We begin with man. The human race is of recent origin. The
proof is in geology and paleontology. Remains of man and traces
of his agency are found only in a very recent geological period;
and the principles of the science determine the impossibility of an
earlier existence.

We proceed with the lower forms of life, animal and vegetable.
Science traces their history, classifies their orders, and marks their
succession in the times of their appearance. Through these suc-
cessions science reaches a beginning of life, and back of it an azoic
state, and a condition of the world in which the existence of life
was impossible.

The nebular cosmogony, the latest and, scientifically, most

---

[1] Mozley. *Faith and Free Thought,* pp. 29–31.

[2] Porter. *The Human Intellect,* pp. 569–592 ; Hamilton. *Metaphysics,* lects.
xxxix, xl, McCosh. *Intuitions of the Mind,* pp. 228–244, Cousin. *History of
Modern Philosophy,* lect. xix, Bishop Foster. *Theism,* pp. 167–250 ; Diman.
The Theistic Argument, lect. iii; Mozley: *Faith and Free Thought,* pp. 3–48,
Randles. *First Principles of Faith,* part ii, Calderwood: *Philosophy of the
Infinite,* chap. vii.

approved theory, finds a beginning of worlds. When we speak of the nebular cosmogony as, scientifically, the most approved theory, we mean simply as an order of world-formations. Many would see in it the method of the divine working instead of the working of purely natural forces. The theory starts with the assumption of a vastly diffused fire-mist as the primordial condition of the matter out of which the solar system and the universe were formed. By the radiation of heat and the force of gravitation this mass was subject to a process of condensation. To this is added a rotary motion as upon an axis. The rapidity of this motion caused many diremptions—one, of a mass sufficient for the solar system. This mass was subject to the same laws as the original whole, and in process of time dropped off a fragment which formed itself into the remotest planet, and thus successively all the planets were formed. In this same order the universe was formed. This is the theory. It is simple in idea, however difficult of any rationale on purely natural grounds. If the theory be true, all matter once existed in a worldless state; so that there must have been a beginning, not only of all living orders and of life itself, but a beginning of worlds and systems of worlds.

We reach a beginning in another mode. Cosmical facts arise in an order of succession. This is a truth of science. It is in the facts which conclude the time-origin of the cosmos; in cosmogony; in geology; in evolution. All theories which assume to build the cosmos through an order of succession in cosmical facts primordial forces of nature must admit an order of succession in cosmical facts. This succession postulates a beginning. It gives us successive measures of time, not in equal but in veritable periods of limited duration. These, however numerous and extended, can never compass eternity. The cosmical past must be finite in time. There was a beginning of all things.

In all beginning there is dependence. A beginning is an event which must have a cause. All that begins or becomes is thus dependent. This includes all that constitutes the cosmos from the lowest forms of physical order up to man; for the dependence upon causation lies not only in an original beginning, but equally in all new beginnings and in all higher becomings.

3. *Inadequacy of Natural Forces to its Formation.*—We must not under this head anticipate what belongs to the scope of the argument teleological and anthropological arguments, though all would be in proper order here. The inadequacy of the forces of nature to the formation of the cosmos appears the clearer and stronger in the light of these arguments. It is also true that they

7

lift us to higher theistic conceptions than the cosmological argument. Still the distinction of these arguments is proper, and in the result profitable. But when this distinction is made it should not afterward be overlooked; nor should the cosmological be the subject of adverse criticism because it does not attain to all the revelation of God that is possible only to the three arguments. "It is only when we have completed and perfected the idea, and when we return to it with the results of further inquiry, that the idea of a first cause becomes clothed with religious significance. Yet, incomplete and unsatisfactory as is the mere abstract conception of a first cause, it is still an essential part of that complex and comprehensive reasoning on which, as we have seen, the argument for the divine existence rests; and it is a point of no small importance thus to ascertain, at the outset of our inquiry, that recent science, instead of dismissing the hypothesis, has supplied us with a striking evidence of the impossibility of excluding it from rational thought."[1]

Mill, in his criticism of the "argument for a first cause,"[2] really MILL'S CRITI-   admits the principle of causation, though the admission CISM OF THE   is contradictory to the determining principles of his ARGUMENT   philosophy. What, then, is the cause in which Mill finds the origin of the cosmos? Not in any thing or being back of the cosmos or above it, but in matter and force as permanent elements in the cosmos, and as eternal existences. "There is in nature a permanent element, and also a changeable: the changes are always the effects of previous changes; the permanent existences, so far as we know, are not effects at all." "There is in every object another and a permanent element, namely, the specific elementary substance or substances of which it consists and their inherent properties. These are not known to us as beginning to exist: within the range of human knowledge they had no beginning, consequently no cause; though they themselves are causes or concauses of every thing that takes place." "Whenever a physical phenomenon is traced to its cause, that cause when analyzed is found to be a certain quantum of Force, combined with certain collocations. And the last great generalization of science, the Conservation of Force, teaches us that the variety in the effects depends partly upon the *amount* of the force, and partly upon the diversity of the collocations. The force itself is essentially one and the same; and there exists of it in nature a fixed quantity, which (if the theory be true) is never increased or diminished. Here

[1] Duran · *The Theistic Argument*, p 97.
[2] *Three Essays on Religion*, pp. 142–154.

then we find, even in the changes of material nature, a permanent element; to all appearance the very one of which we were in quest. This it is, apparently, to which, if to any thing, we must assign the character of First Cause, the cause of the material universe." [1]

In this manner, fairly given in the citations from Mill, he attempts the refutation of the cosmological argument for the existence of God. It is regarded as a most skillful attempt. If he has found in matter and physical force a sufficient cause of the cosmos, then our proposition, that the forces of nature are inadequate to the formation of the cosmos, is not true, and this necessary link fails us; and with it the whole argument fails. It should here be observed that, if the cause of the cosmos which Mill REQUIREMENTS offers is the true and sufficient one, it must answer for OF MILL'S AR- the cosmos not only in its purely physical plane, but GUMENT also for all its wonderful adjustments, for all its forms of life, and for man himself with his marvelous endowments of mind. In a word, it must answer for all the requirements of the teleological and anthropological arguments as well as for the cosmological. Mill himself recognizes this implication, and makes some little attempt to meet its requirements, but with no confident tone or strength of logic. But we must not yet anticipate the teleological and anthropological arguments, though with them will come the most thorough refutation of Mill.

If any one should think that in all this contention Mill proceeds upon purely scientific grounds, and with rigid limita- MILL'S CAUSE tion to scientific facts, he would greatly err, and con- OF THE COS- sequently accord to his reasoning a conclusiveness to MOS UTTERLY INADEQUATE. which it has no rightful claim. Mill as really deals in metaphysics as ever did Plato or Anselm, Leibnitz or Kant. The eternity of matter and physical force, the conservation of energy, the eternal sameness of force in quantity and kind are no scientific facts empirically verified, but metaphysical notions, or deductions from assumed facts. For instance, if it be assumed that matter and force are the original of the universe as an orderly system, their eternity must be assumed, because they could not arise from nothing. This is precisely the method in which theism reaches the existence of an eternal being as the cause of the cosmos. When Mill admits the principle of causation he is in a region of thought as purely metaphysical as the theist when building upon that principle his argument for the divine existence. Hence we are right in denying to the argument of Mill that kind of certainty which scientific verities impart.

[1] *Three Essays*, etc., pp. 142-145.

The theory is open to an analytic testing. How is the world
ANALYTIC   constructed by the operation of physical force?
TESTS   Through a process of change. There is a long succession of changes. The cause of each change is itself a previous
change. "The changes are always the effects of previous changes."
This must be the process, if the theory is true. There is no spontaneity in physical causation; and every change must have its cause
in a previous change. But trouble thus arises for the metaphysics
of the theory. Such changes constitute a series; and for such a
series there must be a first change. But the theory asserts, and
consistently, that every change in the series is the effect of a previous change. There can be no first under such a law; and the
theory falls helplessly into the unthinkable and self-contradictory
infinite series. The principle of causation, and physical changes
as the whole of causality, will not co-operate in the same theory,
and the attempt to work them together must end in a destructive
collision.

There are further testings. The theory is that matter and force
are the first cause, and the original of the cosmos. Matter is concerned in the theory simply as the ground of force and the material
with which it builds. Respecting this force there may be two suppositions: one, that it was eternally active; the other, that after an
eternal quiescence it began its own activity. Against the former
supposition there is this determining fact: the cosmical work of
this force is wholly within the limits of time. As previously
shown, the cosmos is of temporal origin; and therefore the building it could be only a work of time. The eternal activity of such
a force and its formation of the cosmos only in time are inconsistent ideas. If we admit the eternity of force as a potentiality of
matter, still it must have been quiescent in all the eternity ante-
ceding its cosmical work.

It may be assumed that this force was eternally active, but operative as cosmical cause only in time. Assumption has large liberty,
and in this instance needs the largest. The eternal activity of such
a force and its production of cosmical results only in time are contradictory ideas. The new results could have no account in causation. A long preparatory process before any appearance of cosmical results may readily be conceded, but the notion of an eternal
preparatory process is excluded as self-contradictory. If this force
was eternally active without any cosmical production, it must have
been eternally without tendency toward such production. How
then could it move out upon a different line and begin its cosmical
work? This would be a new departure which could have no

account in physical causation. There remains to the theory the old notion of a fortuitous concursus of chaotic elements into cosmical forms.

Again, it may be assumed that the present universe is only one of an indefinite or infinite series. An indefinite series is such only for thought, and, however extended, is finite in fact, and still leaves us with an eternity ante- NO INFINITE SERIES OF UNIVERSES ceding the building of the first universe, which could have no beginning in physical force. An infinite series of universes is a contradiction—unthinkable and impossible. Hence, if cosmical causation is in physical force, that force must have begun its own activity.

There is no spontaneity in physical force. This is too sure a truth, and too familiar, to meet with any contradiction. It is the truth of the inertia of matter. All activity of NO BEGINNING IN PHYSICAL FORCE physical force is absolutely conditioned on the proper conjunction or collocation of material elements. Mill recognizes this principle in the part which he assigns to collocation as a determining law of the action of force. When such a force is within the proper collocations it must act; when out of them it cannot act. We have seen that physical force, even if an eternal potentiality of matter, must have been eternally out of the collocations necessary to any cosmical work. How then could it ever get into such collocations? This getting in means some action. But the conditions necessary to the action are wanting. A cosmical beginning in such a force is impossible—as absolutely impossible as the springing of the universe out of nothing. And the attempt to find in matter and force the first cause and the original of the cosmos is an utter failure.

4. *Theistic Conclusion.*—The principle of causation remains true. Every event must have a sufficient cause. The universe is of temporal origin and its existence must have an adequate cause. There is no such cause in matter and physical force. The sufficient cause must have power in spontaneity; must be capable of self-energizing; must have an omnipotent will. These facts do not in themselves give us the plenitude of the divine attributes as necessary to the sufficient cause of the cosmos, but they do point clearly and strongly to the personality of this cause. Even the physical cosmos points to a rational intelligence as well as to a power of will in its cause. The principle of causation requires for the existence of the universe a personal God. Such a causation does not imply the quiescence of God anterior to his cosmical work. With an eternal activity in himself, it means simply a beginning of that form of agency by which he created the universe. There must

have been such a beginning, whether the universe had its origin in the personal agency of God or in the forces of nature operating in the mode of evolution.

The theistic conclusion is very sure, though not a demonstration.

CONCLUSION.

It cannot be strictly such, because with the axiomatic principle of causation we combine the dependence of the cosmos and the inadequacy of natural forces to its formation. These are not axiomatic truths, but truths which address themselves to the logical reason. Yet the theistic conclusion is in its certainty little short of a demonstration.

III. THE TELEOLOGICAL ARGUMENT.

1. *The Doctrine of Final Cause.*—Teleology is composed of the words τέλος and λόγος, and means the doctrine of ends, or of rational purpose.[1] In the theistic argument it is the doctrine of rational purpose or design in the construction of the cosmos, as exemplified in the foresight and choice of ends and the use of appropriate means for their attainment. There are many exemplifications of the idea in human mechanisms.

EXEMPLIFICA-
TIONS OF THIS TE-
OLOGY.

The microscope and the telescope have each a chosen end, while each is wisely adapted to its attainment. The purpose is the clearer observation of things but dimly seen, or the discovery of things which the unaided eye cannot reach. The idea of divine finality is of frequent occurrence in the Scriptures. Here is an instance : " He that planted the ear, shall he not hear ? he that formed the eye, shall he not see?"[2] The special manifestation of the divine knowledge is in the purpose of the ear and the eye, and the adaptation of each to its chosen end.

This argument does not depart from the principle of causation, but builds upon it in the special sphere of rational ends.

LOGICAL PRIN-
CIPLES.

As the dependent cosmos requires an eternal being possessing spontaneity and omnipotence of will as the only adequate cause, so the many instances of adaptation to ends in the construction of the cosmos require the agency of a divine intelligence as the only sufficient cause.

2. *Rational Ends in Human Agency.*—This is so certain a truth that it is in little need of either illustration or verification.

ILLUSTRATIVE
FACTS

The history of the race is full of its products and proofs. The crude implements of the paleolithic and neolithic ages were the chosen means for the attainment of chosen ends. The rudest hut provided as a shelter from the rains of summer and the inclemency of winter is the production of human purpose. In

---

[1] Krauth-Fleming . *Vocabulary,* p 510   [2] Psa. xciv. 9.

a higher civilization, the building and furnishing of houses, the implements of agriculture, the tools and machinery used in manufacture, the products of the manufacture, the construction and form of the ship, the rudder for steering, the sails hung from the yards to catch the winds for propulsion, the telegraph, telephone, and locomotive all mean the attainment of rational ends.

We are conscious of such an agency, and easily trace the mental process. Conceiving an end, electing its attainment, MENTAL PROC- and using appropriate means for the attainment—these ESS are the facts in the process, and the facts of final cause. Each one is sure of such a mental process in others; and his certainty has a deeper ground than mere empiricism—a ground in reason itself. For such agency we require personal mind, and on the principle that every event must have an adequate cause.

3. *Rational Ends in the Cosmos.*—In the construction of the cosmos there is an orderly and pervasive plan, correlations of part to part, adaptations of means to ends which evince and require a divine intelligence as the only sufficient cause. There are two aspects of nature concerned in this argument. One appears in the orderly processes of nature; the other, in the special adaptations of means to ends. In this distinction some find two arguments, while others find one argument in two spheres [1] The distinction of arguments does not seem important, but the distinction of spheres is clearly useful. This distinction is often made without any formal notification.

An orderly constitution of nature is as necessary to a knowledge or science of nature as the rational intelligence of mind. ORDERLY CON- "If, then, knowledge be possible, we must declare STITUTION OF that the world-ground proceeds according to thought- NATURE laws and principles, that it has established all things in rational relations, and balanced their interaction in quantitative and qualitative proportion, and measured this proportion by number. 'God geometrizes,' says Plato. 'Number is the essence of reality,' says Pythagoras. And to this agree all the conclusions of scientific thought. The heavens are crystallized mathematics. All the laws of force are numerical. The interchange of energy and chemical combination are equally so. Crystals are solid geometry. Many organic products show similar mathematical laws. Indeed, the claim is often made that science never reaches its final form until it becomes mathematical. But simple existence in space does not imply motion in mathematical relations, or existence in mathematical

[1] Diman: *The Theistic Argument*, pp. 105, 106; Flint: *Theism*, p. 133; Janet: *Final Causes*, p. 12.

forms. Space is only the formless ground of form, and is quite compatible with the irregular and amorphous. It is equally compatible with the absence of numerical law. The truly mathematical is the work of the spirit. Hence the wonder that mathematical principles should be so pervasive, that so many forms and processes in the system represent definite mathematical conceptions, and that they should be so accurately weighed and measured by number.

"If the cosmos were a resting existence, we might possibly content ourselves by saying that things exist in such relations once for all, and that there is no going behind this fact. But the cosmos is no such rigid monotony of being; it is, rather, a process according to intelligible rules; and in this process the rational order is perpetually maintained or restored. The weighing and measuring continually goes on. In each chemical change just so much of one element is combined with just so much of another. In each change of place the intensities of attraction and repulsion are instantaneously adjusted to correspond. Apart from any question of design, the simple fact of qualitative and quantitative adjustment of all things, according to fixed law, is a fact of the utmost significance. The world-ground works at a multitude of points, or in a multitude of things, throughout the system, and works in each with exact reference to its activities in all the rest. The displacement of an atom by a hair's-breadth demands a corresponding re-adjustment in every other within the grip of gravitation. But all are in constant movement, and hence re-adjustment is continuous and instantaneous. The single law of gravitation contains a problem of such dizzy vastness that our minds faint in the attempt to grasp it; but when the other laws of force are added the complexity defies all understanding. In addition we might refer to the building processes in organic forms, whereby countless structures are constantly produced or maintained, and always with regard to the typical form in question. But there is no need to dwell upon this point.

"Here, then, is a problem, and we have only the two principles of intelligence and non-intelligence, of self-directing reason and blind necessity, for its solution. The former is adequate, and is not far-fetched and violent. It assimilates the facts to our own experience, and offers the only ground of order of which that experience furnishes any suggestion. If we adopt this view all the facts become luminous and consequent.

"If we take the other view, then we have to assume a power which produces the intelligible and rational, without being itself intelligent and rational. It works in all things, and in each with

RATIONAL PROCESSES OF NATURE

INTERPRETATION IN INTELLIGENCE

exact reference to all, yet without knowing any thing of itself or of the rules it follows, or of the order it founds, or of the myriad products compact of seeming purpose which it incessantly produces and maintains. If we ask why NO ACCOUNT IN BLIND FORCE

it does this, we must answer, Because it must. If we ask how we know that it must, the answer must be, By hypothesis. But this reduces to saying that things are as they are because they must be. That is, the problem is abandoned altogether. The facts are referred to an opaque hypothetical necessity, and this turns out, upon inquiry, to be the problem itself in another form. There is no proper explanation except in theism." [1] This citation possesses great logical force, and in our brief discussion will answer for the argument from the orderly system of nature.

The adaptations of means to ends, of organs to functions, in organic orders are so many, so definite, and so mani- ADAPTATIONS fest that there is little need of elaborative illustra- TO ENDS.

tion. The ground has often been occupied, and the facts presented with the clearness of scientific statement and the force of eloquent expression. No optical instrument equals the eye in the complexity and combination of parts. The organs for the functions of hearing, respiration, nutrition, locomotion, infinitely transcend all human mechanisms. The organ of the human voice in like measure excels all artificial instruments of sound. The venous system with the heart is a wonderful provision for the circulation of the blood.

Are the functions of such organs the purposed ends of their formation, or the unpurposed effects of their existence? The grossest materialism can neither question their seemingly skillful construction, nor their peculiar fitness for the functions which they fulfill. But materialism denies any and all finality in their formation. Eyes were not made for seeing, nor ears for hearing, nor feet for walking, nor hands for any of the mechanical and artistic ends which they serve. We have eyes, and so we see; ears, and so we hear; feet, and so we walk; hands, and so we use them in the service of many ends. But in no instance is there any foresight or purpose of the function in the formation of the organ. What is thus held of the organs specified is affirmed of all organs in the realm of living orders. Here is the point of issue between theism and materialism or any science or philosophy which denies a purposive divine agency in the adaptation of organs to their respective functions.

A divine finality must not here be assumed either because of the

[1] Bowne · *Philosophy of Theism*, pp. 66–69.

seemingly skillful construction of organs or because of their peculiar fitness for the functions which they fulfill. It is a question for DEFINITIVE inductive treatment; and we need a statement of the STATEMENT OF grounds upon which the induction should proceed. FINALITY. We cite the following statement: "When a complex combination of heterogeneous phenomena is found to agree with the possibility of a future act, which was not contained beforehand in any of these phenomena in particular, this agreement can only be comprehended by the human mind by a kind of pre-existence, in an ideal form, of the future act itself, which transforms it from a result into an end—that is to say, into a final cause."[1] The principles here given may be set in a clearer light by the use of illustrations. The hull of a ship, masts, sails, anchors, rudder, compass, chart, have no necessary connection, and in relation to their physical causalities are heterogeneous phenomena. The future use of a ship is not contained in any one of them, but is possible through their combination. This combination in the fully equipped ship has no interpretation in our rational intelligence except in the previous existence of its use in human thought and purpose. The use of the ship, therefore, is not the mere result of its existence, but the final cause of its construction. We give illustrations from the same author.

"The external physical world and the internal laboratory of the FURTHER IL- living being are separated from each other by impene- LUSTRATIONS trable veils, and yet they are united to each other by an OF FINALITY incredible pre-established harmony. On the outside there is a physical agent called light; within, there is fabricated an optical machine adapted to the light: outside, there is an agent called sound; inside, an acoustic machine adapted to sound: outside, vegetables and animals; inside, stills and alembics adapted to the assimilation of these substances: outside, a medium, solid, liquid, or gaseous; inside, a thousand means of locomotion, adapted to the air, the earth, or the water. Thus, on the one hand, there are the final phenomena called sight, hearing, nutrition, flying, walking, swimming, etc.; on the other, the eyes, the ears, the stomach, the wings, the fins, the motive members of every sort. We see clearly in these examples the two terms of the relation—on the one hand, a system; on the other, the final phenomenon in which it ends. Were there only system and combination, as in crystals, still, as we have seen, there must have been a special cause to explain that system and that combination. But there is more here; there is the agreement of a system with a phe-

[1] Janet · *Final Causes*, p. 85

nomenon which will only be produced long after and in new conditions,—consequently a correspondence which cannot be fortuitous, and which would necessarily be so if we do not admit that the final and future phenomenon is precisely the bond of the system and the circumstance which, in whatever manner, has predetermined the combination.

"Imagine a blind workman, hidden in a cellar, and destitute of all intelligence, who, merely yielding to the simple need of moving his limbs and his hands, should be found to have forged, without knowing it, a key adapted to the most complicated lock which can possibly be imagined. This is what nature does in the fabrication of the living being.

"Nowhere is this pre-established harmony, to which we have just drawn attention, displayed in a more astonishing manner than between the eye and the light. 'In the construction of this organ,' says Trendelenburg, 'we must either admit that light has triumphed over matter and has fashioned it, or else it is the matter itself which has become the master of the light. This is at least what should result from the law of efficient causes, but neither the one nor the other of these two hypotheses takes place in reality. No ray of light falls within the secret depths of the maternal womb, where the eye is formed. Still less could inert matter, which is nothing without the energy of light, be capable of comprehending it. Yet the light and the eye are made the one for the other, and in the miracle of the eye resides the latent consciousness of the light. The moving cause, with its necessary development, is here employed for a higher service. The end commands the whole, and watches over the execution of the parts; and it is with the aid of the end that the eye becomes the light of the body.' " [1]

TRENDELENBURG ON FINALITY.

Any denial of final cause in human agency would justly be thought irrational, or even insane. On what ground, then, shall we deny final cause in the adaptations of nature? Certainly not on the ground that organic structures are any less skillfully wrought, or with less fitness for their ends. "If it be supposed that the adaptations of external nature are less striking than the purposive actions of men, and give, therefore, less convincing indications of design, let the following remarkable passage from Mr. Darwin's work on the *Fertilization of Orchids* furnish the reply: 'The more I study nature, the more I become impressed with ever-increasing force with the conclusion, that the contrivances and beautiful adaptations

HIGHER ADAPTATIONS IN NATURE THAN IN HUMAN ARTIFICE

[1] Janet. *Final Causes*, pp. 42, 43.

slowly acquired through each part occasionally varying in a slight degree but in many ways, with the preservation or natural selection of those variations which are beneficial to the organism under the complex and ever-varying conditions of life, transcend in an incomparable degree the contrivances and adaptations which the most fertile imagination of the most imaginative man could suggest with unlimited time at his disposal.'" [1] Darwin elaborately illustrates these adaptations, and thus justifies their assignment to a place infinitely transcending all adaptations of human invention. That he accounts them to purely natural causes, and thus theoretically denies them all finality, does not in the least affect the sense of the passage in its application to the present question. There is still the indisputable fact, and to which Darwin is witness, that the adaptations of nature, of organs to functions in the orders of life, infinitely transcend all the adaptations of human mechanisms. If there is finality or purposive intelligence in the latter, how much more in the former.

It may be objected that, while mind is open to observation in FINALITY human mechanisms, it is not open or observable in the NONETHELESS organisms of nature. There is really no ground for MANIFEST BE- CAUSE NON- such an objection. Beyond the consciousness of one's PHENOMENAL. own agency, the evidences of finality in divine and human agency stand in the same relation to our intelligence. We have no direct insight into the working of other minds. If one were present with the maker of a microscope through the whole process of its construction, nothing would be open to his observation but the physical phenomena of the work. The whole evidence of design would be given in the constructive character of the microscope and its adaptation to the end for which it was made. In the realm of life we have the same kind of evidence, and vastly higher in degree, of a purposive divine intelligence in the construction of organs and their wonderful adaptation to the important functions which they fulfill. Whatever light one's own consciousness of a designing agency may shed upon the works of others, so as to make the clearer a designing agency therein, must equally shine upon the works of nature as the manifestation of a purposive divine intelligence. The objection damagingly recoils. The denial of a designing intelligence in the organic works of nature because it is not open to observation requires the denial of such intelligence in all human works except one's own.

4. *Objections to Finality in Organic Nature.*—It is objected that there are in organic structures instances of malformation, of mon-

[1] Herbert: *Modern Realism*, pp. 215, 216.

strosity even, which are inconsistent with a purposive divine agency. The objection can have no validity except against a **ABNORMAL** false view of that agency, and therefore is groundless **FORMATIONS.** as against the true view. The doctrine of divine finality does not exclude secondary causes. The forces of nature are still realities, and operative in all the processes of organic formation. Hence, that these forces in their manifold interactions should, in rare instances, so modify their normal working as to produce abnormal or even monstrous formations is no disproof of a purposive divine agency. Modern science, however materialistic its ground, holds firmly the uniformity of nature—even such a uniformity as can allow no place for a divine agency. This uniformity is held for the organic realm of nature just as for the inorganic. Hence such science can give no better account of these abnormities than we have given—indeed, must give the very same account. Doubtless there are formative forces which determine the several orders of organic nature; but aberrancies of development are still possible. " Limitations and malformations may occur, for each living thing is not only subject to the law of its kind, but is under the dominion of other forces indifferent to the end and purpose of the organic individual."[1] " As to the difficulty caused by deviations of the germ, it would only be decisive against finality if the organism were presented as an absolute whole, without any relation to the rest of the universe—as an empire within an empire, the *imperium in imperio* of Spinoza. Only in this case could it be denied that the actions and reactions of the medium have brought about deviations in the whole. The organism is only a relative whole. What proves it is that it is not self-sufficient, and that it is necessarily bound to an external medium ; consequently the modifications of this medium cannot but act upon it ; and if they can act in the course of growth, there is no reason why they should not likewise act when it is still in the state of germ. There result, then, primordial deviations, while the alterations taking place later are only secondary ; and if monstrosities continue to develop as well as normal beings, it is because the laws of organized matter continue their action when turned aside from their end, as a stone thrown, and meeting an obstacle, changes its direction and yet pursues its course in virtue of its acquired velocity."[2]

A further objection is made on the ground of useless and rudimentary organs. Seemingly, there are organs of the former class ; certainly there are of the latter. Nor are they entirely without

[1] Muller : *Christian Doctrine of Sin*, vol. ii, p. 57.
[2] Janet : *Final Causes*, p. 131.

perplexity for the doctrine of finality. Any adequate discussion of the question would lead us far beyond our prescribed limits.[1]

Respecting useless organs : " The first are few in number in the

USELESS OR- present state of science. Almost all known organs have
GANS their proper functions ; only a few oppose this law. The
chief of these organs in the higher animals is the *spleen*. It seems, in effect, that this organ does not play a very important part in the animal economy, for numerous experiments prove that it can be extirpated without seriously endangering the life of the animal. We must not, however, conclude from this that the spleen has no functions; and physiologists do not draw this conclusion from it, for they are seeking them, and are not without hope of finding them. An organ may be of service without being absolutely necessary to life. Every thing leads to the belief that the spleen is only a secondary organ ; but the existence of subordinate, auxiliary, or subsidiary organs involves nothing contrary to the doctrine of finality."[2] The case is thus put in view of the chief organ whose special function or definite part in the economy of animal life is not apparent.

Respecting the rudimentary : " There are only two known expla-

RUDIMENTARY nations of the rudimentary organs : either the theory of
ORGANS. the unity of type of Geoffroy Saint Hilaire, or the theory of the atrophy of the organs by default of habit of Lamarck and Darwin. But neither of these two explanations contradicts the theory of finality. We have seen, in fact, that there are two sorts of finality—that of use and that of plan. It is by no means implied in the theory that the second should necessarily be sacrificed or even subordinated to the first. The type remaining the same, one can understand that nature, whether by amplifying it, by inverting it, or by changing its proportions, variously adapts it according to different circumstances, and that the organs, in these circumstances rendered useless, are now only a souvenir of the primitive plan—not certainly that nature expressly creates useless organs, as an architect makes false windows from love of symmetry, but, the type being given, and being modified according to predetermined laws, it is not wonderful that some vestiges of it remain intractable to finality.

" As regards the second explanation, it can equally be reconciled with our doctrine ; for if the organs have ceased to serve, and have thereby been reduced to a minimum, which is now only the re-

---

[1] We refer to McCosh *Typical Forms*, pp. 420–439; and especially to Janet : *Final Causes*, pp. 222–247

[2] Janet : *Final Causes*, p. 223.

mains of a previous state, it does not follow that they cannot have been of use at a former time, and nothing conforms more to the theory of finality than the gradual disappearance of useless complications." [1]

We have thought it well to present these questions mostly in the treatment of a theist who is familiar with the facts concerned, and both candid and capable in their logical treatment. The defense of a divine finality in the organic realm is satisfactory.

Another objection takes the form of an inference from the working of instinct. Animal instinct is viewed as a blind impulse, without prevision or plan, and yet as working WORKING OF INSTINCT. to ends. The inference is, that the adaptations of organs to functions in organic nature neither evince nor require the agency of a divine mind. This inference is the objection to the doctrine of divine finality. In meeting this objection we are not concerned to dispute either the characterization of instinct as a blind impulse, or that it works to ends. Instances of the latter are numerous and familiar. One, however, must go to the naturalists for the fuller information.

The inference here opposed to the doctrine of final cause is just the opposite of an *a fortiori* inference. An animal is a far higher order of existence than mere matter. Animal instinct is a far higher quality or force than any quality or force of mere matter. That animal instinct works to ends is no ground of inference that material forces, once potential in the primordial fire-mist, could found the orderly system of the universe, construct the organic world with all its wonderful adaptations to ends, and create the realm of mind with its marvelous powers and achievements. Indeed, animal instinct, instead of warranting any inference adverse to the doctrine of finality, demands finality as the only rational account of the many offices which it so wonderfully fulfills in the economy of animal life.

The denial of rational intelligence in animal mechanisms is a corrected or second judgment. It is at once manifest that mere material forces could no more perform such work than they could wield the pencil of Raphael or the chisel of Angelo. The immediate judgment accounts such work to intelligence in the worker. This a second judgment corrects; not, however, in view of the work wrought, but simply in view of the animal worker as incapable of such intelligence. This fact requires, for any validity of the inference adverse to a law of teleology in the constitution of nature, the discovery that no being capable of such agency is operative therein.

[1] Janet : *Final Causes*, pp. 229, 230.

But this is the very question in issue. The necessary discovery has not been made; nor can it be made. Hence the inference drawn from the working of animal instinct against the doctrine of final cause in the cosmos is utterly groundless.

Animal mechanisms have an artificial form, not a growth form; and therein they have a special likeness to human mechanisms. Hence, if these works of instinct may warrant an inference adverse to finality, first of all they should so warrant in the case of human mechanisms to which they bear such special likeness. Can this be done? Never, as every sane mind knows. No more can they disprove a purposive intelligence in the constitution of organic nature.

The teleological argument remains in its validity and cogency. NO DISPROOF The orderly system of nature, the manifold adaptations OF TELEOLOGY. of means to ends in the organic system, infinitely surpassing all the contrivances of human ingenuity, show the purposive agency of a divine mind This is the only ground for any rationale of the cosmos. Short of a divine mind we have, at most, only matter and physical force, without any pretension of intelligence in either. No new characterization of matter can change these facts. Assuming for matter a second face, as some scientists do, is not endowing it with intelligence. This is not pretended, not even allowed. With its two faces it remains as blank of thought as the old one-faced matter of Democritus. Blind force must transform a chaotic nebula into the wonderful cosmos. Nor can it be allowed any pause with the formation of the orderly heavens and the wonderful organic world. Man, with all that may be called the mind of man, must have the same original. Then all his mechanisms, all his creations in the realms of science and philosophy and art, must be accounted to the same blind force. All purposive agency in man must be denied. If any one should here be stumbled by his own consciousness of such an agency, let him account this consciousness a delusion, and gladly, because such an agency is really out of harmony with the continuity of physical force, which, at any and all cost, must hold its way in the phenomena of mind, just as in the phenomena of matter. But the truth of a purposive agency in man will hold its place against all adverse theories of science. And so long as a human finality is admitted in the sphere of civilization the denial of a divine finality in the realm of nature must be irrational. The truth of such a finality is the truth of the divine existence.[1]

---

[1] For illustrations of finality in the cosmos—Paley . *Natural Theology;* Flint . *Theism,* lects. v, vi; Argyll · *The Reign of Law;* Chadbourne · *Natural Theology;* Tulloch . *Theism;* McCosh . *Typical Forms;* Janet . *Final Causes*

IV. The Anthropological Argument.

This argument is sometimes called the psychological, and often the moral argument. As it may properly deal with other matters than the distinctively psychological and moral nature and history of man, anthropological, as broader in its application, is preferable to either.

This argument differs from the cosmological and teleological more in its sphere than in its logical principles. In proceeding with the nature and endowments of mind to the proof of the divine existence, the principle is the same as in the cosmological argument. Then in proceeding with the adaptations of mental endowment to our manifold relations, the principle is the same as in the teleological argument. Further, there are facts of man's moral nature which clearly reveal a moral nature in the author of his being

1. *Special Facts of Organic Constitution.*—In his organic nature man belongs to the sphere of the teleological argument. But there are some special facts of his constitution which furnish special illustrations and proofs of divine finality, and may therefore properly be included in the present argument.

In complexity and completeness of structure and symmetry of form the human body stands at the head of organic existences. so far as known to us The harmony of these facts with his higher mental nature is the reflection of a rational intelligence in the author of his being. His erect form becomes his higher plane of life and fits him for the many offices which minister to his well-being. The hand is admirably fitted for its manifold uses. It is true that many useful and ornamental things are now made by machinery, but back of the machinery is the hand, without which it could not have been made. So that back of all the material products of our civilization is this same wonderful hand. Sometimes the skeleton of this hand and that of an ape are sketched side by side, and in the interest of evolution it is suggested that the seeming difference is but slight. The idea is that, if the primordial fire-mist could through a succession of differentiations and integrations construct the ape's hand, then by a little further advance on the same line it could produce the slightly varying human hand. But the Duke of Argyll has well observed that to get the real difference between the two we must compare the work of one with that of the other. In this view the difference is almost infinite. It might be said that the superior brain of man accounts for this difference; but this would

8

not give the real truth. With only an ape's hand only the rudiments of civilization could ever have been attained. The brainwork of the great inventors could have had but little outcome without the skill of the hand. What could the mental genius of Raphael and Angelo ever have achieved without the cunning hand to set in reality their ideal creations? The voice goes most fittingly with the human mind. Such a voice could have no special function even in the highest animal orders. The intelligence is wanting for the special uses of which it is capable. That a parrot may articulate a few words or a bullfinch pipe a few notes of a tune is in no contradiction to this statement. For man this voice has many uses, and uses of the highest value. It is the ready means of intelligent intercourse in human society. It serves for the intelligent and intelligible expression of all the inner life of thought and feeling and purpose, and from the simplest utterances up to the highest forms of eloquence and song. The organ which makes possible this voice in all its high uses is as wonderful as the voice itself.

It is impossible to account for the perfect harmony of these facts without a ruling mind. These notable facts, the erect HARMONY OF THE FACTS ONLY FROM IN- TELLIGENCE posture, the cunning hand, and the voice, with the organ which makes it possible, how else could they come separately and into such happy harmony with the mental grade of man? In the absence of such a mind the only resource is in matter and force, and a process of differentiations and integrations, and the influence of the environment. But down in this plane every force is blind, utterly blind. Here there can be no purposive agency. Then fortuity or necessity is all that remains. Fortuity is too absurd for any respectful consideration. To allege such a necessity is to assume for matter and physical force qualities utterly alien to their nature. A ruling mind is the only rational account of the special facts we have found in the organic constitution of man.

2. *Rational Mind a Spiritual Essence.*—Phenomena must have a ground in essential being. Outright nihilism is outright hallucination. All qualities, properties, attributes, all process, change, motion, force, must have a ground in being. Idealism may question or even deny the reality BEING THE NECESSARY GROUND OF PROPERTIES. of a material world, but on such denial must posit something essentially real as the ground of the sensations which seemingly arise from the presence and influence of such a world. In the definition of matter as the permanent possibility of sensations Mill really admits the necessity of some substantial ground of

such sensations. The agnosticism which posits the infinite or absolute as the ground of finite existences, and then pushes it away beyond all reach of human knowledge, must still hold the essential reality of such ground. We have no immediate insight into being, but our reason affirms its reality as the necessary ground of phenomena. We could just as reasonably deny the fact of a phenomenal world as to deny to it an underlying reality of being. Whatever else we may question or deny, unless utterly lost in the hallucinations of nihilism, we must concede reality of existence to the conscious subject of sensations and percipient of phenomena. Extension, form, inertia, divisibility, thought, sensibility, spontaneity must have a ground in being.

Being and its predicates, whether of properties, agency, or phenomena, must be in scientific accordance. The same principle may be put in this form: Being and its predicates cannot be in contradictory opposition. There may be such opposition simply in one's affirmation, but cannot be in the reality of things. This is not a truth empirically discovered, but is a clear and certain truth of the reason. The mind to which it is not clear and certain is incapable of any processes of thought properly scientific. It follows from the same principle that all predicates of the same subject must admit of scientific consistency, and must exclude all contradictory opposition. ·If two predicates of the same thing are in such opposition, then what is affirmed in the one is really denied in the other. To say of the same thing that it is at the same time both cubical and spherical in figure is to violate the law of contradiction as completely as to say that a thing is and is not at the same time. To predicate inertia and spontaneity of the same subject is to affirm of it contradictory properties, which must refuse all scientific consistency. These principles are intimately related to the question concerning the nature of the ground of mental facts.

NECESSARY AGREEMENT OF PREDICATES

We have what we may call physical facts or phenomena, and also what we may call mental facts or phenomena. The most groveling materialism can hardly deny a very marked difference between the two classes. In those related to matter we have the properties of extension, figure, inertia, divisibility, chemical affinity. In those relating to mind we have thought, reason, sensibility, consciousness, spontaneity. The two classes have nothing in common, and must refuse all combination in either physical or mental science. If any one denies or doubts this, let him attempt the combination. Will thought combine with extension, reason with figure, sensibility

NO COINHERENCE OF MATERIAL AND MENTAL FACTS

with divisibility, consciousness with chemical affinity, spontaneity
with inertia in any scientific construction? No material elements
or animal orders differ so widely as do the facts of mind from the
facts of matter.   Material elements and animal orders do not differ
so much.   Optics and acoustics are different sciences, and must
be because of the difference of phenomena. Chemistry and zoology
are different sciences, and must be for the same reason.   So the
facts of mind cannot be scientifically combined with the facts of
matter, not even in the utmost generalization of science.   Their
difference is not a mere unlikeness, but a face-to-face opposition.
For this reason the two classes cannot become predicates of the
same subject.   They are in contradictory opposition, and therefore
what one class would affirm of the subject the other would deny.
Mental facts cannot be the predicates of matter because they are
contradictory to its nature as revealed in its physical properties.
Spiritual mind must be the ground of mental facts.

It is beginning to be conceded that matter as traditionally known
cannot be the ground of mental facts.   Respecting naturalistic
CONCESSION OF evolution: "For what are the core and essence of this
TYNDALL.   hypothesis? Strip it naked, and you stand face to face
with the notion that not alone the more ignoble forms of animal-
cular or animal life, not alone the noble forms of the horse and lion,
not alone the exquisite and wonderful mechanism of the human
body, but that the mind itself—emotion, intellect, will, and all
their phenomena—were once latent in a fiery cloud. Surely the
mere statement of such a notion is more than a refutation."
"These evolution notions are absurd, monstrous, and fit only for
the intellectual gibbet, in relation to the ideas concerning matter
which were drilled into us when young."[1]   It follows that either
naturalistic evolution must be abandoned or matter must be newly
defined.   Spirit and matter must be considered "as two opposite
faces of the self-same mystery."   "Any definition which omits life
and thought must be inadequate, if not untrue."[2]

Here is a demand for a far more radical change in the definition
of matter than is required in the interpretation of Gen-
DEMAND FOR esis in order to adjust it to the discoveries of modern
A RADICAL science.   But what is gained by the new definition?
CHANGE OF
MATTER.   The difficulties of materialism are not diminished.   If
life and thought must be included in order to provide for naturalistic evolution, then they must be original and permanent qualities
of matter, and must have belonged to it just as really in the primordial fire-mist of science as in the present living organism and

[1] Tyndall: *Fragments of Science*, pp. 453, 454.   [2] *Ibid.*, pp. 454, 458.

the thinking mind. Of course there could be no actual or phe-nomenal existence of either. The substitution of a latent or poten-tial form for an actual form would not relieve the case, because they must none the less have been real properties of matter in that primordial state in order to their development into actual form. The notion of a double-faced matter is equally fruitless of any re-lief. One face represents the mental facts; the other, the physical facts. According to this view the two classes of facts must have the very same ground—that is, must be predicates of the same essence of being. But their contrariety makes this impossible. As we previously pointed out, some of them are in contradictory op-position. The same subject cannot possess the qualities of spon-taneity and inertia. There is no relief in any resort to a mere po-tential or latent state. Mental facts must have a ground in spirit-ual being.

3. *Material Genesis of Mind an Impossibility.*—Nothing can arise out of matter not primordially in it. This is really conceded by the call for a new definition of matter which shall include in it the ground of mental facts. The notion that any thing not primordi-ally in matter should arise out of it is contradictory to all rational thinking, and equally contradictory to the deepest principles of natu-ralistic evolution. How then shall we account for mind ? There might be assumed an eternally existent spirit-ual essence, just as there is assumed an eternally exist-ent material nature. This would avoid the direct dif-ficulty of deriving mind from matter, or of finding in matter the ground of mental facts, but the new position would be open to much perplexing questioning. Did this assumed spiritual essence originally exist in separate portions or in a mass ? If the latter, how comes its individuations into distinct personalities ? If the former, how comes their mysterious union with human bodies ? What is the law of affinity whereby a portion of the spiritual es-sence assumes each newly forming human body, or each body ap-propriates a spiritual mind ? It would be easy to answer that on any theory the facts of mind are a mystery. It is just as easy to reply, and with all the force of logic, that the facts of mind are not contradictory and absurd on the ground of theism as they must be in any purely naturalistic theory. With a divine Creator of mind we have a sufficient account of its origin and personality. This is the only sufficient account. Human minds, with their only pos-sible origin in a creative agency of God, affirm the truth of his ex-istence.

The impossibility of a material genesis of mind is deeply empha-

(margin note:) SUPPOSITION OF AN ETERNAL SPIRITUAL EX-ISTENCE.

sized by the character and grade of its powers. We have previously
LOFTY GRADE shown that there are not only marked differences, but
OF MENTAL face-to-face contrarieties between these powers and
POWERS the properties of matter. When studied in their in-
tellectual and moral forms and traced to the height of their own
scale, the more certain is the impossibility of a material source, and
with the deeper emphasis do they affirm the existence of a personal
God as their only sufficient original.

There is no occasion to expatiate upon the intellectual powers.
The history of the race is replete with their achievements. In the
multiform mechanisms which minister to our present life, in the
inventions which give us power over the forces of nature and make
them our useful servants, in the sciences which so broaden the
knowledge of nature and open its useful resources, in literature and
philosophy, in the creations of poetic and artistic genius, we see
their wonderful productions. These achievements spring from
powers which can have no basis in physical nature.

If we deny the reality of mind as a spiritual essence, separate and
SUCH POWERS distinct from matter, then we must hold the potential
NOT FROM MAT- existence of the mental faculties, with all their achieve-
TER ments, in the primordial fire-mist, and as one in nature
with the physical forces therein latent or operative. This is the
assumption of naturalistic evolution. "But the hypothesis would
probably go even farther than this. Many who hold it would
probably assent to the position that, at the present moment, all our
philosophy, all our poetry, all our science, and all our art—Plato,
Shakespeare, Newton, and Raphael—are potential in the fires of the
sun."[1] Surely this is a case of great credulity. Nor can we see
that the believers in such potentialities of the primordial fire-mist
are any less credulous. There is no support of empirical proof in
either case. It is accepted as the implication or requirement of a
mere hypothesis. In the light of reason our philosophy, and
poetry, and science, and art are not now potential in the fires of
the sun. Nor were they potential in the primordial fire-mist of science. In either case matter and physical force are the whole content. The force is of the nature of its material basis. Can this force
transmute itself into intelligence, sensibility, and will—into personality—and betake itself to the study of philosophy, and the construction of the sciences, so as to trace its own lineage back through an
unbroken series of physical causalities to the fire-mist of which it
was born? This transcends the utmost reach of theistic faith, however possible it may seem to the faith of naturalistic evolutionists.

[1] Tyndall *Fragments of Science*, p. 433.

"The question is this: How, in a nature without an end, does there appear all at once a being capable of pursuing an end? This capacity, it is said, is the product of his organization. But how should an organization, which by hypothesis would only be a result of physical causes happily introduced, give birth to a product such that the being thus formed could divine, foresee, calculate, prepare means for ends? To this point the series of phenomena has only followed the descending course, that which goes from cause to effect; all that is produced is produced by the past, without being in any way determined, modified, or regulated by the necessities of the future. All at once, in this mechanical series, is produced a being that changes all, that transports into the future the cause of the present—that is capable, for instance, having beforehand the idea of a town, to collect stones conformably to mechanical laws, yet so that at a given moment they may form a town. He is able to dig the earth, so as to guide the course of rivers; to replace forests by crops of grain, to bend iron to his use—in a word, to regulate the evolution of natural phenomena in such a way that the series of these phenomena may be dominated by a future predetermined phenomenon. This is indeed, it must be confessed, a final cause. Well, then, can it be conceived that the agent thus endowed with the power of co-ordinating nature for ends is himself a simple result that nature has realized, without proposing to itself an end? Is it not a sort of miracle to admit into the mechanical series of phenomena a link which suddenly should have the power to reverse, in some sort, the order of the series, and which, being itself only a consequent resulting from an infinite number of antecedents, should henceforth impose on the series this new and unforeseen law, which makes of the consequent the law and rule of the antecedent? Here is the place to say, with Bossuet: 'One cannot comprehend, in this whole that does not understand, this part that does, *for intelligence cannot originate from a brute and insensate* thing.'"[1]

That this lucid and logically cogent passage deals so directly with the question of final cause does not make it less applicable to the present point. It proceeds and concludes with the impossibility of a material genesis of our faculties of intelligence.

The moral faculties rise to the highest grade of mental endowment. As rational intelligence rises above the highest forms of sentience and instinct, so the moral nature rises above the purely intellectual nature. The moral reason, the conscience, the sense of God and duty are the crown of

[1] Janet: *Final Causes*, pp. 149, 150.

mental endowments. When the life is ordered according to moral principles and in obedience to moral motives, it rises to its highest form. This fact commands the assent and homage of mankind. Such a life is possible, and has often been exemplified. In many instances conscience and duty have been supreme—supreme over all the allurements of the world, and even at the cost of life. Such lofty souls belong to a higher realm than the physical. Their lives have no limitation to an earthly horizon; their clear vision grasps the infinite and the divine. The life of such souls is a free and holy obedience to the law of duty, not the determination of physical force. Yet such souls live simply according to the moral nature with which they are endowed, nothing above it. Such a moral nature belongs to the constitution of man; and our life is true to this nature, and therefore true to ourselves, only when it takes this higher form. Now, is such a life possible on materialistic ground? We have seen how utterly impossible it is to account for our intellectual life on such ground. Much less can we thus account for this higher moral life, or for the mental endowments which render it possible. The ground of such endowments must be a spiritual mind, with its only possible origin in a divine creation. The moral facts of mind are thus the proof of the divine existence.

4. *Mental Adaptations to Present Relations.*—That knowledge is possible is one of the most wonderful of known facts. PROVISIONS FOR KNOWLEDGE. That it is possible we know as a fact. The deep mystery lies in the mode of our knowing. Yet this mystery does not conceal the fact that we have faculties of knowledge in wonderful adaptation to our present relations. A little study of the facts concerned in the question must lead us up to a divine intelligence as the only sufficient original of these provisions.

We proceed on the assumption of a spiritual mind in man. This mind which is the knowing agent is in essence and attributes the opposite of matter. It is enshrined in a physical organism which shuts it in from all direct contact with the outer world. Here we meet the provisions for such contact as renders knowledge possible. Here are the sense-organs and the brain, with their relation to each other, and the relation of the mind to both. The sensations necessary to knowledge are thus rendered possible. Any material change in any of those provisions might prevent the sensations or so modify them as to render knowledge impossible. Further, the mental faculties must be capable of so interpreting those sensations as to reach a knowledge of the external world. What is the original of these adjustments? Their very remarkable character cannot be questioned. Nothing can seem more complex or difficult. The fitting of part to part in the most elaborate and complicated mechanism is too open and simple to be brought into any comparison. The only alternative to a divine original of these wonderful provisions is a blind physical force. Its utter inadequacy is manifest in the light of reason. Only a divine intelligence can be the original of such facts.

There are other facts which vitally concern the possibilities of knowledge. Here is a profound fact. The mental faculties must be in proper adjustment to the realities of nature. The mind might have been so constituted as to be capable of knowing only individual things. In this case no scientific knowledge would have been possible. Nor could any relief come from all the orderly forms of nature. On the other hand, rational faculties could not of themselves make any science possible. For any such result the orderly and rational forms of nature are just as necessary as the proper rational cast of the mental faculties. Hence the necessity for the proper adjustment between these faculties and the realities of the world. No science could else be possible. For knowledge every thing would be purely individual. There could be no genera or species, classes or families; no abstraction or generalization; no philosophy. The Comtian positivism, low as it is, is a lofty height compared with such a state. Any noble manhood of the race would be impossible. If subsistence were possible, the merest childhood of the race would be perpetual. The harmony of our rational faculties with the rational forms of nature is the possibility of science in its many spheres. Thus comes the elevation of man, the broad knowledge of nature, the sciences with their manifold utilities in our civilization, and the philosophy which underlies all true knowledge. There is a cause for all these facts—the rational cast of mind, the rational forms of nature, and the harmony of the one with the other, so that knowledge in its manifold forms is possible. Again, there are the only two alternative resources: blind force, or a divine intelligence. The utter inadequacy of the former excludes it. The facts prove the existence of a divine intelligence as the only rational account of themselves.

The sensibilities are as remarkable for their adaptation to ends as the mental faculties or the bodily organs. Mere intellectual faculties could not fit us for the present life. The springs of action are in the sensibilities. In them are the impulses to forms of action necessary to the present life. Inquisitiveness and acquisitiveness both have their impulse in the appropriate sensibilities. Without the former there could be but little attainment in knowledge; without the latter, no necessary accumulation

[marginal notes: POSSIBILITY OF SCIENCE AND PHILOSOPHY. THE SENSIBILITIES FOR ENDS.]

of property. The domestic affections are the possibility, and the only possibility, of the family. Neither wealth, nor station, nor intellect, nor culture, nor all combined can make the home. Love makes the home. The home is the profoundest necessity and the crowning benediction of human life. Some good agency, with wise intent, must have ruled the deep implanting of that love in the human soul which creates and blesses the family, and blesses mankind in this blessing. Society and the State are possible only through the appropriate sensibilities. These are richly provided in the constitution of human nature. There is the social affection which finds satisfaction in the fellowship of others. There are all the kindly affections which are the life and beauty of society. Patriotism, native to the human soul, is the life and strength of the State. The æsthetic sensibilities open to us a world of beauty and pleasure in the forms of nature and the creations of artistic genius. Is all this mere fortuity, or the work of physical force ? It cannot be. In these endowments of mind which so widely and beneficently provide for so many interests of human life we see the purposive agency of a divine intelligence.[1]

5. *Proofs of a Moral Nature in God.*—In natural theology the chief proofs of a moral nature in God are furnished in the moral constitution and history of man. There is some light from a lower plane : for instance, in the provisions for happiness in the sentient, intellectual, and social forms of life. As provisions above all the requirements of subsistence, happiness must be their end. Hence their author must be of benevolent disposition and aim. We could not assert an absolute impossibility of benevolence apart from a moral nature. Conceivably, there might be generous and kindly impulses in a nature without moral endowment. But in the facts of human history we see that benevolence, especially in its higher forms, is ever regarded, not only as praiseworthy, but as morally good. This is certainly the case when we recognize benevolence as the constant and ruling aim. Such we must think the benevolence of God in the many provisions for the happiness of his creatures. Thus in God, as in man, we find in a moral nature the source of such benevolence. However, it is still true that in the moral constitution and history of man we find the chief expression and proof of a moral nature in God. Of course, we here view the question entirely apart from the Scriptures as a supernatural revelation from God.

In the present argument we require the proof of two things :

[1] Chalmers. *Moral and Intellectual Constitution of Man*, part ii; McCosh: *Typical Forms*, pp. 440–492.

first, that man is constituted with a moral nature ; and, second, that the moral nature of man is the proof of a moral nature in God.

REQUIREMENTS OF THE ARGU-MENT.

We study the mind in its phenomena, and thus reach a knowledge of its endowments. This is the common method of science. We thus find the mind to be rationally constituted. This is one of the certainties of psychology. In like manner we determine the several forms of intellectual faculty. In the same manner we find the mind to be constituted with sensibility, and distinguish the different

ASCERTAIN-MENT OF MEN-TAL ENDOW-MENTS

forms of feeling. Further, we find the choosing of ends and voluntary endeavors toward their attainment, and determine the mind to be endowed with a faculty of will. The several classes of mental phenomena are conclusive of these several forms of mental endowment. No phenomena of mind are more real, or constant, or common than the phenomena of conscience. But conscience means a moral nature, and can have no psychological explication without such a nature. Thus with the utmost certainty of scientific induction we reach the truth of a moral constitution of the mind. The phenomena of rational intelligence, of feeling, and of volition, which reveal themselves in the consciousness, no more certainly determine the mental endowments of intellect, sensibility, and will than the phenomena of conscience determine the moral constitution of the mind. Further statements may set this truth in a yet clearer light.

The history of the ages, the religions of the world, philosophy and poetry witness to the profound facts of conscience in human experience. The profoundest students of our

PROOFS OF A CONSCIENCE

mental nature unite in this testimony. Conscience is present in all minds, and asserts its right to rule all lives. This right is not disputed, however its authority may be resisted. In the sensibilities there are many incitements to action, and, in the absence of a supreme law, the question as to which should prevail would be merely a question of secular prudence. "But there is a superior principle of reflection or conscience in every man, which distinguishes between the internal principles of his heart, as well as his external actions ; pronounces determinately some actions to be in themselves just, right, good ; others to be in themselves evil, wrong, unjust : which, without being consulted, without being advised with, magisterially exerts itself, and approves or condemns him, the doer of them, accordingly." "Thus, that principle by which we survey, and either approve or disapprove, our own heart, temper, and actions, is not only to be considered as what is in its turn to have some influence ; which may be said of every passion, of the lowest appetites · but likewise as being superior ; as from its very nature manifestly claiming superiority over all others : insomuch that you cannot form a notion of this faculty, conscience, without taking in judgment, direction, superintendency.   This is a constituent part of the idea, that is, of the faculty itself, and, to preside and govern, from the very economy and constitution of man, belongs to it. Had it strength, as it has right ; had it power, as it has manifest authority, it would absolutely govern the world." [1]   "Every man has conscience, and finds himself inspected by an inward censor, by whom he is threatened and kept in awe (reverence mingled with dread) ; and this power, watching over the law, is nothing arbitrarily (optionally) adopted by himself, but is interwoven with his substance." [2]

While conscience is thus at once the central fact and the proof of THE PROOF OF a moral nature in man, it is the clear proof of a moral A MORAL NAT- nature in God.   "Hence, while the direct function of URE IN GOD. conscience is to discriminate the right and wrong in actions, while its immediate sphere is the human will, it goes far beyond this.   In fact, it can perform those functions only in this way. It carries the soul outside of itself, and brings the will before a bar independent of its own impulses. It inevitably awakens in the soul the perception of a moral law, universal, unchangeable, binding under all circumstances ; in short, of a moral order of the world analogous to the physical order which it is the province of science to trace and illustrate. The moral consciousness of man refuses to stop short of this conclusion.   Man feels himself, not merely related to physical laws, but even more closely and more vitally related to moral laws, laws which not only enter into the structure of his own being, and go to form the frame-work of human life, but laws which extend beyond himself and his own hopes and struggles, and assert themselves as every-where supreme.   Such recognition of the moral order of the world is not only the highest, but the only conclusion that can satisfy the educated moral consciousness of mankind." [3]

"Now it is in these phenomena of Conscience that Nature offers to us far her strongest argument for the moral character of God. Had he been an unrighteous being himself, would he have given to this, the obviously superior faculty in man, so distinct and authoritative a voice on the side of righteousness ? . . . He would never have established a conscience in man, and invested it with the

[1] Butler : *Fifteen Sermons*, sermon ii.
[2] Kant : *Metaphysic of Ethics*, p. 245
[3] Diman : *The Theistic Argument*, pp. 248, 249

authority of a monitor, and given to it those legislative and judicial functions which it obviously possesses ; and then so framed it that all its decisions should be on the side of that virtue which he himself disowned, and condemnatory of that vice which he himself exemplified.   This is an evidence for the righteousness of God, which keeps its ground amid all the disorders and aberrations to which humanity is liable."[1]

Thus in the moral consciousness of man there is the recognition of a moral law of universal obligation, and also of a supreme moral ruler to whom we are responsible.   The moral nature of man is thus the manifestation of a moral nature in God.   In the cosmological argument we found in the existence of the cosmos, as a world originating in time, conclusive proof of the existence of an eternal and infinitely potential being as its only sufficient cause. On the same grounds we found that this being must possess the power of self-energizing—must indeed possess an infinite potency of will.   In the teleological argument we found in the adaptations of means to ends the proofs of a divine intelligence as their only sufficient cause.   Then in grouping these truths thus attained we already have the proof of the divine personality.   This same truth is confirmed by the nature and faculties of the mind as presented in the anthropological argument   The moral nature of man is his highest endowment and the crowning proof of his divine original. It is specially the manifestation of a moral nature in God ; and the truth of a moral nature in God is the truth of his holiness, justice, goodness.

[1] Chalmers : *Moral and Intellectual Constitution of Man*, vol. i, pp. 85, 86.

CHAPTER III.

ANTITHEISTIC THEORIES

THEISM means the existence of a personal God, creator and ruler of all things. Any theory, therefore, which excludes or omits these contents of the doctrine is thereby determined to be antitheistic. There are differences in the analysis and classification of such theories. We think that all may be properly classed under five terms: atheism, pantheism, positivism, naturalistic evolution, agnosticism. This omits materialism, one of the most common terms in the usual classifications. There is a sufficient reason for its omission in the fact that two or three of the theories named are grounded in materialism. This is openly true of atheism. It is really true of naturalistic evolution. The attempt of some evolutionists to change the definition of matter so as to provide for vital and mental phenomena rather concedes than disputes this fact. Positivism would be materialistic but for its rigid self-limitation to the sheerest phenomenalism. It is certainly nothing higher. Secularism is so closely kindred to positivism that it requires no separate classification. No elaborate discussion or refutation of these several theories is intended. The chief aim is to point out their antitheistic elements. Mostly, their refutation lies in the proofs of theism, as previously adduced.

Side notes: CLASSIFICA-TION OF THE-ORIES. OMISSION OF MATERIALISM

I. ATHEISM.

1. *Meaning of Atheism.*—After the analysis and classification of antitheistic theories each should have its own place in the further treatment. Atheism should thus be restricted, and none the less so because other theories may have atheistic elements. They still possess some peculiar characteristics as antitheistic theories, and which differentiate them from outright atheism. This is the form of atheism with which we are now concerned. It means the open and positive denial of the existence of God. There may be a skeptical atheism, and there is often such a designation of atheism; but in such a state of mind there is the absence of any proper theistic faith rather than the presence of any positive disbelief of the divine existence. Such a state of mind goes with other antitheistic theories rather than with atheism in its own distinct-

ive sense. Dogmatic atheism, such as we here consider, must be thoroughly materialistic, or must lapse into the merest phenomenalism.

It is still a question in dispute whether there are now, or ever were, any real instances of speculative or dogmatic atheism. ACTUALITY OF ATHEISM. Such atheism is not a mere ignorance of the divine existence, as in a state of mind in which the idea has never been present. A dogmatic atheist is one to whose mind the idea is present ; one who assumes to have considered the evidence in the case, and who still positively denies the existence of God. Profound thinkers, and profound students of questions directly relating to this issue, deny that there ever was an instance of such atheism. Others dissent. We think their position the true one. In the possible aberrancies of the mind there is the possibility of atheism. Yet the instances are either rare or transient. Atheism is mostly sporadic, and cannot broadly possess the mind of a community except in such favoring conditions as were furnished in the frenzy of France in the time of the Revolution. If the history of the past throws light upon the future, atheism must ever be sporadic, or only a transient mania. The moral and religious sentiments, native to the soul and never permanently repressible, must rise in resentful protest against it. The inevitable results of its prevalence must become so repugnant and shocking, even to such as are whelmed in the frenzy of the hour, as speedily to work its own cure. The battle of Christianity is not with dogmatic atheism.

2. *Negations of Atheism.*—Primarily and directly, atheism is the negation of God. Of all negations, this in itself is EXTREME OF NEGATIONS. the greatest that the human mind can think or utter. It cannot remain alone, but must carry with it many others, and others of profound moment. Atheism is a system of negations. The negation of the divine existence is the negation of all Christian truth. If there is no God, there can be no Son of God ; and, hence, no incarnation, no atonement, no salvation. There can be no spiritual existence. Matter must be all. There is no mind in nature, no intelligence that planned the earth and the heavens, and no omnipotent will that set them in order, or that preserves their harmonies. There are no intuitions nor absolute truths ; for atheism is as thorough a negation of our reason as of our God. There can be no spontaneity or freedom of mind. There is no mind. Mental phenomena are a mere physical process determined by mechanical force. There can be no moral obligation or responsibility. Morality is no duty. Whatever expediency may urge in behalf of secular interests, without God there can be no

ground of moral duty.   There is no future existence.   Death is the oblivion of man just as it is the oblivion of a beast.

3. *Dialectic Impotence of Atheism.*—In the issue with atheism the affirmative is with theism.   Atheism should regard this fact with favor, especially for the reason of its inevitable impotence for any direct support of its own position.

Atheism cannot reply to the proofs of theism.   Its impotence lies

NO REPLY TO THEISTIC PROOFS

in its own philosophy, or, rather, in its utter negation of philosophy.   Atheism grounds itself in sensationalism.   Sensationalism is really no philosophy   It repudiates all the deeper principles which must underlie a philosophy, all the intuitions of the reason which are necessary to the construction of a philosophy   The bald and skeptical sensationalism of atheism furnishes no principles upon which it can reply to the proofs of theism—proofs which are grounded in a true and deep philosophy.   If atheism possessed equal logical data with theism it could only balance proof with disproof, with the result of skepticism, not atheism   It possesses no such data.   A denial of the principle of causation is no answer to the theistic argument so strongly builded upon that most certain principle.   The denial of a teleological agency in the adaptations of nature is no answer to the argument from design, since such agency renders the only rational account of these adaptations, just as the teleological agency of mind is the only rational account of the facts of human civilization.   The denial of a moral nature in man is no answer to the argument constructed upon that ground, so long as the moral consciousness of the race affirms its reality.   The shallow sensationalism of atheism must deny the higher faculties of our rational intelligence, and the atheist is thereby rendered helpless against the proofs of theism, just as a blind man is helpless for any contention against the perceptions of vision.

The negation of a God is not the annihilation of the universe.

NO ACCOUNT OF THE COSMOS.

The earth and the heavens are still realities of existence, worlds of order and beauty.   Atheism can give no rational account of these things.   After ages of effort, and with all the resources of science and philosophy at command, it utterly fails.   No real advance has been made since Democritus and Epicurus theorized about the tumultuous atoms at last tumbling into orderly forms.   The notions of an eternal series of systems like the present, or of an accidental concursus of discrete elements into cosmical forms, or of physical forces eternally latent in matter and the source of evolutions in time have no scientific warrant, and make no answer to the logical demand of the facts concerned

Most of all is the dialectic impotence of the atheist manifest in his utter inability to bring any support to his own position. All such endeavor is rendered utterly fruitless by the nescience of his own philosophy. His sensationalism denies him all the higher forms of knowledge, and all the principles which must underlie such knowledge. He can know only the facts given in sensation, and may easily doubt their reality. Now, with such narrow limits of knowledge, and such uncertainty of any true knowledge, how can the atheist know that there is no God, or disprove his existence ? It is only on an assumption of knowledge infinitely transcending all human attainment that he can deny the existence of God. "The wonder then turns on the great process, by which a man could grow to the immense intelligence that can know that there is no God. What ages and what lights are requisite for this attainment ! This intelligence involves the very attributes of Divinity, while a God is denied. For unless this man is omnipresent, unless he is at this moment in every place in the universe, he cannot know but there may be in some place manifestations of a Deity, by which even *he* would be overpowered. If he does not know absolutely every agent in the universe, the one that he does not know may be God. If he is not himself the chief agent in the universe, and does not know what is so, that which is so may be God. If he is not in absolute possession of all the propositions that constitute universal truth, the one which he wants may be that there is a God. If he cannot with certainty assign the cause of all that he perceives to exist, that cause may be a God. If he does not know every thing that has been done in the immeasurable ages that are past, some things may have been done by a God. Thus, unless he knows all things, that is, precludes another Deity by being one himself, he cannot know that the Being whose existence he rejects does not exist. But he must *know* that he does not exist, else he deserves equal contempt and compassion for the temerity with which he firmly avows his rejection and acts accordingly."[1]

NO DIRECT PROOF OF ATHEISM.

VIEW OF JOHN FOSTER

II. PANTHEISM

1. *Doctrinal Statement of Pantheism.*—A history of pantheism would be necessary to the presentation of all its phases. Variations of the theory seem very natural, we might say inevitable, in view of the wide place it has occupied in both

VARIATIONS OF PANTHEISM

[1] John Foster : *Essays*, essay i, letter v.

References . Buchanan *Modern Atheism*, chap. i , Flint : *Antitheistic Theories*, lect. 1 ; Pearson : *On Infidelity*, pp 6-21.

time and territory. It flourished in Hindu philosophy long before the Christian era, and also in the earlier Greek philosophy, particularly in the Eleatic school. It appears in the Christian thought of the Middle Ages, in the speculations of the scholastics, and more fully in German philosophy. It was indeed inevitable that minds so widely separated, and of such variant speculative tendencies, should construct the doctrine in different forms. The outcome appears in some radical variations. There is a materialistic pantheism —so called—in which matter is all ; and life and thought are forces of matter developed through its organizations. In this view matter is God, and life and thought are modes of his operation. There is an ideal pantheism, according to which God and the universe are merely mental creations. This theory logically leads to absolute egoism. Such mental creation must be the work of each individual mind, and each should account all others its own mental production, and then assert for itself the sum of existence. What then is God ?

Spinoza, of the seventeenth century, is the representative of SPINOZAN PANTHEISM. modern pantheism. He treated the subject in a philosophic manner never before attempted, and wrought it into a more exact and definite form than it had ever received. "Assuming the monistic doctrine, he laid down the proposition that the one and simple substance is known to us through the two attributes of infinite thought and infinite extension. Neither of these attributes implies personality, the essential elements of which are denied to the substance. The latter is self-operative, according to an inward necessity, without choice or reference to ends. All finite existences, whether material or mental, are merely phenomenal."[1] This brief passage leads us to the central facts of the Spinozan pantheism. The facts, however, are simply placed side by side ; not skillfully articulated ; not scientifically combined. Thought is an act of personal mind, not an attribute of being ; and the denial of personality to the being denies the possibility of the infinite thought. Extension is a spatial quality and must have a ground in spatially extended being. It thus appears that the two attributes are not coherent. Nor do the attributes seem integral to the one substance, but rather to hang loosely from it, and to give no expression of either its reality or nature. Indeed, the one substance and the two attributes are pure assumptions of the theory.

We may easily give the central and determining facts of the doctrine in its more exact form. Pantheism is rigidly monistic in principle. There is one substance or being. This principle is so fun-

[1] Fisher : *Essays*, pp. 549, 550.

damental that materialistic pantheism must speculatively transform matter into a sense of oneness, or fail to be pantheism. FACTS OF THE The one substance is without intelligence, sensibility DOCTRINE. or will, consciousness or personality. The one substance is blindly operative from an inward necessity. There is neither creation nor providence. In these facts pantheism is thoroughly antitheistic. The purely phenomenal character of all manifestations, whether in material, organic, or mental forms, is determined by the monistic principle of pantheism. The one substance is neither divisible nor creative, so that it can neither part with any thing nor produce any thing to constitute real being in any form of finite existence. All finite things, therefore, are mere modes of the one infinite substance, and have a merely phenomenal existence.

2. *Monistic Ground of Pantheism.*—The mind by a native tendency seeks to combine the manifold into classes, and even into unity. This is a fortunate tendency, and the beneficial results of its incitement appear in science and philosophy. But the mental process in such work has its imperative laws which must be observed ; for, otherwise, instead of any valid result, we have mere hypothesis or assumption. This is the error of pantheism. Monism is not a truth of the reason ; nor is it inductively MONISM AS- reached and verified through a proper use of the rela- SUMED, NOT tive facts. As we have elsewhere shown, the phys- PROVED. ical and mental facts known to us in experience and consciousness absolutely require distinct and opposite forms of being as their ground. Nor can matter and mind both be modes of the monistic ground which pantheism alleges. Both may be the creation of the one omnipotent personal being ; but a mere nature, without personality and operative through a blind necessity, cannot manifest itself in such contradictory modes. The monistic ground of pantheism can no more account for the two classes of physical and mental facts than the material atoms of Democritus. Further, such a ground of the cosmos, a mere *natura naturans,* is disproved by the arguments adduced in proof of theism. The monistic ground of pantheism is a pure assumption, and an assumption contradicted by the facts of nature.

The utter erroneousness of pantheism is manifest in this, that the monism which it maintains determines all finite ex- UTTER ERRO- istences to be mere modes of the one infinite substance, NEOUSNESS mere phenomena without any reality of being in themselves. The physical universe becomes as unsubstantial as in the extremest form of idealism. Mind becomes equally unreal. Neither can be thus dismissed from the realm of substantial existence. In the physical

universe there is very real being.   Not all is mere appearance.
And every personal mind has in its own consciousness the absolute
proof of real being in itself.   Personal mind is not a mere phenomenon.   The monism of pantheism is utterly false in doctrine.

3. *Relation of Pantheism to Morality and Religion.*—It is mostly
LITTLE BETTER admitted that pantheism is something more for the re-
THAN ATHE- ligious nature of man than atheism.   We think this
ISM.   the case only with some minds.   Pantheism is as really
blank of all objective truth which can minister to the religious
cravings of the soul as atheism itself; and only the devout whose
religious fervor clothes God with many perfections which this doctrine denies him—only such souls can find spiritual nourishment
in their conception of him.   But so far they replace pantheism
with theism.   With most minds pantheism must be as really without
God as atheism itself—just as it is in fact.   There is no personality of God, no divine majesty for the soul's reverence, no love for
the inspiration of its own adoring love, no providence over us, no
place for prayer, no knowledge of us, no heart of sympathy with
us, no hand to help us, no Father in heaven.   There can be no religious helpfulness in the idea of a being so utterly blank of all that
the soul craves in God.

In the doctrine of pantheism man is nothing in himself, a phenom-
MAN A MERE enon only, a mere mode of the infinite, appearing for a
MODE OF THE while, and then vanishing forever.   But such totality of
INFINITE.   God and nothingness of man are utterly exclusive of both
morality and religion.   Nothing in us called religion or irreligion,
morality or immorality, is from any agency of our own.   All is the
operation of the infinite which manifests itself in such modes.
"One essential and constituent element of pantheism is the sup-
pressing of all particular causes, and the concentrating of all causality in a single being; that is, in God.   This arises from another
element of pantheism, yet more essential, which consists in suppress-
ing all particular beings, and concentrating all existence in one sole
being, which is God.   If there is but one substance, there is but
one cause; for without substance there can be only phenomena;
and phenomena can only transmit action; they cannot produce it
Pantheism, laying down the principle, therefore, that there can be
only one being and one cause, and that the universe is only a vast
phenomenon, necessarily concentrates in God all liberty, even if it
attributes liberty to him, and necessarily denies it every-where else.
Man and all other beings, therefore, lose their quality of *being* and
of *cause,* and become only attributes and acts of the divine substance and cause.   Deprived thus of all proper causality, man is

also deprived, at the same time, of all liberty, and, consequently, can have neither a law of obligation nor a controlling power over his own conduct. Such are the evident and necessary consequences of pantheism; and the pantheist, who does not adopt them either does not comprehend his own opinions or is voluntarily false to them." [1]

If God is not thus all, then he must be an utter blank. Pantheism must hold the one side or the other. The tend- OF ATHEISTIC ency is toward the blankness, which is not other than TENDENCY atheism. "In conceiving of God, the choice before a pantheist lies between alternatives from which no genius has as yet devised a real escape. God, the pantheist must assert, is literally every thing; God is the whole material and spiritual universe; he is humanity in all its manifestations; he is by inclusion every moral and immoral agent; and every form and exaggeration of moral evil, no less than every variety of moral excellence and beauty, is part of the all-pervading, all-comprehending movement of his universal life. If this revolting blasphemy be declined, then the God of pantheism must be the barest abstraction of abstract being; he must, as with the Alexandrian thinkers, be so exaggerated an abstraction as to transcend existence itself; he must be conceived of as utterly un-real, lifeless, non-existent; while the only real beings are these finite and determinate forms of existence whereof 'nature' is com-posed. This dilemma haunts all the historical transformations of pantheism, in Europe as in the East, to-day as two thousand years ago. Pantheism must either assert that its God is the one only ex-isting being whose existence absorbs and is identified with the uni-verse and humanity; or else it must admit that he is the rarest and most unreal of conceivable abstractions; in plain terms, that he is no being at all." [2] Whichever alternative is taken, all grounds of morality and religion disappear. When pantheism is divested of all false coloring and set in the light of its own principles it is seen to be much at one with atheism. [3]

III. Positivism.

1. *The Positive Philosophy.*—Positivism, considered as a philoso-phy, is much newer in its name than in its determining principles.

---

[1] Jouffroy : *Introduction to Ethics*, vol. i, p 193.

[2] Liddon : *Bampton Lectures*, 1866, lect viii

[3] Saisset . *Modern Pantheism ;* Plumptre *History of Pantheism ;* Hunt *Es-say on Pantheism ;* Buchanan *Modern Atheism*, chap. iii ; Jouffroy · *Introduc-tion to Ethics*, lects. vi, vii ; Flint: *Antitheistic Theories*, lects. ix, x ; Thomp-son *Christian Theism*, book i, chap. vi.

The term came into this use with the system of M. Comte, in the earlier part of this century.[1] This use of the term positive has been sharply criticised; with which fact, however, we are here little concerned. The meaning could not be simply an affirmative system in distinction from negative systems. There was no place for any such distinction. The real meaning of M. Comte seems to be that his system dealt only with facts certainly known, while opposing systems admitted many delusions.

The system of Comte is a most pretentious one. "The positivism which he taught, taken as a whole, is at once a philosophy, a polity, and a religion. It professes to systematize all scientific knowledge, to organize all industrial and social activities, and to satisfy all spiritual aspirations and affections. It undertakes to explain the past, to exhibit the good and evil, strength and weakness, of the present, and to forecast the future; to assign to every science, every large scientific generalization, every principle and function of human nature, and every great social force its appropriate place; to construct a system of thought inclusive of all well-established truths, and to delineate a scheme of political and religious life in which duty and happiness, order and progress, opinion and emotion, will be reconciled and caused to work together for the good alike of the individual and of society."[2]

PRETENSIONS OF POSITIVISM

What then are the facts with which M. Comte deals, which may be so certainly known as to preclude all mistake, and with which so mighty a structure is to be builded? With such high pretension one might reasonably expect the fullest recognition of all the powers and resources of the mind, not only in observation and experience, but equally in the profoundest intuitions of the reason. Indeed, the view is very narrow. The only facts to be known and used are facts of phenomena. Even here there is a narrow restriction. All facts of consciousness are excluded. Only external phenomena, only facts outward to the senses, are admitted into the circle of positivist verities. Nor are these facts to be known in either ground or cause. For positivism they have neither ground nor cause. They are simply sensible facts, or facts of change, to be observed and known in the order of their succession, and in their likeness or unlikeness.

NARROWNESS OF THE SYSTEM

Positivism is an extreme phenomenalism, and must have its psychological ground in a narrow form of sensationalism. We know that Comte utterly repudiated psychology, and no doubt would have resented any suggestion of such a

MERE PHENOMENALISM

<hr>

[1] *Philosophie Positive.*   [2] Flint: *Antitheistic Theories*, pp. 178, 179.

ground of his philosophy. This could not have changed the facts in the case. A phenomenon means, not only something to appear, but also a mind to which it appears—a fact which Professor Bowne has pointed out with special force. External things make no appearance to our sense-organs. These outward facts of change can have no phenomenal character until perceived by the mind. How shall the mind reach them? It has no power of immediate vision; and there is required, not only the mediation of the sense-organs, but also the sensations resulting from the impression of external things. The mind must be conscious of these sensations, or still there could be no perception of any thing external. Not a single phenomenon would otherwise be possible. And what would positivism do without phenomena, since it has nothing else with which to build its mighty structure? But the sensations necessary to phenomena are facts of mind, and hence it is utterly futile for the system to deny for itself a ground in psychology. That the system is grounded in a purely sensational psychology, and of the very narrowest type, is manifest in this, that external phenomena are the only really knowable facts. Even the facts of consciousness are denied to knowledge. There are no truths of the reason, no ontological realities. Properties mean nothing for substance; events, nothing for cause. Neither has any reality for knowledge. Both are excluded by the narrow limitation of knowledge to external phenomena. Neither substance nor cause is such a phenomenon. If only phenomena can be known, sensations are the only lights of knowledge. Such sensationalism is not new. It is certainly as old as the earlier Greek philosophy, and probably has never since failed of representatives. It has flourished in more modern times, particularly in the eighteenth century. Positivism is therefore only a new name for a system which is not new in the determining principles of its philosophy. No philosophy constructed upon the ground of this narrow sensationalism can ever satisfy the demands of our rational intelligence.

Two things have special prominence in the system of Comte: the law of the three states, and the classification of the sciences.

The three states are three forms of human thought respecting the phenomena of nature. In the first state all facts of LAW OF THE change are attributed to some supernatural agency: this THREE STATES. is the theological state. In the second the facts of change are attributed to the intrinsic forces of nature: this is the metaphysical state, with the ruling ideas of substance and cause. The third state is the positivistic, in which the ruling ideas of the first and second are dismissed, and science deals only with the phenomena of nature.

Here no account is given of the origin and course of nature. The question is excluded as delusive and unscientific. For positivism there is no reality of nature back of phenomena. Nothing has any account in causation. The *law* of the three states means that the human mind passes successively through the three, or through the first two into the third, beyond which it cannot advance. This then is the doctrine of the three states. The mind's first ideas are in the theological state; then in the metaphysical state; and finally in the scientific or positivistic state. This is the uniform and necessary law of mental movement, for both the individual and the race. It is a part of the doctrine that each state is exclusive of the others, so that the mind must leave the first in order to enter the

FACTS DIS-
PROVE THIS
LAW.

second, and the second in order to reach the third. The facts in the case do not warrant any such law. It is neither true of the individual mind nor of the race. The ideas of the child respecting the things about it are far more positivistic than either metaphysical or theological. The ideas of the barbarian mind are a mixture of theology and positivism—in open contradiction to this law of the three states. A higher mental development may eliminate many superstitions assigned to the theological state, and discover in the forces of nature the causes of many events previously accounted to supernatural agency; but there is no necessary parting with either theology or metaphysics on the most thorough entrance into the sphere of science. The proof of this statement is in the fact that many very eminent scientists are true believers in God and his providence, in the law of causation, and in the intrinsic forces of nature. Positivism does not dominate the higher mental development of the times. With all the advancement of science the truths of both religion and metaphysics are still firmly held.

In the classification of the sciences the ruling principle is, to

CLASSIFICA-
TION OF THE
SCIENCES

begin with the least complex, to proceed in the order of increasing complexity, and so ending with the most complex. The sciences, as given in this order, are mathematics, astronomy, physics, chemistry, biology, sociology. As this philosophy admits into its service only facts of external phenomena, it is compelled so to characterize the facts of mathematics. This is a dire necessity. In none of its principles or processes has mathematics any such quality. There is nothing outward for the organic eye; all is for the inner eye of the mind. And, on its ruling principle of classification, how can this philosophy begin with mathematics as the more simple, and then proceed to astronomy as more complex, when the very complexity of astronomy arises from the profound problems of mathematics which are its necessary ground? Then biology is made to include the whole man, just as it includes the animal and the plant. The mind has no distinct place in this grand hierarchy of the sciences. It cannot have any in a system which repudiates all the inner facts of consciousness. Mind belongs to our physiological constitution and must be studied in the convolutions of the brain. This is not the way to any true classification of the sciences. Yet mostly the disciples of Comte specially admire this part of his work. It has not escaped severe criticism, even from some who sympathize with many CRITICISM OF THE CLASSIFI- of his views. Spencer and Mill and Huxley are in this CATION. list. In this criticism there is at times a mingling of contempt. Of course, open inaccuracies in matters of science are specially glaring and offensive in any one of such lofty pretensions.

M. Comte did a queer thing, and a thing very offensive to most of his admirers, when he proceeded to construct upon A NEW RELIG- the ground of his positivism a new religion. They ION. naturally thought that in a system so utterly atheistic there was no place for religion. The offense was the deeper because of the character of the new religion. Indeed, it is a very queer affair. There are ceremonies and sacraments, a priesthood and a supreme pontiff. Collective humanity, symbolized by a woman, is the enthroned idol. Society must be absolutely subject to the new social and religious *régime*. No individual liberty nor rights of conscience can be tolerated. No wonder that the new religion gave BITTERLY great offense. Huxley bitterly styles it "Catholicism CRITICISED *minus* Christianity." It could not be so much the absence of Christianity as the Romish cast of this religion that so deeply offended Mr. Huxley. Mill joins in this severity of criticism; hardly, however, because this new religion was purposely constructed "sans Dieu," since he ventures for himself the opinion that a religion is possible without a God, and such a religion as may be, even to Christians, an instructive and profitable subject of contemplation. M. Comte sharply resented these criticisms, and denounced his followers who accepted his philosophy, but rejected his religion, as deficient in brains. It is a quarrel in which we have little concern. The new religion is enshrined in—ink. Its devotees are very few.

2. *The Philosophy Antitheistic.*—The heading of this paragraph might suffice for all the necessary content. Positivism is openly and avowedly antitheistic. It was purposely constructed without God. In the low plane of its principles there is no need of God, and no proof of his existence. If knowledge is limited to

external phenomena, there can be no knowledge of God, for he is not
such a phenomenon. We can readily believe La Place
that, on surveying the heavens with a telescope, he saw
no God. He could thus discover only physical phenomena, and God is not such a phenomenon. It is on such ground
that for positivism he can have no existence. If there is no truth
in either efficient or final causation, nothing in nature leads up to
God. Positivism is thus determined to an antitheistic position by
the low form of its phenomenalism. Its weakness as against theism
arises from this low plane of its philosophy. A position which can
be held only by a limitation of knowledge to external phenomena,
and a virtual denial of our rational intelligence, cannot be strongly
held. That intelligence will assert for itself a much larger sphere.
Nor will reason, with its absolute truths, and conscience, with its
sense of God and duty, vacate their rightful place in our consciousness to the occupancy of positivism.[1]

POSITIVISM INTRINSICALLY ATHEISTIC

3. *The Kindred Secularism.*—Mr. Holyoake is the acknowledged
leader in the propagation of the modern atheistic secularism. His
theories are set forth and advocated in various publications.[2] The
late Mr. Bradlaugh was in the same leadership, but not in full accord with Mr. Holyoake. The former was a dogmatic and openly
avowed atheist; the latter repudiated the term on account of the opprobrium associated with it, and assumed merely a skeptical or agnostic position respecting the divine
existence. "The theory of secularism is a form, not of *dogmatic,*
but of *skeptical,* atheism; it is dogmatic only in *denying the sufficiency of the evidence* for the being and perfections of God. It does
not deny, it only does not believe, his existence. There may be a God
notwithstanding; there may even be sufficient evidence of his being,
although some men cannot, or will not, see it. 'They do not deny
the existence of God, but only assert that they have not sufficient

A SKEPTICAL ATHEISM

---

[1] Comte : *Philosophie Positive,* condensed in an English translation by Miss
Martineau ; *Politique Positive,* translated by English admirers ; Littré : *Au-
guste Comte et la Philosophie Positive,* Congreve : *Essays, Political, Social, and
Religious ;* Bridges : *Unity of Comte's Life and Doctrines*—a reply to Mill ;
Lewes · *History of Philosophy,* vol ii, pp. 590–639 , Morley : *Encyclopædia
Britannica,* art. "Comte," Spencer : *Genesis of Science ; Classification of the
Sciences ;* Mill : *Auguste Comte and Positivism ;* Huxley : *Lay Sermons,* vii,
viii , McCosh : *Christianity and Positivism ;* Flint : *Antitheistic Theories,*
lect. v , Martineau : *Essays,* vol. i, pp. 1–62 ; Morell : *History of Modern
Philosophy,* pp 354–362

[2] *Paley Refuted ; Trial of Theism ; Townly and Holyoake ; Grant and Holyoake,* and other public debates ; *The Reasoner,* a periodical edited by Mr. Holyoake, and the chief organ of the modern Freethinkers of England.

proof of his existence.'[1] 'The non-theist takes this ground. He affirms that natural reason has *not yet* attained to (evidence of) Supernatural Being. He does not deny that it *may do so*, because the capacity of natural reason in the pursuit of evidence of Supernatural Being is not, so far as he is aware, fixed.' 'The power of reason is yet a growth. To deny its power absolutely would be hazardous; and in the case of a speculative question, not to admit that the opposite views may in some sense be tenable is to assume your own infallibility, a piece of arrogance the public always punish by disbelieving you when you are in the right.'[2] Accordingly, the thesis which Mr Holyoake undertook to maintain in public discussion was couched in these terms: 'That we have *not sufficient evidence* to believe in the existence of a Supreme Being independent of Nature,' and so far from venturing to deny his existence, he makes the important admission that '*denying implies infinite knowledge as the ground of disproof.*'"[3]

Secularism is the practical application of positivism to the conduct of the present life. While less pronounced in its atheism, it equally denies all present knowledge of God, and all sufficient proof of his existence. If there is no God, there is no future existence; certainly no proof of such an existence. The present world and the interests of the present life we know. Therefore we should wholly dismiss from our thought and care both God and religion, and give our whole attention to the interests of the present life. A divine providence must be substituted by the providence of science. A practical atheism should thus rule the present life.

A PRACTICAL APPLICATION OF POSITIVISM.

This secularism must be more thoroughly atheistic at heart than in open profession, for otherwise it could not thus enforce the lesson of practical atheism. It often occurs in our secular interests that prudence imperatively demands attention to the slightest chance of certain contingencies. How much more should this be the case respecting interests which may stretch away into eternity! Secularism admits that there may be a God and a future life; that it is impossible to prove or know the contrary. It is a principle admitted by all thoughtful minds that questions of interest should receive attention according to their importance. Then, with the admissions of secularism respecting the divine existence and a future life, it opposes itself to all the dictates of prudence, and is utterly without rational warrant. It takes this position against the common faith of the race in the

REALLY ATHEISTIC

---

[1] *The Reasoner*, xii, pp 24, 376   [2] *Ibid.*, New Series, pp. 9, 130.
[3] Buchanan · *Modern Atheism*, p. 365.

existence and providence of a divine being, and the future existence of man; against the universality of religion, and against its necessity as arising from the constitution of the mind, which, with rare exceptions, is now admitted by all students of the question; against the conclusion of the profound thinkers of the ages that in the works of nature and the endowments of mind there are conclusive proofs of the existence of God.

Secularism is not content to be merely a theory; it becomes a propaganda. That from such merely skeptical ground any one should draw for himself the lessons of practical atheism is unreasonable enough. That he should feel impelled to a propagandism for the purpose of indoctrinating the masses into a life without God, or religious duty, or thought of a future state leads us again to an atheism far deeper at heart than in the open profession, as the only account of such a propagandism. Its method is most skillful. So much must be conceded to secularism. Dogmatic atheism is not winsome. A merely skeptical atheism, quite concealed in the appeals to secular interests, encounters far less opposition in the common moral consciousness. Then the propagation is attempted among the masses, the men of toil whose secular lot is often a hard one. Secularism is not for men of affluence. Little need is there for preaching to such the paramount duty of exclusive attention to the interests of the present life. The common toilers suffer many privations, and, with open professions of sympathy and a purpose of helping them, it is not difficult to get their attention. Advantage is easily taken of the state of unrest or discontent with the laboring class, and their prejudices turned to practical account in favor of secularism.

The improvement of the condition of the laboring classes is a worthy aim. Whether secularism has any such honest aim is uncertain. Its leaders may think so, and yet be self-deceived. An unsuspected depth of atheism and intensity of prejudice against Christianity may rule them in a measure unknown to themselves. No unperverted mind can think that the secularism which they preach can improve the temporal condition of the laboring masses. It is not secularity that they need. Mostly this is already dominant. The need is for its wise direction. Such direction can never come from an atheistic secularism. The deepest need is for higher ideas of life; pre-eminently for moral and religious ideas. These ideas are the best practical forces for even the present life. They nourish higher aims and purposes, preserve from vice and waste, inspire industry and economy, patience and hope. Atheism utterly blanks these ideas, opens the flood-gates of

vice and waste, and breeds discontent and despair. It is a shallow
assumption of this atheistic secularism that religion, even that
Christianity is a detriment to the present life—an assumption utterly irrational on the face of it, and utterly disproved by the facts
of history.[1]

IV. NATURALISTIC EVOLUTION.

1. *Theory of Evolution.*—The theory of evolution has become so
familiar, even to the popular mind, that for our own discussion it
needs no very exact statement. The theory involves two questions:
one, a question of fact respecting the origin of species in the mode
of evolution, the other, respecting the law of the process, or the
force or forces which determine the evolution. Respecting these
forces there are among evolutionists marked differences of opinion;
with which, however, we are not here concerned.

Respecting the question of fact, the theory is that species arise in
the mode of evolution, the higher being evolved out of MODE OF EVO-
the lower The process is from a beginning up to man LUTION
The ascension is either in the mode of slight, insensible variation
and improvement, as maintained by Darwin, or by leaps, as others
hold. In one or the other mode, or in both. higher species are
held to have been successively evolved from the lower. Thus from
some incipient form or forms of life, and through successive evolutions into higher organic orders, the human species has been
reached. Man is the last and the highest result of the process.
Whether he is the highest possible evolution, the theory does not
inform us. On the principles of the theory, there is no reason
why the process should terminate with man, unless the evolving
forces are already exhausted. If these forces are purely and exclusively natural, they can possess only a finite potency, and must
therefore reach a point of elevation above which they cannot ascend.
The evolution of an order as high above man as man is above mol-
lusk would be a grand result Mere naturalistic evolution can
hardly promise so much.

Naturalistic evolution requires a preparation in the inorganic
world for the inception and development of the organic. PROCESS OF
It is admitted that life could not exist in the primor- PREPARATION.
dial state of matter as known to science. Only through a long
process of change could the necessary conditions be provided for
the origin and progress of life. The nebular cosmogony covers
much of this preparation, and is really a part of the theory of nat-

[1] Buchanan : *Modern Atheism*, chap. ix ; Flint . *Antitheistic Theories*, lect.
vi ; Pearson · *On Infidelity*, Appendix.

uralistic evolution. We previously explained that theory of world-building. In the beginning all matter existed in a state of intensest heat, in the form of a fire-mist. By the operation of natural forces a process of change began therein, and has continued without interruption through the formation of the world, the origin of life, and the evolution of species. Thus the inception of change in the primordial fire-mist was theoretically the real beginning of this form of evolution.

2. *Distinction of Theistic and Naturalistic Evolution.* — Theistic evolution means a divine agency in the process. There are differences of opinion respecting the measure of this agency. Some posit special interpositions, as in the origin of life and in the origin of mind. Others hold the nebular cosmogony and the evolution of species, not as a process carried on by the forces of nature, but as the method of the divine agency in creation. In the view of such the divine agency is just as real in the origin of a new species as it would be in its original or immediate creation. Such theories might modify the proofs of the divine existence, but could not void nor even weaken their force. Some would claim an enhancement of their cogency. Even Darwin's narrow limitation of the divine agency to an incipient vitalization of a few simple forms leaves the ground of theistic proofs in its full strength. In the light of reason, that agency which could endow a few simple organic forms with potencies for the evolution of all living orders is possible only in a personal being of infinite wisdom and power. The view is false to the divine providence, and to the true sense of creation, but leaves the cosmological, the teleological, and the moral arguments in their full strength.

DIFFERENCES IN THEISTIC THEORY.

The theory of a purely naturalistic evolution is in the nature of it antitheistic. It allows no divine agency at any point in the whole process, and asserts an absolute continuity of the physical forces which initiated the movement in the primordial fire-mist. Such a theory cannot be other than antitheistic.

ANTITHEISTIC THEORY

No repudiation of materialism or atheism, or of both, can change this fact. Instances of such repudiation are not wanting; but they mean little or nothing contrary to either materialism or atheism. Materialism is denied under the cover of a new definition of matter which classifies the phenomena of mind with the phenomena of matter. The result is not the elevation of the latter to a spiritual ground, but the reduction of the former to a material ground. The mental facts are thoroughly merged into the physical process, under an absolute

REPUDIATION OF MATERIAL-ISM AND ATHE-ISM.

continuity of force. There is no escape from materialism in this mode. Sometimes the denial of materialism means simply a denial of the reality of matter, or means our utter ignorance of any such reality. After a long discussion of "the physical basis of life," thoroughly materialistic in its process and outcome, even to the inclusion of all mental facts, Huxley says: "I, individually, am no materialist, but, on the contrary, believe materialism to involve grave philosophical error."[1] That we correctly stated the ground of this denial appears in his words which follow. "For, after all, what do we know of this terrible 'matter,' except as a name for the unknown and hypothetical cause of states of our own consciousness? And what do we know of that 'spirit' over whose threatened extinction by matter a great lamentation is arising, like that which was heard at the death of Pan, except that it also is a name for an unknown and hypothetical cause, or condition, of states of consciousness? In other words, matter and spirit are but names for the imaginary substrata of groups of natural phenomena."[2] This is pure phenomenalism, and, instead of an ascent to the spirituality of mind, is a descent to the lowest level of the Comtian positivism. This level is most thoroughly antitheistic. The denial of atheism often means a nescience of God rather than any faith in his existence. This is certainly the case with some evolutionists who confess to many mysteries of nature which have no solution in any empirical mode. "They have as little fellowship with the atheist who says there is no God as with the theist who professes to know the mind of God."[3] Such a separation from atheism means no acceptance of theism.

Much of the modern antitheism allies itself with the theory of naturalistic evolution. The theory itself is thoroughly antitheistic. We must not here overlook the distinction of this theory from the theistic theory. The facts upon which the theory is professedly constructed are not in the line of our studies, and hence we have no preparation for its scientific discussion. Yet some questions which deeply concern the theory are open to fairly intelligent minds. Such we may briefly consider.

CHIEF ALLIANCE OF ANTITHEISM.

3. *Perplexities of the Naturalistic Theory.*—As we have seen, this theory begins with the nebular cosmogony. Its only material is the primordial fire-mist; its only agencies, the physical forces latent therein. With such material, and through the operation of such forces, it must build the world and originate all the forms of

---

[1] *Lay Sermons*, p. 139.   [2] *Ibid.*, p. 143.
[3] Tyndall · *Fragments of Science*, p. 457.

life, including man himself. The results are before us. Such are
the assumptions of the theory. Surely they are extravagant enough to perplex the shrewdest and appall
the boldest. In the light of reason insuperable difficulties beset
the theory at many points.

ASSUMPTIONS

What account can the theory give of the primordial fire-mist?
If it be granted that the indices of geology and cosmogony point to such a prior state of matter, unanswered questions still remain. The fire-mist, primordial
with science, is not primordial with reason. Whence the fire-mist?
Reason demands the real beginning, and a sufficient cause for it,
as for every transition in the upward cosmical movement. The
primordial fire-mist makes no answer to these demands. The
hypothesis of evolution gives us no light. "It does not solve—it
does not profess to solve—the ultimate mystery of this universe.
It leaves, in fact, that mystery untouched. For, granting the nebula and its potential life, the question, whence they came, would
still remain to baffle and bewilder us. At bottom, the hypothesis
does nothing more than 'transport the conception of life's origin
to an indefinitely distant past.'"[1] The granting a potential life
in the fire-mist is a pure gratuity, without any ground or proof in
empirical science. The hypothesis of evolution, with its beginning
in the nebular cosmogony, is, for any rationale of the cosmos, confessedly an utter blank.

NO ACCOUNT
OF THE FIRE-
MIST.

No theory could be in profounder need of the most certain and
most certainly verifying facts than this of naturalistic
evolution. On the face of it the theory is most irrational. As previously stated, there is for a beginning
only the nebula or fire-mist. Through the operation of physical
forces this fire-mist goes to work, forms itself into worlds and sets
them in the harmony of the heavens, just as if directed by an omniscient mind. For our own world, as probably for many others,
it provides the conditions suited to living beings, originates life in
the many forms which swim in the waters, fly in the air, roam in
forest and field. A wonderful ascent is this, but a mere starting
compared with the culmination. In the process of evolution this
fire-mist mounts to the grade of man and invests itself with the
high powers of personality. Now it legislates in the wisdom of
Moses, sings in the psalmody of David, reasons in the philosophy of
Plato, frames the heavens in the science of Newton, preaches in the
power of Paul, and crowns all human life and achievement with the
divine life of the Christ. All this is in the assumption of natural-

NECESSITY FOR
VERIFYING
FACTS.

[1] Tyndall: *Fragments of Science*, p. 455.

istic evolution. "Surely the mere statement of such a notion is more than a refutation. But the hypothesis would probably go even farther than this. Many who hold it would probably assent to the position that, at the present moment, all our philosophy, all our poetry, all our science, and all our art—Plato, Shakespeare, Newton, and Raphael—are potential in the fires of the sun. We long to learn something of our origin. If the evolution hypothesis be correct, even this unsatisfied yearning must have come to us across the ages which separate the unconscious primeval mist from the consciousness of to-day. I do not think that any holder of the evolution hypothesis would say that I overstate or overstrain it in any way. I merely strip it of all vagueness, and bring before you, unclothed and unvarnished, the notions by which it must stand or fall. Surely these notions represent an absurdity too monstrous to be entertained by any sane mind."[1] In this exigency Tyndall seeks relief in a new definition of matter. His effort is utterly fruitless, and leaves in all its strength his characterization of the hypothesis of naturalistic evolution. All this, however, could not disprove the theory in the presence of clearly ascertained facts sufficient for its verification, but it clearly points to an absolute necessity for such facts. Their absence must be fatal to the theory.

The origin of life is a crucial question with this theory. A wide gulf separates the living from the lifeless. How shall this gulf be crossed? Can this theory bridge it? It must, if it would itself live. The bridge must answer for the crossing. CONCERNING THE ORIGIN OF LIFE. Abiogenesis, the origin of living matter from lifeless matter, is a necessity of the theory. Hence no mere speculation, conjecture, or illogical inference will answer at this point. Only the veritable facts will answer. What is the present state of the question? Comparatively recently, and after reviewing the relative facts, Professor Huxley said: NO PROOF OF ABIOGENESIS. "The fact is, that at the present moment there is not a shadow of trustworthy direct evidence that abiogenesis does now take place, or has taken place within the period during which the existence of life on the globe is recorded."[2] There is no better witness to this state of the case. Huxley is familiar with all the facts concerned, and has said many things which clearly mean that he is a reluctant witness.

The bent of Huxley's mind is so strongly toward a purely naturalistic evolution that he could not close the case with such a statement. Hence he proceeds: "But it need hardly be pointed out

[1] Tyndall: *Fragments of Science*, pp. 453–454.
[2] *Encyclopædia Britannica*, "Biology."

that the fact does not in the slightest degree interfere with any
ASSUMPTION
OF DEDUCTIVE
PROOF. conclusion that may be arrived at deductively from
other considerations that, at some time or other, abiogenesis must have taken place." Indeed, we think this
pointing out very urgent, and, moreover, that this abiogenesis must
be proved as a fact, because it is a necessary part of naturalistic
evolution. Without the proof of that fact the theory must utterly
fail. The proof is attempted. How? Thus: "If the hypothesis of
evolution is true, living matter must have arisen from not-living
matter; for, by the hypothesis, the condition of the globe was at one
time such that living matter could not have existed in it, life being
entirely incompatible with the gaseous state. . . . Of the causes
which have led to the origination of living matter, then, it may
be said that we know absolutely nothing. But postulating the existence of living matter endowed with that power of hereditary
transmission, and with that tendency to vary which is found in all
such matter"—why, then Darwin could show how the process of
evolution went on.

This is jumbling logic, and in a case where exactness is needed.
JUMBLING
LOGIC. Its fallacies are easily pointed out. On the hypothesis
of evolution, living matter must have arisen from not-
living matter, because there could have been no life in the primordial fire-mist. This is the deductive process, suggested in the first
citation, by which abiogenesis is to be proved. But abiogenesis is
not a necessary part of evolution. Evolution might be a process in
nature, while at the beginning life originated in a divine fiat. No
doubt a majority of evolutionists hold this view. Hence abiogenesis is necessary only to the purely naturalistic theory of evolution.
It is absolutely necessary to this theory. How, then, is abiogenesis
proved as a fact? From the hypothesis of naturalistic evolution
Huxley deduces the reality of abiogenesis. If the hypothesis be
true, abiogenesis must be true. But this "must be" is merely a
consequence in logic, not a reality in nature. And it is a consequence that hangs upon a mere hypothesis. Here is queer logic.
Abiogenesis is deduced as a fact in nature from evolution as a mere
hypothesis. This is the sheerest fallacy. Then life thus surrepti-
tiously got is postulated as a reality in possession of high endowments. "But postulating the existence of living matter endowed
with that power of hereditary transmission, and with that tendency
to variation which is found in all such matter"—then we may accept the hypothesis of naturalistic evolution.

Any theory could be proved in this way. It is a short and easy
process. Make your hypothesis; deduce its logical consequence;

transform this consequence into a reality in nature; make this reality the proof of your hypothesis, and the work is done. This is really the way in which Huxley proves the naturalistic theory of evolution. By a saltative process of logic he constructs a science of evolution. The structure tumbles in the presence of the facts. Abiogenesis is an essential part of naturalistic evolution, the very ground of the theory, and must be verified as a fact before the theory can have any standing. The verification must proceed in an inductive mode, with the support of the necessary facts. But the necessary facts are not at hand. There is not a shadow of proof in favor of abiogenesis. We know absolutely nothing about any such origin of life. This is the open confession. In such a case there is absolutely no proof. Had there been any, Huxley would certainly not have resorted to such fallacies of logic, and to a method utterly unscientific. In no other hands could the theory have fared any better. The warranted conclusion is that naturalistic evolution is utterly groundless. It must remain groundless until proof is furnished of a material genesis of life.

If naturalistic evolution could prove a material genesis of life, it might claim an open way up through all organic orders —certainly through all below man. In the utter failure of this proof, the theory must verify itself in every grade of the assumed evolution. There are openly confessed perplexities at many points. However, we leave these questions to scientists. The proof of evolution up to man could not conclude his origin in the same mode. He is too distinct in his constitution, and too high in his grade, for any such conclusion This view is widely accepted Many evolutionists separate man from all lower orders, and account his origin, particularly in his mental and moral nature, to the creative agency of God.

In bodily form, in organic structure, in volume of brain, man is so widely separated from all other orders, so elevated above all, that his immediate evolution from any known order clearly seems impossible. This may be said in the presence of all the determining principles which underlie the theories of evolution. In the distinctive facts which place man at such a height, he was the same in his earliest existence that he is now. No discovered remains represent him in the beginning as far down the scale in approximation to the ape. Mr. Huxley has closely examined this subject, and with special view to the question of man's origin in the mode of evolution. In this investigation he critically studied the notable Engis and Neanderthal skulls, among the very oldest human fossils yet discovered. His conclusion is that man

ANY THEORY SO PROVABLE

CONCERNING THE EVOLUTION OF MAN

NO EARLY APE-LIKE MAN

was man then as he is man now. Respecting the Engis skull, he says: " It is, in fact, a fair average human skull, which might have belonged to a philosopher, or might have contained the thoughtless brains of a savage." The Neanderthal skull represents a man of somewhat lower type, but still a man as widely separated from the ape as the lower races of the present. " In conclusion, I may say that the fossil remains of man hitherto discovered do not seem to me to take us appreciably nearer to that lower pithecoid form, by the modification of which he has probably become what he is." [1] Dawson confirms these views, and even adds to their strength by the study of other fossil remains.[2] The meaning of all this is that the wide separation of living man from the ape is not in the least narrowed by any discovered remains of fossil man.

These facts render the evolution of man simply in his organic RESPECTING nature a very difficult question for thorough-going evo-MAN'S ORGANIC lutionists. Of course, there is no pretension to any NATURE. knowledge of actual instances of such evolution. Where, then, are the proofs? If in the evolution of lower orders instances could be shown of as wide a variation by a single bound as that which separates man from the ape, some proof of his evolution might therein be claimed; but there are no such instances. Besides, the Darwinian theory excludes the saltatory mode of evolution, and therefore must pronounce such instances an impossibility. The only other resource, if any, is in transitional links. If some paleontologist should uncover the fossilized remains of anthropoids successively ascending from the ape into a higher likeness to man until the last transition seemed possible, much proof would be claimed for his evolution. Confessedly, these links are still missing. Evolutionists are looking in the direction just pointed out. " Where, then, must we look for primeval man? Was the oldest *homo sapiens* pliocene or miocene, or yet more ancient? In still older strata do the fossilized bones of an ape more anthropoid, or a man more pithecoid, than any yet known await the researches of some unborn paleontologist?" [3] That no such discovery has yet been made is much against all hope of the future. Evolutionists may continue looking, but they should not meantime claim the evolution of man just as though the necessary proofs were on hand. " No remains of fossil man bear evidence to less perfect erectness of structure than in civilized man, or to any nearer approach to the man-ape in essential characteristics. The existing man-apes belong to lines that reached up to them as their ultimatum; but

[1] Huxley. *Man's Place in Nature*, pp. 181, 183.
[2] *Nature and the Bible*, lect. v.   [3] *Man's Place in Nature*, p. 184.

of that line which is supposed to have reached upward to man. not the first link below the lowest level of existing man has yet been found. This is the more extraordinary in view of the fact that, from the lowest limits in existing man, there are all possible gradations up to the highest; while below that limit there is an abrupt fall to the ape-level, in which the cubic capacity of the brain is one-half less. If the links ever existed, their annihilation without trace is so extremely improbable that it may be pronounced impossible. Until some are found, science cannot assert that they ever existed."[1]

Other difficulties than the wide separation of man from all lower orders beset the theory of his evolution. We should not be misled by all that we hear about the anthropoid ape, nor lured into the notion of some one family specially man-like. Nor should we admit the notion of an ascending scale of man-likeness through a succession of ape families until the higher points of similarity converge in a single family. There is in these families no such prophecy of the evolution of man. That the ape families do not in any order of succession represent a growth of anthropoid quality an eminent scientist clearly points out.[2] In his careful study of the question, Mivart shows that the points of likeness to man are widely distributed among the ape families, and in a very miscellaneous way. Thus there is no gathering of anthropoid qualities into any one family, and no ascension through the several families toward a higher man-likeness. "In fact, in the words of the illustrious Dutch naturalists, Messrs. Shroeder van der Kolk and Vrolik, the lines of affinity existing between different primates construct rather a network than a ladder."[3] There can be no ascent toward man through such a state of facts. Hence the perplexity of evolutionists in locating the parentage of man, whether in the chimpanzee, or in the gibbon, or in the gorilla, or in the orang, or in some other ape family. Of later years the gorilla has been in much favor. Mivart, however, sends him to the rear and denies him all chance of appropriating the high honor of fatherhood to mankind. It seems impossible for evolutionists to construct a ladder out of such a web, so as to gain any ascent toward man.

Wallace studied this same question, and recognized its perplexities. "On the whole, then, we find that no one of the great apes can be positively asserted to be the nearest to man in structure. Each of them approaches him in certain

Marginal notes: NO APE FAMILY SPECIALLY MAN-LIKE. TESTIMONY OF WALLACE

[1] Dana: *Geology*, 1875, p. 603.   [2] Mivart: *Man and Apes*, part iii.
[3] *Ibid.*, pp 175, 176

characteristics, while in others it is widely removed, giving the idea, so consonant with the theory of evolution as developed by Darwin, that all are derived from a common ancestor, from which the existing anthropoid apes as well as man have diverged." [1] The ape-parentage of man is thus abandoned, while an earlier parentage common to ape and man is assumed. The present tendency of evolutionists is strongly toward this view. Clearly, the reason for it arises from the insuperable difficulties which beset the theory of an ape-parentage of man. How are they less in the new view? There is no reason to think a remoter ancestor more anthropoid than the ape. No evidence is given of such a fact. Thus, too, the line is lengthened, instead of shortened, along which the missing links must be found, in order to any proof of the evolution of man. There is really no proof of the evolution of man's organic nature.

Naturalistic evolution assumes the burden of proving the evolution of the whole nature of man. No exception can
NO ACCOUNT
OF MIND   be made in respect to his mental and moral nature. A theory which begins with the fire-mist as its only material, and the forces latent therein as its only agencies, must proceed to the end with such equipment. No other essence or agency can be admitted or assumed at any point in the evolutionary process. The naturalistic evolution of man's mental nature involves infinitely greater difficulty than the evolution of his organic nature. This is the reason for the imperative demand for a new definition of matter. We already have Tyndall's view of the absurdity of evolution on the definition current in science since the time of Democritus. Others join him in the demand for a new definition which shall thoroughly transform matter. If only they had the power of transubstantiation, success might crown their endeavor. However, a new name does not change an old nature. Matter is still the very same. Some adopt a Hylozoistic view of nature. Others are forced into idealism or agnosticism. Matter is nothing substantively, or a mystical something about which we know nothing. All this makes full concession that matter as we know it, and as it really is, cannot be the source of mind, and that the higher nature of man could not have its origin in naturalistic evolution.

As previously stated, many evolutionists, and some who hold the evolution of the organic nature of man, do not admit the origin of his higher faculties in this mode. They deny its possibility on the very principles of evolution. Wallace is an instance, and his view may have the greater weight because he is a Darwinian, and might fairly have claimed to share with Darwin the originality of his

[1] Wallace. *Darwinism*, pp. 452, 453.

theory. But with the conclusion of Darwin, "that man's entire nature and all his faculties, whether moral, intellectual, or spiritual, have been derived from their rudiments in lower animals," he joins issue. We need not follow his discussion; but he shows the impossibility of such an evolution of our higher faculties, such as the mathematical, musical, artistic, and moral.[1]

WALLACE DISPROVES THE EVOLUTION OF MIND

4. *No Disproof of Theism.*—Only in its extreme form is evolution antitheistic. We have seen that eminent scientists hold the nebular cosmogony and the evolution of species as a method of the divine agency in creation, and hence in the fullest accord with theism. So that the proof of evolution as a process in nature would not in itself prove any thing against theism. But the theory of evolution is yet in an hypothetic state. It is not yet an established science. The diversities of theory among evolutionists deny it a scientific position. There are many gaps yet to be closed;[2] many facts not yet adjusted to the theory, and serious deficiencies of direct proof. "Those who hold the doctrine of evolution are by no means ignorant of the uncertainty of their data, and they only yield to it a provisional assent. They regard the nebular hypothesis as probable, and, in the utter absence of any evidence to prove the act illegal, they extend the method of nature from the present into the past."[3] Evolution then is an inference from a mere hypothesis. This is not the method of science. Hypothesis is an utterly insufficient ground for any science. No theory can claim a scientific position until it has verified itself by facts.

EVOLUTION ONLY AN HYPOTHESIS

In some instances there are generalizations from a few observed facts. Thus from the observed co-existence of certain characteristics in a few animals their invariable co-existence is inferred. This inference, however, is not in itself a scientific principle, and becomes such only on the warrant of the uniformity of nature. But the theory of evolution has the warrant of no such law. Production in kind rules the propagation of life. This is a most certain generalization. But it is one which gives no support to the theory of evolution. Indeed, it is in direct opposition to the origin of species in the mode of evolution.[4]

Much more is the evolution of man a mere hypothesis. The sci-

[1] Wallace: *Darwinism*, pp. 461–478.
[2] McCosh. *Christianity and Positivism*, pp. 343–345.
[3] Tyndall: *Fragments of Science*, p. 456.
[4] Winchell: *Evolution*, p. 54; Dawson: *Story of the Earth and Man*, p. 327; Quatrefages. *The Human Species*, p. 80.

entific proof of it is hardly a pretension. It is an inference from
PURELY HY- the hypothesis of evolution in the lower forms of life.
POTHETIC RE- We have already seen how Huxley attempted its deduc-
SPECTING MAN. tion from such an hypothesis. It is really in the same
way that Wallace maintains the origin of man's organic nature in
evolution.[1] It is a very common method. The method, however,
is utterly unscientific. The truth is that the deductive method
is wholly inapplicable to such a science. It is the method of
mathematics and metaphysics, to which evolution is foreign, and
not of the natural sciences, which include evolution.[2] The origin
of man in the mode of evolution is without proof. And this resort
to deductive proof, at once utterly unscientific and in open violation of logical method, is a confession that the theory is without
the facts necessary to its scientific verification. Opposed to such
an unwarranted inference of the evolution of man are the over-
whelming disproofs of such an origin. Surely such a state of facts
can make nothing against the proofs of theism.

If the origin of new species in the mode of evolution were of
NATURALISTIC present occurrence, and open to the most searching ob-
EVOLUTION UN- servation, a purely naturalistic evolution could neither
PROVABLE be known nor proved. A supernatural agency in the
process would not be open to sense-perception, but would be manifest in our reason   This accords with the theory of many evolutionists. Scientific authority is very largely against a purely
naturalistic evolution. This fact means the more because it arises
from scientific or philosophic grounds, not from religious predilec-
tion. What is the conclusion? As evolution is yet in an hypothetic
state; as a purely naturalistic evolution is in the nature of it unprovable; and as scientists are by a very weighty preponderance
against such a doctrine, there is nothing in the theory which in the
least discredits the proofs of theism.[3]

[1] *Darwinism*, p 446.   [2] Krauth-Fleming . *Vocabulary*, "Deduction."
[3] Darwin : *The Origin of Species ; The Descent of Man*, Professor Gray :
Darwiniana, Haeckel · *History of Creation , History of the Evolution of Man ,*
Mivart · *On the Genesis of Species ; Man and Apes ; Lessons from Nature ;*
Schmidt : *Doctrine of Descent and Darwinism ;* Wallace *Contributions to the
Theory of Natural Selection , Darwinism ;* Wilson . *Chapters on Evolution ;*
Conn . *Evolution of To-day ,* Hodge · *What is Darwinism ?* Winchell : *Evo-
lution ,* Joseph Cook . *Biology ,* lects. II, III, "Concessions of Evolutionists ;"
Dawson *Nature and the Bible ,* lects. iv–vi ; *Story of the Earth and Man ,*
chaps xiv, xv , Quatrefages *The Human Species*

CHAPTER IV.

ANTITHEISTIC AGNOSTICISM.

THAT form of agnosticism with which we are here concerned will appear in the discussion. It belongs to pantheism, on the one hand, and, on the other, has its special representatives in Sir William Hamilton and Herbert Spencer.

I. DENIAL OF DIVINE PERSONALITY.

1. *Assumption of Limitation in Personality.*—The pantheistic view is stated as follows: " Personality only exists on PANTHEISTIC condition of a limitation, that is to say, by a negation. VIEW. From this it follows that Infinite Being, excluding all negation and all limit, excludes also all personality. To conceive God as a person, we must attribute to him the forms of human activity, thought, love, joy, will. But thought supposes variety and succession of ideas. Love cannot exist without want, nor joy without sadness, nor will without effort, and all this implies limitation, space, and time. A personal God is therefore limited, mutable, imperfect. He is a being of the same species as man, more powerful, wiser if you will, but like him imperfect, and infinitely below an absolute principle of existence. "[1] It will not be overlooked that Saisset has thus given, not his own doctrine, but that of pantheism—a doctrine which he treats with a masterly analysis and refutation.

The following passage from Spencer gives the substance of his doctrine: " Those who espouse this alternative position SPENCER'S —of an ultimate personal cause—make the erroneous DOCTRINE. assumption that the choice is between personality and something lower than personality; whereas the choice is rather between personality and something higher. Is it not just possible that there is a mode of being as much transcending intelligence and will as these transcend mechanical motion? It is true that we are utterly unable to conceive any such higher mode of being. But this is not a reason for questioning its existence; it is rather the reverse."[2] What would Spencer think of a theologian who should so reason about the Trinity? He has an unquestioning faith in such a " higher

[1] Saisset : *Modern Pantheism*, vol. 1, pp. 11, 12
[2] *First Principles*, p 109

mode of being," but loyalty to his nescience of the Infinite permitted only an hypothetic statement of it. The passage cited, especially as taken in connection with his doctrine of the Absolute, plainly denies the divine personality as a limitation and imperfection. In the same connection he declares the ascription of personal attributes to God a degradation of him. Then follows a homily upon "the impiety of the pious" who meanly worship God as a person instead of reverently worshiping the Unknowable Absolute. There is the charitable concession of a contingent good, an element of truth even within the impious creeds of theology: "that while these concrete elements in which each creed embodies this soul of truth are bad as measured by an absolute standard, they are a good as measured by a relative standard."[1] The standard is relative with a personal God; absolute with an unknowable Somewhat. But how can the nescience of Spencer reach an absolute standard? If this Absolute is utterly unknowable, there can be no knowledge of an absolute standard of religion. The fountain of charity still flows. Toleration for the impious creeds is a duty because "these various beliefs are parts of the constituted order of things; and not accidental but necessary parts. Seeing how one or other of them is every-where present, is of perennial growth, and when cut down redevelops in a form but slightly modified, we cannot avoid the inference that they are needful accompaniments of human life, severally fitted to the societies in which they are indigenous. From the highest point of view, we must recognize them as elements in that great evolution of which the beginning and the end are beyond our knowledge or conception—as modes of manifestation of the Unknowable; and as having this for their warrant."[2] A solace for the Christian conscience in an impious worship. There is still a grave question which the charity of Spencer has strangely overlooked. It is the question whether this palliation may continue in the higher light of his own philosophy of the Unknowable. On the other hand, we may even suggest a doubt whether he might not have made a more gracious use of the fact that the impious creeds are necessary parts in the evolution of the great Unknowable. It was clearly open for him to say that, as necessary parts in this evolution, they could not be impious even in the worship of a personal God. Enough has been

LIMITATIONS OF PERSONALITY. said to show that in the doctrine of Spencer personality is a limitation and in contradiction to the Infinite. That such is the doctrine of Hamilton and Mansel will appear under the next head.

[1] *First Principles*, p. 121.   [2] *Ibid.*, pp. 121, 122.

2. *Erroneous Doctrine of the Infinite and Absolute.*—As these terms are used in an abstract form, they are not properly definitive, but terms in need of definition. The definition which renders them essentially contradictory to personality gives a sense for which there is no need in human thought, no evidence of truth in reality, and certainly not the true sense of the divine infinity and absoluteness. In order to reach the truth in the case we require, first, the sense of the terms in the philosophy which makes them contradictory to personality, and, secondly, their true sense in application to God.

To the terms infinite and absolute Sir William Hamilton adds the term unconditioned as of special significance in his philosophy. He notes their distinction, and holds the first two to be related to the third as species to genus.[1] THE INFINITE OF AGNOSTICISM. Hence the unconditioned is with him the deepest term. These distinctions, however, do not specially concern the relation of the doctrine embodied in the terms to the question of the divine personality.

The doctrine of Hamilton, as given in the definition of these terms, denies to the unconditioned, and hence to the infinite and absolute, causal agency, or, at least, holds such agency to be a contradiction in thought to the unconditioned. WITHOUT CAUSAL AGENCY "A cause is a relative, and what exists absolutely as a cause exists absolutely under relation. Schelling has justly observed that 'he would deviate wide as the poles from the idea of the absolute who would think of defining its nature by the notion of *activity*' But he who would define the absolute by the notion of *cause* would deviate still more widely from its nature; inasmuch as the notion of a cause involves not only the notion of a determination to activity, but of a determination to a particular, nay, a dependent, kind of activity—an activity not immanent, but transeunt."[2] If the absolute cannot be a cause, or if the notion of causation is contradictory to the absolute, then either God cannot be the absolute, or his personality must be contradictory in thought to his absoluteness; for the power of causal agency is central to the notion of personality. The sense of the absolute or unconditioned thus appears in the doctrine of Hamilton as contradictory to the divine personality.

Mansel is properly the expositor of Hamilton, and more fully sets forth the implications of his doctrine of the unconditioned as contradictory to the notion of divine personality. DOCTRINE OF MANSEL It is proper to cite a few passages from his treatment of this question.

---

[1] *Discussions*, pp. 20, 21. [2] *Ibid.*, p. 40.

"To conceive the Deity as he is, we must conceive him as First Cause, as Absolute, and as Infinite. By the *First Cause* is meant that which produces all things, and is itself produced by none. By the *Absolute* is meant that which exists in and by itself, having no necessary relation to any other Being. By the *Infinite* is meant that which is free from all possible limitation; that than which a greater is inconceivable; and which, consequently, can receive no additional attribute or mode of existence, which it had not from all eternity." [1] Little exception need be taken to these definitions so far as the true sense of the terms is concerned, but exception must be taken to the erroneous inferences drawn from them or the false sense given in further statements. "The metaphysical repre-

PANTHEISTIC IMPLICATION sentation of the Deity, as absolute and infinite, must necessarily, as the profoundest metaphysicians have acknowledged, amount to nothing less than the sum of all reality. 'What kind of an Absolute Being is that,' says Hegel, 'which does not contain in itself all that is actual, even evil included?' We may repudiate the conclusion with indignation; but the reasoning is unassailable." [2] The reasoning is unassailable only on an extreme and false sense of the absolute, which is contradictory to the co-existence of the finite, and equally contradictory to the personality of God. This consequence appears in the further words of Mansel: "A cause cannot, as such, be absolute: the Absolute cannot, as such, be a cause. . . . How can the Infinite become that which it was not from the first? If causation is a possible mode of existence, that which exists without causing is not infinite; that which becomes a cause has passed beyond its former limits." [3] A power of causation may be reckoned an intrinsic mode of being, but the becoming a cause is not such a mode. Hence becoming a cause is not the acquisition of any new quality of being. These obvious and valid distinctions bring to naught the logic of the above passage. But the sense of the infinite and absolute as therein given is openly contradictory to the divine personality; for personality and the power of causal agency are inseparable truths The same contradictory sense runs through the further treatment of the question. A necessary causation is contradictory to the infinite and absolute. A voluntary causation is equally contradictory, because it implies consciousness.[4] The same contradictory sense is thus manifest; for it is needless to say that consciousness is an essential fact of personality.

Thus, in the doctrine of the infinite and absolute as maintained

---

[1] *Limits of Religious Thought*, p 75   [2] *Ibid*, p. 76.   [3] *Ibid*, p 77.
[4] *Ibid.*, pp. 77-79.

by Hamilton and Mansel, personality is not only an inevitable limitation in human conception, but must be intrinsically PERSONALITY a limitation. The reasoning proceeds in this manner: DENIED THE Consciousness can only be conceived under the form INFINITE of a variety of attributes; and the different attributes are, by their very diversity, conceived as finite. The conception of a moral nature—even as we must think of a moral nature in God—is in itself the conception of a limit.[1] But God cannot be a person without a distinction of attributes, nor a moral personality without a moral nature. If such facts are contradictory to the infinite and absolute, does it not follow that we must either deny these qualities to God or deny his personality? It certainly follows that so far as in religious thought God is conceived as a person he is neither infinite nor absolute. Thus from Mansel: " But personality, as we conceive it, is essentially a limitation and a relation." [2]

Herbert Spencer maintains substantially the same doctrine of the Absolute, as the ground of contingent existences. SPENCER'S How must we think of the First Cause, if we can think DOCTRINE THE of it at all? "It must be independent. If it is not SAME independent it cannot be the First Cause; for that must be the First Cause on which it depends. . . . But to think of the First Cause as totally independent is to think of it as that which exists in the absence of all other existence. . . . Not only, however, must the First Cause be a form of being which has no necessary relation to any other form of being, but it can have no necessary relation within itself. There can be nothing in it which determines change, and yet nothing which prevents change. For if it contains something which imposes such necessities or restraints, this something must be a cause higher than the First Cause, which is absurd. Thus the First Cause must be in every sense perfect, complete, total: including within itself all power, and transcending all law. Or, to use the established word, it must be absolute." [3] How causation, as necessary to finite existences, can arise in such an absolute is a question for Mr. Spencer to answer. The only modes of action are in spontaneity or necessity; but both are denied to the absolute. Yet there can be no causation without action.

The doctrine of Spencer is further given thus. " The objects and actions surrounding us, not less than the phenom- MUST BE A ena of our own consciousness, compel us to ask a cause; FIRST CAUSE. in our search for a cause, we discover no resting-place until we arrive at the hypothesis of a First Cause; and we have no alternative

[1] *Limits of Religious Thought*, p. 127.   [2] *Ibid.*, p. 102.
[3] *First Principles*, p. 38.

but to regard this First Cause as the Infinite and Absolute." [1] No exception could be taken to these positions, but for the false doctrine of the Infinite and Absolute, which equally with that of Hamilton and Mansel excludes the divine personality. Indeed, Spencer appropriates their doctrine, and freely cites their discussions in its support.

It should be said that Spencer adheres to this doctrine with a consistency which can scarcely be accorded these eminent Christian philosophers. In his own philosophy there was no need, as in their theology, to dispose of the doctrine in consistency with Christian theism. He repudiates their appeal to faith in God as an immediate and necessary datum of the religious consciousness. If a personal God is thus saved to their theology, it is difficult to see in what consistency with their doctrine of the infinite and absolute. This faith, even if a reality, cannot cancel the contradiction of that doctrine to the divine personality. What, then, is God as thus saved in theology? He cannot be both a person and the infinite and absolute. Or if held to be both, it is against the contradiction of thought. This cannot be satisfactory.

Such an absolute and infinite as appears in the doctrine under notice is no immediate truth, and no requirement of THE TRUE CAUSE NOT GIVEN. the mind. In the activities of thought the finite may suggest the infinite, the conditioned the absolute, the temporal the eternal, the changeable the immutable; but the truth or objective reality of these suggestions is not thus either given or required. Much less is such an infinite and absolute as posited in the doctrine under notice either given or required. The necessity of thought, the only necessity, and comprehensive of the whole, is for a cause of finite and dependent existences. The necessity is definitely and only for such a cause as will account for the finite and dependent. Such a cause is no impersonal infinite and absolute. The original or first cause which answers to the necessity of thought must possess the power of a beginning, and an intelligence equal to the order and adjustments of the cosmos; must be equal to the origination of rational and moral personalities. A personal God, and only a personal God, can answer to this necessity of thought.

There is no such an infinite and absolute as that posited in the doctrine of Hamilton and Spencer; certainly no need NO SUCH AN INFINITY of it in human thought, and no proof of it in human reason. There must be an eternal being; for otherwise present existences must have sprung from nothing, which is unthinkable.

[1] *First Principles*, p. 38.

An eternal being is by no necessity eternally the totality of being. Nor need it be such an infinite and absolute that it must at once exclude all distinction of attributes and modes, and yet necessarily include all actualities and possibilities of both. The infinite which must forever be the totality of being is an infinite in the sense of magnitude or bulk, and so space-filling as to allow no room for any other existence. "To think of the First Cause as finite is to think of it as limited. To think of it as limited, necessarily implies a conception of something beyond its limits: it is absolutely impossible to conceive a thing as bounded without conceiving a region surrounding its boundaries. What now must we say of this region? If the First Cause be limited, and there consequently lies something outside of it, this something must have no First Cause—must be uncaused. . . . Thus it is impossible to think of the First Cause as finite. And if it cannot be finite it must be infinite." [1] With all the use of causal terms, the First Cause is here treated simply as being, not as causal agency. The being is an infinite magnitude, a bulk filling all space. It is a very crude notion. It is only such an infinite that can allow no room for the finite. God is not such an infinite. There is no such an infinite. The absolute which is, and must forever be, so unrelated that it cannot be a cause—such an absolute being, if an existence at all, must be a dead existence, and therefore utterly useless for any requirement of thought or any rational account of the universe.

The doctrine of Hamilton and Mansel was maintained in the interest of Christian theology, as against the German transcendentalism, the drift of which was into rationalism and pantheism. It is true, however, that the contention of Hamilton was more directly with Cousin, who held with the German transcendentalists the capacity of the soul for an immediate cognitive vision of the Infinite, though with the rejection of its pantheistic implication. The refutation of this transcendentalism should in itself be reckoned a valuable service; but the method of it involves a detriment not less than the gain. There was no necessity for the nescience of the Infinite which the method involved, or for the representation of personality as contradictory to the divine infinity. In the doctrine of an immediate and necessary faith in the divine personality there is little relief from the agnosticism which, for our reason, sinks the personality of God in his infinity. It is not pretended that this faith either changes the sense of the Infinite or replaces the consequent

[margin note: A MERE BULK INFINITE]

[margin note: AIM OF HAMILTON AND MANSEL]

[1] Spencer: *First Principles*, pp. 37, 38.

nescience with any true knowledge of God. Hence God is still beyond the reach of cognitive thought. We may affirm his personality as an immediate datum of the religious consciousness, but for rational thought personality is still a limitation. Hence God can be the Infinite for faith only by a divorcement of faith from rational thought; indeed, only against the contradiction of thought. "It is greatly to be lamented that men should teach that the only way in which it is possible for us to form any idea of God leads to no true knowledge. It does not teach us what God is, but what we are forced against reason to think he is."[1]

3. *The True Infinite and Absolute.*—In the true sense of these terms in application to God we shall find their consistency with his personality.

The true sense of these terms must be determined in view of the subject of their predication. Only in the observance of this principle can we reach any definite or clear result. There may be an infinite and absolute without relevancy to any question respecting the co-existence of the finite, or the consistency of causation and personality with itself. Or these terms may be used in a false sense, and are so used in the doctrine of the unconditioned.

Space is infinite and absolute—without either limitation or relation. Yet it is neither the ground nor cause nor quality of any existing thing. There are what we call the spatial qualities of being, but these are purely from the nature of the being, and are in no sense caused or affected by the nature of space. A body may occupy space, or rest or move in space, and undergo great change, so that a chaos shall become a cosmos, but space itself is ever the same, and without any effect upon that which occupies it or transpires in it. Hence the questions whether the infinite and absolute must be the totality of being, and unrelated, and impersonal, can have no relevancy to such an infinite and absolute as space.

The same is true of duration, also infinite and absolute—without limit and unrelated. Successional events and uniform revolutions of bodies which mark off periods of time to us do not affect duration itself: neither does duration affect them. The power of time to affect existences and to work changes is purely a figure of speech. All such changes are from interior constitution or exterior influence, in neither of which has duration any part. It is without influence upon any thing, and is itself unaffected by any. Hence there can be no relevancy in the questions whether such an infinite

[1] Hodge: *Systematic Theology*, vol. i, p. 344.

and absolute can admit the co-existence of the finite and become the relative through causal agency.

We have previously noted the crude and contradictory notion of the infinite in the sense of quantity or space-filling being, and so space-filling as to preclude all other exist- CRUDE NOTION
ences—a sense which certainly can have no application OF A QUANTI-TATIVE INFI-NITE
to God.   Yet this sense ever appears in the transcend-
ental philosophy of the infinite, and is too often present in the doctrine of Hamilton and Mansel.   "The very prevalent tendency in philosophic speculation on this subject, to argue as if 'our idea of infinity arises from the contemplation of *quantity*, and the endless increase the mind is able to make in quantity, by the repeated additions of what portions thereof it pleases,' has led to various uses of the term 'infinite,' which are not only inapplicable to the Divine Being, but even contradictory of his nature.   Such, for example, are these: 'an infinite line,' 'an infinite surface,' and 'an infinite number.'   All such expressions have obviously been used from a tacit admission that 'our idea of infinity arises from the contemplation of *quantity*.'   But, as I have said, the terms 'infinite' and 'unlimited,' while they apply to the nature of God, do not explain what that nature is, and as soon as the nature of the Deity is indicated all these expressions immediately disappear. When it is declared that God is a *spirit* it is affirmed that God is not extended, and that all references to quantity are inapplicable to him."[2]   A being infinite in the sense of quantity, and therefore preclusive of finite existences, must be infinite in spatial extension. Thus the notion inevitably becomes materialistic with respect to both the infinite being and the finite existences in question; for otherwise the question of co-existence could not arise.   NO BULK IN-FINITE
There is no such an infinite.   Whatever is extended in
space in the manner of material bodies must be actually divisible into parts, and nothing thus divisible can be infinite.   The parts must be finite, and yet equal to the whole; therefore the whole cannot be infinite, because the finite parts, however many or great, cannot make an infinite.   There is no actually infinite line, or surface, or number.   The crude and contradictory notion of the infinite in any sense of quantity should be eliminated from this question.   Martineau, having cited from Mansel a passage in which there is too much of that notion, says with force: "Now what does all this prove?   This, and this only: that if we take the words 'Absolute' and 'Infinite' to mean that he to whom they are ap-

---

[1] Locke: *Essay*, book ii, chap. xvii, sec. 7.
[2] Calderwood : *Philosophy of the Infinite*, pp. 183, 184.

plicable *chokes up* the universe, mental and physical, and prevents
the existence of every one else, then it is nonsense and clear contradiction for any one else, who is conscious of his own existence,
to use these words of God at all. Surely this might have been said
without so much circumlocution. And what does Mr. Mansel
thereby gain? Simply, so far as we can see, that he has established the certain non-existence of any Being *in this sense* 'absolute ' or ' infinite.' " [1]

The summary method which posits an infinite and absolute
DIVINE PER-
SONALITY NOT
TO BE NEGA-
TIVED BY A
FALSE DEFINI-
TION.
ground of things, and then denies its consistency with
personality, cannot be admitted. It has no claim to
admission on the ground of either a priori or inductive
truth. The inconsistency alleged is in the definition
of the terms, not in their true sense as predicates of the
First Cause. The inference of inconsistency may be legitimate to
the premise as determined by definition, but the premise itself is
an instance of the sheerest material fallacy. The question of the
divine personality cannot be thus negatively concluded. It is the
great question of the divine reality, and cannot be disposed of by
a false definition. God is what he is. As an eternal being, there
is no cause of his existence, and no reason for his being what he is
or other than he is. Hence no a priori assumption can be valid
against his personality. The reality of a ground of finite and dependent existences is given as a necessity of thought, and only the
boldest phenomenalism or positivism can question its truth. But,
as we previously found, the same law of thought requires by an
equal necessity the personality of the First Cause.

The true sense of the infinite and absolute in their application
THE TRUE IN-
FINITY IN PER-
SONAL PERFEC-
TION.
to God is given in the perfection of his personal attributes. This accords with the principle previously
noted, that the sense of these terms must be determined by the nature of the subject of their application.
God in personality is here the subject. We must not anticipate,
further than the requirement of the present question, what more
properly belongs to the treatment of the divine attributes; but we
cannot conclude the present question without reference to these attributes. We need not include all.

God is infinite in knowledge and power. Omniscience and omnipotence are his personal attributes. It may be objected that objects of the divine knowledge and products of the divine power are
finite, and therefore no conclusive manifestation of an infinite knowledge and power. Things known to God are mostly finite; yet they are

[1] *Essays, Philosophical and Theological,* vol. i, pp. 291, 292.

such in number, complexity, and relation, especially as we include the possible with the actual, that only an omniscient mind can know them as he knows them. God has perfect knowledge of himself, and this is infinite knowledge of the infinite. Dependent existences are finite; yet the power which produced them, and, according to their nature as physical or spiritual, set them in their order or endowed them with intellectual and moral reason, must be infinite. There is an infinite love of God.

It will be easy for the doctrine of the conditioned as the utmost limit of human thought, with its inevitable nescience DISTINCTION of God, to attempt a criticism of this view. With a OF ATTRIBUTES CONSISTENT ready relapse into the crude and contradictory notion of WITH INFIN- a quantitative infinity, it must object to a triplicity of ITY. infinites, with the implication of a fourth—an infinite God with three infinite attributes. But the criticism falls with the false and contradictory notion of an infinite magnitude or quantity. God is a spiritual being, and, with a distinction of attributes, a simple unity of being, without any spatial or quantitative quality. His measureless personal perfections are not preclusive of finite existences. Infinite knowledge, power, and love are neither reciprocally preclusive nor a limitation of each other. The divine knowledge is not the less for all the knowledge of finite minds, nor the divine power less for all the forces of physical nature or power of finite wills, nor the divine love less for all the love of human and angelic spirits.

God is the absolute. The absolute is the self-sufficient, the un-conditioned, the unrelated, except as voluntarily re- GOD THE TRUE lated. Any sense of the absolute which excludes even ABSOLUTE. the possibility of relation must be false to the ground or cause of finite and dependent existences. Causal agency is the only original of the finite and dependent; but such original must come into relation to its own agency and effects. An absolute, therefore, which cannot become related cannot be the ground of the finite and dependent. God as an eternal personal being, with the perfections of infinite knowledge and power and the free determination of his own agency, is absolute in the truest, deepest sense of the term. We challenge a comparison with the transcendental absolute which precludes personality. Such an absolute must forever remain unrelated, and therefore can account for nothing. Otherwise, the finite, and self-conscious personalities, as really as material forms of existence, must be accounted as purely phenomenal, with the result of a monism which at bottom is pantheism. Far truer and grander is the view of a personal God,

infinite in his perfections. with the power of free causal agency.
God is the true absolute.

Thus we find the divine personality consistent with the truest,

voluntary relations consistent with the absolute. deepest sense of the infinite and absolute. The true sense is not in being itself, but in the perfection of being or the perfection of attributes. "The infinite is not to be viewed as having an independent being, it is not to be regarded as a substance or a separate entity; it is simply the quality of a thing, very possibly the attribute of the attribute of an object. Thus we apply the phrase to the Divine Being to denote a perfection of his nature; we apply it also to all his perfections, such as his wisdom and goodness, which we describe as infinite."[1] "We cannot think of God as the unconditioned Being conditioning himself, without conceiving him as *Reality, Efficiency,* and *Personality.* These constitute the conception of the divine essence whereby it is what it is. When we think of the attributes of such a Being we must necessarily conceive them as *Absolute, Infinite,* and *Perfect.*"[2] "In particular, Mansel sought to show that God could not be thought of as cause, because as cause it must be related to its effect. He cannot, then, be creator, because as such there must be a relation between God and the world. But this objection overlooks the fact that relation in the abstract does not imply dependence. The criticism would be just if the relation were necessary and had an external origin. But as the relation is properly posited and maintained by himself there is nothing in it incompatible with his independence and absoluteness."[3] As we thus expose and eliminate the contradictory notion of a quantitative infinite and absolute, and find the true sense of the terms in the perfection of personal attributes, their consistency with the divine personality is manifest. Only a personal God, infinite and absolute in the perfection of his attributes, can answer in human thought for any rationale of finite and dependent existences. God in personality is the true infinite and absolute.

4. *Personality the Highest Perfection.* — This we confidently maintain against the assumption of pantheism, and against the theistic nescience which posits an infinite and absolute inconsistent with personality. The question may be appealed to the clearest logical judgment and to the profoundest intuitions of the reason. In the orders of existence directly known to us man is the highest, and the highest by virtue of the facts of personality. If this be not

[1] McCosh : *Intuitions of the Mind,* p. 197.
[2] Cocker : *Theistic Conception of the World,* p. 41.
[3] Bowne : *Metaphysics,* p. 131.

the truth, then judgment and reason are no longer trustworthy and we are incapable of any rational treatment of the question. Judgment and reason are trustworthy, and the truth we stated is above question. With this basis of truth. we may rise to the thought of God. and find in personality the highest conception of his perfection. In all the range of being, finite and infinite, personal attributes are the highest. What impersonal terms can replace the personal with any comparable idea of God? In the vague and contradictory use of the terms infinite, absolute, unknowable, inscrutable, in application to the original cause of finite and dependent existences, with personality lost in the confusion, there is an infinite descent from the notion of God as personal cause.

PERSONALITY AT THE HEAD OF EXISTENCE.

There is a false principle underlying all the speculations in which personality is held to be a limitation It is the principle that all determination, predication, or distinction of attributes is a limitation, or, in the extreme form of Spinoza, a negation. We cannot know the infinite and absolute, because as such it exists out of all limitation and relation. If we predicate intelligence, will, affection, causal agency of God, we so distinguish his attributes and bring him into relation to the products of his agency as to deny his infinity and absoluteness. This denial is on the principle that all predication is limitation or negation. This point is so admirably treated by another that the citation of his words should be heartily approved.

FALSE PRINCIPLE OF LIMITATION IN PERSONALITY

" If I do not mistake, the whole system of those reasonings rests on an error common to skepticism and pantheism, which formerly misled, and still deceives, many a superior mind. This error consists in maintaining that every determination is a negation. *Omnis determinatio negatio est*, says Hamilton after Spinoza. Nothing can be falser or more arbitrary than this principle. It arises from the confusion of two things essentially different, namely, the limits of a being, and its determinate and constitutive characteristics. I am an intelligent being, and my intelligence is limited; these are two facts equally certain. The possession of intelligence is the constitutive characteristic of my being, which distinguishes me from the brute being. The limitation imposed on my intellect, which can only see a small number of truths at a time, is my limit, and this is what distinguishes me from the Absolute Being, from the Perfect Intelligence which sees all truths at a single glance. That which constitutes my imperfection is not, certainly, my being intelligent; therein, on the contrary, lies the strength, the richness, and the dignity of my being. What constitutes my weakness and my nothingness is that this intelligence is inclosed in a narrow circle. Thus, inasmuch as I am intelligent, I participate in being and perfection; inasmuch as I am only intelligent within certain limits, I am imperfect.

"It follows from this very simple analysis that determination and negation, far from being identical, differ from each other as much as being and nothing. According as a being has more or less determinations, qualities, and specific characteris-

THE GRADE OF BEING AS ITS DETERMINA- TIONS. tics, it occupies a rank more or less elevated in the scale of existence. Thus, in proportion as you suppress qualities and determinations, you sink from the animal to the vegetable, from the vegetable to brute matter. On the other hand, exactly in proportion as the nature of beings is complicated, in proportion as their bodies are enriched with new functions and organs, as their intellectual and moral faculties begin to be displayed, as more delicate senses are added to their grosser senses, to sensation, memory, to memory, imagination, then the superior faculties, reasoning, and reason, and will, you rise nearer and nearer to man, the most complicated being, the most determined and the most perfect in creation. . . . God is the only being absolutely determined. For there must be something indetermined in all finite beings, since they have always imperfect powers, which tend toward their development after an indefinite manner. God alone the complete Being, the Being in whom all powers are actualized, escapes by his own perfection from all progress, and development, and indetermination. It would be a pure illusion to imagine that different determinations could, by any chance, limit or contradict each other. Could intelligence prevent liberty? or the love of the beautiful extinguish the love of the good? or truth, or beauty, or happiness be any hinderance, the one to the other? Is it not evident, on the contrary, that these are things perfectly analogous and harmonious, which, far from excluding, require each other, which always go together in the best beings of the universe, and, when they are conceived in their eternal harmony and plenitude, constitute the living unity of God?

"Now, let us hear our skeptics. They say the Absolute excludes

PERFECTION OF DETERMINA- TION THE PER- FECTION OF GOD. all limits, and, consequently, all determination. I reply, the Absolute has no limits, it is true, that is to say, that his being and the powers that are in him are all full, complete, infinite, eternal; but far from these determinations limiting his being, they characterize and constitute it."[1]

[1] Saisset: *Modern Pantheism*, vol. ii, pp. 69-72.

Unity is a perfection of being; but the highest unity lies in the harmony of differentiated qualities. Man, most complex of creaturely orders directly known to us, is yet a higher unity than any other. This higher unity is in personality; and personality is the highest perfection. In the plenitude and harmony of personal attributes in God there is an infinite perfection of unity. Herbert Spencer was far astray from truth and reason in saying that the question of personality in the First Cause was not a question between personality and something lower, but one between personality and something higher. There is nothing higher. Personality is the highest perfection. Being without quali- PERSONALITY THE PERFECTION OF GOD. ties or attributes is a blank in itself, and a blank for thought. "Also, it must be added, that it is a strange perversion of thought which takes this *caput mortuum*, this logical phantom, and gives it the place of the highest reality, the object of profoundest veneration, in bowing down to which science and religion are to find their ultimate reconciliation. For, in so doing, we are simply turning away from all the concrete wealth of the world of thought and being, and deifying the barest, thinnest abstraction of logic. It is not too much to say that almost any object of reverence would be more worthy than this, and that in nature-worship, animal worship, even the lowest fetichism, there is a higher cultus than in the blind veneration of the philosophic Absolute." [1]

If we compare the Absolute of pantheism, or as posited in the doctrine of Hamilton and Spencer, with the theistic BIBLICAL CONCEPTION OF GOD. conception of Moses and the prophets and apostles, the infinite transcendence of the latter must be manifest. Can any impersonal somewhat, however styled, be comparable with the divine Father as revealed by the divine Son? Personality is the highest perfection of the Absolute. [2]

II. DENIAL OF DIVINE COGNOSCIBILITY.

1. *The Infinite Declared Unthinkable.*—It is the doctrine of Hamilton and Mansel, as also of others, that the Infinite is unknowable and unthinkable. As in relation to God, this is the doctrine of theistic nescience. God may be the object of faith, but is beyond the reach of cognitive thought. This consequence is inevi-

[1] Caird. *Philosophy of Religion*, p. 38.
[2] Cooker: *Theistic Conception of the World*, pp. 42, 43; Martineau: *Essays*, vol i, pp 292, 293; Fisher: *Grounds of Theistic and Christian Belief*, pp. 69-71, Herbert: *Modern Realism*, pp. 408-426; Mansel: *Limits of Religious Thought*, pp. 103, 104; Christlieb: *Modern Doubt and Christian Belief*, Third Lecture, iii, iv.

table, if the principles of the doctrine be true. Religious thought,
LIMITATION OF just as thought in any other sphere, is conditioned by
RELIGIOUS the mental capacity. There might be a revelation of
THOUGHT. truths undiscoverable by the mind itself, or a divine
illumination which should raise the power of thought to its highest
capacity, but this power would still be conditioned by the mental
capacity. Nor is there for us any immediate vision of God wherein
we may grasp him in a comprehensive knowledge. These facts
disprove the transcendentalism which Hamilton controverted, but
they neither imply nor prove the nescience of God which he maintained.

The analysis of this doctrine will place it in a clearer view.
ANALYSIS OF Thought is finite and relative; therefore it can have no
THE DOCTRINE. cognitive apprehension of the infinite and absolute.
The only movement of thought toward the infinite is in thinking
away the finite. The thinking is thus purely negative, and the
infinite forever reachless. In denying the qualities of the finite to
the infinite the finite supplies the whole content of thought. The
absolute is both unrelated and infinite, while thought is conditioned by relations or a distinction of qualities, both of which are
declared to be contradictory to the absolute. With such elements
of the doctrine, it follows that, if God is such an infinite and absolute, he is unknowable and unthinkable.

Such a doctrine of theistic nescience is spread widely upon the
pages of Hamilton and Mansel in the treatment of this question.
The culmination of the doctrine is in these words· " The Divinity,
in a certain sense, is revealed; in a certain sense is concealed;
CULMINATION he is at once known and unknown. But the last
IN WORSHIP and highest consecration of all true religion must be
an altar — Αγνώστῳ Θεῷ — ' To the unknown and unknowable
God '" [1]

Such an altar Paul found in Athens. Was this the last and
highest consecration of all true religion? It was such in style, if
not in truth. However many and great the errors and superstit-
tions of the Athenians, it seems that this altar signified no defect
of either truth or worship. Yet Paul assumes a very serious defect in both. Plainly in his mind the ignorance of their worship
was in their ignorance of the true God. Him therefore he would
declare or make known, that they might worship him in truth.
Paul had not attained to this theistic agnosticism Hence in the
declaration of the true God there is not a word about an unthinkable infinite, or an absolute blank for thought; there is the declara-

[1] Hamilton · Discussions, p. 22.

tion of a personal God, Creator and Lord of all, and whose off-spring we are.[1]

2. *Concerning the Limitation of Religious Thought.*—As pre-viously stated, religious thought, just as thought on other ques-tions, is conditioned by the mental capacity and the laws of think-ing. The mind does not become divine by the study of divine things. The thinking is still human, however divine the subject, or whatever the divine revelation or illumination. Christianity makes no pretension to a comprehensive knowledge of God. Such a pretension is the extravagance of the transcendentalism which professedly grasps the Infinite in the mode of an immediate vision, but mostly loses the divine personality in the pretended knowledge. Along the Christian centuries it has been the wont of theologians to confess the inadequacy of thought to the full comprehension of God. It was very easy, therefore, for Hamilton, as for others, to array such eminent Christian authors —Tertullian, Cyprian, Augustine, Chrysostom, Grotius, Pascal, and others—as witnesses to this limitation of religious thought. He could hardly claim their authority for his own doctrine of theistic nescience. Surely such a doctrine was far from their thought. Their meaning was simply the divine incomprehensibility—a very familiar truth in Christian theology. Hence their utterances are valueless for the doctrine of theistic nescience as against the doc-trine of a true knowledge of God in religious thought.

NO COMPRE-HENSION OF GOD

3. *God Truly Knowable.*—There may be a true knowledge—true in the measure of it—which is not fully comprehensive of its subject. It is easy to embody the contrary doctrine in a definition of thinking If such definition be true, God must be unthinkable and unknowable. Cognitive thought must fully compass the subject But human thought can-not compass the infinite. Thinking is possible only under condi-tions of limitation, which must place the infinite beyond the reach of thought. Such is the summary method of this doctrine. " *To think is to condition ;* and conditional limitation is the fundamental law of the possibility of thought."[2] Mansel[3] and Spencer[4] hold the same doctrine. The meaning is that only the conditioned and limited is thinkable. The law may be valid against the com-prehension of God in thought, but is not valid against all cognitive thought of God.

AGNOSTIC DEF-INITION OF THOUGHT

The central position of this doctrine is that all thought of the infinite is purely negative, and only of the finite which is denied to

<hr/>

[1] Acts xvii, 22–31.   [2] Hamilton · *Discussions*, p. 21.
[3] *Limits of Religious Thought*, pp. 98, 99.   [4] *First Principles*, pp. 81, 82.

the infinite. "The unconditioned is incognizable and inconceivable; its notion being only of the conditioned, which last can alone be positively known or conceived."[1] If this be true, the terms infinite and unconditioned have no positive meaning, signify no positive content of thought. Yet, while negative in form, they are predicates in fact, and therefore must have a positive sense. There can be no predication without a subject, and no subject except in positive thought. The full comprehension of a subject in thought is not necessary to predication, but the cognitive apprehension of it is absolutely necessary. We cannot affirm the infinity and absoluteness of God without the apprehension of God in thought; for this would be predication without a subject, which the laws of thought render impossible. Such is the fallacious outcome of the doctrine which places God beyond the reach of cognitive thought.

THOUGHT OF THE INFINITE NOT WHOLLY NEGATIVE.

It is not true that the notion of the unconditioned or infinite is "only negative" of the finite, and the finite the only content of thought. We appeal the question to consciousness itself. Infinite space and infinite duration are more for thought than the mere negation of finiteness. Consciousness is indeed witness that we cannot comprehend either in thought; but consciousness is equally witness of a form and content of thought which are not merely of the finite. The same is true in our thought of God. We cannot indeed fully comprehend God, but our thinking is not purely negative, with only the finite for content. The Infinite is reached in cognitive thought. We rest this issue on the testimony of consciousness.[2]

APPEAL TO CONSCIOUSNESS.

So far, we have maintained the issue against the nescience of the Infinite as it is interpreted in this antitheistic agnosticism. In this view of the question the result is entirely satisfactory. Our position is much clearer and stronger with the true notion of God as the Infinite. We have previously shown the erroneousness of the doctrine which denies the knowableness of the Infinite; that there is no such an Infinite as this agnosticism maintains; no demand for it in reason; no proof of its existence; no use for it in the universe. Most of all is God not such an Infinite. God, the true Infinite, is a personal being, with the attributes of personality in absolute perfection. The essential attributes of all personality, intellect, sensibility, and will are realities known in our own consciousness. That these attributes

THE TRUE INFINITE TRULY KNOWABLE.

---

[1] Hamilton. *Discussions*, p. 19.

[2] Calderwood: *Philosophy of the Infinite*, pp. 266–268; Martineau: *Essays*, vol. i, pp. 295–298.

are infinite in God does not render them unthinkable or unknowable.   Through his moral government and providential agency God is truly knowable.   In the view of Spencer, the Absolute is too great for any apprehension in cognitive thought.   The real difficulty for knowledge in his Absolute is in its utter blankness, not in its greatness.   When the false Infinite is replaced with the true, the personal God, the Infinite is manifestly thinkable and knowable.

In the results of this discussion it is clearly seen that this form of antitheistic agnosticism is without force against the truth of theism.[1]

[1] Calderwood : *Philosophy of the Infinite ;* Fisher : *Grounds of Theistic and Christian Belief,* pp. 85–102 ; Harris . *The Self-Revelation of God,* pp. 172–182 , Porter . *The Human Intellect,* part IV, chap. VIII ; Martineau . *Essays, Philosophical and Theological,* vol I, pp. 224–243 , Bascom : *Philosophy of Religion,* chap iv ; Herbert . *Modern Realism,* pp. 430–141.

General reference . — Theistic literature has become so voluminous that only a selection can be given in such a reference   We shall not be careful to omit all works previously referred to, or from which citations have been made.

Cudworth : *The Intellectual System of the Universe ;* Howe . *The Living Temple,* part i ; Paley . *Natural Theology, The Bridgewater Treatises ;* Hickok . *Creation and Creator ;* Saisset . *Modern Pantheism ;* Diman . *The Theistic Argument ;* Argyll . *The Reign of Law,* Chadbourne . *Natural Theology ;* Randles : *First Principles of Faith ;* Harris . *Philosophical Basis of Theism ; The Self-Revelation of God,* Tulloch : *Theism ;* Bowne . *Studies in Theism ; Philosophy of Theism ;* Thompson : *Christian Theism,* Buchanan . *Modern Atheism ;* Blakie . *Natural History of Atheism ;* Flint . *Theism ; Antitheistic Theories ;* Cocker . *Theistic Conception of the World ,* Janet . *Final Causes ;* Bishop Foster . *Theism*

PART II.

THEOLOGY.

THEOLOGY.

This part is for the discussion of truths relating directly to God. For the representation of these truths we place at its head the single term theology. Some think that its modern use in a much wider sense renders it inappropriate for such representation. Hence we often find with it some interpretative phrase or limiting word. We thus have, in form, theology—doctrine of God; oftener, theology proper. This is neither graceful in style nor definitive in sense. Appropriateness still lies in the etymological sense. Theology thus means a doctrine of God, and may properly represent all the truths more directly relating to him. Primarily it was used in this sense. We so use it here; and we thus secure a symmetry of terms not otherwise attainable for the several parts of systematic theology.

CHAPTER I.

GOD IN BEING.

I. Being and Attribute.

1. *Definitive Sense of Attribute.*—In a general sense an attribute is any thing which may be affirmed of its subject. This wider sense may include what is accidental as well as what is essential. In the more definite sense an attribute is any quality or property which is intrinsic to the subject, which characterizes and differentiates it, and by virtue of which the subject is what it is.

Attribute, property, quality, faculty, power, are in common use much in the same sense, though mostly with some distinction in application. Thus extension, solidity, divisibility are properties or qualities of body; intellect, sensibility, will are faculties or powers of mind; omniscience, goodness, omnipotence are attributes of God. We do not allege an invariable uniformity in such distinctions of application, yet we think them common. We certainly do not use the term faculty in application to either body or God, while it is the common term in application to the human mind.

2. *Distinctive Sense of Being.*—Qualities are neither possible nor thinkable as separate or self-subsisting facts. For both thought and reality body is more than its properties, mind more than its faculties, God more than his attributes. Sensationalism or positivism may, in a helpless agnosticism, be content with the surface of things or with the merest phenomenalism; but for deeper thought, the thought without which there is neither true science nor philosophy, properties, faculties, attributes must have a ground in essential being. The necessity is as absolute as that of a subject to its predicate in a logical proposition.

The essence of being is a truth of the reason, not a cognition of experience. The reality is none the less sure because BEING A TRUTH OF THE REA-SON. such a truth. Physical properties must have a ground in a material substance. Reason equally determines for the mental faculties a necessary basis in mind. For the divine attributes there must be a ground in essential divine being. Reason is in each case the indisputable authority. The distinctive sense of being in God is that it is the ground of his attributes.

3. *Connection of Attribute and Being.*—We are again within the sphere of reason, not in that of experience. As there is no empirical grasping of essential being, so there is no such grasping of the connection of attribute and subject. Even reason cannot know the mode of this connection. But reason can and does affirm it to be most intrinsic. The connection is in no sense a loose or separable one. Being is not as a vessel in which attributes may be placed and from which they may be withdrawn; not as a ground on which they may repose as a building upon its foundation or a statue upon its pedestal, and which may remain after their removal.

The connection must be most intrinsic, so that neither BEING AND ATTRIBUTE INSEPARABLE is nor can be without the other. Being and attribute are separable in abstract thought, but inseparable in reality. Neither can exist without the other. While extension must have a basis in material body, such body must exist in extension. While intellect must have a ground in mind, mind must have the faculty of intelligence. In the present conditioning relation of a nervous organism to the activities of the mental powers their normal working may be interrupted or temporarily suspended, but they must ever exist potentially in mind, because necessary to the very notion of mind. In the very being of God are all his attributes. Without them he would not be God.

4. *True Method of Treatment.*—While attribute and being are correlatives of thought and inseparable in fact, they are separable in abstract thought, and for clearness of view must be so separated.

Only thus can we attain to the truer notion of attribute and subject respectively, and in the unity of being.

What is thus generally requisite to a true method is specially requisite in the study of the truths now in question. A right view of God as subject is necessary to the truer notion of his attributes, and therefore to the truer notion of himself. It is only in a distinctive view of God as subject that we can reach the ground of a scientific classification and category of his attributes.

5. *Common Error of Method.*—The common error in the treatment of these questions is in the omission of all distinction between the being of God and his attributes—such an error as would appear in the omission of all distinction between subject and predicate, which must render impossible any logical process or result. The truths which directly relate to God as subject are drawn into the circle of his attributes. For instance, spirituality, the very essence of his being, is classed and treated as an attribute. But an attribute of what ? There is nothing deeper than essential being of which it may be an attribute. With such an error of method, it is not strange that the classification of the attributes is felt to be most difficult. The result is that mostly the modes of classification are purely arbitrary. With a proper distinction between subject and attribute in God, most of all, with the deepest and most determinative truth of God as the ground of his own attributes, a scientific classification is clearly attainable. But this question may be deferred for the present, as it must recur with the distinct treatment of the attributes.[1]

II. Spirituality of Being.

1. *Notion of Being through Attribute.*—As the essence of being is a truth only of the reason, but cognizable only on some knowledge of its qualities, so a rational notion of the nature of being must be conditioned in a like manner. This law of the notion of being may seem to require a study of properties previous to any inquiry into the nature ORDER OF THE QUESTIONS OF BEING AND ATTRIBUTE of the substance in which they are grounded. It would so require in the case of an entirely new question. But the present is not a new question; and we may so far anticipate the more direct treatment of the divine attributes as to appropriate our present knowledge of them in a previous inquiry into the divine nature. There are two other facts which legitimate this course. One is that we are here directly within the sphere of revelation, pre-eminently the

[1] Sir William Hamilton. *Lectures on Metaphysics*, pp. 104–106 ; D. H. Hamilton: *Autology*, part 1, chap. ii ; Porter: *The Human Intellect*, pp. 619–630.

12

sphere of truth respecting the nature of God as well as of his attributes. The other is that the real question of the divine attributes is not so much the question of their kind as that of their perfection. A complete analysis of this question finds the attributes of God to be distinctively and exclusively personal in kind. But as such they are involved in the profound question of the personality of God. The truth of his personality carries with it the truth of his personal attributes. The question of their perfection still remains; and this is distinctively the question of the divine attributes. The question of personality may, therefore, properly precede this question of the attributes. Personality is related to spirituality as its necessary ground. It is true that neither personality nor spirituality can be properly treated without a forward glancing at the personal attributes. But with the distinctive sense of the question of the divine attributes it is in the order of a proper method to treat previously the questions of both spirituality and personality.

2. *Requirement for Spiritual Being.*—As the notion of essential being is conditioned on some knowledge of properties, so the notion of a distinction of subjects must be through some known distinction of properties. As an attribute requires a subject, so it requires a subject answering in kind to its own distinctive quality. The latter requirement is as absolute as the former. For the two kinds of facts classed as the properties of body and the faculties of mind reason must imperatively determine essentially distinct and different subjects. Empirical science can allege nothing of any weight against this position. It may gratuitously deny any real distinction between the two classes of facts or assert the identity of the mental with the physical; or it may pronounce for agnosticism in respect to the nature of matter, and then by the covert assumption of a most pretentious gnosticism proclaim a new face of matter which accounts for the facts of mind. No assumption could be more gratuitous, no assertion more groundless. It is a dogmatizing which would shame the method of the most positive theology. Reason is still the decisive authority. While a material ground can answer for the properties of body, only a spiritual ground can answer for the faculties of mind. The divine attributes must have their ground in spiritual being.

Margin note: NECESSARY CONSISTENCY OF ATTRIBUTE AND BEING

3. *Truth of Divine Spirituality.*—The theistic conception of the race, while often very crude and low, is without rational explication except with the notion of divine spirituality. The mere idol is rarely the whole mental conception of the devotee.[1] Mostly

[1] Caird: *Philosophy of Religion*, p. 177.

it is but the symbol of a being whom he apprehends, however dimly and feebly, as cognizant of his life, with power to help or to harm, and in whose regards, whether of approval or reprehension, he is deeply concerned The divine spirituality is the rational implication of these conceptions. The once prevalent notion of God as the life of nature or the soul of the world, now known as Hylozoism, has no sufficing ground in either materialism or pantheism Even fetichism so far recognizes a conscious intelligence and agency in the many gods resident in many things as to rise above both materialism and pantheism in a high advance toward the conception of a divine spiritualism. Monotheism, now recognized by the most thorough students of the question as the primitive faith of the most ancient races, must be grounded in a divine spirituality [1]

IN THE THEISTIC CONCEPTION OF THE RACE

The arguments of theism, while conclusive of the divine existence, are equally conclusive of the divine spirituality. Spontaneity or the power of personal will is an absolute requirement for the original cosmical cause. The adjustments of the world and the universe evince the teleology of a divine intelligence. The anthropological argument finds in a divine mind the only possible original of human minds, with their vast and varied powers, while their moral constitution is conclusive of a moral personality in their author. These facts require and evince the divine spirituality

IN THE PROOFS OF THEISM.

On this question the sense of Scripture is uniform and clear. The recorded agency of God in creation and providence, his manifestations in patriarchal history and the Jewish theocracy, the theistic conceptions of the sacred writers, the thoughts and affections which they ascribe to God, their conception of his transcendence above nature—all these facts carry with them the sense of the divine spirituality.

A TRUTH OF THE SCRIPTURES.

There are more explicit utterances. God is not only our Creator, but the Father of our spirits. We are his offspring.[2] The truth of spirituality in God is thus revealed in our own spiritual being. The same truth is deeply wrought into the second commandment.[3] The full sense of Scripture is completed in the explicit words of our Lord: "God is a Spirit: and they that worship him must worship *him* in spirit and in truth."[4]

EXPLICIT UTTERANCES.

4. *God Only in Spirituality.*—If there is no divine spiritual being there is no God. The inevitable logic of materialism is atheism. The absolute monistic principle of pantheism, however set forth as

---

[1] Gillett. *God in Human Thought.*

[2] Num. xvi, 22; xxvii, 16; Acts xvii, 28; Heb xii, 9.

[3] Exod. xx. 4   [4] John iv. 24.

the cause of all phenomenal facts, is not God. The case is not other with the alleged attributes of infinite thought and infinite extension. These are purely hypothetic in pantheism, and in no proper sense intrinsic to the being of God. The former can have no meaning except as the predicate of an infinite personal mind. With these hypothetic attributions, the monistic principle is still without consciousness or intelligent agency; a mere force, working without ends or aim. No mere force, though it were omnipotence itself, can answer to the theistic demands of the human soul. It requires an overseeing conscious intelligence, a ruling providence and a fatherly love. There must be the assurance of sympathy and helpfulness in the trying exigencies of life. These imperative requirements are absolutely impossible except in a divine spiritual being.

5. *Immutability of Being.*—The question of immutability may · have in relation to God a twofold application: one as a predicate of his essential being; the other as a predicate of his personality, or, more broadly, of his personal attributes and the principles of his providence. The latter is the real question of the divine immutability, but properly belongs to the treatment of the divine attributes. There is truth in the former application. God is immutable in his essential being. There is no proof of any change in the essence of the human spirit. The question is not open to any empirical testing. The unity of consciousness and the persistence of personal identity through the extremest changes of the most prolonged life are conclusive against any such change. There is no proof of any change even in the essence of matter, however common and great the changes in its chemical combinations and organic forms. There is no quality of spirit which can become a law of essential change. What is true of the human spirit is profoundly true of the absolutely perfect Spirit. With any law of change in his essential being, he could not be the true and eternal God.

TWOFOLD QUESTION OF IMMUTABILITY

6. *Question of Divine Infinity.*—The real question of the infinity or omnipresence of God is a question of the perfection of his personal attributes, and will be treated in its proper place. The divine infinity has proved itself a most perplexing question, even to the profoundest thinkers. We must think that much of this perplexity arises from an error of method, or, rather, from a mistaken sense of the question. The mistake is in treating the question in the sense of an infinite essence, not in the sense of infinite personal attributes. The ubiquity of God is a ubiquity by virtue of his personal perfec-

MISTAKEN VIEW OF THE DIVINE INFINITY

tions. The question of an infinite divine essence is for rational thought an abyss of darkness. It is the question of an infinite magnitude or extension of essential being. Spatial ideas thus inevitably arise, but only for the deeper confusion and helplessness of thought. But the divine Spirit has no spatial qualities. Hence there is no place for the question of an infinitely present divine essence.

CHAPTER II.

GOD IN PERSONALITY.

I. PERSONALITY.

THE question of personality must be studied first of all and
KNOWLEDGE chiefly in the light of one's own consciousness.   There
OF PERSONAL- is no other way to a knowledge of other personalities,
ITY   whether human or angelic, or even the divine.   We
have no immediate knowledge of the facts in others which constitute personality.   When these facts are known in one's own consciousness, then the personality of others is revealed to him through
a manifestation of the same facts.   This is a true mode of knowledge ; and the knowledge is validated by the deepest and most
determining principle of science   The generalizations and constructions of science would be groundless if things which manifest
the same qualities were not the same in fact.

Personality is a unity in the deepest sense of the term.   The
facts of consciousness are manifold and diverse, but consciousness
itself, the very center of personality, is one.   Consciousness and
memory, but memory as a fact of consciousness, reveal to one's self
his personal identity.   The unity of personality is in the truth of
personal identity.

With the deepest sense of the unity of mind, its faculties are
CONSTITUENT open to analysis and classification.   Otherwise there
FACULTIES OF could be no mental science.   Personality, while a unity
PERSONALITY. in itself, admits of scientific treatment because it con-
sists, not in a single principle or power, but in a complex of powers.
Analysis may open this complex and discover its content of powers.
This process is necessary to a clear insight into personality itself,
and the way to a truer view of the divine personality.   The first
thing, then, in the opening of this question is to find the necessary
facts of personality.

1. *Determining Facts of Personality.*—There are mighty forces
in physical nature; but they can act only on the proper adjustment
or collocation of material things, and thereon must necessarily act.
Their action is without consciousness or aim as well as under a law
of necessity.   Such forces, however great in potency or wonderful

in operation, can have no quality of personality. Life, with its marvelous agency in the vegetable kingdom, still makes no advance beyond the purely physical realm toward any intrinsic personal quality.

In the animal orders, notably in those of the higher grades, there are instinctive impulses toward ends, and a voluntary power for their attainment, but no evidence of other essential requisites of personality. We cannot study the psychology of animals as we can that of minds like our own, because we cannot place the facts of the former in the light of our own consciousness as we can the facts of the latter. Yet strong instinctive impulses and strong voluntary power are manifest facts in animal life. But there is no evidence of such rational intelligence in the conception of ends and such freedom in the choice of ends as must combine in the constitution of personality.

Pure intellect, intellect without any form of sensibility, however great, could not constitute personality. Conceptually, PERSONALITY such an intellect is a possibility, though its sphere of NOT IN PURE knowledge could not be universal. A deeper analysis INTELLECT must find in the sensibilities a necessary element of knowledge in many spheres. Such a mind might have great intuitive power and a clear insight into the abstract sciences, but it could have no interest in their study. Neither could there be for it any eligibility of ends. For such a mind the mightiest potentiality of will would be useless for the want of all motive or reason of use. The only possible action would be purposeless and purely spontaneous. Personality is intrinsically a free rational agency. This is impossible in pure intellect, however great—impossible even with the complement of a will potentially very strong.

Rational or moral motives are a necessity to personal agency, and therefore to personality. Such motives are not mere RATIONAL MO- instinctive impulses toward action, but forms of con- TIVITY A NE- scious interest in ends of action, which may be taken CESSITY. up into reflection and judgment. Motives are possible only with a capacity for conscious interest in ends. This capacity is broader and deeper than can well be expressed by the term sensibility. The profounder motives arise from the rational and moral nature rather than from what we usually designate as the feelings. There can be for us no eligibility of ends, and therefore no rational choice, except through motives arising in some form of conscious interest in ends. But rational choice is the central fact of rational agency, and the only difference between rational agency and personal agency is a difference of verbal expression. With the power of personal agency there is personality. It follows that for the constitution of personality an emotional nature, with a capacity for rational interest in ends, must combine with rational intelligence.

Will is the central power of personal agency, and therefore a
WILL IN PER- necessary constituent of personality. Without the will
SONALITY there could be no voluntary use or direction of the mental faculties, no voluntary action of any kind. In such a state man would be as incapable of personal agency as an animal or even as any force of physical nature.

The result of the previous analysis is that rational intelligence,
FREE AGENCY sensibility, and will are essential requisites of person-
NECESSARY ality. But such a complex of faculties does not in itself complete the idea of personality. There must also be the freedom of personal agency. Such agency means, not merely the freedom of external action, but specially the free rational choice of the ends of action. The freedom of external action requires simply the freedom of the bodily organism from interior impotence and exterior restraint, and may be as complete in an animal as in a man. The bodily organism is merely instrumental to the external action, and can be free only as a freely usable instrument. The mere freedom of external action can have no higher sense. The true freedom must lie back of this in the personal agency, and must consist in the power of free rational choice. With this there is true personality.

There is still a profound question which vitally concerns the
DETERMINING reality of personality. It is the question of the relation
MOTIVE CON- of motive to choice, or, more properly here. the decision
TRADICTORY
TO PERSONAL- of the mind with respect to an end—more properly,
ITY. because whether such decision be a choice or not depends upon the relation of the motive to the mental action. That motive is a necessary condition of choice is a plain truth—so plain that the maintenance of a liberty of indifference may well seem strange. Any voluntary decision in a state of indifference must be a purely arbitrary volition, and therefore cannot be a choice.[1] Choice in the very nature of it is the rational election of an end. For its rationality there must be a motive. But what is the action of the motive upon the elective decision? This is the question which vitally concerns the reality of personality. If the motive is simply a solicitation or inducement which may be taken up into reflection and weighed in the judgment, personality is secure. But if the motive is a causal efficience which determines the decision to

[1] Kant. Metaphysic of Ethics, p. 204; Miley: "The Freedom of Choice," Methodist Quarterly Review, July, 1881.

the end, then there is no choice, nor the possibility of one, and personality sinks with personal agency beneath an absolute law of determinism.

Only as rational intelligence, sensibility, and will combine in the constitution of free personal agency is there the reality of personality. There must be rational intelligence for the conception of ends, sensibility as the source of motives with respect to ends, and will in combination with intelligence and sensibility as the complement of power in choosing between ends. With these facts there is personality. Our own personality is in this complex of powers.

With moral reason and a capacity for moral motives, motives sufficient for the choice of the good against the evil, there is a moral personality. Conceptually, there MORAL PERSONALITY might be a rational personality without the necessary powers of a moral personality. These powers might be an original omission, or the rational might remain after the moral were sunken beneath a law of necessitation. Moral personality must sink under a moral necessity to evil, just as rational personality must sink in the want of its essential requisites. There is no deeper moral necessity, none more exclusive of moral personality, than an incapacity for the motives necessary to the choice of the good. For complete moral personality there must be free moral agency.

2. *Requisites of All Personality.*—There can be neither human nor angelic personality, nor even a divine personality, without this complex of essential requisites. There is no need and no purpose of asserting a complete parallelism in all personalities. There is no such implication. As we ascend through the orders of higher intelligences, angels and archangels, even up to God himself, there may be, and in the divine must be, large variations from such a parallelism. The variations may be not only in the grade of faculties, reaching to the infinite in the divine, and particularly in the forms of sensibility, but there may be other powers, now wholly unknown to us. The position is that the complex of requisites in our own personality is a necessity for all personality. Neither angel nor archangel is or can be a person in the true, deep sense of the term without these powers, whatever their grade in such higher intelligences, whatever variation in the forms of sensibility, or whatever other powers they may possess. The same law of requisites must hold for the divine personality. But this application must be treated under a distinct heading.

II. THE DIVINE PERSONALITY.

1. *In the Light of the Human.*—Any conception of the divine personality irrespective of our own is for us impossible. It does not follow that our own must be the measure of the divine. We have previously disclaimed any necessary complete parallelism between human and angelic personalities, and pointed out how profoundly this is true as between our own and the divine. Still there may be a likeness between the former with its finite powers and the latter with its infinite perfections which is greatly helpful toward a truer and clearer notion of the divine. There is a deep truth in our creation in the image of God.[1] With the revelation of this truth, there is no rashness in looking into our own personality for the likeness of the divine. Nor is it, after a recognition of the difference in the grade of powers and the forms of sensibility between the two, open to the reprehension: "Thou thoughtest that I was altogether such a one as thyself."[2] Personality is the deepest truth of our likeness to God. Our vision of his personality is in the reflection of his image in our own.[3]

HUMAN PERSONALITY THE IMAGE OF THE DIVINE.

2. *Same Complex of Powers Requisite.*—There must be in God the three forms of power which constitute personality in us. In the lack of any one he could not be a person. Such perfections as omniscience, omnipotence, and immutability, in however complete a synthesis, could not of themselves constitute a divine personality. There must be even for God the eligibility of ends and freedom in the choice of ends These are an absolute requirement of personal agency, which is the central fact of personality. But, as we have previously seen, the eligibility of ends can arise only with some form of conscious interest in them. This conscious interest cannot arise either from pure intelligence or from the will—not even from an infinite intelligence or an omnipotent will. There must be motivities of the divine nature, as in distinction from intellect and will —rational and moral motivities as the necessary ground of interest in ends. With the powers of intellect, sensibility, and will, and the freedom of rational and moral self-determination with respect to ends, there is a divine personality. The question of the divine freedom will be treated elsewhere.

3 *Personality Manifest in Proofs of Theism.*—Theism is the doctrine of a personal God. The arguments for the truth of theism are conclusive of personality in the original cause of the dependent cosmos. A glance at these arguments, as previously given,

[1] Gen 1, 27   [2] Psa. 1, 21.
[3] Fisher: *The Grounds of Theistic and Christian Belief,* pp. 1, 2

will make this manifest. We recur to them in the order of theistic discussion, not as the facts of personality arise in the method of psychological treatment.

We begin with the cosmological argument. On the principle of causation, with the dependence of cosmical facts, there is manifest in the existence of the cosmos the power of will. IN THE COSMO-LOGICAL. Only in a self-energizing will is there an adequate cause for the beginning and ongoing of cosmical formations. This is not in itself conclusive of personality, but the argument goes so far as to give us one essential attribute of personality in the original cosmical cause.

In the teleological argument there is in the formation of the cosmos a manifestation at once of both intelligence and sensibility. The adjustments of the cosmos are the IN THE TELEO-LOGICAL. work of intelligence. As these adjustments appear in the harmony of the heavens, in the wonders of vegetable and animal organism, in the formation of man, only an omniscient mind could have planned them. Thus another essential attribute of personality in the original cause is given us.

But teleology is not complete in the mere intellectual conception of ends and the adjustment of means to their attainment. The choice of ends is an essential element. This choice, essentially rational in its nature, must be for a reason—for a reason in the sense of motive. The ends chosen must have possessed a rational eligibility for the divine mind; for otherwise its whole work in the formation of the cosmos must have been purely arbitrary. But, as we have previously shown, the actual eligibility of ends is dependent upon some form of conscious interest in the electing mind. Such interest is possible neither from pure intellect nor from will, but only in a subjective motivity combined with those powers in the constitution of personality. This subjective motivity is of the nature of feeling; and we thus find in God the third essential attribute of personality.

The anthropological argument for theism proves that a material genesis of mind is impossible; that God is the only sufficient original of mind. The adaptations of mental endowment to our manifold relations and duties, secular and moral, clearly evince the highest form of divine teleology. IN THE AN-THROPOLOG-ICAL. In such teleology there is manifest at once all the essential attributes of divine personality. In the provisions for the happiness of sentient life, provisions above the mere necessities of existence, there is the proof of a rational benevolence which must be a personal quality in the author of such life. In the moral endowments of the soul there is the proof of a moral nature and a moral agency in its divine original.[1] A moral nature, with its agency in the creation of beings morally constituted, is possible only in a divine personality.

4. *The Sense of Scripture.*—It seems quite needless to carry this question into the Scriptures. No attempt need be made to cite the multitude of texts expressive of personal attributes in God. Little TESTIMONY OF more is required than to note and emphasize the fact THE SCRIPT- that from beginning to end, without the slightest halt- URES ing or variation, the Scriptures utter the one great truth of the divine personality. The theistic conception of patriarchs, prophets, and apostles is ever the conception of a personal God. The personal divine Son is the revelation of the personal divine Father. In the sublime words which open the Scriptures— "In the beginning God created the heaven and the earth"—there is the profound truth of a personal God, eternally before the beginning. In the giving of the law, notably in the contents of the ten commandments, the same deep truth is manifest. The Lord's Prayer is replete with the truth of the divine personality. We breathe its petitions to the Father in heaven, devoutly recognize his will, pray for the daily ministries of his providence, for his gracious forgiveness and heavenly guidance. This prayer is useless and without meaning for any one who does not believe in a personal God.

If the texts which openly express or clearly imply the sense of ALL THE POW- divine personality were properly classified, they would ERS OF PER- be found ascribing to God the three forms of attribute SONALITY which constitute personality. There is first the ascription of intelligence or omniscience.[2] Again, there is the ascription of feeling or affection. The Lord loves righteousness and hates iniquity. He is pitiful and of tender mercy.[3] One great fact might well suffice for the present truth. The great redemption originated in the divine love.[4] In this love there is an infinite fullness of feeling. "God is love."[5] This is the deepest truth of God; and it is the truth of an emotional nature. This does not imply the excessive or passionate forms of emotion as in ourselves, but it does mean the reality of affections in God. Finally, there is ascribed to God the attribute of will as the power of personal agency.[6] Thus distinctly and definitely the Scriptures ascribe to

[1] Mansel · *Limits of Religious Thought,* p. 122
[2] Psa. cxlvii, 5; Prov. xv, 3; Acts xv, 18; Heb. iv, 13.
[3] Psa. xxxii, 5; xlv, 7; Jas. v, 11.   [4] John iii, 16; 1 John iv, 10.
[5] 1 John iv, 16.   [6] Psa. cxv, 3, Isa. xlvi, 10; Dan. iv, 35; Matt. xix, 26.

God the three attributes, intelligence, feeling, will, which constitute personality.

5. *God Only in Personality.*—If God is not a personal being, the result must be either atheism or pantheism. It matters little which. The dark and deadly implications are much the same. There is no God with self-consciousness or the power of rational and moral self-determination, no personal divine agency in the universe. A blind, necessitated force is the original of all. The existence of the world and the heavens is without reason or end. There is no reason for the existence of man, no rational or moral end. God has no interest in him, no rational or moral rule over him. The universal sense of moral obligation and responsibility must be pronounced a delusion. There should be an end of worship, for there is wanting a truly worshipful being. All that remains is the dark picture of a universe without divine teleology or providence.[1]

[1] Hamilton: *Autology*, part v; Strong: *Systematic Theology*, pp. 121, 122; Harris: *Philosophical Basis of Theism*, pp. 98, 99; *The Self-Revelation of God*, part iii; Olssen: *Personality, Human and Divine.*

CHAPTER III.

GOD IN ATTRIBUTES

WE have previously given the definite sense of attribute, the distinction of attribute and essential being, and the immanence of attribute in being. In treating the question of divine personality we unavoidably anticipated the divine attributes. But they were then brought into notice only incidentally, and only so far as that discussion required, and their proper treatment we still have on hand. This discussion should proceed on a scientific analysis and classification. A neglect of this method allows various divine predicables to be classed and treated as attributes which are not distinctively such. There are many instances of this error. These divine verities should not be omitted, but we should avoid the artificial method of classing them as attributes, and should treat them separately.

I. CLASSIFICATION OF THE ATTRIBUTES.

1. *Method of Classification.*—There are peculiarities in the classification of the attributes, as compared with the classifications in the sciences of nature, which should not be overlooked. In these sciences the classifications are made under terms which express general conceptions, not realities of existence. Such are the terms mollusca, vertebrata, mammalia, ruminantia. The attributes have no such a conceptual ground. God as their subject is the deepest reality of existence. It was an egregious error of Mill to assert the contrary: "God is as much a general term to the Christian or Jew as to the polytheist."[1] With the polytheist to whom there are many gods the term might express a general conception, but with the Christian or Jew, to whom there is only one God, it cannot have such a sense. If this term expressed a mere conception or general notion, no ground would remain for the attributes as concrete realities in the divine personality. But God is a personal term, with the definite and concrete sense of a proper term. As the subject of the attributes he is the infinite reality of being. In this fact lies one peculiarity in the classification of the attributes as compared with the classifications in the sciences of nature.

[1] *Logic*, p 94.

There is another peculiarity of this classification. Under the common terms or general conceptions, as above stated, the things classed are essential, individual existences; whereas the attributes are neither essential nor individual existences, but are concrete realities of the divine personality.

With these profound differences, we may still observe a scientific method in the treatment of the divine attributes. Such THE METHOD a method requires their classification on the ground of SCIENTIFIC. what is the deepest in God as their subject. This law must exclude all predicables which, however true of God, are not distinctively attributes. It follows that a catalogue of divine predicables, however complete and true, is not a classification of the divine attributes. Nor is any division on grounds which do not thoroughly differentiate the several groups a proper classification. A neglect of these principles results in artificial distinctions—of which there are many instances.

2. *Artificial Classifications.*—It will help us to a clearer view of the question if we notice a few instances of such artificial distinctions and groupings.

Such is the division of the attributes into the natural and the moral. Instances of the kind are so common that it is AS NATURAL needless to give any special reference. It might be AND MORAL. proper to distinguish the spheres of the divine agency into the natural and the moral, but such a distinction of the attributes is groundless. God acts in the physical and moral spheres, but not by two distinct sets of powers. Such a distinction in the spheres of his operation cannot be carried back into the powers of his agency.

A grouping of the attributes as positive and negative is equally artificial. It is artificial because this distinction in the AS POSITIVE terms marks no real distinction in the attributes. The AND NEGA- negative terms have just as positive a sense as the class TIVE. of positive terms. Infinity and immutability express the reality of the limitless and changeless in God just as omniscience and omnipotence express the absolute plenitude of his knowledge and power. It thus appears that there is no ground for this classification of the attributes. It is a grouping without any real distinction. It will further appear that the divine predicables which we express negatively are not distinctively attributes.

There is no scientific advance on the ground of a distinction between what God is in himself and in his manifestations: "the *Majesty* which he has in himself, and the glory which he *outwardly* manifests; the inner brightness, consequently, and the outward radiance of the light; the attributes which relate to *his mode of existence*, and those which become known to us in *his mode of operation.*[1] There is no ground for such a distinction. In any proper sense in which some attributes are related to the mode of the divine existence all must be so related. Hence they cannot be thus divided into distinct classes. Further, all are eternally complete in God; hence no manifestation of a part in the mode of his operation can constitute a ground of classification.

AS INNER GLORY AND OUTER MANI-FESTATION.

Dr. Hodge accepts the classification of the Westminster Catechism. He thinks that, while open to speculative objection, it has the advantage of simplicity and familiarity.[2] He does not commend it, as certainly he could not, for any exact analysis or scientific construction. However complete as a catalogue, it is not in any strict sense a classification.

We may present together two instances of analysis and classification which, with verbal differences, are substantially the same. Dr. Pope gives, as the result of his analysis, "First, the attributes pertaining to God as absolute or unrelated being; then, those arising out of the relation between the Supreme and the creature, which indeed require the creature for their manifestation; and, finally, those which belong to the relation between God and moral beings under his government, with special reference to man."[3] Dr. Cocker gives the result of his analysis and the grounds of his classification thus: "1. As related to our intuition of real being; by abstraction from all other being or personality—the *immanent* attributes of God. 2. As causally related to finite, dependent existence; by elimination of all necessary limitation—the *relative or transitive* attributes of God. 3. As ethically related to finite personality; by elimination of all imperfection—the moral attributes of God."[4] It will readily appear, on a comparison of these two instances, that the three divisions of the one are the same in principle and method as the three divisions of the other. They are both specially formal endeavors toward a scientific attainment. We must think the method a mistake and the aim a failure. In the grouping of the attributes according to the three divisions, certain divine predicables are placed in the first which are not distinctively attributes. We may instance *spirituality*, which is of the very essence of God and not an attribute of his being; *eternity*, which

BY POPE AND COCKER

---

[1] Van Oosterzee: *Christian Dogmatics*, vol. i, p. 254.
[2] *Systematic Theology*, vol. i, p. 376.
[3] *Christian Theology*, vol. i, p. 291.
[4] *Theistic Conception of the World*, p. 50.

is in no proper sense an attribute of the absolute being of God, and no truer of his absolute being than of his personal attributes which are grouped in the second and third divisions ; *immutability,* which is not distinctively a truth of the essential being of God, as it is equally true of all his attributes ; *self-sufficiency,* which, instead of being a distinct truth of the very essence of God, can be a reality only with his omniscience and omnipotence. In the second and third groupings, on a distinction of relations to the creature and to moral beings, with a resulting distinction of attributes as the transitive and the moral, it was impossible to complete the second division without placing in it some attributes which are necessary to the third—impossible, because that distinction is scientifically insufficient for the separate groupings Omniscience, omnipotence, wisdom, goodness, which could not be omitted from the relation of God to the creature, are equally necessary in his relation to moral government. The insufficiency of these distinctions may be further noted, particularly in the analysis of Cocker. The transitive attributes of his second division are as immanent in God as the attributes of the first, and no more transitive than those of the third. In both instances, the distinction between the second and third divisions is really the same as that, previously noticed, between the natural and moral attributes, and is open to the same insuperable objections.

It was not our purpose to review comprehensively the many methods in the classification of the attributes, but to notice a few instances as illustrative of an artificial method. What we have given may suffice for this purpose. *PURPOSE OF THESE INSTANCES.*

3 *Classification on the Ground of Personality.*—In the true method of science classification is on the ground of what is most determinate in the subject. This is the natural method in distinction from the artificial. The same method should be observed in the classification of the divine attributes. Personality is the most determinate conception of God, and the truest, deepest sense in which he can be viewed as the subject of his own attributes. Personality is the only *PERSONALITY THE TRUE GROUND OF CLASSIFICATION* conception of God which immediately gives his attributes. Any other ground of classification must result either in a mere catalogue in which subject and attribute are confusedly jumbled, or in groupings without any sufficient ground of distinction. Personality gives all attributes which are properly such in distinction from what God is as their subject. This will appear on their direct treatment, while the attributes themselves will thus open into a clearness of view not otherwise attainable.

12

4. *Category of the Attributes.*—Our method omits from this cat-egory certain divine predicables usually classed as attributes. Of these there are several classes. Some belong to God as subject, not as attributes. Some, however true of God, are in no proper sense his attributes. Others result from the perfection of attributes, but are not distinctively attributes themselves. We have previously noted spirituality as belonging to the first class. Eternity and unity belong to the second. Immutability and omnipresence be-long to the third. For the present it may suffice thus to name the several classes, as all must be treated in the proper place. It may be further stated that one attribute, as we shall find the category, includes what are usually treated as several attributes.

As God in personality is the subject of his own attributes, so therein we must find their true category. This cat-egory must be determined by the constitutive and essen-tial facts of the divine personality. These essential facts are the divine attributes. There are no single terms for their complete expression, and the best will require explication. The requirement is specially from the perfection of the powers which constitute the divine attributes. The terms which express these powers in the human personality require ex-plication; and the requirement must be far deeper in their use for the divine attributes. A proper analysis gives us the essential powers of the human personality as intellect, sensibility, and will. For the present we shall use the same terms for the designation of the constitutive powers of the divine personality. We said for the present, because these terms must be left open for such modifi-cation or substitution as may be required by the plenitude and perfection of these powers in the divine personality.

Intellect is in both common and philosophic use for the power or capacity of rational intelligence in the human mind. It includes all the cognitive faculties, but signifies simply the capacity for knowledge, while knowledge itself must be an acquisition through their proper use. There is the reality of intellect in God; and, so far, there is a likeness of powers in the human and the divine personalities. Knowledge in God, however, is not an acquisition, but an eternal possession. This profound distinction requires the use of another term for the expression of the whole truth in God. Intellect well expresses the power of knowl-edge in the human mind, but cannot express the plenitude of the reality in the divine mind. No term is more appropriate than omniscience—the one long in theological use. Omniscience implies the profoundest sense of intellect as a power of knowledge, but

THE TRUE CATEGORY IN PERSONAL AT-TRIBUTES

INTELLECT, OM-NISCIENCE

omits all implication of a process of acquisition, while it expresses the infinite plenitude of the divine knowledge.

Sensibility is the term in philosophic use for all forms of mental feeling.   It is also used without any qualification for all forms of divine feeling.   It seems more appropriate for a philosophy grounded in sensationalism than for a SENSIBILITY, DIVINE SENSIBILITY philosophy which gives a proper place to the higher rational powers and to original truths.   The profoundest motives of life arise with the activities of the philosophic and moral reason.   Sensibility seems but a poor term for the expression of these higher motivities. Yet it is the term in philosophic use ; nor have we another with which to replace it   It seems still more inappropriate and insufficient for the expression of the forms of feeling in the mind of God, and necessary to his personality   But the difficulty of replacing it with a better still remains.   The term feeling is deficient in definiteness, and includes much of human sensibility which can have nothing analogous in the divine consciousness.   Affection and emotion are in philosophic use for distinct forms of sensibility, and hence are respectively too specific and narrow for the present requirement.   Even love, while the deepest truth of the divine nature, does not include all the forms of divine feeling.   It seems necessary still to use the term sensibility.   But we here use it only in the sense of the higher forms of feeling, particularly the rational and moral, which render man the image of God.   These feelings are the response of his motivities to the objects of his conception, and constitute the motives of his providence.   Without such motives he could have no reason for any action.   Neither teleology, nor justice, nor love could have any place in the operations of his providence.   There could be no divine providence.   Neither could there be a divine personality.

Will is the third and completing attribute of personality.   It is the necessary power of personal agency, of rational self-determination, of rational action with respect to motives and ends.   The will is not sufficient for personality simply as WILL, OMNIPOTENCE. a power of self-energizing for the attainment of the ends of one's impulses and appetences.   Such a power is no higher than the self-energizing of an animal.   It must be central to the personality, that it may be the working-power of the rational personal agency. It is thus the power of election with respect to ends, and the executive power whereby one may give effect to his choices.   The will is thus a necessary attribute of personality.   It is such an attribute in God.   The truth of such a divine attribute is in the Scriptures, and in the reality of the divine personality. The power of personal agency in God, whether in creation, providence, or grace, is the power of his will. It has the plenitude of omnipotence. Hence will and omnipotence in God are the same attribute. For this reason we may properly use the term omnipotence.

II. DIVINE OMNISCIENCE.

As previously noted, we use the term omniscience instead of either intelligence or intellect for the reason that knowledge in God is immediate and infinite. The reality of intellect is given with his personality, while omniscience expresses the plenitude of its perfection. .Such perfection is the real question in the treatment of this attribute.

1. *Sense of Omniscience.*—In the measure of agreement between the mental concept and the object of conception there is knowledge, in whatever mind. The fact is the same whatever the mode of the conception or the extent of the knowledge. Omniscience must be God's perfect conception of himself, and of all things and events, without respect to the time of their existence or occurrence. Any limitation in any particular must be a limitation in the divine knowledge.

Omniscience must be an immediate and eternal knowing. The AN IMMEDIATE knowledge which is not immediate and eternal must be AND ETERNAL an acquisition. For the acquisition there must be time KNOWING. and a mental process. Such knowledge must be limited. An acquired omniscience is not a thinkable possibility. The ideas are too alien for any scientific association in rational thought. Hence we must either admit an immediate and eternal knowing in God or deny his omniscience. These alternatives are complete and absolute.

Omniscience, in the truest, deepest sense of the term, must be prescient of all futuritions, whatever their nature or causality. Future free volitions must be included with events which shall arise from necessary causes. Only with such prescience can there be a true omniscience. Such a divine omniscience is the common Christian faith. There are exceptions; and the issue raised should not be entirely omitted.

2. *Respecting Future Free Volitions.*—The divine nescience of future free volitions as now maintained is, apparently, quite different from the doctrine of Adam Clarke, who held on the part of God a purely voluntary nescience. The difference, however, is THE DOCTRINE rather apparent than real. The doctrine of Clarke OF CLARKE. must assume for God simply a faculty of knowledge, potentially existent in him and for his voluntary use, in analogy to

his power. He did recognize this analogy, but plainly without apprehending its implication respecting the mode of the divine knowledge. A faculty of knowledge for voluntary use is simply a faculty for the acquisition of knowledge. An immediate and eternal knowing is thus precluded. But, as previously noted, such acquisition requires time and a mental process. Further, there must be the conditions necessary to the mental process. Such conditions might exist in relation to all necessary futuritions, as a knowledge of them might be reached through their necessitating causes, but no such conditions could exist in relation to future free volitions. The divine nescience of such volitions would, therefore, be a necessity, not a free choice. The outcome is thus contradictory to the doctrine of the divine nescience which Clarke maintained. With this result, we scarcely need add the usual adverse criticism, that a voluntary nescience in God must imply a knowledge of the things which he chooses not to know.

The doctrine now specially maintained denies the possibility of a divine prescience of future free volitions. Thus the PRESENT DOC-TRINE OF NES-CIENCE. same ground is here openly asserted which we found as an implication of the doctrine previously noticed, but as contradictory to the particular form in which it was maintained. In addition to this deeper ground on which a doctrine of nescience is maintained, various other arguments are adduced as corroborative of the doctrine. Some of these arguments we shall briefly notice, though our chief aim is to analyze the doctrine and set it in a clear light.

The doctrine itself is not entirely new. Along the Christian centuries it occasionally appears in theological speculation. The earlier Socinianism openly avowed it. Some of the Remonstrants held the same view, though it does not appear with Arminius himself. The principle must be in the Calvinism which grounds the prescience of God in his decrees and denies the con- TREATMENT BY McCABE tingency of foreknown events. But the doctrine itself has more recently been treated with a definiteness and thoroughness and supported with a force of argument which are quite new.[1] It is much easier to pronounce the arguments of Dr. McCabe a nullity than to answer them in a process of lucid and conclusive logic. Divine omniscience, with prescience of future free volitions, however sure as a truth of Scripture, has real difficulty for rational thought. We need but instance the relation of the question to the freedom of choice. Some deny omniscience as contradictory to

[1] McCabe: *The Foreknowledge of God; Divine Nescience of Future Contingencies.*

freedom. Some deny freedom as contradictory to omniscience.
Many, while holding both, regard their reconciliation as above the
power of human thought. But this is only one of many facts
which seriously perplex the question.

Whatever the perplexities which may arise with the doctrine of
omniscience, they must be as real respecting the futuri-
RESPECTING tions of the divine agency as of the human. Indeed,
FUTURITIONS
OF THE DI- there are difficulties which more directly concern the
VINE AGENCY
divine agency. It might be said that God freely pre-
determines his own future volitions, and therefore may foreknow
them in entire consistency with their freedom. This, however, can
relieve no difficulty of the question—indeed, simply avoids the real
question. Such future volitions must be purely executive for the
attainment of previously chosen ends. In the mind of God they
must be subject to his predetermination, and therefore cannot stand
in the attitude of future free choices. If future free volitions are
unknowable because free, or unknowable for any other reason, then
such volitions of God are as completely beyond the reach of his prescience as the future free volitions of men. If he cannot foreknow
our free volitions, neither can he foreknow his own, which, in a
wise dealing with us, must, in many instances, be shaped in adjustment to such as we put forth.

Whether the divine foreknowledge is consistent with the freedom
of choice is a question which may be more appropriately treated in
another place.

It is strongly urged against the doctrine of prescience that God
deals with men, particularly with the wicked, in the
PRESCIENCE
AND GOD'S use of means for their salvation, just as though he
DEALINGS did not foreknow their decisive moral choices. This
WITH MEN
statement is, at least, apparently true. That is, there
would be no apparent reason for a change of procedure if God did
not foreknow the final moral choices of men. Is such a procedure
so contradictory to the doctrine of prescience that both cannot be
true? If this be the case, omniscience would disqualify God for
the administration of a moral government over the human race.
The only apparent alternative would be a divine allotment of final
destinies on the foresight of what would be the decisive moral
choices of men if placed in a probationary life. Such a doctrine of
the divine procedure actually appears in theological speculation.
In the many attempts to solve the perplexing dogma of Adamic sin
as the common penal desert of the race, the position has been taken
that God, foreknowing that every man, if placed in the same state
as Adam, would sin just as he did, might justly and did actually

account the same sin to every man. Of course this doctrine can have no place in a true theology. Nor can it be true that omniscience would disqualify God for the administration of a moral government. If we were under a law of necessity, the divine use of means for our salvation would be without reason. This is manifestly true in the case of necessitation to evil. That we are free and salvable renders the use of means consistent with the divine prescience. Otherwise the total omission of means of salvation would be justified in all cases of a foreknown final sinful choice. Such an omission could not be reconciled with the requirements of a divine moral government. With the truth of prescience, God may consistently, and must in fatherly rule and love, deal with us in the use of means for our salvation just as though he did not foreknow our final moral choices.[1]

It is objected that the creation of souls with prescience of a sinful life and a final penal doom is irreconcilable with the goodness of God. This is a weighty objection—so weighty that we might well prefer the doctrine of nescience if it could obviate the difficulties which beset the question of sin. But this it cannot achieve. Insoluble perplexities would still remain. The creation of souls for the moral responsibility of free personalities must be with the known possibility of a final sinful choice and penal doom. This is a fact which our reason cannot fully adjust to the goodness of God, and a fact which remains in all its force with the nescience of future free volitions. Further, even with the nescience of future choices, we must admit the divine knowledge of all actual choices, and therefore the knowledge that, up to the present time, many through the choice of evil have incurred the penal doom of sin. Yet, with this knowledge, and with the forecast of such results in the future, God still perpetuates the race. The difficulty in this case seems quite as inexplicable for our reason as that which arises with the doctrine of the divine prescience. The real difficulty is the existence of moral evil under the government of God. This still remains with the doctrine of nescience.

> CREATION OF SOULS WITH PRESCIENCE OF A PENAL DOOM

An argument against the prescience of future free volitions is brought from their present nihility. Such volitions are nothing until their actuality, and therefore cannot be the object of any previous knowledge. The validity of this argument is not above question. Moreover, if properly analyzed, its implications must be found of very difficult adjustment to the realities of the divine knowledge. A future

> A FUTURE CHOICE AN UNKNOWABLE NOTHING

[1] Bledsoe: *Theodicy*, pp. 241, 242.

eclipse is as much a present nihility as a future free choice. What then is the difference between the two as it respects the divine prescience? The answer is obvious. For the former there is a necessitating cause: for the latter, a free cause. This is the only difference. Hence the implication of this argument is that the divine foreknowledge of any futurition is conditioned on a present knowledge of its necessitating cause. It follows that God foreknows an eclipse just as an astronomer foreknows it. His knowledge may be more ready and perfect, but cannot be other in its mode. Thus the divine knowledge is conditioned and must be an acquisition through a mental process. These facts cannot be adjusted to the perfection and plenitude of the divine knowledge as clearly revealed in the Scriptures.

Further, a present free choice is in itself a purely metaphysical fact, and, even with complete ethical quality, may be without any cognizable sign. Hence it may be rationally questioned whether a mind incapable of foreknowing a future free choice could know a present free choice in its pure metaphysical self. On the other hand, if it be true, as the Scriptures so fully declare, that the divine mind is ever cognizant of the most central and secret facts of the human mind, we may rationally think its vision so immediate and absolute as clearly to foresee our future free choices.

The most difficult question of omniscience concerns its relation to the divine personality. This, however, must go forward to a more appropriate place for its treatment. So far we have specially aimed to place the doctrine of nescience in the light of its implications respecting the divine knowledge. We think these implications irreconcilable with the plenitude of this knowledge as it is clearly revealed in the Scriptures, and as it must be in the truth of theism. We have not treated the question of nescience with any profound apprehension for the truth. Its doctrinal and practical bearing may easily be overestimated The divine nescience of future free volitions, if accepted as a truth, is not necessarily revolutionary in theology. The Calvinism which grounds foreknowledge in the divine decrees would remain the same. It can freely admit the divine nescience of future volitions as pure contingencies. This position it already occupies. But for it there are no such future volitions. The long-time debate on the question of freedom would still be on hand, and it would be necessary to carry this question convincingly against Calvinism before the doctrine of nescience could disturb its foundations Nor would this doctrine be any more revolutionary in the system of Arminianism. Every vital doctrine would remain just the same.

IMPLICATIONS OF THE DOCTRINE OF NESCIENCE.

The chief perceivable result would be to free the system from the perplexity for freedom which arises with the divine prescience. The very serious difficulty in the attainment of this result is that we require the reality of freedom as the necessary ground of the doctrine of nescience. Only through the proved reality of the former can we reach the truth of the latter. This is their logical and irreversible order. If the truth of nescience were established or accepted, it would be as little revolutionary within the sphere of practical truth as in that of doctrinal truth. Certainly it could not in the least abate any of the moral forces of Christianity. God would still be immediately and perfectly cognizant of all the actualities of our moral life. Our responsibility would be just the same; all divine promises and penalties the very same.[1]

3. *Truth of Omniscience.*—There is for us no direct or complete knowledge of omniscience. We can no more fully grasp it in thought than we can grasp the omnipotence of the divine will or the infinitude of the divine love. If there be such a reality, only omniscience itself can absolutely know it. We may listen to the united utterances of nature and revelation and receive the great truth in faith, but cannot receive it in a comprehensive knowledge.

In the fitness of materiale lements for cosmical uses, in the manifold and marvelous adjustments of nature, in the sim- TESTIMONY OF plicity and far-reaching sway of the laws of nature, in the SCRIPTURE wonders of organic life, in the realm of rational intelligences there are manifestations of a mind which we must rationally think omniscient. These thoughts are in accord with the utterances of Scripture. "O Lord, how manifold are thy works! in wisdom hast thou made them all."[2] "The Lord by wisdom hath founded the earth; by understanding he hath established the heavens"[3]

There are more explicit words of Scripture respecting the infinite plenitude of the divine knowledge. Even in special MORE EXPLICIT applications the expression of the knowledge is so com- WORDS plete that its infinite comprehension is an inevitable implication. "O Lord, thou hast searched me, and known me. Thou knowest my downsitting and mine uprising; thou understandest my thoughts afar off. Thou compassest my path and my lying down, and art acquainted with all my ways. For there is not a word in my tongue, but, lo, O Lord, thou knowest it altogether. Thou hast beset me behind and before, and laid thine hand upon me. Such knowledge is too wonderful for me, it is high, I cannot attain unto it. Whither

[1] Martensen : *Christian Dogmatics*, p. 219 ; Dorner : *Christian Doctrine*, vol i, p. 336.
[2] Psa civ, 24.   [3] Prov. iii, 19.

shall I go from thy Spirit? or whither shall I flee from thy presence? If I ascend up into heaven, thou art there. if I make my bed in hell, behold, thou art there. If I take the wings of the morning, and dwell in the uttermost parts of the sea; even there shall thy hand lead me, and thy right hand shall hold me. If I say, Surely the darkness shall cover me; even the night shall be light about me. Yea, the darkness hideth not from thee; but the night shineth as the day: the darkness and the light are both alike to thee."[1] This passage is so replete with the deepest truth of the divine knowledge that we may well cite it in full. There is nothing in the life of man, nothing in his deeds or words, nothing in his most secret thoughts and feelings which is not perfectly known to God. This is the truth respecting all the multitudes of the race. Only an immediate and absolute knowing is equal to such knowledge. Neither height nor depth nor distance can impose any limitation. For it the night is as the day, the darkness as the light

We may add a few texts: "Great is our Lord, and of great FURTHER TES- power. his understanding is infinite."[2] "The eyes of TIMONY. the Lord are in every place, beholding the evil and the good."[3] The truth of each of these texts is the truth of the other. If God's understanding is infinite, he must every-where behold the evil and the good. If he every-where beholds the evil and the good, his understanding must be infinite. "Neither is there any creature that is not manifest in his sight: but all things are naked and opened unto the eyes of him with whom we have to do."[4] The divine knowledge is beforehand with the future. "Behold, the former things are come to pass, and new things do I declare before they spring forth I tell you of them."[5] These texts reveal the infinite plenitude of the divine knowledge. In the sense of the former, all things, in the fullest sense of all, are in the open vision of God. The connection shows the inclusion of the most central and secret life of all men. The latter text brings the future with the past into the comprehension of the same knowledge.

It might be objected that all the texts which we have cited in SUCH KNOWL- proof of omniscience, with one exception, reveal simply EDGE GRASPS the divine knowledge of the present, the truth of which THE FUTURE no theist questions. It might further be said that the one text which embraces the future may not include free choices, but only such futuritions as shall arise from predetermining causalities. If all this should be conceded, the proof of omniscience must still lie in these texts. The plenitude and the mode of the divine

---

[1] Psa. cxxxix, 1-12.   [2] Psa. cxlvii, 5.   [3] Prov. xv, 3.
[4] Heb iv, 13.   [5] Isa. xlii, 9.

knowledge which they reveal warrant the inference of omniscience in the truest, deepest sense of the term. We need not dwell upon the extent of the universe which, in all its magnitudes and minutiæ, even to every atom, is perfectly known to God. Nor need we specially speak of higher intelligences, with lives replete with the deepest intensities of thought and feeling and action, all which are comprehended in the divine knowledge. Suffice, that God knows what is in man; all that is in man; all that is in all men. This is what the Scriptures declare, and what no theist can question. The knowledge is perfect. It embraces all the interior activities, all the springs of action, all the impulses and aims of every life. The knowledge is so complete that God can perfectly adjust his ministries to the exigencies of every life; so complete that he can finally be the perfectly righteous Judge of each life. Such knowledge must be immediate and absolute in its mode. Its plenitude can admit no process of acquisition, no conditions of space or time. The future, even in its ethical volitions, must be open to the vision of such absolute knowledge.

The prophecies cannot be interpreted without the divine prescience of morally free and responsible volitions in men. We speak of the prophecies generally. Even if some could be interpreted on deterministic ground, the many require freedom in the responsible human agency so widely operative in their fulfillment. We need not enter into details or into the citation and unfolding of particular prophecies. A general view may suffice. Prophecy began its utterances in the earliest history of the race, and continued to multiply them through all the progress of revelation, while the times of their application still stretched far down the centuries, even unto the final consummation. In a general way, we may instance the Jews and neighboring nations—Egypt, Nineveh, Babylon, Tyre—as the subjects of prophecy. Not only are their future fortunes severally sketched in bold outline, but the reason of their fortunes is given specifically in their own moral conduct. The various forms of vice and crime are depicted in their incipiency, progress, and repletion, as the prelude and provocation of the providential doom which successively befell them. These prophecies, so specific in facts, and often long antedating the fulfilling events, could not have been uttered and verified by the result without the divine prescience of the morally responsible conduct of these people severally and individually. This is the prescience of free choices.

The Messianic prophecies should receive a separate notice in their relation to this question. Students of these prophecies find in

them much of the life of Christ as it is given in the gospels. Moreover, the responsible conduct of others respecting him is
equally foretold. The rejection and persecution which
he should suffer from his own people; the heinous offense
of his betrayal by Judas and his denial by Peter, his crucifixion,
with singular detail of particulars in the cruel treatment which he
should suffer, and the fearful sin of the authors of these cruelties—all
this is in these prophecies. They equally disclose the providential
doom of this people for the willful and wicked rejection of the
Christ. How could all this be without the divine prescience of the
free and responsible action of men? These prophecies were not the
utterance of a mere judgment of the future in view of the drift of
the present, but divine predictions of clearly foreseen events, in the
production of which the free and responsible agency of men should
be efficiently operative. Prophecy in its fulfillment seems conclusive
of the divine prescience of free, ethical volitions.

SPECIALLY IN THE MESSIANIC PROPHECIES.

4. *Distinctions of Divine Knowledge.*—There are certain distinctions in the knowledge of God which may be helpful toward
an adjustment of omniscience to his personal agency. The originality of these distinctions is accorded to Fonseca and Molina,
Spanish theologians of the Jesuit order. Naturally, they were
formulated in the technical manner common at the time: *scientia
Dei necessaria; scientia Dei libera; scientia Dei media.* Dorner
gives a very full and clear statement of these distinctions.[1] Dr
Hodge also gives a clear statement, particularly of the third—
scientia Dei media—from which, however, his stanch Calvinism
dissents.[2] A summary statement in simpler terms may render
these distinctions clearer.

God's knowledge of himself is necessary and eternal. This is an
inevitable implication of his eternal personal existence.
Personality is unreal without self-consciousness, which
must include self-knowledge. The infinite perfection of the divine mind must imply the absolute plenitude of self-knowledge.
In the perfection of this knowledge God must know his own potentialities, and therefore all possibilities with respect to his own
immediate agency. Further, all rational and ethical truths which,
with the personality of God, must be eternal realities, may properly be placed in the content of his necessary knowledge. There
is thus a sphere of necessary knowledge, which is intrinsic to the
divine personality.

SCIENTIA DEI NECESSARIA.

But as the universe is the creation of God on his own free

[1] *Christian Doctrine,* vol. i, pp. 325–328
[2] *Systematic Theology,* vol. i, pp. 398–400

choice,[1] a knowledge of it cannot be included in his necessary self-knowledge. The fact is the same even with an eternal SCIENTIA DEI prescience of his creative work. It is still the work of LIBERA. his free agency, and therefore need not have been. In this case it could have been an object of knowledge only as a possibility, which belongs to the distinction of necessary knowledge. It follows that God's knowledge of the universe, whether as a purposed futurition or an effectuated reality, is conditioned on his own free agency, and may properly be designated *scientia Dei libera*—a knowledge within his own power or dependent upon himself.

In the reality of our free moral agency, God must adjust the ministries of his government to the manner of our con- SCIENTIA DEI duct as arising from our freedom There is nothing MEDIA surer than this. To deny it is to deny the reality of our own free agency. With freedom, human conduct is often other than it might have been. One man is bad who might have been good, and another good who might have been bad. The divine dealings with each must, as wise and good, be shaped according to his conduct, and would be different with a difference of conduct. In all such cases God's prescience of his own agency is conditioned on the foreseen free action of men. There is this logical mediation even with immediateness in the mode of the divine knowledge. *Scientia Dei media* is therefore no erroneous or misleading formula.[2]

5 *Omniscience and Divine Personality.*—The scientific adjustment of omniscience to the divine personality and personal agency is no easy attainment. The real difficulty has not re- REAL DIFFI-ceived its proper recognition. It should not be over- CULTY OF THE looked, even if without solution in our reason. The QUESTION discussion respecting the consistency of foreknowledge and freedom has been conducted with little apprehension of the profound truth that free agency and personal agency are but different formulas for the same reality, and that, if free agency falls by the logic of foreknowledge, personality must fall with it, and the divine personality no less than the human. There can be no true personality or personal agency except in freedom. The necessary freedom is the freedom of choice. For the freedom of choice there must be the eligibility of ends — eligibility in the reality of motives to choice Can there be the eligibility of ends for an omniscient mind? This is the real question of difficulty. It is far deeper than the usual question of consistency between fore-

[1] Isa. xxix, 15 ; Matt. vi, 32 ; Acts xv, 8.
[2] Usual reference for illustration : 1 Sam. xxiii, 9-13 ; Jer. xxxviii, 17, 18 ; Ezek. iii, 6 , Matt. xi, 21-24.

knowledge and freedom, which concerns only the relation of fore-knowledge in God to freedom in man, while the question in hand concerns the consistency of omniscience and freedom, both being in God himself.

We cannot in rational thought separate God's conception of realities, even as futurities, from his motive-states respecting them. For our thought the latter must co-exist with the former and be as the former. If his conception is eternally complete in his eternal prescience, does it not follow that his motive-states are eternally the same respecting all realities? Seemingly, no distinction can be made between futurities and actualities. How can any thing take on a new form or appear in a new light of interest in the view of an absolute prescience? If all is eternally the same in that view, how can we avoid the consequence of an eternally fixed and changeless mental state, both cognitive and emotional, in God respecting all objects of his conception? Hence there would seem to be no reason for any choice or agency which was not eternally the same in the divine mind. In this case only an unthinkable eternal choice would seem possible. There could be no eligibility of ends arising in time, no specific choices in time; and therefore only a divine operation eternally predetermined. Such facts do not seem consistent with either a true personality in God or a true personal agency in his providence. It thus appears how far deeper this question is than the question of consistency between divine prescience and human freedom. How shall the necessary adjustment be attained? The manifest truth of omniscience will not allow us to replace it with the divine nescience of all free and responsible futuritions, and thus eliminate the difficulty—if indeed this would eliminate it.

There is no clear way out of this perplexity. Yet we should not concede its utter hopelessness of all explication. Doubtless the moral principles of the divine procedure are eternally the same in the divine consciousness; but the divine feelings in view of moral conduct in the free subjects of moral government are not eternally the same, as seemingly implied in omniscience. Otherwise they would either be false to the truth of facts, or in many instances involve a contradictory dualism in the divine mind. Such would be the case in all instances of a radical change of moral conduct in human life. A very wicked man may become truly saintly—of which there are many instances. If respecting such there were eternally the same feelings in God, they could not be true to the facts. This possibility is precluded by the great change in moral character. If from eternity such are regarded with reprehension as bad and with approval as good, then the unthinkable dualism must exist in the divine mind. These implications are conclusive against an eternally changeless emotional state in the mind of God respecting the free subjects of his moral government.

It is the clear sense of Scripture that the divine feelings are not eternally the same nor yet dualistic respecting the responsible conduct of men, but in forms answering in time to the moral quality of their action: feelings of displeasure against their wickedness; of clemency and forgiveness on their true repentance; of approving love for their genuine piety. The truth of divine displeasure against the wicked, whatever the subsequent change in their moral conduct, is given in many texts; but it is a truth so familiar and sure that a few references may suffice.[1] It is in the nature of God as holy and just that this must be so. It is equally sure on the same ground of his holiness that he does not and cannot so regard any others than the wicked. The truth of the divine propitiousness on a true repentance is also given in many texts.[2] The whole truth of an approving love on a genuine piety may be given in a single text: "He that hath my commandments, and keepeth them, he it is that loveth me: and he that loveth me shall be loved of my Father, and I will love him, and will manifest myself to him."[3] It is thus clear that God's personal regards of men ever answer in time to the moral quality of their personal conduct. Those who hold the doctrine of divine nescience, as previously noticed, may say that this precisely accords with their doctrine, and is therefore the proof of it. We admit the agreement, and would also admit the proof were it not for the paramount proof of the divine prescience. But the facts which we have found do not yet bring us the adjustment of omniscience to the divine personality and personal agency.

Even with the doctrine of prescience, it is still open for us to say that futurities of human conduct may not be the same for the divine conception and feeling as in their actuality. There is some ground for this position in the distinctions of the divine knowledge previously considered. The self-intuition of God is eternal and absolute. But the universe is the creation of his free agency, and therefore was eternally foreknown only as a futurity or as a freely purposed futu-

Marginal notes: DIVINE FEELING NEITHER DUALISTIC NOR ETERNALLY THE SAME

Marginal notes: FUTURITIES AND ACTUALITIES DIFFERENT FOR THE DIVINE MIND.

---

[1] Num xxxii, 14, Deut. vii, 4; 2 Kings xvii, 17, 18; Psa. vii, 11; lxxviii, 40.
[2] Isa. xi, 1; lv, 7; Dan. ix, 16-19.   [3] John xv, 21.

rition, and known in its actuality only when by the free act of creation this purpose was set in reality. Even as a purposed futurition it could not be the same to the divine conception and consciousness as in its actuality. What is thus true respecting the universe as a creation may be specially true respecting the moral choices of free and responsible personalities. While eternally foreknown, they are yet different in their actuality for the divine conception, and therefore different for the divine feeling. There may thus be a sphere of free personal agency for God. There is no other apparent reconciliation of omniscience with either his personality or his personal agency in providence. If the distinctions in the knowledge of God may not be claimed as absolutely valid for the sphere of his personal free agency, they yet appear reasonably sufficient; and this is about all that we could expect in so difficult a question. But further, than this: it is surely possible that the plenitude of personality in God may place him above any law of determinism which may seem to us an implication of his omniscience; so that there is for him all the reality of a free personal agency which seems so manifest in the history of his providence.

There is a providence of God, with ministries in time. Nor can MINISTRIES OF all this be regarded as merely executive of eternal pre-
PROVIDENCE IN determinations. The field of this providence is an his-
TIME. toric world developing in time. Its successive facts can be actual for the divine conception only on their actuality. What is thus true respecting all must be specially true respecting the free ethical action of men. The interests of both morality and religion require the ministries of providence in the ever-living personal agency of God. There must be the ever-actual discrimination of human conduct in his moral judgment; the reprehension of the evil and the loving approval of the good in the very depths of his moral feeling. Without these facts there is for the moral and religious consciousness no living relation of God to the present life, and our theism must be practically as empty of vital content as deism or pantheism. If the ministries of providence in the free agency of God, with all the emotional activities of such ministries, be not consistent or possible with his foreknowledge, then foreknowledge cannot be true. If there must be for us an alternative between the prescience of God, on the one hand, and his true personal agency in the ministries of his providence, on the other, the former doctrine must be yielded, while we tenaciously cleave to the latter, because it embodies the living reality of the divine moral government. With all the difficulties of the question, we have not

found any contradictory opposition of the two doctrines, and therefore hold both in a sure faith.[1]

6. *Divine Wisdom.*—The wisdom of God is so closely related to his knowledge that the former may properly be treated in connection with the latter. Yet there are elements of wisdom which do not belong to mere knowledge. For wisdom ELEMENTS OF WISDOM there must be the practical use of knowledge. For the deepest truth of wisdom there must be the practical use of knowledge for benevolent ends. In the apt use of means for the attainment of evil ends there may be ingenuity or skill which requires knowledge, but there cannot be wisdom. Hence in wisdom there must be an element of goodness, a benevolence of aim. Benevolence requires affection. There can be no good end, either as a conception or an aim, without the emotional nature. Hence wisdom is not purely from the intellect, but from the intellect and the sensibility in co-operation. The wisdom of God appears in the co-operation of infinite knowledge and love.

For the present life, even in its providential aspects, there is a mixture of good and evil; so that for our view the wisdom of God does not stand in the clearest light. The WISDOM AND THE MAGNITUDE OF EVIL circle of our vision is but a narrow one, while often much of it lies in the shadow of cheerless clouds.[2] For our faith there is sunshine above and upon the vast fields beyond the circle of our vision, where the wisdom of God is revealed in the brightness of its own divine light. It is in truth deeply wrought into the wonders of creation, providence, and grace, however hidden from our present view. So the Scriptures witness. Wisdom was with God in determining the marvelous adjustments and laws of nature.[3] "O Lord, how manifold are thy works! in wisdom hast thou made them all: the earth is full of thy riches."[4] The wisdom of God assumes its divinest form in the manifestation and work of Christ, "in whom we have redemption through his blood, the forgiveness of sins, according to the riches of his grace; wherein he hath abounded toward us in all wisdom and prudence."[5] Thus is made known, even unto the principalities and powers in heavenly places. "the manifold wisdom of God, according to the eternal purpose which he purposed in Christ Jesus our Lord."[6] The perfections of knowledge and love are here co-operative. "O the depth of the riches both of the wisdom and knowledge of God!"[7]

---

[1] Dorner: *Christian Doctrine*, vol. i, pp 329-337.
[2] Butler: *Analogy*, part i, chap vii; Bowne: *Metaphysics*, p. 547.
[3] Job xxviii, 20-27   [4] Psa. civ, 24   [5] Eph. i, 7, 8.
[6] Eph. iii, 10, 11.   [7] Rom. xi, 33.

14

III. DIVINE SENSIBILITY.

1. *Sense of Divine Sensibility.*—As previously noticed, sensibility is in philosophic use for even the highest forms of human feeling; for the rational and moral as for the lower appetences and impulses. Theology has no better term for substitution, and must still use the same, even in application to the divine feelings. There is an emotional nature in God. This nature is active in various forms of feeling respecting the objects of his conception. There may be feelings of approval or aversion, of pleasure or displeasure, of reprehension or love. There is the reality of such emotional states in the mind of God, as in the mind of man. This is the sense of divine sensibility. There are certain differences between the human and the divine which may be noted in the proper place.

2. *Truth of Divine Sensibility.*—An emotional nature is necessary to the divine omniscience; that is, there are forms of knowl-
RELATION OF SENSIBILITY TO KNOWLEDGE
edge which would be impossible even to the divine mind if totally without sensibility. It has not been properly considered how much the sensibilities have to do with human knowledge. In empirical knowledge our conception or notion of things could not be what it is without the element furnished by sensation. In the higher spheres of truth the feelings are necessary to knowledge. Without the correlative emotions we could have no true notion of friendship, or country, or kindred, or home. Without the moral feelings there could be no proper knowledge of a moral system; no true conception of moral obligation, of right or rights, of the ethical quality of free moral action. There must be such a law even for the divine knowledge. Certainly there is no apparent reason to the contrary. Without an emotional nature in God, his omniscience, in the truer, deeper sense of the term, would be impossible.

The Scriptures freely ascribe to God various forms of feeling—
PROOFS OF DIVINE SENSIBILITY
abhorrence, anger, hatred, love, patience, compassion, clemency. It is very easy to pronounce all this pure anthropopathism, carried into the Scriptures in accommodation to the modes of human thought and feeling. If these forms of feeling are not such a reality in God as to have a truthful reflection in our own, these terms of Scripture are but empty or deceiving words. Then divine holiness, justice, goodness, mercy, faithfulness, are meaningless or misleading. Why this perversion of the deepest truth of the divine nature? Too long has theology, in its deeper speculative form, arrayed the living God of the Scriptures in the apathetic bleakness of deism or pantheism. The

endeavor to represent God as pure intellect or pure action may be
reverent in aim, but is no less a sacrifice of the most vital truth
Without emotion God cannot be a person: cannot be the living God
for the religious consciousness of humanity No longer could we,
in the profound exigencies of life, look up to him as the heavenly
Father. There is no heavenly Father without an emotional love.
There is the truth of an emotional love of the Father in the deep
words of the Son: "For thou lovedst me before the foundation of
the world;"[1] and also in those other deep and gracious words:
"God so loved the world."[2] If there is reality in one form of divine sensibility there is reality in other forms. In the revelations
of God by word and deed there is as clear and full a manifestation
of sensibility as of intelligence or will. One knows his own emotional states in his own consciousness. Another's he can know only
through the modes of their expression; but his knowledge is greatly
aided by reading these expressions, as he can, in the light of his
own experience. Hence he is quite as sure, though in a different
mode, of emotional states in other minds as in his own He is just
as sure of their sensibilities as of their intelligence or voluntary
power. We thus know the mind of God, and as surely in its emotions as in its intellections and volitions. His words and deeds
which express emotions are the sign of divine realities. Otherwise
they have for us no meaning and serve only to delude.

There are certain differences between the human and the divine
sensibilities which may be noted, though seemingly open
to the common view. We have forms of sensibility, as
arising through our physical organism or in the circle
of our peculiar relationships in life, which can have no analogies in
the divine mind. Also our higher motive-states which arise with
our rational and moral cognitions may have an intensity of excite-
ment and a passionate impulsiveness which can have no place in
the divine emotions.

DIFFERING
FROM THE HU-
MAN

3. *Distinctions of Divine Sensibility.*—There is not an absolute
unity or oneness of feeling in God. His sensibilities are active in
forms answering to the distinctions of their objects. The activities
of our own higher sensibilities are conditioned on the mental apprehension of their appropriate objects, either as actual existences or as
ideal conceptions. This must be a law for the divine
sensibilities. It is no sign of limitation in God that for
knowledge he requires the objects of his cognitions, or
that for the activities of his sensibilities he requires their appropriate
objects. It follows that his sensibilities must differ according to

DISTINCTIONS
AS THE OB-
JECTS DIFFER

[1] John xvii, 24.   [2] John iii, 16.

the distinctions of their objects. The law which requires an object for an affection must determine the quality of the affection according to the character of the object. Objects of the divine affection are very different. There is the profound distinction between the physical and the moral realms; in the former, between the chaotic and the cosmic states; in the latter, between the ethically evil and the ethically good. It is impossible that God should regard these profoundly diverse objects with the same affection. It is in the Scriptures, as in the philosophy of the facts, that he does regard them with distinctions of affection answering to their own profound distinctions. We might enter more largely into details, but, while the ground would be valid, the method might prove an unseemly attempt at a divine psychology. We may with propriety note some general distinctions.

There is in God a rational sensibility. We mean by this a con-
RATIONAL SEN- scious interest in the rational order and constitution of
SIBILITY.   existences. The world is a cosmos, a world of order.
This is the possibility of a rational cosmology. For science and philosophy, we require not only rational faculties, but also an order and constitution of existences which render them susceptible of scientific and philosophic treatment. There is such an order of existences. Both in reality and for rational thought law reigns in the realms of nature. Physics, chemistry, botany, zoology, astronomy are possible because the rational order of existences places them in correlation with rational mind. For the reason of this correlation the rational order and constitution of existences elicit an interest in all who have any proper notion of them. Gifted minds study them with a profound interest. That interest ever deepens with the clearer insight into this rational order. Thus in the spheres of study usually regarded as purely intellectual there is an intense conscious interest which can arise only from a profound rational sensibility.

From this view we rise to the notion of God as the original of our own minds, and also of the forms of existence which constitute the subjects of our scientific study. He is the author of their rational correlation; the author of the rational constitution of existences in all the realms of nature. That orderly constitution must have been with him, not merely an intellectual conception, but also an end of conscious interest and eligibility. These facts evince a profound rational sensibility in God. While he pronounces the successive orders of the newly rising world "very good," his words no more express the conception of a divine thought than the pleasure of a divine emotion.

There is a divine æsthetic sensibility. The world, the universe, is as richly wrought in the forms of beauty as in the forms of rational order. The beautiful is so lavished upon the ÆSTHETICSEN-earth and the heavens that all are recipients of its SIBILITY grateful ministries. It is the fruitage of the divine constitution of the soul within us and the divine formation of existences without and above us. Such a correlation of the forms of nature to the constitution of the mind could not have been a mere coincidence, but must have been the divinely instituted means to a divinely chosen end, just as in the case of a master in the science and art of music, who through the harmonious combination of parts reaches the chosen end of a great symphony. The beautiful in its manifold forms was with God a chosen end in the work of creation. Therefore it was with him more than a mere mental conception. There is no eligibility for pure intellection, not even for the divine. The eligibility of the beautiful could arise in the mind of God only with the activity of an æsthetic sensibility. God loves the beautiful. In the following citation we have really the presentation of both a rational and an æsthetic sensibility in God, but especially the latter. "I must hold that we receive the true explanation of the *man*-like character of the Creator's workings ere man was, in the remarkable text in which we are told that 'God made man in his own image and likeness.' There is no restriction here to moral quality: the moral image man had, and in large measure lost; but the intellectual image he still retains. As a geometrician, as an arithmetician, as a chemist, as an astronomer—in short, in all the departments of what are known as the strict sciences—man differs from his Maker, not in kind, but in degree—not as matter differs from mind, or darkness from light, but simply as a mere portion of space or time differs from *all* space or *all* time. I have already referred to mechanical contrivances as identically the same ● the divine and human productions; nor can I doubt that, not only in the pervading sense of the beautiful in form and color which it is our privilege as men in some degree to experience and possess, but also in the perception of harmony which constitutes the *musical* sense, and in that poetic feeling of which Scripture furnishes us with at once the earliest and the highest examples, and which we may term the *poetic* sense, we bear the stamp and impress of the divine image " [1] Thus in the æsthetic element of our mental constitution, the source of pleasure in music and poetry and art, in all forms of the beautiful, we see the likeness of an æsthetic sensibility in God, who created man in his own image.[2]

[1] Hugh Miller. *Testimony of the Rocks*, pp 259, 260.
[2] Le Conte : *Science and Religion*, lect. iii.

In the constitution of a moral personality there is moral reason,
MORAL SENSI- and also moral feeling. The moral personality could
BILITY.   not be complete without the latter. For the true conception of a morally constituted personality and the true judgment of ethical conduct, whether one's own or another's, there
must be the activity of a moral feeling. Pure intellection is not
sufficient for either the conception or the judgment. This must be
a law for even the divine mind. Without a moral consciousness
in God the creation of moral beings must have been without eligibility, and therefore without reason or end. If there is any divine
teleology in the universe the creation of the highest order of beings
could not have been purposeless. The Scriptures freely express the
reality of moral feeling in the divine judgment of human conduct.
For the good there is loving approval; for the evil, displeasure and
wrath. These facts manifest the reality of moral sensibility in
God.

We have thus presented the divine sensibility in three distinc-
FURTHER   tions. The moral, however, must receive further treat-
TREATMENT OF ment. Pure thought, pure intuition, pure intellection
MORAL SENSI- does not give the complete view of the divine mind.
BILITY.   Infinite feeling completes the view. "We hold, therefore, that God is not only pure thought, but he is also absolute
intuition and absolute sensibility. He not only grasps reality in his
absolute thought, but he sees it in his absolute intuition, and enjoys
it in his absolute sensibility. We cannot without contradiction
allow that there is any thing in the world of the thinkable which is
excluded from the source of all thought and knowledge. Our notion
of God as pure thought only would exclude the harmonies of light,
sound, and form from his knowledge; and limit him to a knowledge of the skeleton of the universe instead of its living beauty.
The notion of God as sensitive appears as anthropomorphic only
because of mental confusion. To the thoughtless, sensibility implies a body; but in truth it is as purely spiritual an affection as
the most abstract thought. All the body does for us is to call forth
sensibility; but it in no sense produces it, and it is entirely conceivable that it should exist in a purely spiritual being apart from
any body. There can hardly be a more irrational conception of the
divine knowledge than that which assumes that it grasps reality
only as it exists for pure thought, and misses altogether the look
and the life of things. On the contrary, just as we regard our reason as the faint type of the infinite reason, so we regard our intuitions of things as a faint type of the absolute intuition; and so also
we regard the harmonies of sensibility and feeling as the faintest

echoes of the absolute sensibility, stray notes wandering off from the source of feeling and life and beauty."[1]

IV. Modes of Divine Moral Sensibility.

As there are distinctions of divine sensibility in the general or comprehensive sense of the term, so there are distinctions of moral sensibility. Moral feeling in God respects profoundly different subjects, and reveals itself in distinctions of mode answering to that difference of subjects. We may reach the clearer view by studying the question in the light of these several modes. However, there is a truth of moral feeling in God which is deeper than the more definite distinctions of mode—the moral feeling which is intrinsic to the holiness of the divine nature. This is the first truth to be noticed.

1. *Holiness.*—The Scriptures witness to the holiness of God with the deepest intensities of expression. A few passages may be cited for exemplification. "Who is like unto thee, O Lord, among the gods? who is like thee, glorious in holiness, fearful in praises, doing wonders?"[2] The glory of the divine holiness appears in its manifestation, but the manifestation leads the thought to its plenitude in the divine nature. "Holy and reverend is his name."[3] The perfection of holiness in God is the reason for the holy reverence in which all should worship and serve him. "Holy Father," and "O righteous Father,"[4] express in the words of Christ the deep truth of divine holiness. "Who shall not fear thee, O Lord, and glorify thy name? for thou only art holy."[5] These words are responsive to words previously cited: "Who is like thee, glorious in holiness?" In the deepest, divinest sense, God only is holy. The seraphim before the heavenly throne cry one to another, "Holy, holy, holy, is the Lord of hosts;" "and they rest not day and night, saying, Holy, holy, holy, Lord God Almighty, which was, and is, and is to come."[6]

The holiness of God is not to be regarded simply as a quality of his nature or a quiescent mental state, but as intensely HOLINESS AND active in his personal agency, particularly in his moral RIGHTEOUS- government. In this view holiness is often called right- NESS eousness. Hence the righteousness of God is expressed with the same intensity as his holiness. The precepts of moral duty and the judgment and reward of moral conduct spring from his holiness and fulfill its requirements. Through all the forms of instrumental agency he ever works for the prevention or restraint of the

---

[1] Bowne. *Metaphysics*, pp. 201, 202   [2] Exod. xv, 11.   [3] Psa. cxi, 9.
[4] John xvii, 11, 25.   [5] Rev. xv, 4.   [6] Isa. vi, 3; Rev. iv, 8.

evil and the promotion of the good. In every form and in the deepest sense God is righteous. Abraham apprehended this truth in his profound question, "Shall not the Judge of all the earth do right?"[1] There was a special case in question; but there is no sense of a local or temporary limitation in the meaning of the words. There is a universal and eternal righteousness of the divine agency. "He is the Rock, his work is perfect; for all his ways are judgment: a God of truth and without iniquity, just and right is he."[2] "Thy righteousness is an everlasting righteousness, and thy law is the truth."[3] These texts express the same deep sense of an ever-present holiness in the divine moral government. "The law of the Lord is perfect"[4]—"perfect as the expression of the divine holiness; perfect therefore as the standard of right; perfect in its requirements; perfect in its sanctions. All this is summed into one sentence by St. Paul: ' The law is holy, and the commandment holy, and just, and good.'[5] Returning back, however, to the attribute of the Lawgiver, we are bound to believe that all ordinances are righteous: first, with regard to the constitution and nature of his subjects; and, secondly, as answering strictly to his own divine aim."[6] The means and the ministries of his moral government are ever in accord with his holy law; and, however his righteousness may for the present be obscured or hidden even, it shall yet be made manifest, and receive a common confession.

PRESENT OB-SCURITY, FUT-URE MANIFES-TATION. God will place his providences in the clear, full light. These ideas of a present obscurity and a future manifestation are in the Scriptures. "Clouds and darkness are round about him: righteousness and judgment are the habitation of his throne." "Even so, Lord God Almighty, true and righteous are thy judgments."[7]

MORAL FEEL-ING IN DIVINE HOLINESS It should be specially noted here that in the holiness of God as operative in moral government there is the activity of moral feeling. This is the distinctive fact of his moral agency. If the plan of God had terminated with the creation of a mere physical universe there would still have been a great sphere for the activities of intelligence and will, and also for the rational and æsthetic sensibilities, but no place for moral feeling. Such a feeling could have no office in a mere physical universe. God would still be the same in his holy nature, with the possible or actual activity of moral sensibility in the conception and purposed creation of moral personalities, with the known possibility of ethically

[1] Gen. xviii, 25.   [2] Deut. xxxii, 4   [3] Psa. cxix, 142.   [4] Psa. xix, 7.
[5] Rom. vii, 12   [6] Pope: *Christian Theology*, vol i, p. 336.
[7] Psa. xcvii, 2 ; Rev. xvi, 7.

good and ethically evil action. On this supposition, however, there is a reaching of the divine plan far beyond a mere physical universe, and, therefore, it remains true that an original limitation to such a universe would require no activity of moral feeling in its creation and government. There was no such original limitation. In the building of the world, even from the beginning, man was the divinely destined occupant, just as other moral intelligences were destined for the occupancy of other worlds. Creation, therefore, was from the beginning the work of God in his complete personality. There was the activity of his moral sensibility, just as of his intelligence and will. It is specially this truth which discredits the distinction of the attributes into the natural and moral. As we thus find the ultimate purpose and completion of the creation in the existence of free and responsible personalities, so we find a moral realm as really as a physical one. Certainly in the moral God rules in his complete personality, and no more really through the agency of his intelligence and will than in the activities of his moral feeling. There is as absolute a requirement for the latter as for the former. A holy love of the ethically good and a holy hatred of the ethically evil are intrinsic to the divine agency in moral government. We cannot think them apart. To separate them in thought would require us to think God apathetically indifferent as between righteousness and sin. So to think God would be to think him not God. Holiness of action is impossible, even in God, without the proper element of moral feeling. An act may formally square with the law, but can be right- HOLY FEELING NECESSARY TO HOLY ACTION. eous only through the feeling from which it springs or the motive which it fulfills. The sense of moral feeling in God, as active in his regards of human conduct and in the ministries of his providence, is a practical necessity to the common religious consciousness. It is only the sense of an emotional displeasure in God that can effectively restrain the wayward tendencies to evil ; only the sense of an affectionate love that can inspire the filial trust which may become the strength of a loving obedience. There is great practical force in the commands, "Be ye holy; for I am holy," and "Be ye therefore merciful, as your Father is merciful,"[1] but only with the sense of true feeling in his holiness and mercy. Divest them of true feeling, and let them stand to the religious consciousness simply as pure thought, emotionless intellections, and they become practically forceless. In the divine holiness there is the intensity of holy feeling.

2 *Justice*—The more appropriate place for the treatment of

[1] 1 Pet. i, 16 ; Luke vi, 36.

justice is in the discussion of atonement. For the present, the treatment is specially in reference to the reality of an element of holy feeling in the divine justice. Justice itself is broadly operative within the realm of moral government, so that the discussion of its offices therein must include much more than belongs to it simply as a question of the divine attributes.

The office of justice is the maintenance of moral government in THE OFFICE OF the highest attainable excellence. The aim is the pre-JUSTICE. vention or restraint of sin, the protection of rights, the defense of innocence against injury or wrong, the vindication of the government and the honor of the divine Ruler.

Divine legislation is for the attainment of these great ends. But ENDS OF DI- however great and imperative the ends, they cannot VINE LEGIS- justify any arbitrariness of judicial measures for their LATION. attainment. Justice has no license of departure from the requirements of the divine holiness and righteousness. Indeed, justice itself is but a mode of the divine holiness. In legislation justice must respect the nature and condition of subjects. Laws must be within their power of fulfillment, whether that power be a native possession or a provision of the redemption in Christ. The sanctions of law in the form of reward and penalty must have respect to the ethical character of subjects. Emphasis should be placed upon this principle in respect of penalty, specially for the reason, first, that the demerit of sin is more manifest than the merit of righteousness, and, secondly, because penalty without demerit or beyond its measure would be more manifestly an injustice than any reward above the merit of righteousness.

In the study of the Hebraic theocracy we must admit the presence THE HEBRAIC of measures of expediency, and not only in ritualistic THEOCRACY. forms, but also in administrative discipline—as in the entailment of both good and evil upon children in consequence of the moral conduct of their parents. Such entailments, however, were not the ministries of distributive justice, but the measures of economical expediency for the attainment of the great ends of the theocracy. Like measures often appear in human governments. In terms of law the high crimes of parents are visited in certain alienations or disadvantages upon their children; certainly not, however, that they are reckoned guilty and punishable in any proper sense of distributive justice, but that the highest good of the government may be attained. That the Hebraic government was a theocracy did not change the character of the people as its subjects. They were still men, with all the tendencies of men under the forms of human government. It was expedient, therefore, that God should use the necessary policies of human governments for the attainment of the great ends of the theocracy. In this mode the entailments of parental conduct upon the children took their place as measures of economical expediency, and not as the ministries of distributive justice, which must ever have respect to the grounds of personal conduct.

Distributive justice is divine justice in the judicial ministries of moral government It regards men in their personal character, or as ethically good or evil, and rewards or punishes them according to the same. Any departure LAW OF DIS-
TRIBUTIVE
JUSTICE from this law must require an elimination of all that is distinctive and essential in distributive justice Nothing vital can remain by which to characterize or differentiate it. We have previously said that the demerit of sin is more manifest than the merit of righteousness. The former reveals itself in the moral and religious consciousness in a clearer and intenser form than the latter. Still the rewardableness of righteousness approves itself in that consciousness. Also, the fact of rewardableness is thoroughly scriptural. Further, it is both clear and scriptural that rewards must have respect to personal righteousness. There may be other blessings, and of large measure, but they cannot be personal rewards, and therefore cannot be accounted the ministry of distributive justice. But sin has intrinsic demerit, and on its own account deserves the penalties legislated against it. Demerit is the only ground of just punishment. There are great ends of penalty in the requirements of moral government, but, however great and urgent, they could justify no punishment except on the ground of demerit. The demerit must be personal to the subject of the punishment. Penalties are therefore in the strictest sense the ministry of distributive justice.

Reward and penalty thus fall in with the judicial or rectoral office of justice, which is the conservation of moral government in the highest attainable excellence. They are means to this high end ; just means because of the rewardableness of righteousness and the demerit of sin; and proper means because of fitness for their end.

Distributive justice which thus deals with men on the ground of personal conduct is no abstract principle or law, but a concrete reality in the divine personality. Justice has its seat in the moral being of God, and apart from him is but an ideal conception. The law of moral duty is the transcript of his mind; the sanctions of the law the expression of his judgment of the rewardable excellence of righteousness and the punitive demerit of sin. MORAL FEEL-
ING IN DIVINE
JUSTICE. This judgment is not a mere apathetic mental conception, but includes the intense activity of moral feeling. God lovingly approves the righteousness which he rewards with eternal blessedness, and reprobates with infinite displeasure the sin upon which he visits the fearful penalty of his law. The Scriptures are replete with utterances which express or imply these truths. There is a discriminative judgment of men according to their character : "For there is no respect of persons with God."[1] Respecting the divine regard for the righteous, it is said : "For God is not unrighteous to forget your work and labor of love."[2] Over against these words of an affectionate and faithful friendship may be placed the words of displeasure against the wicked : "For the wrath of God is revealed from heaven against all ungodliness and unrighteousness of men, who hold the truth in unrighteousness."[3] In the divine wrath there is an emotional displeasure. This is the terrifying sense of those who would have the rocks and mountains fall on them and hide them "from the face of him that sitteth upon the throne, and from the wrath of the Lamb."[4] "For thou art not a God that hath pleasure in wickedness : . . . thou hatest all workers of iniquity."[5] Just the opposite is the divine regard for the righteous · "For the righteous Lord loveth the righteous ; his countenance doth behold the upright."[6] In the final ministries of distributive justice there are the activities of divine sensibility : in the "Come, ye blessed of my Father," an emotional love ;· in the "Depart from me, ye cursed," an emotional wrath.[7] It is thus manifest that we find the justice of God only in his personality, and only with an element of moral feeling.

3. *Love.*—No theistic truth is more deeply emphasized in the Scriptures than love. No truth has a fuller or more grateful recognition in the Christian consciousness, nor, indeed, with any who have a proper conception of the personality of God and the plenitude of his perfections. Neither the apathetic God of deism, nor the unconscious God of pantheism, nor the God of agnosticism, without any law of self-agency either in his own holy personality or in the responsible freedom of his human subjects, is the God of the Scriptures. "God is love."[8] This is the profound truth which they give us. But, while love is so profound a truth in God, it is never disrupted from his holiness. Indeed, love, as justice itself, is but a mode of his holiness, and in moral administration justice as well as love still has its offices.

Any notion of God without love is empty of the most vital content of the true idea. The very plenitude of other perfections, such as infinite knowledge and power and justice, would, in the absence of

[1] Rom. ii, 11. [2] Heb. vi, 10. [3] Rom. i, 18. [4] Rev. vi, 16.
[5] Psa. v, 4, 5. [6] Psa. xi, 7. [7] Matt. xxv, 84, 41. [8] 1 John iv, 16.

love, invest them with most fearful terrors—enough, indeed, to whelm the world in despair. The holiness of God is the implication of love. Neither benevolence nor goodness is possible in any moral sense without love. A deed might confer a great benefit, but could not be ethically beneficent without the impulse and motive of love. In all the benefits which God may lavish upon the universe, he is truly beneficent only with the motive of love. Holy love is the deepest life of all holy action. *ETHICAL GOODNESS ONLY WITH LOVE.*

It must be admitted that the love of God is for theism, simply in the light of reason, a perplexing question. The perplexity arises in view of the magnitude of physical and moral evil under the providence of an omniscient and omnipotent Creator and Ruler. John Stuart Mill has given the strength of the issue on the side of skepticism.[1] It is easy to point out a false and misleading assumption which underlies his discussion. It is that the question of evil, and of moral as of physical evil, is purely a question of the divine knowledge and power. The holy personality of God and the moral personality of man, both of which must be a law of the divine agency, are thus entirely omitted from the discussion. This omission must vitiate the argument. However, the pointing out of this fallacy comes far short of eliminating all the difficulties of the question. Great perplexity still remains. We have no theodicy of our own; certainly none simply in the light of reason. Nor have we received any through the work of others. Few questions have been more earnestly and persistently discussed. We find the discussion mostly in works on systematic theology, or in treatises on natural theology. Among the authors who have made special endeavor toward the attainment of a theodicy we might name Leibnitz,[2] King,[3] Bledsoe,[4] Whedon,[5] Naville,[6] McCabe.[7] Some of these discussions mostly proceed on the grounds of Arminianism as against the determining principles of Calvinism. But the great problem is still on hand; nor do we think its solution possible simply in the resources of the human mind. Revelation does not give the solution. *PERPLEXITY RESPECTING THE DIVINE LOVE*

The world, with the human race, must have a personal author. The author must possess infinite knowledge and power; for otherwise he could not be a sufficient cause to such dependent existences. He cannot be of malevolent disposition, else the constitution of his creatures would evince a malevolent purpose, and evil be manifold more than it is. That con- *EVIDENCE OF DIVINE GOODNESS.*

---

[1] *Three Essays on Religion.*   [2] *Théodicée.*   [3] *The Origin of Evil.*
[4] *A Theodicy*   [5] *Freedom of the Will*   [6] *The Problem of Evil.*
[7] *Divine Nescience of Future Contingencies.*

stitution really expresses a benevolent purpose. The provisions for
the happiness of animal life above the requirements for mere subsistence are many and manifest. The happiness of animal life
immeasurably exceeds its suffering. The comparatively trivial evils
may not be wholly avoidable. They must be a liability in a constitution of life with such provisions for its happiness. Clearly, the
constitution might have been such that suffering would have been
greatly in excess. The real facts in the case are a manifestation of
the divine goodness.

Human suffering is greater than mere animal suffering, and
MUCH SUFFER-   therefore creates a greater perplexity in the question of
ING FROM OUR-   the divine goodness. But here other elements appear
SELVES.   in the question. In his physical nature man still
touches the plane of animal life, but in his rational and moral
nature constitutes a higher realm of existence. His life in respect
of both good and evil is largely conditioned on his own free and
responsible agency. Most of the evil, both physical and moral, that
he suffers is from himself, not from his constitution, and might be
avoided.

So far as one's suffering arises from his own responsible agency,
HERE PROVI-   or might be avoided without omission of duty to others,
DENCE EASILY   the divine goodness needs no vindication. The asser-
VINDICATED   tion of such a need is really the denial of all self-
responsibility for one's own condition in life. The assumption is
that God should secure the same common well-being to the idle and
wasteful as to the industrious and provident, to the vicious as to the
virtuous, to the criminal as to the upright. This neither should be
nor can be. The false assumption re-appears that the providential
treatment and condition of men is simply a question of the divine
power. But God is a moral Ruler, and men his free, responsible
subjects. Justice, therefore, must have its offices in the divine
administration. Otherwise the interests of the virtuous and upright
would deeply suffer—just as in the case of a human government
which should provide for the idle, the vicious, and the criminal all
the immunities and blessings of life usually enjoyed by the upright
and deserving. This would violate the common sense of justice,
and in the result sacrifice all the rights and interests which the government should sacredly protect. Such a policy would be utterly
subversive of any government, human or divine. In the divine it
would be a departure from all the laws of life, physical, rational,
and moral, and the substitution of a purely supernatural agency,
particularly in providing for the well-being of all such as are reckless of these imperative laws. Nothing could be more extravagant

or false in the notion of divine providence. God is the rational
and moral Ruler of men as rational and moral subjects. This is
the only light in which to view his providence. It follows that
neither the secular nor the moral well-being of men is possible
against their own agency. Much of human suffering thus arises,
and for its existence the divine goodness needs no vindication.
Nor is any special defense needed in the case of suffering which
arises with the fulfillment of duty to others. To assert such a
need is to question or even deny the obligation of duty in all such
cases. But the truest and the best ever hold this obligation most
sacred, and its fulfillment the highest excellence.

Not all suffering, however, is avoidable. The interaction of life
upon life, inseparable from the providential relations
of humanity, is the source of evil to many. But there
is also a counterbalancing good to many through the
same law. The law of heredity in like manner works both good
and evil. The constitution of humanity renders inevitable the
results of these laws. The consequence is that the offices of the
present life are largely vicarious. The good suffer from the deeds
of the evil, and in turn serve them in the ministries of good.[1]
Such is the providential state of facts; but the facts are not self-
explicative so as to clear the question of perplexity respecting the
divine goodness.

STILL MUCH
UNAVOIDABLE
SUFFERING·

There is no solution of the problem through the solidarity of the
race, as this doctrine has been wrought into theology.
It is on this ground specially that Naville, previously
referred to, attempts to deal with the problem of evil.

NO LIGHT IN A
SOLIDARITY OF
THE RACE.

This is the common Calvinistic position, whether the solidarity of
the race is held on the ground of a realistic or a representative oneness. The position is that all are sinners by participation in the
sin of Adam, and that, consequently, the evils of this life are a
just retribution on the ground of that common sin. There is no
light in this doctrine. The realistic view requires an impossible
agency of each individual of the race in the sin of Adam. We did
not, and could not, so exist and act in Adam as to be individually
responsible for that original sin. The representative view concedes
the common personal innocence of that sin, but alleges a common
guilt of the sin through immediate imputation on the ground of a
divinely instituted federal headship in Adam. There is still no
light for our reason. Between the conceded personal innocence of
the Adamic sin and the common infliction of punishment there
intervenes only the immediate imputation of guilt—that is, the

[1] Butler: *Analogy*, part ii, chap. v.

accounting to us the guilt of a sin in the commission of which we had no part. It is the doctrine of a common guilt and punishment, without any personal demerit. Personal demerit is a sufficient explanation of the suffering involved in its just punishment; but the merely imputed guilt of another's sin is no explanation of such suffering.

The attempt is often made to reconcile human suffering with the divine goodness on the ground that it is a necessary and most valuable discipline of life. That it is a valuable discipline can scarcely be questioned. There are wayward tendencies which it may hold in check or often correct. The graces of gentleness, patience, kindness, and sympathy are nurtured and matured. The fortitude and heroism developed through suffering and peril have been the molding forces in the formation of the best and noblest characters. We have examples in Abraham, and Job, and Moses, and Paul. Neither could have attained the sublime height of his excellence without the discipline of sore trial and suffering. Many of the better and higher graces receive the most effective culture in the necessary and dutiful ministries to the suffering. It is thus plain that in suffering there is a large mixture of good; and the good is of the highest excellence and value. Nor can it be questioned that often the good exceeds the evil. Of course, it is still open for the skeptic to say that, while all this is true, the real difficulty lies in such a providential constitution of human life as to need this severe discipline of suffering. Simply in the light of reason there is strength in this position; but the logical implication is atheistic. Atheism, however, explains nothing, and affords no ground for either faith or hope. An inexplicable mystery of suffering is far more endurable than the hopeless darkness of atheism. There is manifestly great value in the discipline of suffering, but this fact does not clear up the mystery for our reason.

There is light for our faith. The light is in the Gospel. Over against the Adamic fall and moral ruin of the race the Gospel places the redemption of Christ; over against abounding sin, the much more abounding grace of redemption;[1] over against the suffering of this life, a transcendent eternal blessedness.[2] This blessedness is infallibly sure to all who in simple faith and obedience receive Christ as their Saviour and Lord. Nor shall any fail of it who in sincerity and fidelity live according to the light which they may have.[3] The condition of this blessedness is most easy, and in its fruition the mystery of suffering will utterly disappear. It is clearly thus with those who through great tribula-

SUFFERING AS A DISCIPLINE OF LIFE.

LIGHT IN THE GOSPEL

[1] Rom. v, 15, 20.   [2] Rom. viii, 18; 2 Cor. iv, 17.   [3] Acts x, 34, 35.

tion have reached the blessedness of heaven.[1] Dark as the picture of the world may be for our reason, for our faith there is light in the Gospel. The darkness is but the background of that picture, while in the light of the forefront the cross is clearly seen. "God so loved the world." "Herein is love." "God is love."[2] The cross is the very outburst of his infinite love.

4. *Mercy.*—Mercy is a form of love determined by the state or condition of its objects. Their state is one of suffering and need, while they may be unworthy or ill-deserving. Mercy is at once the disposition of love respecting such, and the kindly ministry of love for their relief. This is the nature of all true love—true in the reality and fullness of benevolence. It is profoundly the nature of the divine love.

There are other terms, kindred in sense with mercy, which are equally expressive of the gracious disposition and kind- KINDRED ness of love. We may instance compassion or pity, TERMS. propitiousness or clemency, forbearance or long-suffering. All true love regards its suffering objects with compassion or pity. This is profoundly true of the divine love. It is exemplified in the compassion of Jesus for the multitudes, faint, and scattered abroad, as sheep having no shepherd; and for the poor leper whom he touched and healed.[3] Such is the compassion of God for the suffering; even for the unworthy and the ill-deserving.[4] So the Scriptures emphasize the pity of the Lord, which, equally with his compassion, has respect to the suffering and need of man. Pity is expressed in words of pathetic tenderness.[5] Propitiousness or clemency is the divine disposition to the forgiveness and salvation of the sinful and lost.[6] The forbearance or long-suffering of God manifests the fullness and tenderness of his clemency. He is reluctant to punish, and waits in patience for the repentance of the sinful, that he may forgive and save them.

Thus the Scriptures emphasize these terms which are kindred in sense with mercy. In numerous texts they are grouped with mercy, so that all are emphasized together. Still mercy receives its own distinct expression, and often, in terms of the deepest intensity. God is the Father of mercies; his tender mercies are over all his works; and his mercy endureth forever.[8]

[1] Rev. vii, 13–17.   [2] John iii, 16, 1 John iv, 10, 16.
[3] Matt. ix, 36, Mark i, 41.
[4] Psa. lxxxvi, 15; cxi, 4; cxlv, 8, Lam. iii, 22.
[5] Psa. ciii, 13; James iii, 11.   [6] Psa. lxxviii, 38; Isa. lv, 7; Heb. viii, 12.
[7] Exod. xxxiv, 6, Rom. ii, 4, 2 Pet. iii, 9, 15.
[8] 2 Cor. i, 3; Psa. cxlv, 9, cxvii, 1.
    15

There is an emotional element in mercy, and in all kindred forms
of the divine disposition.   Mercy, pity, clemency,
long-suffering—these are not mere forms of divine
thought, but intensities of divine feeling, and would
be impossible without an emotional nature in God.   Divest them
of this sense and they become meaningless, and must be powerless
for any assurance and help in the exigencies of suffering and
need.

AN EMOTIONAL ELEMENT IN MERCY.

5. *Truth.*—Truth in God may be resolved into veracity and
fidelity.

Veracity is the source of truthfulness in expression, whether in
the use of words or in other modes.   It is deeper than
mere intellect; deep as the moral nature.   With all
true moral natures veracity is felt to be a profound obligation.
Veracity is revered, while falsehood, deceit, hypocrisy are abhorred.
In the truest, deepest sense of veracity there is profound moral
feeling.   The divine veracity is more than truthfulness of expression from absolute knowledge ; it is truthfulness from holy feeling.
As God solemnly enjoins truthfulness upon men, and severely
reprehends its violation, in whatever forms of falsehood or deceit,
so his own words and ways ever fulfill the requirements of the most
absolute veracity.

AS VERACITY.

This is the guarantee of truthfulness in the divine revelation,
though not the requirement of a revelation of all truth.   There
may be much truth above our present capacity of knowledge ; much
that does not concern our present duty and interest.   Nor does
the divine veracity require such a revelation that it can neither be
mistaken nor perverted.   Certainly we are not competent to the
affirmation of such a requirement.   Otherwise we might equally
pronounce against all the tests of a probationary life—which is the
same as to pronounce against probation itself.   Whether we shall
rightly or wrongly interpret the Scriptures in respect to our faith
and practice, according to the light and opportunity which we may
have, is one of the tests of fidelity to duty in the present probation,
and in full consistency with other tests.[1]   Errors in respect to
moral and religious truth are mostly the fruit of perverting feeling—such feeling as we responsibly indulge, and might correct or
replace with a better disposition toward the truth.   With simplicity
of mind and a love of the truth we may find in the Scriptures all
the lessons of moral and religious duty requisite to a good life and
a blessed immortality.[2]

[1] Butler · *Analogy*, part II, chap. vi.
[2] Matt. vi, 22 ; John vii, 17 ; viii, 31, 32 ; Eph. i, 17, 18 ; James i. 5.

Fidelity in God specially respects his promises, and is the guarantee of their fulfillment.   There are contingencies of
failure in human promises.   A promise may be deceit-
fully given.   Unforeseen events may effect a change of disposition
respecting fulfillment.   With abiding honesty in the promise, new
conditions may render fulfillment impossible.   These contingencies
of failure arise out of the possible dishonesty and the actual limitations of men.   No such contingencies can affect the divine fidelity.
The holiness of God is the infinite sincerity of his promises, and
the plenitude of his perfections the absolute power of fulfillment.
The Scriptures emphasize these truths.[1]

Fidelity in God is thus a truth of priceless value.   It is the absolute guarantee of his "exceeding great and precious promises."[2]
These promises, in the fullness and fitness of their content, are
sufficient for all the exigencies of life, and are absolutely sure of
fulfillment to all who properly meet their terms.

In the faithfulness of God there is an element of holy feeling.   A
certain measure of fidelity with men may be a matter
of conventional pride or personal honor.   It is truer
and deeper just as it is grounded in moral feeling, and
finds its ruling motive in a sense of moral duty.   It is the stronger
and surer just in the measure of this moral feeling.   Fidelity in
God is the more assuring to us with the deeper sense of his holy
feeling as its essential element and ruling principle.

V. DIVINE OMNIPOTENCE.

As previously noted, we use the term omnipotence in preference
to personal will for this attribute, because it better expresses the
plenitude of the divine power.   However, we shall not thus be led
away from the true nature of this attribute.

1. *Power of Personal Will.*—As God is a purely spiritual being
his power must be purely spiritual.   This, however, does not deny
to him power over physical nature.   As he is both a spiritual and
personal being his power must be that of a personal will.   This is
at once the logic of the relative facts and the sense of Scripture.
This sense will clearly appear in treating the omnipotence of the
divine will.

Nothing is more real in one's consciousness than the exertion of
energy.   The energizing is of the personal self through
the personal will, with power over the mental faculties and the physical organism.   How there is a voluntary self-energizing, with power over the physical organism, and

[1] Num. xxiii, 19; Tit. i, 2; Heb. vi, 17, 18.   [2] 2 Pet. i, 4.

through it over exterior physical nature, is for us an insoluble mystery. The facts, however, are most real, and the mystery cannot in the least discredit them. There is an equal mystery in the power of the divine will, but it can no more discredit the reality of this power than in the case of the human will. If for any power over exterior physical nature the human will is now dependent upon a physical organism, this may be simply the result of a present conditioning relation of such an organism to the personal mind, and not an original or intrinsic limitation. Indeed, there must be an intrinsic power of the will, else there could be no voluntary self-energizing with power over the physical organism. There must be an immediate power of the will over the physical organism; or, at most, the contrary is mere assumption so long as we cannot show either the reality or the necessity of any mediation. Even with the necessity of such mediation for the human will, it would not follow that the divine will is so conditioned. Omnipotence is self-sufficient.

2. *Modes of Voluntary Agency.*—As God is a personal being, he must possess the power and freedom of personal agency. The freedom of personal agency is the freedom of choice. In complete personal agency there must be a distinction between the elective volition in the choice of ends and the executive volition in giving effect to the choices. There must be this distinction in the modes of the divine agency.

If personality and personal agency be realities in God, he must ELECTIVE DI-VINE VOLI-TIONS. freely choose his own ends and determine his own acts. Any sense of his absoluteness preclusive of specific choices and definite acts in time is contradictory to his personal agency, and therefore to his personality. The assumption that knowledge in God must be causally efficient and immediately creative or executive is utterly groundless. With omniscience as an immediate and eternal knowing in God and immediately creative or executive, there could be no personal agency. The two are in contradictory opposition. With the truth of the former, all predication of personal agency would be false. For God there could be no rational ends, no eligibility or choice of ends, no purpose or plan. Then the universe must be a necessary evolution, but without divine teleology or one act of divine personal agency. By the supposition of knowledge in God, he might passively know the ongoing of the evolution, but could have no active part in the process. There could be no divine providence. These inevitable implications are false to reason and the sense of Scripture. As a personal being God must freely elect his own ends and determine his own acts. His personal will completes the power of such agency.

We must also distinguish between the elective and executive agency of the divine will. The choice of an end is not executive divine volitions its producing cause. If such a cause, the effect must be instant upon the choice. In this case there could be for God no plan or method of his agency, no futurition of his own deeds. But God has chosen ends, and plans for their effectuation through future deeds. This is the requirement of a divine teleology and a divine providence. The truth of such a mode of personal agency is in the Scriptures. Promise and prophecy, so far-reaching in their scope, are full of such facts. The futurities of promise and prophecy, so far as dependent upon the immediate agency of God, must have their future effectuation by the causal energy of his personal will. There is thus determined for the divine will an executive office in distinction from its elective office.

3. *Omnipotence of the Divine Will.*—Will as a personal attribute is an infinite potency in God. As a voluntary power it is operative at his pleasure. The contradictory or absolutely impossible is in no proper sense contrary to the omnipotence of his will. These statements are in full accord with the Scriptures. God is the Almighty.[1] God is in the heavens: he hath done whatsoever he hath pleased.[2] His counsel shall stand, and he will do all his pleasure.[3] He has made the heavens and the earth by his great power, and there is nothing too hard for him.[4] He doeth according to his will in the army of heaven, and among the inhabitants of the earth.[5] With God all things are possible.[6]

The omnipotence of God is manifest in his works of creation and providence. The concentration of all finite forces into a single point of energy would be infinitely insufficient omnipotence in creation and providence for the creation of a single atom. In the sublime words, "In the beginning God created the heaven and the earth," there is the agency of an omnipotent personal will. Only such a will is equal to the creation of the universe, and to the divine providence which rules in the universal physical and moral realms.

| [1] Gen. xvii, 1. | [2] Psa. cxv, 3. | [3] Isa. xlvi, 10. |
| [4] Jer. xxxii, 17. | [5] Dan. iv, 35. | [6] Matt. xix, 26. |

CHAPTER IV.

DIVINE PREDICABLES NOT DISTINCTIVELY ATTRIBUTES.

As previously noted, classifications mostly include truths respecting God which are not properly attributes. These truths are important and should not be omitted, but we think it far better to treat them separately than in a wrong classification. Their own distinctive sense can thus be more clearly given, while confusion is avoided in the treatment of the attributes.

It is unnecessary to notice all the truths, or all the terms for truths, which have been thus wrongly classed. Some are only a repetition of others in sense. For instance, immensity, as thus used, can add nothing to the sense of infinity or omnipresence, specially as it is usually given. Self-sufficiency, another of these terms, is profoundly true of God, but the whole truth is given in his eternal personality, omniscience, and omnipotence. Other truths, however, are so definite in themselves, or so special in their relation to the attributes, that they should be properly considered. Such are the eternity, unity, omnipresence, and immutability of God.

I. ETERNITY OF GOD.

1. *Sense of Divine Eternity.*—In its simplest sense, the eternity of God is his existence without beginning or end; in its deepest meaning, his endless existence in absolute unchangeableness of essence or attribute.

Eternity of being must be accepted as a truth, however incom-

ETERNITY OF BEING. prehensible for thought. The only alternatives are an absolute nihilism or a causeless origination of being in time. Nihilism can never be more than the speculative opinion of a few. Self-consciousness ever gives the reality of self, and is the abiding and effective disproof of nihilism. A causeless origination of being in time is absolutely unthinkable. We must accept the truth of eternal being. Hence the eternity of God encounters no peculiar difficulty; for there is no more perplexity for thought in the eternity of a personal being than in the eternity of matter or physical force.

The question arises respecting the relation of God to duration or time. It is really the question whether he exists in duration or in an eternal now. There is no eternal now. The terms are contra-dictory. The notion of duration is inseparable from RELATION OF the notion of being, just as the notion of space is GOD TO TIME inseparable from the notion of body. Being must exist in dura-tion. God is the reality of being, and none the less so because of his personality. The perplexity arises with the divine personality, particularly with the divine omniscience. Can there be mental succession in omniscience? The real question here concerns the personality of God rather than his relation to time. This we have previously considered, with full recognition of its difficulty. We cleave to the reality of personality in God, and could not surrender it for the satisfaction of thought respecting his omniscience, or the consistency of the one with the other. In the previous treatment we could not clear the question of all perplexity, but found no such contrariety between personality and omniscience as to discredit either.

2. *Eternity of Original Cause.*—Science may find an unbroken succession of physical phenomena, in which each is in turn effect and cause, but it cannot find the initiation of the series in physical causation. In the absence of a personal cause, the only alterna-tives are an infinite series and an uncaused beginning. Neither is thinkable or possible. Reason requires a sufficient cause for a beginning and for the marvelous aggregate of results. God in personality is the only sufficient cause. He must therefore be an eternal personal existence. This sublime truth is in the opening words of Scripture: "In the beginning God created the heaven and the earth."

3. *Truth of the Divine Eternity in Scripture.*—The Scriptures give frequent and sublime utterance to the divine eternity. Abra-ham calls upon the name of the everlasting Lord.[1] God proclaims himself the I AM THAT I AM,[2] which embodies the deep truth of his absolute eternity. The same truth is in the sublime words of the psalmist: "Before the mountains were brought forth, or ever thou hadst formed the earth and the world, even from everlasting to everlasting, thou art God."[3] He is the high and lofty One who inhabiteth eternity;[4] the King eternal.[5]

The eternity of God is simply the absolute duration of his exist-ence, and in no sense a quality or attribute of his be- DURATION NO ing, just as space is no quality or property of body. QUALITY OF We may speak of the spatial properties of matter, but BEING we can only mean such as appear or project in space. But such

---

[1] Gen xxi, 33.   [2] Exod. iii, 14.   [3] Psa. xc, 2.
[4] Isa. lvii, 15.   [5] 1 Tim. i, 17.

properties are purely from the nature of matter, and in no sense either constituted or modified by space. Being must exist in duration, because being must abide, and is being only as it abides. But its abiding is purely from its own nature, not from any quality or influence of time. Many forms of existence are temporal, but from their constitution or condition, not from any influence of time. Time is no quality of any existing thing. Eternity is no attribute of God; no quality either of his essential being or of his personal attributes. His absolute eternity is no less a profound and sublime truth.

II. UNITY OF GOD.

1. *Sense of Divine Unity.*—Unity does not well express the theistic truth for which it has long been in common use, though it may not be easy to replace it with a better term. Its deficiency arises from its applicability to any thoroughly individuated body, however many its elements or complex its organism. Thus a stone is one, a tree is one, a man is one. God is one in perfect simplicity and unchangeableness of being, one in an absolute, eternal unity. There is still a deeper sense of the divine unity, and one which the term still more signally fails properly to express. A stone, a tree, a man—each is one of a kind. They belong to specifical orders. God is not one of a kind. He is infinitely above all the categories of species. He exists in absolute soleness of essential divinity. This is the deepest sense of his unity. For the expression of this sense we have from Dorner the word *solity.*

2. *Rational Evidence of Divine Unity.*—With all the diversities of nature, there are such harmonies as evince a unity of divine original. The more complete the discoveries of science, the fewer and simpler are found to be the laws of physical nature. It is even claimed that the various distinctions of force express simply modes of the one force. Certain it is that the elements of physical nature are so few and in such correlation that a few simple laws determine the cosmic order of the earth and the heavens. If the light of this order reveals a divine Creator, it certainly reveals only one. Organic structures are formed upon such a unity of plan and in such a harmony of orders that there must be one Creator of all. Rational intelligence and moral reason are the same in all men, and the profoundest reason must determine one divine original of all. The three orders of the physical, the animal, and the rational are so diverse that they might seem to point to diverse originals; but they all so blend in man that in the light of this union it is manifest that there is one, and only one, Creator of all.

3. *Unity of God in the Scriptures.*—The Ten Commandments

embody the profound truth of the divine unity.[1] This truth is their transcendent moral and religious power. The Lord declares himself God in heaven and earth, besides whom there is no other; and on this ground claims the reverent and unreserved obedience of his people.[2] The Lord our God is one Lord. Therefore we must love him with the whole heart.[3] With slight variations of expression, this same truth of the unity of God is often declared. The Lord says, " I, even I, am he, and there is no God with me."[4] "Thus saith the Lord the King of Israel, and his Redeemer the Lord of hosts; I am the first, and I am the last; and beside me there is no God."[5] " We know that an idol is nothing in the world, and that there is none other God but one."[6] Thus is given the Scripture sense of the divine unity. There is only one God, Creator, and moral Ruler. He only must be worshiped, because he only is God. In perfect agreement with these truths is the sublime *monotheism* of St. Paul.[7]

4. *No Requirement for Plurality.*—Polytheism is the result of a vicious perversion of the intuitive and rational notion of God. This is the account of it given by St. Paul.[8] It is also in complete accord with the moral grounds upon which he had just based the responsibility of the Gentile world.[9] Polytheism can have no co-existence in any mind with the true notion of God. If there are any facts which seem contrary to this view, it is only in appearance, not in reality. No other God can be admitted to the faith and worship of the soul while in possession of the unperverted notion of the true God. There is no demand for another. The one true God satisfies the most searching logic of the question, the clearest intuitions of the reason, and the profoundest religious feeling. In the clear vision of the true God there is no place for another.

Unity is not in any sense determinative of what God is in himself. Just the reverse is the truth. God is the deep- UNITY NOT AN est unity because he only is absolute spirit, existing in ATTRIBUTE eternal personality, with the infinite perfection of personal attributes. This deepest unity is, therefore, in no sense constitutive or determinative of what God is in himself, but is purely consequent to the infinite perfections which are his sole possession. Unity is therefore in no proper sense an attribute of God.

III. Omnipresence of God

1. *Notion of an Infinite Essence*—The omnipresence of God, however sure in its reality, has been regarded as very difficult for

[1] Exod. xx, 3-17.   [2] Deut. iv, 39, 40.   [3] Deut. vi, 4, 5.
[4] Deut. xxxii, 39.   [5] Isa. xliv, 6.   [6] 1 Cor. viii, 4.
[7] Acts xvii, 22-31.   [8] Rom. i, 21-25.   [9] Rom. i, 18-20.

speculative thought. Much of this perplexity, however, arises from a misconception of the question; particularly from the rather common theological opinion that an essential omnipresence of God is the necessary ground of his omniscience and the potency of his will. This will appear as we proceed.

The doctrine of an infinite essence of being should be carefully guarded in both thought and expression. Otherwise it ERRONEOUS VIEWS OF DIVINE UBIQUITY. may become the foundation of pantheism. In all true theism the divine essence is pure, absolute spirit. All sense of magnitude or spatial extension is alien to such a nature, and should be excluded from our notion of the divine ubiquity. Much of our experience is a hinderance to this exclusion. As so many existences known to us in sense-perception appear in the form of magnitude or spatial extension, it is the more difficult for us to dissociate the notion of such extension from any form of essential being. Thus if we think of God as essentially present in all worlds we tend to think of his essence as a magnitude reaching all in a mode of extension, and as filling all the interspaces. The notion is utterly inconsistent with pure spirituality of being. If, however, we still assert the essential ubiquity of God, but hold our thought rigidly to the notion of pure spiritual being, we must at once be conscious of an utter incapacity to form any conception of the manner in which he is thus omnipresent. Shall we deny the essential ubiquity because of its mystery, or hold fast to it notwithstanding the mystery? We shall find that the question of such a presence of God possesses very little interest when we attain the real truth of his ubiquity.

The real truth is not in the sense of a ubiquitous divine essence. NOT A UBIQUITY IN DIVINE ESSENCE. In such a view the essence is considered simply in itself, without the personal attributes. As such, it cannot exercise the agency which must ever be a reality of the divine presence. Indeed, personal agency is for us the only vital reality of this presence. A mere essential presence is not only without agency, but must be without any distinction with respect to places or existences: must be the same with forms of physical nature as with morally constituted personalities; the same with the ethically evil as with the ethically good; the same in the empty space as in the living Church; the same in hell as in heaven. Nothing could be more aberrant from any rational or scriptural sense of the divine ubiquity.

The notion of an omnipresent divine essence as the necessary ground of omniscience and omnipotence involves insuperable difficulty. Omniscience and omnipotence are purely personal attributes. Hence the necessity of an essential ubiquity to these attributes can be asserted only on the assumption that God perplexities of that view. can have knowledge and exert energy only where he is locally present. If this be true, then personality in God must itself be so broadened in extension as to be omnipresent. Nothing could be more inconceivable or more contradictory to the nature of personality. In the light of reason and consciousness, as in the nature of its constitutive facts, personality is self-centered and above all spatial quality or relation. Neither knowledge nor the energy of will can have any dependence on so alien a quality as extension in spiritual essence and personality. The truth of the divine ubiquity must lift it above all spatial quality and relation and hold it as a purely personal reality.

2. *Omnipresence through Personal Perfections.*—We have previously stated that the personal agency of God is the vital reality of his presence. This truth is so obvious that it requires neither elucidation nor proof. There is an infinite plenitude of personal agency in the omniscience and omnipotence of God. His omniscience embraces the universe of realities, and all are subject to his omnipotence, according to his wisdom and pleasure. In the plenitude and perfection of these personal attributes God is omnipresent in the truest, deepest sense of the term. This doctrine obviates the insuperable difficulties of an extensive or spatial ubiquity, and, instead of grounding omniscience and omnipotence in the omnipresence of God, finds the reality of his omnipresence in the plenitude of those attributes.[1]

This doctrine easily adjusts itself to the divine agency, which is operative in all the realms of existence, and in modes answering to their distinctions. While operating in all, accords with the divine agency. it is in no pantheistic sense of a monistic infinite necessarily developing in mere phenomenal forms, but in the manner of a personal agency which secures the transcendence of God above all the realms of created existence. Such an agency adjusts itself to the profoundest distinction of the physical and moral realms, and equally to the profoundest ethical distinctions of the moral.

3. *The True Sense of Scripture.*—The Scriptures repeat the sublime utterances of the divine ubiquity. These utterances are the expression of a personal ubiquity through the omnipresence in personal agency. perfection of knowledge and the plenitude of power. "Whither shall I go from thy Spirit? or whither shall I flee from

[1] Martensen : *Christian Dogmatics,* pp. 93, 94 ; Venema . *System of Theology,* p 193 , Van Oosterzee *Christian Dogmatics,* vol. 1, 258 ; Dorner . *Christian Doctrine,* vol. 1, pp. 240, 241 ; Bowne . *Metaphysics,* p. 203.

thy presence?"[1] These words are the center of a long passage
which expresses the omnipresence of God in terms of the deepest
intensity. In these terms we find the reality and the absoluteness
of this omnipresence in the omniscience of God and the omnipotence of his will. While God dwells in heaven, he also dwells with
the contrite and humble in spirit to revive and comfort them.[2]
These are purely personal ministries, and, therefore, signify a presence of God with the contrite and humble in his personal agency.
"Thus saith the Lord, The heaven is my throne, and the earth is
my footstool "[3] Here is first the expression of the greatness and
majesty of God; then the expression of his kingly government. He
is enthroned in heaven and rules over all the realms of existence.
In the representation God is personally local, but his personal
agency is every-where operative. Thus he is present in all the
universe in the comprehension of his knowledge and the infinite
potency of his will. "Am I a God at hand, saith the Lord, and
not a God afar off? Can any hide himself in secret places that I
shall not see him? saith the Lord. Do not I fill heaven and earth?
saith the Lord."[4] There is no interpretation of the omnipresence
of God as here expressed except through the infinite perfection of
his personal attributes. "For in him we live, and move, and have
our being "[5] This text is central in St. Paul's sublime expression
of the being and providence of God. He is Creator and Ruler of
all—Lord of heaven and earth. He giveth to all life, and breath,
and all things. The sense of the broader and more detailed statements centers in the words cited. How is it that we live, and move,
and have our being in God? Only through his personal agency.
Any departure from this sense may run into the extravagance of
mysticism, on the one hand, or into the bleakness of pantheism, on
the other. There is no *hylozoism* in the theism of the Scriptures.
The agency of God, in whatever realm, is purely and solely a personal agency. The immanence of God in the universe must leave
his personal transcendence complete. Through the infinite efficiencies of his personal agency all systems of worlds and all orders
of rational and moral intelligences were created ; through the same
agency all are preserved. God is present with all—omnipresent in
his personal agency.

NOT DISTINCT-
IVELY AS AT- The omnipresence of God is a great truth; but as it is
TRIBUTE. solely through the perfection of his personal attributes
and in the efficiencies of his personal agency, it cannot
itself in any distinctive sense be classed as an attribute.

[1] Psa. cxxxix, 7.   [2] Isa. lvii, 15.   [3] Isa. lxvi, 1.
[4] Jer xxiii, 23, 24.   [5] Acts xvii, 28.

IV. IMMUTABILITY OF GOD.

1. *The Truth in Scripture.*—This great truth also receives its intensely forceful expression in the Scriptures. "I AM THAT I AM "[1] is at once the truth of the divine eternity and of the divine immutability, and of the latter in as profound a sense as of the former. " The counsel of the Lord standeth forever, the thoughts of his heart to all generations."[2] Here the thought rises from God in himself to the principles of his providence and asserts his immutability therein. The very heavens, seemingly so changeless and eternally permanent, are, in comparison with God, but as a fading, perishing garment, while he is eternally the same.[3] "I am the Lord, I change not:"[4] a truth of his providence, as of his being and attributes. God is " the Father of lights, with whom is no variableness, neither shadow of turning."[5] These words express a lofty conception of the divine immutability.

2. *Immutability of Personal Perfections.*—We previously pointed out the truth of immutability in the essential being of God. It is the truth of his eternal absolute identity of being. He is immutable in the plenitude and perfection of his personal attributes. His omniscience, holiness, justice, love, considered simply as attributes, are forever the same. Definite and varying acts of personal agency, and new facts of consciousness, such as must arise with the personal energizing of will in his creative and providential work, are entirely consistent with such immutability. The earth and the heavens, as temporal forms of existence, are ever in a process of change ; but even this ceaseless change arises from changeless laws, which point to an unchangeable divine original. In the perfection of his personal attributes God is forever the same.

3. *Immutability of Moral Principles.*—Sacred history discloses a changing frame-work of expediency in the older dispensations of revealed religion, and a great change from the elaborate ceremonials of Judaism into the simple forms of Christianity, but the same moral principles abide through all these economies. Change within the sphere of expediency is entirely consistent with the unchangeableness of God, while the changeless moral principles are a profound reality of his immutability. That he regards the same person now with reprehensive displeasure, and again with approving love, is not only consistent with his immutability, but a requirement of it in view of the moral change in the object of his changed regards.

The immutability of God is a great truth in the Scriptures, and

[1] Exod. iii, 14. [2] Psa. xxxiii, 11. [3] Psa. cii, 25–27.
[4] Mal. iii, 6. [5] Jas. i, 17.

a truth vital to morality and religion ; but as it arises from the
NOT A DISTINCT perfection of his personal attributes, and is equally a
ATTRIBUTE reality of each, it is not itself an attribute in any dis-
tinctive sense.[1]

[1] Works on theism more or less discuss the questions of the nature, personality, and attributes of God ; hence, much of the literature given in connection
with theism is appropriate for present reference.

Systems of theology very uniformly discuss these same questions. Works of
the kind are so well known that no detailed reference is necessary. It will suffice that we name a few authors : Knapp ; Nitzsch ; Watson ; Hodge ; Pope ;
Breckinridge ; Raymond ; Martensen ; Shedd ; Van Oosterzee ; Dorner ; Smith ;
Strong.

Special reference.—Samuel Clarke : *Being and Attributes of God*, Boyle Lect-
ure, vol. ii ; Charnock : *The Existence and Attributes of God ;* Bates : *Harmony
of the Divine Attributes ;* Pearson : *Exposition of the Creed,* article i ; Barrow :
Works, vol. ii, " The Apostles' Creed," sermons x–xii ; Saurin : *Sermons,* " The
Divine Attributes," sermons ii–xi ; Christlieb : *Modern Doubt and Christian
Belief,* lects. iii, iv ; Howe : Works, " Oracles of God," lects. xi, xii, xvii–xxv ;
Macculloch : *Proofs and Illustrations of the Attributes of God ;* Robert Hall :
Spirituality of the Divine Nature, Works, vol. iii, pp. 295–310 ; Dwight : *The-
ology,* vol. i, sermons iv–xiii ; Harris : *The Self-Revelation of God,* part iii ;
Muller : *Christian Doctrine of Sin,* vol. ii, pp. 13–30 ; Smith : *Existence and
Nature of God ;* Thompson : *Christian Theism,* book iv.

CHAPTER V.

GOD IN TRINITY.

In the doctrine of the Trinity there are questions of fact, and also a question of harmony in the facts. The latter is the chief question in the construction of the doctrine. It is a **DIFFICULTIES** very difficult question. We do not think it open to **OF THE QUESTION** full explication in human thought It is not wise to attempt more than is attainable. Yet the manifest prudence of this law has often been violated in strivings after an unattainable solution of this doctrine. We shall not repeat the error. Still, the divine Trinity is so manifestly a truth of Scripture, and so cardinal in Christian theology, that the question cannot be omitted. If a full solution cannot be attained, the facts may be so presented as not to appear in contradictory opposition. With this attainment, nothing hinders the credibility of the doctrine on the ground of Scripture.

It is proper to open the discussion with a distinct statement of the constituent elements of the doctrine. Following this, the doctrine itself, as held in the faith of the Church, should be so far treated as to present it in its proper formulation. Then before the completion of the discussion the essential divinity of the Son of God, and the personality and divinity of the Holy Spirit, must receive distinct and special treatment. This treatment is necessary because these questions involve essential elements of the doctrine.

I. Questions of the Trinity.

1. *The Unity of God.*—This is the first question of fact, but really a question not in issue. Trinitarianism is not tritheism; nor are trinitarians less pronounced on the unity of God than unitarians. The sense of this unity is embodied in the term designative of the personal distinctions in the Godhead. It follows that the unity of God is the basal truth in the doctrine of **BASAL TRUTH** the Trinity. But as this question is not in issue as be- **OF THE DOCTRINE.** tween trinitarianism and unitarianism, and especially as we have previously considered it in its distinctive application to God, it requires no further treatment here.

2. *Trinal Distinction of Divine Persons.*—The doctrine of the
Trinity asserts the personal distinctions of the Father, and the Son,
and the Holy Spirit, and the essential divinity of each.

Of course, there is no issue respecting the Father. With all
THE DIVINE theists his personality and divinity are above question.
FATHERHOOD. However, the real sense of the divine Fatherhood must
be determined by the doctrine of the Son. If the Son is only human in his nature, then, however rich his endowments, the relation of God to the human gives the fullest sense of his Fatherhood.
Arianism may raise this sense to a higher significance, but the
plenitude of its meaning can be given only with the essential divinity of the Son. Only this can give the full meaning of the Father's love of the Son;[1] the full sense in which he is the only begotten Son;[2] the infinite significance of the Father's love in the
redemption of the world.[3] The sublimest theistic truth of the
Scriptures is embodied in this definite reality of the divine Fatherhood. For the religious consciousness it possesses a fullness of truth
and grace far above all the creative work of God. His fatherly relation to man and to all intelligences is a great and grateful truth:
but the truth of his Fatherhood most replete with benedictions is
given only with the divine Sonship of the Saviour.

The doctrine of the Trinity encounters little issue respecting
RESPECTING the personality of the Son. Even Sabellianism and
THE SON. Swedenborgianism, which hold a mere modal Trinity,
admit his personality, though both deny to him any personal distinction from the Father. It is in this that both depart from
the true doctrine of the Trinity. The antagonism to the divinity of the Son, as posited in the doctrine of the Trinity, represents different grades of doctrine respecting his nature, ranging
all the way from Semi-Arianism down to the mere human Christ
of Socinianism.

The issue against the doctrine of the Holy Spirit, as embodied
RESPECTING in the doctrine of the Trinity, is in the denial of both
THE SPIRIT. his personality and divinity, but mostly the former.
But if the Spirit is not a person, neither can he be divine in any
sense necessary to the doctrine of the Trinity. The forms of
this antagonism may be more conveniently brought into view,
so far as necessary to this discussion, when treating the doctrine of the Spirit in its relation to the Trinity. Enough has
already been stated to show that the questions respecting both
the Son and the Spirit are vital to this doctrine. Without the

[1] Matt. iii, 17; John xvii, 24.   [2] John i, 14, 18.
[3] John iii, 16; Rom. viii, 32; 1 John iv, 10.

personal distinction of the Son and the Spirit from the Father, and the essential divinity of each, there is for theology no question of the Trinity.

3. *Union of the Three in Divine Unity.*—This is the question of harmony in the constituent facts of the Trinity, and, as previously noted, the very difficult question of the doctrine. It is the point which the adversary mostly assails. The defense is not in a clear philosophy of the doctrine, for there is no such a philosophy. For our reason the unity of God in Trinity is a mystery. There is, however, a profound difference between a mystery and a contradiction. The latter is utterly incredible, while the former may be thoroughly credible, as many mysteries are. The GROUND OF strength of the doctrine for Christian faith lies in its THE DOCTRINE. sure Scripture ground, and not simply in the completeness of its constituent facts as therein given, but especially in its complete articulation with the cardinal truths of Christianity. With the strength of this ground, we simply require such a statement of the facts as shall at once be sufficient for the doctrine and yet place them above all contradictory opposition. With this attainment, the assaults of the adversary are futile.

It is not assumed that such a statement is easily made. The difficulties are serious, though we do not think them REAL DIFFI-insuperable. For speculative thought the ground seems CULTY OF THE narrow between unitarianism, on the one hand, and DOCTRINE. tritheism, on the other. This is the real difficulty. In the treatment of the question there are not wanting instances in which this middle ground is lost, sometimes on the one side, and sometimes on the other. The predication of both unity and plurality in exactly the same view of God is a contradiction, and there must be error respecting either the unity or the plurality. God cannot be one person and three persons in the same definite sense of personality. Hence there must be a ground of unity below the trinal distinction of persons, or personality in this distinction must be held in a qualified sense. If we find a ground of unity below personality we must still confront the question whether such ground will answer for the unity of God as given in the Scriptures. Whatever the qualification in the sense of personality, it must still remain sufficient for the trinal distinction of persons, while the unity and the trinality must not be in contradictory opposition. Otherwise there is no question of the Trinity. The necessary elements of the doctrine disappear, with the result of either unitarianism or tritheism. It may thus be seen that we have not disguised the difficulties of the question.

16

II. Treatment of the Trinity.

1. *Incipiency of the Doctrine.*—In speaking of this incipiency
we distinguish between a doctrine as formally wrought out in
Christian thought and the elements of the doctrine which are given
in Scripture, but given simply as elements, not in doctrinal synthesis. The cardinal doctrines of Christian theology are mostly
the construction of Church councils—councils less or more general

BEGINNING IN in their representation. But the incipiency of a doc-
INDIVIDUAL trine ever anticipates the work of a council. Certainly
MINDS. this is true respecting all the leading doctrines of Christian theology. As the elements of such a doctrine are given in the
Scriptures they must be taken up into the thought of the religious
teachers, and through their ministry become the thought of the
Church. There are always minds of such philosophic cast that
they will study the elemental truths in their scientific relation, and
seek to combine them in doctrinal form. Thus it is that leading
doctrines of theology have ever taken form more or less definite
in individual minds. Such is specially the case respecting the
doctrine of the Trinity. The Scriptures are replete with truths
respecting the Father, and the Son, and the Holy Spirit. These
truths are specially central to the salvation in Christ and the life
in the Spirit, and must therefore have been in the daily thought of
the Church. Thus through the vital interest of its elemental
truths the doctrine of the Trinity soon began to take form, especially in leading minds. Such a process is always hastened, and
was specially in this instance, by the incitement of dissident opinions which are regarded as harmful errings from the truth. There
was such a preparation for the work of the great council which constructed the doctrine of the Trinity. Indeed, in this case the
groundwork had received a definiteness of form, as in the Apostles' Creed, which scarcely appears in the preparation for any other
leading doctrine.

2. *The Great Trinitarian Creeds.*—There are three creeds which
may properly be designated as great: the Apostles', the Nicene, the
Athanasian. Formulations of the same doctrine follow in the symbols of different Churches, but mostly they are cast in the molds
of these earlier creeds, which have continued to shape the doctrinal thought of the Church upon this great question. Yet only
one of these creeds has a clear historic position in respect to its
original formation. The Apostles' is not an apostolic production,
and must be dated from a later period. The Athanasian is later
than the time of Athanasius, but doubtless received much of its

inspiration and cast from his teaching on this great question. It is mostly an amplification of the Nicene Creed, in the formation of which Athanasius had so large a part, and was probably a work of the school of Augustine. This is the more prevalent opinion.[1]

3. *Content of the Creeds.*—The position of these creeds in the history of doctrines, and their determinative work in this central truth of Christian theology, may justify a very free citation, particularly from the Nicene and Athanasian. In no other way can we place the doctrine of the Trinity more clearly before us.

The Apostles' Creed is so familiar that citations may be omitted, particularly as it contains nothing which is not equally or more fully expressed in the others. THE APOSTLES'.

The Nicene: "We believe in one God, the FATHER Almighty, Maker of all things visible and invisible. THE NICENE.

"And in one Lord JESUS CHRIST, the Son of God, begotten of the Father, Light of Light, very God of very God, begotten, not made, being of one substance with the Father; by whom all things were made.

"And in the Holy Ghost."

The mere declaration of faith in the Holy Ghost made no advance beyond the Apostles' Creed, and was quite insufficient for a doctrine of the Spirit either in the full sense of the Scriptures or as required for a doctrine of the Trinity. The question was thus left in a very unsatisfactory state. It was too great a question, and too intimately related to the doctrine of the Trinity, for the indifference of the Church. Agitation followed. Opposing views were advocated. Error flourished. The truth was not so definitely formulated or placed in such commanding position that the better thought of the Church might crystallize around it. It was needful, therefore, that a doctrine of the Spirit should be formulated for its own sake, and also for the completion of the doctrine of the Trinity. The Council of Constantinople was convened, A. D. 381, for this purpose. Some additions were made to the doctrine of the Son, which, however, it is not important here to note. The doctrine of the Spirit is given thus:

"And [we believe] in the HOLY GHOST, the Lord and Giver of life, who proceedeth from the Father, and with the Father and the Son together is worshiped and glorified, who spake by the prophets."

This addition was held to complete the doctrine of the Trinity, and is often viewed simply as a part of the Nicene Creed.

---

[1] Pearson. *Exposition of the Creed:* Schaff. *Creeds of Christendom*, vols. i, pp. 14–41, ii, pp. 45–71 ; Shedd. *History of Doctrines*, vol. i, pp. 306–375.

The Athanasian Creed, while not the formation of any Church
THE ATHA-   council and of unknown authorship, has yet been quite
NASIAN.   as influential and authoritative on the doctrine of the
Trinity as any other.   Hence it is proper to cite from this creed
also.

"And the Catholic faith is this : That we worship one God in
Trinity, and Trinity in Unity; neither confounding the persons,
nor dividing the substance.   For there is one Person of the Father ;
another of the Son ; and another of the Holy Ghost.   But the Godhead of the Father, and of the Son, and of the Holy Ghost, is all
one ; the Glory equal, the Majesty co-eternal. . . . So the Father
is God : the Son is God : and the Holy Ghost is God.   And yet
there are not three Gods : but one God. . . . The Father is made
of none : neither created, nor begotten.   The Son is of the Father
alone : not made, nor created : but begotten.   The Holy Ghost is
of the Father and of the Son : neither made, nor created, nor begotten : but proceeding. . . . And in this Trinity none is afore, or
after another : none is greater, or less than another.   But the whole
three Persons are co-eternal, and co-equal.   So that in all things,
as aforesaid : the Unity in Trinity, and the Trinity in Unity, is to
be worshiped."

It would be easy to cite many highly appreciative views of this
ITS PROMI-   creed.   Hagenbach says : "The doctrine of the Church
NENCE   concerning the Trinity appears most fully developed
and expressed in its most perfect symbolical form in what is called
the *Symbolum quicunque* (commonly, but erroneously, called the
Creed of St Athanasius).   It originated in the school of Augustine,
and is ascribed by some to Vigilius Tapsensis, by others to Vin-
centius Lerinensis, and by some again to others.   By the repetition
of positive and negative propositions the mysterious doctrine is
presented to the understanding in so hieroglyphical a form as to
make man feel his own weakness.   The consequence was that all
further endeavors of human ingenuity to solve its apparent contra-
dictions by philosophical arguments must dash against this bul-
wark of faith, on which salvation was made to depend, as the
waves against an impregnable rock."[1]

These great creeds give their own doctrinal contents.   It would
be difficult, perhaps impossible, to find words more definite or explicit for the expression of the same truths.   The history of doctrinal expression on this great question confirms this view.   Few
subjects have more deeply engaged the thought of the Church.   Not
only have great synods profoundly studied and carefully formulated

[1] *History of Doctrines*, vol. 1, pp 288, 289.

the doctrine, but all along the Christian centuries the most learned and gifted theologians have given to the subject the highest powers of discussion and expression which they could command. The success has been in the measure of accordance with the great creeds. Any thing less must lose some element of the doctrine ; any thing more must bring the constituent truths into discord.

4. *The Doctrinal Result.*—The creeds are simply a careful statement and combination of the elements of truth which constitute the doctrine of the Trinity. There is no solution of the doctrine for our reason. This was not attempted, and could not have been attained. The human mind to which the whole subject of the Trinity seems clear surely does not see it at all. Difficulties must arise with any close study of the doctrine, and the more as the study is the profounder. We should no more disguise or deny them than attempt a philosophy of the Trinity. We previously pointed out the central difficulty of the question. It is in finding between unitarianism and tritheism sure and sufficient ground for the doctrine of the Trinity. However sure the several truths of the doctrine as given in the Scriptures, it must yet be admitted that for speculative thought this middle ground is seemingly but narrow and not very real. If we posit for the Trinity one intelligence, one consciousness, one will, seemingly we are very close upon unitarianism. If, on the other hand, we assume for each personal distinction all that constitutes personality as directly known to us, we seem equally close upon tritheism. The real difficulty is in finding the whole truth of the Trinity between these extremes ; and we have again brought it into notice, not for any solution, but rather as a caution against attempting a philosophy of the doctrine.

Such perplexities were present to the minds most active in the formation of the great creeds. This is manifest in the careful selection and use of terms for the expression of the truths combined in the doctrine of the Trinity ; particularly in the qualified sense of personality, that it might be at the same time consistent with the unity of God, on the one hand, clear of tritheism, on the other, and yet sufficient for the trinal distinction of persons in the sense of the doctrine. This was their high aim ; which, however, is far short of a philosophy of the doctrine. They sought to avoid contradictory statements ; and to this they did attain. They neither denied the unity of God nor asserted three Gods, but did most explicitly deny the latter and assert the former. The trinal distinction of persons implies no division in the essential being of God. The unity of his being is guarded and preserved in most explicit terms. There is in the doctrine no distinct nature for each person of the Trinity. The distinction is of three personal subsistences in the unitary being of God.

"What then is this doctrine? It is that God is one being in
THE DOCTRINE. such a modified and extended sense of the language as
to include three persons in such a modified and restricted sense of the terms that he is qualified, in a corresponding restricted sense, for three distinct divine personal forms of phenomenal action. Now what presumption is furnished by this doctrine against its truth? Does it assert that one God is three Gods, or that there are more Gods than one? It admits of no such construction, for it expressly affirms that there is but one God, and that the three persons, *as persons*, are not three beings or three Gods. Does the doctrine then exclude from the conception of God the ordinary, necessary phenomenal conception of a being? So far from it, that in asserting that God is one being, it includes this conception. Does the doctrine then include more in the conception of God as one being than is comprised in the ordinary, necessary phenomenal conception of being? But allowing this, what presumption does it afford against the truth of the doctrine? What shadow of evidence can the mind of man discover that the eternal, self-existent God should not subsist in a mode peculiar to himself, and quite diverse from that of creatures? Rather, what evidence can man possess that nothing more enters into the full and true conception which is formed by his own infinite mind of himself than is comprised in the ordinary, phenomenal, and very limited conception which man forms of the same being? What evidence has man, or can he have, that this limited phenomenal conception of his own being comprises all that is true, and all that God, who made him, conceives and knows to be true? If there is nothing like evidence to his mind that more is not, in this respect, true of himself, what presumption can there be that more is not true of the self-existent God, even that which constitutes three persons in one God?"[1] We have not cited this passage as an explication of the doctrine in the light of reason. This is not really its aim, though the author had more faith in such a possibility than we have. The passage is admirable as a defense against much of the hostile criticism which the doctrine encounters, and it is for this reason that we have cited it. It not only successfully defends the doctrine against the accusation of contradictory opposition in the facts which constitute it, but clearly points out the extravagant pretension to a knowledge of being, even of the divine Being,

[1] Taylor: *Revealed Theology*, pp. 54, 55.

necessary on the part of any one who denies the possibility of the divine Trinity.

With this effective defense against hostile criticism, difficulties for our reason still remain. In the lesson of these difficulties we may still learn the unwisdom of attempt- RESOURCE OF CHRISTIAN ing a philosophy of the Trinity. The chief resource of THOUGHT AND FAITH. Christian thought and faith is in a close adherence to the several truths of the Trinity as given in the Scriptures. The constituent elements of the doctrine are clearly given therein, but simply as truths, not with any explication. The incomprehensibility of the doctrine is only one of many incomprehensibilities in God. In the trinal distinction of persons in the Trinity, personality itself must not be interpreted too rigidly after the notion of our own. In this notion personality is an instance of the purest unity, and a distinction of persons is simply a distinction of such unities, with complete individuality in each. But while we are created in the image of God, we are not individually the measure of his Being. Hence a trinality which might well seem contradictory to unity in man may yet be consistent with unity in the plenitude of God. Any warranted denial of such a possibility as much transcends our reason as a philosophy of the Trinity, because only a comprehensive knowledge of the being of God could warrant such a denial on rational ground.[1]

[1] Schaff . *Creeds of Christendom*, vol. i, chap. ii; Harvey: *History and Theology of the Three Creeds;* Shedd: *History of Christian Doctrine*, book iii; Cunningham: *Historical Theology*, vol. i, chaps. iii, ix; Hagenbach: *History of Doctrines*, vol. i, pp. 258-290; Sir Peter King: *The Apostles' Creed*; Forbes: *The Nicene Creed*; Waterland . *The Athanasian Creed*, Works, vol. iii.

CHAPTER VI.

THE SON OF GOD.

As previously noted, the essential divinity of the Son is a necessary element in the doctrine of the Trinity. Hence this doctrine is vitally concerned in the question of the Sonship, and requires

FILIATION OF
THE SON.

for it a ground in the divine nature. If the full sense of filiation is given in the miraculous conception of Christ, or in his Messianic offices, there is no truth of the Sonship sufficient for the doctrine of the Trinity. If, on the other hand, filiation respects the personality of the Son in a higher nature than the human, it must include the sense of an essentially divine Sonship. The indefiniteness of Semi-Arianism respecting the higher nature of the Son may properly rule it out of any issue on this question. As Arianism holds the Son to be a creation of God, it allows no true sense of filiation respecting his higher nature. Creation is not a mode of the truest filiation. Certainly Arianism cannot give the filiation of the Son in the sense of the Scriptures. It follows that the issue of this question, as it respects the nature of the Son, is solely between the divine sense of the Nicene Creed and the mere human sense of Socinianism. If there be a filiation of the Son in a higher sense than the latter, it must be in the full sense of the former. It thus appears that the filiation of the Son so vitally concerns the doctrine of the Trinity as to justify its treatment separately from the more direct question of his divinity. If, however, the Scriptures clearly give the higher sense of the former, so far they affirm the latter.

I. DOCTRINE OF THE SONSHIP.

1. *Fatherhood and Sonship.*—The divine Fatherhood is in its deepest sense purely correlative with the filiation of the Son; though in a lower sense it is vastly broader. God is "the Father of spirits,"[1] and in a sense inclusive of all intelligences. This broader relation, however, is simply from creation, and its real meaning is the loving care of God for his rational creatures, such as a father cherishes for his children.[2] There is still the profound distinction between a Fatherhood through generation, as in relation

[1] Heb. xii, 9.   [2] Psa. ciii, 13.

to the Son, and a Fatherhood on the ground of creation, as in relation to men and angels. Christian sonship through regeneration, or being "born of God,"[1] rests on the deeper ground, and signifies the fullness of the Father's love for his spiritual children. The divine Fatherhood, even in relation to the divine Son, should have a special depth of meaning for us through the fatherly and filial relations in our own life.

The Fatherhood of God in relation to the Son is so frequently expressed in the Scriptures, and must so fully appear in the treatment of the Sonship, that it requires no separate statement.

2. *Lower Sense of Filiation.*—A lower and a higher sense is a very common fact in the use of words. It appears in such cardinal terms of theology as redemption and atonement. In no such case, however, does either sense exclude the other, unless they be in contradictory opposition. Hence the Nicene doctrine of the Sonship has no dialectic interest in denying a lower sense of filiation. If a proper exegesis gives such a sense of Scripture, it is simply a result to be accepted; and if such an exegesis gives the higher sense, it is none the less true on account of the lower, because the two are in no opposition. The filiation of the Son as expressed in Scripture is not always in the exclusive sense of his divinity.[2] Sometimes the more direct reference is to a lower ground. Such is the case in the salutation of the angel to Mary.[3] Here is the announcement of the miraculous conception and birth of a holy child who should be called "the Son of God." We would not even here deny to this formula the sense of essential divinity. The profound truth of the incarnation forbids it. But in this instance the Son of God is the Son incarnate, and the filiation must include the human nature with the divine; and, while the meaning transcends the human, the more direct reference is still to a filiation through the miraculous conception of Christ. It thus seems clear that the filiation of the Son is not always in the exclusive sense of his divine nature.

Sometimes the Sonship has more direct reference to the Messianic and kingly offices of Christ.[4] The sense of a divine filiation may be present even here; but as the SON AS MESSIAH. Son fulfills these offices through his incarnation and exaltation in our nature, the filiation must include this lower element. This psalm is clearly the seed of other passages of like import. In one it is declared that the promise of God unto the fathers was fulfilled unto their children in the resurrection of Christ.[5] Reference

[1] John i, 12, 13.   [2] Pearson: *On the Creed*, art. ii.
[3] Luke i, 31-35.   [4] Psa. ii, 7-12.   [5] Acts xiii, 32, 33.

is made to the second psalm, with a citation of the words, "Thou art my Son; this day have I begotten thee." The resurrection of Christ may here mean his advent as the Messiah. But if taken in the ordinary sense, the filiation of Christ simply through his resurrection would give a very narrow sense of the text; but even if the true one, it would have no doctrinal consequence against the higher sense of filiation, which, without any contradiction to the lower, would still securely stand in other texts of Scripture. In a truer view, the resurrection of Christ is not in itself a filiative fact, but a central fact in proof of his Messiahship and kingly power,[1] and thus represents a filiation inclusive of these elements. This is the same sense of filiation as given in the second psalm.

"For unto which of the angels said he at any time, Thou art my Son, this day have I begotten thee?" "So also IN KINGLY AND Christ glorified not himself to be made a high-priest; PRIESTLY but he that said unto him, Thou art my Son, to-day OFFICES have I begotten thee."[2] The sense of Sonship in these texts is much the same as in the second psalm, from which they are informal citations. The mere citation, however, does not determine the sameness of the meaning. The sense of this day or to-day, which relates to the filiation, may not be easily determined. It must be either indefinite or definite in meaning. If the former, it has no time-limit and means an eternal filiation; if the latter, as first uttered it must have been prophetic of some future fact or facts which contain the lower sense of filiation. If the exegesis of these texts should hold us rigidly to the sense of a temporal filiation, fulfilled in the kingly and priestly offices of Christ, it would simply place them in accord with texts previously noticed, and without in the least affecting the truth of an eternal Sonship as given in others. In the coming of the end, or in the consummation, the Son shall deliver up the kingdom to the Father, and shall himself be subject to the Father, that God may be all in all.[3] There is a relative subordination of the Son in the doctrine of the Nicene Creed; but there is here a surrender of functions and a subjection of the Son which find their fulfillment only in connection with Messianic or kingly offices. Powers of government were vested in Christ, the incarnate and redeeming Son. All power in heaven and in earth was given to him.[4] To him was committed the office of judgment; and he shall finally judge all men.[5] He was exalted in Headship over the Church, and in Lordship over the angels; and it was the Son incarnate, the Christ in our nature, in whom such powers of govern-

[1] Rom. i, 4   [2] Heb. i, 5; v, 5.   [3] 1 Cor. xv, 24-28.
[4] Matt. xxviii, 18.   [5] John v, 22, Acts xvii, 31, 2 Cor. v, 10; 2 Tim. iv, 1.

ment were invested.[1] In the consummation the Son will deliver up the kingdom and be subject to the Father with respect to these powers of his mediatorial office, which will then have been fulfilled. Thus all that appears as temporal in respect to the Son appertains to his mediatorial office, and is without any contrary opposition to his own eternal Sonship.

3. *A Divine Sonship.*—A full treatment of the divine Sonship would anticipate much that properly belongs to the more direct question of the divinity of Christ. But as the proof of the latter must confirm the truth of the former, there is the less occasion for its full treatment as a separate question.

"The Son," as this name is placed in the formula of baptism, must be both a personal and a divine being.[2] His association with the Father in this sacrament can mean nothing less. To deny the personality of the Son is to preclude all rational account of baptism in his name. To deny his divinity is equally preclusive of any rational interpretation. We have previously shown that Arianism allows no ground of filiation in Christ higher than his human nature. Hence if we deny a divine filiation of the Son as the sense of the baptismal formula, there remains no higher ground of Sonship than the human nature of Christ. We are brought down to the low ground of Socinianism. Can such a doctrine explain the association of the Son with the Father in the sacrament of baptism? Can it give any sufficient reason for the baptism in the name of the Son? Baptism signifies the remission of sins, the regeneration of the moral nature, and the initiation of the soul into the kingdom of grace. Hence when the risen Lord, invested with all power in the kingdom of God, charged his apostles with the great commission, "Go ye therefore and teach all nations, baptizing them in the name of the Father, and of the Son, and of the Holy Ghost," his words must mean a personal agency of the Son, as of the Father, in the great works which the baptism signifies, and an agency to which only divinity itself is equal. Hence the filiation of the Son must be in the sense of essential divinity.

The true doctrine of the Sonship appears in a conversation of Christ with the Jews, in which he defends himself against the charge of violating the Sabbath by a miracle of mercy wrought upon that sacred day.[3] For his vindication he claims for himself a perpetual work of providence in co-operation with the Father: "My Father worketh hitherto, and I work." There was a definite work of creation from which the

IN THE FORMULA OF BAPTISM

IN HIS OWN WORDS OF FILIATION.

---

[1] Eph. i, 20–23 ; Phil. ii, 9–11 ; 1 Pet. iii, 22
[2] Matt. xxviii, 19   [3] John v, 16–23.

Father rested, but his providential agency in the maintenance of the universe ever continues. In this agency the Son ever works with the Father. With these words the Jews were intensely offended. In their minds Christ had not only broken the Sabbath, but had said also that God was his Father, making himself equal with God. In this crimination they might have emphasized the association of himself with the Father in the work of his providence, which clearly implies an equality with God. The Jews were not authorities in the interpretation of the words of Christ. However, they could express their own sense of his meaning; and this is all that concerns us here. With this fact the noteworthy point is, that in no sense does Christ question or correct their inference, that the Sonship which he asserted for himself implied an equality with God. The rather do his further words confirm their interpretation. We may specially note the conclusion. "For the Father judgeth no man, but hath committed all judgment unto the Son : that all men should honor the Son, even as they honor the Father." "Whatever form that honor may take, be it thought, or language, or outward act, or devotion of the affections, or submission of the will, or the union of thought and heart and will into one complex act of self-prostration before infinite Greatness, which we of the present day usually mean by the term adoration, such honor is due to the Son no less than to the Father. How fearful is such a claim if the Son be only human ; how natural, how moderate, how just, if he is in very deed divine."[1] The filiation of the Son as set forth by himself in this self-vindication must contain the sense of essential divinity.

The creative work of the Son is conclusive of a divine filiation. IN HIS WORK OF CREATION The Word by whom all things were made[2] is not the reason or creative energy of God in a mere attributive sense, and personified in the work of creation, but a divine person. The personality is clearly given in the identification of the Word with the incarnate Son: "And the Word was made flesh, and dwelt among us, (and we beheld his glory, the glory as of the only begotten of the Father,) full of grace and truth."[3] "The only begotten of the Father" ever means the Son of God. The Son is the Word. The Word is personally and essentially divine. This is the truth of a divine Sonship. A revelation of the same truth through the creative work of the Son is given with equal clearness and fullness in other texts of Scripture. The Son through whose blood we have redemption and remission of sins is the Creator of all things.[4] Hence the Sonship must antedate the incarnation and the Messiahship of

---

[1] Liddon : *Our Lord's Divinity*, p. 182.
[2] John 1, 1-3.   [3] John 1, 14.   [4] Col. i, 13-17.

Christ. In the text under notice it is declared to antedate all created existences. Again, it is declared that the Son by whom God has spoken unto men in the times subsequent to the prophets is the Maker of worlds and the Upholder of all things.[1] In the sense of these texts there is a divine Sonship. The filiation of the Son is not in its deepest sense through the supernatural generation of his human nature, nor on the ground of his Messianic offices, nor by the creative act of God, but by an eternal generation in consubstantiality with the Father.

4. *Generation of the Son.*—There are repeated utterances of Scripture which express or imply the generation of the Son. He is "the only begotten of the Father;" "the only begotten Son;" "the only begotten Son of God."[2] On the ground of these words of Scripture, generation is in proper theological use for the expression of a fact distinctive of the Son in the doctrine of the Trinity. It requires no forced interpretation to read out of the words of St. Paul, "Who is the image of the invisible God, the first-born of every creature,"[3] the same distinctive fact of generation respecting the Son. "As the εἰκών, Christ is the πρωτότοκος πάσης κτίσεως: that is to say, *not* the first in rank among created beings, *but* begotten before any created beings. That this is a true sense of the expression is etymologically certain; but it is also the only sense which is in real harmony with the relation in which, according to the context, Christ is said to stand to the created universe."[4] The distinction of the Son from the created universe is profound. His existence is, not by creation, but by generation, and before all created existences. Not only is he distinguished from all creatures in the mode of his own existence, but is himself the Author of all creation.[5] With these determining facts of distinction, "the first-born of every creature"—πρωτότοκος πάσης κτίσεως—cannot be classed with created existences either as first in the order of time or as highest in the order of rank. The Son is born or begotten of God before creation and time.

The fact of generation is peculiar to the Son in the personal distinctions of the Trinity. There is no sense of generation respecting either the Father or the Holy Spirit. The ground of the fact as distinctive of the Son is given GENERATION PECULIAR TO THE SON in the Scriptures, but without any explanation. But as the Scriptures give the distinctive fact they warrant the use of generation as a theological term. The use of the term, however, is rather for doctrinal expression than for any explication of the doctrine. The

[1] Heb. i, 2, 3. [2] John i, 14, 18; iii, 16, 18; 1 John iv, 9
[3] Col i, 15. [4] Liddon. *Our Lord's Divinity.* p. 318. [5] Col i, 16, 17.

creeds state the fact of generation very much as the Scriptures do, and without any advance toward an explanation. The words of the Nicene Creed are· "The only begotten Son of God, begotten of the Father before all worlds, God of God, Light of Light, very God of very God, begotten, not made, being of one substance with the Father;" of the Athanasian: "The Son is of the Father alone not made, nor created: but begotten . . . of the substance of the Father; begotten before the worlds."

If the generation of the Son is for us an insoluble mystery, still GUARDED USE it may be guarded against erroneous interpretation. OF GENERA- This is necessary to preserve its consistency with other TION elements in the doctrine of the Trinity. Two or three points may be specially, though briefly, noted.

The generation of the Son must exclusively respect his personality, and in no sense his nature. The communication of the divine nature, and of the whole divine nature, to the Son, as also to the Holy Spirit, is a form of expression very current in the Trinitarian discussion subsequent to the Nicene Council, and still continues in substance, if not so much in more exact form. The aim was at once to guard the unity of the divine nature and yet to assert in the fullest sense the divinity of the Son. The aim was according to truth, and therefore good. Still the method of the aim may be questionable. The communication of the divine nature to the Son naturally implies his previous personal existence without this nature, and that his divinity is the result of the communication. Yet this was not the intentional meaning, and it would be entirely false to the doctrine of the Trinity. The seeming error is avoided by holding the generation of the Son simply and exclusively in relation to his personality. In the progress of the Trinitarian discussion this came to be the definite view of the question. As a personal subsistence in the divine nature, and in possession of divine attributes, the Son is divine in the deepest sense of divinity.

Generation must not be interpreted in any close analogical sense. NO CLOSE As the Sonship is eternal, it cannot be the result of any ANALOGICAL definite divine act, such as a creative or providential act. INTERPRETA- Such an act must be in time, and its product of tem- TION. poral origin. We should thus determine for the Son an origin in time. Further, such a personal divine act must in the nature of it be optional, and hence might not be at all. Therefore the Son might never have been. These implications are utterly contradictory to the divine predicables of the Son, and therefore a temporal and optional generation cannot be the truth. In this profound mystery we can account the generation of the Son only to an eternal and necessary activity of the divine nature.

5. *Consubstantiality with the Father.*—The sense of consubstantiality is that the essential being of the Son is neither different in kind nor numerically other than the substance of the Father, but the very same. This doctrine was formally decreed by the Council of Chalcedon : " We, then, following the holy fathers, all with one consent, teach men to confess one and the same Son . . . ὁμοούσιον τῷ πατρὶ κατὰ τὴν θεότητα—consubstantial with the Father according to the Godhead." [1] The definition was intended to be most exact. The council used ὁμοούσιος in sharp discrimination from ὁμοιούσιος, which means a distinct substance, and may mean a substance lower in kind. Both Arianism and Semi-Arianism were thus excluded, while the true and essential divinity of the Son was affirmed.

6. *Doctrine of Subordination.*—In the divine economies of religion, particularly in the work of redemption, there is a subordination of the Son to the Father. There is, indeed, this same idea of subordination in the creative and providential works of the Son. However, the fullness of this idea is in the work of redemption. The Father gives the Son, sends the Son, delivers up the Son, prepares a body for his incarnation, and in filial obedience the Son fulfills the pleasure of the Father, even unto his crucifixion.[2] The ground of this subordination is purely in his filiation, not in any distinction of essential divinity.

II. DIVINITY OF THE SON.

This is a question of revelation. The faith of the Church even from the beginning affirms its truth. But we must go back of this faith, and back of all formulations and creeds of councils, to the Scriptures themselves as the only authority in Christian doctrine. An exposition of all the texts, or even most of the texts, which concern the divinity of our Lord would require an elaboration running into a volume. This method is entirely proper in a separate or monographic treatment of the question, but is neither the usual nor the better method in a course of doctrinal discussions. Nor is it necessary to a conclusive argument for the divinity of Christ. A summary grouping and application of Scripture proofs may give the argument in a conclusive form, and with a strength against which the fallacies of logic and the perversions of exegesis are powerless.

A TRUTH OF
SCRIPTURE.

[1] Schaff : *Creeds of Christendom*, vol. ii, p. 62.
[2] John iii, 16, 17 ; Rom. viii, 32 ; Psa. xl, 6–8 ; Heb. x, 5–7 ; Phil. ii, 8.

The principle in which this argument may be grounded underlies
all science. Every thing is for science what its own
qualities determine it to be. This law must rule the
classifications of science in all realms of existence.
Otherwise no science is possible. In the crudest forms of matter,
in the spheres of chemistry, botany, zoology, in the realms of intellectual and moral life, every thing must be for science what its
own distinctive qualities determine it to be. The same principle is
equally valid for theology. It must be valid for theology, because
it is the necessary and universal ground of rational and cognitive
thinking.   Hence, if it is not true in all spheres that existences
are what their distinctive facts determine them to be, it cannot
be true in any. With such a result, mind would sink far below
skepticism into the starkest nescience. As, on this necessary and
universal law, gold is gold by virtue of its determining facts, so God
is God by virtue of the essential and distinctive facts of divinity.
There is for thought no other law of differentiation between the
finite and the Infinite, or between things and God. The principle is equally valid in the question of the divinity of Christ. If
the Scriptures in an unqualified sense attribute the essential facts
of divinity to the Son, then on the ground of their authority and
in the deepest sense of the term he is divine.

It may thus be seen that the strength of the argument for the
divinity of Christ may be given without any great elaboration. Proceeding on the principle which we have
laid down, all that is required is a grouping of the essential and
distinctive facts of divinity as clearly attributed to Christ in the
Scriptures. These facts may be classed under four heads : titles,
attributes, works, worshipfulness. There is nothing novel in this
division or grouping of these facts. It is so simple and advanta-
geous that it has been very customary, and in this sense is the prescriptive method.

1. *Divine Titles.*—There are titles which in their primary or full
sense are expressive of divinity and belong only to God. Yet such
titles are given in the same sense to the Son.

God is such a title. It is at once expressive and distinctive of
divinity. This is none the less true because it is not
always used in this higher sense. Even in the Script-
ures the term is often applied to idols.[1] It is not necessary to multiply references. This name is given also to princes, magistrates,
and judges.[2] In this lower sense Moses was a god : "And the
Lord said unto Moses, See, I have made thee a god unto Pha-

[1] Exod. xxii, 20 ; Judg. xi, 24.   [2] Exod. xxii, 28 ; Psa. lxxxii, 1, 6.

raoh."[1] Even Satan himself is called god—"the god of this world."[2]
In all these instances, however, the partial or figurative use of the term
is open and clear. Idols are gods as representing the objects of
heathen worship. Princes, magistrates, judges are gods as the
ministers of God in government, or as exercising functions in some
likeness to the divine agency. Moses was a god to Pharaoh as the
minister and representative of God himself. Satan is a god as
exercising a ruling power over the world. Such a qualified use of
terms is very common, and without any effect upon the primary or
full meaning. In this higher sense God is still the expressive and
distinctive title of divinity. As in the beginning God created the
heaven and the earth ;[3] as God is great and doeth wondrous things,
and he only is God ;[4] as God is the only object of supreme worship,[5] so is the term expressive and distinctive of divinity.

In this higher sense Christ is God, and therefore divine. It may
suffice to adduce a few instances. "And many of the THE SON TRULY
children of Israel shall he turn to the Lord their God."[6] GOD
This is the mission fulfilled by John as the forerunner of Christ.
Unto him the hearts of many were turned ; and he it is who is
called "the Lord their God." This application is confirmed by the
words immediately following : "And he shall go before him in the
spirit and power of Elias, to turn the hearts of the fathers to the
children, and the disobedient to the wisdom of the just; to make
ready a people prepared for the Lord." There is no restricted or
qualified sense of the divine name in this use of it. Any issue
would be joined, not against the deepest sense of the term, but
against its application to Christ. Such an issue, however, must
concede the fullest sense, because there is no other possible reason
for denying its application to him. With this concession, we need
but point again to the clear and full proof of this application. It
is thus true that Christ is God in the deepest sense of divinity.
"In the beginning was the Word, and the Word was with God, and
the Word was God."[7] In the fourteenth verse of this chapter the
Word is identified with the personal Son in the incarnation. The
Son is the Word, and the Word is God. There is no limitation of
the term in this application to the Son. There is no reason in the
connection for any limitation, but conclusive reasons for its deepest
sense. The eternity and creative work of the Son, as here clearly
given, justify his designation as God and require its deepest sense
for the expression of his nature.

"And Thomas answered and said unto him, My Lord and my

[1] Exod. vii, 1.   [2] 2 Cor. iv, 4.   [3] Gen. i, 1.   [4] Psa. lxxxvi, 10.
[5] Matt. iv, 10 ; Rev. xxii, 9.   [6] Luke i, 16.   [7] John i, 1.

17

God."[1] Thomas not only refused faith in the resurrection of
FURTHER TES-   Christ simply on the testimony of his brother-disci-
TIMONY   ples, but demanded the sight of his own eyes and the
touch of his own fingers in a definitely specified manner.[2] Christ
freely offered him all that he required. Then it was, as Christ
stood before him in living form and with all the required tokens of
his identity, that Thomas addressed him in these words of adoring
faith : "My Lord and my God." It is easy to declare these words
a mere ejaculation, addressed to God the Father, if to any one. If
addressed to no one, they must have been profane, and therefore
could in no sense have received the approval of Christ. A mere
ejaculatory rendering is not consistent with the temper of Thomas.
Besides, the words themselves are definite respecting the person addressed : "And Thomas answered and said unto him"—unto Jesus
—"My Lord and my God." Eliminate from these words the sense
of adoring worship, and they become profane. They were not profane, for Thomas received the approval and blessing of Christ in
their use. So sure is it that he is God in the deepest sense of the
term.

"Take heed therefore unto yourselves, and to all the flock over
TESTIMONY   which the Holy Ghost hath made you overseers, to feed
OF PAUL   the Church of God, which he hath purchased with his
own blood."[3] So Paul addressed the elders of the church in
Ephesus, whom he met at Miletus. We know that some dispute
the genuineness of Θεοῦ in this text, and would replace it with
Κυρίου; but the preponderance of critical authority is strongly in
favor of the former. As Christ is frequently called God in the
Scriptures, and often by St. Paul himself, such an application of
Θεός is nothing against its genuineness in this text. In all fair-
ness, it must stand with the preponderance of critical authority.
It is an instance in which, in the deepest sense of the term, Christ
is called God. "Whose are the fathers, and of whom, as concerning the flesh, Christ came, who is over all, God blessed forever.
Amen."[4] St. Paul had just been enumerating the great privileges
LIDDON'S   of Israel. "To these privileges he subjoins a climax.
EXEGESIS   The Israelites were they, ἐξ ὧν ὁ Χριστὸς τὸ κατὰ σάρκα,
ὁ ὢν ἐπὶ πάντων Θεὸς εὐλογητὸς εἰς τοὺς αἰῶνας It was from the
blood of Israel that the true Christ had sprung, so far as his human nature was concerned; but Christ's Israelitic descent is, in
the apostle's eyes, so consummate a glory of Israel, because Christ
is much more than one of the sons of men, because by reason of
his higher pre-existent nature he is 'over all, God blessed for-

[1] John xx, 28.   [2] John xx, 25.   [3] Acts xx, 28.   [4] Rom. ix, 5.

ever.' This is the natural sense of the passage. If the passage occurred in a profane author and there were no antitheological interest to be promoted, few critics would think of overlooking the antithesis between Χριστὸς τὸ κατα σαρκα and Οεὸς εὐλογητὸς. Still less possible would it be to destroy this antithesis outright, and to impoverish the climax of the whole passage, by cutting off the doxology from the clause which precedes it, and so erecting it into an independent ascription of praise to God the Father. If we should admit that the doctrine of Christ's Godhead is not stated in this precise form elsewhere in St. Paul's writings, that admission cannot be held to justify us in violently breaking up the passage, in order to escape from its natural meaning, unless we are prepared to deny that St. Paul could possibly have employed an ἅπαξ λεγόμενον. Nor in point of fact does St. Paul say more in this famous text than when in writing to Titus he describes Christians as 'looking for the blessed hope and appearing of the glory of our great God and Saviour Jesus Christ, who gave himself for us.' [1] Here the grammar apparently, and the context certainly, oblige us to recognize the identity of 'our Saviour Jesus Christ' and 'our great God.' As a matter of fact, Christians are not waiting for any manifestation of the Father. And he who gave himself for us can be none other than our Lord Jesus Christ." [2] This citation, while addressed more directly to the proof of Christ's divinity, is conclusive of our specific point in proof of the same truth, that in the profoundest sense he is called God

"But unto the Son, he saith, Thy throne, O God, is forever and ever: a scepter of righteousness is the scepter of thy kingdom." [3] In this connection the subject is the greatness of the Son, and the particular view, his greatness above the angels. He has a higher inheritance and name than they. ✦ No one of them is ever styled, as the Son himself, the begotten Son of the Father. The Son is their Creator and Ruler, and the object of their supreme worship. They are servants and ministering spirits, while the Son is enthroned in the supremacy of government. He is God. The facts call into thought the words of the prophet: "For unto us a child is born, unto us a son is given: and the government shall be upon his shoulder: and his name shall be called Wonderful, Counselor, The mighty God, The everlasting Father, The Prince of Peace.' [4] When the incarnate Son is thus called God, it must be in the sense of his divinity.

Jehovah is a distinctive name of the Deity. It is also a Scripture

[1] Titus ii, 13, 14. [2] Liddon: *Our Lord's Divinity*, pp. 313–315.
[3] Heb. i, 8. [4] Isa. ix, 6.

appellation of the Son, and therefore a proof of his divinity.   God
made known this name to Moses in a manner which
emphasizes its profound meaning. "And God spake
unto Moses, and said unto him, I am JEHOVAH: and I appeared
unto Abraham, unto Isaac, and unto Jacob, by the name of God
Almighty; but by my name JEHOVAH was I not known to them."[1]
It is restrictively the name of God: "That men may know that
thou, whose name alone is JEHOVAH, art the Most High over all the
earth."[2]   It is the expression of an infinite perfection and inalien-
able glory: "I am the Lord [JEHOVAH]; that is my name: and
my glory will I not give to another, neither my praise to graven
images."[3] In the plenitude of its meaning this name signifies the
eternal and immutable being of the Deity.

JEHOVAH A DIVINE TITLE.

There is nothing in the combination of this name with terms of
finite import which contradicts or even modifies its profound meaning.   Hence it is groundless to object,
"that it is sometimes given to *places*.   It is so; but
only in composition with some other word, and not surely as indic-
ative of any quality in the places themselves, but as MEMORIALS
of the acts and goodness of JEHOVAH himself, as manifested in
those localities.   So 'Jehovah-jireh, in the mount of the Lord it
shall be seen,' or, 'the Lord will provide,' referred to HIS interposition to save Isaac, or, probably, to the provision of the future
sacrifice of Christ."[4]   There is no use of this term in combination
with others which restricts or modifies its profound meaning as the
distinctive and expressive name of the Deity.

ITS USE IN COMBINA- TIONS.

This name is given to the Son, and in the fullness of its meaning
as a divine title.   The Scriptures open with the name
of God in plural form.   These terms may have in
themselves but little force for the proof of the Trinity; but as seen
in the light of a fuller revelation of God they properly anticipate
the personal distinctions in the theophanies of a later period.   In
these theophanies there are the personal designations of Jehovah
and the Angel of Jehovah.   The same person appears, sometimes
with the one title, sometimes with the other, and in some instances
with both, and with the distinctive facts of divinity.   A few references will verify these statements.[5]   The Angel of Jehovah, as revealed in these theophanies, is a divine person.   The powers
which he exercises and the prerogatives which he asserts are dis-

THE SON IS JEHOVAH.

---

[1] Exod. vi, 2, 3.   [2] Psa. lxxxiii, 18.   [3] Isa. xlii, 8.
[4] Watson: *Theological Institutes*, vol i, p. 506.
[5] Gen. xvi, 7–13; xvii, 1–22; xviii, 1–33; xxii, 1–18; xxviii, 10–22; xxxii,
24–30, with Hosea xii, 3–5; Exod. iii, 2–15.

tinctive of the Deity. Yet when styled Jehovah it is clearly with personal distinction from the Father. He cannot be the Angel of Jehovah and Jehovah the Father at the same time; though he can be Jehovah the Son and the Angel of the Father. This is the sense of these theophanies as we read them in the light of later revelations, especially in the clear light of the New Testament. The Angel of Jehovah, the Jehovah of these theophanies, is the Son of God. "The angel, who appeared to Hagar, to Abra- DR. HODGE. ham, to Moses, to Joshua, to Gideon, and to Manoah, who was called Jehovah and worshiped as Adonai, who claimed divine homage and exercised divine power, whom the psalmists and prophets set forth as the Son of God, as the Counselor, the Prince of Peace, the mighty God, and whom they predicted was to be born of a virgin, and to whom every knee should bow and every tongue should confess, of things in heaven, and things in earth, and things under the earth, is none other than He whom we now recognize and worship as our God and Saviour Jesus Christ. It was the Λόγος ἄσαρκος whom the Israelites worshiped and obeyed; and it is the Λόγος ἔνσαρκος whom we acknowledge as our Lord and God." [1] This is the summation after a full review of the relative facts; and the facts fully warrant the conclusion.

"From all that has been said, it is now manifest on how great authority the ancient doctors of the Church affirmed that it was the Son of God who in former times, under BISHOP BULL. the Old Testament, appeared to holy men, distinguished by the name of Jehovah, and honored by them with divine worship. . . . He who appeared and spoke to Moses in the burning bush and on Mount Sinai, who manifested himself to Abraham, etc., was the Word, or Son, of God. It is, however, certain that he who appeared is called Jehovah, I am, the God of Abraham, of Isaac, and of Jacob, etc., titles which clearly are not applicable to any created being, but are peculiar to the true God. And this is the very reasoning which the fathers all employ to prove that in such manifestations it was not a mere created angel, but the Son of God, who was present; that the name of Jehovah, namely, and divine worship are given to him who appeared; but that these are not communicable to any creature, and belong to the true God alone; whence it follows that they all believed that the Son was very God." [2]. This is the conclusion of the learned author from a thorough treatment of the appropriate texts, and after a thorough review of the Antenicene fathers, with free citations from their writings.

[1] Hodge. *Systematic Theology*, vol. i, p. 490.
[2] Bishop Bull. *Defense of the Nicene Creed*, book i, chap. 1, 20.

It is clear that the argument for the divinity of Christ, as thus constructed, goes far beyond the fact that he is called Jehovah in its deepest sense as a title of the Deity. In the divine manifestations of Jehovah, the Son, in the earlier revelations of God, he appears in the possession of divine attributes and prerogatives, performs divine works, and receives supreme worship. He is called Jehovah in the deepest sense of the term, and this fact is in itself the proof of his divinity. That he is thus called Jehovah is clear in the texts of the theophanies, previously given by reference.

2. *Divine Attributes.*—The more exact analysis and classification of the attributes, as previously treated, may here be omitted. Such a method would prove a hinderance to the simplicity of the argument, without adding any thing to its strength. Certain divine predicables which we treated as true of God and distinctive of divinity are equally true of the Son, and as conclusive of his divinity as the possession of the divine attributes which are distinctively such.

As the words, " In the beginning God created the heaven and the earth," [1] infold the truth of his absolute eternity, so the words, " In the beginning was the Word. . . . All things were made by him," [2] infold the truth of the absolute eternity of the Son. There are more explicit utterances of the same truth. The Son is Alpha and Omega, which is, and which was, and which is to come ; the first and the last ; the beginning and the end.' In these predicates of the Son we have an informal citation from Isaiah : " Thus saith the LORD the King of Israel, and his Redeemer the LORD of hosts ; I am the first, and I am the last; and besides me there is no God." [4] No proper interpretation is possible in either case without the absolute eternity of the subject of such predication.

The Son by an immediate insight knew all men, even their most secret thoughts and deeds ; [5] searches the reins and the heart of men.[6] A close and keen observer may acquire a pretty clear insight into the character of one with whom he is in daily intercourse. Yet even in this case the interior active life, the thoughts, desires, aspirations are hidden from the sharpest gaze. The knowledge of Christ infinitely transcends all the possibilities of such knowledge. It has no limitation to such facts as are in some mode expressed, but apprehends the most secret life. Nor is it in the least conditioned on any personal acquaintance or special study, but is an immediate and perfect insight into the most

ETERNITY.

OMNISCIENCE.

SCOPE OF THIS ARGUMENT.

[1] Gen. i, 1.   [2] John i, 1–3.   [3] Rev i, 8, 17 ; xxii, 13.
[4] Isa. xliv, 6.   [5] John ii, 24, 25.   [6] Rev ii, 23.

secret facts of the life ; and not only of one man, or of a few familiar friends, but equally of all men. "Lord, thou knowest all
things ; thou knowest that I love thee,"[1] is the witnessing of
Peter to his immediate knowledge of the inmost life of men.
"Now we are sure that thou knowest all things,"[2] is the testimony of the disciples to his omniscience. The same truth receives
the very strongest expression in the words of our Lord himself:
"As the Father knoweth me, even so know I the Father."[3] The
infinite depth of such a knowledge of the Father is possible only
with omniscience. This may suffice for the present, as the same
truth must re-appear in treating the final judgment of all men as the
work of Christ.

However, we must not entirely omit an objection which is ever
at hand with those who dispute the divinity of our Lord. SEEMINGLY, A
This objection is based on his own words—whether re- CONTRARY
specting the destruction of Jerusalem or the final judg- TEXT.
ment concerns not the present question : "But of that day and hour
knoweth no man, no, nor the angels which are in heaven, neither
the Son, but the Father."[4] In the discussion respecting the divinity of Christ these words have been much in issue. This appears in
the repeated and persistent efforts of the fathers to bring the text
into harmony with that doctrine, or, at least, to obviate all disproof of it. All along the Christian centuries the champions of the
Nicene Creed have taken up the question for the same purpose. In
his masterly work on the divinity of our Lord, Canon Liddon renews the endeavor with all the resources of his rare ability and
learning. Seemingly, little remains to be added on this side of
the question. Indeed, this has been the case for a long time.

The genuineness of the text has been questioned, or, at least, the
question has been raised, but that genuineness has not ATTEMPTED
been discredited. It has been attempted to obviate SOLUTIONS.
the difficulty by rendering the words as relating to the Son, in the
sense of not making known, instead of not knowing. This, however, is purely arbitrary, and inadmissible. Man, the angels, and
the Son, as disjunctively placed in the text, stand in precisely the
same relation to the one verb, οἶδεν. If, with the negative term,
we render this verb in the sense of nescience in relation to man and
the angels, and then abruptly change to the sense of not making
known in relation to the Son, the transition is so arbitrary that
laws of interpretation must forbid it. Further, if οὐδὲ ὁ υἱός
(οἶδεν) means that the Son doth not reveal or make known, then
εἰ μὴ ὁ πατήρ (οἶδεν)—words which immediately follow—should mean

[1] John xxi, 17.　　[2] John xvi, 30.　　[3] John x, 15.　　[4] Mark xiii, 32.

that the Father doth make known. This, however, would contradict the plain sense of the text. The only escape from this contradiction would require another abrupt transition back to the sense of the verb in its relation to man and the angels. There is no light in this view.

Mostly, a solution of the question has been attempted on the
LEADING   ground of a distinction between the divine and the
ATTEMPT.   human consciousness of Christ. On this ground it is
assumed that, while as God he knew the time of the judgment, as man he did not know it. This is the method of Athanasius himself, and for it he claims the consensus of the fathers. The great defenders of the Nicene Creed are mostly in his following. Canon Liddon joins them.[1] We specially refer to him because he is among the most recent and most able upon this question, as also upon the whole question of the divinity of Christ. Of course, the assumed distinction between the divine and the human consciousness of Christ is open to the pointed criticism that it is inconsistent with the unity of his personality in the union of his divine and human natures. In the terse putting of Stier, "Such knowing and not knowing at the same time severs the unity of the God-human person, and is impossible in the Son of man, who is *the Son* indeed, but emptied of his glory."[2] Seemingly, such a distinction involves the doctrinal consequence of Nestorianism, in which the human nature of Christ is a distinct human person, in only sympathetic union with the divine Son. It is a rather curious fact that, for the explication of a perplexing text, so many truly orthodox in creed should make a distinction in the consciousness of Christ which seems like a surrender to the Nestorian heresy. Of course, this is not intended. There are, indeed, many facts in the life of Christ which seemingly belong to a purely human consciousness; but if they are made the ground of a distinct human consciousness the same Nestorian consequence follows. Such facts lie within the mystery of the incarnation, where they unite with the facts of divinity manifest in Christ. The personality of Christ must be determined, not from any one class of facts, whether human or divine, but from a view of both classes as clearly ascribed to him in the Scriptures.

What is the result? The perplexity arising from this text is
THE RESULT.   not obviated by any of the methods previously noticed.
                 Nor is there any method by which this result can be
attained. Any inference from this fact that Christ is not divine

---

[1] *Our Lord's Divinity,* pp. 458–461
[2] *The Words of the Lord Jesus,* vol. iii, p 296.

would be hasty and unwarranted. The many conclusive proofs of his divinity still remain in the Scriptures. The subordination of these many proofs to one seemingly adverse text would, for its method, be against all the logic of science and all the laws of biblical exegesis. That text must remain as a perplexity for our exegesis, and may remain without any weakening of our faith in the divinity of our Lord.

As this attribute must be clearly manifest in treating the works of Christ, a very brief statement may suffice here. He has absolute power over nature. This is manifest in OMNIPOTENCE many of his miracles. In the feeding of thousands to satiety with a few loaves and fishes, in giving sight to the blind and hearing to the deaf, in raising the dead, in calming the storm, we see the efficiencies of omnipotence in its absoluteness over all the forces of nature. By his mighty power he is able to subdue all things to himself.[1] He upholds all things by the word of his power.[2] He is the Almighty.[3] Such attributions of power and agency can be true of Christ only on the ground of his true and essential omnipotence

Respecting the attributes of Christ, one truth is given in another truth. The truth of his omnipresence is given in the truth of his universal providence. which has already OMNIPRESENCE appeared in the fact of his upholding all things by the word of his power, and will further be shown in a more direct treatment. The providence of Christ is through his personal agency, in all the realms of nature. That personal agency is the reality of his omnipresence in its truest, deepest sense—an omnipresence in the infinitude of his knowledge and power. We may cite two promises of Christ, which can receive no proper interpretation without the truth of his omnipresence. "For where two or three are gathered together in my name, there am I in the midst of them."[4] These words are in the form of assertion, as of a fact, but with the sense and grace of a promise. The fact is of his presence with all who meet in his name, wherever and whenever it may be. As a promise of grace, his presence means a personal agency for the spiritual benediction of his worshiping disciples. Again, when he commissioned his apostles for the evangelization of all nations, he said, "Lo, I am with you alway, even unto the end of the world. Amen."[5] Again the words in form assert the fact of his presence, but in the sense and grace of a promise. The fact of his presence is for all his ministers, in all the world and for all time, as for his chosen apostles

<hr>

[1] Phil. iii, 21.   [2] Heb. i, 3.   [3] Rev. i, 8.
[4] Matt. xviii, 20.   [5] Matt. xxviii, 20.

whom he immediately commissioned to the work of evangelization. As a promise of grace, it is for all true ministers of Christ, as for the apostles, an assurance of his helpful agency. He seals this assurance with his own "Amen." Only an omnipresent Being—omnipresent with the infinite efficiencies of a personal agency—could truthfully assert such facts and give such promises.

Mutations of estate with the divine Son are the profoundest.

IMMUTABILITY. He was rich, and became poor;[1] in the form of God, with an equal glory of estate, but divested himself of this glory and assumed instead the form of a servant in the likeness of men, and humbled himself even to the death of the cross; and again he was exalted of the Father in Lordship over all intelligences.[2] Still, there is the deep truth of his immutability. "Jesus Christ the same yesterday, and to-day, and forever,"[3] immutable in divine personality through all his mutations of estate. As pointed out in treating the immutability of God, its strongest and sublimest expression is given in the words of the psalmist.[4] Yet these very words, without any variation affecting their sense, or any qualification, are applied to the Son. "And, Thou, Lord, in the beginning hast laid the foundation of the earth; and the heavens are the works of thine hands. They shall perish, but thou remainest: and they shall wax old as doth a garment; and as a vesture shalt thou fold them up, and they shall be changed· but thou art the same, and thy years shall not fail."[5] If the reality of immutability is expressible in words, it is expressed in these words. Then the Son of God is immutable.

The possession of the attributes of eternity, omniscience, omnipotence, omnipresence, and immutability, as thus grounded in the truth of Scripture, concludes the divinity of Christ.

3. *Divine Works.*—There are works of such a character that they must be as expressive of divinity in the personal agency which achieves them as the possession of its essential and distinctive attributes. Does Christ perform such works? This question we must carry into the Scriptures. They will not leave us in any reasonable doubt as to the truth in the case.

The Scriptures open with the creative work of God. With simplicity of words, the lofty tone at once lifts our thoughts
CREATION to the infinite perfections of his being. In the beginning God created the heaven and the earth. And God said, Let there be light· and there was light. And God said, Let there be lights in the firmament of heaven; let the earth bring forth grass

---

[1] 2 Cor. viii, 9.   [2] Phil. ii, 6-11.   [3] Heb. xiii, 8.
[4] Psa. cii, 25-27.   [5] Heb i, 10-12

and herb and fruit-tree, and let the waters bring forth abundantly the moving creature that hath life: and it was so.[1] Verily God is God. Creation is his work; the expression of his infinite perfections. The same truth runs through all the Scriptures. The heavens declare his glory, and the firmament showeth his handiwork.[2] God who made the world and all things therein, he is Lord of heaven and earth.[3] His works of creation reveal his eternal power and Godhead.[4]

Creation is the work of Christ. A few texts may suffice for this truth. "All things were made by him; and without CREATIVE WORK OF CHRIST. him was not any thing made that was made."[5] The Word who was in the beginning with God, and was God, and is in the fourteenth verse of this chapter identified with the incarnate Son, he it is who created all things. Futile is the attempt to resolve this work of creation into a moral renovation of the world. The words of John are so much like the opening words of creation in Genesis, to which one's thought is immediately carried, that only an original creation will answer for their full meaning. "For by him were all things created, that are in heaven, and that are in earth, visible and invisible, whether thrones, or dominions, or principalities, or powers: all things were created by him, and for him."[6] It is the Son of God, as the connection determines, who is thus declared the Creator of all things. No admissible in- CREATION IN ITS DEEPEST SENSE. terpretation can eliminate from this text the idea of an original creation—a creation of all things in the sense in which the Scriptures ascribe their creation to God. The notion of setting things in order, or of a moral renovation, is utterly precluded by the amplification of the text. If the former sense were admissible, very little would be gained even for an Arian Christology; nothing certainly for the Socinian. A setting of all things in order could mean nothing less than the reduction of chaotic materials into cosmic forms, and the collocation of worlds so as to secure the order of systems and the harmonies of the universe. God only is equal to such a work. There is the same inevitable implication, if with the text we carry up the thought to all higher intelligences, even to thrones and dominions, principalities and powers Any limitation to an institutional ordering, as in the Christian economy, is senseless for this text. The amplification includes in the creative work of Christ all things in earth and heaven, visible and invisible, material and rational, all the ranks and orders of celestial intelligences This is infinitely too broad

[1] Gen. i, 1-20.   [2] Psa. xix, 1.   [3] Acts xvii, 24
[4] Rom. i, 20.   [5] John i, 3.   [6] Col. i, 16.

and high for any institutional work of a merely human Christ. In the deepest meaning of the term, and with limitless comprehension, the Son is the creator of all things. The words of Bishop Bull are not too strong for this sense of the text: "But if these words of the apostle do not speak of a creation, properly so called, I should believe that Holy Scripture labored under inexplicable difficulty, and that no certain conclusion could be deduced from its words, however express they might seem to be." [1] We add a single text, without comment: "And, Thou, Lord, in the beginning hast laid the foundation of the earth. and the heavens are the work of thine hand." [2]

These three texts prove the creative work of Christ. "If God the Father were here substituted for Christ, no man would ever think of denying that the work of creation is attributed to him in the most proper sense." [3] The creative work of Christ is conclusive of his divinity.

The question of a divine providence is not here to be treated PROVIDENCE. any farther than in application to the present argument. There is a providence of God which is conservative of all existences, material and rational. "Lift up your eyes on high, and behold who hath created these things, that bringeth out their host by number; he calleth them all by names by the greatness of his might, for that he is strong in power; not one faileth." [4] The preservation of all worlds in their orderly existence is thus revealed as the work of a divine providence, and classed with the work of their creation. In the monotheism which St. Paul preached to the men of Athens on Mars' Hill there is the same creative work of God, only with broader comprehension, and the same providence in the preservation and government of his works. [5] Here again the work of providence is classed with the work of creation. God only can preserve and rule the works of his hands.

Such a work of providence is ascribed to the Son. After that remarkable passage, previously cited, in which the creation of all things is attributed to him, it is added: "And he is before all things, and by him all things consist." [6] Here the providence of the Son in the preservation of all things is classed with his work in their creation, just as in the texts previously noticed the preserving providence of God is classed with his creative work. "Upholding all things by the word of his power" [7] strongly expresses

[1] *Defense of the Nicene Creed*, book 1, chap. 1, 15.   [2] Heb. i, 10.
[3] Wood: Works, vol. i, p. 351.   [4] Isa. xl, 26.   [5] Acts xvii, 22–28.
[6] Col. i, 17.   [7] Heb. i, 3

the providence of the Son. He sustains all things, and rules them in an orderly manner. "By the word of his power" signifies a personal agency of infinite efficiency. In a like manner the personal agency of God in creation and providence is expressed.[1] So by the word of his power, his immediate, omnipotent personal agency. the Son upholds all things, and rules them in an orderly manner. In the providential work of the Son there is the truth of his divinity.

It is the clear sense of Scripture, and the common unperverted moral judgment, that God only can forgive sin, in its strictly ethical sense. Yet Christ forgave sin in the deepest sense of divine forgiveness.[2] This is decisive proof of his divinity. FORGIVENESS OF SIN

The theory of the resurrection does not concern the present argument. There is in the Scriptures the doctrine of a final, general resurrection of the dead. This is a great work of the future—so great as to suggest a doubt of its possibility. WORK OF THE RESURRECTION. The sacred writers neither deny its greatness nor attempt to modify the sense of the resurrection, so as to obviate the objection. Instead of this, they make answer simply by appealing the question to the infinite power of God.[3] The resurrection is a great work to which God only is equal; but he is equal to its achievement. This is their only answer. Yet it is the explicit truth of Scripture that Christ by his own power shall raise the dead.[4] If God only can accomplish this work, Christ, who shall accomplish it, must possess the infinite efficiencies of God, and, therefore, must be divine.

The final judgment must be perfectly righteous both in its decisions and rewards. It must be such respecting every person judged, and respecting every moral deed of every person. FINAL JUDGMENT. For such a judgment, a perfect knowledge of every life, even in its every moral deed, is absolutely necessary. Every life in its constitutional tendency and exterior condition, in all its susceptibilities and allurements, in its most hidden thoughts and feelings, motives and aims, must be perfectly known. There must be such knowledge of each individual life, and of every life of all the generations of men. There is such knowledge only in omniscience. If we might compare works, each of which requires an infinite agency, the final judgment is a greater one than the general resurrection. Not all the divine teleology in the construction of the universe requires a more absolute omniscience. Yet that final judgment is the

---

[1] Gen. i, 3; Psa. xxxiii, 6, 9.   [2] Luke v, 20-24.
[3] Matt. xxii, 29; Acts xxvi, 8.   [4] John v, 28, 29; Phil. iii, 21.

work of the Son. This is an explicit truth of the Scriptures.[1] We have given only a few references out of many. What we have given are of themselves sufficient for the truth which they so clearly express. The Son of God who shall finally judge all men must be omniscient, and, therefore, truly and essentially divine.

Each of the works of Christ, five in number, which we have brought into the argument is conclusive of his divinity. In their combination the argument is irresistible.

4. *Divine Worshipfulness.*—God only is supremely worshipful. Such worship consciously rendered to any lower being is idolatry. Many texts of Scripture witness to these truths. Reference to a few may suffice.[2]

Christ claims and receives supreme worship. It is divinely com-
SUPREMELY   manded. The Scriptures witness to these truths, as a
WORSHIPED.   few texts may show.

"The Father judgeth no man, but hath committed all judgment to the Son : that all men should honor the Son, even as they honor the Father. He that honoreth not the Son honoreth not the Father which sent him."[3] In the connection Christ speaks of God as his Father in a sense expressive of his own divinity. So the Jews understood him. He offers no correction, but proceeds with words replete with the same truth. He is co-operative with the Father in the perpetual work of his providence, and ever doeth the same things which the Father doeth. Such words lead up to the rightful claim of a supreme worshipfulness with the Father, as expressed in the words which we have cited. Men honor the Father only as they supremely worship him. Yet it is made the duty of all men to honor the Son, even as they honor the Father. "And again, when he bringeth the first begotten into the world, he saith, And let all the angels of God worship him."[4] Only a supreme worship of the incarnate Son can fulfill the requirement of this command.

In many instances of prayer and forms of religious service supreme
INSTANCES OF   worship is rendered to Christ. In filling the place in
THE WORSHIP.   the apostolate made vacant by the treason of Judas
the apostles "prayed, and said, Thou, Lord, which knowest the hearts of all, show whether of these two thou hast chosen."[5] Stephen in the hour of his martyrdom prayed, "Lord Jesus, receive my spirit," and also prayed for his murderers, "Lord, lay not this sin to their charge."[6] Thrice did Paul beseech the Lord for the

[1] Matt xxv, 31–46 , John v, 22 ; 2 Cor v, 10.
[2] Exod xx, 3–5 , Isa. lxii, 8 , Matt. iv, 10 ; Rev. xix, 10.
[3] John v, 22, 23.   [4] Heb. i, 6.   [5] Acts i, 24.   [6] Acts vii, 59, 60.

removal of that thorn in the flesh, that buffeting messenger of Satan.[1] The connection shows that it was the Lord Jesus to whom he thus devoutly and persistently prayed. "The grace of the Lord Jesus Christ, and the love of God, and the communion of the Holy Ghost, be with you all. Amen."[2] This benediction is the devout prayer of Paul for the divine gift of the largest spiritual blessings to the members of this Church. For these blessings he prays to the Lord Jesus, just as he prays to God the Father. Only a divine being could bestow such blessings. No other could be associated with the Father in such a supplication by one so fully enlightened in Christian truth as St. Paul. No such prayer could be truly offered except in a spirit of devout and supreme worship. Thus did Paul worship the Lord Jesus in this prayer. In two given instances he prays in like manner for the church in Thessalonica.[3] As Paul thus prayed, so did the other apostles pray, and so did the saints in every place call upon the name of the Lord Jesus.[4] To deny them the spirit of a devout and supreme worship of Christ in these prayers is to accuse them of superstition or idolatry.

Christ is exalted and enthroned in supreme lordship and worshipfulness over saints and angels. He is seated on the right hand of God, far above all principalities and powers, while all are made subject to him.[5] To him is given a name which is above every name, that at the name of Jesus every knee should bow, and every tongue should confess that he is Lord.[6] There shall thus be rendered to him the supreme homage which God in most solemn form claims of all.[7] As this homage is claimed of God, and due to him only because he is God, Christ must be truly divine; for else it could not be claimed for him. Yet, even angels and authorities and powers are made subject to him, and must render him supreme homage.[8] If Christ is not supremely worshipful, Christianity becomes a vast system of idolatry for both earth and heaven. He is supremely worshiped. There is such worship in the grateful and joyous doxology: "Unto him that loved us, and washed us from our sins in his own blood, and hath made us kings and priests unto God and his Father; to him be glory and dominion for ever and ever. Amen."[9] He is supremely worshiped in heaven. Even the angelic hosts join in this worship, saying, "Worthy is the Lamb that was slain to receive power, and

(marginal note: SO WORSHIPED IN HEAVEN.)

[1] 2 Cor. xii, 7, 8.
[3] 1 Thess. iii, 11-13; 2 Thess. ii, 16, 17.
[5] Eph. i, 20-23.   [6] Phil. ii, 9-11.
[8] 1 Pet. iii, 23.   [9] Rev. i, 5, 6.
[2] 2 Cor. xiii, 14.
[4] 1 Cor. i, 2.
[7] Isa. xlv, 22, 23.

riches, and wisdom, and strength, and honor, and glory, and blessing." The strain is prolonged : " Blessing, and honor, and glory,
and power, be unto him that sitteth upon the throne, and unto the
Lamb for ever and ever."[1] If in this adoring service the Father
is supremely worshiped, so is the Son. His supreme worshipfulness is the proof of his divinity.

The unqualified ascription of the distinctively divine titles, attributes, works, and worshipfulness to the Son is conclusive of his
true and essential divinity, as the sense and doctrine of the Holy
Scriptures. The proof is in the highest degree cumulative and
conclusive.

[1] Rev. v, 12, 13.

General reference.—Athanasius : *On the Incarnation* ; Burton : *Testimonies
of the Antenicene Fathers to the Divinity of Christ* ; Pearson · *Exposition of the
Creed*, article 11 ; Waterland : *Defense of the Divinity of Christ; A Second Defense of Christ's Divinity*, Works, vol. ii ; *Princeton Essays*, essay ii, " The Sonship of Christ ," Whitelaw *Is Christ Divine ?* Perowne · *The Godhead of Jesus*,
Hulsean Lectures, 1866 ; Liddon : *Our Lord's Divinity*, Bampton Lectures, 1866.

CHAPTER VII.

THE HOLY SPIRIT.

THE questions requiring special attention in the present discussion are the personality and the divinity of the Holy Spirit. Both questions involve necessary elements in the doctrine of the Trinity. Both must have sure ground in the Scriptures, or this doctrine cannot be maintained. The history of doctrines shows a persistent disputation of both; yet their Scripture ground remains clear and sure. After the conclusive proof of the personality and divinity of the Son, objections to the personality and divinity of the Holy Spirit have the less weight. The two questions are so one in their deepest ground that mere rational objections must be the same against both. Hence, as all such have spent their force and proved themselves powerless against the former, they are already proved groundless against the latter. In a word, the conclusive proof of the distinct personality and essential divinity of the Son clears the way for the Scripture proof of the distinct personality and essential divinity of the Holy Spirit. However, in this case particularly, the two questions of personality and divinity require separate treatment.

CLOSELY RELATED QUESTIONS.

I. PERSONALITY OF THE SPIRIT.

1. *Determining Facts of Personality.*—These facts were sufficiently given in our discussion of the divine personality. As in all instances the same facts are necessary to personality, and in all determinative of personality, a reference to the previous discussion may here suffice.

2. *The Holy Spirit a Person.*—The Scriptures are replete with references to the Spirit, the Spirit of God, the Spirit of Christ, and the Holy Spirit. This reference is in the first chapter of the Bible and in the last. But it is not necessary, nor would it be judicious or wise, to assume in every such instance a personal distinction of the Spirit in the sense of Trinitarianism. It suffices for the doctrine that there are sufficiently numerous texts which give the sense of this distinction, and which cannot be rationally interpreted without it. There are enough such; even many above the need. The clearer texts are in

REFERENCES TO THE SPIRIT.

18

the New Testament, but there are many in the Old which, especially as read in the light of the New, give the same meaning.

In the brooding of the Spirit upon the face of the waters, bring-
FACTS OF PER- ing cosmic forms out of the chaotic mass;[1] in the striv-
SONAL AGENCY. ing of the Spirit with men;[2] in his gift of wisdom to
Bezaleel and Aholiab, and to other artisans of special skill;[3] in
his illumination and guidance of Othniel, the son of Kenaz, in the
leadership and government of Israel, securing to them the conquest
of their enemies, and rest for forty years;[4] in giving a pattern of
the temple to David—a pattern which he gave to Solomon;[5] in the
gracious baptism of Christ, as foretold in prophecy and fulfilled in
the Gospel,[6]—in all these operations, as in many others like them,
there are forms and qualities of agency which clearly signify the
personality of the Spirit.

The association of the Holy Spirit with the Father and the Son
PERSONAL AS- in the form of baptism gives the sense of his own per-
SOCIATIONS. sonality.[7] The personality of neither the Father nor
the Son can be questioned, so far as the meaning of these words is
concerned. Any such denial respecting the Spirit is utterly arbitrary and groundless. If it be not so, then the Holy Spirit must
signify some nameless impersonal energy of the Father. In this
case, baptism would be in the name of the Father, and in the name
of some indefinite form of his personal energy. So irrational a
sense cannot be read into these words of Christ. The Father
must here mean the plenitude of his Deity. Hence baptism in
his name must be in the full sense of this plenitude. No impersonal somewhat can remain, in the name of which baptism
may be solemnly performed, just as though it stood in the same
infinite plenitude of divinity with the Father himself. In the
form of apostolic benediction there is a like association of Father, Son, and Holy Spirit.[8] For like reasons we must here find
the personality of the Spirit. This benediction is not a mere form
of words, but an earnest prayer, an outbreathing of the soul in supplication for the richest spiritual blessings. These blessings can be
conferred only through personal divine agency. This love of God
the Father is the personal bestowment of the gifts of his love.
This grace of Christ is the personal gift of the benefits of his
redemptive work. Hence this communion of the Spirit must signify his personal agency in our spiritual life. The personality of
the Spirit is as real as that of the Father and of the Son.

[1] Gen. i, 2.   [2] Gen. vi, 3.   [3] Exod. xxxi, 2-6.   [4] Judg. iii, 9-11.
[5] 1 Chron. xxviii, 11, 12.   [6] Isa. lxi, 1-3; Luke iv, 18-21.
[7] Matt. xxviii, 19.   [8] 2 Cor. xiii, 14.

'There are many words of Christ respecting the offices of the Spirit which can have no rational interpretation without the sense of his personality. The disciples were taught that, when arraigned before magistrates, they need not be anxious respecting their answer, for the Holy Spirit would teach them in the same hour what they should say, and in this manner answer for them.[1] Again, Christ promised the mission of the Spirit as another Comforter, who should abide with the disciples, teach them in all things, reprove the world of sin, guide the disciples into all truth, and glorify the Son.[2] These are strange forms of expression if the Spirit is not a person. Strictly personal terms are used, with pronouns just as usual in other instances of personal antecedents. The agency of the Spirit in the several forms of its expression is strictly personal—such as only a person can exercise. There can be no mere personification. The facts of this agency preclude it. The personality of the Spirit is given in these facts.

The diverse gifts of the Spirit, as expressed by St. Paul, are conclusive of his personality. The Spirit gives wisdom, knowledge, faith, the power of healing and working miracles, of prophesying, discerning of spirits, speaking with divers tongues, and interpreting tongues.[3] Here again is the use of strictly personal terms, and the expression of a strictly personal agency. These diverse gifts signify the diverse forms of this agency: "But all these worketh that one and the self-same Spirit, dividing to every man severally as he will." Nowhere has St Paul expressed himself in so strange a personification as this would be. The meaning of his words cannot admit such a mode. We must give them a strictly personal sense, and with that sense the personality of the Spirit.

We may group a few significant and decisive facts. The Holy Spirit suffers blasphemy;[4] witnesses to our gracious adoption, and helps us in our prayers;[5] is lied to, and resisted;[6] is grieved;[7] is despited;[8] searches and knows all things;[9] chooses ends and orders the means of their attainment.[10] These facts are distinctive of personality, and thus prove the personality of the Holy Spirit. There is significance for the present question in the very common qualitative appellation, Holy Spirit, or Holy Ghost. This appellation occurs so frequently in the New Testament, and is so familiar, that references are quite

[1] Mark xiii, 11.
[2] 2 John xiv, 16, 17, 26; xv, 26; xvi, 8, 13, 14.
[3] 1 Cor. xii, 4–11.
[4] Luke xii, 10.
[5] Rom. viii, 16, 26.
[6] Acts v, 3; vii, 51.
[7] Eph. iv, 30.
[8] Heb. x, 29.
[9] 1 Cor. ii, 10, 11.
[10] Acts xiii, 2–4.

needless. We find it also in the Psalms and in Isaiah.[1] If, instead of a personal title, we find with this appellation only a personification, we are brought back to some indefinite energy of God. Why should such an energy be thus specially qualified? Holiness is distinctively a personal quality. Deeds may be holy, but only as the deeds of a person in holy action. Even a subjective holiness can be such only as its tendencies are to holy personal action. Holy, as a qualitative term in the appellation of the Spirit, must signify the personality of the Spirit.

3. *Procession of the Spirit.*—With the distinction between generation in respect to the Son and procession in relation to the Spirit, each of which is a mystery for our thought, the treatment PROCESSION of the latter is much the same as that of the former. RESPECTS Procession respects purely the personality of the Spirit, PERSONALITY. and, as the generation of the Son, is designated as eternal. Procession is not from an optional act of the Father, for this would place the origin of the Spirit in time, which is contradictory to his true and essential divinity. An optional act of the Father as original to the existence of the Spirit will answer for Arianism or Semi-Arianism, but will not answer for the true doctrine of the Trinity. It only remains to say that the procession of the Spirit is from a necessary and eternal activity of the Godhead. Like other truths of the Trinity, it is inexplicable for human thought.

The procession of the Spirit from the Father is a definite truth PROCESSION of Scripture. This truth, while omitted in the Apos-FROM THE tles' Creed, was distinctly affirmed in the Nicene. FATHER So far there was no reason for disputation among those who accepted this Creed. All could agree in its affirmation that the Spirit proceedeth from the Father, as this is so definitely RESPECTING a truth of Scripture. It might still be questioned THE FILIOQUE whether this gave the whole truth in the case. Such a question did arise. Soon after the Nicene Council it came to be hotly disputed whether the procession of the Spirit was from the Father only, or from the Father and the Son. The former view prevailed in the East; the latter in the West. A provincial Council, convened at Toledo, A. D. 589, and representing the Western view, added to the Nicene Creed the notable *Filioque*, so that the procession of the Spirit should be expressed as from the Father and the Son. The friends of this addition thought it a logical requirement of the true and essential divinity of the Son; that if the Son is ὁμοούσιος τῷ πατρί—of one substance with the Father—the

[1] Psa. li, 11; Isa. lxiii, 10.

procession of the Spirit must be from the Son as from the Father. The question is thus carried into a sphere of speculation which seems too subtle for any very positive assertion of doctrine. However, this issue respecting the procession of the Spirit was a chief influence which led to the separation between the East and the West, or to the division of the Church into the Greek and the Roman. Evangelical Churches hold the *Filioque*.

The procession of the Spirit from the Father is, as we have stated, explicitly scriptural: "But when the Comforter is come, whom I will send unto you from the Father, even the Spirit of truth, which proceedeth from the Father, he shall testify of me."[1] The procession from the Son is not an explicit truth of Scripture; yet it is held to be derived from the Scriptures, but only in an inferential mode. This mode is legitimate; and a doctrine thus obtained may be as validly scriptural as if explicitly given. Many leading doctrines are so derived; notably, the doctrine of the Trinity, and the doctrine of the person of Christ. The only question is whether the grounds are at once thoroughly scriptural and conclusive of the inference. This is the vital question concerning the procession of the Spirit from the Son.

There are certain relationships between the Father and the Spirit which imply, and, for their full truth, require, the pro- PROOFS OF cession of the Spirit from the Father. But the same THE FILIOQUE. relations exist between the Son and the Spirit, which, therefore, prove the procession of the Spirit from the Son. For the proof of this procession, these facts of relationship must be presented. The Holy Spirit is the Spirit of the Son, just as he is the Spirit of the Father.[2] This fact of a common relationship seems clearly stated, without any qualification or reserve. If it be true, as maintained in this argument, that the Spirit is the Spirit of the Father on the specific ground of procession, and that this is the only ground of the relation, he must be the Spirit of the Son on the same ground. Therefore the procession of the Spirit is from the Son, as from the Father. This is one Scripture proof of the *Filioque*. Again, the mission of the Holy Spirit in the economy of redemption is from the Son, just as it is from the Father.[3] Here also is a fact of common relationship, clearly expressed, and without any distinction. But the mission of the Spirit from the Father implies a subordination, the only ground of which is in his procession from the Father. Therefore his mission from the Son implies a subordination which must have its ground in a procession from the Son. This is the

[1] John xv, 26.   [2] Rom. viii, 9; Gal. iv, 6; 1 Pet. i, 11.
[3] John xiv, 16, 26; xvi, 7; Acts ii, 33.

second argument. The two give, in substance, the more direct Scripture proof of the *Filioque*, or of the procession of the Spirit from the Son.

II. DIVINITY OF THE SPIRIT.

The argument in this case is much the same as for the divinity of the Son. It is grounded in the same principle, which underlies all science, that every thing is what it is by virtue of its essential and distinctive qualities. As on this principle we found the proof of the divinity of the Son in his possession of the distinctive facts of divinity, so in the same method we prove the true and essential divinity of the Spirit.

1. *Attributes of Divinity.*—These attributes are not so fully ascribed to the Spirit as to the Son; yet the ascription is entirely sufficient for the argument. If only one were so ascribed, all must be included; for they cannot be separated. More than one is in the ascription.

The eternity of the Spirit must be manifest in his creative agency, which will be separately treated. It may here suffice ETERNITY that the Spirit is plainly declared eternal.[1]

The attribute of omniscience must be manifest in the offices which the Spirit fulfills. In the declaration of his OMNISCIENCE. knowledge of God there is a profound expression of his omniscience· "For the Spirit searcheth all things, yea, the deep things of God. For what man knoweth the things of a man, save the spirit of man which is in him? even so the things of God knoweth no man, but the Spirit of God."[2] No man can know the secret things in the mind of other men, but the Spirit searcheth and knoweth all things. The deepest emphasis is in the fact that he searcheth and knoweth the mind of God. The searching is the absolutest knowing. This is the sense of ἐρευνᾷ, as the term is used in other texts.[3] There is no stronger expression of an absolute omniscience in the Scriptures. This is the omniscience of the Holy Spirit.

"Whither shall I go from thy Spirit?"[4] is a central question in a long passage, which, in the strongest sense, expresses OMNIPRES- ENCE. the absolute omnipresence of God. That omnipresence is as strongly expressed by interrogation as by affirmation. The question respecting the Spirit is in the affirmative sense of his absolute omnipresence. The same truth will appear in the works of the Spirit.

[1] Heb. ix, 14.   [2] 1 Cor. ii, 10, 11.
[3] Rom. viii, 27; Rev. ii, 23.   [4] Psa. cxxxix, 7.

2. *Works of Divinity.*—The works of the Spirit are manifold, and of such a character that they can be possible to his agency only on the ground of his essential divinity.

The moving of the Spirit upon the face of the waters [1] signifies a creative agency, which brought order out of chaos, clothed the world with light, and produced the forms of organic life. [2] The symbolical inbreathing of God into the nostrils of Adam, as yet a lifeless bodily form, signifies an agency of the Spirit in quickening him into life. The action of God, as figuratively expressed, was in this case as the action of the risen Lord and Saviour, when he breathed on his disciples, as a sign of the gift and power of the Holy Spirit. [3] As in this case the sign-act of the Saviour signified the agency of the Spirit as the source of their spiritual life and the power of their ministry, so that sign-act of God meant the agency of the Spirit as the original of life in Adam. There are other expressions of the work of the Spirit in creation. The garnishing of the heavens is his work. [4] This carries one's thought back to the beginning, when, as we saw, the Spirit transformed the chaotic mass into a cosmos. So he clothes the heavens in their light and beauty. In respect to this world, the Spirit is ever and every-where operative as the source of life. [5] This may suffice for the creative work of the Spirit. [6] Such works are conclusive of his divinity.

The Spirit is the source of prophetic inspiration : " For the prophecy came not in old time by the will of man : but holy men of God spake as they were moved by the Holy Ghost." [7] In a more specific application, the prophecies respecting the sufferings of Christ and the glory that should follow were the utterance of the Spirit. [8] Many of his sufferings, long foretold, sprang from free causalities in the volitions of men. Were these the only prophecies of the Spirit, they would prove his absolute prescience. Only an omniscient mind could unerringly predict such events. The vastly broader scope of prophecy, comprehending all the predictive utterances of the Spirit, deeply emphasizes the requirement and the proof of his omniscience.

Christianity is replete with the agency of the Spirit. The Gospel, in distinction from the law, is designated " the ministration of the Spirit." [9] This accords with the prophecy of Joel and the promise of Christ respecting the fuller presence and

---

[1] Gen. i, 2.   [2] Lewis. *Six Days of Creation*, pp. 63–67.
[3] John xx, 22.   [4] Job xxvi, 13.   [5] Psa. civ, 30
[6] Morgan. *Scripture Testimonies to the Holy Spirit*, pp. 5–8.
[7] 2 Pet. i, 21.   [8] 1 Pet. i, 10, 11.   [9] 2 Cor. iii, 8.

power of the Spirit.[1] Fulfillment of both the prophecy and the promise began on that memorable day of Pentecost—only began, because this was the initiation of a fuller ministry of the Spirit permanently distinctive of the Gospel. The outward signs which attended this manifestation, with some extraordinary gifts, might cease, but the presence and power of the Spirit must abide. The life of the Church and the saving efficiency of the Gospel are in his presence and power. Hence the agency of the Spirit in the many forms of his operation is fully expressed in the New Testament. This agency is conclusive of his divinity. We may group a few facts for the illustration and proof of our statements.

The saving efficiency of the Gospel is in the power of the Spirit. This truth is in the promise of Christ to endow his disciples with power for their work of evangelization;[2] and this truth they ever recognized and exemplified.[3] It is definitely the office of the Spirit to make the truth a convincing power in the conscience of men.[4] Regeneration, that mighty transformation of the soul out of a state of depravity into a true spiritual life, is the work of the Spirit.[5] Also, the Spirit is an assuring witness to the gracious adoption and sonship attained through regeneration.[6] All the graces of the new spiritual life are the fruitage of his renewing power and abiding agency in the soul.[7] Through the power of the Spirit we are transformed into the image of Christ.[8] He is a Helper and Intercessor in all truly earnest and availing prayer;[9] the source of all strength in the inner spiritual life;[10] the necessary helping agency in all gracious access to the Father.[11] The union of believers, the unity of the Church, is through the gracious work of the Spirit.[12]

These manifold and great works require an infinitude of personal A DIVINE perfections. Giving efficiency to the ministry of the PERSON. Gospel, applying the truth with convincing power to the conscience of men, renewing depraved souls in true holiness after the image of God, sustaining the life of the Church through a quickening influence in the mind and heart of believers individually—these are works which God only can perform. In this agency the Spirit must be operative through the whole Church, in the mind of every believer. Indeed, the sphere of his agency is vastly broader; for he is a light and influence in every mind of the race. His personal agency must therefore be every-where operative. This is

[1] Joel ii, 28, Luke xxiv, 49, Acts i, 4, 5   [2] Luke xxiv, 49.
[3] Acts iv, 31; 1 Thess. i, 5.   [4] John xvi, 8–11.   [5] John iii, 5, 6.
[6] Rom. viii, 16.   [7] Gal v, 22, 23; Eph v, 9
[8] 2 Cor. iii, 18.   [9] Rom. viii, 26, 27.   [10] Eph. iii, 16.
[11] Eph. ii, 18.   [12] 2 Cor. xii, 18.

conclusive of his omniscience and omnipotence; for it is only through such attributes that a personal agency can be omnipresent. Hence, in every view of the work of the Spirit in the economies of religion, and especially in Christianity, he is truly and essentially divine.

3. *Supreme Worshipfulness.*—The worship of the Holy Spirit is not so fully revealed as that of the Son. It is neither so explicitly enjoined as a duty nor so frequently exemplified in instances of worship. Yet there are facts of Scripture which clearly give the sense of his supreme worshipfulness. Such is FACTS IN PROOF the fact that he may be the subject of the deepest blasphemy.[1] Blasphemy is the use of reproachful or impious terms respecting God or against God. Its specially deep impiety arises from the infinite perfections of God and his supreme claim upon our devout homage. When, therefore, we find in the Scriptures a blasphemy against the Holy Ghost of the very deepest turpitude and demerit the fact must mean his supreme claim upon the reverence and worship of men. The sanctity and responsibility of an oath arise from the perfections of God, in whose name alone it must be taken, and ever with reverence.[2] Otherwise an oath is profane and impious. Yet there is an asseveration of Paul in the presence of the Holy Spirit which is of the very essence of an oath : "I say the truth in Christ, I lie not, my conscience also bearing me witness in the Holy Ghost."[3] "This being an appeal to Christ and to the Holy Ghost, as knowing the apostle's heart, is of the nature of an oath."[4] "This is one of the most solemn oaths any man can take. He appeals to Christ as the Searcher of hearts that he tells the truth; asserts that his conscience was free from guile in the matter, and that the Holy Ghost bore him testimony that what he said was true."[5] "The best commentators are agreed that this is a form of solemn protestation partaking of the nature of an oath. . . . The full sense of the words is . 'I protest by Christ that I speak the truth. I take the Holy Spirit, who knoweth my heart, to witness that I lie not.'"[6] Thus did Paul asseverate in the name and presence of the Holy Spirit, with all that constitutes the substance and solemnity of an oath, just as elsewhere he more formally made oath in the name of God.[7] Such an oath is utterly irreconcilable with the religious faith and life of Paul, except with devout reverence for the Holy Spirit, such as is central to the supreme worship of God.

The Holy Spirit occupies the same position in the form of bap-

---

[1] Matt. xii, 31.
[2] Deut. vi, 13; Matt. v, 33–36.
[3] Rom. ix, 1.
[4] Macknight: *On the Epistles,* in loc.
[5] Clarke: *Commentary,* in loc.
[6] Bloomfield: *Greek Testament,* in loc.
[7] 2 Cor. i, 23.

tism as the Father and the Son.[1] This sacrament has a profound

IN BAPTISM AND BENEDIC-TION religious significance, and its administration is a very real religious service. In this service the faith of the Church embraces the central truths of the Gospel, and her prayers are poured forth for the great spiritual blessings which the baptism signifies. Truly there is profound worship in this service. In the light of Scripture, as in the deepest consciousness of the Church, even from the beginning, these great blessings come more immediately from the Holy Spirit. Did our Lord in the institution of this sacrament mean that the Holy Spirit should be omitted from the supreme worship in its proper administration? Surely not. Else, he has very strangely enjoined the administration in the name of the Holy Spirit, just as in the name of the Father and of the Son. What is true of the form of baptism is equally true of the apostolic benediction. This benediction is an invocation of blessings from the Holy Spirit, just as from the Father and the Son.[2] It is an invocation, with adoration of the Spirit, just as of the Father and the Son. The divine attributes, divine works, and supreme worshipfulness of the Holy Spirit are conclusive of his divinity.

4. *Relative Subordination.*—The Spirit is of one and the same substance with the Father and the Son. Any divergence from this doctrine must be either tritheistic, or Arian, or purely Unitarian. Yet the Church early accepted, and still holds, the doctrine of an economical or relative subordination of the Spirit to the Father. This subordination appears in the offices which the Spirit fulfills in the divine economies of religion, particularly in Christianity. After the adoption of the *Filioque*, the procession of the Spirit from the Son also, there was for the Western Church the same sense of subordination to the Son. There is a mission of the Spirit from both the Father and the Son, and in this mission appears the subordination of the Spirit. The subordination, however, is purely on the ground of procession, not from any distinction in true and essential divinity.

---

[1] Matt. xxviii, 19.   [2] 2 Cor. xiii, 14.

General reference.—Owen : *Discourses on the Holy Spirit;* Pearson : *Exposition of the Creed,* article viii ; Smeaton : *On the Holy Spirit;* Morgan : *Scripture Testimony to the Holy Spirit;* Walker : *Doctrine of the Holy Spirit,* Hare : *The Mission of the Comforter;* Parker : *The Paraclete, Essays on the Personality and Ministry of the Holy Spirit;* Heber : *Personality and Office of the Comforter,* Bampton Lectures, 1816 ; Buchanan : *Office and Work of the Holy Spirit;* Daunt . *Person and Offices of the Holy Spirit,* Donnell Lectures, 1879 ; Cardinal Manning : *Internal Work of the Holy Ghost;* Stowell : *The Work of the Spirit,* Congregational Lectures, 1849 , Moberly : *Administration of the Holy Spirit in the Body of Christ,* Bampton Lectures, 1868.

CHAPTER VIII.

TRUTH OF THE TRINITY.

THE doctrine of the Trinity, as formulated in Christian theology, is exclusively a question of revelation. Hence the question of its truth has respect simply to the reality and sufficiency of its Scripture ground. The Scriptures neither formulate the doctrine nor directly express it. The one text most nearly approaching such an expression is no longer accredited as genuine, and therefore is dismissed from the discussion.[1] The Scriptures clearly give the elements of the doctrine. These elements in proper combination truly constitute the doctrine. Therefore the doctrine itself is a truth of the Scriptures. This is the method of proof. It will thus readily appear that but little remains for our discussion. We have sufficiently treated the primary questions of the Trinity, and it only remains so to bring the results together as to render clear and conclusive the Scripture proofs of the doctrine.

GROUND OF THE DOCTRINE.

I. PROOFS OF THE TRINITY.

1. *Omission of Questionable Proofs.*—The argument for the Trinity from the Scriptures is so full and clear that there is no need of questionable proofs. Yet some long in use may be so classed. We may instance the plural form of the divine name; the threefold priestly benediction; the *tersanctus* or trinal ascription of holiness to God; the manifestation of Father, Son, and Spirit at the baptism of Christ. These facts were pressed into the argument for the Trinity by leading fathers of the Church, and have continued to be so used by very eminent divines. Yet others, not inferior either in the exegesis of the Scriptures or in teaching their doctrinal content, fail to find any direct proof of this doctrine in these facts. With this opposition of views between the friends of the doctrine the facts in question can hardly be of any use in a polemic with its opponents.

The plural divine name, אלהים—Elohim—occurs in many places. Only an overstrained definition, however, could give it the sense of a trinal distinction of persons in the Godhead. Elohim is placed in apposition with יהוה[2]—Jehovah—and in

PLURAL DIVINE NAME.

[1] 1 John v, 7.   [2] Deut. iv, 35; 1 Kings xviii, 21.

such instances a plural sense of the former would be inconsistent
with the latter.   Therefore Elohim has no fixed plural sense which
PRIESTLY   can give the personal distinctions of the Trinity.   There
BENEDICTION.   is a threefold priestly benediction in the one divine
name, Jehovah.[1]   With those who use the fact for the proof of the
Trinity, stress is laid upon the definite trinal form of benediction
and the distinction of blessings, as at once indicating and distinguishing the three persons of the Trinity.   It is only as the text is
read in the light of later and fuller revelations that any such meaning appears.   Hence this form of priestly benediction is not in itself
THE TER-   any proof of the Trinity.   There is in the Scriptures a
SANCTUS.   thrice-holy predicate of God.[2]   But, as in the previous
case, it is only as we read this *Trisagion* in the light of a fuller revelation of the Trinity that we find in it any suggestion of the doctrine.   It is therefore in itself without proof of the doctrine.   Fathers of the Church were wont to say : " Go to the Jordan and you
shall see the Trinity."   They had in view the manifestation of the
THE BAPTISM.   Father, the Son, and the Spirit at the baptism of Christ.[3]
In the clear light of the New Testament, and with the
doctrine constructed out of the truths which it reveals, we do recognize the three persons of the Trinity in this divine manifestation.
But apart from this fuller revelation very little truth of the Trinity
is given ; for these manifestations, simply in themselves, might stand
with the Arian or Semi-Arian heresy.

2. *Verity of the Constituent Facts.*—The unity of God, the personal distinctions of Father, Son, and Spirit, the divinity of the
Son, and the personality and divinity of the Spirit we have found
to be clear and sure truths of Scripture.   The result is not tritheism, but a triunity of persons in the Godhead—the doctrine of the
Trinity.

3. *The Facts Determinative of the Doctrine.*—The argument for
the Trinity centers in the requirement of the doctrine for the in-
SCIENTIFIC   terpretation and harmony of the Scripture facts.   It is
METHOD OF THE   in the method of science, which accepts as a principle
ARGUMENT.   or law whatever will interpret and unite the relative
facts; and the more when such principle or law is the only means
of explaining and uniting them.   Such a result is the inductive
verification of the principle or law.   The Trinity is the only doctrine which can interpret and harmonize the trinal distinction
of divine persons in the unity of God.   It is therefore the doctrine of Scripture.   We proceed in precisely the same method in
Christology, so far as it respects the person of Christ.   While the

[1] Num. vi, 24–26.   [2] Isa. vi, 3; Rev. iv, 8.   [3] Matt. iii, 16, 17.

Scriptures reveal him as one person, they freely ascribe to him both human and divine facts. The facts are interpreted and harmony attained through a union of the human and divine natures in the unity of his personality. This doctrine of his personality is thus inductively verified as a truth of Scripture. In the same method we have maintained the doctrine of the Trinity. The method is legitimate and the proof conclusive. The doctrine is a truth of the Scriptures.

II. Mystery of the Trinity.

1. *Above our Reason.*—The Scriptures give the facts of the Trinity, but without any doctrinal combination, and without any explanation of their seeming contrariety. There is no solution of the mystery for our reason. Whoever attempts an explication of the doctrine must treat it either superficially or in a fruitless speculation. The highest attainment is in a scriptural and accordant statement of the constituent facts, with the doctrinal result.

2. *Without Analogies.*—The mystery of the doctrine naturally incites an outlooking for illustrations which may bring it into the apprehension of thought. In the literature of the question we find the results of such incitement. Attempts at illus-   <small>SEARCH FOR</small>
tration began with the early Christian fathers and have   <small>ANALOGIES</small>
continued to the present time. Joseph Cook, following the example of so long a line of predecessors, gives an illustration in his own impressive mode of thought and expression.[1] Christlieb, also recent in the treatment of the doctrine, is elaborate in the use of analogies.[2] Our criticism of such illustrations, whether of ancient or modern use, is that they are without sufficient basis in analogy, and therefore useless for both reason and faith. The notice of a few instances may suffice for the force of this criticism.

The triple facts of intellect, sensibility, and will unite in the personality of mind. True; but no ground remains   <small>ATTEMPTED IL-</small>
for any personal distinctions either in the mind or in   <small>LUSTRATIONS</small>
the powers which constitute its personality. No possible distinction between personal mind and its constitutive powers or between these powers can have any analogy to the personal distinctions of the Trinity. Thesis, antithesis, and synthesis are so related in thought as to constitute a trinity in unity. Perhaps not. For such a result the three must completely co-exist in thought, and the possibility of such a co-existence is far from sure. Further, analysis holds as closely with these forms of thought as they do

[1] *Boston Monday Lectures,* "Orthodoxy," pp. 62, 68.
[2] *Modern Doubt and Christian Belief,* pp. 275-278.

with each other. With this fact, the four might combine in as complete a unity of "thought as the three. All analogy of the three with the Trinity is thus shown to be fallacious. Besides, modes of thought can have no analogy to the personal subsistences of the Trinity. There is a trinity of dimensions in the unity of space, and a trinal distinction of past, present, and future in the unity of time. These dimensions and distinctions, however, are purely relative, and without any reality in the absolute unities of space and time. Even if realities, they still could have no likeness to the Trinity. We think in propositions, and cannot else think at all. A proposition is a trinity of subject, predicate, and copula. All this is true; but the distinction of parts in a proposition has no analogy to the distinction of persons in the Trinity, and for the obvious reason that in the former case there are no personal qualities as in the latter. Man in personality is a trinity of body, soul, and spirit. This trichotomic anthropology is not settled as a truth. If it were, the instance would still be useless. Body and soul, as apart from mind, have no personal quality. Hence the distinction of natures in the unity of man can have no analogy to the distinction of persons in the unity of God. Luminosity, color, and heat combine in the unity of light. But light is no such a unity as personality Nor have its properties any personal quality. There is no analogy to the Trinity. Such illustrations are really useless for both reason and faith, and we think it better to omit them.

There is a widely prevalent trinitarianism in pagan philosophy and religions, but it is valueless for the Christian doctrine, TRINITY IN PAGAN PHILOSOPHY. except as an indication that trinitarianism is rather attractive than repulsive to speculative thought. It is valueless because so very different in its contents. The doctrine of the Platonic philosophy, and of Brahmanism and Zoroastrianism, so far as representing a trinal distinction of divine persons, is rather tritheistic than trinitarian. There is in neither a union of the divine persons in the unity of God. The doctrine of emanation, so prevalent in these systems, carries with it the sense of inferiority or a lower grade in the emanations. Hence, so far as in these systems we find a trinal distinction of divine persons, they are neither truly and essentially divine, nor yet a trinity in any proper sense of the Christian doctrine.[1] This doctrine, without any antecedent in philosophy, or in the speculations of pagan religions, has its sure and only ground in the Scriptures.

[1] Knapp : *Christian Theology*, p. 145 , Shedd : *History of Christian Doctrine*, vol. 1, pp. 243–245.

3. *A Credible Truth.*—The objection most commonly urged against the doctrine of the Trinity is its mystery; whereas this is in itself no valid objection. If all mysteries were incredible, the sphere of truth would be infinitely narrowed. The world within us and without us is replete with mystery. The facts of nature which are combined in the many forms of science are open to observation, but the laws of nature, without which there is no true science, are realities only for rational thought, and in themselves a profound mystery. What do we know of cohesive attraction? or of the forces of chemical affinity? or of gravitation, acting across the measureless spaces that separate the stars, and binding all systems in the harmony of the heavens? or of life in the manifold forms of its working? or of the power of the will, which in all voluntary agency reveals itself in our own consciousness? We know forces in their phenomena, and in the laws of their action, but forces themselves are for us an utter mystery. If we must dismiss all mysteries, the higher truths of science and philosophy must go with the higher truths of religion as no longer truths for us. But mystery is no limit of credibility. The principle is as valid for the doctrine of the Trinity as for science and philosophy. Were the constituent facts of the doctrine in contradictory opposition, it would be incredible, but for that reason, and not because of its mystery. Unitarianism may assert their contradictory opposition, and even make a plausible case, but only on such a modified statement of the facts as violates polemical justice. The facts as posited by Trinitarians are not contradictory. Hence, the doctrine, however profound a mystery, is properly accepted as a truth of the Scriptures. It has the credibility of the Scriptures themselves.

MYSTERY NO VALID OBJECTION.

CONSISTENCY OF CONSTITUENT FACTS.

4. *A Vital Truth of Christianity.*—The doctrine of the Trinity is no speculative abstraction, but a central truth of the Gospel, and closely articulated with all that is evangelical in Christian theology. Without it the religion of Christ falls away into a mere moral system.

The divine Fatherhood is largely the theology of professedly Christian Unitarianism, however rationalistic it may be. Its frequent utterance is in a tone of fondness and assurance. Reference to expressions of Christ cannot be omitted, even though all that is supernatural be denied him. No other ever put such meaning into the words, "The Father," "Your Father," "My Father," "Our Father." Unitarianism may pervert their meaning, but cannot overstate their plenitude of truth and grace. As we previously pointed out, the divine Fatherhood is given only through the divine Sonship. Our own existence

TRUTH OF THE DIVINE FATHERHOOD.

is through the creative work of God; and we are his offspring only in a figurative sense. No higher sense of his Fatherhood is given simply through our creation. The divine Fatherhood, with its plenitude of grace and love, is given only through the divine filiation of the Son. It cannot be given in any form of professedly Christian Unitarianism or Rationalism. It was not given in the older Socinianism, though it held so strongly the miraculous conception of Christ, for in any rational sense of this fact the divine agency was operative simply in a creative mode. Arianism has no other mode of the Son's existence. Semi-Arianism, *homoiousian* as to the nature of the Son, is too indefinite respecting both his nature and mode of existence to give any true sense of the divine Fatherhood in correlation with the divine Sonship. These deepest truths are given only with the doctrine of the Trinity. The divine Fatherhood is at once real and revealed through the divine filiation of the Son. Christianity could not part with this truth without infinite loss. Our religious consciousness needs it, and the more with the truer sense of sin and the deeper exigencies of our moral and spiritual life. In the intensest expressions of God's love emphasis is placed on the Sonship of Christ, through whose mediation he achieved our redemption.[1] The divine Fatherhood as revealed in the divine Sonship is the only sufficient pledge of his grace and love. Hence for this pledge we are carried into the central truths of the Trinity.

The atonement is bound up with the doctrine of the Trinity, as TRINITY AND ATONEMENT. it is groundless without the true and essential divinity of the Son. It is not meant that Arianism formally rejected the atonement, but that, with such a Christology, it was illogically retained. It is true that Arianism represents the Son as very great—so great as to be the Creator of all things. If, however, as this doctrine holds, the Son was himself a created being, he could not create the heavens and the earth, nor any part of them ; and this representation of his greatness must be an extreme exaggeration. A created being cannot create other existences. His powers, however great, must still be finite, and therefore infinitely short of creative energy. Neither could a created being, and therefore finite and dependent, redeem a sinful race. Only the divine Son could make an atonement for sin. It is noteworthy that the sacred writers present the infinite greatness of Christ in connection with his redeeming work, as though the former were a necessary assurance of his sufficiency for the latter. It was the Word, who was God, and maker of all things, who was incarnated in our nature for the purpose of our redemption.[2] The

[1] John iii, 16 ; Rom. viii, 32 ; 1 John iv, 10.   [2] John i, 1-3, 14.

Son, through whose blood we have redemption and remission of sins. created all things in heaven and earth, visible and invisible, thrones, dominions, principalities, powers—all things.[1] There is significance in such association of these truths. The divinity of the Son is to be understood as the necessary ground of his atonement and the assurance of its sufficiency. Without his divinity there is no atonement for sin. But his divinity is a central and determining truth of the Trinity ; so that the atonement is indeed bound up with this doctrine. It is therefore a vital doctrine in Christianity.

The offices of the Holy Spirit in the economies of religion, and particularly in Christianity, as previously pointed out, are manifold and profound. It must follow that the character of Christianity as a religion is largely involved in the question of his personality and divinity. Without these truths the agency of the Spirit cannot stand in the same light as with them. Neither can the fruits of his agency stand in the same light. Conviction for sin, regeneration, assurance of a gracious sonship through the witness of the Spirit, the help of the Spirit in the duties of life and his consolations in its sorrows, the graces of the Christian life as the fruits of the Spirit—these cannot have the same meaning without their source in the personal agency of the divine Spirit. There is a falling away of Christianity into a mere moral system. Christ is a wise teacher and a good example, but not a divine Saviour. The personal agency of the Spirit in the Christian life lapses into the motives of the Gospel and the moral culture of one's self. So vital is the doctrine of the Holy Spirit, and with it the doctrine of the Trinity in Christianity. *TRINITY AND THE HOLY SPIRIT.*

The sacrament of baptism, so significant of our moral and spiritual need, and so assuring of all needed help from the Father, and the Son, and the Spirit, in whose name we are baptized, would be quite meaningless without the truths which we combine in the doctrine of the Trinity. The apostolic benediction, which invokes for Christians the love of God, and the grace of Christ, and the communion of the Holy Spirit, would be equally meaningless. The formula of baptism and the invocation of the benediction are not meaningless, but profoundly significant of the deepest truths of Christianity. With these truths the doctrine of the Trinity is given. *BAPTISM AND BENEDICTION.*

The vital offices of the Son and the Spirit in the economy of redemption and in the salvation which the Gospel reveals may be further emphasized by a brief but significant text: "For through him we both have access by one *VITAL OFFICES OF SON AND SPIRIT.*

[1] Col. 1, 14-16

Spirit unto the Father." [1]   This one great privilege is for both Jews
and Gentiles.   The privilege is great because there is salvation for us
only in this access to the Father.   It is attainable only through the
redemptive mediation of the Son for us, and the gracious work of
the Spirit within us.   Each office requires a personal divine agency,
and both the Son and the Spirit must be divine persons.   These
truths are simply central to the all-pervasive sense of Scripture respecting the offices of the Son and the Spirit in our salvation.   In
their combination we have the doctrine of the Trinity.   It follows
that the rejection of this doctrine is the rejection of these vital truths.

The doctrine of the Trinity deeply concerns the Christian life.
Bishop Butler clearly points out the obligations of duty
arising from the relations in which the Son and the
Holy Spirit stand to us in the economy of redemption
and salvation.   These duties arise from moral grounds,
just as the duties which arise with the relations in which we stand
to each other and to God.   As related to others, we are under the
obligations of justice, truth, kindness, charity ; as related to God,
we are under the obligations of reverence, obedience, and love : so,
as related to the Son and Spirit, we are under obligations of " reverence, honor, love, trust, gratitude, fear, hope.   In what external
manner this worship is to be expressed is a matter of pure revealed
command ; as perhaps the external manner in which God the
Father is to be worshiped may be more so than we are ready to
think.   But the worship, the internal worship itself, to the Son and
Holy Ghost, is no further matter of pure revealed command than
as the relations they stand in to us are matter of pure revelation ;
for the relations being known, the obligations to such internal worship are obligations of reason, arising out of those relations themselves.   In short, the history of the Gospel as immediately shows
us the reason of these obligations as it shows us the meaning of
the words Son and Holy Spirit." [2]

As the duties of the Christian life are thus concerned with the
doctrine of the Trinity, so, with this doctrine, there are
the weightier truths for our faith and experience, and
indeed for the whole practical life of religion.   Whether
in comparison with pure Unitarianism or even the highest form of
Arianism, there is an infinite fullness and depth of truth in the
true and essential divinity of the Son and the Spirit, with the
incarnation and atonement of the one, and the vital agency of
the other in our spiritual life.   These distinctive truths of the
Trinity embody the weightiest motives of the Gospel, and thus give

---

[1] Eph. ii, 18.   [2] *Analogy*, part ii, chap. i, sec. 2.

to the faith which truly embraces them the greatest practical efficiency, while at the same time they deepen and intensify the experiences and practical forces of the inner Christian life. Hence it is that in the history of the Church we find with the doctrine of the Trinity the most spiritual, practical, and evangelistic type of Christianity. Trinitarians may fall short, and far short, of their faith in both the inner and outer life. Still for them there are the highest possibilities of both. There are not such possibilities with any anti-trinitarian creed. As the religious faith departs from the doctrine of the Trinity it must in a like measure lose the significance of the mediation of Christ and the agency of the Holy Spirit in the religious life. By so much does Christianity fall away from its true evangelical form toward a mere moral system. In pure Unitarianism this fall is quite complete. From this ground no evangelical development of Christianity is possible. It is an open truth that the deepest and most earnest Christian life of the present, whether as an inner experience and practical force, or as an outward endeavor toward the evangelization of the world, is with the Trinitarian Churches.

We have attempted no philosophy of the Trinity. There is for us no present solution of the doctrine. There is, however, a philosophy of its profound significance for the spiritual and practical Christian life. This philosophy we have clearly indicated. God in Christianity is God in Trinity. This doctrine underlies the most vital forces of the Gospel, and on the ground of Scripture we hold it in a sure faith, whatever its mystery for our thought. "That which remains a cross for our thinking is thus at the same time the crown of the Christian conception of God."[1]

A PHILOSOPHY FOR THE CHRISTIAN LIFE.

---

[1] Van Oosterzee: *Christian Dogmatics*, vol. i, p. 293.

General reference.—Hooker: *Ecclesiastical Polity*, book v, secs. 51–56, Usher: *Body of Divinity*, chap. iv; Cudworth *Intellectual System*, chap. iv, Waterland: *Importance of the Doctrine of the Holy Trinity*, Works, vol. iii; Burton: *Antenicene Testimonies to the Doctrine of the Trinity;* Howe: *The Oracles of God*, lects. xiii–xvi; Bull: *Defense of the Nicene Creed;* Owen *God the Father, Son, and Holy Ghost; Vindication of the Doctrine of the Trinity*, Works (Goold's), vol. ii; Edwards: *Observations on the Trinity;* Bickersteth: *The Rock of Ages;* Cook: *Boston Monday Lectures*, "Orthodoxy;" Taylor: *Revealed Theology, The Trinity;* Graves: *Select Proofs of the Trinity*, Works, vol. iii; Christlieb: *Modern Doubt and Christian Belief*, lect. iv; Kidd: *On the Trinity;* Treffrey: *The Trinity;* Dorner: *Doctrine of the Person of Christ, Nicene Trinity*, vol. ii, pp. 181–346.

Unitarian view.—Clark: *Orthodoxy*, chap. xvi; Norton: *Statement of Reasons;* Wilson: *Unitarian Principles;* Eliot: *Unity of God;* Forrest: *On the Trinity.*

CHAPTER IX.

GOD IN CREATION.

IN opening this question certain points should be noted, certain
PRELIMINARY distinctions made, as preliminary to the main discus-
DISTINCTIONS. sion. This is necessary to clearness, for the reason that
the question concerns several spheres of creative work. The distinctions between matter simply as being, matter in its orderly
physical forms, and matter in its organic forms, give rise to different
questions respecting the work of creation. Then there is the distinction between material and spiritual existences. This distinction
is so profound that the creation of matter and the creation of mind
are two separate questions. We have thus indicated the points
which must be more formally discriminated in their discussion.

I. THE QUESTION OF CREATION.

1. *Several Spheres of Creative Work.*—There can be no actual
MATTER AND separation between matter as substance and its primary
ITS ORDERLY qualities, though there is a real distinction for abstract
FORMS thought. But there is no such inseparable connection
between matter and its orderly forms. The latter we may think
entirely away from the former. They are actually separable. The
fact is manifest in many instances. Cohesive attraction loosens its
grip and solid bodies disintegrate and dissolve. Chemical com-
pounds are resolved into their discrete elements. Organic forms
decay and fall again into dust. The earth was once a chaos, formless and void. This is a truth of Scripture,[1] and a truth of science
as well. It was the same in substance then, as now with its plenitude of orderly forms. But while the substance may exist without
these forms it must ever be present in them. Idealism may speculatively question or even deny the reality of substantial being in the
cosmos, but must ever practically confess it. Positivism may ignore
this reality, but, with its confessed agnosticism, retains no right to
dispute it. But as matter and its orderly forms stand apart in the
manner stated, they constitute distinct spheres respecting the question of creation.

The reality of being is given us through its properties as appre-

[1] Gen. i, 2.

hended in sense-perception, or through its activities as apprehended in consciousness. That which is extended in space and divisible into parts, which has form and color, is more than its properties, is indeed substantial being as the necessary ground of such properties. That which thinks and feels, which reasons and constructs the sciences and philosophies, which is creative in æsthetic spheres, which is personally active in a moral and religious life, is more than its faculties, more than its manifold forms of thought and feeling, of rational and moral agency, is indeed the reality of being as the necessary ground of these multiform powers and activities. There is equally the reality of being under both the properties of body and the activities of mind. But as these properties and activities unerringly point to the reality of being, so they equally point to an essential distinction of being. The two classes of properties and activities, the one of body and the other of mind, have nothing in common. The cognition of them is in totally different modes. With these profound distinctions, there must be an essential difference between material and spiritual being. Hence the eternity of the former could be no proof of the eternal existence of the latter. Even if both have their original in the creative work of God, it must be through distinct energizings of his will. It thus more fully appears that the distinction between material and spiritual being deeply concerns the question of the creative work of God.

2. *Question of Creation Threefold.*—All that is here required is to bring together the distinctions previously made, and to point out the result respecting the work of creation. The question whether matter is eternal or a creation is distinct and complete in itself. The question respecting the creation of the orderly forms of matter, as they stand in the cosmos, is equally distinct and complete in itself. Further, if the eternity of matter were conclusively proved, neither the eternity of the cosmos nor its naturalistic origination could follow as a consequence. Finally, the essential distinction of mind from matter, and of its faculties and activities from the properties and orderly forms of matter, separates the question of its creation from that of both the others. Neither the eternity of matter nor the naturalistic evolution of the world in all its lower orderly forms could give any account of the existence of personal mind. Thus the question of the creative work of God has respect to three distinct spheres. We might still make a further distinction inclusive of all living forms of existence below man, which would raise the three to four.

These distinctions are so real and obvious, and the separation of

the question respecting matter itself from the other spheres of creation so complete, that a sweeping contrary may well
be thought strange. Yet there is such a contrary.
"If the first cause is limited, and there consequently
lies something outside of it, this something must have no first
cause—must be uncaused. But if we admit that there can be something uncaused, there is no reason to assume a cause for any thing." [1]
Dr. Cocker takes the same position. Indeed, he indorses the view
of Spencer, or, rather, he indorses his own with that of Spencer.
"With what reason can we admit that some things do exist that
never were created, but others cannot so exist? If substances are
eternal, why not attributes? If matter is self-existent, why not
force? If space is independent, why not form? And if we concede
the eternity of matter and force, why not admit the eternity of law
—that is, uniformity of relations? And if so much is granted, why
not also grant that a consequent order of the universe is also eternal?" [2] In speaking of "things" supposed to exist without having
been created, there is reference to space, and time, and number, as
well as to matter; and the position is that an admission of the
eternity of any one "tends to the invalidation of every proof of the
existence of God." Neither space, nor time, nor number is a cre-
atable entity in any proper sense of the term. Nor
could their eternity in any sense or measure invalidate
the proofs of theism. The existence of space and the
existence of orderly forms in space are entirely separate questions.
Law has no ontological existence, but is simply an expression of the
order of things. Hence to speak of an eternal law is to assume an
eternal order of existences. Whether the universe as an orderly
existence is eternal or of time-origin is a question of fact, and one
the decision of which is in no sense contingent upon the creation of
matter. The time-origin of the universe is a truth of science as
well as of Scripture. There is no surer truth of science. As an
origination in time, it is dependent, and must have a sufficient
cause. God only is such a cause. Therefore God is. The eternity
of matter could not invalidate this proof.

DISTINCTIONS
REAL AND
CLEAR

THEISM NONE
THE LESS
SURE.

II. CONCERNING THE CREATION OF MATTER.

For the present discussion this question is still on hand. We
have not, certainly not intentionally, intimated any doubt that
matter is a creation in the sense of a divine origination. So far,
we have simply aimed to discriminate the spheres of God's creative

[1] Spencer: *First Principles*, p. 37.
[2] *Theistic Conception of the World*, pp. 67, 68.

work, and for two ends: that we might attain a clearer view of his
work; and that the proofs of theism, while not here to   AIM OF PREVI-
be repeated, might remain secure on their distinctive   OUS DISTINC-
grounds, and especially that they might not illogically   TIONS
be made contingent upon the most difficult question respecting the
creation of matter.   That we hold this creation as a fact does not
commit us to all the proofs alleged.

1. *The Question on A Priori Ground.*—The position is often
taken that the eternity of matter is contradictory to the absoluteness of God.   Hence its origination in his creative agency is an
immediate datum of his absoluteness.   " The doctrine of creation
flows from the infinite perfection of God.   There can   A PRIORI AR-
be but one infinite being.   If any thing exists inde-   GUMENTS.
pendent of his will, God is thereby limited."[1]   " However perplexing the thought of a properly so-called creation from nothing may
be, yet it flows with absolute necessity from belief in an absolutely
almighty Creator.   Nay, matter without any form cannot be conceived of; an eternal matter must also be an independent matter,
another God; of which it would be hard to explain why it ought or
should need to yield to the will of an almighty Fashioner."[2]   " If
we admit that any thing besides God is self-existent, that any thing
exists independent of God as ' the *condition* of the divine agency
and manifestation,' then God is not the unconditioned absolute Being."[3]   These citations are given as instances of this position, and
as examples of its expression.   There is a false sense of the Infinite
and the Absolute, such as we previously considered, which would
have the consequences here alleged.   That sense, however, neither
of these authors admits.   With the true sense, which they fully
hold, the logic of their position is overstrained.

Common as the notion is in philosophic thought, it is not an
a priori truth that " there can be but one infinite be-   CRITICISM OF
ing."   With the false sense of a quantitative, space-filling   THE ARGU-
infinite, there could be but one.   God is not infinite in   MENTS
such a sense, but infinite in the plenitude of his personal perfections; nor would he be less infinite, though another existed.
Moreover, if matter is eternal, it is not therefore an infinite being.
The eternal existence of matter as finite is just as conceivable as
the eternal existence of God as infinite   If matter is eternal, it is
independent of the creative and preserving agency of God ; but he
is not thereby limited.   His perfections and sovereignty would be

<hr/>

[1] Hodge : *Systematic Theology*, vol. i, p. 561.
[2] Van Oosterzee . *Christian Dogmatics*, vol. i, p. 302.
[3] Cocker : *Theistic Conception of the World*, p. 68.

just the same as with the origination of matter in his creative
agency. It is true that "matter without any form cannot be conceived of," but it can be conceived without any orderly or cosmical
form   Whether created or eternal, this is the primordial state of
matter in the view of both Scripture and science. Hence the eternity of matter neither concludes the eternity of the cosmos nor the
power of its naturalistic evolution. When it is said that "an eternal matter must also be an independent matter, another
God," logic is strained even to breaking. It would be
independent of God's creative agency, but might else be
as completely subject to his will as though his own creation. If
he could have created matter as it is, so could he annihilate it
and replace it with another, and none the less so on the supposition of its eternity. Hence, even on this supposition, there is no
independence of matter in contradiction to the true infinity and
absoluteness of God. The utmost extreme is reached in the assumption that, if matter is eternal, "it must be another God."
Why another God because eternal ? Plainly, it is not God in any
sense, whether created or eternal. Duration itself has no determining influence upon the quality of any being. If we assume
that matter, if eternal, must be another God, we assume that the
eternity of its existence determines its quality as divine. Such an
assumption, however, is excluded as utterly groundless. As that
which is eternal has no cause of existence, neither has it any determining cause of its quality. It simply is what it is. There is no
a priori necessity that an eternal being must be a divine being. God
is God in what he is, and from no determinate consequence of his
eternity. If matter were eternal, it would simply be what it is,
without any determining cause. The explanation of "why it
ought or should need to yield to the will of an almighty Fashioner"
is sufficiently given in his almightiness. Nor could the admission
"that any thing besides God is self-existent" involve
the consequences that he "is not the Absolute Being,"
unless such thing should be of a nature to limit or
condition him. As we have previously explained, matter itself
could exert no such power. In the further assumption that if
"any thing exists independent of God as 'the *condition* of the
divine agency and manifestation,' then God is not the unconditioned
Absolute Being," there may be truth ; indeed, we might say there
must be truth, as the members of the proposition are identical   It
is a truth, however, which has no weight against the eternity of
space, and time, and number, for in no sense can these condition the
divine agency. It is equally invalid against the eternity of matter.

ETERNAL MAT-
TER ONLY
MATTER

GOD NONE THE
LESS THE AB-
SOLUTE.

We think it clear, as the result of the previous criticism, that there is no *a priori* proof of the creation of matter. Certainly that proof does not appear in the arguments which we have reviewed. We know not any of greater strength.

2. *On Cosmological Ground.*—A necessary link in the cosmological argument for theism is the dependence of the cosmos. The proof of this dependence centers in the manifest fact of its time-origin. This time-origin, however, has respect simply to the orderly forms of the cosmos, and leaves open the question respecting matter itself. To prove the creation of matter by the logic of the cosmological argument, it would be necessary to prove its dependence or time-origin. This is the vital point of the question. It is mainly a question of physical science. CONCERNING THE DEPENDENCE OF MATTER. While great progress has been made in physics, and rapidly in recent years, it is not yet a completed science. Its diverse schools are conclusive of its incompleteness. " Many scientists of to-day are of the opinion expressed by Grove,[1] that ' probably man will never know the ultimate structure of matter ' " [2] Others may look for such knowledge, but no one claims its attainment. If there are as yet no data of the science conclusive of the time-origin of matter, neither are there any conclusive against it. It is hardly in the nature of the science that there ever should be such, while the former, if not yet sufficient, may be attainments of the future.

Some scientists claim the present attainment and possession of facts sufficient to prove the time-origin and creation of matter. " Chemical analysis most certainly points to an origin, and effectually destroys the idea of an external PROOF OF DEPENDENCE CLAIMED self-existent matter, by giving to each of its atoms the essential character, at once, of a *manufactured article* and a *subordinate agent.*" [3] " None of the processes of nature, since the time when nature began, have produced the slightest difference in the properties of any molecule. We are therefore unable to ascribe either the existence of the molecules or the identity of their properties to the operation of any of the causes which we call *natural*. On the other hand, the exact equality of each molecule to all others of the same kind gives it the essential character of a manufactured article, and *precludes the idea of its being eternal and self-existent.*" [4]

[1] *Correlation of Physical Forces*, p. 187.

[2] Cocker : *Theistic Conception of the World*, p. 122.

[3] Sir John Herschel : *Dissertations on the Study of Natural Philosophy*, sec. 28

[4] Professor Clerk Maxwell : *Nature*, vol. viii, p. 411, these citations in Cocker . *Theistic Conception of the World*, pp. 125, 126.

Respecting the more direct point, the only difference between Herschel and Maxwell is that what the former alleges of the atoms the latter alleges of the molecules.

3. *On Teleological Ground.*—The central and necessary fact in the teleological argument for theism is the manifestation of rational intelligence in the conception of ends and the adjustment of means for their attainment. With the cosmos as an end, there is the use of matter in its formation. There can be no question of a marvelous adaptation of matter to this end. Does this adaptation lead us certainly to its creation for this end? The answer little concerns the question of a divine teleology in the cosmos. With a negative answer, such teleology would still have sure ground and ample room. The mechanical use of a machine may so determine the material for its construction as to allow but little skill in its selection. The material of a locomotive is not only well suited to its mechanical use, but a practical necessity. Hence the sphere of skill in its selection is very narrow; yet the rational teleology in the conception of its use, and in its construction for that use, is not thereby diminished. In like manner, even if matter were an eternal existence, the conception of the cosmos as an end and the constructive use of matter in its formation would still be conclusive of a divine teleology.

ADAPTATIONS OF MATTER.

Whether the ground of teleology can carry us any further depends upon the scientific discovery of an inner constitution of matter which evinces its origin in time, and its creation for cosmical uses. Some claim such a discovery, as we have recently seen, but without any decisive concurrence of scientific authority. Such opinion, therefore, cannot be conclusive of the creation of matter. Further, as previously noted, the facts which mark the molecules or even the atoms as "manufactured articles" may not be primordial with matter itself, but a product of the divine agency in its preparation for cosmical uses. The molecules are not the ultimates of matter, and therefore not necessarily original with it. Even if matter itself is eternal, it is easily conceivable that God in the process of his creative agency should cast it in its molecular forms, or even endow its atoms with affinities and potencies not originally theirs.

NOTHING IN SCIENCE DE-CISIVE

The conclusion is that the creation of matter is no *a priori* truth, and that, while nothing appears in the light of science as contradictory to its creation, neither does any thing yet appear as conclusive of it.

4. *In the Light of Scripture.*—Here the question may be studied either in the more specific terms of creation or in the informing

idea of passages which beyond a mere verbal sense express the work of creation.

The more specific terms in the Hebrew are יָצַר, עָשָׂה, בָּרָא.   The second and third have rarely been given the definitive sense of immediate or originative creation of matter.   There is nothing in the root-sense or biblical use of the words to warrant such a definition. The same is true of the first.   " The best critics understand them as so nearly synonymous that, at least in regard to the idea of making out of nothing, little or no foundation for that doctrine can be obtained from the use of the first of these words.   They are used *indifferently* and *interchangeably* in many passages ; as, for example, in Isa. xliii, 7, where they all three occur applied to the same divine act.   The Septuagint renders בָּרָא indifferently by ποιεῖν and κτίζειν.   But especially in the account of the creation in Gen. i, the verbs are used irrespectively in verses 7, 16, 21, 25, etc. ; and in comparing Gen. i, 27, and ii, 7, man is said to have been *created*, yet he is also said to have been *formed out of the ground*.   Again, in the decalogue (Exod. xx, 11) the verb is עָשָׂה, *made*, not created." [1]   " The Hebrew word בָּרָא, rendered *create*, has nothing abstract or metaphysical about it. It is as clearly phenomenal as any word in the language.   Its primary meaning is to *cut*, hence to *shave*, shape, form, or fashion." [2] The result is, not that the primitive act of creation was not originative of matter itself, but that there is no conclusive proof of such origination on purely philological ground.

The result is the same in the mere verbal study of κτίζειν and ποιεῖν, the terms of creation in the New Testament, and in common use in the Septuagint for the rendering of the Hebrew words previously considered.   Κτίζειν, " literally, to make habitable, to build, to plant a colony. . . . Then, in general, to set up, to establish, to effect any thing.   In the Septuagint it answers mainly to the Hebrew בָּרָא, though this word in Genesis is always rendered by ποιεῖν, and afterward by either ποιεῖν or κτίζειν, and, indeed, more rarely by ποιεῖν, but not (as has been said) exclusively by κτίζειν." [3]   An originative creation of matter does not appear in the mere verbal sense of these words.   It could not have been an original sense, because such a creation had no place in the Greek mind which originated and used these terms

It does not follow that the sense of an originative creation of matter is not in the Scriptures.   All exegesis is not purely philo-

[1] Kitto · *Cyclopædia of Biblical Literature*, " Creation."
[2] Lewis . *The Six Days of Creation*, p 48.
[3] Cremer : *Biblico-Theological Lexicon.*

logical. There are other laws of interpretation, and must be, for the reason that philology alone cannot always give the full meaning or even the true meaning of an author.

OTHER LAWS
OF INTERPRE-
TATION.

Any such etymological restriction would deny to the words of the Hebrew Scriptures the reception of any new or varied meaning in the advancement of revelation, and equally to Christianity the introduction of any new ideas into the Greek of the New Testament. Nothing in either case could be more false to the facts. While, therefore, an originative creation of matter cannot be determined from the Scriptures on purely verbal grounds, such a sense of creation may be clearly given through other laws of interpretation.

It is an obvious principle of interpretation that often the connections of a word, rather than its etymology, determine its meaning. By such a law we may find in the first biblical use of בָּרָא the sense of an originative creation of matter.

CONNECTIONS
OF TERMS OF
CREATION.

This is really the method of interpretation and the chief resource of such as claim for the word itself the sense of such a creation. We may notice a few instances; not so much for exemplification, however, as for the proof thus given of the creation of matter. On Gen. 1, 1, as containing this sense of creation: " This is also shown in the connection between our verse and the one which follows· '*And the earth was without form, and void ;*' not before, but when, or after, God created it. From this it is evident that the void and formless state of the earth was not uncreated or without a beginning. At the same time it is evident from the creative acts which follow (vers. 3–18) that the heaven and earth, as God created them in the beginning, were not the well-ordered universe, but the world in its elementary form; just as Euripides applies the expression οὐρανὸς καὶ γαῖα to the undivided mass (μορφὴ μία) which was afterward formed into heaven and earth." [1] " But whatever weight may be due to the usage of the term, it is to be noted that the question turns not so much on the sense of the verb, taken alone and apart from the context, as on the way in which it is to be viewed in such a peculiar collocation as, ' *In the beginning* God *created* the heavens and the earth.' Granted, that in itself the term does not absolutely deny or affirm the presence of pre-existing matter, and that this can be inferred only from the context or subject treated of, the question comes to be, What can be the meaning of the term here? The expression, ' In the beginning,' evidently refers to the *beginning* of created existence, in contradistinction to the eternal being

FURTHER VIEW
OF THESE CON-
NECTIONS.

[1] Keil and Delitzsch : *On the Pentateuch*, pp. 47, 48.

of the Creator, and is thus an *absolute* beginning in and with time."[1] There is still another or further decisive connection of this verb. It lies in the conjunctive transition to the state of the earth. "Verse 2 begins, '*And the earth*,' etc.; but no history can begin with the Hebrew *vav*, whether taken in the sense of *but* or *and*."[2] It follows that verse 2 is an historic continuation of verse 1; and hence, that the meaning must be the creation of the earth as a void and formless mass. With this result, the meaning must be an originative creation of matter. The void and formless state of the product precludes the sense of a cosmical formation and leaves only the sense of origination.

The following words are treated by some as the most direct Scripture testimony to the creation of matter: MORE DIRECT PROOF. "Through faith we understand that the worlds were framed by the word of God, so that things which are seen were not made of things which do appear."[3] The former part of the text seems rather to give the sense of a formative creation of worlds. This is the more natural sense of the words, "the worlds were framed by the word of God"—κατηρτίσθαι τοὺς αἰῶνας ῥήματι Θεοῦ. Special account is made, however, of the latter part: "So that things which are seen were not made of things which do appear"— εἰς τὸ μὴ ἐκ φαινομένων τὰ βλεπόμενα γεγονέναι. There may be a question respecting the construction of these words. Such a question is raised, but it is one which does not materially affect the sense. Bloomfield, after treating the construction, says: "Thus the sense is that 'the world we see was not made out of apparent materials, from matter which had existed from eternity, but out of nothing; so that, at His fiat, the material creation was brought into existence, and formed into the things we see."[4] Dr. Hodge holds much the same view. After a review of the construction, he concludes: "Whatever is real is phenomenal; that is, every substance, every thing which really exists, manifests itself somewhere and somehow. The proper antithesis, therefore, to φαινομένων is οὐκ ὄντων. 'The worlds were not made out of any thing which reveals itself as existing even in the sight of God, but out of nothing.'"[5] There is another text classed with this one as at once illustrative and affirmative of the same sense of creation: "God, who quickeneth the dead, and calleth those things which be not as though they were."[6] His calling things which are not as though they were may be taken in the sense of his divine fiat which

[1] Macdonald : *Creation and the Fall*, pp. 64, 65.
[2] *Ibid.*, p 245.   [3] Heb. xi, 3   [4] *Greek Testament*, in loc.
[5] *Systematic Theology*, vol. i, p. 580.   [6] Rom. iv, 17.

causes or can cause them to exist and serve his purpose. "God calls τὰ μὴ ὄντα just as he does τὰ ὄντα; things that do not now exist are at his disposal as really and truly as things that do exist —that is, they can be made to exist and to subserve his purpose, in the same manner as things do which now already exist. If any one still feels a difficulty, he may solve the sentence in this simple way, namely, καλοῦντος τὰ μὴ ὄντα ὡς [ἐκάλεσεν] ὄντα—that is, calling into existence (Gen. 1, 2; Psa. xxxiii, 6) things that are not, as [he called into existence] things that are. The sense would be for substance the same."[1] "For example, the centurion says to his servant, . . . Do this; but God says to the light, whilst it is not in existence, just as if it were, Come forth, γενοῦ, come into existence. Think of that often-recurring and wonderful יהי, Gen. i; it expresses the transition from *non-existence to existence,* which is produced by God *calling.*"[2]

This interpretation cannot claim decisive authority, and for the reason that some able expositors do not find in the words the sense of an originative creation. Still, there is nothing forced or inconsistent in the interpretation, and the text may fairly be claimed in support of the creation of matter.

There is another significant fact. There are in the Scriptures

NO CONTRARY INTIMATION OF SCRIPTURE

many references to the creative work of God; many sublime descriptions of the greatness of that work, and of the greatness of God in its achievement; much of detail in these descriptions; lofty expressions of his majesty and the absoluteness of his power, of his eternity in distinction from the temporariness of all other existences; but in all this there is not the slightest reference to any eternally existing matter which he used in framing the heavens. This total omission is out of all consistency with such an existence.

In other spheres of existence, particularly in those of life and mind, the proof of an originative creation is clear and full. Science can give no account of the origin of either life or mind. In the light of reason, as in the light of revelation, both originated in the creative agency of God. With this clear truth, there is the less reason to question the creation of matter; or, rather, the former facts of an originative creation should be accepted as quite decisive of the latter.

III. Several Spheres of Creation.

Our discussion of Theism unavoidably anticipated much that might properly be treated under the present heading. Hence little

[1] Stuart: *On Romans,* in loc.
[2] Bengel: *Gnomon of the New Testament,* in loc.

more is here required than to present the several questions in
the light of Scripture.   This limitation will avoid unnecessary
repetition.

1. *The Physical Cosmos.*—Out of a primordial chaos came orderly worlds and systems.   The transformation was the work of
God in a formative creation.   This is the sense of the Scriptures in
many passages.   They open with the account of such a creation.[1]
God spreadeth out the heavens; maketh Arcturus, Orion, and
Pleiades, and the chambers of the south.[2] The heavens declare
the glory of their Creator, and the firmament showeth his handiwork.[3] By the word of the Lord were the heavens made; and all
the host of them by the word of his mouth.[4] Of old he laid the
foundations of the earth; and the heavens are the work of his
hands.[5] He stretcheth out the heavens as a curtain, and spreadeth them out as a tent to dwell in; and as we lift our eyes to the
heavens we behold the worlds which he created.[6] He hath made
the earth by his power, he hath established the world by his wisdom, and hath stretched out the heavens by his discretion.[7] The
same truth is in the New Testament.   The earth and the heavens
are the creation of God, and therefore the manifestation of his perfections.[8] We have given the substance of a brief selection of texts
which present the creative work of God in the orderly constitution
of the earth and the heavens.   What we have given may suffice,
especially as the same truth must appear in other texts of creation
which include the living orders of existence.   After the creation of
matter, the work of God within the physical realm is simply formative in its mode.   The discrete and confused elements are set in
order; chaos is transformed into a cosmos.   In this there is no
originative creation, but only a constitution of orderly forms.

2. *Living Orders of Existence.*—The divine creation of these
orders is the explicit word of Scripture.   "And God said, Let the
earth bring forth grass, the herb yielding seed, and the fruit-tree
yielding fruit after his kind, whose seed is in itself, upon the
earth; and it was so."   "Let the waters bring forth abundantly
the moving creature that hath life, and fowl that may fly above
the earth in the open firmament of heaven."   "Let the earth bring
forth the living creature after his kind, cattle, and creeping thing,
and beast of the earth after his kind. and it was so."[9]   These
were successive creative fiats of God; and the living orders were the
product of his own divine energizing.   "Thou, even thou, art

[1] Gen. i, 1–8. [2] Job ix, 8, 9. [3] Psa. xix, 1.
[4] Psa. xxxiii, 6. [5] Psa. cii, 25. [6] Isa. xl, 22, 26.
[7] Jer. x, 12. [8] Rom. i, 20. [9] Gen. i, 11, 20, 24.

LORD alone; thou hast made heaven, the heaven of heavens, with all their host, the earth, and all things that are therein, the seas, and all that is therein." [1]   " Lord, thou art God, which hast made heaven, and earth, and the sea, and all that in them is." [2]   These verses, written in far later periods, are cast in the mold of the Mosaic cosmogony, and clearly express the truth of creation respecting the living orders of existence.

In organic structure these forms of existence are profoundly dis-
THE LIVING tinct from all crystalline and chemical forms, and con-
HIGHER THAN stitute a higher order.   Life is a profound differentia-
THE LIFELESS tion. Sentience and instinct still deepen the distinction.
They constitute higher orders of existence than any mere physical forms.   It is entirely consistent with these facts that their origin is in distinct and specific acts of creation.   The creative work which brought the physical elements out of confusion into order was not in itself the origination of these organic and living orders. This is the sense of Scripture, as manifest in the texts previously given.   Only by further and distinct energizings of the divine will did they receive their existence.

Life is a mystery.   All concede this.   Neither the scientist nor
LIFE A REALITY. the philosopher has any more insight into its inner
nature than the rustic.   Its reality, however, is above question.   Its energy is great, its activities intense.   So effective an agent must be a profound reality.   Science gives no account of its origin.   Whatever the arrogance of assumption a few years ago, for the present there is little pretension to any merely physical or naturalistic origin.   The origin of life is accounted for in the creative agency of God.   In the light of reason, as in the light of Scripture, this is its only original.   The case is only the stronger with the sentience and marvelous instincts of the animal orders. Hence the divine creation of the living orders of existence was more than a mediate or merely formative creation; it was an immediate or originative creation, which gave existence to life, with its distinctive facts in the higher orders of animal existence.

3. *Man.*—The origin of man is in a further distinct act of crea-
tion.   It is accompanied with forms of expression and action which mark its significance.   After the completion of all other works, the sacred record is: " And God said, let us make man in our image, after our likeness: and let them have dominion over the fish of the sea, and over the fowl of the air, and over the cattle, and over all the earth, and over every creeping thing that creepeth upon the earth.   So God created man in his own image, in the

[1] Neh. ix, 6.   [2] Acts iv, 24.

image of God created he him; male and female created he them." [1]
The separate creation of man is further expressed in the more
definite statement of its manner. "And the LORD God formed
man of the dust of the ground, and breathed into his nostrils the
breath of life; and man became a living soul." [2] Here are the two
modes of creation: one mediate in the formation of the body; the
other immediate in the origination of the mind. There are in the
Scriptures many references to this distinct creation of man. The
sense is really the same whether his origin is referred to the creative agency of God or to his Fatherhood. [3]

Materialism, in whatever form of evolution, exposes its weakness
in any and every endeavor to account for the origin of
man and the faculties of mind. It is only by the unwarranted and unscientific assumption of missing links
that even his physical evolution from lower orders can be alleged.
The difficulties are infinitely greater in respect to mind. The
powers of mind so differentiate it from all else in the realm of nature, so elevate it above the plane of all other forms of existence,
that its naturalistic evolution is a manifest impossibility. Only the
creative agency of God can account for the origin and existence of
mind. This question, however, properly belongs to the anthropological argument for theism, where its fuller discussion may be
found.

MAN AN IM-
MEDIATE CREA-
TION

4. *Angels.*—Science, as such, knows nothing of angels. They
have no connection with any sphere which brings them within her
observation. The question of their existence and origin, as of
their character and rank, is purely one of revelation. It is reasonable to think that the limits of living and rational existences are far
wider than this world, which is but a speck among the magnitudes
of the physical universe. Spectrum analysis discloses a physical
composition of other worlds similar to our own. With this fact of
likeness, it is not to be thought that all those worlds lie forever
waste—without form and void. It is reasonable to think many of
them are the homes of living orders; and of the higher as of the
lower. The lower forms point to the higher. As in this world man
completes the orders of life, and is their rationally necessary culmination, so we must think of rational beings as completing the scale
of living existences in other worlds. In a universe originating in
the wisdom and power of God the existence of angels, such as appear in the light of revelation, is entirely consistent with the
highest rational thought.

[1] Gen. i, 26, 27   [2] Gen. ii, 7.
[3] Num. xxvii, 16; Eccl. xii, 7; Acts xvii, 29; Heb. xii, 9.

All that we know of the angels we learn from the Scriptures. Many interesting facts are given. For the present, however, their creation is the definite point. Their nature and offices, with their distinction as good and evil, will be treated elsewhere.[1]

ANGELS KNOWN ONLY IN THE SCRIPTURES.

On the ground of Scripture, their origin in a divine creation is a manifest truth. Yet of this there is no definite statement. It is, however, a clear implication. As finite existences originating in time, they could have no other origin. Their creation is implied in the fact that they are angels of God, and particularly in the definite and impressive manner in which this fact is expressed in the Scriptures.[2] It is equally implied in their own adoring worship of God as the Creator of all things.[3] The same truth is given in those comprehensive texts which attribute to God the creation of all things in earth and heaven. There is one more direct text: "For by him were all things created, that are in heaven, and that are in earth, visible and invisible, whether they be thrones, or dominions, or principalities, or powers: all things were created by him and for him."[4] The creation of the angels is here included in the all things in heaven, and particularly in the all invisible things, which expression discriminates them from the visible forms of existence in this world. It is still more definitely given in the specific terms, thrones, dominions, principalities, powers, which clearly designate angelic orders of existence.[5]

WHEN CREATED.

When the angels were created is a question on which the Scriptures are silent. If their creation has any place in the cosmogony of Moses, it must be in the first verse of Genesis. To place it there would require the sense of the verse to be so broadened as to include the whole work of creation. This is hardly permissible, because it would break the proper historic connection with the following verses. Neither the time of their creation nor its inclusion in the Mosaic record is in any sense necessary to the interpretation of Scripture. It is neither unscriptural nor unreasonable to think of the angels as created long before the formation of this world. Such a view is not without Scripture ground. It seems no forced interpretation that the morning stars and the sons of God which sang together over the founding of the world were the holy angels.[6]

---

[1] The deeply interesting facts of Scripture respecting the angels should not be omitted. Yet they neither directly concern any vital doctrine of theology nor claim any place in a logical order of doctrines. The question of the angels is therefore assigned to an appendix to the second volume.

[2] Gen. xxviii, 12, Luke xv, 10; Heb. i, 6.   [3] Rev. iv, 11.

[4] Col. i, 16.   [5] Eph. i, 21; 1 Pet. iii, 22.   [6] Job xxxviii, 4–7.

Whenever the creation of the angels took place, it must have been a creation in the deepest sense of origination. We must not anticipate their nature and qualities beyond the requirement of this particular point; but as they appear in the light of Scripture it is manifest that they are specially spiritual beings, with very lofty intellectual and moral powers. As such, they are not a formation out of existing material, but a divine origination in the very essence of their being.

IV. THE MYSTERY OF CREATION.

1. *Mystery of Immediate Creation.*—A mediate or formative creation is so common in the history of civilization, so manifest in its manifold works, and, indeed, so deeply wrought into our experience, that the sense of mystery is mostly precluded. The great achievements in mechanics may often surprise us as to the powers of man, but without perplexity as to the modes of his operation. With this familiarity of a merely formative creation through our own agency, there is the less perplexity for our thought of such an agency in God. Yet for our deeper thought there is still a profound difference in FAMILIAR WITH FORMATIVE CREATION. the two cases. We mostly work through mechanical means; whereas God as a purely spiritual being must work by an immediate power of personal will. There is still some light for our thought in the facts of consciousness. We surely know the immediate energizing of our personal will. This energizing is not the less immediate for the reason that the action is first upon our bodily organism, and then through it upon exterior nature. With the simple spiritual essence of mind, we must at some initial point exert an immediate power of will upon the physical organism. To deny this is to assume for all forms of our personal action an absolute mechanical law. Reflective thought, with the facts of personal consciousness in clear view, must ever reject this law. It is true that we thus reach an immediate power of will only upon our own bodily organism, and without the faintest insight into its mode; yet even so much is of value for our thinking of the formative creations of God. With the distinctive fact of a physical organism, we may yet see in the light of our own immediate power of will the reality of an immediate power of the divine will which can so act upon the elements of matter as to set them in their orderly forms. With this power, the formative creations of God are clearly possible.

The profound mystery is in the notion of an immediate creation of essential being. If we but think a little, it must appear that

any notion of such being as an actual existence is a profound mystery.   With the thought of such a reality, the alterna-
MYSTERY OF
ORIGINATIVE   tives of an eternal existence or an origination in time
CREATION.   inevitably present themselves.   Neither is comprehen-
sible in thought.   Yet we are shut up to the reality of eternal
being.   There is no escape either in the extremest idealism or in
the baldest positivism.   Eternal being is for us an absolute truth.
This alternative, however incomprehensible, has ever been accepted
in reflective thought.   So constant and thorough is this conviction
that the possibility of an originative creation never appears in
human thought apart from the light of revelation.   In all heathen
thought, even in its profoundest philosophic forms, matter itself is
either eternal or in some inexplicable mode an emanation of the
very nature of God.   Even with the light of our biblical theism,
we need have no reserve in conceding the utter mystery of an originative creation of matter.   Objectors, who must admit the utterly
incomprehensible reality of eternal being, are in no position to
question the possibility of such a creation.   The mystery for our
thought is no disproof of the possibility.

2. *Deeper Mystery of Emanation.*—The profound mystery of an
originative creation of essential being has induced not a few minds,
and even some Christian minds, to accept the notion that things
which appear as real and individual existences are an emanation or
evolution out of the very nature of God.   Sir William Hamilton
IDEA OF EMA-   may represent this view.   With him the annihilation of
NATIVE CREA-   being is just as inconceivable as its origination: "We
TION.   are utterly unable to construe it in thought as possible
that the complement of existence has been either increased or
diminished.   We cannot conceive, either, on the one hand, nothing becoming something, or, on the other, something becoming
nothing.   When God is said to create the universe out of nothing,
we think this by supposing that he evolves the universe out of himself; and, in like manner, we conceive annihilation only by conceiving the Creator to withdraw his creation from actuality into power."[1]
All this is grounded in the principle that nothing can come from
nothing, and nothing be reduced to nothing—for the forcible expression of which the author cites the words of Lucretius and Persius.[2]
The ancient and familiar formula, *ex nihilo nihil fit*—from noth-

[1] *Philosophy* (Wight's), pp. 493, 494.
[2] "Nil posse creari
De Nihilo, neque quod genitu 'st ad Nil revocari;"
"Gigni
De Nihilo Nihil, in Nihilum Nil posse reverti."

ing nothing is or can be—is true in its principle, but may be false in its application. It is true in respect to all events; APPLICATION OF EX NIHILO NIHIL FIT. and in such application it is thoroughly validated by the law of causation. Whether this law so validates Hamilton's doctrine of creation is the very question in issue. The creation of the universe out of nothing never can mean, and is never intended to mean, that nothing is in any sense wrought into the material of the new existence. Further, the creation of the universe out of nothing is, in the sense of Christian theism, totally different from the notion of its springing from nothing. In the antecedents for thought there is the infinite difference between an absolute void and the omnipotent God. The notion of an originative creation through his agency is in no violation of the law of causation. The sufficient cause of the new existence is given in the potential plenitude of the Creator.

The notion of an absolute complement of being, forever without possible increase or diminution, from which the doctrine NO ABSOLUTE COMPLEMENT OF BEING is deduced of an emanation or evolution of the universe out of the very nature of God, must be monistic in principle. Otherwise, it must involve an eternal dualism, or even an eternal pluralism of existences, according to the distinctions of essential being. Materialism is monistic, but, as utterly atheistic, it has no part in this question. Monism is the ground-principle of pantheism. Nor is the deduction of a mere phenomenal character of all sensible forms of existence illogical. Hamilton admitted no such an implication of his doctrine of creation, but it is much easier to deny than legitimately to escape such an implication. A doctrine of creation which lies so near the deepest and most determining principle of pantheism cannot give the true sense of the Scriptures respecting the origin of the universe. Further, if this doctrine of an evolutionary creation be true of matter, it must be equally true of mind, whether human or angelic. Mind is thus reduced to a merely phenomenal mode of existence, without any reality of being in itself. For otherwise the very being of God must be divided into many parts. It thus appears that this doctrine lies close to the emanation of souls out of the nature of God as maintained in Brahmanism—entirely too close to be true to the Scriptures.

The heading of these paragraphs signifies a deeper mystery of an evolutionary than of an originative creation. With the THE DEEPER MYSTERY OF EMANATIVE CREATION. pure spirituality and infinite personal perfections of God, such must be the fact. True, we cannot think how either matter or mind is originated. Can we think how either can be evolved out of the very nature of God? If we know any thing, we know the reality of our own personal being. We cannot be such through a mode of evolution except by a division of the divine nature. If matter is an evolution, either it must express the eternal nature of God or be the subject of an essential mutation, which is equivalent to an originative creation. These facts fully justify our heading. As one turns back from the mystery of an originative creation to the evolution of the universe out of the nature of God, he does but plunge into a deeper mystery.

3. *Evil Tendency of Emanative Doctrine.*—The doctrine of an emanation or evolution of finite existences out of the nature of God is not new to speculative thought. In its deeper principle, as we have seen, it underlies pantheism. In widely prevailing pagan religions, souls are an emanation of God, and destined to a re-absorption into his nature. Such an evolution of matter was deeply wrought into the gnosticism which appeared as a malign heresy in the early history of the Church. There was a long series of emanations, on a scale of degradation, and terminating in matter. Matter was thus viewed as intrinsically evil, and the inevitable source of moral evil. In these latter facts, matter was much the same in the Greek philosophy; in which, however, it was held to be a distinct eternal existence, not an evolution out of the nature of God.

OF ASCETIC OR VICIOUS TENDENCY. The tendency of the doctrine in both was evil, and only evil. In religion, its tendency is to asceticism, but with an easy diversion into a life of vicious indulgence. Apart from religion, the primary tendency is to such a life. With an intrinsically evil nature and a consequent absolute helplessness, there is a ready excuse for the grossest vices; and only the more ready with this evil nature as an emanation of God.

CHRISTIAN THEISM NOT A FULL CORRECTIVE With a true Christian theism, of course such consequences are denied. It is hardly thinkable that, with the evolution of finite existences out of the nature of God, such a theism can be maintained or held in any clear view. In any case, the law of moral duty and responsibility may be greatly weakened. If in our whole being, as consisting of soul and body, we are an evolution out of the being of God, and therefore of his very nature, why should not such a nature be the law of our life? The clear view and deep sense of God as revealed in Christianity would reject such an implication; but that view and sense may easily be obscured and weakened; and the direct tendency of such an origin of our nature in God must be toward such obscurity and weakness.

4. *Mode of Divine Agency in Creating.*—The question thus raised specially concerns the providence of God, but is also properly

in place here. Forces, and the power of God as well, are in their deeper nature still secret to our thought, but there are clearly noticeable distinctions in their operation. The mode of agency must in all cases be determined by the nature of the agent. We may thus distinguish between personal agency in man and physical agency in matter. If we cannot reach the secret of physical forces, we yet know their reality in the energy of their operation, and that, on the proper collocation of material elements, they act immediately and necessarily. Such is the law through all the forms of physical force. In distinction from this law, personal agency in man is through an optional energizing of the will. Still, in our present condition there can be no putting forth of power to act upon exterior nature except through our physical organism. There are exigencies of experience when we are deeply conscious of this inability. Such, however, is simply the fact of a present limitation, and it does not follow that in an unbodied state we can have no such power. Much less could such limitation of the divine will thus follow. God is a purely spiritual being, and, hence, whatever power he puts forth, whether in an originative A PURELY PERSONAL AGENCY or in a formative creation, must be purely spiritual, and, therefore, only through the energy of his personal will. Any other sense of creative agency in God is contradictory to both his spirituality and personality, and must sink into some form of pantheism.

Such a mode of the divine agency in the work of creation is widely pervasive of the Scriptures. We read it in the forms of the divine *fiat* as given in the narrative of creation;[1] in THE SENSE OF SCRIPTURE all the texts which attribute the work of creation to the word of God.[2] This view of the divine agency is profoundly important in both a doctrinal and practical sense. It is the only view which can secure for our faith and religious consciousness the personality of God and his transcendence above the realm of nature.

5. *Freedom of God in Creating.*—There is observable in both philosophical and theological thought a strong tendency toward the necessitation of God in his creative work. Various grounds are alleged for this necessitation, some of which may properly be noticed.

The ground with some is that some form of existence objective to God was necessary to his personal consciousness. God could not come to the knowledge of himself except in this mode. Therefore creation was for him a necessity. NO NECESSITY TO HIS CONSCIOUSNESS. This assumption is beyond any warrant of our reason. Personal

[1] Gen. i, 3, 6, 9, 11, 14, 20, 24
[2] Psa. xxxiii, 6, 9; Heb. xi, 3; 2 Pet. iii, 5.

consciousness in man may be conditioned on some distinct and objective existence. If it be true, as mostly accepted, that the inception of our own consciousness is in sensation, seemingly an objective existence, as the condition of sensation, is necessary to our consciousness. This, however, may be a requirement only for our present embodied state. We cannot affirm it as a law for all intelligences. Much less can we affirm it as a necessary law for the divine consciousness. The difference between the finite and the infinite precludes such an affirmation. Further, there are weighty objections to this assumed necessity for the work of creation. The assumption implies a purpose of God in creating—a purpose that through an objective existence so created he might come to self-consciousness. These ideas are inconsistent. There can be no such purpose without personal consciousness. This leads to further objection. If an objective existence was necessary to the coming of God into a personal consciousness, it follows that such consciousness could not arise until after his creative work. Therefore creation could not be his personal work, for there can be no personal agency without consciousness. Neither could there be intelligence, motive, or aim in the work of creation. In a word, the existence of the world and the universe must be without a divine teleology. We should thus surrender all that is distinctively theistic in the conception of creation.

Some find the necessary source of finite existences in a plenitude of the divine nature which must overflow, and which does overflow in the creation of such forms of existence. Such a view is utterly irreconcilable with any teleological conception of creation. The personal agency of God is whelmed in the necessary activities of his nature. Nor can such a view be reconciled either with the time-origin of the universe or with definite instances of origination. Such a plenitude in God, if assumed at all, must be assumed as eternal. Therefore there should have been an eternal outflow of finite existences, while in fact they are clearly of time-origin.

NO NECESSITY OF THE DIVINE PLENITUDE.

Many, especially in the line of theological thought, find in the nature of God a moral necessity for his creative work. It is wise and good to create; therefore God as eternally wise and good must create. "By far the most common opinion from the beginning has been that the creation is to be referred to the *bonitas*, the goodness, benevolence, or, as the modern Germans at least generally express it, the love of God. As God is love, and the nature of love is to communicate itself, as it must have an object to be enjoyed and rendered blessed, so God created

NO MORAL NECESSITY OF CREATION.

the world that he might rejoice in it and render it blessed."[1] If
the wisdom and goodness of God necessitated the work
of creation, it follows that this world, and every other
as well, must be the best possible. This was definitely

IMPLICATIONS OF SUCH NECESSITY.

the doctrine of Leibnitz,[2] and in complete logical consistency
with such a stand-point. The whole view is open to criticism. It
is open to the same insuperable objection as previously alleged
against another assumed ground of necessitation. Wisdom and
goodness, as of the very nature of God, must be eternal in him.
Therefore, if they are assumed to necessitate his creative work, there
must be conceded an eternal necessitation. This is utterly irreconcilable with the time-origin of the world, and especially with
the very recent origin of man. Farther, if God must create that
he may communicate his love to his creatures and render them
blessed, it follows that his creative efficiency should be the only
limit of his work. We are in no position to affirm any such implied extension. Finally, if, as an implication of the ground-principle, this is the best world possible, it further follows that every
other world must be precisely the same. There is no proof of any
such sameness, but decisive indications of the contrary. Clearly,
the angelic orders are very differently constituted from mankind.
The reasoning which we thus criticise seems plausible, but it proceeds upon lines which run out far beyond the possible reach of
our thought, and hence we cannot be sure of the conclusion. The
facts which we can grasp seem decisive against it. If no sentient being, or no rational being, with capacity for higher blessedness, had ever been created, there would have been no wrong to
any. Nonentities have no rights.

The freedom of God in creating is a requirement of his personal
agency therein. Personal agency and free agency are
really the same; and there is no clearer truth in Scripture than the personal agency of God in the work of

REALITY OF THE DIVINE FREEDOM.

creation. Creation has a purpose and a plan. All things were
created in the divine pleasure, and for the manifestation of the
divine glory,[3] to the end that men might know God and live to
him as their supreme good.[4] Personal agency in such work must
be free agency. Hence no necessity could have determined the
creative work of God. His freedom therein was absolute.[5]

[1] Hodge : *Systematic Theology*, vol. i, p. 566.
[2] *Théodicée*.
[3] Rev. iv, 11 ; Psa. xix, 1.
[4] Acts xvii, 24–28 ; Rom. i, 19, 20.
[5] Cocker : *Theistic Conception of the World*, pp. 62–66

V. Mosaic Cosmogony and Science.

1. *Historic Character of the Mosaic Narrative.*—So ancient and remarkable a document could not escape a most searching criticism. A chief aim of such criticism has been to discredit its historic character. Thus it has been treated as a compilation of more ancient documents, which contained the traditional notions of creation; as a poetic effusion; as a mythical or allegorical composition; as a philosophical speculation of a devout Hebrew upon the origin of the world. In such modes it has been attempted to discredit the Mosaic narrative of creation.

There are no decisive proofs of a compilation. Nor would such QUESTION OF A a fact affect the character of the narrative, unless it COMPILATION. could be proved to have only a pagan source. There is no proof of such a source, but much disproof. In some pagan cosmogonies there are points of likeness to the Mosaic, but also points of very marked difference. The pagan, as Tayler Lewis points out, have a pantheistic cast, and are as much theogonies as cosmogonies.[1] The definite and lofty theistic conception of the Mosaic determines for it a distinct and higher source. The question of a compilation is quite an indifferent one with those who maintain the historic character of this narrative. This is the position of thoroughly orthodox and conservative divines. A compilation, while not complete in originality, may be thoroughly genuine and historical.

Nor is this narrative a poetic effusion. It might be poetic, and NOT A POETIC yet truly historical. It is not a poem either in form or EFFUSION style. "But every thorough Hebrew scholar knows that in all the Old Testament there is not a more simple, straightforward prose narrative than this first chapter of Genesis."[2] "There is certainly poetry in other parts of the Bible, and the opening account might have been in the same style, designed like all other poetry, to excite strong emotion—to impress us feelingly with the thought of the wisdom and goodness and greatness of the First Cause, without claiming exact credence for the literal prosaic truth of the representations employed for such 'an emotional purpose. But the opening narrative of the Bible has not the air and style of poetry, although the subsequent Hebrew poets have drawn largely upon this old store-house of grand conceptions, and thereby thrown back upon it something of a poetical tinge."[3] Dr. Strong

[1] *The Six Days of Creation*, p. 287.
[2] Terry : *Biblical Hermeneutics*, p. 548.
[3] Lewis : *The Six Days of Creation*, pp. 18, 19.

says: "The first chapter of Genesis lacks nearly every element of acknowledged Hebrew poetry."[1]

Against the assumption of a mythical or allegorical cast of this narrative we may place the decisive evidences of an historical character. "We have no difficulty in detecting these styles—the mythical and parabolical—in the Scriptures wherever they may occur. When we meet with such a passage as this—'The trees said to the bramble, Rule thou over us'—or, 'Thou hast brought a vine out of Egypt and planted it'—or, 'My beloved had a vineyard in a very fruitful hill'—or, 'A sower went forth to sow, and as he sowed some seed fell by the way-side'—we have no trouble in determining its character. Every intelligent reader, whether learned in the original languages or not, says at once, if he understands the terms, this is myth—this is parable—this is allegory—this is poetical or figurative language. We fail to detect any of these well-known marks of style in the account of the creation. It professes to narrate the order of facts, or the chronological steps, in the production of our present earth. It is found in Scriptures well known to have existed in our Saviour's day—Scriptures with which he was familiar, which he styled holy, and to which He, the Light of the world, appealed as of divine, and, therefore, unerring, authority. Whatever, then, be its fair meaning, that meaning, we say again, is for the believer the actual truth, the actual fact or facts, the actually intended teaching; and is to be received as such in spite of all impertinent distinctions between the natural and the moral, or any arbitrary fancies in respect to what does or does not fall within the design of a divine revelation."[2]

NOT A MYTH OR ALLEGORY.

"If we pass to the *contents* of our account of the creation, they differ as widely from all other cosmogonies as truth from fiction. Those of heathen nations are either hylozoistical, deducing the origin of life and living beings from some primordial matter; or pantheistical, regarding the whole world as emanating from a common divine substance; or as mythological, tracing both gods and men to a chaos or world-egg. They do not even rise to the notion of a creation, much less to the knowledge of an almighty God, as the Creator of all things. . . . In contrast with all these mythical inventions, the biblical account shines out in the clear light of truth, and proves itself by its contents to be an integral part of the revealed history, of which it is accepted as the pedestal throughout the whole of the sacred Script-

PROOFS OF HISTORIC CHARACTER.

---

[1] McClintock and Strong: *Cyclopædia*, "Cosmology."
[2] Lewis · *The Six Days of Creation*, p. 19.

ures."[1] "Not a few, as Eichhorn, Gabler, Baur, and others, have here found a so-called *philosophical myth*, wherein a highly cultured Israelite has given us the fruit of his reflections as to the origin of all things, clothed in the form of history. That, however, neither the contents, nor the tone, nor the place of the narrative of creation speaks in favor of this construction is at once apparent to every one. By all later men of God, as also by Jesus and his apostles, the contents thereof are manifestly regarded as history. The form in which the genesis of all things is here clothed can be just as little explained from the mythical standpoint as can the particular object contemplated by the anonymous thinker. . . . By what fatal accident came the thinker on the genesis of the world, who stood so much higher than the most renowned philosophers, to remain unknown to posterity? Assuredly, ' the historical account which is given there bears in itself a fullness of speculative thoughts and poetic glory; but it is itself free from the influences of human philosophemes: the whole narrative is sober, definite, clear, concrete.' "[2]

The facts thus given respecting the Mosaic narrative are decisive of its historic character. There could be no other intention than to give the facts of creation in an orderly form. Any other view severs the connection of this narrative with the remainder of the book, which is clearly intended for history. Indeed, the whole stream of biblical history is cut off from its fountain. Its similarities to some other cosmogonies may point to an earlier record more or less common to itself and them, but its own profound distinctions and incomparable superiority assert for itself a divine original which the others cannot claim.

THE AIM CLEARLY HISTORICAL.

2. *Theories of Mosaic Consistency with Science.*—With the historical character of the Mosaic narrative, the question arises respecting its consistency with science, particularly with geology. It is now above question that geology discloses a process of cosmogony running back through measureless ages; whereas the Mosaic cosmogony is seemingly brought within a few thousand years of the present time. This apparent discrepancy in time is the real question of adjustment. When the great age of the world, and not only as a physical body, but in manifold forms of life, came to be manifest in the light of geology, Dr. Chalmers met the issue with the declaration that "the writings of Moses do not fix the antiquity of the globe; and that if they fix any thing at all, it is only the antiquity of the human species." At a later period, and with the

[1] Keil and Delitzsch. *On Genesis*, pp. 39, 40.
[2] Van Oosterzee: *Christian Dogmatics*, vol. i, p. 319.

work of the six days in view, he said : " The first creation of the earth and the heavens may have formed no part of that work. This took place at the *beginning*, and is described in the first verse of Genesis. It is not said when the beginning was."[1] This position was not wholly new, though mainly so to modern Christian thought. The chief merit of Chalmers, as concerned in this question, lies in his ready apprehension of the issue involved, and in his prompt and confident enunciation of the principle of adjustment. There is no other principle. Yet, while the only one, it is open to different modes of application. It is only in the application that a distinction of theories appears in the reconciliation of Genesis with geology.

One mode of adjustment, and the one that Chalmers propounded, proceeds on a distinction of creations as expressed in THEORY OF the first verse of Genesis, and in the account of the six TWO CREA- days. There was " in the beginning " a creation of the TIONS. heavens and the earth. This is the creation the date of which is not fixed, but which is assumed to provide for all the ages of geology. Then there was a second and more recent creation; so recent as to accord with biblical chronology. In the further development of the theory it is maintained that, after long ages of geological history, a cataclysmic disturbance reduced the world to a formless and void mass. All forms of life perished. Some at least hold this view, while others may be less positive of so utter a desolation. Then followed a second and modern creation, the products of which are man and the forms of life cotemporary with him. This creation was the work of six literal days, as detailed in Genesis, and within the reach of biblical chronology.[2] Such is one mode of reconciling the Mosaic cosmogony with geology. If the facts are as posited, the reconciliation is complete.

There is another theory of reconciliation, which, however, is but a modification of the previous one. The same facts of THEORY OF A two creations are posited, but the desolation which LOCAL, MOD- preceded the modern creation of the six days was only ERN CREATION. local. After the long ages of geological history arising out of the first creation, with all the actualities of life which this history discloses, a portion of the earth, most likely in south-western Asia, suffered an inundation which destroyed all forms of life therein, and reduced it to a state of chaos. This local section was the scene of the second creation as detailed in the six days of the Mosaic record. These were literal days, and man, with the forms of life more directly related to him, the product of this creative work.

[1] Cited by Macdonald : *Creation and the Fall*, pp. 82, 83.
[2] McClintock and Strong : *Cyclopædia*, " Cosmogony."

Again the reconciliation is complete, if the facts are as given in this modified view.[1]

There is a third mode of reconciliation, which agrees with the previous ones in that the Scriptures do not fix the an-
THE DAYS VIEWED AS GEOLOGICAL AGES. tiquity of the earth, but differs from them in other leading facts. This theory holds the Mosaic and geological cosmogonies to be the same, and provides for the harmony of the two records in the element of time by an extension of the days of creation into geological ages. Such is the distinctive fact in this third mode of adjustment. If such extension is warranted, or even permissible, the adjustment may be accepted as entirely satisfactory. We know not any other than these three modes of bringing the two records into harmony. There are attempts in fanciful methods, which may be passed without notice.

3. *Concerning a Second and Modern Creation.*—Most that can be said for this mode of adjustment is that it preserves the literal sense of the days of creation, which, upon the face of the record, seems to be their true sense, and, further, that it answers to the reason for the Sabbath as given in the fourth commandment. It will hardly be pretended that there are interior facts of the records which require such an interpretation. The theory is open to the question whether the interior facts, and the facts of geology as well, are not against the interpretation.

It is surely difficult to read the ideas of this interpretation
DIFFICULTIES OF THE FIRST THEORY. into the Mosaic narrative, or into the many references of Scripture to the work of creation. Through the whole there runs the sense of an original and completed work, with an unbroken continuity. The absolute silence of Scripture respecting the long ages of life between the creation of the first verse of Genesis and the chaos of the second, the complete overleaping of these ages, and the introduction of a second and modern creation, while the narrative reads just like a history of unbroken continuity, are facts which it is most difficult for the theory to dispose of on any admissible laws of interpretation. There are also very serious difficulties for the theory in the facts of geology, particularly in the unbroken continuity of life since its first inception in the creative work of God.

Against the modified form of the theory, which posits a local chaos,
DIFFICULTIES OF THE SECOND THEORY. and a local second and modern creation, there are insuperable objections. The continuity of the history is sundered. The grand march of the narrative perishes in the disruption. The sublime work of a universal creation sinks

[1] Pye Smith: *Scripture and Geology;* Murphy: *On Genesis*, chap. i.

into the narrow limits of a local one.   The creative *fiat*, " Let there be light," has no higher meaning than a clearing up of the local atmosphere, so that the rays of the sun might again reach the local scene of the second creation.   This narrow sense cannot be reconciled with the narrative which places the creation of light and appoints the sun as its perpetual source before the creation of the higher forms of life.   Such is the order of facts in the narrative and in the requirement of geology.   The theory robs the creation of light of its profound meaning and lofty sublimity.   Hugh Miller might well say : " I have stumbled, too, at the conception of a merely local and limited chaos, in which the darkness would be so complete that, when first penetrated by the light, that penetration could be described as actually a *making* or creating of light." [1]

The theory requires unwarranted and inadmissible changes in the use of הָאָרֶץ—the earth.   In the first and second verses of Genesis the word clearly means the same whole earth, whereas for this theory it means in the second only a small section, reduced again to a state of chaos.   Then the theory must force the same narrow sense upon the term in other places which utterly refuse it.[2]   " The heavens and the earth, and all the host of them," of the former, and "heaven and earth, the sea, and all that in them is," of the latter, are clearly the creation of the six days, and such expressly in the latter.   It is impossible to reduce such a creation to the narrow sense of this theory.[3]

FURTHER DIF-FICULTY.

4. *Mosaic Days of Creative Work.*—The question is, whether these are literal days, as now measured to us, or indefinite and prolonged periods.   The latter are the proper alternatives of the former; for if we depart from the literal sense, the length of the days becomes entirely subordinate to the order of divine works in the process of creation.

Mostly the Christian interpretation of these days has given them the literal sense.   Recently, however, there are many exceptions.   It may gratify the rancor of infidelity to attribute this change to an exigency created by the disclosures of modern science.   Such an occasion may readily be admitted, while all sense of serious perplexity is denied.   While the Scriptures are divine, their interpretation is human, and new facts may help to a truer rendering.   However, the new rendering is new only to the common view of the later Christian centuries.   All along the centuries, and without any exterior pressure, such a sense has been given, and by most eminent Christian authors — for instance,

COMMON IN-TERPRETATION OF DAY.

[1] *Testimony of the Rocks*, p. 156.   [2] Gen. ii, 1 ; Exod. xx, 11.
[3] Macdonald : *Creation and the Fall*, pp. 86-91.

Augustine and Aquinas. Other names are given by Mivart,[1] and also by Cocker.[2] An indefinite and prolonged duration of these days is not therefore a new meaning forced upon Christian interpreters by the discoveries of modern science, but an earlier one which, in the view of many, the interior facts of the narrative required.

On a casual reading of this record, the days of creation would be taken in a literal sense. In this case, however, as in DIFFERENT MEANINGS OF DAY. many others, a deeper insight may modify the first view. The question has no decision on purely philological ground, for the reason that םוי—*yom*—is used in both a definite and indefinite sense. Respecting the former use there is no question. A few instances by reference may suffice for the latter.[3] As *yom*—day—is so frequently used in both senses, we must look to the connection for its meaning in any particular place. In the verse where the word first appears it is used for different periods: one, the period of light; the other, the period of the darkness and the light.[4] For the first three days there was no ruling office of the sun to determine their time-measure. Nor is there any apparent law of limitation to a solar measure. There is nothing in the direct account of these three days against the sense of indefinite and long periods. This is the most rational interpretation. With this fact, it seems clearly permissible so to interpret the remaining three days.

5. *The Six Days and the Sabbath.*—The reason for the Sabbath, as given in the fourth commandment,[5] is specially urged against an indefinite sense of the days of creation. The point is made that the force of the reason for the Sabbath lies in the literal sense of the days of God's working. If this be valid, the literal sense must be true of all the six. It is impossible, however, as we have seen, to fix this sense in the first three. Further, if this reason for the Sabbath requires definite solar days of God's working, it must equally require such a day of his resting, and also a resumption of his work at its close; for his resting as much concerns this reason as his working. Such a consequence proves the groundlessness of this argument for the literal sense of the days of creation.

If the grounds of the Sabbath were the same for God as for man GROUNDS OF THE SABBATH. there might be some force in this argument. There is, however, no sameness, not even a similarity, of grounds in the two cases. We need the Sabbath on both physiological and

----

[1] *Lessons from Nature*, pp. 141, 142.
[2] *Theistic Conception of the World*, pp. 150, 151.
[3] Con. ii, 4 ; Job xiv, 6 ; Isa. xli, 1 ; Micah iv, 1.
[4] Gen. i, 5.   [5] Exod. xx, 11.

moral grounds—not to name many others. There is no such need in God. Work does not weary him. His resting has no sense of recuperation or repose. Nor is the Sabbath any requirement of his moral nature. Hence the reasons for its observance arising out of his example cannot require a limitation of the days of his working and resting to a definite solar measure. That God wrought through six periods in the upward progress of his creative work and then ceased, however indefinite or long the days of his working and resting, gives all the reason for the Sabbath, as arising out of his example, which is expressed in the fourth commandment.

6. *Consistency of Genesis and Geology.*—We have presented the three leading modes of reconciling the Mosaic narrative of creation with the disclosures of geology. While we much prefer the third, and think the others open to objection, we know that they have the preference and support of some leading minds. Were they the only resource of Christian exegesis, it would not be forced into any very serious strait. With the sense of ages for the Mosaic days, which we have found clearly permissible, the reconciliation is complete. Scientists find an accordance between the two records which, beyond the attainment of consistency, proves the divine original of the Mosaic.

It may be objected that scientists are rarely philologists, and the objection might have weight if this were purely a question of philology. It is not such. Nor is any profound attainment in philology requisite to an intelligent treatment of the question. Only one word is directly involved. As it is used in different senses, its meaning in any particular place must, as we have seen, be found in its connections. These connections are open to clear eyes, even without a profound philology. It is not thus conceded that the learned in biblical philology are generally against the age-sense of day in the Mosaic record. Far from it. Neither is proficiency in science generally, or in geology in particular, necessary to an intelligent treatment of this question. The leading fact to be known is that the geological history of the world is a record of long ages, and, with this, some clear view of the successive stages of its upward progress. One may know all this without being a geologist in any scientific sense. Hence Dr. Cocker, with the requisite knowledge of science and philology, though skilled in neither, might with propriety treat the question as a philosopher. This he has done with rare ability, and with a result which leaves no apparent conflict between science and the Mosaic cosmogony.[1]

REQUIREMENTS FOR TREATING THE QUESTION.

[1] *Theistic Conception of the World,* chap. v.

21

Macdonald and C. H. Hitchcock have treated the question rather
as theologians or expositors, but with an intelligent apprehension of the facts concerned, as embodied in the
cosmogony of science.   The former, after a comparison of the two
cosmogonies, says : " It is not too much to assert that the harmony
above traced, and the peculiarities of the Mosaic narrative of creation, both as regards manner and matter, are explicable only on the
principle that the Creator of the earth, of its rocks and mountains,
its rivers and seas, plants and animals, is also the Author and
Source of this record of the wonderful production of his almighty
power." [1] Dr. Hitchcock holds, with many others, the rather poetic
view of a revelation of the Mosaic cosmogony through a process of
daily visions.   This allowed him a primary literal sense of the days ;
which, however, he holds in a symbolical form.   Time-symbols
frequently occur in Scripture.   There is such a use of day or days
and other time-measures in prophetic utterance. [2] As future events
were prophetically expressed in a symbolical use of days, so in a
like use the successive stages of creation were retrospectively expressed   Further, as the events which fulfill the prophecies reveal
the symbolical sense of their time-measure, so the age-sense of day
in the narrative of creation is revealed in the light of modern science.   It is this sense which enables the author to find in Genesis
the cosmogony of science.   "A review of the work of creation as
described in nature and revelation convinces us of the essential
harmony of the two records." [3] This is the conclusion after a full
comparison of their respective contents.

Eminent scientists, proceeding with the sense of geological ages
in the days of creation, not only find no serious contrariety between Genesis and geology, but do find a marvelous accordance in the cardinal facts of the two records.   Such
facts are placed in parallel columns, that the agreement may at
once be clear to the eye and the clearer in the mind   This is no
" deadly parallel " for Moses, but the proof of a divine original of his
cosmogony.   Its great facts were, in his time, beyond the reach of the
human mind, and remained so until within a century of the present,
Only the divine mind could then have communicated these truths.

Hugh Miller, thoroughly Christian in faith and life, was a man
of rare intelligence, and eminent in geology.   He profoundly studied and compared the cosmogonies of Gen-
esis and geology, so as to command the clearer view of their likeness

(marginal notes: EXPOSITORY TREATMENT. *;* TREATMENT BY SCIENTISTS *;* MILLER*)*

---

[1] *Creation and the Fall*, pp 85, 86.
[2] Dan viii, 14 , ix, 24-26 ; xii, 11, 12 ; Rev ix, 15 ; xi, 2, 3.
[3] *Bibliotheca Saera*, July, 1867.

in the account of the successive stages of the world's creation. We need not follow the author in this discussion, but may give the result as reached in the full persuasion of his own mind. "Now, I am greatly mistaken if we have not in the six geological periods all the elements, without misplacement or exaggeration, of the Mosaic drama of creation." "Such seems to have been the sublime panorama of creation exhibited in vision of old to

> ' The shepherd who first taught the chosen seed,
> In the beginning how the heavens and earth
> Rose out of chaos , '

and, rightly understood, I know not a single scientific truth that militates against even the minutest or least prominent of its details." [1]

Professor Winchell was a distinguished scientist, and thoroughly versed in the questions which concern the cosmogony of Genesis. He also instituted a comparison, and found a WINCHELL. wonderful agreement between the two records. The upward progress and completion of the world as detailed in the two is, day for day, substantially the same. "The author of Genesis has given us an account which, when rightly understood, conforms admirably to the indications of latest science." After a further unfolding of the two records, Winchell says · "Now compare the work of these 'days' with the events of the seven 'periods' before indicated, and judge whether the correspondence is not *real*, and, indeed, much greater than we could expect of a history written in an age before the birth of science, and (according to the popular chronology) 2,500 years after the close of the events which it narrates." [2]

The eminence of Dr. Dawson for scientific learning is well known. He, too, finds a "parallelism of the scriptural cosmogony with the astronomical and geological history of the earth," DAWSON. at once illustrative and confirmatory of the former. After a thorough study and lucid comparison of the two histories, he gives the result, modestly, indeed, but clearly without any hesitation in his own mind : "The reader has, I trust, found in the preceding pages sufficient evidence that the Bible has nothing to dread from the revelations of geology, but much to hope in the way of elucidation of its meaning and confirmation of its truth." [3]

On this question Professor Dana has coupled the name of Professor Guyot with his own : "The views here offered, and the following on the cosmogony of the Bible, are essentially those brought

---

[1] *Testimony of the Rocks*, pp 204, 210.
[2] *Reconciliation of Science and Religion*, pp. 358, 361.
[3] *Origin of the World*, p. 359.

out by Professor Guyot in his lectures."[1] Dana repeats this state-

DANA AND
GUYOT. ment in a fuller treatment of the biblical question.[2]
We thus have the common view of two very distinguished scientists.[3] "Professor Dana, of Yale, and Professor
Guyot, of Princeton, belong to the first rank of scientific naturalists; and the friends of the Bible owe them a debt of gratitude for
their able vindication of the sacred record."[4] The details of this
vindication must be passed simply with the references. Both hold
the age-sense of day in the Mosaic record, and in the discussion
there is disclosed a wonderful harmony between the cosmogonies of
science and Genesis; a harmony which is explicable only with the
divine original of the latter. "The order of events in the Scripture cosmogony corresponds essentially with that—of science—which
has been given." "The record in the Bible is, therefore, profoundly philosophical in the scheme of creation which it presents.
It is both true and divine. It is a declaration of authorship, both
of creation and the Bible, on the first page of the sacred volume.
There can be no real conflict between the two books of the GREAT
AUTHOR. Both are revelations made by him to man—the *earlier*
telling of God-made harmonies coming up from the deep past,
and rising to their height when man appeared, the *later* teaching
man's relations to his Maker, and speaking of loftier harmonies in
the eternal future."[5]

[1] *Manual of Geology*, p. 472.

[2] *Bibliotheca Sacra*, January and July, 1856.

[3] Rev. J. O. Means gives a formal statement of Guyot's doctrine in *Bibliotheca Sacra*, April, 1855.

[4] Hodge: *Systematic Theology*, vol. i, p. 573.

[5] Dana: *Manual of Geology*, pp. 744, 746.

General reference.—Much of the literature of theism, as previously given,
relates to the question of creation. The question is discussed in works on systematic theology and commentaries on Genesis; and the later more directly
meet the issues raised by modern science.

Pearson: *Exposition of the Creed*, article i, Howe: *The Oracles of God*, part
ii, sec. 2; Dwight: *Theology*, sermons xvii–xxii; Venema: *System of Theology*,
chap. xix; Martensen: *Christian Dogmatics*, secs. 59–78; Hodge: *Systematic
Theology*, vol. i, part i, chap. x; Van Oosterzee: *Christian Dogmatics*, secs.
56–58; Shedd: *Dogmatic Theology*, Theology, chap. vii; Oehler: *Theology
of the Old Testament*, part i, sec. 2; Ladd: *Doctrine of Sacred Scripture*,
part ii, chap. ii; Hickok: *Creator and Creation;* Macdonald: *Creation and
the Fall;* Lewis: *The Six Days of Creation;* Lange, Murphy, Delitzsch, Dods,
Quarry, severally on Genesis; Buckland: *Bridgewater Treatise;* Miller: *Foot-
prints of the Creator;* Murchison: *Siluria;* Mantell: *Medals of Creation;*
McCausland: *Sermons in Stones;* Cook: *Religion and Chemistry;* Fraser:
Blending Lights; Agassiz: *Structure of Animal Life;* Herschel: *Discourse on
Natural Philosophy.*

CHAPTER X.

GOD IN PROVIDENCE.

A PROVIDENCE of God is very fully revealed as a fact. The Scriptures are replete with expressions of his govern-

AN OPEN TRUTH OF SCRIPTURE

ment. These expressions are given in such terms of universality, and with such detail, that nothing is omitted. God rules in all the realms of nature, and in their minutiæ as in their magnitudes. A few texts will verify these statements. God's power sustains and rules the mighty orbs of heaven.[1] The heavens and all their hosts, the earth and the sea, with all they contain, are the subjects of his preserving and ruling providence.[2] The thunder and the lightning are his; the frost and hail and snow, and the warm winds which dissolve them, are the determination of his hand.[3] His showers water the earth, soften the furrows, and bless the springing corn.[4] He cares for the falling sparrow, and numbers the hairs of our head.[5] Such is the providence of God as revealed in the Scriptures.

The idea of a providence is not in itself an obscure one. It appears in the light of our own experience and observa-

SIMPLE AS A FACT.

tion. We see it in the government of the State, or in the offices of the ruler of the State. This sense of providence is expressed in the New Testament.[6] The idea is yet more clearly and impressively given in the parental care of the family. In the government of the children, in the watch-care over their interests, in the provisions for their good, there is a true parental providence. With such facts ever present in our own life, it is easy to rise to the idea of a divine providence. God is the Creator of all things, our own Creator and Father. He must care for the works of his own hands, even for those without any capacity for either pleasure or pain. Much more must he care for the forms of existence with such capacity. This care must be providential in its offices. We are his offspring and sustain to him the intimate relation of children. Nor are little children in deeper need of the parental care than we are of the providential ministries of the heavenly Father. There is no reason to doubt his care for us. The idea of his provi-

---

[1] Isa. xl, 26.   [2] Neh. ix, 6.   [3] Job xxxvii, 2–11.
[4] Psa. lxv, 9, 10.   [5] Matt. x, 29, 30.   [6] Acts xxiv, 2.

dence is just as simple and assuring as the idea of that parental providence which we see in our human life. We read this meaning in the words of the psalmist: "Like as a father pitieth his children, so the Lord pitieth them that fear him. For he knoweth our frame; he remembereth that we are dust."[1] We read it more clearly and deeply in the words which Christ addressed to his disciples for their assurance in the trying experiences of this life: "Your Father knoweth that ye have need of these things."[2] But the providence of God is thus viewed merely as a fact; and it is only in this view that it is clear and simple.

It is useless to assume for this question a simplicity which is not DIFFICULT FOR real. It is equally useless to attempt a concealment of DOCTRINAL its perplexities. They appear all along the history of TREATMENT. its doctrinal treatment. Nor are they any less in the more recent issues of the question. Difficulties appear in the diversities of doctrinal view.

Questions arise respecting the nature and extent of the divine agency in the preservation and government of the universe. The answers widely differ. In pantheism God is the only operative force, but as a nature without personal agency. The position of theism must consistently be directly the opposite. The providential agency of God is purely and only personal. As personal, it must be through the rational energizing of his will. On this point theists have not always been sufficiently definite. There is a doctrine of the divine immanence which does not keep sufficiently clear of the pantheistic view. While the personality of God is still maintained, the view that his divine nature as a universal presence is a universal energy finds too much place in the doctrine of providence. Answers differ respecting the extent of the divine agency as well as respecting its mode. The differences range along the whole line from the negative position of deism to the position that God is the only force operative in nature. Again, the answers differ as to whether the divine agency always operates in harmony with the laws of nature, or whether it sometimes so departs from these laws as to prevent their natural results, or to attain results which could not otherwise be achieved. The point is not here to discuss these several views, but simply to note them as signs of the difficulties which beset the doctrinal treatment of the divine providence.

The difficulties of a doctrinal treatment have been increased by IMPLICATION its implication with questions of modern science. If, WITH SCIENCE as some scientists maintain, the spheres of animate and rational life are one with the material, and all subject to an

[1] Psa. ciii, 13, 14.   [2] Luke xii, 30.

absolute continuity of physical causality, there is no place for the providence of God as a personal agency. There is in the order of nature, especially within the physical sphere, a uniformity which is seemingly the determination of purely natural forces. The question thus arises whether there are such forces, and, if so, whether their operation may be, and sometimes is in fact, modified by the divine agency. All such questions now concern the doctrine of providence.

Another question of difficulty arises from the relation of providence to our free moral agency. It is clear that with- RELATION TO out such freedom there can be neither moral obligation FREE MORAL nor responsibility. Both, however, are realities above AGENCY any reasonable questioning. Moral freedom must be a reality. Hence the real question is the adjustment of such a freedom to the offices of a divine providence in our human life. To many minds this adjustment may seem very simple and easy, but the history of opinions on the question does not warrant such a view.

There is still the difficulty, and perhaps the most perplexing of all, arising from the magnitude of evil, physical and THE MAGNI- moral. Only a complete theodicy could fully adjust TUDE OF EVIL such evil to the doctrine of providence. There is no present attainment of such a theodicy. However, the truth of a divine providence is not so conditioned for our faith. It is so conditioned only for the full comprehension of our reason. This is not necessary to a fully warranted and very sure faith. While there may be no complete explication of present evils, the proofs of a beneficent providence may be clear and sure. The same is true respecting all other questions of perplexity.

I. Leading Questions of Providence.

The divine providence cannot be formulated under any single law, nor as operative in any single mode. This is obvious in view of the many spheres of its agency. As we found it helpful to distinguish the spheres of God's creative work, so may we find it helpful to distinguish the spheres of his providential work. There is ample ground for such distinction, and for the analysis of the question. In this method we may relieve the doctrinal treatment of much perplexity, and in the end attain a clearer view of providence. We need the statement of some general facts as preparatory to the more definite analysis.

1. *Providential Conservation and Government.*—The doctrinal treatment of providence recognizes both a conserving and a ruling agency. This is the first distinction to be noted, and the broadest

and deepest of all.   There is ample ground for it in the Scriptures,
and also in the nature and relations of created existences.

A conservative providence of God is clearly expressed in the
PROVIDENTIAL Scriptures.   As the creation of all things, and of all
CONSERVATION in the most comprehensive sense, is ascribed to God, so
is their preservation: "And thou preservest them all."[1]   "O
Lord, thou preservest man and beast."[2]   He calleth by name the
hosts of heaven, the stars of the firmament, and upholdeth them
by his great power, so that not one faileth.[3]   "For in him we live,
and move, and have our being."[4]   "And he is before all things,
and by him all things consist."[5]

It is the sense of Scripture, in many places and in many forms
A RULING of expression, that all things are subject to the ruling
PROVIDENCE providence of God.   The earth and the heavens, the
forces of nature, the seasons of the year, the harvests of the field,
the fruits of the earth, the powers of human government, the allotments of human life are all thus subject.   It is needless to cite,
or even to give in substance, the many texts, or even a selection
of the many, which contain this truth.   A brief reference may
suffice[6]

In the reigning and ruling of the LORD there is the sense of a
universal governing providence.   The texts which express this
truth are not merely prophetic of an ultimate universal dominion,
nor restricted to the idea of a distinctively spiritual kingdom, but
give the sense of a present and perpetual government of all things
"Thine, O LORD, is the greatness, and the power, and the glory,
and the victory, and the majesty: for all that is in the heaven
and in the earth is thine; thine is the kingdom, O LORD, and
thou art exalted as head above all.   Both riches and honor come
of thee, and thou reignest over all; and in thine hand is power
and might; and in thine hand it is to make great, and to give
strength unto all."[7]   "He ruleth by his power; his eyes behold
the nations   let not the rebellious exalt themselves."[8]   "The
LORD hath prepared his throne in the heavens; and his kingdom
ruleth over all."[9]   "And I heard as it were the voice of a great
multitude, and as the voice of many waters, and as the voice of
mighty thunders, saying, Alleluia: for the LORD God omnipotent
reigneth."[10]

[1] Neh. ix, 6.   [2] Psa xxxvi, 6   [3] Isa xl, 26   [4] Acts xvii, 28.   [5] Col i. 17.
[6] Job v, 10, ix, 4-10; xxxvi, 26-32; xxxvii, 6-18; Psa lxxiv, 12-17;
civ, 1-30; cxxxv, 6, 7, Isa xlv, 7, Jer v, 23, 24, xxxiii, 20, 25; Joel ii,
21-27; Matt. vi, 25-34; Acts xiv, 17.
[7] 1 Chron. xxix, 11, 12.   [8] Psa lxvi, 7.   [9] Psa. ciii, 19.   [10] Rev. xix, 6

The nature and relations of created existences point to the distinction between the preserving and ruling offices of providence which we find in the Scriptures. Even the conservation of the orderly forms of material existences carries with it the sense of providential government. Otherwise, we must think this perpetual order the determination of original laws of nature, without any perpetual agency of God. This is the baldest deism, false to the Scriptures, and offensive to the religious consciousness. The distinction we make is yet more manifest in the relations of providence to the sentient and rational forms of existence. The uniformities of nature are of great value to both, but absolute uniformities would often be at painful odds with their interests. If the sustenance of the living is with the providence of God, the forces of nature must be subject to his sway. For the interests of the human race there must be a ruling as well as a preserving providence.

2. *Universality of Providential Agency.*—We here need little more than a statement of this universality. It has already appeared, especially in the explicit words of Scripture. If we hold a providence of God in any proper sense, we must rationally think it universal. The special reason for its present statement lies in its intimate relation to the further analysis of the question of providence. The more extended the field of providence the more numerous are the spheres of its agency. A proper distinction of these spheres is necessary to the analysis of the question.

3. *Distinction of Providential Spheres.*—The two spheres of God's preserving and ruling providence are commensurate in their universality, but distinct for thought, and really distinct for the manner of the divine agency therein. There is also the distinction between material being and its orderly forms; and the divine agency in the preservation of the one and in the preservation and government of the other must give rise to different questions in the doctrinal treatment. Again, there is the distinction between the material and animate spheres, wherein there are different questions for the doctrinal treatment of providence. Finally, there is the profound distinction between free and responsible personalities, on the one hand, and all the lower forms of existence, on the other. With such distinctions in the spheres of providence there must be distinctions of mode in the divine agency.

4. *Distinctions of Providential Agency.*—We have prepared the way for these distinctions by the statement of the different spheres of providence. The conservation of matter as being—if there be such an office of providence—and the conservation of its cosmical

forms must be through different modes of the divine agency.   In
the first that agency can have no respect to either the spatial relations or the dynamical qualities of the elements of matter, while in
the second it must have exclusive respect to such relations and
qualities.   There is thus in the second a governing agency which
determines the collocations of matter or directly modifies the working of its forces, while there is no place for such a manner of agency
in the first.   From the purely material, whatever its mechanical
or chemical form, we pass into a new and higher form of existence
in the sphere of the animate.   There is a new and higher force
in the living organism.   The agency of providence must be in adjustment to this new and higher force and to the definite forms in
which it works.   Forces themselves are hidden from our immediate
view, but the manifest difference between the orderly forms of the
merely physical and the organic forms of the living clearly points
to a distinction of providential agencies in the two spheres.   Finally,
there is the profound distinction between personal mind and all the
lower forms of existence.   With this distinction, there cannot be
the same law of providential agency for the former as for any sphere
of the latter.

Nothing is yet concluded or even discussed respecting the working of providence in the different spheres of finite
existence.   The aim has been to justify the position
that the divine providence cannot be formulated under
any single law, nor as operative in any single mode.   It must
be studied and interpreted in view of the manifold and diverse
spheres in which it may be operative.   What may be the truth of
a providence in one may not be the truth in another.   If it should
even appear that in some one sphere there is no evidence of a providence, it would not follow that there is no providence in others.
If it could be made clear that God is the only force operative in
material nature, it would not follow that there is neither power nor
personal agency in the human mind.   Hence an absolute providence in the former would leave the way open for a very different
mode of the divine agency in the latter.   An absolute continuity in
the order of physical sequences could not disprove a divine providence within the realm of mind.   Such facts are of value in the
study and interpretation of providence in the different spheres of
its agency.

II. Providence in the Physical Sphere.

1. *Concerning the Conservation of Matter.*—There is a preserving providence within the sphere of physical nature.   This, as

previously shown, is the clear sense of Scripture. There is for this
sphere a universal conservation. But as so revealed it is simply
the fact of a divine conservation, without any such absolute universality or specific application, that it must hold in being the very
essence of matter as well as preserve its orderly forms. Yet such a
view is prominent in the history of doctrinal opinion. The assumption is that if matter were left without the up- THE COMMON
holding power of God, even for an instant, it would VIEW.
in that instant fall into nonentity. Hence its continued existence
must be through the unceasing conservation of his power. This is
the common view. "The conception of the divine conservation of
the world as the simple, uniform, and universal agency of God
sustaining all created substances and powers in every moment of
their existence and activity is the catholic doctrine of Christendom "[1] It should be noted that this citation includes spiritual
being just as it does the material. This is proper, and not only as
a requirement of accuracy in the statement, but also as a requirement of consistency in the doctrine ; for if the doctrine be true
respecting the essence of matter it must also be true respecting the
essence of mind.

Widely as this doctrine has prevailed, we cannot think it closed
against all questioning. In order to any proper view THE VIEW
we must distinguish between the essence of matter and QUESTIONED.
its orderly forms. The former existed in the primordial chaos ;
the latter are the product of the formative work of God. It may
be very true that but for his preserving power these orderly forms
would quickly relapse into chaos, but it does not follow that the
matter itself must also fall into nonentity. This profound distinction has been overlooked, and the question has been treated
just as though the essence of matter and its orderly forms were in
one dependence upon providence for their continued existence.
That it should be so seems against reason. Being, even material
being, is a profound reality, and must have a strong hold on existence It has no tendency to fall into nothing which only omnipotence can counterwork. Instead of saying that only the power
which created matter can hold it in being, we would rather say
that only such power could annihilate it. What is thus true of the
essence of matter must be equally true of the essence of mind.

There is nothing in this view in any contrariety either to the
sense of Scripture or to a proper dependence of all things upon
God. There is no text which isolates the essence of either mind or
matter and declares the dependence of its continued existence upon

[1] Cocker : *Theistic Conception of the World*, p. 176.

an upholding providence. As we recur to the texts which reveal
DEPENDENCE the conserving providence of God we see that he up-
OF THINGS NOT holds the earth and the heavens, not, however, as mere
QUESTIONED masses of matter, but as worlds of order in the truest
cosmical sense. God "preserves man and beast," but as organic
structures, with life and sentience, and also with personality in
the former. Further, as matter is the creation of God, and continues to exist only on the condition of his good pleasure, and is
wholly subject to his use for the purposes of his wisdom, it is in a
very profound sense dependent upon him. There is also a like
dependence of mind. Such a dependence satisfies all the requirements of both reason and Scripture.

2. *View of Conservation as Continuous Creation.*—From the
notion of a dependence of finite being, which for its conservation
momentarily requires such a divine energizing as originally gave it
existence, there is an easy transition into the notion of a continuous
creation. Such a notion early appeared in Christian thought, and
has continued to hold at least a limited place. Illustrious names
are in the roll of its friends. Augustine is reckoned in the list.
His own words so place him.[1] Aquinas is definitely with Augustine.[2]

We may add the name of Edwards, who has given the real and
VIEW OF ED- full content of this doctrine. "It follows from what
WARDS has been observed that God's upholding created substance, or causing its existence in each successive moment, is
altogether equivalent to an immediate production out of nothing,
at each moment; because its existence at this moment is not
merely in part from God, but wholly from him, and not in any
part or degree from its antecedent existence. For the supposing
that its antecedent existence concurs with God in efficiency, to produce some part of the effect, is attended with all the very same
absurdities which have been shown to attend the supposition of its
producing it wholly. Therefore the antecedent existence is nothing, as to any proper influence or assistance in the affair; and consequently God produces the effect as much from nothing as if
there had been nothing before. So that this effect differs not at
all from the first creation, but only circumstantially; as in first

---

[1] "Deus, cujus occulta potentia cuncta penetrans incontaminabili præsentia
facit esse quidquid aliquo modo est, in quantumcumque est ; quia nisi faciente
illo, non tale vel tale esset, sed prorsus esse non posset."—*De Civitate Dei*, lib.
xii, cap. xxv.

[2] "Conservatio rerum a Deo non est per aliquam novam actionem, sed per
continuationem actionis qua dat esse."—*Summa Theol.*, p. i, qu civ, art. 1.

creation there had been no such act and effect of God's power *before;* whereas, his giving existence afterward follows preceding acts and effects of the same kind in an established order. "[1]

The sense of this passage is open and full. We know what the author means by the conservation of existences as a continual creation. No doubt such a formula has often been adopted without any clear apprehension of its meaning. The true sense is implied in the citations from Augustine and Aquinas, but it is not brought into clear view, and their words might be used with much less meaning. No one can mistake the meaning of Edwards. Nor has he overstated the sense of a continual creation. If we allow the formula any distinctive meaning, it must be taken in the sense of an immediate origination of existences. This is widely different from a divine agency which constantly sustains their being. We must suppose them momentarily to drop out of being and momentarily to be re-created. The supposition may be most difficult, but such are the implications of the doctrine. It must hold, not only for essential being, but also for all orderly and organic forms of existence, and equally for the human mind. In the treatment of Edwards the latter was the special application of the doctrine.

With the full meaning and content of the doctrine thus brought into view, it appears without the support of either reason or Scripture. If the doctrine be true, the present has no real connection with the past. There is CRITICISM OF THE EDWARDS-IAN VIEW no continuity of being. In all the realms of finite existence, nothing of yesterday remains to-day. All such existences of the present moment perish, and new existences take their place in the next. This has been repeated in all the succeeding moments since the original creation. The fact is not other, that the new existences are so like the old as to allow no distinction for sense-perception. The new are absolutely new. Existences may be annihilated; but, once annihilated, they cannot be re-created. Thus in every moment since the beginning a universe has perished and a universe has come into being. Then there was nothing profoundly distinctive of the original creation. The only distinction, as pointed out in the passage from Edwards, is merely circumstantial. The original was merely the first, but not more really an originative creation. When God said, "Let there be light," his creative act was not more real than in the creation of light in the next moment and in every moment since. Such a doctrine of providence cannot be true, and, when fully understood, must sink beneath the weight of its own extravagance.

[1] Works, vol. ii, p. 489.

There is not a word in Scripture which either supports or requires
NO GROUND IN such a doctrine. Many passages express the frailty and
SCRIPTURE transience of some forms of organic existence, but without any intimation that they abide but a moment or momentarily
sink into nothing, while new creations momentarily take their
place. Many forms of nature are described as permanent, abiding
through the centuries of the world's history. There is in the
Scriptures no conservation of finite existences in the sense of a
continuous creation.

3. *Question of Physical Forces.*—The question of natural forces,
such as we call mediate or secondary causes, deeply concerns the
doctrine of providence. Of course, the question here reaches beyond
matter as being, and specially respects its orderly forms. It is
only in these forms that forces emerge for rational treatment. If
there be natural forces, then the mode of providential
RELATION OF agency is in their support, in determining the colloca-
THE QUESTION tions of matter for their efficiency, and in co-working
TO PROVI- with them for the attainment of chosen ends in the
DENCE cosmos. If there be no such forces, then God is the only efficience
within the physical realm. No exception can be made in the case
of human agency. It is true that man has greatly changed the face
of the physical world, but he has no immediate power over material
nature, and can work only through existing forces, which, on the
present theory, are purely modes of the divine energizing. If this
theory be true, then all the forces operative in the physical universe, and none the less so the forces through which man works, are
the power of God. There is a profound distinction between a
divine agency working through natural forces and a sole divine
efficiency which determines all movement and change in the physical universe. So profoundly does the question of natural forces
concern the doctrine of providence.

There is no unity of view on this question. Not a few deny all
PRESENT TEND- secondary causality and find in God the only efficient
ENCY OF agency in material nature.[1] Seemingly the pres-
THOUGHT ent tendency of theistic speculation is toward this
view. There is, however, no determining principle. The names
given in the note represent widely different schools of religious
thought, while among them are theologians, philosophers, and

---

[1] "Dr. Samuel Clarke, Dugald Stewart, John Wesley, Nitzsch, Muller, Chal-
mers, Harris, Young, Whedon, Channing, Martineau, Hedge, Whewell, Bascom,
Professor Tulloch, Sir John Herschel, the Duke of Argyll, Mr. Wallace, Proctor,
Cocker, and many among the ablest recent writers have defended this view."
—McClintock and Strong ; *Cyclopædia*, art. "Providence."

scientists. But others of the same schools hold just the opposite theory. It thus appears that neither theology nor philosophy nor science necessarily determines one's view on this question. It is here that the treatment of providence is implicated with questions of physical science. This implication rather obscures than clears the question. Nothing is more loudly trumpeted than the very great, and recently very rapid, advancement of physical science. Its achievements are specially noteworthy. After all, the uncertainty and diversities of view on the question of physical forces deny us all light on the question of providence. Physical science within its own limit is purely empirical, and therefore cannot reach the secret of force. Reason imperatively affirms an adequate force for all the movements and changes in physical nature, but what that force is, whether intrinsic to matter, or extraneous and acting upon it, or purely of the divine energizing, empirical science cannot know. We think that the question is beyond the reach of metaphysics. It is not clear to our reason that physical nature is in itself, and under all collocations of material elements, utterly forceless.

The theory which denies all secondary causality in material nature, and finds in God the only agency operative in the physical realm, is known in philosophic speculation as *Occasionalism.* The principles were given in the philosophy of Des Cartes, but were more fully developed and applied by his followers. Primarily the doctrine was more directly applied to the bodily action of man The mind could not act upon the body. A volition to move the arm was not the cause of its moving, but only the occasion on which the divine power determined its movement. In its broader application the doctrine denies all interaction between material bodies. No one can determine any change in another. The implication is the utter powerlessness of physical nature, and that all changes therein are from the divine agency.[1]

(margin note: IN PRINCIPLE OCCASIONALISM.)

This question is entirely above the plane of empirical science. Metaphysics cannot resolve it. The Scriptures are silent as to any decisive judgment, though seemingly against the doctrine. Yet the question is open to rational treatment in view of its contents. The doctrine is the utter forcelessness of physical nature, and that God is the only force operative therein. We think it open to weighty objections. We need not urge what others have urged, that it imposes an immense drudgery upon God. The force of this objection is only

(margin note: IMPLICATIONS OF THE PRINCIPLE)

[1] Morell · *History of Modern Philosophy*, p. 120.

seeming. There can be no drudgery for that which cannot weary; hence there can be no drudgery for omnipotence. This occasionalism must not be allowed any office which the doctrine really denies it. The occasions are not only without all force, but are in no proper sense conditions of the divine agency. The two are merely coincident in time. Matter has no instrumental quality, and is really reduced to a blank. It must be denied all the qualities, primary as well as secondary, with which philosophy has been wont to invest it. With these properties it could not be forceless. Gravitation, cohesive attraction, chemical affinity, magnetism, electricity, without force in themselves, are simply coincident with the divine energizing. The lightning can have no part in riving the oak, the projected ball no part in breaching the wall, for any such part is possible only with the possession of force. The massive cables of steel which seemingly uphold the Brooklyn Bridge have no natural strength of support, but are the mere occasion of the divine energizing as the sustaining power, and for which, so far as any natural strength is concerned, threads of cotton might answer as well. Indeed, if this occasionalism be true, there is no natural weight of the bridge, which is possible only with a natural force of gravitation, and but for a mighty downward pressure of the divine hand there would be no weight to sustain.

In the implications of this doctrine there is no natural fitness of FURTHER IM- physical conditions for vegetable production, none in PLICATIONS organic structures for any function of animal life. The " tree planted by the rivers of water " has no natural advantage of growth and fruiting over the tree planted in the most arid and barren earth. The richest harvest might spring as readily from the sand of the desert as from the field of richest soil. The stomach has no more natural fitness for the digestion of food than the dish in which it is served. The system of nerves and ligaments and muscular tissue, so wonderfully wrought in the living body, has no natural fitness for animal movement. The structure of the eagle gives no natural strength for flight, while there is no reaction of the air against the stroke of his wings. All this must be true if there be no forces of nature. There is no proof of such a doctrine; and in the light of rational thought the extravagance of its implications is conclusive against it.

The mystery of natural forces is no valid objection against their reality. We know not how they act. This, however, is no peculiar case, but a common fact respecting the operation of force, whatever its nature. How there can be interaction between material entities, or how gravitation can act across the spaces which separate the planets from the sun, we know not. Our own personal energizing through the will is specially distinct and clear in the light of our consciousness, but only as a fact. How we thus act is as hidden as the action of gravitation across such vast spaces. Surely we cannot know how God puts forth power. There is no profounder mystery than that the energizing of his will in the purely metaphysical form of volition should act as a ruling force in the physical universe. We escape no mystery by denying all natural force and finding in God the only agency operative in the material realm.

It is a weighty objection to this occasionalism that it leads to idealism and pantheism. As a forceless world can have no effect upon our experiences, for us it can have no reality. "The outer world is posited by us only as the explanation of our inner experiences; and as, by hypothesis, the outer world does not affect us, there is no longer any rational ground for affirming it."[1] The logical result is idealism. "In this one affirmation, *that the universe depends upon the productive power of God not only for its first existence, but equally so for its continued being and operation*, there is involved the germ of the several doctrines of pre-established harmony, of occasional causes, of our seeing all things in God, and, finally. of pantheism itself, the ultimate point to which they all tend."[2]

4. *Providence in the Orderly Forms of Matter.* —The reality of physical forces does not mean their sufficiency for either the origin or the on-going of the cosmos. There is still an ample sphere for the divine agency in supporting these forces, and in determining the collocations of material elements which are the necessary condition of their orderly efficiency. A true doctrine of providence must accord with such facts—the reality of natural forces, and their dependence upon God for their orderly working. Hence, as previously noted, the true doctrine must widely differ from any one constructed on the assumption of an utter forcelessness of physical nature For the true doctrine we shall appropriate the statement of a recent excellent work It contains a few words seemingly not in full accord with our own views, but is so good as a whole that we omit all exceptions "The theory which seems most consistent with all we know of God and nature is that which supposes the Creator to have constituted the world with certain qualities, attributes, or tendencies, by which one part has a causal influence on another, and one state or combination of parts

(marginal notes:) TENDENCY TO IDEALISM AND PANTHEISM

(marginal notes:) THEORY OF PROVIDENCE

[1] Bowne ; *Metaphysics*, p. 116
[2] Morell · *History of Modern Philosophy*, p. 120

22

produces another, according to what we call laws of nature, the result being the co-ordination and succession of events which we call the operations of nature. At the same time all nature is pervaded by the living presence of God, sustaining the being and operations of the world he has made and governs, retaining a supreme control which may at any point supersede or vary the usual course of natural causation. Ordinarily he neither sets aside the causal qualities of nature nor leaves them to themselves. This is the reconciliation, if any were needed, of the primary and secondary causes. God is immanent in natural causation, as truly and necessarily as in natural being, in the operations as in the existence of matter or mind."[1]

Any inference from the uniformity of nature against a providential agency within the sphere of physical forces is

PROVIDENCE AND THE UNIFORMITY OF NATURE

utterly groundless. The two are not only entirely consistent, but the latter is the only rational account of the former. The denial of such consistency must either assume an absolute uniformity of nature as the determination of physical forces which leaves no place for the divine agency, or that such agency must be capricious and the cause of disorder. There is no ground for either assumption. If the processes of nature are wholly from the energizing of a blind and purposeless force, there is no guarantee of an absolute uniformity. For aught we know there may have been great variations in the past, and the near future may bring an utter reversion of the present order of things. We could know the contrary only by a perfect knowledge of the blind and purposeless nature assumed to determine the order of existences, which is for us an impossible attainment. "Whether the members of the system will always continue, or whether they will instantaneously or successively disappear, are questions which lie beyond all knowledge We do not know what direction the future will take in any respect whatever. The facts in all these cases depend upon the plan or nature of the infinite. and unless we can get an insight into this plan or nature, our knowledge of both past and future must be purely hypothetical."[2]

Such result is inevitable if the infinite or ground of the finite is

UNIFORMITY NOT FROM NATURE

assumed to be a blind and purposeless nature. There is no a priori necessity of uniformity in the working of such a nature. When Mr J S Mill says, " I am convinced that any one accustomed to abstraction and analysis, who will fairly exert his faculties for the purpose, will, when his imag-

[1] Randles . First Principles of Faith, pp. 232, 233.
[2] Bowne · Metaphysics, p. 139.

ination has once learned to entertain the notion, find no difficulty
in conceiving that in some one, for instance, of the many firma-
ments into which sidereal astronomy now divides the universe
events may succeed one another at random, without any fixed
law,"[1] he fully admits that the orderly course of nature is no necessity of physical causality, and hence that such order is entirely
consistent with the agency of a divine providence. When by such
a putting of the question Mill would unsettle the law of causation,
that every event must have an adequate cause, he utterly fails.
In the necessity of thought the movement of worlds at random, or
without any fixed law, would no less imperatively require a cause
than the movement of worlds in the order of a system. However,
the axiomatic truth of causation is only a formal truth, valid for
all events but without the determination of any, while events
themselves, with their respective causes, are matters of empirical
or logical knowledge. It remains true that there is no absolute
uniformity of nature which must exclude the agency of a divine
providence.

In the light of reason, as in the sense of Scripture, the providence
of God is the ground and guarantee of the uniformities
which the system of nature requires. The requirement
is specially for the adjustment of the physical sphere to
the living and rational spheres. The physical, however

PROVIDENCE
THE GROUND
OF UNIFORM-
ITY

complete its mechanical order, has no rational end in itself, and
must find such an end in the interest of sentient and rational life.
"There only, where the possession, the preservation of being is
felt, can existence be considered as a good, and consequently as an
end to which a system of means is subordinated. What does it
really matter to a crystal to be or not to be ? What does it matter
to it whether it have eight angles in place of twelve, or be organized
geometrically rather than in any other way ? Existence having no
value for it, why should nature have taken means to secure it ?
Why should it have been at the expense of a plan and a system of
combinations to produce a result without value to any one, at least
in the absence of living beings ? So, again, however beautiful the
sidereal and planetary order may be, what matters this beauty, this
order, to the stars themselves that know nothing of it ? And if
you say that this fair order was constructed to be admired by men,
or that God might therein contemplate his glory, it is evident that
an end can only be given to these objects by going out of themselves,
by passing them by, and rising above their proper sphere."[2] As in
the plan of God the physical system was constituted as preparatory to

[1] *Logic*, book iii, chap. xxi, sec. 1.   [2] Janet : *Final Causes*, pp. 156, 157.

the coming of sentient and rational existences, so its orderly preservation is for their sake. "Physical and mechanical things being in a general manner connected with finality by their relation to living beings, we conceive that there may thus be in the inorganic world a general interest of order and stability, conditions of security for the living beings."[1] With such an original purpose in the constitution of the physical system, there is a manifest reason for the providence of God in its orderly conservation.

Thus the providence of God, so far from being in any contrariety ERROR OF CON- to the orderly course of nature, is in fact the ground of TRARY VIEW. its uniformities. The contrary view arises from the false notion that a divine agency within the course of nature must be capricious and disorderly. Nothing could be more irrational. Nothing could be more utterly groundless than any inference from the orderly course of nature that there can be no providential agency therein. "For when men find themselves necessitated to confess an Author of nature, or that God is the natural Governor of the world, they must not deny this again, because his government is uniform; they must not deny that he does all things at all, because he does them constantly; because the effects of his acts are permanent, whether his acting be so or not; though there is no reason to think it is not."[2] We may add the noble words of Hooker, as replete with the same ideas: "Now, if nature should intermit her course, and leave altogether, though it were but for a while, the observation of her own laws—if those principal and mother elements, whereof all things in this lower world are made, should lose the qualities which they now have—if the frame of that heavenly arch erected over our heads should loose and dissolve itself—if celestial spheres should forget their wonted motions, and, by irregular volubility, turn themselves any way as it might happen—if the prince of the lights of heaven, which now as a giant doth run his unwearied course, should, as it were, through a languishing faintness, begin to stand still and rest himself—if the moon should wander from her beaten way, the times and seasons blend themselves by disorder and confused mixture, the winds breathe out their last gasp, the clouds yield no rain, the earth be defeated of heavenly influence, the fruits of the earth pine away as children at the withered breast of their mother, no longer able to yield them relief—what would become of man himself, whom these things do now all serve?"[3] All such dissolutions in the physical system

[1] Janet: *Final Causes*, p. 159.
[2] Butler: *Analogy*, part i, chap. ii.
[3] Hooker: Works (Oxford ed., 1793), vol. i, pp. 204, 205.

would be utterly indifferent but for the interest of sentient and rational existences; and God, who constituted that system for the sake of such existences as its finality, ever maintains its uniformities in their interest. This is the work of his providence in the conservation of the orderly forms of matter.

III. Providence in Animate Nature.

1. *Reality and Mystery of Life.*—In passing from the lifeless to the living we reach a higher order of existence. From the highest chemical and crystalline forms of matter there is still a high ascent to the lowest forms of life. In the living organism there is a new element or force, and one far higher than any force of nature previously operative in the physical history of the world. Life is at once a reality and a mystery. The mystery cannot conceal the reality, nor the reality unfold the mystery.

Whatever be the nature of life, it is too subtle for any empirical cognition. Neither the scalpel nor the microscope can reach it. Yet it is not on this account any less a reality. It is a reality for our reason, just as other forces *no empirical cognition of life* which, however manifest in their effects, never reveal themselves to any sense-perception. Gravitation, cohesion, chemical affinity, magnetism are such hidden forces. There can, however, be no question respecting their reality. They are every-where operative in nature, and the aggregate of effects ever resulting from their agency allows no such question. So the vast aggregate of vital phenomena, so manifold and marvelous in form, can allow no question respecting the reality of life. As by an imperative law of thought we require a force of cohesion for the compacting of solid bodies, a force of chemical affinity for the compounding of discrete elements into concrete forms, and a force of gravitation for the orderly ruling of the heavens, so do we require a vital principle or force for the many facts ever appearing in the sphere of animate nature. This requirement gives us the reality of life.

The reality of a vital element or force is not the explanation of its nature. The mystery remains. This fact, however, *all force a mystery.* is not peculiar to life, but is common to all the forces of nature. No one pretends to any explanation of the inner nature of either gravitation, or cohesive attraction, or chemical affinity, or magnetism. "Astronomers consider gravitation the unknown cause of the movement of the stars; I consider life as the unknown cause of the phenomena which are characteristic of organized beings. It may be that both gravitation and life, as well as the other general forces are merely as x, of which the equation has not yet been discovered." [1] In all these cases, however, the mystery is still the nature of the cause, not its reality.

2 *Providence in the Sphere of Life.*—As the cosmos itself, so life must take its place under the law of dependence. Neither its spontaneous origin nor its self-sufficiency for the continued facts of vital phenomena is in any sense an implication of its reality. For the existence of life and the realm of its activities, reason requires the interposition of a divine agency. Spontaneous generation has often been asserted, not, however, as a fact proved, but as the implication and requirement of a purely naturalistic theory of evolution. The absence of all proof of such an origin of life is admitted. There is still for mere science the impassable gulf between the lifeless and the living. God who said, "Let there be light," must also have said, "Let there be life." Only in such a divine fiat could life have its origin.

Even such an origin of life does not give us any insight into its NO SELF-SUF- nature; though it does give us the idea of a living or-
FICIENCY OF ganism, even if in its germinal incipiency. We can
LIFE have no idea of life apart from an organism. It is the sense of Scripture that the beginning of life was in organic forms. It is equally the sense of Scripture that life was to be perpetuated through a law of propagation [2] Such is the divine law for the realm of life. But it does not mean that life itself as thus initiated should be sufficient for all the future of this realm. We should rather find in the facts the proof of a divine agency than the intrinsic sufficiency of life itself for such a marvelous outcome. This view is fully warranted by the wonderful complexities and correlations of part with part in the living organism. It is not thinkable that life itself, without any higher directive agency, could weave the elements of matter into such marvelous forms. There must be a divine providence in the realm of life.

3. *The View of Scripture.*—It is the clear sense of Scripture that God is the Author of all orderly forms of existence, and not only by an original creative act, but by a perpetual providential agency through which such forms are perpetuated. It is also the sense of Scripture that there is a providence of God over living orders of existence and operative for their preservation. The living creatures of the sea wait upon God for their meat, and receive it in due season. Their life is in his hand, and they live or die according to his pleasure. He sends forth his Spirit, and life in manifold forms is created, and the face of the earth renewed.[3]

[1] Quatrefages *The Human Species.* p 7
[2] Gen. i, 11, 22, 28.   [3] Psa. civ, 27–30.

"The eyes of all wait upon thee; and thou givest them their meat in due season. Thou openest thine hand, and satisfiest the desire of every living thing "[1] "He giveth to the beast his food, and to the young ravens which cry."[2] "Behold the fowls of the air: for they sow not, neither do they reap, nor gather into barns; yet your heavenly Father feedeth them."[3] The same doctrine of a divine providence in the realm of life, especially in the sphere of sentient existences, is given by Paul in his great words to the men of Athens. God is the Creator of all living orders, and gives to all life, and breath, and all things. Men are his offspring, and in him live, and move, and have their being.[4]

IV. Providence in the Realm of Mind.

1. *Reality of Power in Mind.*—Any proper interpretation of providence over mind must keep in view the qualities which differentiate it from all lower orders of existence. In his present constitution man partakes of much in common with the lower orders. So far he may be the subject of a common providence with them With the powers of a personal agency, he is placed in relation to higher laws of government. Nature without spontaneity is subject only to a law of force. This is true of the entire physical realm. With sensibility and instinct, as in the animal orders, there is spontaneity, but no law of freedom. For such the method of providence must be according to their nature. There are powers in man which distinguish him, not only from mere physical nature, but from all other living orders. With many, matter in itself is utterly forceless. With not a few, animals are mere automata. As such they could possess no power of spontaneity, and would in this respect be reduced to a level with mere matter. Man cannot be so reduced. Spontaneity cannot be denied him. The proof of such power is given in every man's consciousness, and in every instance of free voluntary action. There is not only the power of voluntary action, such as an animal may put forth, but the power of rational action. Such action must be from rational motive, and in freedom. So different is man from all the lower forms of existence as a subject of providence and law. The rational inference is that the mode of providence in his government must be widely different from that in the government of the lower orders.

2. *Profound Truth of Personal Agency.*—The significance of the power in man for the question of providence requires further statement. Analysis of the mind gives us the powers of a personal agency, rational, moral, and religious. There is the freedom of action in

[1] Psa. cxlv, 15, 16.   [2] Psa. cxlvii, 9.   [3] Matt. vi, 26.   [4] Acts xvii, 22–28.

obedience to the laws of his personal constitution, or against them. In the secular sphere he is capable of a rational life with respect to present interests and duties. He is thus largely responsible for his present estate. It is better for him to be thus responsible, even with the contingencies of secular evil, than to be the subject of necessity. Man has still a higher nature, and the powers of higher action. Conscience and moral reason, the sense of God and religious duty belong to his personal constitution. As so constituted he is properly MORAL LAW a subject of moral law, and to be governed by moral FOR PERSONAL motives. He cannot else be governed at all according AGENCY to his moral and religious nature. He can be so governed only in freedom. This is significant for the mode of his providential government. He cannot be subject to any such determining law as rules in physical nature, or even in the animal orders. He must be left in freedom, even with the contingency of moral evil. The proof that he is so left is in all the history of the race.[1] Man, in common with all other finite existences, is ever in DEPENDENT, a state of dependence. "But this natural dependence YET FREE upon the divine omnipotence is only the groundwork of a moral and religious dependence, which allows ample room for the exercise of self-determination. In the moral order of the world God's power does not avail itself merely as natural omnipotence— as the all-generating, world-creating, and world-sustaining will— but as a *commanding* and reminding will, speaking to us 'at sundry times, and in diverse manners,' by the law and the prophets within us as well as without; and likewise as the permissive will (*voluntas permissiva*), which permits even 'darkness' to have its hour and its power.' Viewed then in the light of the *holy law* of God, the course of this world is not only a working together with God, but a working against him also; and the words of Scripture are realized, 'man's thoughts are not God's thoughts, neither are man's ways God's ways;'[3] 'the people imagine a vain thing;' the truth is held 'in unrighteousness:' the spirits of time and the powers of the darkness of this world oppose God and the kingdom of his holiness.[4] It is only a false optimism which regards the actual as in and for itself necessary."[5]

3. *Providence over Free Personalities.*—With the reality of freedom, there is still an ample sphere for the providence of God over man. Only, in the moral sphere the agency of providence must

---

[1] Butler . *Analogy*, part I, chaps. ii–v.
[2] Luke xxii, 53   [3] Isa. lv, 8.
[4] Psa. ii, 1–3 ; Rom. i, 18 ; Eph. vi, 12.
[5] Martensen : *Christian Dogmatics*, p. 216.

accord with this freedom. That it does so accord is a truth previously set forth as manifest in all the history of the race. If such is not the truth, the evil deeds of men, as really as the good, must result from a determining divine agency. A theory of providence which must either render moral action impossible or make God the determining agent in all evil can have no place in a true theology.

In the constitution of our moral and religious nature there are spontaneous activities which warn us from the evil and prompt us to the practice of the good. There is the sense of God and duty, the sense of spiritual need, spontaneous outgoings of the soul for the grace and blessing of the heavenly Father. In many ways God may address himself to such feelings and quicken them into a higher state of practical force. He may do this through events of his providence, through the words of godly men, through the clearer manifestation of religious truth, or by an immediate agency of the Spirit within the religious consciousness. The mind may be thus enlightened, the moral and religious nature quickened and strengthened, the deep sense of sin awakened, the freeness and blessedness of the divine favor made manifest. In such ways, as in many others, God may deal with men in the ministries of his providence. Regarded as in their moral and religious nature, such are specially the offices of his providence over them. Therein is the chief sphere of his providence in dealing with men. Plainly, such offices are in full accord with our freedom.

PROVIDENCE IN ACCORD WITH FREEDOM.

4. *The Sense of Scripture.*—We need no large collection of texts, nor any elaborate and profound exegesis, to find in the Scriptures a sense of providence in accord with the law previously stated. There is still a providence over man determinative of many things in his life quite irrespective of his own agency. Yet even in his secular life he is mostly treated as a personal agent, at once rational, responsible, and free. The many promises of secular good, the many threatenings of secular evil have respect to human conduct, and clearly with the sense of freedom and responsibility therein. Specially is this so within the moral and religious sphere. Man begins his life under a law of duty, with the sanctions of life and death.[1] His history proceeds with divine appeals to his moral and religious nature in favor of a good life and against an evil one, with the sanction of reward or retribution according as he is good or evil. Through all the economies of religion divine providence proceeded in the same manner. Under the law and the prophets, under the mission of Christ and the

MAN FREE AND RESPONSIBLE.

[1] Gen. ii, 16, 17.

ministry of his apostles, appeals are made to man as a free and responsible subject of moral government. The righteousness of the final rewards of this life is grounded in the same law. Such facts belong to the divine providence over men. They are all in strict accordance with our personal agency and freedom. Such are the facts of providence as they openly take their place in the process of the divine revelation. There must be the same law for the less open facts of providence in its usual course.

This truth must be of value in the question of theodicy. If the OF VALUE FOR agency of providence must be absolute, even in the ANY THEODICY moral and religious sphere, there can be no approach toward a theodicy. All evil, physical and moral, must be directly placed to the divine account. Man can have no personal or responsible agency in either. For good and evil he is but the passive subject of an absolute providence. In the light of reason, and conscience, and Scripture there is no such a providence over man.

V. FORMULAS OF PROVIDENTIAL AGENCY.

In the doctrine of providence there is mostly recognized a distinction between the uniform agency of God in the course of nature and his occasional interpositions, with results exceptional to that uniformity. There is ground for such a distinction, and its clear expression would be helpful to clearness of doctrine. The distinction itself is not obscure for thought; yet its proper formulation is not an easy attainment. There is no one formula in common use. All are open to criticism. A brief notice of such formulas may help us to a clearer view of the distinction which they are intended to express, and also to a clearer view of providence itself.

1. *As General and Special.*—Sometimes the word particular is used in the place of special, but without distinction of sense. Neither the primary sense of these terms nor their usual interpretation in this formula marks any distinction between the uniform agency of providence in the course of nature and its exceptional interpositions, with results apart from that uniformity. The sense of providence as general is that it sustains and rules all things; as special or particular, that it is concerned with all the parts, even NO REAL DIS- the smallest parts of the whole. There is thus no real TINCTION distinction between the general and the special, and the only service of the latter term is to emphasize the comprehensive sense of the former. Here is an instance of such interpretation: "There have been disputes among thinking minds in all ages as to whether the providence of God is general or particular. Philosophers, so called, have generally taken the former view, and

divines the latter. There has been a wide difference between the views of these two parties, but there is no necessary antagonism between the doctrines themselves. The general providence of God, properly understood, reaches to the most particular and minute objects and events, and the particular providence of God becomes general by its embracing every particular." [1] It thus appears that the most vital question of providence never comes into view under this formula. That question respects interpositions of God apart from his agency in the uniformities of nature, and above the course of nature, and which in special instances prevent the results of that course, or produce results which it would not reach. This is the real question of the supernatural in providence and in religion. No formula of providential agency is adequate which does not bring this truth into clear view.

2. *As Immanent and Transcendent.*—This formula is in frequent use, and, seemingly, growing in favor. "We must distinguish between the *immanent* and the *transcendent* DISTINCTION OF THE TERMS. in the operations of the providence of God. We call those of its workings immanent wherein the divine providence incloses itself in the laws of this world's progress, and reveals itself in the form of *sustaining* power in the moral order of things. We call those of its operations transcendent wherein the course of history is interrupted, and the divine will breaks forth in creative or commanding manifestations." [2] The real and vital distinction between the uniform operations of providence in the order of nature and its supernatural interpositions which in special instances depart from that course is here rather intimated or implied than expressed. Yet this distinction is the very truth which should be most clearly expressed. Further, the above statements are open to the inference that as between an immanent and a transcendent providence God operates in different modes: in the former by the activities of his nature; in the latter purely by the energizing of his will. There is no ground for any such distinction. All the providential agency of God is purely through his will, and no less so in the maintenance of the orderly course of nature than in those occasional supernatural interpositions which produce results apart from that course.

This distinction between the immanence of God in nature and his transcendence above nature is one that should be A DISTINCTION TO BE CAUTIOUSLY MADE. cautiously used. It is true that so long as his personality stands clearly with his transcendence his immanence in nature cannot consistently be held in any contradictory sense.

[1] McCosh : *The Divine Government*, p 181
[2] Martensen : *Christian Dogmatics*, pp. 219, 220.

But we are not always logical in our thinking. Inconsistency is ever a liability. With the immanence of God as the only force operative in nature, we are formally close upon pantheism. Expressions of this force inconsistent with the divine personality are pretty sure to follow. "God is not simply the *transitive* but the *immanent* cause of the universe. He is in nature, not merely as a *regulative* principle impressing laws upon matter, but as a *constitutive* principle, the ever-present source and ever-operating cause of all its phenomena. . . . Nature is more than matter: it is matter swayed by the divine power, and organized and animated by the divine life. . . . The will of God is the one primal force which streams forth in ever-recurring impulses with an immeasurable rapidity at every point in space—an incessant pulse-beat of the Infinite Life." [1]

Dr. Cocker has not left us in any doubt of his theism; yet many

REMARKS ON COCKER'S VIEW.

of these expressions are more consistent with pantheism. They spring from an extreme and unguarded view of the divine immanence in the processes of nature. The providential agency of God, in whatever sphere of its operation, is purely through his personal will. This cannot be expressed as an organizing and animating divine life in nature. Nor can it be expressed as a force ever streaming forth at every point in space, as with censeless and infinitely rapid pulsations—an incessant pulse-beat of the Infinite Life. God is not operative in his providence as a nature, but only as a person. He is in no sense a *natura naturans*. It follows that the providential agency of God is as purely personal and supernatural in his immanence as in his transcendence. Nor does this formula properly distinguish between the uniformity of providence in the course of nature and its exceptional variations

3. *As Natural and Supernatural.*—Others may have used this formula, though we do not remember any instance. On first view, it must seem highly objectionable; and the more so if, as maintained, the agency of providence is as verily supernatural in the uniformities of nature as in its exceptional variations from such uniformity.

With Bishop Butler's sense of natural, such objection is obviated

THE SENSE OF NATURAL.

and the formula approved. "But the only distinct meaning of the word is, *stated, fixed,* or *settled ;* since what is natural as much requires and presupposes an intelligent agent to render it so—that is, to effect it continually, or at stated times—as what is supernatural or miraculous does to effect it for

[1] Cocker : *Theistic Conception of the World,* pp. 141, 142

once."[1] In this sense, natural expresses, not the causal force in the cosmos, but the uniformity of its operation. Physical causality as the whole account of the cosmos is no implication of the order of uniformity. Such may be the order of an intelligent, personal cause. Order itself, for which mere physical causality is inadequate, is the proof of an intelligent cause. This then is the sense of providence as natural—a providence which operates uniformly, as in the orderly processes of nature. For the attainment and maintenance of a cosmos there must be uniformity of causal agency, and for the personal as for the physical. Order is the central reality of a system. Any assumption that personal causality must be capricious is the sheerest gratuity. The perfections of the divine personality are the only sufficient cause and the only guarantee of the uniformities of nature. There is such a providence of God, in the maintenance of the orderly processes of nature, which from its uniformity we call his natural providence.

But such a providence, because it is personal, may, in given instances and for sufficient reasons, so vary its agency as to prevent the results of its uniform operation, or attain results which otherwise would not be reached. SENSE OF THE SUPERNATURAL. Such interpositions we call a supernatural providence. The real distinction, however, is one of order, not of agency. In both the agency is supernatural, and equally in both, as in distinction from mere physical forces, but in the one it operates with uniformity, and in the other with occasional and varying interpositions.

4. *Illustrations of the Natural and the Supernatural.*—We shall directly point out the difficulty of distinguishing between the natural and the supernatural modes of providence, as events usually arise in the history of the world. We turn therefore for illustrations to sacred history. If any object to such instances, they may be regarded simply as suppositions. They will in this view equally answer for illustration.

Palestine has its meteorology, the usual phenomena of which are well known. It has its former and latter seasons of rain as yearly occurring. These are facts under the natural providence of God. IN THE PHYSICAL REALM. Then under his ordering there is a drought and a famine for three years and six months; and then in answer to prayer there is, out of season and coming suddenly, a mighty rain. These are facts of a supernatural providence. God has so interposed within the laws of nature or the order of his natural providence as to achieve these supernatural results. Under a natural providence sun and moon run their appointed course, and

[1] *Analogy*, part i, chap. i.

give us the orderly measures of day and night. But God so interposes in the working of his natural providence that the sun stands still in Gibeon and the moon is stayed in the valley of Ajalon; and thus arise the facts of a supernatural providence. For the illustration we need not assume a literal standing still of either sun or moon. A phenomenal staying will answer as well for the Scripture account. The limited localization of the facts requires a purely phenomenal mode. As such they were easily within the power of God, and were the product of his supernatural providence.

The realm of mind is specially, and chiefly, the sphere of a super-natural providence. The human mind possesses the powers of personal agency under a law of freedom. God is the author of its powers, with the laws of their action. These laws, together with the providential allotments of life, have much to do with our action, even under a law of freedom. We must therefore be the subjects of a natural providence. Often there are in human life the facts of a supernatural providence. Ahasuerus comes to the throne of Persia. His administration proceeds according to the laws of the kingdom. His daily life is employed in the exercise of the powers with which he is endowed. So far it proceeds in the order of a natural providence. But on a certain night the king is strangely sleepless and restless. A divine influence has touched the sources of thought and feeling. His mind is put upon a process of reflection which it would not have reached in its own working. In this new mood he calls for a reading of the chronicles of the court. Thus in a crisis of profound interest the king discovers the hidden wickedness of Haman—which leads to his speedy and merited destruction, and to the deliverance of the Jews whose utter ruin he had so craftily and cruelly plotted.[1] Here are the facts of a supernatural providence. In his missionary tour St. Paul comes to Mysia, intending to go hence into Bithynia. He is proceeding upon a plan formed in his own judgment. So far he is acting under a natural providence. Here his plan is changed. Through an impression of the divine Spirit he goes, not into Bithynia, but into Macedonia.[2] Here again are the facts of a supernatural providence.

5. *The Mode of Providence often Hidden.*—The events of a supernatural providence are as really supernatural as the miracles of Scripture. Miracles, however, have a distinct office as the credentials of God's messengers, and therefore must have an open manifestation. Providential events have no such office, and therefore need no such manifesta-

---

[1] Esth. vi, vii.   [2] Acts xvi, 7–10.

tion. They are none the less supernatural on that account. Any divine interposition which modifies the working of a natural force, in however slight a measure, is as truly supernatural as all the miracles of Moses in Egypt. Any divine influence which induces new movements of thought and feeling, however unconsciously to the mind itself, is as really supernatural as the inspiration of Isaiah and Paul, as the mission of the Spirit at the Pentecost. But as such providence has no office requiring an open manifestation it is rarely self-identifying.

The two modes of providence work in the fullest harmony, but because both are without open manifestation the actual mode in any given instance is hidden. In marked cases, even in great catastrophes, it is not in human wisdom to know whether they arise from a natural or a supernatural providence. NEITHER MODE OF PROVIDENCE MANIFEST. For illustration we recall an event already more than thirty years past, but one still living in the memory of such as then received its fuller impression. The *Arctic*, freighted with much precious life, sailed from Liverpool for New York. Onward she moved, day after day, until she reached the Banks of Newfoundland. Meantime a French ship sailed from a Canadian port, on a course which brought her to the same Banks, and upon a line crossing the path of the *Arctic*. There was a collision, and the *Arctic* quickly perished. It was a fearful catastrophe. Whether this was a natural or a supernatural providence only God could know. If we assume the former, then how easy for the interposition of the latter! A few seconds earlier or later sailing; a very slight change of speed; the turning of a pilot-wheel, even to a spoke or two, half an hour before—on any such change in the case of either ship they would have safely cleared each other. How easy for God to effect such a change through any ruling mind in the management of either! Or, if we assume a supernatural providence in this memorable event, the means were just as ready to the divine hand for its inducement as for its prevention. On either view we must recognize a divine providence in such an event. Whether a natural or a supernatural providence, the heart of God was with the fated *Arctic* in every league and knot of her voyage. This is sure to our faith, however dark the event to our reason. From our low level we look up as into an investing fog, such as covered the scene of this fatal collision. God is in the light, and for him all events are in the light, and he looks down upon them with the eye of his own wisdom and love. We know that his eye marks the falling sparrow. Nor should we question that with an infinitely deeper regard he beheld this fearful event.

As the mode of providence is so hidden from our view, we should
THE PROPER not hastily assume a supernatural interposition in
INFERENCE. bringing about every event which specially concerns
the interests of men. There is no warrant for such an assumption.
On the other hand, we are assured that the divine providence, in
one mode or another, is present in all such events. We are ever
in the view of God, and under his watchful care.

VI. TRUTH OF A SUPERNATURAL PROVIDENCE.

1. *A Truth of Theism.*—In a true sense of theism the causal
ground of finite existences is a personal being, with the essential
attributes of personality. As a personal being, his agency must
ever be under a law of freedom. Therefore it must not be fet-
tered with the laws of either materialism or pantheism. Both systems are utterly fatalistic. Of course there can be no freedom
under either. From the beginning, and through all its process,
the course of nature must be absolutely determined, and by the
blindest necessity. The order of nature must be natural in the
lowest sense of materialism or pantheism. There can be no variation from such absolute determinism. Consistently with such
principles, the supernatural is utterly denied. Agnosticism is
equally exclusive of freedom, as every system must be which has
no place for the divine personality. Theism is the opposite extreme
FREEDOM OF to such systems. God is a personal being, with the
THE DIVINE freedom of personal agency. Such truths are central
AGENCY to theism, and to surrender them is to surrender all
that is most vital in the doctrine. It is not for a personal God to
fetter himself with a chain of absolute sequence in the processes of
nature. He is free to modify these processes, and in the interest
of sentient and rational existences must modify them in exceptional
cases. Without a supernatural providence we sink into the bleakness of deism, and might as well sink into materialism or pantheism. Theism is supernaturalism. If there is a personal God there
is a supernatural providence.

2. *A Truth of Moral Government.*—There is a moral government
over man. The moral consciousness of the race affirms its truth.
There is in this consciousness a sense of God, of duty, of responsibility. For the consciousness of the race God is a supernatural being; one who is concerned with human affairs, and in whose regards
men have a profound interest. With all the crudities of polytheism,
the elements of such convictions still abide. Duty, however neglected, is yet confessed to be paramount. Responsibility, however
forgotten or resisted in the interest of present appetence and pleasure.

still asserts itself and constrains the confession of its importance. With these convictions there is consistently the sense of a supernatural providence. If they are groundless, the deepest and most imperative consciousness of the race is a delusion. If they are grounded in truth, as we must rationally think them, there must be a moral government, and therefore a supernatural providence. Without such a providence all that is real in such a government falls away.

On the ground of theism there must be a moral government. With the Christian conception of God there is, and there must be, such a government; and with the truth of a moral government there must be a supernatural providence. It is not to be thought that God, as our moral ruler, would leave us wholly to the guidance of conscience and experience. If we should except the physical realm from all supernatural interpositions, we cannot rationally close the moral against such agency. A supernatural providence is the requirement and complement of a moral government.

PROVIDENCE IN MORAL GOVERNMENT.

3. *A Truth of the Divine Fatherhood.*—The religious consciousness of the race longs for something more than a blind force, even though it were omnipotent, back of finite and dependent existences. The profoundest reason imperatively requires something more. Both require personality in the causal ground of such existences. The common religious consciousness, with the deep and abiding sense of dependence and need, requires sympathy and love in the Creator and Lord of all. Nothing less can satisfy it, or give assurance of needed help in the exigencies of life. The assurance of sympathy and love is reached in the idea of the divine Fatherhood. The light of reason leads up to this idea. The doctrine of Paul, as delivered to the men of Athens, cannot mean less. Revelation, opening with the more special view of the power of God, advances to the idea of his sympathy and love, and on to that of his Fatherhood. The divine Son sets this truth in the clearest, divinest light. He came to show us the Father. His mission was marvelously fulfilled. He has revealed the Father in the richness of his grace and the pathos of his love. The prayer of humanity may now begin with " Our Father."

We found it to be against all rational thinking that God as moral ruler over men should leave them, with their profound obligation and responsibility, wholly to the guidance of conscience and experience. How much less could the heavenly Father so leave his dependent and needy children! He must often interpose by an immediate agency for their good. The truth of the divine Fatherhood is the truth of a supernatural providence.

23

4. *A Clear Truth of the Scriptures.*—As we previously pointed out, the agency of God in the uniformities of nature is in itself, and in distinction from any mere natural force, as strictly supernatural as in those special interpositions which modify the course of nature and constitute what we distinctively call a supernatural providence. The Scriptures are replete with both ideas. However, we are here specially concerned with the latter.

There are many facts of Scripture which can neither be reduced ILLUSTRATIVE to the uniformity of nature nor accounted for by any FACTS. known or unknown law of nature. Any such interpretation is false to the truth and life of the facts. In the history of creation, in the life of Enoch, in the call of Abraham, in the segregation and history of the Hebrews, in the ministry of Moses, in the inspiration of prophets, there were interpositions of the divine agency apart from the order of nature, and results above any mere law of nature. There is like truth respecting many facts of the New Testament. In the birth and life of our Lord, in his lessons of truth and miracles of power and grace, in the ministry of his apostles, in the new spiritual life through the grace of the Gospel and the power of the Spirit, there are again the interpositions of a distinctively supernatural agency of God. Theology finds in the power of God the sufficient cause of such facts, and in his wisdom and grace their sufficient reason. There is no law of thought which requires more; certainly none which demands either their subjection to natural law or the denial of their reality. Theology has no issue with science respecting the reign of law in the realm of nature; but regards the demands of science, that the spiritual realm, if there be such, shall be subject to the same law, as the height of arrogance. Any attempted elimination of the supernatural from the Scriptures in the interest of theology is at once a perversion of the truth and a cowardly surrender to the adversary. Theism is supernaturalism. Revelation is supernaturalism. Christ himself is supernatural. Every true spiritual life is supernatural. We shall hold fast the supernatural in the interest of theology and religion.

It is the clear sense of Scripture that the divine agency in its supernatural interpositions reaches beyond the distinctively spiritual realm into the natural. These instances, however, are neither so frequent nor so radical REALMS. as to hinder the interests of science or unsettle the laws of our secular life. Still there are real instances of a supernatural agency within the lower sphere in the interest of the higher; within the lifeless in the interest of the living; within the natural in the interest of the spiritual. It is a rational law, and one ever observable in the process of nature, that the lower may be used in the service of the higher. Thus the divine agency is supernaturally operative within the lower forms of existence in the service of the higher. There is no true interpretation of the Scriptures without the truth of the supernatural.

5. *Providence the Privilege of Prayer.*—Were there no providence with a supernatural agency there could be no place for prayer. With the reality of such a providence, prayer is a common privilege, and the means of blessings not otherwise attainable. Hence objections to the efficacy of prayer are mostly the same as those urged against a supernatural providence, and so far require no separate review. They will be considered in the proper place. However, this may be said now, that all the proofs of a supernatural providence go to the refutation of these objections. The refutation is already quite sufficient.

Prayer is the supplication of the soul, offered up to God for his blessing. The forms of need may be many, and the answers may vary accordingly, but still with a blessing. PRAYER. The presuppositions of prayer are the personality and providence of God, his power over nature and mind, his interested watch-care over us, his kindly regard for our good, his gracious readiness to help us. The impulse to prayer arises from a sense of dependence and need. Beyond this, as the soul enters into the truer religious life prayer is imbued with the spirit of worship, is full of praise and love. There is the grateful sense of blessings received in answer to prayer. Hence the deeper ideas of prayer are the same in the thanksgiving as in the supplication.

The instinct for prayer is a part of our religious nature. We have a religious nature, and one as real and ineradicable as AN IMPULSE OF any other intrinsic quality. This is rarely questioned. OUR RELIGIOUS Thinkers who deny all supernaturalism in religion NATURE. openly confess this reality.[1] The logic of religious facts constrains this confession. The time when unbelief would banish all religion is forever past. Conscience and moral reason, the sense of God and duty, of dependence and need, are confessedly characteristic facts of our nature. With these facts, there is the instinctive impulse to prayer. This impulse must be active in the deeper exigencies of experience. The fact has often been exemplified, even with such as usually deny all religious faith. In the hour of painful suspense, in the presence of calamity, no unbelief can repress this impulse.

[1] Spencer: *First Principles*, pp. 13-15; Tyndall: *Preface to Belfast Address*, seventh edition.

The sense of Scripture on the question of prayer is very full and clear.[1] Prayer is a common duty and privilege.[2] Prayer should be offered for national blessings.[3] Intercessory prayer, prayer of one for another, is a requirement of the Scriptures.[4] Our prayer should be with persistence.[5] The help of the Spirit in our prayers is graciously promised.[6] There are many instances of timely and gracious answer to prayer. The blessings for which we may pray, and which are in the promised answer, are specially of a spiritual nature, but are far from being exclusively such. Secular blessings are included with the spiritual. God, who commands our prayer and promises the answer, is sovereign in the natural as in the spiritual realm. Our interests lie in both, though chiefly in the latter. Yet profound exigencies arise in the former. Both alike are known to our heavenly Father, who careth for us in all our wants. Prayer for temporal blessings has a divine warrant in the prayer of our Lord: "Give us this day our daily bread."

A few words may properly be added for the sake of the truth, and as a caution against fanaticism. Two facts are worthy of special notice. One is that the Jewish theocracy specially abounded in secular blessings. So far the truth holds, however false the view which denies to that economy all outlook beyond the present life. There were rich promises of such blessings, and these promises were often fulfilled in answer to prayer. We, however, are not warranted in the common expectation of answers so full and so openly supernatural under an economy so distinctly spiritual as the Christian in its blessings. The other fact is that the initial period of Christianity was specially supernatural, miraculous even, and that within the natural realm. What thus belonged distinctively to that period can have only a qualified application in subsequent ages. For instance, we are not warranted to expect the healing of the sick in a manner so openly supernatural as in that initial period. Nor have we reason to expect instant or even speedy release from bodily ills or other forms of trouble simply in answer to prayer. Certainly there should be limit to such expectation. Submission to the will of God must always qualify our faith in praying for such blessings. There is in the Scriptures

SENSE OF SCRIPTURE ON PRAYER.

CAUTION AGAINST FANATICISM.

---

[1] Paley: *Moral Philosophy*, book v, chap. iii.

[2] Matt. vii, 7, 11, Luke xxi, 36; Rom. xii, 12; Phil. iv, 6; 1 Thess. v, 17; 1 Tim. ii, 8.

[3] Psa. cxxii, 6; 1 Tim. ii, 1-3.

[4] Exod. xxxii, 11; Acts xii, 5; Rom. i, 9; xv, 30; James v, 16.

[5] Matt. xxvi, 44; Luke xviii, 1-8; 2 Cor. xii, 8.   [6] Rom. viii, 26, 27.

the lesson of patience in suffering. There are promises whose special grace is for such as endure suffering. These facts do not bar the privilege of prayer for temporal blessings, but should moderate the expectation of supernatural interpositions in a manner specially open and manifest. They should teach us the lesson of humble submission to the divine will. "Father, if thou be willing, remove this cup from me: nevertheless, not my will, but thine, be done."[1] How profound is this lesson! With this spirit, there is still a wide place for prayer in the seasons of temporal affliction. God may answer in our deliverance, or in the mitigation of our affliction. Or he may answer us as he answered Paul respecting the thorn in the flesh.[2] Our prayer shall not be in vain.

    LESSON OF PATIENCE

6. *Review of Leading Objections.*—A supernatural providence and the efficacy of prayer are so linked in principle that the same objections are common to both. Any distinction is so slight that it may be omitted in the present review. Certain things are alleged as the disproof of such a providence.

The divine perfections are assumed to be the ground of such an objection. We require some detail in order to a proper review of this objection. There are indeed several objections on the ground of these perfections, as severally viewed.

    THE DIVINE PERFECTIONS.

One objection is based on the divine immutability. The idea of a supernatural providence, with answers to prayer, is the idea of a temporal agency of God above the order of nature. The objection is that such an agency is contradictory to the divine immutability. There is no issue respecting the truth of immutability. Is such an agency contradictory to this truth? An affirmative answer must reduce our Christian theism to the baldest deism. Whatever the agency of God in the realms of nature and mind, it must be exercised through the personal energizing of his will. If such a personal providence is consistent with immutability, so are the definite acts of a supernatural providence. Only a false sense of immutability can require the same divine action toward nations and individuals, whatever the changes of moral conduct in them; the same toward Christian believers, whatever the changes of estate with them. A true sense of immutability requires changes of divine action in adjustment to such changes in men. It seems strange that any one who accepts the Scriptures can for a moment give place to this objection.

    IMMUTABILITY.

Another objection is based on the divine omniscience. This objection is made specially against the efficacy of prayer. God foreknows all things, knows from eternity the state and need of every

[1] Luke xxii, 42.   [2] 2 Cor. xii. 7-9.

soul.   Hence prayer is not necessary, nor can it have any influence upon the divine mind.   These inferences are not warranted.   If it were the office of prayer to give information of our wants, it is surely needless, and must be useless.   Prayer has no such office.   It is required as the proper religious movement of a soul in its dependence and need, and thus becomes the means of God's blessing.   The soul is doubly blest through such a condition of the divine blessing.   This will further appear.

OMNISCIENCE.

Again, objection to the need and efficacy of prayer is urged on the ground of the wisdom and goodness of God   He is wise and good, and, therefore, will give what is good without our asking.   We appropriate an answer : "This objection admits but of one answer, namely, that it may be agreeable to perfect wisdom to grant that to our prayers which it would not have been agreeable to the same wisdom to have given us without praying for. . . . A favor granted to prayer may be more apt, on that very account, to produce good effects upon the person obliged.   It may hold in the divine bounty, what experience has raised into a proverb in the collation of human benefits, that what is obtained without asking is oftentimes received without gratitude. It may be consistent with the wisdom of the Deity to withhold his favors till they be asked for, as an expedient to encourage devotion in his rational creation, in order thereby to keep up and circulate a knowledge and sense of their dependency upon him.   Prayer has a natural tendency to amend the petitioner himself ; and thus to bring him within the rules which the wisdom of the Deity has prescribed to the dispensation of his favors."[1]

WISDOM AND GOODNESS.

Some attempt an adjustment of providential events to the order of nature through the mediation of some higher, unknown law.   Such events would thus stand in harmony with nature, though above it as known to us.   There are weighty objections to this view   Such a higher law is the merest assumption, and therefore useless for the proposed adjustment. The weight of the objection to a supernatural providence is tacitly conceded, while this hypothetic law brings no answer   No difficulty is obviated or in the least relieved.   Further, how could such a law of nature be on hand just in the time of need, or wisely minister to us in the exigencies of our experience, or make timely answer to our prayers ?   There is no answer to such questions.   Nor can the theory admit any divine application of the law, for this would be the very supernaturalism which it assumes to displace.

NO HIGHER LAW OF NATURE

There is another mode in which it is attempted to place the facts

[1] Paley : *Moral Philosophy*, book v, chap. ii.

of providence in accord with the order of nature. It is that in the original constitution of nature God provided for the foreseen wants and prayers of men. Thus the plan of providence is supernatural, but the mode of its minis-tries is purely natural. NO ORIGINAL PROVISION OF NATURE. The theory must hold the reality of natural forces. Otherwise God is the only force in nature, and the original provisions of his providence must mean simply a determination of the modes of his own future agency on the contingency of human exigencies and prayers. This, however, is the extremest form of supernaturalism, and therefore out of all consistency with the theory. With the reality of natural forces, the difficulties of the theory become insuperable. It is assumed that such forces act with absolute uniformity. This is the principle on which a super-natural providence is denied. How, then, can original provision be made for answers to future prayers through the agency of such forces ? If human actions were a part of the processes of nature and subject to the same necessity, such provision might be made. With the freedom of human action, it is impossible. The forces of nature, which in themselves ever act in accord with their own laws, can never turn aside to meet the exigencies of our experi-ence or to answer our prayers. This is the work of a supernatural providence.[1]

The uniformity of nature is often asserted in objection to a super-natural providence. So far as this objection is con-cerned, such uniformity is simply a question of fact, and therefore must be proved before the objection can be valid. UNIFORMITY OF NATURE. The actual uniformity of nature is no *a priori* truth. The con-trary is clearly thinkable and possible. The Author of nature can vary the working of its laws, and may often have reason for such interposition. Hence the question of an unvaried uniformity re-quires proof, just as any other question of fact. It never has been proved; nor can it ever be.[2] It might appear that nature, so far as open to our observation, is uniform; but such observation reaches only to a small segment of the whole. Further, the causal force is never open to sense-perception, and an event which might seem to arise from natural forces might in fact arise from the supernatural agency of God. He could so alter the meteorological conditions in a given place that a storm should quickly replace the calm. In such a case there would appear only the signs of natural force, but the affirma-tion of unvaried uniformity would be false to the deepest truth. It might be assumed that the forces of nature are always uniform in

[1] Buchanan : *Modern Atheism*, pp. 283–301 ; Mozley : *On Miracles*, lect. vi.
[2] Jevons : *Principles of Science*, pp. 149–152, 765.

their own working, but an unvaried uniformity would not follow.
For such a consequence it would still be necessary to prove that
they are the only forces operative in nature. Of this there is no
proof. The agency of mind is conclusive of the contrary. Mind
is an agency above that order of forces of which uniformity is alleged, and often so modifies their working as to vary their results.
So, there may be, and there is, a divine mind operative within the
realm of nature, and in a manner to modify the results of mere
natural force.

This objection advances beyond the previous ground, and denies
ABSOLUTE UNI- the possibility of a supernatural providence. The posi-
FORMITY   tion would be valid upon the ground of both materialism and pantheism ; but neither of these theories is verified, and
so far the position is groundless. As previously pointed out, personal mind acting under a law of freedom is an agency above the
forces of nature, and, in distinction from them, strictly supernatural.[1] This is the disproof of an absolute naturalism. The
only ground of such a naturalism is atheism; but atheism is not
proved. If there be a personal God, a supernatural providence is
surely possible. So plain a truth must be clear to all minds with
sufficient intelligence to understand the proposition. John Stuart
Mill deserved no praise, though he has been praised, for saying that
if there be a personal God a miracle is possible. Of course it is;
and the denial of so plain a truth would betoken the most willful
blindness. The possibility of a miracle is the possibility of a supernatural providence through a divine variation of the working of
natural forces. The truth of theism is the refutation of this objection to a supernatural providence.

It is objected to a supernatural providence that it must prove
VIOLENCE AND   itself a disorderly and disruptive agency within the
DISRUPTION   order of nature. "Without a disturbance of natural law, quite as serious as the stoppage of an eclipse, or the
rolling of the St. Lawrence up the Falls of Niagara, no act of
humiliation, individual or national, could call one shower from
heaven, or deflect toward us a single beam of the sun." "Assuming the efficacy of free prayer to produce changes in external
nature, it necessarily follows that natural laws are more or less at
the mercy of man's volition, and no conclusion founded on the assumed permanence of those laws would be worthy of confidence."[2]
These statements are without logical warrant, and are plausible only
through exaggeration and distortion. The efficacy of prayer does

[1] Bushnell · *Nature and the Supernatural*, chap. ii.
[2] Tyndall · *Fragments of Science*, pp. 361, 362.

not subject the course of nature to the caprice of men. Nor is the
agency of providence subversive of the order of nature. Representations more false to the sense of a supernatural providence are
scarcely possible.

A supernatural providence is the agency of God within the realm
of his own works. The laws of nature are his own or-   PROVIDENCE
dination. His supernatural agency is not the disrup-   AN   ORDERLY
tion of nature, not a suspension of the laws of nature,   AGENCY.
but an interposition which in particular instances produces new
results. By new adjustments and combinations within the sphere
of nature we often modify the results, and without any violence or
disorder. The mechanist so constructs his machinery that its
movement may be adjusted to changing conditions. Its higher
perfection appears in this fact. There is no disorder in the varied
movement. We should not think less of the wisdom of God in
the constitution and government of nature. As a chemist may
vary results by new combinations, or an engineer hasten or slacken
the speed of his train, or a father recast the thought and impulse of his child, so may God interpose the agency of a supernatural providence within the realm of his own creation and government.

The miracles of Scripture, just as they stand in the several narratives, involve no disruption of the constitution of   ILLUSTRA-
nature. A mighty rain in answer to the prayer of   TIONS.
Elijah is phenomenally the same as if arising in the regular course
of nature, and just as free from violence or disorder. God could
so change the local conditions of the atmosphere without any
change of the laws of nature. Suppose it true that through his
immediate agency an ax-head rose from the bottom of the Jordan to the surface of the water : the fact involved no violence or
disruption of nature. The law of gravitation was not suspended.
The river did not take to the hills. No mountain trembled or
toppled. Iron ores remained quiet in their beds. There was no
reeling of the earth nor falling of the stars. Suppose Elisha had
recovered the ax-head with a grapple: even more gently and orderly
did the agency of God lift it to the surface of the water. The word
of Christ which calms the storm and the sea is no more a disorderly
agency than the oil which quiets the beating waves. Dietetics
remain the same after the miraculous feeding of thousands with a
few loaves and fishes. The common laws of life and death are the
same after the resurrection of Lazarus as before it, yea, the very
same in the instant of his reviviscence. The violence and disruption of a supernatural providence are the picturings of a distorted

imagination, and no part of the reality. Nature remains the same for science and all the practical interests of life.

Mind is the chief sphere of a supernatural providence; and there INSTANCE IN is here the same absence of disorder. The divine agency MIND. acts upon individual minds, and in a manner accordant with the laws of mental action. Personal agency and moral freedom remain complete. It is often the case that one man influences the thought and feeling of another, and thus indirectly influences his action. In like manner the teacher influences the pupil, the parent the child. Here indeed is a law of great potency in human life, but so far as it operates in accordance with the laws of personal agency it is free from all violence. By an immediate agency operative within the mind God can move man's thoughts and feelings in like accordance with his mental constitution and personal agency, yet so as to induce new forms of action. So orderly is this agency of providence within the realm of mind.

The facts of a supernatural providence differ from miracles in FURTHER IL- their office, and therefore in respect to manifestation. LUSTRATIONS It is the special function of the latter to accredit God's messengers of truth; therefore they must be open to sense-perception. The former, while no less supernatural, have no such special mission, and therefore require no such manifestation. In accordance with this fact the end of a supernatural providence may often be reached as readily through the laws of mind as through the forces of nature. Hence, if it could be determined that events which have answered great ends were purely natural within the physical realm, it would not follow that there was no supernatural agency connected with them. Were the timely storms which destroyed the invincible Armada the immediate work of God? Whether such or not, a true faith sees the hand of God in the great event. There was a simpler and more rational mode of the divine agency than in the origination of these storms for the hour; and the recognition of such an alternative would have been quite as creditable to Macaulay as his rather flippant criticism of the popular judgment in the case.[1] Just when the Armada should reach the place of its disaster was not the determination of natural law. In the contingency of human agency its arrival might have been earlier or later. How easy for the divine agency, acting upon a few minds, or even upon one controlling mind, to hasten or delay the sailing, so that the fleet intended for the destruction of England should encounter the whelming storms which arose purely in the order of nature! Surely the profound interests contingent upon the result justify the

[1] *History of England*, chap. ix.

faith in such a providence. In a few questions Pope embodies the objections, whether on philosophic or scientific grounds, to a supernatural providence.[1] Shall God reverse his laws for his favorites ? Shall gravitation cease when one may be passing a mountain just ready to fall ? The only apparent force of these questions is in the false assumption that physical nature is the exclusive sphere of a supernatural providence. Then this false assumption is infinitely exaggerated in the view that such an interposition of providence must be only through a universal suspension of some law of nature. We have previously shown the falsity of this view. A man stays a falling rock till his imperiled friend escapes ; but surely he does not repeal the law of gravitation. It suffices that, for the time, he counterworks its force in the impending rock. What man so does God may do. But, as previously pointed out, there is still a simpler mode of the divine agency in any such case. God can accomplish his pleasure through the laws of mind.[2]

The question of so much evil in human life must arise in connection with several points in the course of theological discussion. Only a theodicy could fully dispose of its perplexities. That there is a theodicy we have no doubt; but we are quite as sure that for us it is an impossible attainment. While righteousness and judgment are the habitation of God's throne, clouds and darkness are round about him.[3] With these facts before us, a few words may here suffice. MAGNITUDE OF EVIL.

There is no solution of the question in the principle of Optimism —that the universe, and therefore the world as a part of it, is the best that could be created. The principle must be a deduction from the absolute righteousness of God as its only possible ground. The issue is thus closed against all objections arising from the magnitude of evil, but only by the assumption of the righteousness against which they are urged. There is no light for our understanding in such dialectics. For such illumination we would require not only the primary truth of an absolute divine righteousness, but also a comprehension of the present world as the best possible. We have no such power; and any attempt to solve the perplexities of sin and suffering in such a mode is but a vain endeavor. It is far better not to attempt the impossible. For our understanding, human ills do perplex the question of a supernatural providence. The righteousness of God, clearly manifest despite these ills, is the vindication of his providence for our faith. This is the utmost attainment for the present life. NO SOLUTION IN OPTIMISM.

---

[1] Essay on Man.   [2] McCosh. The Divine Government, pp. 182, 183.
[3] Psa. xcvii, 2.

Life is a moral probation. This is the paramount fact of our
LIFE A PROBA- present existence, the fact in which our deepest inter-
TION. ests center. The ministries of a supernatural providence must be in adjustment to such a probation. It does not
follow that freedom from all present evil is a requirement of its
offices. Sin is a possibility of such probation, and has become actual. This is the source of human ills. With the fact of sin and
its attendant ills, our moral probation still remains, with its profound contingencies. Providence must deal with us in view of all
these facts. Our highest good must be its aim. What shall be its
method? We dare not say that its wisest method is in the prevention of all present suffering, or in its reduction to the smallest possible measure. Our moral interests are paramount; and it may be
the case, and no doubt is, that the wiser method of providence in
their favor is in the permission and use of present suffering. What
seems to us an evil may be a good. We rashly assume a knowledge
of what would be the wisest ministries of providence, and thus involve ourselves in perplexity and doubt. A little child knows not
its own interests, and therefore knows not the wisest parental treatment. No more can we know what measures and ministries of
providence shall best accord with its wisdom.

With the deepest mystery of suffering, what would be gained by
NO GAIN IN the denial of a supernatural providence? The denial
ATHEISM would not lessen the ills of life, but would deprive us
of the divinest inspiration of trust and patience and hope. God
would no longer be for the soul an assured "refuge and strength,
a very present help in trouble."[1] From the persuasion of a supernatural providence springs the heroism of faith. With this truth,
Paul could say, even in the deepest trouble, and with the profoundest sense of security, "I know whom I have believed;"[2] and
Job could say, "Though he slay me, yet will I trust in him."[3] If
we read with the Revised Version, "Yet will I wait for him," the
sense appears little changed, especially in view of the context. Such
a faith is the strength of the soul, and the formative power of the
noblest life.

The ills of life, however, are not all in utter darkness. When
punitive they have an explanation in the demerit of sin, and no
SOME LIGHT ground of complaint remains. Often afflictions have
a disciplinary office, and are ministries of love. We
need their correcting and restraining force, and are the better for
their patient endurance. Thus the chastenings of the heavenly
Father proceed from his love, with the aim of our highest good.

[1] Psa. xlvi, 1.   [2] 2 Tim. i, 12.   [3] Job xiii, 15.

Though for the present grievous, and not joyous, they are fruitful of righteousness.[1] This whole lesson on the ministry of suffering is replete with the deepest truth. If such afflictions fail of their proper results, the fault is our own. We may pervert them just as we may pervert the most direct blessings of life. It suffices for the vindication of providence, that they are wisely and graciously intended as the means of our greatest good. When rightly endured their fruitage is in blessedness. "Behold, we count them happy which endure. Ye have heard of the patience of Job, and have seen the end of the Lord; that the Lord is very pitiful, and of tender mercy."[2] In the instances of Abraham, and Joseph, and Moses, and Daniel, and Paul, life is tested in the furnace of affliction, and the gold is only the purer for the trial. In addition to their own personal good, how valuable the lesson of their patience and piety! That lesson has been the inspiration of many a true soul. Nor have all the passing centuries exhausted its helpful influence. It is still working for good, and will continue so to work through all the coming centuries.

For Christian thought the truth of a supernatural providence stands in the clear light of the cross. This is the great fact of such a providence in behalf of the world and the interests of moral government. It is the crown- LIGHT FOR CHRISTIAN FAITH ing fact of blessing through suffering; of blessing for the many through the suffering of the One. It is replete and radiant with the divine wisdom and love. In it center the divinest moral truths. There is no murmur upon the lips of Christ, as against a dark and afflictive providence, that he should so suffer for the good of others. In the presence of the cross there should be with us no murmurings against the ills of life, no doubt of a good providence over us, but patience and faith, and the inspiration of the truest, best life

---

[1] Heb xii, 5–11.   [2] Jas. v, 11.

General reference.—Sherlock: *On Providence*; Young: *The Providence of God Displayed*; Flavel: *Divine Conduct, or the Mystery of Providence*; Croly: *Divine Providence*; Pilkington: *Doctrine of Providence*; Proclus: *Essay on Providence*; Wood: *Works*, lects. xlii–xlv; Hodge: *Systematic Theology*, vol. i, part i, chap. xi; Knapp: *Christian Theology*, secs. 67–72; McCosh: *The Divine Government*, book ii; Dorner: *System of Christian Doctrine*, vol. ii, pp 44–62; Shedd: *Dogmatic Theology*, Theology, chap. viii; Van Oosterzee: *Christian Dogmatics*, secs. lix–lxiv; Smith: *System of Christian Theology*, pp. 102–114; Strong: *Systematic Theology*, pp 202–220.

PART III.

ANTHROPOLOGY.

ANTHROPOLOGY.

THE one term, anthropology, has both a theological and a scientific use. Theological anthropology deals with the facts of man's moral and religious constitution and history as related to Christian doctrine, while scientific anthropology deals with his specifical characteristics. However, in the latter case there are wide variations. With naturalists anthropology means the natural history of the race With German philosophers the term is so broadened as to include psychology, sociology, and ethics, together with anatomy and physiology.[1] Hence in works with the common title of anthropology there is a great difference in the range of topics. In the wider range some things are included which belong also to theology. However, enough difference still remains for the division into a scientific and a theological anthropology.

It should be noted that this distinction simply differentiates topics, not methods of treatment. It is not meant that the treatment of scientific anthropology is any more scientific than the treatment of theological anthropology

In a philosophy of religion all the facts which concern the moral and religious constitution and history of man might properly be called anthropological. This would greatly broaden the term, as we found it broadened in the scientific sphere In an evangelical theology, however, the view of anthropology is largely determined by its relation to the mediation of Christ. Man is thus viewed as in need of redemption and salvation. This need arises from the fact of sin, or the common sinful state of man This state is the chief question of doctrinal anthropology. It is, in accordance with theological formulation, the doctrine of sin. But a proper treatment of this doctrine requires a previous treatment of primitive man, his probation and fall, and the consequence of that moral lapse to the race. With this question of consequence the further question of our relation to the Adamic probation arises—whether it was such as to involve us in the guilt and punishment of Adam's sin. There is still a further

ANTHROPO-LOGICAL DOC-TRINES

[1] Krauth-Fleming · *Vocabulary of the Philosophical Sciences*, Anthropology.

21

question—whether the common native depravity, as consequent to the Adamic fall, has in itself the demerit of sin. We have thus indicated, in a summary way, the leading questions of anthropology in a system of Christian doctrine. In their discussion they will appear in their proper order, and with more exact formulation.

These questions are not simply of speculative interest, or merely CARDINAL IN incidental to a system of Christian theology, but in-THEOLOGY. trinsic and determining. In any system, whether evangelical or rationalistic, the anthropology and soteriology must be in scientific accordance. If we start from the side of anthropology, our soteriology must follow accordingly. If we proceed in the reverse order, a like consequence must follow for our anthropology. If our present state is the same as our primitive state, if there is no moral lapse of the race, and no common native depravity, there can be no need of a redemptive mediation in Christ, nor of regeneration through the agency of the Holy Spirit. To allege any such necessity is to assume an original constitution of man in a state of moral evil and ruin. No theory of Christianity can rationally admit such an implication. With a moral lapse of the race and a common native depravity, we need the redemptive mediation of Christ, and the offices of the Holy Spirit in our regeneration and spiritual life. For the reality of these facts we require the divinity of the Christ, the personality and divinity of the Holy Spirit. With these truths we require the truth of the divine Trinity. On a denial of the primitive lapse and moral ruin of the race, all these great truths may be dismissed. They can have no proper place in theology. So intrinsic and determining is the doctrine of anthropology in a system of Christian theology. " Original sin is the foundation upon which we must build the teaching of Christian theology. This universal evil is the primary fact, the leading truth whence the science takes its departure; and it is this which forms the peculiar distinction of theology from sciences which work their own advancement by the powers of reason." [1]

CHAPTER I.

PRELIMINARY QUESTIONS.

THE origin of man, the time of his origin, and the unity of the race are open questions of science, and, with the wide study of anthropology, could not fail to be brought into scientific treatment. These same questions are also related, more or less intimately, to

[1] *Melanchthon.*

theological anthropology. Instances of divergence in scientific and doctrinal opinion are not to be thought strange. With the extreme views of some scientists, certain points of issue arise, more especially respecting the origin of man and the time of his origin. On the side of revelation these questions specially concern the offices of exegesis and apologetics; yet they are so related to systematic theology that we cannot pass them without some notice. A summary treatment will suffice.

I. THE ORIGIN OF MAN.

1. *In Theories of Evolution.*—Theories of evolution widely differ in the account which they give of the origin and progress of life in its manifold forms. The variations range from a materialistic ground up to a form held to be consistent with biblical theism. With this wide range of theories, and with the marked characteristics of man which differentiate him from all other forms of organic being, evolutionists specially differ respecting his origin. We may notice three views.

First, then, there is the theory which is purely materialistic and atheistic in its principles. Matter is the only real being, and is eternal. Primordially, it existed in the condition of a vastly diffused fire-mist. The inception of evolution was from the nature of matter in such a state. Such was the beginning. The whole process has been equally naturalistic. There is no other force than such as in some way belongs to matter. Man is the product of this force, not immediately in the order of sequence, but none the less really; for, according to this doctrine of evolution, all the force ever operative in the universe existed potentially in the original fire-mist. Such is the origin of man in this theory. He is the outcome of a long process in the ascending scale of evolution, but none the less a product of mere material force. There is such a theory of evolution. Its advocates are not the many, yet it has its representative names. We have no occasion again to controvert the theory. THE ATHEISTIC THEORY.

Another theory admits the interposition of a divine agency, but only in a very restricted measure. Originally Mr. Darwin attributed the inception of living orders to such an agency. But the primary endowment of one or, at most, a few simple forms with life is with him the sum of that agency. There is no divine interposition at any other point. From this inception the whole process of evolution is purely naturalistic. Man is the outcome of this process. His origin is the same and one with the lowest forms of life. There is no provision for any essential distinction of mind. THE THEISTIC THEORY.

In a third view, God was not only operative in the inception of life, but has continued his agency through the whole process of evolution. Some regard evolution simply as the method of his creative work. Hence in the evolution of new species mere natural force is replaced by the divine agency. Special account is made of this agency in the evolution of man. From this point, however, opinions may widely diverge. The divergence is into different views of the nature of man. There may be no profound distinction between his physical and mental natures. Mind itself may be regarded as a product of evolution, and without any essential distinction from the body. With others there is a profound distinction between the two; and, while the body is an evolution, the mind is an immediate creation of God.

2. *In the Sense of Scripture.*—We turn to the sacred narratives of man's creation for the Scripture sense of his origin. The whole account is given in comparatively few words. "And God said, Let us make man in our image, after our likeness."[1] In these words, with their connection, a few facts are specially noteworthy. In the process of this narrative we have the several phrases, "Let there be;" "Let the earth bring forth;" "Let the waters bring forth."[2] These words signify the divine energizing in the work of creation. Any interpretation which limits the sense to an agency of nature is utterly false to the deeper truth. "The earth" and "the waters" mean the fields of the divine agency rather than any creative agency of their own. While these forms of expression are entirely consistent with the use of secondary causes in the method of creation, they never can be interpreted satisfactorily without the divine agency.

DIVINE AGENCY IN CREATION

There is a notable change in the form of words respecting the creation of man. He is the last in the successive orders, and the crown of the whole. There is a change in the divine procedure; no longer an immediate word of creative energy, but deliberation, preparatory counsel. "Let us make man." The truth of the Trinity, implicit in these words, becomes explicit as we read them in the light of the more perfect revelation. The grade of man in the scale of creation is marked with the deepest emphasis: "Let us make man in our image, after our likeness." All the deep meaning of these words is not for present inquiry. Their most open sense places man above all other orders as a spiritual, personal being. We read the same meaning in the dominion assigned him over all other orders.[3] He was created in the likeness of God to this end, and with qualification

MAN AN ORIGINAL CREATION

<hr/>

[1] Gen. i, 26.   [2] Gen. i, 3, 11, 20.   [3] Gen. i, 26, 28.

for this headship. These facts place the origin of man in an immediate divine creation.[1]

In the second narrative of man's creation we read: "And the Lord God formed man of the dust of the ground, and breathed into his nostrils the breath of life; and man became a living soul."[2] There is no contradiction, not even discrepancy, between these two narratives. The second is more specific respecting a few facts, but in entire consistency with the more general account. In the second there is a distinction of soul and body. Even without this second narrative, the same distinction would have been read into the first. Otherwise, the body rather than the soul would have been omitted from the meaning, because, without the latter, in no proper sense could man be the image of God. The formation of the body from the dust of the ground, or out of existing material, is also a more specific fact of the second narrative. With only the first narrative, such would have been the more rational inference. So consistent are the two respecting this fact. Again, in the first narrative we learn that God created man male and female; but only the general fact is stated.[3] Then in the second the specific manner of woman's creation is given.[4] Thus through and through the two narratives are in full accord. Man is still so distinct from all other orders that we must assign his origin to an original creation.

3. *Relation of the Question to Theology.*—With a purely naturalistic evolution, and inclusive of man as of all lower orders, no place remains for a theological anthropology or for any form of theology. Outright materialism is the only ground of such an evolution; and outright materialism is outright atheism. With atheism, atheology.

The second theory, which admits a divine agency in the inception of life, but finds no place for that agency in the whole process of evolution, not even in the origin of man, leaves no ground for a doctrinal anthropology as related to other central doctrines of Christianity. Man remains thoroughly implicated in the course of nature. Indeed, he is but a part of nature, down in the dead level of the whole, and without any essential distinction in himself. The theory pushes God so far from the course of nature, and so utterly away from man, that for religion and theology it is practically atheistic. No theory of evolution which denies an immediate and transcendent agency

THE SECOND NARRATIVE.

[1] Macdonald · *Creation and the Fall*, pp. 287–291 ; Laidlaw: *Bible Doctrine of Man*, pp. 277–279.

[2] Gen. ii, 7   [3] Gen. i, 27.   [4] Gen. ii, 21, 22.

of God in the origin of man can be consistent with Christian theology.

The third form of evolution, which excepts the mind from the process of nature and accounts its origin to the transcendent agency of God, stands in a very different relation to theology. The evolution of man in his physiological constitution, if established as a truth, would raise new questions of exegesis, but would not unsettle the grounds of Christian doctrine. Some theologians and expositors, with thorough loyalty to the Scriptures, hold this view. The position is that, while the Scriptures account the origin of the human species, even in its physical constitution, to the divine agency, they leave it an open question whether the method of that agency was by a mediate or immediate creation. Whether God formed the body of primitive man immediately from the ground or mediately through a long process of genetic derivation does not in itself affect either his complete constitution as man or his place in Scripture, as related to theological anthropology.

AN EVOLUTION CONSISTENT WITH THEOLOGY.

The modern hypothesis of evolution should cause no alarm for Christian theology. Evolution itself is as yet a mere hypothesis, unverified as a theory. A purely naturalistic evolution is not only unproved, but in the very nature of the case is unprovable. With the evolution of the human body, the human mind would still stand apart from the physical process, with the only account of its origin in the creative agency of God. There is no urgency for haste in making terms with modern evolution. It is only an hypothetic structure, without the substance of a science. With limitless assumption and dogmatism, it lacks the material for the foundation of a science. There must be long waiting for the superstructure. The evolution of the human race is wholly without proof, and the sheerest assumption. There is the broad margin between man and the highest order below him—confessedly too broad for crossing by a single transition in the process of evolution. All search for connecting links is utterly fruitless. That broad margin remains without the slighfest token of successive stages in the transition across to man. The Bible account of his origin in the creative agency of God remains, and will remain, the only rational account. The grounds of a theological anthropology remain secure.

THEOLOGY NOT IN PERIL.

II. TIME OF MAN'S ORIGIN.

The question of the antiquity of man could not fail of prominence in the discussions of modern science. As students of nature trace the marks of change in the spheres of cosmogony, geology, zoology, archæology, the question of time must con- INTEREST OF stantly arise. The division of geology into periods THE QUESTION keeps the question ever present in that study. Period will be compared with period in respect to length of duration. A fuller knowledge of nature is possible only with some insight into the measures of time occupied in the processes of change. This question, so constantly present, could not fail of special interest in its application to man. Even for the extremest evolutionist his appearance must have an interest above every other event in the course of nature. Very naturally, therefore, the signs of his presence have been carefully traced, and deeply studied in connection with such other facts as might be helpful toward a proximate measurement of his time in the natural history of the world.

Scientists are agreed that, of all living orders in the world's history, man came last. They are equally agreed that his WIDELY DIF-origin is comparatively recent. But a comparative FERING VIEWS. recency in geological time may be very long ago—so long as to dwarf the centuries of biblical chronology into mere hours. Such measurements are made. An issue thus arises, for the thorough discussion of which only a large volume would answer. We can do little more than state the question. It may be said here that these measurements of man's time on earth vary almost infinitely, and that this fact denies to scientists infallibility on the question. Not only are they at such variance, but some measure a time in no serious issue with biblical chronology, on a permissible extension of its centuries.

1. *In the View of Biblical Chronology.*—It is well known that biblical chronology remains, as it ever has been, an NO DOCTRINE open question. Individuals may have been very posi- OF BIBLICAL tive respecting the exact years of the great epochal CHRONOLOGY events in the world's history, but there is no common concurrence in such a view. The profoundest students of the question find different measures of time, not varying so widely as between scientists, yet sufficiently to be of value in the adjustment of the seeming issue with facts of science. The leading views are well known and easily stated. The origin of man preceded the advent of our Lord by 4,004 years, as reckoned by Usher on the ground of the Hebrew Scriptures; by 5,411 years, as reckoned by Hales on the ground of the Septuagint Version. Here is a margin of 1,407 years, which might cover many facts of science respecting the presence of man in the world, and bring them into harmony with biblical chronology. The acceptance of this reckoning requires no cunning

device. While through the Vulgate Version the shorter period gained ascendency in the Western Church, in the Eastern the longer period prevailed. With the whole Church it has been quite as common; and, while a lower estimate than that of Usher has rarely been made, a longer reckoning than that of Hales has not been rare.

The uncertainty of biblical chronology is of special value in its UNCERTAINTY OF THE DATA. adjustment to the reasonable claims of science respecting the time of man's origin. That uncertainty is no recent assumption, no mere device which the exigency of an issue with science has forced upon biblical chronologists, but has long been felt and openly expressed. The many different and widely varying results of the most careful reckoning witness to the uncertainty of the data upon which that reckoning proceeds. The tables of genealogy are the chief data in the case, and their aim is to trace the lines of descent, not to mark the succession of years. Hence the line of connection is not always traced immediately from father to son, but often the transition is to a descendant several generations later—which answers just as well for the ruling purpose, however it may perplex the question of time. "Thus in Gen. xlvi, 18, after recording the sons of Zilpa, her grandsons and her great-grandsons, the writer adds, 'These are the sons of Zilpa, . . . and these she bare unto Jacob, even sixteen souls.' The same thing recurs in the case of Bilha, verse 25, '*she* bare these unto Jacob: all the souls were seven.' Compare verses 15, 22. No one can pretend that the author of this register did not use the term understandingly of descendants beyond the first generation. In like manner, according to Matt. i, 11, Josias begat his grandson Jechonias, and verse 8, Joram begat his great-grandson Ozias. And in Gen. x, 15–18, Canaan, the grandson of Noah, is said to have begotten several whole nations, the Jebusite, the Amorite, the Girgasite, the Hivite, etc. Nothing can be plainer, therefore, than that, in the usage of the Bible, 'to bear' and 'to beget' are used in a wide sense to indicate descent, without restricting this to the immediate offspring."[1] It would be easy to give many other instances of a like presentation of facts. Such facts justify the prevalent uncertainty respecting biblical chronology. Indeed, the tables which furnish the chief data for its construction are purely genealogical, and in no proper sense chronological. With such uncertainty of data, no biblical chronology can have either fixed limits or doctrinal claim. It follows that the usual reckoning may be so

[1] Green. *The Pentateuch Vindicated from the Aspersions of Bishop Colenso*, p. 132.

extended as to meet any reasonable requirement of scientific facts respecting the time of man's origin, without the perversion of any part of Scripture or the violation of any law of hermeneutics. Such are the views of theologians thoroughly orthodox in creed and most loyal to the Scriptures.[1]

2. *Scientific Claim of a High Antiquity.*—While scientists are agreed that man is the latest of living orders, and com- VIEWS OF SCI-paratively very recent, there is with them a wide range ENTISTS. of opinion respecting the time of his origin. Many are agreed in assigning him a high antiquity. However, beyond this point of agreement the range is from a comparatively moderate reckoning, say 100,000 years, up to millions, and even hundreds of millions. Figures, however, are rarely given, but alleged facts are assumed to measure vast ages. Lyell thinks he can trace the signs of man's existence up to the post-pliocene era, and anticipates the finding of his remains in the pliocene period.[2] LYELL. Only an immense reach of time can carry us back to that period. Again, he thinks that the facts of geology "point distinctly to the vast antiquity of paleolithic man."[3]   After a review of some of the evidences of man's antiquity Huxley puts the question of time thus : " Where, then, must we look HUXLEY. for primitive man ? Was the oldest *Homo sapiens* pliocene or miocene, or yet more ancient?"[4]   Without the "yet more ancient," he had already gone back into the midst of the tertiary period. By so much does he transcend Lyell   On the truth of evolution Huxley is sure that " we must extend by long epochs the most liberal estimate that has yet been made of the antiquity of man."   Sir John Lubbock is quite up with Lyell ; indeed, we may say, quite up with Huxley. The relative facts of geology "impress us with a vague and overpowering sense of an- LUBBOCK. tiquity. . . . But it may be doubted whether even geologists yet realize the great antiquity of our race."[5]   Lubbock believes in miocene man, but rather as an implication of evolution than from any discovered sign of his presence in that ancient geologic age.[6] Wallace is comparatively very moderate, but reaches out for a long time   " We can with tolerable certainty affirm WALLACE that man must have inhabited the earth a thousand centuries ago, but we cannot assert that he positively did not exist, or that there

---

[1] Hodge : *Systematic Theology*, vol. 11, pp 40, 41 ; Pope : *Christian Theology*, vol. 1, pp 219, 434 ; Strong : *Systematic Theology*, p 106
[2] *Antiquity of Man*, p. 399   [3] *Principles of Geology*, vol. 11, p 570.
[4] *Man's Place in Nature*, p. 184.   [5] Lubbock : *Prehistoric Times*, p. 419.
[6] *Ibid* , p 423.

is any good evidence against his having existed, for a period of ten thousand centuries."[1]   We have given a few instances.   Many scientists of like views might be added to the list.

3. *Review of Alleged Proofs.*—The sources of evidence for a high antiquity of man are well defined, and appear with much uniformity in the fuller treatment of the question.   However, the treatment is often partial, when the evidence from only a few sources, perhaps from only one, is adduced.   This is the method of Huxley, who treats the question simply in view of fossil remains of man, particularly of fossil skulls.[2]   A summary of the sources of evidence in a comprehensive treatment is given by Southall,[3] and also by the Duke of Argyll.[4]   These summaries, while varying in words, are much the same in their facts.   The comprehensive discussions of the question by Sir Charles Lyell[5] and Sir John Lubbock[6] are substantially in the method of these classifications.

We may state the evidences of a high antiquity of man in the
SUMMARY OF   following order : 1. History, with special reference to
PROOFS   the antiquity of nations.   2. Archæology, including
many forms of fact which show the early presence and agency of man.   3 Geology, with special reference to drift deposits. 4 Language—the time necessary for its growth and multiplication into so many forms.   5. The distinction of races in color and feature.   Our brief review cannot fully adhere to this order.

The evidence from history centers in the proof of an early exist-
HISTORY   ence of separate nations or kingdoms.   Contemporary
with the earliest history of Abraham, twenty centuries before the Christian era, Chaldea and Egypt appear as strong and flourishing kingdoms.   Kings with separate realms are already numerous, mostly with small dominion, but some perhaps, as appeared a little later in the case of Chedorlaomer, king of Elam, with broad sway.   So much may fairly be gathered from the Scriptures.[7]   The evidence of history and archæology seems conclusive that in the time of Abraham Egypt was a strong kingdom, with a high form of civilization.   Such a kingdom could not be the growth of a few years ; and we may add an antecedent history of from five to seven centuries.   Renouf would add many more,[8] but the number named will suffice.   There were other kingdoms and civilizations, the Babylonian, Persian, Indian, and Chinese, of about the same antiquity.   They also came into history about the time of Abraham,

[1] *On Natural Selection*, p 303.   [2] *Man's Place in Nature*, p. 140.
[3] *The Recent Origin of Man*, p. 86.   [4] *Primeval Man*, pp. 76–78.
[5] *Antiquity of Man.*   [6] *Prehistoric Times.*
[7] Gen xi–xiv.   [8] *The Religion of Ancient Egypt*, lect. ii.

but, with Egypt, required previous centuries of growth. "So far, then, we have the light of history shining with comparative clearness over a period of two thousand years before the Christian era. Beyond that we have a twilight tract of time which may be roughly estimated at seven hundred years—a period of time lying in the dawn of history, at the very beginning of which we can dimly see that there were already kings and princes on the earth."[1]

It thus appears that history, with its clear implications, carries the existence of distinct nations back to the time of the flood—as that time is usually reckoned We have three alternatives : either a narrow limitation of the flood, or a plurality of human origins, or an extension of our biblical chronology anterior to the call of Abraham. No sufficient limitation of the flood is permissible. If consistently with the Scriptures we might in this mode account for the existence of the distant nations of India and China, we could not so account for the equally early, rather earlier, nations in the regions of the Tigris and the Euphrates These regions could not have escaped the flood. A plurality of human origins is contrary to the Scriptures and to the facts of science, and inconsistent with the deepest truths of Christian theology. The third alternative may be accepted without the slightest hesitation. There is no fixed chronology of the Scriptures before the time of Abraham. Hence there is nothing against the addition of all the time—say two or three thousand years—which the facts of human history may require

Many facts adduced in evidence of a high antiquity of man may be grouped under the heads of archæology and geology. In some classifications the two terms represent distinct sets of facts. The distinction, however, is but slight, and may be omitted in our brief discussion. Under these headings we have several classes of facts, and many particulars of each class—altogether too many for present notice We may name as classes— megalithic structures and tumuli ; lake-dwellings ; shell-mounds ; peat-bogs ; bone-caves ; drift-deposits. The point of the argument in each is that the remains of man and the products of his agency appear in conditions which prove his high antiquity.[2] This argument is fully elaborated by the authors named

We shall give a very brief reply in the words of an eminent scientist "The calculations of long time based on the gravels of the Somme, on the cone of the Tinière, on the peat-bogs of

[1] Argyll Primeval Man, p 95.
[2] Lubbock Prehistoric Times; Lyell Antiquity of Man; Jeffries Natural History of the Human Races; Quatrefages: The Human Species, pp. 129-153.

France and Denmark, on certain cavern deposits, have all been
shown to be more or less at fault; and possibly none of these
reach further back than six or seven thousand years which, according to Dr. Andrews,[1] have elapsed since the close of the bowlder-
clay deposits in America. . . . Let us look at a few facts.
CONE OF THE Much use has been made of the 'cone' or delta of the
TINIÈRE Tinière, on the eastern side of the Lake of Geneva, as an
illustration of the duration of the modern period. This little stream
has deposited at its mouth a mass of *débris* carried down from the
hills. This being cut through by a railway, is found to contain
Roman remains to a depth of four feet, bronze implements to a
depth of ten feet, stone implements to a depth of nineteen feet. The
deposit ceased about three hundred years ago, and, calculating
1,300 to 1,500 years for the Roman period, we should have 7,000
to 10,000 years as the age of the cone. But before the formation
of the present cone another had been formed twelve times as
large. Thus for the two cones together a duration of more than
90,000 years is claimed. It appears, however, that this calculation
has been made irrespective of two essential elements in the question.
No allowance has been made for the fact that the inner layers of
a cone are necessarily smaller than the outer; nor for the further
fact that the older cone belongs to a distinct time (the pluvial age
already referred to), when the rainfall was much larger, and the
transporting power of the torrent greater in proportion. Making
allowance for these conditions, the age of the newer cone, that
holding human remains, falls between 4,000 and 5,000 years. The
ABBEVILLE peat-bed of Abbeville, in the north of France, has grown
PEAT-BED at the rate of one and a half or two inches in a century.
Being twenty-six feet in thickness, the time occupied in its growth
must have amounted to 20,000 years; and yet it is probably newer
than some of the gravels on the same river containing flint implements. But the composition of the Abbeville peat shows that it is
a forest peat, and the erect stems preserved in it prove that in the
first instance it must have grown at the rate of about three feet in a
century, and after the destruction of the forest its rate of increase
down to the present time diminished rapidly almost to nothing.
Its age is thus reduced to perhaps less than 4,000 years. In 1865
GRAVELS OF I had an opportunity to examine the now celebrated
ST. ACHEUL. gravels of St. Acheul, on the Somme, by some supposed
to go back to a very ancient period. With the papers of Prestwick
and other able observers in my hand, I could conclude merely that
the undisturbed gravels were older than the Roman period, but how

[1] *Transactions*, Chicago Academy, 1871.

much older only detailed topographical surveys could prove ; and that taking into account the probabilities of a different level of the land, a wooded condition of the country, a greater rainfall, and a glacial filling of the Somme valley with clay and stones subsequently cut out by running water, the gravels could scarcely be older than the Abbeville peat. . . . Taylor[1] and Andrews[2] have, however, I think, subsequently shown that my impressions were correct

"In like manner, I fail to perceive—and I think all American geologists acquainted with the prehistoric monuments SUNDRY OTHER of the western continent must agree with me—any evi- FACTS. dence of great antiquity in the caves of Belgium and England, the kitchen-middens of Denmark, the rock-shelters of France, the lake-habitations of Switzerland. At the same time, I would disclaim all attempt to resolve their dates into precise terms of years. I may merely add that the elaborate and careful observations of Dr. Andrews on the raised beaches of Lake Michigan—observations of a much more precise character than any which, in so far as I know, have been made of such deposits in Europe—enable him to calculate the time which has elapsed since North America rose out of the waters of the glacial period as between 5,500 and 7,500 years. This fixes at least the possible duration of the human period in North America, though I believe there are other lines of evidence which would reduce the residence of man in America to a much shorter time. Longer periods have, it is true, been deduced from the delta of the Mississippi and the gorge of Niagara ; but the deposits of the former have been found by Hilgard to be in great part marine, and the excavation of the latter began at a period probably long anterior to the advent of man."[3]

In this brief survey instances of the several classes of archæological and geological facts adduced in proof of a high THE RESULT antiquity of man are reviewed. Among them are in- SATISFACTORY stances regarded as most decisive of the question The criticism of Dawson at least places their conclusiveness in uncertainty ; and if it is not proved beyond question that the time of man's presence in the world must be limited to from 8,000 to 10,000 years, neither is it proved that his time is greater. In his elaborate discussion of this question Southall reviews all these instances, and finds them inconclusive of a high antiquity of man.[4] Such, likewise, is the conclusion of Winchell from the same facts.[5]

The argument from the growth of language is far less in use than

[1] *Journal of Geological Society*, vol. xxv   [2] *Silliman's Journal*, 1868.
[3] Dawson . *Story of the Earth and Man*, pp. 292–296.
[4] *The Recent Origin of Man.*   [5] *Pre-adamites*, pp. 421–426.

others.　Argyll distinctly names it in his classification, as pre-
TIME REQUIRED　viously given by reference, but the use he makes of it is
FOR LAN-　rather to prove the unity than the antiquity of man. He
GUAGE.　points out the now familiar fact that comparative philology furnishes a law by which widely diverse races may be traced
back to a common ethnic unity.[1]　There is still an indirect argument for the high antiquity of man.　With the unity of the race
through a common parentage, there was originally but one language.
Hence there must be time in the existence of the race for the formation of this original language, and of all the languages in the
use of man.

The doctrine of evolution requires a brutal character of primitive
ON THE　man, with the merest rudiment of that rationality
GROUND OF　which came with his higher development.　Such a
EVOLUTION　man might well be accounted speechless; and the
creation of a language would indeed require a long time.　But the
evidence of such a brutal character of primitive man is still wanting.　The facts in the case refuse to satisfy the exigency of the
doctrine.

There is nothing in science to discredit the Mosaic account of
man's origin.　In the sense of this account he was created in the
maturity of manhood, and in respect to his whole nature.　A
mature body and an infantile mind would have made him a
monstrosity, with the slightest chance of survival.　His mind was
created in the same maturity as his body, and with mental powers as
ready for normal action as the physical.　It is also entirely consistent with this account—indeed, we think it a rational requirement—
that primitive man was supernaturally aided in his mental acquire-
ments.　He did not have to wait upon the slow process of experience, but by divine inspiration came quickly to a knowledge of
nature and language.　In this rational view, the original acquisition
of language required no measure of time which must push back the
origin of man into a high antiquity.

The immediate offspring of Adam acquired language in the same
ONLY ONE　manner as children of the present day, and in as brief
ORIGINAL　a time.　Such continued to be the law through all the
LANGUAGE.　antediluvian centuries.　Under the same law the post-
diluvian race started anew.　Language was already a possession,
and continued to be a transmission from generation to generation.
In all divisions into separate communities each division went out
with a language.　Hence the multiplication of languages was by
variation, not by origination.　There are no facts in the history of

[1] *Primeval Man*, pp. 109-112.

the race which require the pure originality of more than one. Comparative philology clearly traces many widely variant languages back to a few sources, and might reach a common source of all did not the marks of an ultimate unity become invisible in the dimness of antiquity. It thus appears that the assumption of a vast extent of time as necessary to the successive originations of many languages is utterly groundless.

Languages, however, are very many, and there must have been time in the existence of the race for their formation. But in estimating the necessary time we must not overlook the distinction between origination and variation. In the former case we assume a speechless community in an infantile mental state. With such facts, the necessary time could hardly be measured. Even the possibility of a purely human creation of language in such a state is not yet a closed question. In the other view, which accords with Scripture and is without the opposition of scientific facts, language was a speedy acquisition through a divine inspiration, with such mental development as must go with the knowledge and use of language. All were thus early in the possession of rational speech. Henceforth the formation of new languages was by variation. This is often a rapid process, as the facts of history prove. There are exceptional cases. With a common education, a common literature, and a free intercourse in the use of a common speech, there may be little change through long periods of time. It is not under such conditions that languages have been multiplied. It is when a larger community, with a common language, separates into distinct communities, and each begins a new life under changed conditions, that through a process of variation the one language is soon multiplied into as many as these separate communities.

The facts of history show that this process is often a rapid one. No long age is required for the formation of a new language. The formation of many may proceed at once. The relative facts are sufficiently presented by Lyell,[1] and also by Southall.[2] It is worthy of note that the two are in substantial agreement respecting these facts, though the former maintains a high antiquity of man, and the latter a recent origin. The material point in which they agree, and which the facts verify, is that under changed conditions new languages are rapidly formed. Thus on the breaking up of the Roman Empire and the distribution of the people into separate nationalities their common language was soon transformed into the Romance—such as the French, Italian,

---

[1] *Antiquity of Man*, chap. xxiii. [2] *Recent Origin of Man*, pp. 25–30.

Spanish, and Portuguese. These languages, now spoken by so many peoples, are not a thousand years old, and only the fraction of a thousand was required for their formation. This is simply one instance out of many given by the authors named.

This rapid formation of new languages is the material fact of the question. It is the conclusion of Southall that of some five thousand languages now spoken only a half-dozen are a thousand years old. If such is the work of ten centuries, the formation of languages requires no stretch of time conclusive of a high antiquity of man.

Another argument is based on the distinction of races. It does RACIAL DIS- not require a detail of all the facts open to its use, but TINCTIONS may be given in its full strength on such general distinctions of race as the Caucasian, Mongolian, and Negro. The argument is in two alleged facts: first, that such distinctions appear with the dawn of history ; second, that only a very long time could have produced them. Greater apparent strength must be conceded to this argument on the theory of a unity of the human race. With a plurality of origins such distinctions might have existed from the beginning, and no time would be required for their origination, while with the unity of the race the necessary time must be conceded. The early date of such distinctions cannot be disputed. For instance, the Negro, with his clearly marked characteristics, appears in Egyptian archæology fifteen or twenty centuries before the Christian era. It must be agreed that many other facts are adduced which prove the first part of the argument—a very early appearance of race distinctions.[1]

The second part, that only long ages could produce such varia- NO LONG TIME tions, is disputed. Many facts in natural history prove REQUIRED the contrary. Fortunately, such facts have fallen within historic times, particularly in the settlement of America, where the process of change could be more accurately measured. "In the domesticated races of animals, and the cultivated tribes of plants, the phenomena of variation have been most remarkably displayed."[2] Dr Prichard cites many instances which illustrate and verify his position. The discussion runs through many pages.[3] The force of these facts is not affected by their limitation to domesticated animals and cultivated plants. The domestication and cultivation merely furnish the new conditions under which these

---

[1] Lyell · Antiquity of Man, pp. 385, 386; Lubbock · Prehistoric Times, pp. 587, 588; Argyll. Primeval Man, pp 97-102, Winchell. Pre-adamites, chap. xiii

[2] Prichard · Natural History of Man, p. 27.   [3] Ibid, pp 23-50

changes naturally arise Further, such instances are more readily open to observation ; and their selection is for this reason and not because they exemplify any peculiar susceptibility to change.

It is a rational inference, and one supported by the strongest analogies, that under new conditions man is subject to COMMON LAW like change, and in many respects, as the new con- OF CHANGE ditions may greatly vary. "Races of men are subjected more than almost any race of animals to the varied agencies of climate Civilization produces even greater changes in their condition than does domestication in the inferior tribes. We may therefore expect to find fully as great diversities in the races of men as in any of the domesticated breeds. The influence of the mind must be more extensive and powerful in its operations upon human beings than upon brutes. And this difference transcends all analogy or comparison." [1]

Nor could the conditions of physiological variation be wanting in the earlier state of man. As the race multiplied, broader territories would be required for its occupancy. Besides, the natural disposition of many would anticipate this exigency and push them out into new and distant regions. It appears, accordingly, in the beginning of history, and back of this in the relative facts of archæology, that at a very early day men occupied extensive reaches of territory. With this wide distribution there were great changes of climate and new habits of life. Thus at a very early day there were all the new conditions necessary to the variations which appear in the distinctions of race.

Physiological changes have occurred in historic times, and in comparatively brief periods.[2] There are many such INSTANCES OF instances. They do not equal some of the deeper race CHANGE distinctions, but, with the brevity of their own period, are sufficient to discredit the assumption of vast ages as necessary to such variations. Hence we need no vast time to account for the distinctions of race which appear in the early history of man A permissible extension of biblical chronology to eight or ten thousand years will suffice for the whole account.

4. *Relation of the Question to Theology.*—The antiquity of man concerns the Scriptures in the matter of chronology. The question might thus become one of exegesis or apologetics However, with the uncertainty of the earlier data for a biblical chronology and the absence of any authoritative doctrine, there is little occasion for such a question, except in issue with extreme assumptions

[1] Prichard . *Natural History of Man*, p. 75.
[2] Southall *Recent Origin of Man*, pp. 26-28.

25

respecting the antiquity of man. The question mostly concerns doctrinal theology through its relation to the unity of the race. Theology is deeply concerned in this question, and, therefore, in the question of antiquity with which it is very closely connected. With a limit of six thousand years for the time of man on the earth, the unity of the race cannot be maintained. This is rendered impossible specially by the very early appearance of some of the deepest variations of race. Only a plurality of origins could account for these early distinctions. It is hence fortunate that the data of biblical chronology do not commit us to a period so limited. The higher the antiquity of man. the more certain is the unity of the race. This position will scarcely meet with any scientific dissent. Therefore the evidences of a higher antiquity than the usual reckoning of biblical chronology, instead of causing anxiety, should be accepted with favor It thus appears that the antiquity of man is specially related to theology through the unity of the race. "And precisely in proportion as we value our belief in that unity ought we to be ready and willing to accept any evidence on the question of man's antiquity. The older the human family can be proved to be, the more possible and probable it is that it has descended from a single pair. My own firm belief is that all scientific evidence is in favor of this conclusion ; and I regard all new proofs of the antiquity of man as tending to establish it on a firmer basis."[1]

AS RELATED TO THE UNITY OF MAN.

III. The Unity of Man.

1. *Question of a Unity of Species.*—As the unity of man is definitely the question of a unity of species, we require for its proper treatment a definite view of species. Seemingly, this is no easy attainment, for definitions greatly vary. However, we may pass with slight notice the polemics of the question, and present in a brief statement all that our own discussion requires.

For any true sense of species we require its fundamental idea or ideas This principle will hardly be questioned ; and yet it cannot bring definitions into unity, for the reason that these ideas differ in the view of different minds. We appropriate the following · "Species is a collection of individuals more or less resembling each other, which may be regarded as having descended from a single primitive pair by an uninterrupted and natural succession of families."[2] There are in this definition two fundamental facts—resemblance and genetic connection. We should

SENSE OF SPECIES

[1] Argyll · *Primeval Man*, p. 128.
[2] Quatrefages : *The Human Species*, p. 36.

state more strongly the principle of filiation or genetic connection, but not more strongly than the author holds it, as appears elsewhere.

The doctrine of species varies as it makes more fundamental the one or the other of these ideas, or as it omits the one VARIATIONS OF or the other. There are both forms of variation; but DOCTRINE mostly both ideas are embodied in definitions. After a statement of the definitions by Ray and Tournefort, that of the former embodying only the principle of filiation, and that of the latter only the principle of resemblance, Quatrefages proceeds to say : " Ray and Tournefort have had from time to time a few imitators, who, in their definition of species, have clung to one of the two ideas. But the immense majority of zoologists have been aware of the impossibility of separating them. To convince ourselves of this fact it is only necessary to read the definitions which they have given. Each one of them, from Buffon and Cuvier to MM. Chevreul and C. Vogt, has, so to speak, proposed his own. Now, however they may differ in other respects, they all agree in this. The terms of the definitions vary, each endeavors to represent in the best manner possible the complex idea of species ; some extend it still further, and connect with it the idea of cycle and variation ; but in all the fundamental idea is the same." [1] This is the statement of an author at once learned and candid, and who writes in open view of the modern theories of evolution.

Professor Gray holds the same doctrine of species, and also sets it forth as the more common doctrine of naturalists. We DOCTRINE OF may cite a few of his statements : " The ordinary and GRAY generally received view assumes the independent, specific creation of each kind of plant and animal in a primitive stock, which reproduces its like from generation to generation, and so continues the species." [2] " According to the succinct definition of Jussieu—and that of Linnæus is identical in meaning—a species is the perennial succession of similar individuals in continued generations. The species is the chain of which the individuals are the links. The sum of the genealogically-connected similar individuals constitutes the species, which thus has an actuality and ground of distinction not shared by genera and other groups which were not supposed to be genealogically connected." [3] Such is the doctrine of species held

---

[1] *The Human Species*, p. 36.

[2] *Darwiniana*, pp. 11, 12. For the same doctrine of species Gray cites the definition of Linnæus : "Species tot sunt, quot diversas formas ab initio produxit Infinitum Ens; quæ formæ, secundum generationis inditas leges, produxere plures, at sibi semper similes."

[3] *Darwiniana*, pp. 163, 164.

by Professor Gray, and which he sets forth as the more common doctrine of naturalists. His learning and candor, which no one will question, give weight to his statements. Any favorable view of evolution which Professor Gray may hold does not really affect his doctrine of species. His theism is thorough and devout, and for him evolution would simply represent the mode of the divine agency in the origin of species. This would be a variation from the view of an immediate creation of the progenitors of species, but a variation which would not change the fundamental ideas of the doctrine.

While the ideas of genetic connection and resemblance are both
THE DEEPER regarded as fundamental in the doctrine of species, they
IDEA are not so in just the same form or measure. The deeper idea is that of genetic connection. It is the ground of likeness among the individuals. The likeness may be widely variable, while the genealogical connection must be constant and complete. With this connection the species abides, however slight the resemblance.

2. *Theory of Unity with Plurality of Origins.*—It is now a familiar fact that Louis Agassiz, a very eminent scientist of our own country, held distinct origins of the human races. Indeed, he held the same doctrine respecting different races in all the lower forms of life. However, the doctrine of Agassiz had no connection with the Darwinian evolution, for to that he was openly opposed. In his view the several human races originated in separate divine creations. Thus, instead of one original creation of a single pair as the common parentage of man, there were several such creations as the heads of the several races. The doctrine is most thoroughly theistic, and the extreme of supernaturalism respecting the origin of man, and, indeed, of all the lower forms of life.

With such separate creations, the human races might still be one
UNITY WITH in all the facts distinctive or constitutive of species,
SEPARATE ORI- except the one fact of genealogical connection. With-
GINS out this connection God could so constitute the several races that they should possess in common all other characteristics distinctive of species. So far the unity of man could consist with a plurality of origins.

Some naturalistic evolutionists hold to separate origins of the
AS HELD BY several human races. If such an origin of man is pos-
EVOLUTION- sible, there may have been a plurality of origins. If
ISTS the requisite natural conditions could meet in one point, so might they in several, or even in many. In such a case, however, there could be no account of the unquestionable unity of the several races in specifical facts. Such origins are assumed to be widely

separated in time and place, and hence an exact identity of natural conditions could not be the remotest probability. But if the environment is a strongly molding force over all the forms of organic life, the widely different conditions of human evolutions must have caused wide differences in the products. Hence such plurality of human evolutions is disproved by the specifical unity of the several races. This consequence cannot be voided by alleging the distinctions of the several races as the whole account of the different natural conditions of their separate evolutions. These distinctions are merely superficial or incidental, and fully accounted for by differences of environment in the actual life, while in all the intrinsic and constitutive facts of mankind the several races are without distinction.

Mostly such plurality of origins is maintained as a necessary account of the distinctions of race. It might be held as simplifying the question respecting the distribution of mankind, but, with the present knowledge of facts, can AS RELATED TO RACIAL DISTINCTIONS no longer be claimed as necessary to its solution. With the profoundest students of the natural sciences, and particularly of anthropology, a unity of origin makes no serious difficulty in accounting for that distribution. Some of the most diverse and widely separated races are easily traced back to an earlier connection, while decisive facts warrant the inference of an original unity. With such facts already in hand, we need not be perplexed with any questions of distribution which may still wait for their interpretation.

3. *Distinctions of Race and the Question of Unity* —The distinctions of race constitute the chief objection to the specific unity of mankind. There are wide variations of human type, particularly in size, form, and color. Hence the question is, whether such variations are consistent with a common parentage, or whether the several races require separate origins. This is largely a question of science, and so far we must look to scientists for its proper treatment. At least we are dependent upon them for the requisite facts. Scientists are not agreed in a common doctrine. Some hold a plurality of human origins. With such, however, there is no agreement respecting the number, and the scale runs from four or five up to sixty or more. The weight of scientific authority is for a unity of origin.

The question of species is common to the manifold forms of vegetable and animal life. Hence on the ground of analogy the variation of types, as related to the unity of species, is properly studied in these broader spheres. OTHER APPLICATIONS OF THE QUESTION. If variations of race appeared only in the case of man, a fixity of type in the many other species would largely discredit his unity. If in those species there were many variations of type, but only slight in comparison with the distinctions in man, such a difference would place his specifical unity in uncertainty. On the other hand, if variations of type are common to all species, and are often as great or even greater in the spheres of botany and zoology than in the distinctively human sphere, then the objection to the unity of man on the ground of the distinctions of race is discredited and denied all logical force. In the light of natural history many such variations are open and clear. It is in the use of such facts that scientists easily obviate the chief objection to the specifical unity of man.

The tendency of species to diverse and wide variations, and the TENDENCY TO actuality of such variations, are clearly pointed out by VARIATION. Professor Gray.[1] We may cite two brief passages out of the references. "As to amount of variation, there is the common remark of naturalists that the varieties of domesticated plants or animals often differ more widely than do the individuals of distinct species in a wild state : and even in nature the individuals of some species are known to vary to a degree sensibly wider than that which separates related species." "But who can tell us what amount of difference is compatible with community of origin ? " Community of origin is with this author the deepest fact of species. The instances which he adduces as illustrative of actual variation clearly show that a very wide range is compatible with unity of species. Hence the variety of human races is compatible with the specific unity of man.

Quatrefages treats the question in the same method, and reaches THE VIEW OF the same result ; only, his treatment is much fuller, QUATREFAGES. and, by so much, with higher cumulative force. He thus states his own method: "Any one really desirous of forming an opinion upon the unity or multiplicity of the human species should therefore discover what are the facts and phenomena which characterize races and species in plants and animals, then turn to man and compare the facts and phenomena there presented with those which botanists and zoologists have observed in the other kingdoms If the facts and phenomena which distinguish the human groups are those which, in other organized and living beings differentiate *species*, he will then legitimately infer the multiplicity of human species; if, however, these phenomena and facts are characteristic of *race* in the two former kingdoms, he must conclude in favor of specific unity."[2] In this legitimate method the question is fully discussed. Many facts are adduced as instances of

[1] *Darwiniana*, pp 26, 27, 97, 111, 203.   [2] *The Human Species*, pp 41, 42.

wide variations of type within well-known species. It is clearly pointed out that in animal and plant races variations attain limits never exceeded, and rarely reached, by the differences between human groups.[1] Such variations are pointed out in all the particulars of size, color, and form, and are shown to be equal to such as appear in the differences of human races. The conclusion of the author is fully warranted : "The several facts which I have here enumerated seem to me sufficient to justify the proposition which I asserted at the commencement of the chapter, namely, that the limits of variation are almost always more extensive between certain races of animals than between the most distinct human groups. Consequently, however great the differences existing between these human groups may be, or may appear to be, to consider them as *specific characters* is a perfectly arbitrary estimation of their value. It is, to say the least, quite as rational, quite as scientific, to consider these differences only as *characters of race*, and even on that account to refer all the human groups to a single species."[2] If the specific unity of man is not thus fully proved, the chief objection which it encounters in the distinctions of race is thoroughly obviated. But only the full discussion of this author can give the full force of his argument.[3]

Against this account of the distinctions of race, it is alleged that the varieties of type are as remarkable for their fixity as FIXATION OF for their early appearance ; that through all the cent-RACIAL TYPES uries of history and the changes of environment they remain the same. From this alleged persistence of human types it is inferred that they could not have originated in differences of environment. On the validity of this inference, it would follow that each race is a distinct species, with its own separate origin.

There is a persistency of human types through long periods of history, and under great changes of climatical condi-NO DISPROOF tion. So much is readily conceded. However, this OF UNITY concession falls very far short of all that is claimed in the above argument for a plurality of species. That the several types undergo no change, or only the slightest change, is not at all conceded. Many variations have occurred in historic times, and even in comparatively recent times. A selection of such instances is given by Dr. A. H. Strong[4] The brevity of his summary renders it very suitable for citation : "Instances of physio-INSTANCES OF logical change as the result of new conditions · The CHANGE Irish, driven by the English two centuries ago from Armagh and

[1] *The Human Species*, pp. 42, 48.   [2] *Ibid*, p. 55.   [3] *Ibid.*, chaps. iv-vi
[4] *Systematic Theology*, pp. 242, 243.

the south of Down, have become prognathous like the Australians. The inhabitants of New England have descended from the
English, yet they have already a physical type of their own. The
Indians of North America, or at least certain tribes of them, have
permanently altered the shape of the skull by bandaging the head
in infancy. The Sikhs of India, since the establishment of Babel
Nina's religion (1500 A. D.) and their consequent advance in civilization, have changed to a longer head and more regular features,
so that they are now distinguished greatly from their neighbors, the
Afghans, Thibetans, Hindus. The Ostiak savages have become the
Magyar nobility of Hungary. The Turks in Europe are, in cranial
shape, greatly in advance of the Turks in Asia from whom they
descended. The Jews are confessedly of one ancestry; yet we have
among them the light-haired Jews of Poland, the dark Jews of Spain,
and the Ethiopian Jews of the Nile valley. The Portuguese who settled in the East Indies in the sixteenth century are now as dark in
complexion as the Hindus themselves. Africans become lighter
in complexion as they go up from the alluvial river-banks to higher
land, or from the coast; and on the contrary the coast tribes which
drive out the Negroes of the interior and take their territory end by
becoming Negroes themselves."

From such facts it is reasonably inferable that there is no fixity
of human types which disproves their origin in climat-
LOGIC OF THE ICAL conditions. It is true that in the instances cited
ILLUSTRA-
TIONS.   there are no variations equal to the deeper distinctions
of race; but this lack is fully compensated by the difference of
time. In the one case we have, at most, only a few centuries; in
the other, thousands of years. If in the shorter time such physiological variations could arise from changes of environment, the
deeper distinctions of race could so arise in the vastly longer time.

Admitting the slightness of variation under great climatical
change, as claimed in many instances, there is an interpretation
which obviates all inference against the origin of race distinctions from natural causes. This interpretation lies in the fact
CAUSES OF that, with great climatical change, there is in many
CHANGE OBVI- modern instances but slight exposure to the natural
ATED.   causes of physiological change. "There are some
reasons which make it probable that changes of external condition,
or rather of country, produce less effect now than was formerly the
case. At present, when men migrate they carry with them the
manners and appliances of civilized life. They build houses more
or less like those to which they have been accustomed, carry with
them flocks and herds, and introduce into their new country the

principal plants which served them for food in the old. If their new abode is cold they increase their clothing, if warm they diminish it. In these and a hundred other ways the effect which would otherwise be produced is greatly diminished." [1] The facts were very different in many early migrations. Without agriculture or domestic animals, without homes for shelter, with only the rudest weapons, men were wholly dependent upon natural resources, and would be without protection from the natural causes of physiological change in any new climatical conditions. It is thus obvious that such change would be more rapid and extensive than in many modern migrations. It follows that the slightness of change in such modern instances cannot disprove the origin of race distinctions from natural causes under the early conditions of full exposure to their force.

This question is placed in yet another view. It is the view that the infancy of a species is the time of its most rapid PERIOD OF variation into races or types, that such variations soon RAPID CHANGE reach their limit, after which the several types become so fixed as to suffer little further change. Respecting the Negro—the standard instance of an early and persistent type : " What it does prove is a fact equally obvious from the study of post-pliocene mollusks and other fossils, namely, that new species tend rapidly to vary to the utmost extent of their possible limits, and then to remain stationary for an indefinite time." [2] It appears in these statements that such laws are not assumptions to meet a doctrinal exigency, but scientific inductions on the ground of facts. Nor are such facts limited to the human species and races, but are found broadly in natural history. With this wider sphere of inductive facts, the more certain are these laws. Their relation to the distinctions of race is obvious. They account for the variation of species into these distinctions on natural grounds ; for the early appearance of the several human races ; and also for their permanence. It follows that neither the early appearance nor the permanence of the several human types is any disproof of their origin in natural causes. Neither fact, therefore, is any disproof of the specifical unity of mankind. [3]

4. *Scientific Evidences of Specifical Unity.*—A sufficient account of the distinctions of race in natural causes is not in itself conclusive of a specifical unity of mankind. Its direct logical value

[1] Lubbock : *Prehistoric Times*, p. 589.

[2] Dawson : *Story of the Earth and Man*, p. 360.

[3] Prichard : *Natural History of Man*, sec. xlviii , Whedon : *Methodist Quarterly Review*, 1878, p. 565.

is in the refutation of the argument from these distinctions for a plurality of species. There is, however, a large indirect value for the doctrine of unity. In the history of relative facts there is no call for the agency of God in repeated original creations of mankind. Hence a single original creation is the only rational inference. Beyond this inference there is a further value in the refutation of that chief argument for a plurality of species : it clears the way for all the more direct evidences of the unity of men. A summary of these evidences must now be given.

There is a oneness of races in physical characteristics. The distinctions are superficial, and the result of local influences. The oneness in all intrinsic facts of the physical constitution is as real as in any animal species. The human body is intrinsically one among all races : one in chemical elements ; one in anatomical structure ; one in physiological constitution ; one in pathological susceptibilities.[1]

There is among all the different races a oneness of psychological endowment. This oneness appears as the result of a thorough analysis of the facts concerned in the question. Superficially, differences are many and obvious. It is easy to set in wide contrast the barbaric Negro and the cultured, Christianized Caucasian. There are, however, instances of little less difference between one and another of the Caucasian race. But in this case the difference is understood to be only accidental or superficial, while there is still a oneness in all the intrinsic facts of mind. A thorough analysis gives the same result respecting all the races of men. The mental differences are accidental or superficial, while the intrinsic facts of mind are the same in all. There are the same sensibilities, with their marvelous adjustment to the manifold relations of life ; the same intellectual faculties, which constitute the rationality of mind ; the same moral and religious nature, which, while it may sink to barbarism and idolatry in the Caucasian, may rise to the highest moral and Christian life in the Mongolian and Negro.[2]

Prichard carries the discussion of these questions through many pages, and with his characteristic lucidity and candor. Widely diverse races are brought into view, that their oneness in the essential facts of mind may be fairly tested. Any one who follows the author with a mind open to the truth must find

Marginal notes: PHYSIOLOGIC- AL ONENESS. PSYCHOLOGIC- AL ONENESS. ARGUMENT OF PRICHARD.

[1] Quatrefages : *The Human Species*, book ix ; Prichard : *Natural History of Man*, pp. 477–486.

[2] Quatrefages : *The Human Species*, pp. 431–498 ; Dorner : *System of Christian Doctrine*, vol. ii, pp. 92, 93 ; Prichard . *Natural History of Man*, pp. 486–546.

it most difficult to reject his conclusion : " We contemplate among all the diversified tribes, who are endowed with reason and speech, the same internal feelings, appetencies, aversions ; the same inward convictions, the same sentiments of subjection to invisible powers, and, more or less fully developed, of accountableness or responsibility to unseen avengers of wrong and agents of retributive justice, from whose tribunal men cannot even by death escape. We find every-where the same susceptibility, though not always in the same degree of forwardness or ripeness of improvement, of admitting the cultivation of these universal endowments, of opening the eyes of the mind to the more clear and luminous views which Christianity unfolds, of becoming molded to the institutions of religion and of civilized life : in a word, the same inward and mental nature is to be recognized in all the races of men. When we compare this fact with the observations which have been heretofore fully established as to the specific instincts and separate psychical endowments of all the distinct tribes of sentient beings in the universe, we are entitled to draw confidently the conclusion that all human races are of one species and one family." [1]

The sexual union of the most distinct races is just as fruitful as that within the purest and most definite race. The progeny of such union are entirely free from hybridity. ABSENCE OF HYBRIDITY Their fruitfulness is permanent and without decrease. If in some instances it may be less, in others it is greater, so that there is a full average. Here are facts utterly unknown in all the crossings of animal species. It is only from the union of closely allied species that there is any produce. There is only the most limited fruitfulness of such offspring ; never a permanent fruitfulness. Here is the law of hybridity ; a law which is the chief guide of science in the analysis and classification of species. But this law is wholly unknown among human races. It follows that human races are not separate species, but simply varieties of one species.

The law of hybridity which limits the production of a permanently fruitful progeny to the species, and so denies it to the crossing of species, is one of the most obvious A GREAT LAW OF NATURE. laws of natural history. A mere statement of the relative facts must make this plain. " The law of nature decrees that creatures of every kind shall increase and multiply by propagating their own kind, and not another If we search the whole world, we shall probably not find one instance of an intermediate tribe produced between any two distinct species, ascertained to be such. If such a thing were discovered it would be a surprising anomaly. The

[1] Prichard Natural History of Man, pp. 545, 546.

existence of such a law as this in the economy of nature is almost self-
evident, or at least becomes evident from the most superficial and
general survey of the phenomena of the living world : for if, as some
have argued, there were no such principle in operation, how could
the order, and at the same time the variety, of the animal and vegetable creation be preserved ? If the different races of beings were
intermixed in the ordinary course of things, and hybrid races were
reproduced and continued without impediment, the organized world
would soon present a scene of universal confusion ; its various
tribes would become every-where blended together, and we should
at length scarcely discover any genuine or uncorrupted races.   It
may, indeed, be said that this confusion of all the living tribes
would long ago have taken place.   But how opposite from such a
state of things is the real order of nature !   The same uniform and
regular production of species still holds throughout the world ; nor
are the limits of each distinct species less accurately defined than
they probably were some thousands of years ago.   It is plain that
the conservation of distinct tribes has been secured, and that universally and throughout all the different departments of the organic
creation." [1]   It thus appears that the very possibility of a natural
science is conditioned on the law which limits the production of a
permanently fruitful progeny to the species.   Hence the fact of
such a science is the fact of such a law.   The presence of this law
is ever the proof of specifical oneness, however wide the variations
of race.   It follows that the several human races, among which this
law is without any limitation, are one species.

    " The infertility, or, if you will, the restricted and rapidly limited
like the law of gravita-tion. fertility between species, and the impossibility of natural
forces, when left to themselves, producing series of in-
termediary beings between two given specific types, is
one of those general facts which we call a *law*.   This fact has an
importance in the organic world equal to that rightly attributed to
attraction in the sidereal world.   It is by virtue of the latter that
the celestial bodies preserve their respective distances, and complete
their orbits in the admirable order revealed by astronomy.   The
law of the sterility of species produces the same result, and maintains between species and between different groups in animals and
plants all those relations which, in the paleontological ages, as well
as in our own, form the marvelous whole of the *organic empire*.
Imagine the suppression of the laws which govern attraction in the
heavens, and what chaos would immediately be the result.   Suppress upon earth the law of crossing, and the confusion would be

[1] Prichard · *Natural History of Man*, pp. 12, 13.

immense. It is scarcely possible to say where it would stop. After a few generations the groups which we call genera, families, orders, and classes would most certainly have disappeared, and the branches also would rapidly have become affected. It is clear that only a few centuries would elapse before the animal and vegetable kingdoms fell into the most complete disorder. Now order has existed in both kingdoms since the epoch when organized beings first peopled the solitudes of our globe, and it could only have been established and preserved by virtue of the impossibility of a fusion of species with each other through indifferently and indefinitely fertile crossings." [1]

The doctrine here is the same as that given from Prichard. These eminent authors did not rest the question with such summary statement, however decisive in itself. Each carefully and thoroughly studied the relative facts in natural history, and found them in full accord with the doctrine as summarily stated. We have the same conclusion as previously given. With the narrowly limited fruitfulness of all specifical crossings, the unrestricted fruitfulness between all the human races is conclusive of their specifical unity.

So far, we have simply stated as a fact the average and permanent fruitfulness of the progeny from the union of the most distinct human races. No proof has been offered. ABSENCE OF HYBRIDITY There is little need of any formal argument. The fact VERIFIED is too open and too well known to be seriously questioned. It is verified by innumerable instances in modern history. These instances arise specially in the intercourse of Europeans with the Negro and the Indian or Redskin of America. The produce of such intercourse is fruitful without any stint. Hence every-where mixed races have arisen. Their permanence is conclusive of their freedom from the hybridity which suffers only a temporary existence to the progeny of specifical crossings. The facts are amply given, and with scientific clearness, by the authors recently cited. [2] It will suffice to give their conclusion. "It appears to be unquestionable that intermediate races of men exist and are propagated, and that no impediment whatever exists to the perpetuation of mankind when the most dissimilar varieties are blended together. We hence derive a conclusive proof, unless there be in the instance of human races an exception to the universally prevalent law of organized nature, that all the tribes of men are of one family." [3] Quatrefages, having also reviewed the relative facts, says: "Thus, in every case crossings

[1] Quatrefages : *The Human Species*, pp. 80, 81.

[2] Prichard. *Natural History of Man*, pp. 18–26 ; Quatrefages : *The Human Species*, pp. 85–87.

[3] Prichard : *Natural History of Man*, p. 26.

between human groups exhibit the phenomena characteristic of mongrels and never those of hybrids. Therefore, these human groups, however different they may be, or appear to be, are only *races of one and the same species* and not *distinct species.* Therefore, there is but *one human species,* taking this term species in the acceptation employed when speaking of animals and plants."[1] This author is fully warranted in these concluding words: "Now I wish that candid men, who are free from party spirit or prejudices, would follow me in this view, and study for themselves all these facts, a few of which I have only touched upon, and I am perfectly convinced that they will, with the great men of whom I am only the disciple—with Linnæus, Buffon, Lamarck, Cuvier, Geoffroy, Humboldt, and Muller—arrive at the conclusion that *all men belong to the same species,* and that there is but *one species of man."*

BUT ONE HU-MAN SPECIES

Comparative philology is a witness for the specifical unity of man. This recent science is already a chief light in the study of ethnology. Affinities of widely separated races are thus discovered, and these races are traced back to a common origin and a primary ethnic unity. The existence of the same words in different languages is the proof of a primary connection and a common original. No principle of the inductive sciences is more valid. The primary unity of such languages carries with it the ethnic unity of the races which use them. "It is absolutely certain from the character of the French, Spanish, and Italian languages that those nations are in large measure the common descendants of the Latin race. When, therefore, it can be shown that the languages of different races or varieties of men are radically the same, or derived from a common stock, it is impossible rationally to doubt their descent from a common ancestry. Unity of language, therefore, proves unity of species because it proves unity of origin."[2]

COMPARATIVE PHILOLOGY.

Comparative philologists have thus been able to bring back into a primary unity many widely separate and widely diverse peoples. The affinity of languages leads up to a primary unity of language, and hence to the unity of man. "The universal affinity of language is placed in so strong a light that it must be considered by all as completely demonstrated. It appears inexplicable on any other hypothesis than that of admitting fragments of a primary language to exist through all the languages of the Old and New World."[3] "Much as all these languages differ from each other, they appear, after all, to be merely branches of one

UNITY OF DIVERSE LANGUAGES.

---

[1] *The Human Species,* pp. 87, 88.
[2] Hodge: *Systematic Theology,* vol. ii, p. 89.   [3] Klaproth.

common stem."[1] "As far as the organic languages of Asia and Europe are concerned, the human race is of one kindred, of one descent." "Our historical researches respecting AND PEOPLES language have led us to facts which seemed to oblige us to assume the common historical origin of the great families into which we found the nations of Asia and Europe to coalesce. The four families of Turanians and Iranians, of Khamites and Shemites, reduced themselves to two, and these again possessed such mutual material affinities as can neither be explained as accidental nor as being so by a natural external necessity; but they must be historical, and therefore imply a common descent." "The Asiatic origin of all these [American] tribes is as fully proved as the unity of family among themselves."[2] We may add one more testimony: "The comparative study of languages shows us that races now separated by vast tracts of land are allied together, and have migrated from one primitive seat. . . . The largest field for such investigations into the ancient condition of language, and, consequently, into the period when the whole family of mankind was, in the strictest sense of the word, to be regarded as one living whole, presents itself in the long chain of Indo-Germanic languages, extending from the Ganges to the Iberian extremity of Europe, and from Sicily to the North Cape."[3] The sense is that the inheritance of all these languages from a common source proves the original unity of the many widely different peoples which they represent.

Comparative philology thus makes it clear and sure that peoples widely separated in place, and representing very distinct racial types, were originally one family and one RESULTS blood. What is thus proved to be true of a part may be true of the whole. Indeed, in the absence of all disproof, the only rational inference is that all human families were originally one family. More and more is the wider study of comparative philology pointing to this truth. The results already attained render groundless the distinctions of race for a plurality of origins, and prove beyond question that more or less of the several species as held by polygenists are mere varieties of the one species.

5. *The Scripture Sense of Unity.*—The whole human race is lineally descended from Adam and Eve. There is hence A COMMON a genetic connection of all mankind. This is the obvi- PARENTAGE ous sense of the Scriptures. It appears in the more definite state-

[1] Schlegel · *The Philosophy of History*, p 92, London, 1847.

[2] Bunsen . *Philosophy of Universal History*, vol. ii, pp 4, 99, 112; the last three authors as cited by Macdonald : *Creation and the Fall*, p. 381.

[3] Humboldt : *Cosmos*, vol. ii, p. 111.

ments respecting the origin of man and the peopling of the world, and also in various incidental and doctrinal references to the race. There is the creation of a single pair as the beginning of the human species and the progenitors of all mankind. It was for them to be fruitful, and multiply, and replenish the earth.[1] Such was the order of Providence, and the multiplying people down to the time of the flood were in unbroken genetic connection with them.[2] The repeopling of the world was from the sons of Noah, who clearly stand in lineal descent from Adam and Eve.[3] All these facts are openly given in the earlier chapters of Genesis.

The notable words of Paul to the Athenians must mean the genealogical oneness of mankind. "And (God) hath made of one blood all nations of men for to dwell on all the face of the earth."[4] The New Version drops the word blood; so that in its rendering we read simply, "And he made of one every nation of men." The weight of critical authority is against the genuineness of $a\tilde{\iota}\mu a$ in the Greek text. This was the reason for the new rendering. The change strengthens the sense of a genealogical unity. While the words "of one blood"—$\dot{\epsilon}\xi$ $\dot{\epsilon}\nu\dot{o}\varsigma$ $a\tilde{\iota}\mu a\tau o\varsigma$— clearly point to such a unity, they might be claimed to express simply a oneness of nature which is consistent with a plurality of origins. The new rendering is in no sense open to such a claim. We cannot so supplement the words "made of one" as to read, "made of one nature or kind." Of one man, of one father, or of one parentage, is the only permissible rendering. There was reason with Paul for the utterance of such a truth in the presence of his Greek audience. On the notion of autochthonism the Athenians claimed for themselves a distinct origin, and thereon the distinction of a special superiority over other nations. Now as on this great occasion Paul declares all men by their creation to be the offspring of God,[5] so he declares all to be mediately the offspring of a common parentage. This is the meaning of the words, "And he made of one every nation of men for to dwell on all the face of the earth." This is the deepest unity of man; not only that of a specifical oneness of nature, but also that of a genealogical oneness.

There are other words of Paul which give the same sense.[6] In the passages given by reference both the prevalence of sin with all men and the death of all are traced back to a connection with the sin of Adam. These facts involve doctrinal questions which more properly belong to another division of the subject, but irrespective of this have special significance for the

ALL OF ONE

CLEAR TESTIMONY

[1] Gen. i, 27, 28.   [2] Gen. v, 1, 2.   [3] Gen. x, 1, 32.   [4] Acts xvii, 26.
[5] Acts xvii, 28.   [6] Rom. v, 12, 17–19; 1 Cor. xv, 21, 22.

present point. The common sinfulness of the race could not in the deep sense of Paul be consequent on the sin of Adam without a common genealogical connection with him. Neither could there be the consequence of death as common to all without such a connection. So much may be said with the fullest warrant, and quite irrespective of certain doctrinal grounds of such consequences as set forth in theology.[1]

6. *A Special Theory of Pre-adamites.*—This theory is the same in principle as the polygenism which holds a plurality of origins for the more distinct races. It is peculiar in claiming for itself entire consistency with the Scriptures, and even that it is necessary to their proper interpretation. For many centuries there was no question in the Church respecting either the unity of man or the true primariness of Adam. The new theory was initiated by Peyrerius, a Romish priest. His first work[2] —a disquisition on Rom. v, 12–14—appeared in 1655. The existence of men before Adam is maintained as the sense of the passage named. The next year this work was followed by another from the same author, with a fuller discussion of the same theory. The theory encountered strong opposition, and soon sank into silence. This silence continued for two centuries, when the question was revived.

THEORY OF PEYRERIUS.

The occasion for the new discussion was furnished in the discovery of facts which seemingly point to an antiquity of man far beyond the reach of biblical chronology. The aim is to adjust the alleged facts to the limitations of this chronology. The method is to regard Adam, not as the first man, but as the first of a distinct race, which appears in the opening of biblical history. This Adamic race falls within the limits of biblical chronology, while the facts which point to a much higher antiquity of man must be interpreted on the theory of earlier races. The existence of such races is in the fullest consistency with the Scriptures. Such is the theory.

THE THEORY REVIVED.

While the advocates of this theory agree that the Adamic race is distinct from others, and of later origin, they are not agreed as to its ethnic composition. For instance, the Adamic race is with Peyrerius simply the Hebrew race; with McCausland, the Caucasian in distinction from the Mongolian and Negroid, with Winchell, the Mediterranean or white race, but as including Japhetites, Semites, and Hamites.[3]

[1] Van Oosterzee : *Christian Dogmatics,* vol. i, pp. 363, 364; Macdonald *Creation and the Fall,* p. 373 ; Dorner · *System of Christian Doctrine,* vol. ii, p. 89.
[2] *Præ-adamitæ,* etc.   [3] *Pre-adamites,* p. 52.

As this theory claims to be thoroughly scriptural, very natu-

CLAIM OF
SCRIPTURE
GROUND.

rally the proof of it is sought in the Scriptures. Its later advocates go beyond the Scriptures into such facts of ethnology, geology, and archæology as are usually adduced in proof of a high antiquity of man. In this, however, we need not here follow them, as we have previously considered these facts. It could not be overlooked by thoughtful writers who appeal to the Scriptures for proof of this theory that it is in seeming collision with fundamental truths of Christian anthropology and soteriology. Nor could all endeavor toward a reconciliation be omitted. Here the theory encounters insuperable difficulty, as we shall point out in the proper place. Later advocates of the theory on scriptural grounds very properly omit the argument of Peyrerius from the notable passage of Paul in the Epistle to the Romans.[1] So far from being the ground of an argument, the reconciliation of the passage with the new theory is above the power of its advocates.

Much use is made of familiar incidents in the life of Cain. He

INCIDENTS IN
THE LIFE OF
CAIN.

is a fratricide and a fugitive, and suffers the remorse of sin and the severity of the divine judgment. He is seized with the dread of vengeance: "Every one that findeth me shall slay me." God in pity sets upon him a seal of protection, "lest any one finding him should slay him." So Cain went forth from the presence of the Lord, and dwelt in the land of Nod, on the east of Eden. He next appears in married life. There is born to him a son, whom he names Enoch. He builds a city and calls it after the name of this son.[2] In view of such facts the argument for pre-adamites is easily constructed. On the face of the narrative, Adam and Eve and Cain at this time composed the whole Adamic family. Who then were the slayers whose vengeance Cain so dreaded? And where did he find a wife? And how could he so soon build a city without the co-operation of people already existing? And why should a city be built, except for the occupancy of such people? The interpretation of these facts requires the existence of pre-adamites.[3]

The argument is plausible, and seemingly possesses much force.

PLAUSIBILITY
OF THE CASE.

It might be deemed conclusive, if the question hinged entirely upon the incidents here narrated. Such, however, is not the case. Many other facts concern the question, and such as are more decisive of the issue. For any conclusiveness,

---

[1] Rom v, 12-14.　　　　　　　　　　　　　　[2] Gen iv, 8-17.

[3] McCausland: *Adam and the Adamite*, pp. 194-197; Winchell: *Pre-adamites*, pp. 188-193.

the argument requires an unwarranted assumption of fullness in this early Adamic history. For aught we know, the family of Adam may have already multiplied to a very considerable number, at least to one sufficient for the incidents in the life of Cain. The birth of only Cain and Abel previous to that of Seth is, in view of the time given by the manhood of both before this event, an unreasonable supposition. The omission of other names is nothing against the assumption of other births. Neither is the formal naming of the three, which no doubt was for special reasons. Thus, on the reasonable supposition of a considerable increase in the family of Adam beyond the names given, the incidents in the life of Cain are sufficiently provided for without the existence of pre-adamites. In view of very decisive facts of Scripture against this theory, we very much prefer the above solution of the questions arising from such incidents.

The unity of man by genealogical descent from Adam and Eve implies the marriage of brothers and sisters in the initial history of the race; and much account is made of the fact by the advocates of this pre-adamite theory. It is a case in which strong words may be used. Strong words are used.[1] The only avoidance of so repugnant a consequence is in the existence of pre-adamites, with whom the children of Adam might unite in lawful marriage. Such is the view. RESPECTING MARRIAGE.

How would Professor Winchell account for the initial multiplication of the race without the implication which he so strongly reprobates? On his theory, only the coincident evolution of two human beings, respectively male and female, could meet the lowest requirement for the inception of a human race. It might be said that such man and woman, even if born of the same animal parentage, would not be brother and sister, because such a relation has no sufficient ground in such a parentage. However, their children would be brothers and sisters, and there would still be no provision for a human race without their intermarriage. Hence the theory must assume the coincident evolution of distinct human pairs, and, reasonably, from distinct animal parentages, so as to provide for marriage without the consanguinity of brother and sister. Such evolutions must be assumed to be coincident in both time and place; for otherwise their children could never meet in wedlock, and the lawful requirements for a human race would still be wanting. A coincident creation of distinct human pairs, if such were the divine order, would be entirely responsive to rational thought; but such opportune evolutions QUESTION FOR EVOLUTIONISTS.

[1] Winchell Pre-adamites, pp. 190, 191.

to meet the exigencies of this pre-adamitism are not responsive to
such thought. It thus appears that this theory has for itself no
escape from the implication which it so strongly repels, except
through the most unwarranted assumptions.

The requirement of pre-adamites in order to provide lawful
THE QUESTION marriage for the children of Adam carries with it
IN ETHNOLOGY. serious difficulties in the question of ethnology and the
distinctions of race, while the implication so strongly objected
to the Adamic origin of man still cleaves to this theory. On this
theory, the distinctions of race are from separate origins or evolutions, not from differences of environment. Such is the law for
the deeper distinctions of the Negroid, Mongoloid, and Caucasian
races. The Negroid is held to be the oldest. There must be an
oldest, and the case is the same whichever be the race. We proceed on the supposition of the Negroid. For a beginning, the theory requires the coincident evolution of a Negroid man and woman.
But how shall the race be propagated without the marriage of
brothers and sisters ? There are no pre-negroidites with whom
they might intermarry. If the deeper distinctions of race are original, the Negroid must be original, without any mixture of blood
by the marriage of its first family of sons and daughters with an
older race. Otherwise, it is impossible to identify any original
race, and the ethnology of this theory becomes an utter tangle.
Whence the Mongoloid? Some have thought him the mongrel
child of the Negro and the Caucasian. If such be his origin, the
Caucasian race is older than the Mongoloid, while the latter is
clearly of lower grade. Therefore this view is out of accord with
the theory of evolution, which cannot allow the antecedence of a
higher race to a lower. Nor can it agree with many of the alleged
proofs of pre-adamites. Hence Professor Winchell consistently rejects it.[1] On his own theory of the evolution of distinct races, the
IN THE THEORY Mongoloid must be a new type by evolution from the
OF WINCHELL. Negroid stock. How shall the new type be perpetuated except by propagation within itself ? If the first offspring
of the newly evolved type must intermarry with the original stock,
it can have no permanence. But the propagation within itself, as
necessary to its perpetuation as a distinct race, requires the intermarriage of brothers and sisters. Adam appears as a ruddy white
man. His origin is by evolution from an older stock, not by direct
creation. He is the beginning of the Caucasian or white race.[2]
How is this new type to be propagated so as to preserve its distinction as the Caucasian race ? The children of Adam must not inter-

[1] *Pre-adamites*, p. 189.   [2] *Ibid.*, p. 294.

marry. For its avoidance the pre-adamites must be on hand. Cain married a Mongoloid.[1] Other children of Adam, at least the earlier, must have done the same. So the theory requires. It is the union of a very few with a race already numerous. The slight infusion of white blood will readily be absorbed without any noticeable or abiding variation of the Mongoloid type. It cannot be so with the new type. The grandchildren of Adam are half-Mongoloid, and each succeeding generation must be still more conformed to that type. There is here no parentage for the propagation of the distinct Caucasian race. Nor could there be any distinct Adamic race.

While such difficulties cleave to this theory, nothing is gained by thus recasting the traditional interpretation of Scripture. There is in it no avoidance of the special objection under review. On the initiation of a human race NO GAIN IN PRE-ADAMIT-ISM. without the intermarriage of brothers and sisters, science sheds not a ray of light. Hence pre-adamites should not hastily and dogmatically urge such an objection against the primariness of Adam. Any relief for his family can be gained only at the cost of an earlier family. On any theory, there must have been a beginning of mankind ; and at that beginning, whenever placed, such pre-adamites must find their own objection on hand, and with all its force against themselves. For purely naturalistic evolutionists the question has no concern, but for theistic evolutionists it has profound concern ; and it is far better that they should modestly and reverently leave it with the providence of God. Surely the ordering of the matter was wholly within his prerogative. Nor should we judge the question out of our present feelings. The case may have been very different in the first family of the race. God may have given to the sons and daughters of Adam a conjugal cast of the affectional nature rather than a brotherly and sisterly cast. On the ground of theism there is no perplexity in such a view. In the constitution of man nothing is more remarkable than the adjustment of his affectional nature to his manifold relations. It is an instance of the purest divine teleology. Nor shall we hesitate to believe that in like manner God could easily provide for any exigency arising in the initial history of the race.

7. *Doctrinal Interest in the Question of Unity.*—Polygenism, or an original plurality of races, in whatever form of the theory, is in opposition to fundamental doctrines of Christian theology. We instance anthropology and soteriology.

The Adamic origin of mankind ; the sin and fall of the prim-

[1] *Pre-adamites*, p. 295.

itive pair; the consequent moral lapse and ruin of the race; the

IN ANTHROPOL-
OGY AND SOTE-
RIOLOGY redemption of the race by Jesus Christ; the inclusion of all men in the race so ruined and redeemed—these are clear truths of Scripture. A few texts will suffice for the proof. The most explicit is the great passage of St. Paul.[1] It affirms the facts of anthropology and soteriology which we summarily stated. Through the sin of Adam all men suffer the consequence of depravity and death. Then for all men so ruined by the Adamic fall there is a common redemption in Jesus Christ. There is another text which, with its profound implications, gives the same truths: "For since by man came death, by man came also the resurrection of the dead. For as in Adam all die, even so in Christ shall all be made alive."[2] It thus appears again that the death of all men is a consequence of Adamic sin, and that for all as so involved there is a common redemption in Christ.

Neither polygenism in general nor pre-adamitism in particular
NO ADJUST-
MENT. can adjust itself to these truths of Christian theology. Of course, the attempt is made; but its futility is easily exposed. How could races existing long before Adam, and out of all genealogical connection with him, suffer the consequences of his sin? Any affirmative answer must assume a retroaction of Adam's sin. Such retroaction is assumed. The position of Peyrerius is thus stated: "Death entered the world before Adam, but it was in consequence of the imputation 'backward' of Adam's prospective sin; and this was necessary, that all men might partake of the salvation provided in Christ."[3] McCausland regards the pre-adamites as sinners on their own account, and finds in the words of Paul, not the universality of Adamic sin, but the universality of the redemption in Christ: "The Saviour redeemed Adam and his race, as the apostle states; but the redemption extends from the highest heaven to the lowest Hades—from Abel, Enoch, and Noah to 'the spirits in prison,' who were not of Adam's race."[4] The equivalence of great facts, as given in the comparison of Paul, is thus annulled. In this view the redemption in Christ immensely transcends the extent of Adamic sin and death, while in the sense of Paul the two are of the same extent.

Professor Winchell's own argument for the consistency of pre-
VIEW OF WIN-
CHELL. adamitism with Christian doctrine is mostly put in certain questions: Why could not antecedent races share with Noah and Abraham in the plan of salvation? If the atonement was retroactive for four thousand years or more, why

[1] Rom. v, 12–19.　　　　　　　　　　[2] 1 Cor. xv, 21, 22
[3] Winchell: Pre-adamites, p. 458.　　　[4] Adam and the Adamite, p. 294.

not a few thousand years farther? If it reached Adam, why not his ancestry? Why should the limitations of Hebrew knowledge limit the flow of divine grace ?[1] These questions might all be answered in the implied sense of the author, and yet be valueless for the proof of his theory, because, at most, they could give only the inference of a possible extension of redemptive grace, while the real question concerns the actual facts of sin and redemption as given in the Scriptures.

Professor Winchell gives prominence to certain utterances of Dr. Whedon, which, however, were confessedly only tentative or hypothetic, and were subsequently with- WHEDON'S VIEWS. drawn.[2] There was a time when the evidences of a high antiquity of man seemed to Dr. Whedon very strong, and when he thought it possible that further disclosures might prove an antiquity beyond the reach of biblical chronology. In forethought of such a contingency he suggested the admission of pre-adamites as probably the best mode of adjusting Christian doctrine to such antiquity : "Why not accept, if need be, the pre-adamic man ? If Dr. Dawson admits an Adamic center of creation, why not admit, if pressed, other centers of human origin ? The record does not seem to deny other centers in narrating the history of this center. The atonement, as all evangelical theology admits, has a retrospective power. It provides, as St. Paul says, ' remission for the sins that are past '— that is, for those who lived and sinned before Christ died ; and who received ' remission' from God in anticipation of the atonement. It was thus that Abraham was justified by faith, through the Christ that had not yet made the expiation. The atonement thus may throw responsibility and propitiation for sin over all past time, all terrene sections, and all human races. So, too, the sin of Adam may bring all past misdoings of earlier races under the category of sin and condemnation—that is, under the inauguration of a system of retribution which otherwise would not have taken existence. Some theologians have held that the atonement throws its sublime influence over other worlds than ours ; why not then over other human races ? Here, as often elsewhere, science, that seemed to threaten theology, does but open before it broader fields and sublimer elevations. It contradicts our narrow interpretations, and reads into the text worlds of new meaning. With this provisional view we have not the slightest misgiving as to the effect of the demonstration of the pre-adamite man upon our own theology."[3]

[1] *Pre-adamites*, pp. 285, 286.   [2] *Ibid.*, pp. 286–289, 470, 471.
[3] *Methodist Quarterly Review*, 1878, pp. 369, 370.

We cannot share the confidence of Dr. Whedon in such a mode of adjustment, in case the exigency should ever arise.

NO ADJUST-
MENT IN SUCH
A MODE.

We think the mode discredited by the assumptions which it requires. These assumptions were previously indicated, and now more fully appear in the above citation. One is the retroaction of Adamic sin; the other, the retroaction of redemptive grace. In both cases the retroaction must be such as to reach pre-adamic races. In itself considered, the latter assumption involves no serious perplexity. The atonement was in the plan of God the provisional ground of salvation for the Adamic race from the beginning, and, on the existence of prior races, might have been made available for them. So far, however, the putting of the case is purely hypothetic, while such an extension of redemptive grace is purely a question of fact. The other assumption of a retroaction of Adamic sin which brings pre-existent races " under the category of sin and condemnation " seems to us utterly inadmissible. The full consequence of Adam's sin upon his own race in genealogical descent from himself is full of perplexity. Without the genealogical connection any such consequence must be purely arbitrary, and the product of an immediate providential agency. This implication is not avoidable by a derivative connection of the Adamic race with earlier races, as held by Professor Winchell. The reason is obvious. Genealogical relations have no retroactive power. Heredity ever moves forward, never backward. It remains true that any involvement of earlier races in the sin of Adam must have been a purely arbitrary determination. Such a mode of guilt and retribution has no consistency with Christian theology—certainly none with an Arminian system. With Dr. Whedon himself, in his final view, we think it better not yet to accept the pre-adamite, and not to provide for him until his actual coming.[1]

The idea of a broader relation of the atonement than to mankind

SCOPE OF THE
ATONEMENT.

often appears in theological discussion. It was easy, therefore, for Professor Winchell to cite numerous instances.[2] Any service of the idea to the theory of pre-adamites must depend upon its content. Rarely has it been maintained that the atonement is for other sinners than those of mankind.

MEANING OF
CITATIONS.

When viewed as more broadly related, it is simply as a fact of paramount interest, as a lesson of profoundest moral significance, to all intelligences. Such is the whole content of the idea in its usual theological expression. We find nothing more in the instances cited by Professor Winchell. In most of

[1] *Methodist Quarterly Review*, 1878, p. 567.   [2] *Pre-adamites*, pp. 289–293.

them it is beyond question that this is all. We read nothing more in the citations from Bishop Marvin;[1] nothing more in that from Dr. Chalmers.[2] Indeed, we know that he meant nothing more. The citation from Hugh Miller[3] means simply the familiar idea of an original inclusion of redemption in the divine plan of creation and providence, without any intimation of an atonement for other than human sinners. Any further sense of Sir David Brewster must be a mere inference from an hypothetic interrogation.[4] With Professor Winchell we also could heartily appropriate the words long ago uttered by Bentley: "Neither need we be solicitous about the condition of those planetary people, nor raise frivolous disputes how far they may participate in Adam's fall, or in the benefits of Christ's incarnation;"[5] but they shed no light upon this pre-adamitism. There is no ground in Scripture for any notion of a retroaction of sin and grace in the ruin and recovery of pre-adamic races: Nor can we see how the views of authors, as above stated, could be thought of any value in the support of such a theory.

[1] *The Work of Christ*, pp. 10, 70, 74, 78, 137.
[2] *Astronomical Discourses*, discourse iv, p. 134.
[3] *Foot-prints of the Creator*, p. 326.
[4] *More Worlds than One*, English edition, pp. 166, 167.
[5] *Boyle Lectures*, 1724, p. 298.

CHAPTER II.

PRIMITIVE MAN.

THE man we here study is the man of the Mosaic narrative, not the first man of evolution. The two are widely different. If man came by evolution he was in the beginning of brutish mold, and a savage. It is not proved that man so came. Nor are we here concerned to review the question of his origin, which we previously discussed. We begin the study of man as presented in the narrative of Moses. In such a study the first question concerns the narrative itself, whether it should be interpreted according to a literal sense or be treated as mythical or allegorical. Only in the former sense can it give us any clear light on the question of primitive man. However, the interpretation must be determined, not by the exigency of light, but by the evidences in the case. We previously considered the question respecting the Mosaic narrative of creation; and as the narrative respecting primitive man is a part of that broader history it requires the less separate discussion.

I. LITERAL SENSE OF MOSAIC NARRATIVE.

1. *Historic Style of the Narrative.*—When the style is purely historical the contents must be accepted as literal, unless there be determining reasons for a different sense. This is a familiar and fully accepted principle of interpretation. Murphy states it thus: "The direct or literal sense of a sentence is the meaning of the author, when no other is indicated; not any figurative, allegorical, or mystical meaning."[1] The law is just as valid for an extended narrative as for a sentence. The account of primitive man is clearly historic in style. There is no contrary intimation nor any thing in the contents to discredit the literal sense. Therefore the narrative must be accepted as historic. This conclusion cannot

NOT A PHIL- be discredited by regarding the narrative simply as the
OSOPHIC SPEC- philosophic speculation of some devout Jew on the
ULATION.   origin of moral evil Such a view has gained more or less currency, particularly in German thought. "But we cannot adopt this hypothesis, for it requires a much later date to be

---

[1] *On Genesis*, pp. 13, 14. For a very full and able treatment of the question see Holden : *The Fall of Man*, chap. iii.

assigned to the narrative than the language in which it is written—allowing the utmost latitude that modern criticism demands—admits. It would, moreover, be very difficult to understand how the profound piety of a Jew, in dwelling upon the sacred traditions of his people concerning the progenitors of the race, could allow him to represent his theorizings as real history; or how, contrary to his purpose, such a misapprehension could arise." [1]

2. *Historical Connections of the Narrative.*—The narrative of primitive man is not an isolated part of Genesis, but a part thoroughly interwoven with its contents. If the facts which compose the body of the book are historical, so are the facts respecting man. All have a common ground. Any departure from historic verity is a surrender of the whole to allegoric uncertainty. " No writer of true history would mix plain matter of fact with allegory in one continued narrative, without any intimation of a transition from one to the other. If, therefore, any part of this narrative be matter of fact, no part is allegorical. On the other hand, if any part be allegorical, no part is naked matter of fact; and the consequence of this will be that every thing in every part of the whole narrative must be allegorical. . . . Thus the whole history of the creation will be an allegory, of which the real subject is not disclosed; and in this absurdity the scheme of allegorizing ends." [2] With a simple historic style, with nothing to discredit an historical sense, with no intimation of any other, and with such consequences of any departure from that sense, we must adhere to the true historical character of this narrative.

3. *Uncertainty of a Figurative Interpretation.*—This account of primitive man must have been intended for the communication of important truth. In this again it stands in inseparable connection with the fuller contents of Genesis. One may deny such an intention for the whole, but only at the cost of reducing the book to the grade of a mere romance or groundless speculation. The cost is too great. Nor is there any compensation. The book itself would become utterly inexplicable. It could have no rational account as to either its origin or aim. Such a book must have an aim, and the only rational aim is the communication of important truth. With a literal sense such truth is given; without it, only myth or romance remains.

4. *Scripture Recognition of a Literal Sense.*—This recognition is given in clear references to leading events of the narrative. There

[1] Müller · *Christian Doctrine of Sin*, vol. ii, pp. 347, 348.

[2] Bishop Horsley . *Biblical Criticism*, vol. i, p. 9. Cited by Holden : *The Fall of Man*, pp 21, 22.

is such a reference in the words of our Lord respecting the unity
PROOFS OF THE of husband and wife—such a unity as must bar all di-
RECOGNITION vorcement, except for the one reason which he allows.[1]
The reference is determined beyond question by a citation from
the Mosaic narrative.[2] There could be no reference to such events,
and particularly as the ground of so important a doctrine, without
the reality of the events themselves. Such also is the reference to
the serpent as the instrument in the temptation of Eve.[3] Another
instance is in the reference to the order of succession in the formation of Adam and Eve, and also to the facts that the woman was
deceived and first in the transgression.[4] How could these events
be made the ground of such a lesson of economical order unless
they were regarded as real? There are references to still deeper
truths. One is to the introduction of sin and death into the
world by the sin of Adam.[5] His sin and fall are thus brought into
vital relation to the deepest truths of Christianity. Even the
redemptive mediation of Christ is conditioned on the reality of
these events. Without as much fullness of statement, there is the
implication of the same deep truths in another reference of Paul.[6]
The historic character of the Mosaic narrative respecting primitive
man thus stands clearly in the recognition of the Scriptures. This
recognition, with the other evidences adduced, is conclusive of a
literal sense.

II. Primary Questions of Mosaic Narrative.

The simple narrative of creation, even from the beginning,
moves on in sublime strain; but when the creation of man is
reached a deeper tone is heard. Up to this stage there is for rational thought no completeness of nature. The same stars are in
the sky; the same sun illumines the world; there are the same living orders, with all the wonders of organic constitution; but there
is no mind within this scale of nature for the rational cognition of
these orderly forms of existence; none which may rise in thought
to a divine Mind as their only true and sufficient original. Within
their own limitation no sufficient reason for their existence can
be given. Their end is not in themselves.[7] This deficiency is
the prophecy of a rational culmination, and the prophecy is fulfilled
in the coming of man. That distinct and deeper tone is first
heard in the narrative of his creation, and signifies his true head-

[1] Matt. xix, 4-6.   [2] Gen. ii, 24.   [3] 2 Cor. xi, 3.
[4] 1 Tim. ii, 13, 14.   [5] Rom. v, 12-19.   [6] 1 Cor. xv, 21, 22.
[7] Dwight: *Theology*, vol. i, pp. 348, 349; Watson: *Theological Institutes*,
vol. ii, p. 8.

ship.[1] Such completion of the scale is the satisfaction of rational thought.

A few particulars of the Mosaic narrative require brief attention before we come to the deeper questions of doctrinal anthropology.

1. *Constituent Natures of Man.*—On the face of the sacred narrative there are two distinct natures, body and mind, in the original constitution of man. This fact itself decides nothing respecting the theory of trichotomy, but is so far the obvious truth of the Mosaic narrative. Man is certainly dichotomic. " And the LORD God formed man of the dust of the ground, and breathed into his nostrils the breath of life; and man became a living soul."[2] There must here be the sense of two distinct natures.

The body is material like the earth out of which it is formed. The chemical elements combined in its constitution belong to the same earth. The body can easily be resolved into these common elements. Such a resolution is in constant process, as certain particles, having fulfilled their use, are ever being eliminated, while others are ever taking their place by a process of assimilation. While the body possesses all the qualities of matter, it is subject to the same methods of chemical and mechanical treatment. Its purely material nature is thus at once the clear sense of the Mosaic narrative and the determination of physical facts. [A MATERIAL BODY.]

In the formation of Adam there was no such divine operation as man must put forth in working a batch of clay into a human form. There was no divine *manipulation* of material. So crude a notion never entered into any clear theistic conception. Yet we find such a notion urged as an objection to the origin of man in an immediate divine formation " Pre-adamitism . . . admits that Adam was 'created,' but substitutes for manual modeling of the plastic clay the worthier conception of origination according to a *genetic* method."[3] Whether put as an objection to the orthodox conception of man's creation, or as an argument for his evolution, the answer is already given: the crude notion of a " manual modeling of the plastic clay" never appears in that conception. The divine agency in this case, as in all others, is in the energizing of the divine will. The immediate formation of primitive man through this agency is the whole truth of the orthodox theory. [NO MANIPULATORY WORK]

The formation of the body was only a part of the divine work in the creation of man. There followed the divine in-breathing: God " breathed into his nostrils the breath of life; and man became a living soul." The body might have been complete in its organic constitution without the living state, [CREATION OF MIND.]

[1] Gen. i, 26–28.   [2] Gen. ii, 7.   [3] Winchell : *Pre-adamites* p. 285.

and this divine inbreathing might primarily signify its vitalization, with the inception of respiration as necessary to the maintenance of life. Some expositors find this lower sense in the plural form of the original text, as signifying "the breath of lives." There is, however, in this distinct view of vitalization a trichotomic implication which seems mostly to have been overlooked. In the deeper sense the divine operation must mean the creation of the rational mind. The divine inbreathing signifies this creative agency. However, there is no outward form of action. So far the expression is anthropomorphic. The deep and true meaning is none the less clear. There is no impartation of divine essence as constitutive of the human soul. It is an immediate creation in the most originative sense of the term. This is the deeper meaning of the divine inbreathing in the creation of man.

Rational mind is the distinction of man as an order of existence. MIND DISTINCT- Without this distinction he must be classed merely as an IVE OF MAN.   animal. He might still be the highest grade, but could not be a distinct order. The utmost exaltation, exaggeration even, of animal intelligence leaves it in an infinitely lower plane than that of rational mind. The characteristics and achievements of human intelligence are the sufficient proof. The reality of mind is given with its faculties. Such faculties must have a ground in being. The essential distinction of the mind and the body is given in the profound distinction of qualities. In the one we find the properties of matter, with their complete subjection to chemical and mechanical laws; in the other, the faculties of intelligence and personal agency under a law of freedom. The two classes are in such thorough distinction, contrariety even, that they cannot have a common ground in being. Otherwise properties signify nothing as to the nature of their ground. But if they have no meaning for its nature, neither have they any for its reality. We should thus fall into the most abject phenomenalism or positivism. Reason, however, still asserts, and will forever assert, the reality of being as the ground of properties, and equally asserts a distinction of grounds in accord with the fundamental distinction of properties. Thus reason affirms the reality of spiritual being as the ground of mental faculties. Hence the divine inbreathing was the creation of a spiritual nature in man.

2. *The Question of Trichotomy.*—Trichotomy is the doctrine of OBSCURITY OF three distinct natures in man—body, soul, spirit—σῶμα, A THIRD NAT- ψυχή, πνεῦμα. Body and spirit are defined and dis-URE   criminated in the same manner as in the dichotomic view. There is unavoidable indefiniteness respecting the soul when

thus held as a nature distinct from each of the others. We can readily define and differentiate material and mental natures by their respective and essentially different qualities, but we cannot so treat a nature which is neither, and is without definitive and differentiating qualities of its own. Dr. Bush, with others, designates it as a *tertium quid,* and assumes to find the evidence of its reality in a set of qualities in man which are neither material nor mental in any distinctive sense. These qualities appear in what constitutes the animal life in man in distinction from the intellectual or rational life.[1] The use of the indefinite *tertium quid* for the designation of this intermediate nature fully concedes its indefiniteness. Mere indefiniteness, however, is not conclusive against its reality. A thing is definite as its qualities are open to our mental cognition, and indefinite when they are not open. With hidden qualities there might still be the reality of being; though in such case we could not affirm the being. Whether the qualities of the animal or sentient life of man require as their ground a *tertium quid,* a nature neither physical nor mental, is far from self-evident. It may not be possible to prove the contrary. It follows that the question of trichotomy cannot be decided in this mode.

In the early history of the Church trichotomy flourished mostly in the school of Alexandria, and was introduced into TRICHOTOMY IN THEOLOGY. Christian theology through the Platonic philosophy. For a while it seemed fairly on the way to a common acceptance, when adverse influences checked its progress and brought it into disrepute. Tertullian strongly opposed it, and his influence was very great. Even the seeming indifference of Augustine was indirectly much against it; for his influence was so great on all doctrinal questions that nothing without his open support could hold a position of much favor in the more orthodox thought of the Church. Besides these facts, trichotomy was appropriated in the interest of the Apollinarian Christology and the Semi-Pelagian doctrine of sin. Very naturally, though not very logically, the strong antagonism to these heresies turned all its force against the trichotomy so appropriated.[2] The doctrinal relation of trichotomy to these heresies is worthy of brief notice. The pointing out of this relation requires a statement of the heretical elements of the doctrines concerned.

The Christology of Apollinaris denied to Christ the human mind in its distinct rational sense, and provided for its functions in his

[1] Bush. *Anastasis,* p. 78

[2] Delitzsch. *Biblical Psychology,* p. 106; McClintock and Strong: *Cyclopædia,* " Trichotomy."

personality by the presence of the Logos as the divine reason.
IN APOLLINA-   Such a view requires the trichotomic anthropology, for
RIANISM.   the presence of the Logos in the place of the rational
mind could not account for the sensibilities of Christ in the likeness of our own. In the absence of the rational mind, the soul
must have been present as the ground of the manifold affections
which lie below the purely rational life. Therefore the soul must
be a distinct existence, for otherwise it could not be thus present
in the absence of the rational mind. Such being the facts in the
case, the only relation of trichotomy to the Apollinarian Christology is that it is the requirement and the possibility of such a
Christology. On the other hand, this heresy is in no sense the
logical implication or consequence of the trichotomy. Hence,
with entire consistency, many trichotomists are thoroughly orthodox in their Christology. It follows that this heretical appropriation of trichotomy is no evidence against its truth, and no reason
for the disrepute which it suffered in consequence.

The Semi-Pelagian doctrine of original sin, while holding much
IN SEMI-PELA- truth as against pure Pelagianism, fell far short of the
GIANISM   Augustinian doctrine. It specially differed from the
latter, and fell short of it, in excepting the purely spiritual nature
of man from the effect of Adamic sin. Yet his mere physical
nature could not be the ground of all that was suffered. The soul
as a distinct nature is necessary to such sufficient ground. Hence
it must exist in man as a real nature in distinction from his purely
spiritual nature. It thus appears that trichotomy is related to the
Semi-Pelagian doctrine of sin precisely in the manner of its relation
to the Apollinarian Christology. If the spiritual nature is excepted
from the effect of Adamic sin, trichotomy must be true because it
is the requirement of facts in the case of such exception. This
exception, however, is no logical implication of the trichotomy.
Hence trichotomy has no direct doctrinal concern with the Semi-
Pelagian doctrine of original sin. Indeed, it does not seriously
concern any important doctrine of Christian theology. It is a
question of speculative interest in biblical psychology, but has no
doctrinal implications decisive of either its truth or falsity.

A dichotomic view of man is clearly given in the Scriptures.
DICHOTOMY   We give by reference a few texts out of many.[1] The
OF THE SCRIPT- dust and the spirit, body and soul, body and spirit are
URES   the terms of these texts, which seem at once inclusive of
the whole man and thoroughly distinctive of his natures. In this
view man is only dichotomic. Yet we can hardly regard these texts

[1] Eccl. xii, 7; Matt. x, 28; 1 Cor. vi, 20; Jas. ii, 26.

as decisive of the question; and for the reason that, even with an intermediate nature, the very profound and specially open distinction between our bodily and spiritual natures justifies their designation in the same comprehensive sense as if really constitutive of our whole being. It is not the manner of the sacred writers, as it is not that of any writer, to be always thoroughly analytic. In the treatment of subjects it mostly suffices that chief characteristics be set forth, and the more prominent distinctions be made. Usually this is the actual and the better method. This may be the method in these formally dichotomic texts, and hence they are not conclusive against trichotomy.

There are also trichotomic texts—such at least in form. Two are in special favor with the advocates of trichotomy.[1] In the first we have the three distinctive terms "spirit, and soul, and body;" in the other, "soul and spirit," with other terms, "joints and marrow," which clearly signify the body. In this prayer of Paul for the Christians of Thessalonica the central and ruling idea is the entireness of their sanctification and their blameless preservation therein. With his usual force and fullness of expression, naturally, in such a case he would use words comprehensive of the whole man as the subject of the gracious sanctification and preservation. The intentional meaning of three distinct natures in man is no necessary part of such comprehension. Indeed, such a formal analytic view is hardly consistent with the intensity of the ruling idea of a complete wholeness. Such is the case in the great commandment.[2] With the simple idea of loving God with our utmost capacity of loving, this commandment receives its greatest force; while, on the other hand, it must suffer loss of force by any analysis of heart, soul, and mind into ontological distinctions. The other text is open to similar observations. Soul and spirit are here viewed, not as essentially distinct, but as together the seat of thought and affection. In this view a third term, heart, has the same meaning as the other two. As the word of God is quick and sharp, and pierces even to the sundering of soul and spirit, so it comes to discern the thoughts and intents of the heart. This substitution of the one term heart for the two terms soul and spirit denies to them any ontological distinction; for otherwise we must allow a third distinction for the heart, and the three, with the body, would give us a tetrachotomous division of natures in man. Such an outcome would itself be fatal to trichotomy.

If the original terms, נֶפֶשׁ and ψυχή, on the one hand, and רוּחַ and πνεῦμα, on the other, were used with uniformity of discrimina-

[1] 1 Thess. v, 23 ; Heb. iv, 12. [2] Luke x, 27.

27

tion, the former for the ground of the animal life and the latter for
the ground of the rational and religious life, the fact
would constitute a strong argument for trichotomy.
Such, however, is not the case. Indeed, the contrary is the fact.
The former two often signify the ground of the rational life, while
the latter two often signify the ground of the animal life. A few references may suffice for the verification of this position.
We give the leading meanings of נפש : Life ;[1] life or
spirit ;[2] intellect, as manifest in its predicates or functions : joyful
love ;[3] gladness ;[4] piety toward God ;[5] sinning ;[6] faculty of knowledge ;[7] the personal self.[8] It is thus made clear that this term has
no restricted lower sense which can serve the interest of trichotomy,
but is freely used in the highest sense of personal mind. We find
the same meanings in the use of רוח : breath;[9] animal life ;[10] the one
life and spirit respectively of man and beast ;[11] the intellect, understanding ;[12] the immortal spirit.[13] It thus appears that, while
the former term rises to the highest sense of the latter, the latter
sinks to the lowest sense of the former. This absence of all distinction in their application to the animal and rational sides of
human life denies to their use any support of trichotomy. It will
not be questioned that πνεῦμα often signifies the highest
nature of man. Instances of such use are many and
clear. With the *spirit* we rejoice in God our Saviour.[14] Our *spirit*
witnesses jointly with the Holy Spirit to our gracious sonship.[15]
The glorified saints are *spirits* made perfect.[16] Only as the personal
mind can the πνεῦμα be the subject of such predications. This
same term, however, means breath or breathed air ;[17] also the wind.[18]
On the other hand, ψυχή rises to the highest meaning of πνεῦμα.
The *soul* is the man, the personal self.[19] With the *soul* we must
love God supremely,[20] which is the highest form of personal action.
The martyrs already with God are *souls*.[21] We thus find a concurrence of meanings in the Scripture use of *soul* and *spirit* which precludes any essential distinction between them.

It was previously stated that a uniform distinction of Hebrew and
Greek terms for the designation of the animal and the rational life of

[1] Gen. i, 20, 30.   [2] Gen. xxxv, 18 ; 1 Kings xvii, 21.
[3] Isa. xlii, 1.   [4] Psa. lxxxvi, 4.   [5] Psa. ciii, 1, 2.
[6] Lev. iv, 2.   [7] Psa. cxxxix, 14 ; Prov. xix, 2.
[8] Lev. v, 1, 2, 4, 15, 17 ; Job ix, 21 ; Psa. iii, 2 ; Isa. li, 23.   [9] Job iv, 9.
[10] Job xii, 10.   [11] Eccl. iii, 19, 21.   [12] Isa. xxix, 24.   [13] Eccl. xii, 7.
[14] Luke i, 47.   [15] Rom. viii, 16.   [16] Heb. xii, 23.   [17] 2 Thess. ii, 8
[18] John iii, 8.   [19] Acts ii, 43 , iii, 23 ; Rom. ii, 9.   [20] Matt. xxii, 37.
[21] Rev. vi, 9 ; xx, 4.

man would constitute a strong argument for trichotomy. In the total absence of such discrimination there is no such argu- NO SUPPORT OF ment. On the other hand, the indiscriminate and inter- TRICHOTOMY changing use of these terms may fairly be claimed as an argument for the dichotomic view of man. We do not think it conclusive. It follows that we have reached no dogmatic conclusion on the question of trichotomy. We are not concerned for the attainment of such a result, and for the reason previously stated, that the question does not seriously concern any important truth of Christian theology.[1]

3. *Original Physiological Constitution.*—This question must be determined in the light of relative facts as given in the Scriptures. In this view it is clearly seen that in chemical elements, in physiological constitution, and in the provision for subsistence, the body of Adam was much like our own. There must have been lungs for respiration, an alimentary system for the digestion and assimilation of food, an organism of veins for the circulation of the blood, and of nerves for sensation and locomotion. With these facts there must have been the same osteological and muscular systems.

It is a pure gratuity to think that such a body could be naturally exempt from the susceptibilities and liabilities of our NATURAL LIA- own. With the highest degree of bodily perfection in BILITIES Adam, he must still have been naturally liable to the ordinary casualties of our physical life. His bones could be broken, his blood poisoned, his flesh suffer lesion. He would have suffered from any excess of either fasting or eating. Such a bodily constitution is naturally liable to suffering and death. Any exemption in either case must depend upon a specially providential economy. Such an exemption was no doubt available for Adam on the condition of obedience to the divine will. In accord with these views suffering and death are accounted to man through the sin of disobedience.[2]

4. *Intellectual Grade of Primitive Man.*—Here again the truth is to be sought in a rational interpretation of relative EXAGGERATED facts. The popular view has been molded rather by the VIEWS extravagance of Milton than by the moderation of Moses. The theological mind has not been free from much exaggeration. "An Aristotle was but the rubbish of an Adam."[3] In this manner the vigorous South expresses his lofty conception of the mental endowments of primitive man. Mr. Wesley is not less extravagant in his view, that Adam reasoned with unerring accuracy—if he reasoned at all. The supposition is that he possessed the faculties of

[1] Heard · *Tripartite Nature of Man;* Beck · *Biblical Psychology;* Delitzsch : *System of Biblical Psychology,* pp 103–119.

[2] Gen ii, 17; Rom. v, 12.   [3] South : *Sermons,* vol. i, p. 25.

immediate insight into all subjects, and was in no need of either experience or reasoning as a means of knowledge. No doubt he possessed a faculty of immediate insight into primary truths, but there is no evidence of any such insight into truths which we can acquire only through experience and reasoning. We may concede him a very high grade of mental powers, yet they were merely human, just like our own in kind, and operative under the same laws.

NAMING THE ANIMALS. There is nothing in the naming of the animals which, on any proper interpretation, contradicts this moderate view of Adam's mental powers.[1] The perplexity of this case need not be aggravated by the assumption of an absolute universality in the term which designates the number of animals brought to Adam for naming. "The Hebrew word כֹּל, *kol*, it is well known, does not invariably mean *all* in the largest sense, but sometimes *many* or *much ;* and that it was designed to be received with some limitation in the instance under review is evident from the fishes of the sea not being specified, and from the inutility of making a vocabulary of such animals as were to inhabit distant regions of the globe, and which Adam would never see again after his nomination of them. It is also uncertain whether the assemblage consisted of those only which were within the precincts of the garden of Eden, or included others ; inasmuch as the expressions, ' every beast of the field, and every fowl of the air,' may only denote of the field and climate of Paradise."[2] Another mode of limitation may be cited, which obviates the chief objection urged against the narrative when taken in a universal sense : "It will be more satisfactory, however, if it can be shown that the objection rests only on a misapprehension of the narrative, which by no means affirms that all the creatures, or even many of them, were congregated before the man. ' Out of the ground the Lord God formed every beast of the field, and fowl of the air,' and ' *brought to the man,*' not ' brought *them,*' as in the English version, but ' brought to the man,' which is evidently equivalent to *brought of them*, the universal *every* referring only to the formation. Should it, however, be objected that the next verse adds, ' the man gave names to all cattle,' etc., this will admit of easy explanation, for the correct rendering of the passage is, ' to all *the cattle,*' evidently to as many as were thus brought before him."[3]

BY NO MATERIAL ABILITY. With this restricted sense, however, the naming of the animals remains much the same as it respects the original faculties of Adam. The names given might be viewed either as arbitrary or as descriptive. In the former case they

[1] Gen. ii, 19, 20.   [2] Holden : *The Fall of Man*, pp 98, 99.
[3] Macdonald : *Creation and the Fall*, p. 367.

would signify nothing respecting the nature of the animals, while in the latter case they would express severally the natures of the different classes. For an arbitrary naming the requirements would be simply a sufficient vocabulary and a ready use of words. Adam could have had no such qualifications through his faculties, unless we postpone this event for many years after his creation. Language is not gained by intuition. The ready use of words in articulate speech is gained only through long practice. What Adam might have done through divine inspiration is a question quite apart from the present one which concerns his own capacities. By common agreement of the best thinkers the origination of language is a difficult problem ; and not a few have found its sufficient source only in the divine agency.[1] It was simply impossible for Adam in the mere exercise of his own faculties to acquire almost instantly the vocabulary and the use of words necessary to the naming of the animals, however much we may restrict their number. In the view of descriptive names, all the previous difficulty, as it respects the natural ability of Adam, remains, while very much is added. The giving of such names required an insight into the nature of the various NO SUPERHU- animals. Such an immediate insight has been freely MAN INSIGHT attributed to Adam. We give a single instance : "Adam gave names; but how? From an intimate knowledge of the nature and properties of each creature. Here we see the perfection of his knowledge ; for it is well known that the names affixed to the different animals in Scripture always express some prominent feature and essential characteristic of the creatures to which they are applied. Had he not possessed an intuitive knowledge of the grand and distinguishing properties of those animals he never could have given them such names."[2] It is hardly thinkable that such intuition can belong to any finite mind. To attribute it to Adam is to place him out of all proper homogeneity with ourselves. It must mean that the highest and most distinctive power of primitive man is entirely lost to his race. There is no such original unlikeness, no such loss of original faculty; and it is far more consistent with all the relative facts to account this naming of the animals to a divine inspiration. "To suppose it otherwise, and to imagine that Adam at the first was able to impose names on the several tribes of animals, is to suppose, either that he must from the first have been able to distinguish them by their characteristic marks and leading properties, and to have distinct notions of them annexed to their several appellations, or that he applied sounds, at

[1] Magee . On the Atonement, dissertation liii   [2] Clarke · Commentary, in loc.

random, as names of the animals, without the intervention of such
notions.   But the latter is to suppose a jargon, not a language;
and the former implies a miraculous operation on the mind of
Adam, which differs nothing in substance from the divine instruction here contended for."[1]

We thus find in Adam no evidence of a superhuman mental
grade.   However high his intellectual powers, they were not other
in kind than our own ; and, if left to himself, his progress, even in
the rudiments of empirical knowledge, must have been very slow.
There is no evidence that he was so left; and it is far more rational
to think that he was divinely instructed and helped forward, that
he might the sooner be prepared for the throne of the world assigned
him.[2]

5. *Created in the Image of God.*—In the divine ideal of man as
a purposed creation he was to be the image of God.   "And God
said, Let us make man in our image, after our likeness."[3]   The
record of such an actual creation immediately follows.[4]

Very naturally differences of opinion respecting the likeness of
VIEWS OF HIS
LIKENESS TO
GOD.
man to God early appeared in Christian thought.
With a common agreement that man himself was the
image of God, there was still the cardinal question as
to what really constituted man.   Some could not dispense with the
body as an essential part, and therefore assumed for it a likeness to
God.   This required the assumption of some form of corporeity in
God; for it is not to be thought that a physical nature can bear the
likeness of a purely spiritual being.   With the burden of such an
assumption, the notion of a bodily similitude could not command a
wide acceptance ; and the prevalent opinion placed the image of
God in the spiritual nature of man.   Opinions also divided on the
question whether image and likeness, or the original words so rendered, have different meanings or only serve conjunctly to intensify
the expression of the one truth.   Occasion was found for a distinction of meanings.   "As there is a great difference between the
mere natural dispositions and their development by the free use of
the powers which have been granted to men, several writers, among
whom *Irenæus*, and especially *Clement* and *Origen*, distinguished
between the image of God and resemblance to God.   The latter
can only be obtained by a mental conflict (in an ethical point of
view), or is bestowed upon man as a gift of sovereign mercy by
union with Christ (in a religious aspect)."[5]   Such a view is utterly

[1] Magee : *On the Atonement*, dissertation liii.
[2] Gen. i, 26–28.   [3] Gen. i, 26.   [4] Gen. i, 27.
[5] Hagenbach : *History of Doctrines*, vol. i, p. 157.

discredited by the fact that this likeness of man to God was an original creation, not any subsequent attainment through either the free agency of man or the sovereignty of divine grace. A distinction of meanings in the two original terms is again discredited by the fact that in other places only one is used, sometimes one and sometimes the other, and in a manner to give to each the full meaning of both in the primary instance of their conjunct use.[1]

It should be distinctly noted, and the fact should be emphasized, that man was originally *made* in the image of God. Hence this image must lie in what he was originally, just as he came from the creative hand of God We thus exclude every thing extraneous to the man himself, and equally every thing subsequent to his creation, whether from the divine agency or as the fruit of his own action. We thus exclude the dominion assigned to man,[2] which has often been set forth as the great fact of his likeness to God Man was constituted in himself, not in his dominion, the image of God himself, not of his dominion. His dominion was an assignment subsequent to his creation in the image of God, which image constituted his fitness for such dominion. THINGS EX-CLUDED

We may find the true sense of this image rather in a complex of facts than in a single fact. The spiritual nature of man is the deepest fact of this likeness—the deepest because necessary to all other facts of likeness. But we should not place it so deep that it shall stand related to the divine likeness in man just as the canvas is related to the painting which it bears, or merely "as precious ground on which the image of God might be drawn, and formed."[3] The spiritual nature was itself of the original likeness of man to God. Ontologically, spirit is like spirit, though one be finite and the other infinite. The intellectual and moral endowments of primitive man constituted a measure of his likeness to God. Again we are face to face with the profound distinction between the finite and the infinite; but such distinction does not preclude a profound truth of likeness. In God there is an intellectual, an emotional, and a moral nature. Such qualities of nature were in primitive man; in these facts he was the image of God. Personality is the central truth of man's original likeness to God. As a person he was thoroughly differentiated from all lower orders of existence, and in the highest sense lifted up into the image of God. FACTS OF THE LIKENESS

The original image of God in man no doubt had the implicit sense of holiness Hence in the New Testament it came to signify

[1] Compare Gen i, 27 ; v, 1 ; ix, 6.   [2] Gen. i, 28.
[3] Witsius . *The Covenants*, vol. i, p 34.

holiness.   This appears in the fact that the regeneration of man, his transformation from depravity into holiness, is represented as a recreation in the image of God after which he was originally made.[1] But this question of primitive holiness so deeply concerns important doctrinal issues that it requires a separate treatment.

[1] Eph. iv, 24 ; Col. iii, 10.

CHAPTER III.

QUESTION OF PRIMITIVE HOLINESS.

As previously noted, this question deeply concerns important doctrinal issues. The Pelagian anthropology, with its manifold doctrinal implications, takes its place on the one side; the Augustinian anthropology, with all its implications, takes its place on the other. The profoundest dissent from the former does not require the full acceptance of the latter. It is true that any doctrinal anthropology which may be scientifically wrought into a system of evangelical theology must be in open issue with the Pelagian anthropology; but there is sure ground for such a theology without the extremes of the Augustinian anthropology.

I. NATURE OF HOLINESS IN ADAM.

1. *Determining Law of Limitation.*—Holiness is here viewed as a primitive quality of Adam, such as he possessed in the beginning of his existence. Therefore it must have been simply a quality of his nature, or such as might be an accompanying gift of his creation. It certainly could possess no proper ethical element, such as can arise only from free personal action. This is a determining law of limitation respecting the nature of primitive holiness. To pass this limit is to fall at once into the error of thinking that an ethical holiness may be divinely created in man. Directly following this is the error of thinking that a mere nature, the nature with which we are born, can be the subject of an ethical sinfulness and demerit—just such sinfulness and demerit as arise from personal violations of the divine law. An observance of this law of limitation will protect us against such errors.

2. *Fundamental Distinctions of Holiness.*—In a true godly life, such as that of Daniel, in a true Christian life, such as that of Paul, there is personal holiness, the holiness of character, with the ethical qualities of righteous action. Such holiness has ethical worth before the divine law. The quality of holiness and the moral worth arise from free moral action in obedience to the divine will.

In such a godly or Christian life there is an inner life answering to the outer; an inner life of holy aspirations and aims, which indeed are the inspiration and true worth of the outer life. But in these inner activities there is still the free use of personal faculties, and therefore the truest form of ethical action. The holiness of such an inner life is of the truest ethical character, and therein profoundly different from the possible holiness of a primitive nature.

Below this inner life there is the nature, with its spontaneous tendencies. As matter has its properties, so mind has its powers and tendencies. However metaphysical the distinction between the nature and its tendencies, it is yet real for thought. Tendencies of nature are specially exemplified in the animal orders. The natural disposition is the determining law of the animal life. The distinctions of life are from differences of natural tendency. We thus note, at once, the reality and the differences of natural tendency in the lion and the lamb. In like manner we may note the reality, and the differences, of natural tendency in men whose lives are morally opposite. With the one the spontaneous disposition is to the good; with the other, to the evil. Such is the difference between a regenerate or sanctified nature and a nature yet corrupt and vicious. We thus find differences of moral tendency. On the ground of moral tendency we allege a moral quality of the nature; on the differences of such tendency, we qualify the one nature as good and the other as evil, but only in the sense in which a nature may be good or evil. With a spontaneous disposition to the good the nature is holy. There is such a subjective holiness in distinction from all holiness really ethical in its character.

The nature below the life.

3. *Nature of Adamic Holiness.*—After the previous analysis, the truth in this question is close at hand. The holiness of Adam, as newly created and before any personal action of his own, was simply a subjective state and tendency in harmony with his moral relations and duties. But such a state, however real and excellent, and however pleasing to the divine mind, could not have any true ethical quality, or in any proper sense be accounted either meritorious or rewardable. A deeper analysis which reaches the most determinate moral principles must eliminate from theology the ideas of ethical character without free personal action.

A subjective state.

This question should not be confused by any difficulty, or inability even, to fix the exact line where spontaneous tendency passes over into ethical action. Nor should this line be ignored in order to place such quality in something back of it. Theological speculation is not free from such mistakes.

Not strictly ethical.

"Adam was brought into existence capable of acting immediately, as a moral agent, and therefore he was immedi- THE VIEW OF
ately under a rule of *right* action, he was obliged as EDWARDS.
soon as he existed to act right. And if he was obliged to act right
as soon as he existed, he was obliged even then to be *inclined* to act
right. . . . And as he was obliged to act right from the first moment of his existence, and did do so till he sinned in the affair of
the forbidden fruit, he must have had an inclination or disposition of
heart to do right the first moment of his existence; and that is the
same as to be created or brought into existence, with an inclination, or, which is the same thing, a virtuous and holy disposition of
heart." [1] Not only is there here an overlooking of all distinction
between purely spontaneous tendency and proper ethical action, but
it is attempted to prove an original ethical holiness of Adam from
its necessity to the moral obligation which was instant upon his
existence. The assumption of such instant obligation is a pure
gratuity. The requisite knowledge was not a product of the
divine action which gave existence to Adam. Even the gift of mature powers is not the gift of such knowledge. Whether he was at
once so endowed, or placed under training and gradually inducted
into the moral sphere, we do not know. On these questions the
Scriptures are silent. Reasonably, there was sufficient time for the
knowledge and sensibility necessary to moral obligation. The assumption of an active disposition so instant upon the very existence of man as to be beforehand with an instant obligation, and
not only the same in ethical quality as a free moral act, but a necessity to any holy volition, is far more replete with metaphysical
subtlety than psychological and ethical analysis. The profound
distinction between mere spontaneous tendency and personal action
under obligation and law still remains. It is as real as the deepest
ethical principles. It is none the less real for any inability to fix
the exact line of distinction. A mere initial tendency to the good
in Adam could have no ethical character. It could not become an
active disposition until duty in some form was presented. Simply
as spontaneously active it could constitute only a motive, not an
ethical action. Else to be tempted is to sin, and in every instance
of temptation. Motive, whether to the good or the evil, takes on
ethical character only where approved or entertained. Here it is
that personal agency comes into action. Previous to this there is
no ethical character, and the subtleties of Edwards are futile for
the proof of the contrary. [2]

[1] Edwards · Works, vol ii, p 385.
[2] Full argument of Edwards: Works, vol. ii, pp. 381–390.

Both Whedon and Bledsoe very fully and very ably discuss the principles of this question, and both conclude against the possibility of any moral character, such as involves either merit or demerit, previous to free moral action.[1] The application of these principles to the present question is in this manner: "We may suppose a being, like Adam, created with soul perfectly right. His preferential feelings anterior to action accord with the divine law. His sensibilities are so under easy volitional control, his mind is so clear and pure, that all in its primitive undisturbed state is right. His will is able to hold his whole being in subordination to the moral imperative. He is, in his grade of being, perfectly excellent, and his excellence is not mechanical merely or æsthetical, but ethical. It is moral excellence, it is created moral excellence, and perfect in its kind, yet wholly unmeritorious."[2]

A primitive Adamic holiness is not an impossibility because Adam could not, simply as created, be holy in any strictly ethical or meritorious sense. In the fundamental distinctions of holiness we found a sense which is applicable to a nature in distinction from a personal agent. It lies in a spontaneous tendency to the good. The subjective disposition answers to the good on its presentation. It answers as a spontaneous inclination or impulse toward holy action. This is all that we mean by the nature of Adamic or primitive holiness.

4. *Possibility of Holiness in Adam.*—There may be holiness of the moral nature previous to free moral action. If not, such a quality of the nature must forever be impossible. Whatever it might become by good conduct, such it might be constituted in its original creation. This must be clear if we still hold in view the fundamental distinctions of holiness. In ethical character we become by free personal action what we could not be constituted by the divine agency. Only in the former mode can moral merit or demerit arise. The case is different respecting the nature in distinction from the personal agent. Whatever quality the nature might possess subsequent to holy action, or as consequent to such action, with such quality it could be originally endowed. Otherwise all moral quality must arise from personal conduct, and must belong to man as a personal agent, without any possible application to his nature.

It would follow that moral beings, however opposite their lives,

<hr />

[1] Whedon : *Freedom of the Will*, pp. 375–396 ; Bledsoe . *Theodicy*, pp. 113-151.

differ only in deeds, not at all in their natures. Some may love
and worship God, while others blaspheme and hate, but   REAL DIFFER-
such is the only difference between them. Nero may   ENCES OF
MORAL NAT-
be cruel and vile, and Paul consecrated to the best and   URE.
noblest life, but they are without any difference in subjective
quality. There cannot be any difference in respect to holiness,
because such quality can have no place in the nature. Under
such a law even God could not be holy in his nature. A theory
with such implications must be false. With opposite habits of
moral life there must be a difference of natures. In the one case
the spontaneous tendency is to the good; in the other, to the evil.
The tendency to the good we call subjective holiness—holiness of
the nature in distinction from holiness of the life. With such a
nature Adam could be created.

The determining principle of this question is clearly given in
the words of our Lord: " Either make the tree good,   THE TREE AND
and his fruit good; or else make the tree corrupt, and   ITS FRUIT.
his fruit corrupt: for the tree is known by his fruit."[1] In distinction from the fruit the tree has a quality in itself, for otherwise the quality of the tree could not determine the quality of the
fruit. Nor could there be any meaning in making the tree good
and its fruit good, or the tree corrupt and its fruit corrupt. For
the common intelligence, and for the most critical as well, there is
very real meaning in such facts. We know the quality of a tree by
the quality of its fruit. The principle is the same in the case of
man. This indeed is the meaning and application of these words
of the Master. The deeds of men, as good or evil, answer to their
moral nature and express its quality as good or evil, just as in the
case of the fruit and the tree. The same idea of a moral quality
of our nature is present in many texts which set forth the facts of
regeneration. The transformation of the life is through a renewal
of the moral nature. That renovation of the nature is a moral purification, and imparts to it a quality of holiness.[2] It thus appears
that the question of primitive holiness is not a merely speculative
one, but one which vitally concerns the deepest truth and reality of
regeneration. If there be no moral quality of our nature regeneration loses its meaning for the Christian life. Its profound reality
carries with it the reality of such a quality. Hence Adam as newly
created could be holy in his nature.

[1] Matt. xii, 33.
[2] Psa li, 7, 10, Ezek. xxxvi, 25-27; 2 Cor. v, 17; Gal. vi, 15; Eph. iv,
22-24; Col. iii, 9, 10.

II. PROOFS OF PRIMITIVE HOLINESS.

1. *Implication of the Moral Nature.*—Man is a moral being, and was so constituted in the beginning. Conscience, and moral reason, and the sense of God and duty are no mere acquisition through a process of evolution or the association of ideas, but are as original to man as intelligence and sensibility. Without a moral TENDENCIES OF nature man is not man. Such a nature must have A MORAL NAT- moral tendencies. The notion of its indifference as URE between the ethically good and evil is irrational, and contradictory to all relative and analogous facts. Mind is spontaneously active. The sensibilities which so wonderfully adjust us to our manifold relations are thus active. This activity is in the form of tendency or disposition, of inclination or aversion. There is either an outgoing of the sensibility toward its appropriate object or an aversion from it, and the notion of indifference is excluded. There is no indifference as to society, or country, or kindred, or home. In such objects there is a spontaneous interest. There may be instances of repugnance or aversion; but there are none of indifference. What is thus true of the sensibilities in general is equally true of the moral nature. It must be either spontaneously disposed to the good or inclined to the evil. The facts of observation and experience affirm the truth of this position. A state of indifference would betray an abnormal condition. What is thus TENDENCIES IN ever true of man was equally true of Adam in his prim- ADAM itive state. There were spontaneous tendencies or incli- nations of his moral nature. But the new Adam was just what God made him. His spontaneous tendencies were immediately consequent to his nature as divinely constituted. Hence his moral inclination must have been to the good in preference to the evil. Such inclination is at once the characteristic fact and the proof of subjective holiness.

2. *Primitive Man Very Good.*—That primitive man was very good is more than an implicit fact of the Mosaic narrative. "And God saw every thing that he had made, and, behold, it was very good."[1] It is true that these words are general, and are not specifically applied to man, as in other instances like words were so applied to other parts of the new creation;[2] but, as they immediately follow the account of the creation of man, they must as really and fully apply to him as they could in the most direct and specific manner. Any limitation, therefore, which excludes the moral nature of man from this application is contrary to the clear sense of Scripture.

[1] Gen. i, 31.   [2] Gen. i, 10, 12, 18, 21, 25.

Yet such a limitation is assumed : " And as to the divine declaration that 'every thing was very good,' it expressly A CONTRARY refers to all that God had made, and is quite compatible VIEW with the idea of a germ of sin lying hid in man, and having its origin only in man and not in God. It is also plain that the declaration refers to God's non-intelligent creation as well as to man, so that it expresses the general fitness of every thing for the purpose designed, and not moral good."[1] Only in this way could the author attempt a reconciliation of his theory of a germ of sin in primitive man with his divine characterization as very good ; but no such reconciliation is possible. We cannot thus turn away from a specific sense of " very good " to a general sense which shall exclude moral good in the case of primitive man. Every part of creation has its purpose after its own kind, and, if fitted to its purpose, GOOD IN HIS must be good in its kind. Muller really admits this KIND. principle ; and it must be just as true in the case of primitive man as in application to any other part of creation. But man was morally constituted, and divinely purposed for moral ends. God created man for communion with himself, and for blessedness in his own holy service. If originally good, he must have been morally good, for only therein could he have been good in his kind, and fitted for such divine ends. We could as well omit the luminosity of the sun from its characterization as " very good " as to omit the morally good from a like characterization of primitive man

3. *Further Scripture Proofs.*—Under this head we present a few texts which clearly contain the truth of a primitive holiness.

" Lo, this only have I found, that God hath made man upright ; but they have sought out many inventions."[2] The MAN MADE service of the text for the present question hinges upon UPRIGHT the sense of upright. In the frequent use of this term three senses appear : rectitude of posture or form ; rectitude of conduct ; rectitude of the moral nature. The first can have no place in the present text. The context is a disquisition upon man purely in his moral aspects, not at all in his organic structure. The evil inventions of men, so sharply contrasted with an original uprightness. can have no such distinction from a mere bodily rectitude. The second meaning—rectitude of conduct—is more than the term can here admit. In making man upright God did not make for him an upright life. As previously shown, such a life requires man's own personal agency. It thus appears that neither the first nor the second meaning gives the proper sense of upright in the present text. A third sense remains, and must be the true one. The term has a

[1] Muller · *Christian Doctrine of Sin*, vol. ii, p 350   [2] Eccl vii, 29.

deeper meaning than the deeds of an upright life. It reaches down
to the personal agent, and to the principles which underlie his
action. Thus the moral nature with its spontaneous tendencies is
reached. Such is the deeper meaning of upright in its application
to God.[1] Such, too, is its deeper sense in application to man.[2]
This is the proper meaning in the text under treatment. In such
a sense man was originally constituted holy.

"And that ye put on the new man, which after God is created
HOLINESS OF in righteousness and true holiness." "And have put
THE NEW MAN on the new man, which is renewed in knowledge after
the image of him that created him."[3] These texts are so much
alike that we may properly place them together. We require only
the points which concern the question of primitive holiness. The
central truth of the texts is the transformation of man from an evil
to a good life. This transformation is deeper than the life of personal action, and includes a renovation of the moral nature. The
old man with his deeds, which must be put off, is both a corrupt
nature and a vicious life; and the new man, which must be put on,
is both a holy nature and a good life. Hence it is that this moral
transformation requires a renewal in the spirit of the mind and a
creation of the new man. Here is an inner work of the Holy Spirit,
a purification of the moral nature by his gracious and mighty
agency. This purification is a renewal of the soul in the image of
God in which man was originally created. Clearly this is the
thought in the mind of Paul. His words more than imply it.
The fact of such a thought is not in the least discredited by the
use of words—such as righteousness and knowledge—which carry
a sense beyond the moral nature into the actual life. No exact
parallelism is attempted. With an intense practical aim, the apostle connects with the inner purification the good life which should
spring from it; but it is still true to his thought that this inner
purification is a renewal of the soul in the original image of God.
Hence in that image there is the truth of a primitive holiness.

4. *Error of Pelagianism.*—In the great contention between
PELAGIUS AND Augustine and Pelagius, each went to an extreme: the
AUGUSTINE. former in the maintenance of original sin in the sense
of native demerit; the latter in the denial of native depravity.
Both failed to make the proper distinction between moral character
from personal conduct and the subjective moral state. With an
omission of the proper analysis, such as we have previously given,

[1] Deut. xxvii, 4; Psa. xxv, 8; xcii, 15
[2] Job i, 1, 8; xxiii, 7; Psa. xi, 7; xxxvii, 37.
[3] Eph. iv, 24; Col. iii, 10.

to bring out the clear distinction of the two, native depravity was with Augustine native sin and demerit. On the other hand, Pelagius, equally overlooking that distinction, and holding the impossibility of demerit without one's own personal conduct, denied the truth of native depravity. With the proper analysis, the former might have maintained the whole truth of native depravity without the element of sinful demerit; while the latter might have held the same truth of depravity, and yet have maintained his fundamental principle, that free personal conduct absolutely conditions all sinful demerit. We thus point out the opposite extremes, and the opposite errors, of the two parties in this great contention.

Other errors followed in logical consistency. If all men might be sinners, with the desert of punishment, by virtue of an inherited depravity, Adam could have the moral worth and rewardableness of an eminent saint simply by virtue of an original creation. The anthropology of Augustine both with himself and his many followers tends strongly to this view. On the other hand, ERRORS OF PELAGIUS. the denial of primitive holiness on the part of Pelagius was logically consequent to his denial of Augustine's doctrine of original sin. Failing to analyze this doctrine into its separate elements, his denial of native sin carried with it the denial of native depravity. On such a principle there can be no moral quality of a nature, and therefore no primitive holiness. This was the outcome with Pelagius, as may be seen in his own words. "From the first book of Pelagius on free-will, Augustine quotes the following declaration of his opponent (*De Pec. Orig.*, 13): 'All good and evil, by which we are praise or blameworthy, do not originate together with us, but are done by us. We are born capable of each, but not filled with either. And as we are produced without virtue, so are we also without vice; and before the action of his own will, there is in man only what God made.'"[1] This denies all change in the moral state of the race as consequent to the Adamic fall. In his moral nature man is still the same as in his original constitution. Adam was endowed with freedom and placed under a law of duty, but was morally indifferent as between good and evil. We have previously shown that the notion of such indifference in a being morally constituted is irrational and contradictory to decisive facts. The denial of primitive holiness is not a merely speculative error. The principle of this denial carries with it a denial of the Adamic fall and the depravity of the race, and therefore leaves no place for a system of evangelical theology. There is no longer any need of atonement, or regeneration, or justification by faith, or a new spiritual life in Christ.

[1] Wiggers: *Augustinism and Pelagianism*, p. 85.

28

III. Elements of Primitive Holiness.

The acceptance of primitive holiness as a truth does not necessarily determine the view of its elements or nature. Hence in the history of the doctrine opposing views appear. The issue thus arising has been much in debate, and not as a question of merely speculative interest, but as one which deeply concerns the nature of the Adamic fall, of original sin, and of regeneration. Such implications will sufficiently appear in the statement of these opposing views.

1. *The Romish Doctrine.*—The Romish anthropology is so far PURELY A SU- Augustinian as to accept the truth of a primitive holi-
PERNATURAL ness, but widely diverges from the latter respecting the
GIFT.   nature or content of that holiness. What is specially distinctive of the Romish doctrine is that the primitive holiness was purely a supernatural endowment or gift. As such it must have been extraneous to the nature of Adam, and conferred subsequently to his completed creation. "The first peculiarity of the papal anthropology consists in the tenet that *original righteousness is not a natural, but a supernatural, endowment.* The germ of this view appears in one of the statements of the *Roman Catechism* —a work which followed the Tridentine Canons, and is of equal authority with them in the papal Church. 'Lastly,' says the Catechism,[1] 'God formed man out of the clay of the earth, so made and constituted as to his material body that he was immortal and impassible, not indeed by the force of nature itself, but by a divine favor. But as to his soul, he formed him after his own image and likeness, endowed him with free will, and so tempered within him all the emotions of his mind and his appetites that they would never disobey the rule of reason. Then he *added* the admirable gift of original righteousness, and decreed that he should have the pre-eminency over other animals.'"[1] It thus appears that in the papal anthropology the likeness and image of God in primitive man carried the sense of a similarity in the nature and personality of mind, but not the sense of holiness. Place was thus left for primitive holiness as a supernatural endowment.

Consistently with this view of original righteousness, the papal IMPERFECTION anthropology could admit, and did admit, certain im-
OF THE PRIMI- perfections of man as originally constituted. As consist-
TIVE NATURE   ing of flesh and spirit, the appetences of the former might war against the rational dictates of the latter, and thus render

---

[1] *Catechismus Romanus*, P. I, Cap. ii, Q. 18.
[2] Shedd: *History of Christian Doctrine*, vol. ii, pp. 142, 143.

difficult a prudent and good life. There was thus in the very beginning, and before any lapse of man, a profound moral need of the supernatural endowment of grace which the doctrine maintains. And, further, the primary purpose of this endowment was for the relief of this exigency. So Bellarmin, a master in papal theology, states the facts. "In the first place it is to be observed that man naturally consists of flesh and spirit. . . . But from these diverse or contrary propensities there arises in one and the same man a certain conflict, and from this conflict great difficulty of acting rightly. . . . In the second place, it is to be observed that divine providence, in the beginning of creation (*initio creationis*), in order to provide a remedy for this disease or languor of human nature which arises from the nature of a material organization (*ex conditione materiæ*), added to man a certain remarkable gift, to wit, original righteousness, by which as by a sort of golden rein the inferior part might easily be kept in subjection to the superior, and the superior to God ; but the flesh was thus subjected to the spirit, so that it could not be moved so long as the spirit was unwilling, nor could it become a rebel to the spirit unless the spirit itself should become a rebel to God, while yet it was wholly in the power of the spirit to become or not become a rebel to God. . . . We think that this rectitude of the inferior part was a *supernatural* gift, and that, too, intrinsically, and not accidentally, so that it neither flowed nor could flow from the principles of nature (*ex naturæ principiis*)."[1]

These views are open to criticism, and are sharply criticised from the side of the Augustinian anthropology. Such ERRORS OF THE original imperfections of man have no warrant in the DOCTRINE. Scriptures. Nor is there any ground for the exclusively supernatural character of primitive holiness. Further, the doctrine implies that the fall of man was simply a lapse into his primitive state. The fall in its effect upon man, apart from personal demerit, was simply a deprivation of the supernatural endowment of righteousness. His own nature was the same after the fall as before it. But his own nature, while without holiness before the fall, was equally without depravity, and must have remained the same, after the fall. This is a very superficial and false view of the actual state of man in consequence of the Adamic fall. The consequence of that fall was not only a deprivation of the divine communion, but a depravation of the nature of man. For the present we are not concerned with another objection urged against this papal view

---

[1] Bellarminus : *Gratia Primi Hominis*, C. v. Cited by Shedd : *History of Christian Doctrine*, vol. ii, pp 143, 144

on the part of the Augustinian anthropology, that by implication it denies the actual sinfulness and demerit of human nature as fallen. Any view of regeneration in accord with this papal anthropology must be superficial and false. It must mean simply a restoration of original righteousness as a supernatural endowment. Such limitation must omit the interior work of the Holy Spirit in the renewal and purification of the moral nature, which is the central reality of regeneration. Finally, as this anthropology allows the actuality and the innocence of a certain measure of concupiscence in primitive man, so it must allow the same in regenerate man.

2. *The Augustinian Doctrine.*—By the doctrine so designated we mean, not limitedly any definite view of Augustine himself respecting the nature of primitive holiness, but rather the central view of the Augustinian anthropology as interpreted and maintained in the Calvinistic Churches. In this view original righteousness was an intrinsic quality of the nature of man, not something added to his nature. By the divine creative act he was constituted holy, and there was not only no subsequent act, but no separate act by which he was so constituted. It should not be overlooked that we give this as the central or prevalent view, and without any notice of individual divergences. As against the papal view, "the reformers generally, and especially Luther, had strenuously contended that this original righteousness was a quality of man's proper nature, and necessary to its perfection and completeness, and not a supernatural gift." [1] Also in dissent from the papal view of a superadded holiness, "the reformers most justly assert, in opposition to this mechanical view, that '*justitia originalis*' was an original and actual element of our nature as it came from the hand of the Creator." [2]

On this question the Augustinian doctrine thus takes the opposite extreme to the papal view. This was quite natural to the protestant attitude of the reformers and the intensity of their antagonism to much of the papal anthropology. Further, their doctrine of sin logically carried them to this view of original righteousness. As in this doctrine the very nature of man in his fallen state is actually sinful, or sinful in a sense deserving of God's judicial wrath, so the nature of primitive man in itself and without any gracious endowment could be ethically righteous. The rejection of the papal view does not

OPPOSITE TO THE ROMISH VIEW.

---

[1] Cunningham : *Historical Theology*, vol. i, p. 518.
[2] Van Oosterzee : *Christian Dogmatics*, vol. i, p. 376. Also Hodge : *Systematic Theology*, vol. ii, pp. 104, 105.

logically require the acceptance of this Augustinian view. In this case, as in many others, the truth may lie between the extremes.

3. *Elements of the True Doctrine.*—The first element of primitive holiness was the moral rectitude of the Adamic nature as newly created. In our previous discussions we fully maintained the possibility and the reality of such holiness, and set forth the definite idea of its nature or content. That position holds true against the papal denial of such holiness. We agree with the prevalent Augustinian anthropology respecting the reality of primitive holiness, but dissent respecting any proper ethical character of that holiness, and also respecting its limitation to a mere quality of the Adamic nature. In that anthropology Adam often appears in the very beginning, and before any personal action, with the moral worth of ethical righteousness, with the activities of holy affection in the fear and love of God.[1] We omit all this from the content of primitive holiness. The activities of holy affection may be spontaneous to the moral nature, but must be subsequent to its own constitution. Nor can they be the immediate product of the creative agency which constitutes the nature. A thorough analysis must distinguish between the activities of the moral nature in Adam and that nature itself simply as divinely created. That nature was so constituted as to be responsive to the claims of a prudent and good life, not in the sense of a necessary fulfillment of such claims, but in the sense of a spontaneous inclination or disposition toward such fulfillment. This is all that we can properly mean by holiness as a quality of the primitive nature of man.

There was a second element of primitive holiness in the presence and agency of the Holy Spirit. We have previously dissented from the Augustinian limitation of that holiness to a mere quality of the Adamic nature. We have also dissented from the papal doctrine of its purely supernatural character; but the weighty objection, that it implies serious defects in the nature of man as originally constituted, is valid only against so extreme a view. The presence of the Holy Spirit as a constituent element of primitive holiness has no such implication. The Adamic nature could be holy in its own quality and tendency, and yet need the help of the Spirit for the requirements of a moral probation. Augustine himself held this view. "God had given man an assistance, without which he could not have persevered in good if he would. He could persevere if he would, because that aid (*adju-*

RECTITUDE OF ADAMIC NATURE.

PRESENCE OF THE SPIRIT.

[1] Edwards: Works, vol. ii, pp. 386, 387; Wiggers: *Augustinism and Pelagianism*, p. 142.

torium) did not fail by which he could.   Without this, he could
not retain the good which he might will." [1]   Hence the divine plan
might include the presence of the Spirit as an original and abiding
element in the holiness of man.   We need this truth for the proper
interpretation of human depravity.   The fall of man was not only
the loss of holiness, but also the corruption of his nature.   This
corruption we may not ascribe to any immediate agency of God,
but may interpret it as the consequence of a withdrawment of the
presence and influence of the Holy Spirit.   This is the doctrinal
meaning of " depravation from deprivation."   The most thorough
Augustinians so interpret the corruption of human nature, and thus
concede the presence of the Holy Spirit as an element of primitive
holiness. [2]

We thus combine the two elements in the true doctrine.   The
A PRESENCE IN second element brings the doctrine into full accord
ALL HOLY LIFE. with the fact that in the Christian life the Holy Spirit
is not only the agent in the primary renewal and purification of the
soul, but also an abiding presence in aid of its renewed powers.
And we are pleased to think of the immanence of the Spirit in all
holy life whether human or angelic.

[1] Cited by Wiggers : *Augustinism and Pelagianism*, p. 142.
[2] Cunningham : *Historical Theology*, vol. 1, p. 526.

CHAPTER IV.

THE PRIMITIVE PROBATION.

PROBATION is a state of trial under a law of duty. The law in the case is the test of obedience. The duty imposed is enforced by the sanction of rewards. The rewards determine for the subjects of probation permanent states of good or evil; so that probation is a temporary economy. The central reality of probation is responsibility for conduct under a law of duty. Such was the primitive probation; and it should be studied in the light of these facts.

I. PROBATION A REASONABLE ECONOMY.

This proposition is not intended for universal and perpetual application. It is true in application to primitive man. Possibly a primitive state might be so perfect as neither to require nor admit any *testing* law. Such will be the state of confirmed blessedness. Probably no primitive state is such. Certainly that of man was not. For him trial was naturally incident to duty. Obedience, however, was easily within his power, and a moral obligation, while a law of duty was the imperative requirement of his moral constitution and relations. With the truth of these facts, the primitive probation was a reasonable economy. The facts require a fuller and more orderly statement.

1. *Trial as Naturally Incident to Duty.*—The fact of such trial arose from the constitution of primitive man. With a holy nature, there were yet in him susceptibilities to temptation. In temptation there is an impulse in the sensibilities adverse to the law of duty. This is true even where it finds no response in the personal consciousness. Yet, in the measure of it, such impulse is a trial to obedience. Such trial was naturally incident to duty in primitive man. The proof of it is in a primitive constitution with sensibilities which might be the means of temptation; also in the actuality of such temptation. These facts are entirely consistent with the primitive holiness which we have maintained. In such a state primitive man began his moral life. The only way to confirmed blessedness was through a temporary obedience. But obedience requires a law of duty; and, with the natural incidence of trial and the possibility of failure, such a law must be a testing law. It thus

appears that a probationary economy was the only one at all suited to the state of primitive man.

2. *Complete Ability for Obedience.*—Ability for obedience is a rational requirement under a testing law of duty. The question of such ability in primitive man needs no elaborate discussion, and the mere statement of relative facts will suffice. The reality of such ability lies in the rectitude of his moral nature as originally constituted. With susceptibility to temptation through the sensibilities, his spontaneous disposition was yet toward the good and averse to the evil. In this there was strength for obedience. Nor can we rationally think of any divine imposition of duty in this case above the ability of fulfillment. When responsibility with moral inability is maintained, it must be on the ground of a responsible forfeiture of moral ability. There was no such forfeiture in the case of man when duty was originally imposed upon him. God was at once the author of both his nature and the law of his probation, and therefore could not impose any duty which should transcend his strength of obedience. Further, this strength is fully manifest in view of the special test of obedience divinely instituted. If the moral constitution of primitive man was what the Scriptures warrant us to think it, the fulfillment of that duty was easily within his power.

3. *Obedience a Reasonable Requirement.*—As the subject of such munificent endowments, the recipient of so rich an estate and a provisory heirship to eternal blessedness, primitive man owed the consecration of all his powers in holy obedience and love to the Author of all his good. Every principle of reason and duty so determines. With the deepest emphasis, therefore, does every such principle determine the obligation of the probationary duty imposed upon him.

4. *Moral Necessity for a Law of Duty.*—With far less unreason might we object to the creation of man as a moral being than to his probationary trial under a law of duty. As morally constituted and related, with the obligations of holy obedience and love, and with the possibilities of both good and evil action, a law of duty was for him an imperative requirement.

If we now combine the four facts presented under the head of this section it must be clear that for primitive man probation was a reasonable economy.

II. The Probationary Law.

1. *A Matter of Divine Determination.*—The assignment of duty to primitive man in the form of precept or commandment was

purely the prerogative of God. Adam could not determine his own duties, for he knew not sufficiently either himself or the claims of his Creator. Some duties, such as the love and worship of God, might stand in a clear light, and be seen as by intuition; but what in the way of restraint might be requisite to his best moral and religious development could not thus be known. These things could be known only to God; and the whole right of commandment was his. He might impose any duty or any restraint consistent with his own wisdom. When we say consistent with his own wisdom we mean that the perfections of God are a law unto himself, so that he could impose nothing contrary to his own wisdom. This fact, however, does not bring down the ways of God to the measure of our own minds. We cannot judge him as we judge men, for we stand on the same plane with them, while God is in the infinite heights above us. There is here a place for our trust in God, and an infinite warrant for it, even when the light of his wisdom is hidden from our view. Such trust is far wiser in us than any unfriendly criticism of the law whereby he tested the fidelity of primitive man.

2. *The Law as Divinely Instituted.*—This law is plainly given in the sacred narrative · " But of the tree of the knowledge of good and evil, thou shalt not eat of it: for in the day that thou eatest thereof thou shalt surely die."[1] Respecting the knowledge of good and evil, the sense is not that the fruit of this tree could by any virtue of its own give the knowledge of good and evil, but rather that man, as obedient or disobedient to its divine interdiction, should prove himself good or evil, or come to know in his own experience the good or the evil. Such a sense best accords with the testing function of the law.

We can hardly think that this one commandment constituted the sum of duty for primitive man. There are moral A BROADER laws which must exist for all moral beings. From the LAW OF DUTY beginning it must have been the duty of Adam to love and worship God. Such a religious life requires habits of thought and disposition which in themselves fulfill religious duties. Nor is there in the words of that one commandment any exclusion of other duties. There was this specific commandment, and the first sin was in its violation. So far the sacred narrative is clear. There were other duties; but whether of a proper testing character, or whether in case of fidelity under this first trial other tests might have been instituted—on all such questions that narrative is silent. With the obligation of other duties, the fidelity of Abra-

[1] Gen. ii, 17.

ham was yet specially tried by a positive command. Such was the manner of trial in the primitive probation; and, so far as the Scriptures give us any clear light, such was the law of that probation.

3. *A Proper Test of Obedience.*—This law of the primitive probation was a positive law in distinction from a moral law. The MORAL AND obligation of a moral law is intrinsic and absolute; the POSITIVE obligation of a positive law arises from a divine comLAWS mandment. Such a ground of obligation is in no contradiction to the reality of fundamental principles of ethics. Nor is such obligation grounded purely in authority. A divine command always means to the enlightened religious consciousness a sufficient reason for the duty imposed, however hidden that reason may be. There is thus a place for faith as the practical power of obedience. The case of Abraham is an illustration. No reason was given for the command to offer up his son. His faith found the reason for obedience, not in an absolute arbitrary authority of God, but in the wisdom and goodness of his providence. Such is the real ground of obligation in a positive command. For the religious consciousness such obligation is absolute. A positive command of God is not the dictum of an arbitrary will, but the expression of his wisdom and love.

Nor is obedience to a positive command any abject submission NO MERE AR- to an arbitrary absolute will. No such submission BITRARY WILL. could constitute a true obedience. At most it could be only a conformity of outward action to the positive mandate. Such conformity is not in itself obedience, because without the motives of piety. Such was the case under this probationary law. True obedience to its mandate required the motives of religious reverence and love; and disobedience could arise only with an irreligious revolt of the soul from God. It thus appears that a positive command of God is no arbitrary mandate of an absolute will, indifferent to morality and piety, and which the most servile outward observance will satisfy, but the expression and requirement of his infinite wisdom and goodness as our moral Ruler, and which can be fulfilled only with the truest obedience of a devout mind and a loving heart. So closely one in obligation and fulfillment is a positive law of God with a moral law.

With the inexperience of primitive man as he entered the sphere SUITED THE of probation, a positive law may have best suited the PRIMITIVE purpose of a moral trial. There were sufficient reasons STATE. to the divine Mind for its institution, and, as we shall point out, it was most favorable to obedience. After a long experience of Abraham and the practical development of his moral and religious life, God found reason to test his obedience through a positive command. Clearly, then, there might be sufficient reason for such a trial of primitive man, whose conception of moral principles was as yet without any development through experience.[1] Such a command was given him—a command which addressed itself to the deepest moral and religious consciousness, and required for its proper observance the truest motives of a good life. Further, it embodied the great religious lessons, that the will of God is the supreme law of duty, and that the highest good of man must be found in his loving favor, not in any pleasures of sense. Such facts constituted this law of the primitive probation a proper test of obedience.

III. Favorable Probationary Trial.

A few words will suffice to make it clear that the testing law of the primitive probation was most favorable to obedience. We require simply a brief statement of the leading facts concerned in the question.

1. *Law of Duty Open and Plain.*—There was nothing occult or perplexing in the meaning of the duty enjoined. No philosophic acumen or insight was necessary to the fullest comprehension of its meaning. It was simply the duty of abstinence from the fruit of a tree definitely noted. There could be no plainer mandate of duty.

2. *Complete Moral Healthfulness of Man.*—As yet there was no impulse of vicious or inordinate passion; no clouding or perversion of the moral reason; no evil habit which might fetter all endeavor toward the good. There was still the full strength of the primitive holiness, with its spontaneous disposition to the obedience of love.

3. *Ample Sources of Satisfaction.*—The garden which God prepared for man in the eastward of Eden was rich in beauty and plenty. There grew in it "every tree that is pleasant to the sight, and good for food."[2] There was all that could please the eye and gratify the taste, all that could nourish the physical life. Above all, there was the open presence of God and the privilege of communion with him. Surely the forbidden fruit was no necessity to the completest satisfaction of man.

4. *Most Weighty Reasons for Obedience.*—This law of the primitive probation was directly and openly from God, whose authority

[1] Dorner: *Christian Doctrine*, vol. ii, p. 81; Henry B. Smith: *Christian Theology*, p. 261.

[2] Gen. ii, 9.

and majesty went forth with its mandate for the enforcement of obedience.   Man already knew God in his presence and glory, and must have been deeply sensible to the obligation of obedience to his will.   Then the issues of life and death hung on the contingency of obedience or disobedience.   Such consequences were the revealed sanctions of the law, and must have been somewhat apprehended in their profound import—surely sufficiently to render them weighty reasons for obedience.   With such sanctions of a divine mandate, such weighty reasons for its observance, the soul should be the stronger against the solicitations of temptation, and full and prompt obedience most easy.

If now we combine the four facts set forth in this section, and view them in their relation to the primitive probation, it must be manifest that that probation was most favorable to obedience.

CHAPTER V.

TEMPTATION AND FALL OF MAN.

THERE was a temptation and fall of primitive man, with a consequent fall of the race. These facts do not rest simply upon the Mosaic narrative, but are fully recognized in the later Scriptures, and especially in the New Testament. So far the questions of the temptation and fall seem open and plain; but there are perplexities for both exegesis and apologetics in the details of the Mosaic narrative. In consequence of this we have a diversity of interpretations, and some of them specially shaped for the relief of these perplexities. This is permissible so far as it may be consistent with a proper adherence to the historic character of the narrative, and such adherence may allow some variation in the interpretation of certain items. However, caution must be observed, or the whole narrative will be so marred as to lose its historic character. We shall not take much time with questions which must remain obscure, and which belong to apologetics and exegesis rather than to systematic theology.

I. THE PRIMITIVE TEMPTATION.

1. *Concerning an Instrumental Agency.*—On the face of the narrative nothing seems plainer than the fact of an instrumental agency in the temptation—that is, something used as the instrument of a higher agency. There is, indeed, no mention of a higher agency in the narrative itself, but the facts clearly require such an agency.[1] If the serpent which appears in the temptation is to be taken in the literal sense of an animal, there is still no satisfactory identification of it. "*Who* QUESTION OF THE INSTRUMENT. was the *serpent?* of what *kind?* In what *way* did he seduce the first happy pair? These are questions which *remain yet to be answered.*"[2] It is no wrong to the good doctor to say that, after his own learned endeavor to identify this "*nachash*" with the *ape* order, they still remained in the same unanswered state. There is a widely prevalent tradition of the serpent as concerned in a temptation and fall of man, which in some instances is in close accordance with the Mosaic narrative.

[1] Gen. iii, 1–5.   [2] Clarke : *Commentary,* in loc.

With the literal sense of an animal in the temptation, the use of
PANTOMIMIC   speech encounters strong objection, because there is
VIEW.   wanting the necessary organ. In order to avoid this
difficulty the part of the serpent, or other animal, has been interpreted as purely pantomimic in its mode. There is no relief in
this view. Such representative action is as much above the endowment of an animal as the power of articulate speech. As the
mere instrument of a higher agency, an animal could be used in
the latter mode quite as easily as in the former.

There is another view which may be stated. It is, that serpent
SYMBOLICAL   is a symbolical term for the designation of Satan him-
VIEW   self. With this interpretation there is no literal serpent or other animal with any part in the temptation, but Satan is
the immediate and only agent, and the subject of the penal infliction. It is very difficult to adjust the items of the sacred narrative
to this view. It is further suggested that if no animal was present
in the temptation Satan might still have appeared in the semblance
of one.

2. *A Higher, Satanic Agency.*—As an animal could be only an
instrument in the temptation, so the facts of intelligence embodied
therein evince the presence of a higher agency. There is knowledge of the divine command, reasoning about God, the nature of good
and evil, and the virtues of the forbidden fruit. These facts are
possible only to a rational intelligence. Even without the signs of
the deepest craft, there is still the full evidence of such an agency.

There is no open reference to a satanic agency in the narrative
SATAN NOT   of the temptation. The devil is not named therein,
NAMED   but there is the manifestation of a malignance and
craft which clearly points to his agency. The scriptural characterization of the devil and the evil works attributed to him affirm
the same fact. He is the enemy that sowed the tares among the
good seed which the Son of man cast into the field of the world.[1]
He is a murderer and a liar from the beginning, and there is no
truth in him.[2] He is "that old serpent, called the devil, and
Satan, which deceiveth the whole world."[3] In mentioning the
serpent as beguiling Eve the thought of Paul cannot rest with the
mere instrument in the temptation, but must include the agency
of the devil under the same designation.[4]

3. *Manner of the Temptation.*—Under this head we need no
longer any distinction between the instrument and the real agent in
the temptation. For the manner of the temptation we need little
more than the facts as grouped in the sacred narrative. The

[1] Matt. xiii, 37-39.   [2] John viii, 44.   [3] Rev. xii, 9.   [4] 2 Cor. xi, 3.

subtlety of the devil appears through the whole process of the temptation. There was craft in beginning with Eve in the absence of Adam. The two together would have been stronger than either alone, and presumably Eve was understood to be the more susceptible to temptation. The divine command is inquiringly approached, with the stealthy suggestion of an unnecessary restriction of privilege. Then with cunning boldness the penalty of disobedience is denied: "Ye shall not surely die." Suspicion of divine duplicity is insinuated : God himself knows that, instead of evil, only good shall come of eating the interdicted fruit.[1] Thus the apprehension of death and the strength of religious reverence and love were greatly weakened, while the forbidden fruit was set in such false lights as to excite a very strong desire to partake of it.

II. The Fall of Man.

For the present we need only a brief statement of the more open facts of the fall. The deeper questions of depravity and sin will receive their special treatment further on in our discussions.

1. *Entering Into the Temptation.*—The mental process through which Eve entered into the temptation is much more MENTAL MOVEfully given than in the case of Adam. On a colloca- MENT OF EVE tion of the temptation and the result, her own mental movement becomes obvious. The former we have already considered. The latter is seen in the new light in which the prohibited fruit appeared to her. Through the illusive coloring of the temptation it seemed beautiful to the eye, good for food, and desirable to make one wise. Through the impulse of the appetence thus begotten she took of the fruit, and did eat.[2] It was an open violation of the divine command.

She "gave also unto her husband with her ; and he did eat." This is the sum of the account in the case of Adam.[3] CASE OF ADAM. Yet it is hardly to be thought that, without any hesitation or questioning, he at once accepted the fruit simply on the proffer of his wife. There may be omitted facts. Otherwise the entrance of Adam into the temptation is far stranger than that of Eve.

2. *Penalty of the Sinning.*—Death is the penal term of the probationary law, and signifies the punishment of dis- LAWS OF INobedience to the divine command.[4] There is in the TERPRETATION law no explanation of the penal term, and we must find its full meaning in a proper view of man as its subject, and in its subsequent use in Scripture. Nor should that primary sense be modified

[1] Gen. iii, 1–5.   [2] Gen. iii, 6.   [3] Gen. iii, 6, 12, 17.   [4] Gen. ii, 17.

by any partial or provisory arrest of judgment upon the intervention of a redemptive economy. The announcement of such an economy preceded the judicial treatment of the primitive sin.[1]

There is a threefold sense in which man may be the subject of death, and also a corresponding meaning of the term in its Scripture use.

THREEFOLD SENSE OF DEATH.

It is the clear sense of Scripture that perpetual life was the provisory heritage of man. Obedience would have secured his providential exemption from death. This was provided for and pledged in the tree of life—probably through a sacramental use of its fruit, rather than by any intrinsic virtue which it might possess. By the divine judgment, and by expulsion from the tree of life, penalty in the form of physical death was inflicted upon man.[2] St. Paul confirms this sense of physical death in the original penalty of disobedience.[3]

There is also a spiritual death in distinction from the spiritual life—such as man originally possessed.[4] This death is inseparably connected with sin, and must have been the immediate consequence of sin in Adam.[5] His spiritual life was fully realized only in union with the Holy Spirit. Sin was the severance of that union, with the consequence of spiritual death. Such was now the state of Adam and Eve. With the full execution of the penalty this death must have been utter. But it is reasonable to think that in this case, as in that of physical death, there was a partial arrest of judgment, or an instant gift of helping grace, through the redemptive mediation already instituted.

There is still a third sense of the penal term—that of eternal death. This is not the place for the discussion of the question concerning the ultimate doom of sin. Eternal death is the final penal allotment of the unsaved. Beyond this fact of penal allotment, it is rather the full intensity and perpetuity of spiritual death than a distinct form of death. In view of the nature of man as morally constituted and endowed with immortality, and in view of the final doom of sin as revealed in the Scriptures, the penal term in the probationary law meant eternal death.

3. *Fall of the Race.*—This question arises only incidentally in the present connection. The race is fallen and morally corrupt through the sin and fall of its progenitors. These consequences, however, must be interpreted in a sense consistent with determining facts in the case. But for the immediate intervention of a

---

[1] Gen. iii, 15.   [2] Gen. iii, 19, 22-24.   [3] Rom. v, 12.
[4] John v, 24; Rom. viii, 6, 1 John iii, 14
[5] Rom. viii, 2; Eph. ii, 1; Col. ii, 13.

redemptive economy the penalty of death must have been promptly executed according to its own terms. This execution must have precluded the propagation and existence of the race. This preclusion as an actuality could not have been a penalty, because a never-existent race could not suffer a penalty. Hence the race was not liable to the original penalty in the same manner as its progenitors who transgressed the law; yet it is in a state of moral depravity and subject to death in consequence of their sin and fall. This is the sense of the Scriptures. The law of these results is for later treatment.

III. Freedom of Man in Falling.

The question of freedom is here treated simply in relation to our progenitors in the primitive sin. It will be presented in the light of a few facts which seem conclusive of its reality.

1. *Probationary Obedience a Divine Preference.*—This position seems most sure. The infinite holiness and goodness of God affirm his good pleasure against the sin and misery of the fall. Therefore the probationary obedience which was the necessary condition of their prevention must have been his preference. Further, he must have electively preferred obedience to his own command. The contrary is not to be thought, for God's preference of obedience must always go with his command. Obedience to this primitive command would have secured the standing of our progenitors in holiness and happiness. Therefore that standing must have been a divine preference.

2. *Divine Gift of the Power of Obedience.*—No one can wish any action of another without wishing him the requisite ability. This law must be real for God. If he wished the obedience, holiness, and happiness of our progenitors, he must have wished them the power of obedience as the necessary condition of these blessings. Therefore they must have possessed the power of obedience as a divine endowment. In this probationary trial they were just what God made them. He ordained the law of their duty, with perfect knowledge of their constitution, and in full foresight of their trial. It follows that, with an elective preference of obedience, he must have given them the power of obedience.

3. *Power of Obedience Intrinsic to Probation.*—The progenitors of the race were placed on probation under a testing law of obedience. The probationary character of that economy is above question. The power of obedience to the testing law of duty is essential to such an economy. There can be no testing of fidelity under a law of duty where there is not the power of obedience. As it is

29

truly said "that a state of trial supposes of course a capability of falling, and cannot exist without it," [1] so with equal truth it may be said that a state of trial supposes of course a capability of standing, and cannot exist without it. Thus again the power of obedience in the Adamic probation is manifest.

1 *The Facts Conclusive of Freedom in Falling* —The facts treated in this section are conclusive of the power of obedience in the primitive probation. With this power there must have been freedom in the falling.

IV. SINNING OF HOLY BEINGS.

Whatever the perplexities of this question, they are not peculiar to revelation, but must equally concern every philosophy or religion which admits the reality of moral evil. The Mosaic narrative of the sin and fall of man is not the cause of the prevalent moral evil, but simply the account of its origin in the human race. There is no more rational account. The denial of this account abates nothing of either the reality or the magnitude of moral evil.[2] Either man was originally constituted evil, or he has lapsed into evil from a higher and better state. Such a state must have been one of primitive holiness, as previously set forth. As morally constituted in his creation, man could not have been indifferent as between good and evil. A moral nature must have moral tendencies. There is surely no relief of perplexity in the supposition of original evil tendencies. On the rejection of this view, we must accept the only alternative of an origin of moral evil in a race primarily holy. This implies the sinning of holy beings.

1. *The Question in the Light of the Facts* —Conceivably, a primitive state might be such that sinning would seem to be a moral impossibility. With entire freedom, not only from inner tendencies, but also from outward solicitation toward evil, with strong inner tendencies toward the good, and with all exterior influences acting in full harmony with the inner tendencies, holy action would seem to be thoroughly assured. The origin of sin in such a state could have no rational explication. Even the moral possibility of it is beyond the grasp of rational thought. Such, however, was not the primitive state of man. While Adam and Eve were constituted holy in their moral nature, the spontaneous tendencies of which were toward the good, yet in their complete constitution there were susceptibilities to temptation which might be followed into sinful action. The present question concerning the sinning of holy beings must be treated in the light of these facts

[1] Dwight: *Theology*, vol. i, p. 414.   [2] Sherlock: Works, vol. iv, p. 156.

2. *Primitive Susceptibilities to Temptation.*—In the sensibilities of primitive man there was a ground of temptability. Through these sensibilities there could be solicitations, awakened appetencies, not directly toward sinful action as such, but toward forms of action which might be sinful, and even if known to be such. We have an illustration in the case of Eve. Appetencies are awakened for the forbidden fruit as it is set forth in the false light of the temptation. So far as purely spontaneous, these active sensibilities were innocent and entirely consistent with the primitive holiness. Sin could arise only as their solicitations were unduly entertained or followed into some voluntary infraction of the law of probation. But as purely spontaneous, and while yet within the limit of innocence, they could act as an impulse toward a voluntary infraction.

3. *Moral Forces Available for Obedience.*—In the constitution of primitive man there were certain moral forces which might act as a restraint upon any tendency toward evil-doing. If these forces were sufficiently strong, and exerted their full strength in a purely spontaneous mode, they would so fully counteract all tendency toward evil, and so enforce obedience, that sinning might still seem to be a moral impossibility. They were sufficiently strong, and spontaneous under proper conditions, but not irrespective of such conditions. It follows that they were not in any purely spontaneous mode determinative of obedience. The whole question can be set in a clearer light by application to two leading forces in support of obedience—love and fear.

The love of God, for which the soul was originally endowed, is a practical power of obedience. It is an impulse toward obedience, and, unless in some way counteracted, must secure obedience.[1] Hence it might fully restrain all tendencies toward disobedience. It was so available against the primitive temptation. But love is so operative only when in an active state. This state is conditioned on a proper mental apprehension of God. No object can quicken the correlate affection into an active state except when livingly in the grasp of thought. The constitution of primitive man did not necessitate such a constant apprehension of God. A temporary diversion of thought was possible, and without sin. The temptation led to such a diversion, and so clouded the vision of God as to prevent the practical force of love. In this state love could no longer counteract the impulses of awakened appetence, and disobedience might follow.

We named fear as another leading practical force. It is here

[1] John xiv, 23.

viewed, not in the sense of religious reverence, but as the apprehension of penalty. The fear of penalty may act as
a restraint upon any tendencies toward evil. But its
practical force is conditioned on the same law as love,
and hence in the same manner may fail of practical result. This
is illustrated in the case of Eve. The temptation first engendered
doubt of the penalty, and then occupied the attention with the at-
tractions of the forbidden fruit. In this mental state fear could
not act as an effective restraint upon the impulses of awakened ap-
petite. Even a partial doubt or forgetting would void its practical
force. In such a state the solicitations of temptation might be
followed into disobedience.

PRACTICAL
FORCE OF
FEAR.

4. *The Sinning Clearly Possible.*—The sinning of Adam and
Eve is a truth of the Scriptures. The facts presented in this section clearly show the possibility of this sinning, notwithstanding
the original holiness of their nature. We thus have in the Scriptures a thoroughly consistent account, and the most rational account
of the origin of sin in human history.[1]

V. Divine Permission of the Fall.

Moral evil is the common lot of man, whatever its origin. Its existence is a question of profound perplexity. A denial of the Scripture
account of its origin in the Adamic fall neither voids its reality nor in
the least mitigates its perplexity. We shall long wait for a theodicy.
We do not think such an attainment possible in our present state.

The divine permission of the Adamic fall was not in any sense
an expression of consent or the granting of a license.
The deed of sin by which man fell was definitely forbidden, and under the weightiest sanctions. Hence the meaning
of the divine permission must be simply that God did not sovereignly and effectively interpose for the prevention of the fall. It
has often been said that he could not have so interposed consistently with the moral freedom of man. There is truth in this, but
not such truth as fully resolves the question. Other questions are
thus raised respecting the creation and probationary trial of personal beings endowed with responsible moral agency. If God
could not consistently interfere with the free action of primitive
man, so as to prevent the fall, could he rightfully constitute man a
free moral agent and place him on a probationary trial? These
are the questions which first of all concern the divine permission
of the fall. If there be for us any present light, it must come with
the answer to these questions.

NO SENSE OF
CONSENT

[1] Butler: *Analogy,* part 1, chap. v, sec. iv.

1. *The Creation of Moral Beings Permissible.*—A being personally constituted and endowed with free moral agency must be under law to God, and responsible for his conduct. On the truth of theism and the reality of absolute moral principles, this must be so. Even God could not release such a being from moral duty and responsibility. Yet the creation of such a being must be permissible in God. To deny this permissibility is to restrict the creative agency of God to the spheres of material and impersonal existences. Or, if the highest grade might reach the capacity of rational intelligence, there must be no supreme endowment of a moral nature. Only in such a being is the true likeness of God reached ; and yet in no creative fiat must he say, "in our image, after our likeness." Only a most arrogant and daring mind could prescribe such limitations for God, or deny him the rightful privilege of creating moral beings capable of a worshipful recognition of himself.

2. *Permissibility of a Probationary Economy.*—Probation is a temporal, testing economy. There is a law of duty, with the sanction of rewards. For disobedience there must be at least a withholding of some attainable good; for obedience, the bestowment of some blessing. The state of probation may be longer or shorter, with less or greater trial. No exact limit of duration or measure of trial is intrinsic to such an economy. The essential fact of probation under a testing law of duty is moral responsibility. Such was the essential fact of the Adamic probation. If we declare that probation inconsistent with the divine providence, it will be most difficult, impossible indeed, to reconcile any known facts of moral responsibility with such a providence. We should thus deny the permissibility of a moral system under the providence of God. Yet there is such a system, and the moral consciousness of the race is witness to its reality. We are under a law of moral duty and responsibility. We cannot deny the consistency of this law with the providence of God. Therefore we must admit the permissibility of the Adamic probation.

3. *Permissibility of the Fall.*—With the reality of moral obligation and responsibility, the punishment of sin must be just. If the punishment is just, the permission of the sin cannot be unjust. We cannot say less respecting the primary Adamic sin. We have previously pointed out how favorable the primitive probation was to obedience. If justice or even goodness required the divine prevention of sin in such a state, no state is conceivable in which it might be permitted. Then all sin must be prevented ; and such a requirement must forbid the creation of personal beings endowed with free moral agency. There can be no such requirement. It is

entirely consistent with the providence of God that spiritual good as well as secular good should be conditioned on proper conduct in man. The providential means of subsistence are conditioned on a proper industry and prudence. If through idleness and improvidence any come to want, they have no right to impeach this economy. Plentiful industry and beggarly laziness are under the same providential economy. If that economy is just to the one it cannot be unjust to the other. The obedient who reap the rich harvest of spiritual good and the disobedient who suffer the penalty of sin are under the same moral economy. If that economy is right to the one it cannot be wrong to the other. If the moral economy be righteous there can be no requirement of providence sovereignly to prevent the sin which may forfeit its blessings.

4. *The Event Changes Not the Economy.*—If Adam had rendered obedience to the law of his probation, retained his innocence and rich inheritance, and risen to the fuller reward of his fidelity, even the most querulous could hardly object to the economy under which he was placed. That he sinned and fell alters not in the least the character of that economy. If good in the standing and the perpetuated blessedness, it could not in itself be other in the falling and the forfeiture of blessedness.

5. *Redemption and the Permission of the Fall.*—We have omitted
PERMISSION IN ORDER TO RE-DEMPTION. some facts usually set forth for the vindication of providence in the permission of the fall. Among all these facts the chief one is this: God permitted the fall of man that he might provide a redemption for the race so ruined, and through its infinite grace and love bring a far greater good to the moral universe, and especially to the human race. Mr. Wesley strongly supported this view, and thought it quite sufficient to clear the question of the fall of all perplexity, so far as it concerned the divine wisdom and goodness.[1] The argument is that through the atonement in Christ, rendered necessary by the fall, mankind has gained a higher capacity for holiness and happiness in the present life, and also for eternal blessedness. This higher capacity arises with the broader spheres of religious faith and love which the atonement opens. By this revelation of the divine goodness both faith and love may reach a measure not otherwise attainable. Also the sufferings which came with the fall provided a necessary condition for the graces of patience, meekness, gentleness, long-suffering, which contribute so much to the highest Christian life. In a like manner there is for us a higher blessedness in heaven.

There is some truth in the facts so presented, but not enough for the conclusion so confidently asserted. Besides, there are other facts which deeply concern the main question that are nor an explanation entirely overlooked. It is not to be questioned that the gift of the Son for our redemption is the highest manifestation of the divine goodness, and therefore the fullest warrant of faith and the intensest motive of love. But is it not equally true that through the fall we have suffered loss in our capacity for both faith and love? There is in our fallen nature an alienation from God, and so strong that often the weightiest motives of his love are persistently resisted. Further, if it be true that all who accept the grace of salvation are raised to a measure of love and blessedness not attainable in an unfallen state, it is equally true that the fall is the occasion of final ruin to many. The point we make is, that, if this question is to be brought into rational treatment, account must be taken of all these facts. When this is done it cannot seem so clear that the fall is the occasion of an infinite gain to the race.

Any such attempt, not only to vindicate the divine justice, but even to glorify the divine love in the permission of the perplexing implications fall, must proceed on the assumption of its possible prevention consistently with the freedom of man. On such an assumption, the fall itself must have been completely within the disposition of the divine providence; and, if still permissible for the sake of a greater good to the race, why might it not have been procured for the same end? The theory must thus appear in open contrariety to the divine holiness. This result discredits it; for not even the love of God must be glorified at the expense of his holiness. Nor is it within the grasp of human thought that sin, the greatest evil, can be necessary to the greatest good of the moral universe. It is still true that an immeasurable good will arise from the atonement in Christ; but it is not the sense of Scripture that the fall was any part of a providential economy for the sake of that good. The Scriptures glorify the love of God in the redemption of the world, but ever as a love of compassion for a sinful and perishing world, not as an anterior benevolence which must accept moral evil as the necessary condition of its richest blessings. We may surely say that the providential perpetuation of the fallen race without the redemptive mediation of Christ could not be reconciled with the righteousness of God, and so far we have in redemption an element of theodicy, but we have therein no rational account of the divine permission of the fall.

6. *Question of the Fall of Angels.*—The fact of such a fall is clearly the sense of Scripture;[1] but there are no details which give

[1] John viii, 44; 2 Pet. ii, 4, Jude 6.

us any insight into the nature of their temptation or the manner of their entering into it. So far, the fall of angels stands in much greater obscurity than the fall of man. Yet for the possibility of a fall some facts are obvious. The primary state of such angels must have been probationary. There must have been for them a state of trial under a testing law of duty, and also some form of susceptibility to temptation. It may have been very different from that in primitive man, but must have been equally a reality, for otherwise there could have been no fall. Whatever the nature of this susceptibility, it must have been such that it could be consistent with primitive holiness, for, as the immediate creation of God, all angels must have begun their moral life with a holy nature. They must have been endowed with the power of obedience to the requirements of the divine will, for otherwise they could have had no proper moral trial, nor could their penal doom be a just retribution. So far we must find in the fall of angels the same principles which we found in the fall of man. There is one distinction which should be noted. The fall of primitive man was in a profound sense the fall of the race. There was no such race-connection of angels. Each angel that fell must have fallen by his own personal sin. It is entirely consistent with this fact, and the most rational view of the case, that some one led in a revolt from God and by some mode of temptation induced the following of others.

GROUNDS OF THE POSSIBIL-ITY.

NOT AS THE FALL OF A RACE.

CHAPTER VI.

DOCTRINE OF NATIVE DEPRAVITY.

I. FORMULA OF ORIGINAL SIN.

1. *Analysis of the Formula.*—Original sin, as a doctrinal formula, is common to the orthodox creeds for the expression and characterization of native sinfulness. Augustine first brought it into prominence for this purpose, but it is older than Augustine, and its first doctrinal use is ascribed to Tertullian. For any doctrinal formula so long in use, and so fundamental, some might claim a prescriptive authority. Such formulas, however, are human creations, and, while entitled NO PRESCRIPT-IVE AUTHOR-ITY
to most respectful consideration, must be open to questioning respecting the doctrines for which they stand. Especially must their interpretation in doctrinal discussion be open to questioning, for often several questions of doctrine are treated as one question, or as inseparable questions, which a proper analysis and method must separate and treat separately. This is necessary to clearness of doctrinal view. There has been much neglect of such method in the treatment of original sin.

In the Augustinian anthropology, and in the creeds which formulate a doctrine of sin according to that anthropology, IN NEED OF ANALYSIS.
original sin includes a common guilt of Adam's sin, a common native depravity as the consequence of that guilt, and a sinfulness of the depravity which in all men deserves both temporal and eternal punishment.[1] It is further maintained by Augustinians that native depravity is itself a punishment inflicted upon all men on the ground of a participation in the sin of Adam. This account of depravity as a retribution of the divine justice makes that retribution a part of the doctrine of original sin. We thus find in this formula several questions of fact which are without any such logical or scientific connection that the truth of one must carry with it the truth of any other, much less the truth of all the others. It is for the reason of this unification of distinct questions that the doctrinal formula which represents them requires thorough

---

[1] Augsburg Confession, article ii; Belgic Confession, article xv; Articles of the Church of England, article ix; Westminster Confession, chap vi. In Schaff: *Creeds of Christendom*, vol. iii, pp. 8, 400, 492, 615.

analysis. The jumbling method of treating these several questions
as one truth of original sin should give place to their separation and
separate treatment. Clearness of view and truth of doctrine are
not otherwise attainable.

2. *Doctrinal Isolation of Native Depravity.*—The question of
native depravity is simply the question whether man is by nature or
birth morally depraved or corrupt, alien from the spiritual life, and
inclined to evil. Whether on any ground, or under any law, he is
a sharer in the sin of Adam, or in the guilt of his sin ; or whether
depravity as a fact is a divine punishment justly inflicted on
the ground of a common participation in that sin ; or whether
depravity itself is of the nature of sin and deserves the eternal retribution of the divine justice—these are questions distinct and apart
from the one question respecting native depravity. The truth of
this question does not depend upon the truth of the others. In the
further treatment of anthropology these questions must be considered. They hold such a place in doctrinal creeds and theological
discussions that they could not with any propriety be omitted.
Each will find its proper place in our discussion. For the present
we are concerned only with the separate and distinct question of
native depravity.

II. Doctrinal Sense of Depravity.

1. *A Subjective Moral State.*—Depravity is within us and of us,
_{MANIFEST IN} not, however, as a physical entity or any form of essen-
_{ITS ACTIVITIES.} tial existence, but as a moral condition or state. As such,
it is below consciousness, and metaphysical for thought, but reveals
itself in its activities. These activities are conclusive of both its
reality and evil quality. In its purely metaphysical form it is not
easily grasped in thought, but this fact does not in the least hinder
the mental apprehension of its reality. Many things are beyond
apprehension in their mode, yet fully certain in their reality. We
know not the difference in the inner states of the lion and the
lamb, but we know that there is a difference which determines the
ferocity of the one and the gentleness of the other. There are differences in the lives of men which lead to the certainty of a difference of inner states. Some lives are in the works of the flesh, and
others in the fruits of the Spirit, as Paul has drawn the contrast.[1]
Such differences cannot spring from a common inner state of the
soul. What thus appears in different lives is often exemplified in
the same life. There are many instances of great change in individual lives. Sometimes the change is from a kind and gracious

[1] Gal. v, 19-23.

life into a hard and selfish one, but much oftener a secular, selfish, and evil life is transformed into a spiritual, generous, and good one. With such changes of the actual life there must be like changes of the subjective state. The spontaneous impulses and dispositions must be radically changed. There is no other account of such changes in the habits of life. In the light of such facts we may see the possibility, and in some measure the sense, of a subjective state of depravity, a state of the inner nature which is alien from the spiritual life and inclined to evil.

2. *Broadly in the Sensuous and Moral Nature.*—Theologians often locate depravity in the will. This is simply a part of the error of treating the will as a person endowed with the powers of personal agency. Thus intellect and sensibility are ascribed to the will, and also many forms of personal action. There is error in the will, and evil impulse and inclination, while it resists the motives to the good and rebels against the law of duty. These are mistaken views. The will is not a person, not in itself an agent, but simply an instrumental faculty of mind, which completes its power of personal action. There is no impulse or inclination in the will itself. All impulse and inclination are from the sensibilities. The motives of action which arise through the sensibilities address their solicitations to the personal agent, and it is not for his will, but for himself in the use of his will, to refuse or accept these solicitations. In the light of such facts it is clearly a mistake to locate depravity in the will. The ground is entirely too narrow for the characteristic facts of depravity. The willing power, especially within the moral sphere, is deeply involved in the depravity of our nature, but rather through the perversion of the sensibilities and the moral nature than by any direct effect upon the will itself.

NOT DISTINCT-IVELY IN THE WILL

The sensuous nature, as we here use the term, is much broader than the physical nature, and the seat of many other sensibilities than the appetencies regarded as more specially physical. These manifold feelings have their proper functions in the economy of human life. In a healthful tone and normal state of the sensuous nature, these feelings are subordinate to the sense of prudence and the moral reason, and may thus fulfill their functions consistently with the spiritual life. There may be a disordered state of the sensuous nature, with the result of inordinate sensibilities. Thus arise evil tendencies and vicious impulses and appetencies, inordinate forms of feeling—all that may be included in " the lust of the flesh, and the lust of the eyes, and the pride of life." [1] There are in human life many

IN THE SENSU-OUS NATURE.

[1] 1 John ii, 16.

instances of such perverted and inordinate sensibilities as clearly evince a disordered state of the sensuous nature. Such a disordered state is a part of the depravity of human nature.

The moral nature is the seat of conscience and the moral reason. IN THE MORAL There may be a disordered state of the moral nature, NATURE. just as of the sensuous; a state in which the moral reason is darkened or perverted, and the conscience voiceless or practically powerless. In such a state moral duty is neither clearly seen nor properly enforced. God is far away, or so dimly seen that the vision of him has little or no ruling power; for, while in the reality of his existence he might still be apprehended in the intuitive or logical reason, it is only in the apprehension of the moral consciousness that he becomes a living presence. In such a state the soul is morally weak, and the sensibilities, selfish and secular in impulse and tendency, and without proper moral restraint, easily run to excess and dominate the life. There are in human life many instances of such facts. It may be said, and truly, that this moral disorder, especially in its extreme forms, is often the result of vicious habits; but this does not change either the nature or the reality of such a subjective state. So far it has been our special aim to point out the nature and possibility of such a state. There may be, and there is, a disordered condition of our moral nature. Its manifestations often appear so early in life as to evince its congenital character. Such a disordered condition of the moral powers is a part of the depravity of human nature. We thus locate depravity in both the sensuous and the moral nature. There is at once a filthiness of both " the flesh and the spirit." [1]

3. *Meaning of Depravation from Deprivation.*—In the discussion of the primitive holiness we fully recognized the presence of the Holy Spirit as the source of its highest form. We did not accept the Papal view, that original righteousness was wholly a gracious endowment, superadded after the creation of man, but held the Adamic nature just as created to be upright in itself. In entire consistency with this view we held the presence of the Spirit as the source of the fuller strength and tone of that holiness. Provision was thus complete for the more thorough subordination of all sensuous impulses and appetencies, and the complete dominance of the moral and spiritual life. As the result of sin there was a deprivation of the Holy Spirit, and in consequence of this loss a depravation of man's nature. In addition to the more direct effect of sin upon the sensuous and moral nature, there was a loss of all the moral strength and tone immediately arising from the presence and

[1] 2 Cor. vii, 1.

agency of the Holy Spirit. The detriment was twofold, and in consequence the depravation was the deeper. In this view we still find depravity as a disordered state of the sensuous and moral nature.

4. *Characteristic Evil Tendency of Depravity.*—The orthodox creeds uniformly note an inclination to evil or to sin as a characteristic fact of native depravity. In the words of our own creed, man as fallen and corrupt is "of his own nature inclined to evil, and that continually."[1] In the words of another, we are in consequence of the original corruption of our nature "wholly inclined to all evil."[2] This evil tendency is often given as the constitutive fact of depravity. Thus: "The corruption of human nature means its tendency to sin."[3] Again: "Original sin is an inclination born with us; an impulse which is agreeable to us; a certain influence which leads us into the commission of sin."[4] Müller gives the same view in holding that the evidences of a common depravity "fully justify the old theological expression *peccatum originale*, understanding it as simply affirming the existence of an innate tendency or bias toward sin in every human being."[5] This view is not strictly correct. It proceeds with insufficient analysis, and therefore falls short of scientific accuracy. This inclination to evil is the result of native depravity, not its constitutive fact. Depravity itself lies deeper, and the tendency to evil is a mode of its activity and manifestation. The question of this evil tendency will be further treated in connection with the proofs of depravity. So far we have simply aimed to disconnect the question of depravity from the others associated with it under the formula of original sin, and to give its doctrinal sense as a distinct and separate question.

DISTINCTION OF STATE AND TENDENCY

---

[1] Article vii [2] *Confession of Faith*, chap. vi, sec. 4. [3] Chalmers.
[4] Melanchthon. [5] *Christian Doctrine of Sin*, vol ii, p 268.

CHAPTER VII.

PROOFS OF NATIVE DEPRAVITY.

THE proofs of native depravity lie mostly in the Scriptures: partly,
SUMMARY OF   in the more direct testimony of particular texts;
PROOFS   partly, in the impossibility of righteousness and life
by the law, and the necessity for the atonement and spiritual
regeneration.   Further proof lies in the universality of actual
sin.   Both the Scriptures and the history of the race witness to
the truth of this universality, and the common religious consciousness confirms their testimony.   Native depravity, with its
characteristic evil tendency, is the only rational account of universal actual sin, and thus finds its proof in that universality.
The manifold evils of the present life, the mortality of the race in
the Scripture account of it, the small success of providential agencies for the moral and religious improvement of mankind, and the
common spiritual apathy give further proof of a moral lapse of
the race.   We have thus briefly outlined the evidences of native
depravity which we shall present in this chapter.

I. MORE DIRECT SCRIPTURE PROOFS.

1. *Testimony of Particular Texts.*—A few out of very many
will suffice.   In the texts which we shall adduce the truth of
native depravity is mostly given as an implication of their contents,
rather than in the form of direct statement.   There are indeed but
few proof-texts of the latter class, but there are very many of the
former.   The proof in the former is just as conclusive as in the
latter.

"And God saw that the wickedness of man was great in the
THE SOURCE   earth, and that every imagination of the thoughts of
OF SIN   his heart was only evil continually."   "For the imagination of man's heart is evil from his youth." [1]   In both texts
there is reference to the great wickedness which preceded the flood
and provoked its judicial infliction.   This wickedness in all its
forms of violence and crime is traced to its source in the heart of
man, and to the evil tendency of its incipient impulses, its earliest
and most elementary activities.   Such an account is rational and

[1] Gen. vi, 5; viii, 21.

sufficient only with an inclination to evil which is at once the characteristic and the proof of native depravity.

"Who can bring a clean thing out of an unclean? not one." "What is man, that he should be clean? and he which FOUNTAIN AND is born of a woman, that he should be righteous?"[1] STREAM The first text may be taken as proverbial. Its principle is that every thing inherits the quality of its source: the stream, the quality of the fountain; the fruit, the quality of the tree. From a corrupt source there can be no pure issue. The principle applies to man. The fountain of the race was corrupted by sin, and depravity flows down the stream of human life. This accounts for the evil tendencies of human nature The second text illustrates the principle of the first, with special application to man. "What is man, that he should be clean? and he which is born of a woman, that he should be righteous?" Each man inherits the moral state of the race, and hence is corrupt in his nature because the race is corrupt. Hence the appetence for evil, the relish for sin, the drinking iniquity like water.[2]

"Behold, I was shapen in iniquity; and in sin did my mother conceive me" "The wicked are estranged from the TESTIMONY womb: they go astray as soon as they are born, speak- OF DAVID ing lies."[3] With a fully awakened conscience, David came to a very deep sense of his recent sins, and in very earnest words expressed his consciousness of their enormity. Only the utmost intensity of expression could do any justice to the reality. Below these actual sins he found the corruption of his inner nature; and hence his earnest prayers· "Wash me thoroughly from mine iniquity, and cleanse me from my sin." "Purge me with hyssop, and I shall be clean: wash me, and I shall be whiter than snow." In this intense introspection he carries the view of inner corruption back to the very inception of his existence. It would be easy to call this an exaggeration springing from the whelming intensity of feeling, but we should thus destroy this profound and instructive lesson of penitence, for we might in like manner account its whole expression an exaggeration. The truth of native depravity is clearly given in the first text cited in this paragraph, for otherwise there is nothing to justify or even to render permissible the use of its words. The second text further expresses the same truth. The only rational sense of a moral estrangement from our birth, and a straying into sin as soon as we are born, lies in the truth of native depravity. This is the only sense consistent with the Scriptures and the relative facts. The words cannot mean an actual sinning from one's

[1] Job xiv, 4; xv, 14.   [2] Job xv, 16.   [3] Psa. li, 5, lviii, 3.

birth, and therefore must mean a native depravity, the incipient activities of which tend to evil. This is the only consistent interpretation.

"What then? are we better than they? No, in no wise: for we

OF FALL. have before proved both Jews and Gentiles, that they are all under sin; as it is written, There is none righteous, no, not one: there is none that understandeth, there is none that

METHOD OF PAUL'S ARGUMENT. seeketh after God. They are all gone out of the way, they are together become unprofitable; there is none that doeth good, no, not one." [1]   In this strong passage Paul sums up and applies the arguments conducted in the first and second chapters. He had proved in the first the universal sinfulness of the Gentiles, and in the second the universal sinfulness of the Jews. This proof he assumes in the passage just cited. Instances of personal righteousness, even many such, are entirely consistent with his position of universal sinfulness. The ruling purpose of his argument requires this consistency. As sin is universal there can be no personal righteousness simply by the law; but righteousness is still possible through faith in Christ. All are sinners, but many are thus saved from sin. While many are righteous through grace, it is still true that none are righteous on the footing of nature. Paul confirms his position of universal sinfulness by a citation from the Psalms, [2] as we see in the passage now in hand. These texts in the Psalms refer directly to the great wickedness just preceding the flood. St. Paul, however, is not attempting a mere parallelism between widely separate ages, but is maintaining the sinfulness of man in all ages. This is the presupposition and requirement of his doctrine of justification by faith. Such a universality of sin must mean, as we shall more fully point out, a native inclination or tendency to sin. The argument of Paul in proving the universality of sin is replete with the evidences of such native tendency.

There are many texts which incidentally but strongly convey the

THE SENSE OF MANY TEXTS. sense of a disordered state and evil tendency of mankind. We cite from a collection by Mr. Watson. "'Madness is in the heart of the *sons of men*, while they live' (Eccl. ix, 3). 'But they like *men* have transgressed the covenant' (Hos. vi, 7). 'If *ye, being evil*, know how to give good gifts unto your children' (Matt. vii, 11). 'Thou savorest not the things that be of God, but the things that be of MEN' (Matt. xvi, 23). 'Are ye not carnal, and walk as MEN?' (1 Cor. iii, 3.) The above texts are to be considered as specimens of the manner in which the sacred

[1] Rom. iii, 9-12.   [2] Psa. xiv, 1-3; liii, 1-3.

writers speak of the subject rather than as approaching to an enumeration of the passages in which the same sentiments are found in great variety of expression, and which are adduced on various occasions." [1] They fully give the sense of a native quality of evil in man.

2. *Impossibility of Righteousness and Life by Law.*—Full obedience, or the fulfillment of all duty, must be sufficient FULL OBEDI-
for both righteousness and life. If the fulfillment of ENCE SUFFI-
all duty is not sufficient for personal righteousness CIENT
there must be some divine requirement for righteousness above one's whole duty. This, however, cannot be, for any requirement for righteousness must take its place as one's duty. The fulfillment of all duty must be the very reality of personal righteousness. Such righteousness must be sufficient for life—life in the blessedness of the divine favor. If it should be objected that there is no merit in obedience, it may suffice to answer, that the divine economy of reward is not commercial in its ground. Full obedience must be sufficient for personal righteousness and life, for otherwise sin and death would be an original necessity with all moral intelligences.

Yet neither righteousness nor life is possible to man by deeds of law. This is the doctrine of Paul, and underlies his NONE THUS
doctrine of justification. He finds all men guilty before OBEDIENT.
God, and concludes: "Therefore by the deeds of the law there shall no flesh be justified in his sight." [2] This is not because the fulfillment of duty is not sufficient for personal righteousness, but because the obedience is wanting and all have sinned. "For if righteousness come by the law, then Christ is dead in vain." [3] The very necessity for the atonement in Christ was the impossibility of righteousness under law. "For if there had been a law given which could have given life, verily righteousness should have been by the law " [4] But the law could not give life because it could not give righteousness ; so that neither righteousness nor life is possible by deeds of law.

Why this impossibility ? It must lie in the impossibility of full obedience to the law of duty ; for we have previously PROOF OF A
shown the sufficiency of such obedience for both right- MORAL LAPSE.
eousness and life. We do not mean an absolute impossibility, but an impossibility without the grace of redemption and the office of the Holy Spirit in the ministry of that grace. Why such an impossibility ? Either the law of duty must be above the ability of

---

[1] *Theological Institutes*, vol. ii, p. 71.   [2] Rom. iii, 20.
[3] Gal. ii, 21.   [4] Gal. iii, 21.

man as originally constituted, or he must be in a state of moral lapse and disability. The former alternative must be excluded; for a primary law of duty above the power of obedience would involve the necessity of sin. We must accept the alternative of a moral lapse, with its moral disabilities. This is the truth of native depravity.

3. *Necessity for Spiritual Regeneration.*—The ground of this argument is furnished in the doctrine of regeneration as set forth by Christ in his lesson to Nicodemus.[1] The passage is familiar, and we may omit its formal citation. The construction of the argument requires little more than an analysis of the passage and a grouping of its leading facts.

The nature and necessity of regeneration are set forth in con-
NATURE OF THE nection. "Except a man be born again, he cannot
NECESSITY.   see the kingdom of God." "Except a man be born of water and of the Spirit, he cannot enter into the kingdom of heaven." Regeneration is an inner renovation, a purification of the inner nature. This is its sense as signified by the water of baptism, and by the agency of the Holy Spirit, through whose gracious power the work is wrought. We may trace the idea of this work through the Scriptures, and, while we find it under many forms of expression, we find in all this deeper meaning of an inward renewal and purification. Its necessity to our salvation is declared in the most positive manner. Without it we cannot enter into the kingdom of heaven.

The ground of this necessity lies in a native quality of our nature.
GROUND OF THE This is the clear sense of the words of Christ. After
NECESSITY.   the repeated assertion of the necessity of regeneration to salvation, he adds: "That which is born of the flesh is flesh; and that which is born of the Spirit is spirit. Marvel not that I said unto thee, Ye must be born again." Flesh cannot here be taken in any mere physical sense. Such a sense could neither express the necessity for spiritual regeneration nor allow its possibility. The two ideas are utterly incongruous. Through regeneration the spiritual quality replaces the fleshly quality. That which is born of the Spirit is spirit—in the sense of moral quality. Hence the regenerate, while still physically in the flesh, are in moral quality or subjective state no longer in the flesh but in the Spirit, or the spiritual state produced by the Spirit in the work of regeneration.[2] It is thus clear that flesh and spirit stand in contrast, the former meaning a depraved state, the latter, a renewed and holy state. This interpretation is confirmed by the further contrast

----

[1] John iii, 3-7.   [2] Rom. viii, 9; Gal. v, 24, 25.

which the Scriptures draw between the flesh and the Spirit, or the fleshly mind and the spiritual mind, and between the works of the flesh and the fruits of the Spirit.[1] We thus have the sense of flesh as our Lord used the term in his doctrine of regeneration. It must mean a depraved state, a corrupt nature.

The proof of native depravity is right at hand : "That which is born of the flesh is flesh." On the ground of Scripture this one proof is conclusive.

In the proofs of native depravity thus far adduced it is manifest that the question is not a merely speculative one, but A FUNDAMENT- one that is fundamental in Christian theology. We AL DOCTRINE have seen that it underlies the necessity for an atonement, for justification by faith, and for spiritual regeneration. These are distinctive and cardinal truths of Christianity. Native depravity is the presupposition of each and all. Without this deeper truth there is no requirement of any one. If these doctrines are true, the fallen state of man must be a truth. "If he is not a depraved, undone creature, what necessity for so wonderful a Restorer and Saviour as the Son of God? If he is not enslaved to sin, why is he redeemed by Jesus Christ? If he is not polluted, why must he be washed in the blood of the immaculate Lamb? If his soul is not disordered, what occasion is there for such a divine Physician? If he is not helpless and miserable, why is he personally invited to secure the assistance and consolations of the Holy Spirit? And, in a word, if he is not 'born in sin,' why is a 'new birth' so absolutely necessary that Christ declares, with the most solemn asseverations, 'Without it no man can see the kingdom of God?'"[2]

II. Proof in the Prevalence of Sin.

1. *Universality of Actual Sin* —Both sacred and secular history disclose the universal prevalence of sin. Of course it is not pretended that every person of the race is brought distinctly into view and disclosed in the actual sinfulness of his life. This is not necessary to the utmost certainty of universal sinning. The NATURE OF universality is a warranted generalization from the uni- THE PROOF formity in observed individuals. This is the method of science. In no department of nature is it thought necessary to observe and test every specimen or individual in order to the generalization and certainty of the science. After proper observation, the classification is never disturbed by the discovery of new instances so dissimilar as to refuse a scientific incorporation. The method is thoroughly valid in application to man. Now in all the disclosures of history, in all

[1] Rom viii, 1-13; Gal. v, 16, 17, 19-24.   [2] Fletcher . *Appeal*, part i.

the moral and religious consciousness which has received a frank and open expression, a sinless man has not appeared. Of course we except the Son of man. However, he is not strictly an exception, because his unique character will not allow his human classification simply as a man ; and he is as really distinct in his sinlessness as in his unique personality. There is no human exception. It is not GOOD LIVES NO assumed that all are equally sinful, nor that each is DISPROOF. given to the commission of all sins. Nor is it denied that there have been many good men. The grace of redemption and the work of the Holy Spirit, operative in all ages and among all peoples, have not been without result. Many a soul, taking hold upon this divine help, has been lifted up into a thoroughly good life. Perhaps for the want of the fuller light of heavenly truth this has often been done without full consciousness of the doing. But take the testimony of such men, the truest and best of the race, and not one of them will say that his life has been without sin. No man could claim an entirely sinless life without profound offense to the common moral judgment, and that judgment would pronounce such profession itself a sin. The universality of actual sin is so certain that we need not the details of universal history to confirm it.

The Scriptures are in full accord with the testimony of history. TESTIMONY OF The explicit utterances of a few texts may suffice. SCRIPTURE. "For there is no man that sinneth not."[1] This must mean, at least, that at some time sin is a fact in every life. "They are all gone aside, they are all together become filthy: there is none that doeth good, no, not one."[2] Instances of salvation from sin are entirely consistent with these words, but they cannot mean less than the universality of sin. David prays to God : "And enter not into judgment with thy servant : for in thy sight shall no man living be justified."[3] This is the very doctrine of Paul, that no man can be justified by the deeds of the law, because all have sinned. "For we have before proved both Jews and Gentiles, that they are all under sin." "For all have sinned, and come short of the glory of God."[4] As previously shown, this universality of actual sin underlies the Pauline doctrine of justification. As all have sinned, all are under condemnation; for it is the function of the law to condemn the guilty, not to justify or forgive. This is the necessity for the atonement, and for justification by faith in Christ. Paul thus combines the universality of sin with his great doctrines of atonement and justification. In its certainty it stands with these doctrines. "If we say that we have no sin, we deceive ourselves, and the truth is not in us. If we confess our sins, he is

[1] 1 Kings viii, 46.		[2] Psa. xiv, 3.		[3] Psa. cxliii, 2.		[4] Rom. iii, 9, 23.

faithful and just to forgive us our sins, and to cleanse us from all unrighteousness. If we say that we have not sinned, we make him a liar, and his word is not in us."[1] Again, one may be righteous before God, right with the law, and free from the guilt of sin, but only through a gracious forgiveness of sin. This is a necessity with all, because all have sinned. On this fact the testimony of Scripture is above question.

2. *The Proof of an Evil Tendency in Man.*—Natural tendency is manifest in a uniformity of results. "We obtain a notion of such a thing as tendency no other way than by observation; and we can observe nothing but events; and it is the commonness or constancy of events that gives us a notion of tendency in all cases. Thus we judge of tendencies in the natural world. Thus we judge of the tendencies or propensities of nature in minerals, vegetables, animals, rational and irrational creatures."[2] This is the proper method of reaching the notion of a tendency of nature, and the principle so reached is most certain. There must be a tendency of nature under uniformities of action. This is a valid and necessary principle of science. It underlies physics, and chemistry, and natural history. Without it these sciences would be impossible ; and their practical utilities would be impossible.

The same principle is thoroughly valid for the habits of human life. As in the case of all other things open to scientific treatment, so the tendencies of human nature must be determined according to uniformities of human action. Here, then, is a uniformity in sinful action. All have sinned. With all the differences of temperament, social condition, education, moral training, and religious creed, there is this uniformity of action. Whether we view man as a species, or in the multitude of human personalities, this universality of sin is the proof of an evil tendency of his nature. "For it alters not the case in the least, as to the evidence of tendency, whether the subject of the constant event be an individual, or a nature and kind. Thus, if there be a succession of trees of the same sort, proceeding one from another, from the beginning of the world, growing in all conditions, soils, and climates, and otherwise in (as it were) an infinite variety of circumstances, all bearing ill fruit, it as much proves the nature and tendency of the *kind* as if it were only one individual tree, that had remained from the beginning of the world, had often been transplanted into different soils, etc., and had continued to bear only bad fruit. So, if there be a particular family, which, from generation to generation, and through every remove to innumerable different countries and places

[1] 1 John i, 8–10.   [2] Edwards : Works, vol. ii, p. 318.

of abode, all died of a consumption, or all ran distracted, or all murdered themselves, it would be as much an evidence of the tendency of something in the nature or constitution of that race as it would be of the tendency of something in the nature or state of an individual, if one person had lived all the time, and some remarkable event had often appeared to him, which he had been the agent or subject of from year to year, and from age to age, continually and without fail."[1] On such valid principles the universality of actual sin is conclusive of an evil tendency in human nature. This evil tendency is the characteristic fact and the proof of native depravity.

3. *Only Rational Account of Universal Sin.*—In order to invalidate the argument for native depravity from the universality of actual sin, it has been attempted on other grounds to account for that universality, but without success. It will suffice to consider the chief attempts of the kind.

One attempt is, to account for the universality of sin on the
NO ACCOUNT IN EVIL EXAMPLE ground of evil example and education. In any proper use for such a purpose, the distinction between bad example and bad education is not very thorough, indeed is but slight. However, we have no polemical interest in disputing any distinction which the case will allow. Bad example and bad education are both mighty forces in human life. Many minds are thus perverted, many hearts corrupted, many souls led into sin. But before they can even be assumed to account for the universality of sin there must be conceded them a universal presence and evil influence ; for otherwise they could not account for the universal result. But bad example and bad education, every-where present and operative for evil, are simply forms of the universal sin, and therefore must themselves be accounted for. As a part of the universal sin, they must be valueless for any account of that universality. To attempt it is simply the fallacy of making a thing account for itself: worse than that ; it is the egregious fallacy of making the part of a thing account for the whole.

There is another decisive view of this question. While the great
POWER OF EVIL EXAMPLE. power of bad example and education is conceded, it should not be overlooked that such power, like all practical forces, is conditioned by certain responsive susceptibilities or inclinations in man. Without the responsive sensibilities the mightiest practical forces would be utterly powerless. There must be plasticity of substance as well as molding force, else there can be no casting of any form. For the molding power of any

[1] Edwards ; Works, vol. ii, p. 319.

form of example or education there must be a plasticity of our nature which will readily yield to its influence. If bad example and education have such power over human life that they may be claimed to account for the universality of sin, there must be susceptibilities and tendencies of human nature which readily respond to their influence. Such susceptibilities and tendencies are possible only with an evil bias or inclination. Such evil bias or inclination is the characteristic fact and the proof of native depravity. Thus the great power of bad example and bad education, through which it is attempted to invalidate a leading proof of native depravity, becomes itself a proof of that depravity.

Again, it is maintained that free-will, without any evil tendency of human nature, sufficiently accounts for the universal- NO ACCOUNT IN ity of actual sin. If this position is valid, the argument FREE-WILL for native depravity from that universality is answered. The main support of this position is brought from the case of Adam in the primitive sin. Without any evil bias, and against the tendencies of his nature to the good, Adam sinned purely through the freedom of volition. Therefore all may sin, and do sin, in the exercise of a like freedom. This is the argument. Dr. TAYLOR'S AR- Taylor puts it thus: "Adam's nature, it is allowed, GUMENT was very far from being sinful; yet he sinned. And, therefore, the common doctrine of original sin is no more necessary to account for the sin that has been or is in the world than it is to account for Adam's sin. . . . Thus their argument from the wickedness of mankind, to prove a sinful and corrupt nature, must inevitably and irrecoverably fall to the ground." [1]

From the instance of Adam one might in this manner prove the abstract possibility of universal sin from mere freedom WITHOUT of volition, but could not thus rationally account for VALIDITY. its actuality. A single free action may easily be induced without any natural tendency or disposition. We often recognize individual acts of men as quite apart from their known character and habit of life. To account for such acts we do not require any permanent tendency or disposition. But to account for a habit of life, whether good or evil, we do require an inner tendency or disposition in accord with it. The case is infinitely stronger when we go from one man to all men, and especially when we go from a single action of one man to a uniformity of action in all men. We can account for a single act without any natural tendency or disposition thereto, but cannot account for the habit of even a single life without such tendency or disposition. How much less can we account for the

[1] Cited by Edwards Works, vol. ii, p. 361.

universality of actual sin without a tendency to evil in human nature. The fallacy of Taylor's argument thus appears. A single act of sin gives no account of universal sin, and is utterly powerless against the proof of an evil tendency derived from that universality. Native depravity is the only rational account of universal sin, and its reality is thus proved.[1]

4. *Concerning Natural Virtues.*—It is claimed that there are many natural virtues; and on this ground an objection is brought against the doctrine of native depravity. We do not think the objection valid, and therefore have no interest in disputing the fact of such virtues. However, they must not be exaggerated or counted for more than they are. There are natural virtues—virtues which we may call natural in distinction from such as spring from spiritual regeneration, though we do not concede their purely

NATURAL VIRTUES.

natural ground. They appear in personal character, in domestic life, in social life, in civil life, in the many forms of business. All along the centuries, men and women, without any profession of a regenerate life, yet of unquestionable purity, uprightness, and integrity of character, have appeared: some with natures gentle and lovable, and lives full of sympathy and kindness; others, strong and heroic, but true in all things. A doctrine of native depravity which cannot admit the consistency of such virtues with itself must be an exaggeration, and any inference which that inconsistency warrants goes to the disproof, not of the true doctrine, but of a form of it which exaggeration has made erroneous. There is no doctrine of native depravity in the Scriptures which renders the truth of such virtues inconsistent with itself. Native depravity does not make human nature demonian. It is not irredeemably bad. Life begins with evil tendencies, but also with activities of the moral and religious nature which act as a check upon these tendencies. Monsters of wickedness are a growth. Instances of utter badness from early life are comparatively few, and are properly regarded as abnormal. The Scriptures every-where recognize the moral and religious susceptibilities of men, except as they may be stifled by a vicious habit of life. In the absence of a true spiritual life with so many, natural virtues

NECESSARY IN HUMAN LIFE.

are necessary to the domestic, social, and civil forms of human life which actually exist, and which we must think to be in the order of the divine providence. Their providential purpose implies a capacity in human nature for the necessary natural virtues. The Scriptures contain no doctrine of native depravity inconsistent with these facts.

[1] Edwards. Works, vol. ii, pp. 361–365.

We have not conceded to such natural virtues a purely natural ground. We called them natural because actual in sourceofnat- human life without spiritual regeneration. The fallen ural virtues race is also a redeemed race, and a measure of grace is given to every man, and remains with him as a helpful influence, unless forfeited by a vicious habit of life. Human nature is not just what it would be if left to the unrestricted consequence of the Adamic fall. It is not so left. The helping grace of redemption does not await our spiritual regeneration, but a measure is given to every man, that we might be capable of the forms of life providentially intended for us; most of all, that we might be lifted up to a capacity for the moral and religious probation in which we are all placed. We thus have the true source of what we call natural virtues, and a source entirely consistent with the doctrine of native depravity. Further, the many providential agencies for the moral and religious improvement of mankind have ever co-operated with the helping grace of redemption. The virtues necessary to the providential forms of human life are thus nurtured and strengthened. Finally, these natural virtues are mostly of an instinctive character, spontaneous to our nature, and survive all changes and conditions, except that of an utter personal debasement.

They may exist and fulfill their necessary offices in the providential forms of human life, not only in the absence of a without true true spiritual state, but with the presence of an evil state. spirituality. Their functions are fulfilled without any vitalizing moral principle, without any sense of duty to God. They have in themselves no strictly moral or religious quality, and can be carried up into a true moral and religious sphere only by the incoming of a true spiritual life, which subordinates all the powers and activities of the soul to itself and consecrates all to God and duty. These natural virtues therefore may be called virtues only in the most nominal sense. In themselves they are not virtues. And as they may exist, not only in the absence of a true spiritual life, but with aversion to such a life, with propensity to evil, and with actual evil, they give no proof against the doctrine of native depravity.

III. Further Proofs of a Fallen State.

Under this head we group a few facts which are common to the present state of man, but inconsistent with his primitive state. The idea of a primitive state of holiness and happiness is at once a scriptural and a rational idea. Paradise, with its blessings, its freedom from wearying toil, from suffering and death, with its open communion with God and joy in his presence, seems a fitting estate for primitive man, morally constituted as he was, and fashioned in the image of God. The absence of such an estate and the presence of strongly discordant facts give proof of a fallen state. We note a few of these facts

1. *Manifold Ills of Human Life.*—The present state of man may be characterized as one of frailty and suffering. This is the Scripture view, and the common experience, as voiced in many a lament of weariness and pain. Man is born to trouble, as the sparks fly upward. He is of few days, and full of trouble.[1] The comparison of his life is not with strong and abiding things, but with the frail and the quickly vanishing. We are like the grass which flourishes in the morning and in the evening is cut down;[2] like the flower of the field which perishes under the passing wind;[3] like a vapor, appearing for a little while, and then vanishing away.[4] Such a life of frailty and trouble has no accordance with the primitive state of man, and strongly witnesses to his fallen condition.

2. *Mortality of the Race.*—Human death is the consequence of Adamic sin Death preceded the Adamic fall, and from the beginning reigned over all living orders. Nor was there in the physiological constitution of man any natural exemption from such a consequence In this constitution he was too much like the higher animal orders not to be naturally subject to the same law. Yet he was provisionally immortal—that is, he had the privilege of a prov-
A PROVISIONAL idential exemption from death on the condition of obe-
IMMORTALITY. dience to the divine will. This appears in the narrative of the probation and fall of man, and also in the account of the origin and prevalence of human death. The fruit of the tree of life, originally open to the use of man, signifies a provisional immortality. Expulsion from that tree was a deprivation of this privilege, and the subjection of man to death.[5] It is the sense of this passage that human death came by sin. What is thus given in an implicit mode is elsewhere openly declared.

By one man sin came into the world, and death by sin; and
DEATH BY SIN through the universality of sin came universal death.[6]
While the universality of death is thus connected with the universality of sin, it is yet true that the common mortality is consequent to the Adamic sin and fall. "By the trespass of the one the many died." "By the trespass of the one, death reigned through one." "In Adam all die."[7] How shall we explain the universal mortality as consequent to the sin and fall of Adam? The

[1] Job v, 7, xiv, 1. [2] Psa xc, 5, 6 [3] Psa. ciii, 15, 16, Isa xl, 6–8.
[4] James iv, 14 [5] Gen iii, 22–24 [6] Rom. v, 12.
[7] Rom. v, 15, 17; 1 Cor. xv, 22.

assumption of an immediate effect upon the physiological constitution of man could not answer for an interpretation, because the assumed effect is purely of a physical character and, therefore, would be unnatural to the cause. There could be no such immediate physical effect. The theory which accounts physical death a penal retribution, judicially inflicted upon all men on the ground of a common participation in the sin of Adam, is beset with very great difficulties. Yet, as we have previously shown, the common mortality is in some way consequent to that sin. The subjection of Adam to mortality and death was effected through his expulsion from the tree of life, and the withdrawment of that special providential agency through which, on the condition of obedience, he would have been preserved in life. These were penal inflictions on the ground of sin. In consequence of this subjection of Adam to death, mortality is entailed upon the race. The deprivation of the privilege and means of immortality which he suffered on account of sin descends upon his race. There is this connection of the common mortality with the sin of Adam. In this sense death reigns through his offense and in him all die.

There must be some reason for this consequence; some reason why the race of Adam should be denied the original REASON FOR privilege of immortality with which he was favored. THE UNIVI- If each one begins life with the primitive holiness, why SAL DEATH should he not have this privilege? With such a nature he would be morally fitted for the primitive probation. It is plain, however, that he is not thus fitted. The universality of sin proves his unfitness. The impossibility of righteousness and life by deeds of law, as maintained by Paul, proves the same fact. In consequence of the sin and fall of Adam every man has suffered a moral deterioration which disqualifies him for an economy of works, and requires for him an economy of redemption. Such an economy has been divinely instituted for the race. The privilege of immortality belonged to the former ; mortality, with the provision of a resurrection, belongs to the latter. · This change of economy, rendered necessary only by a deterioration of man's moral nature, proves his native depravity. The common mortality, as thus mediated by the common depravity, is, in turn, the proof of this depravity.

3. *Small Success of Moral and Religious Agencies.* — Everywhere there are convictions of duty, with the activities of conscience approving its fulfillment and reprehending its MEANS AND neglect or violation. This is the case even where there RESULTS is little exterior light for the moral judgment. Every-where such

convictions of duty are embodied in public opinion, and often in statutory law, with the sanction of rewards for the restraint of vice and the support of virtue. In the many religions of the world, even with their many errors, there are lessons of moral duty. Philosophy and poetry have joined in the support of the good against the evil. After due allowance for the errors of moral judgment and the elements of evil in legislation and religion, in philosophy and poetry, there is still a large sum of moral agency which, with a responsive nature in man, must have produced a large fruitage of good. The fruitage has been small because the nature of man has strongly resisted these agencies. Every-where the common life has been far below its moral and religious lessons.

Like facts appear under the more direct agencies of Providence in the interest of morality and religion. Such agencies, often in an open supernatural mode, appear through all the history of the race. We see them in the beginning of that history. God is present with men; present with precepts and promises, with warnings against sin, with blessings for obedience and punishment for disobedience. The evil tendencies of men are stronger than these moral restraints. The tide of iniquity rises above all barriers, and so floods the world as to provoke the divine retribution in its destruction. Against all the force of this fearful lesson STRENGTH OF EVIL TENDENCIES. iniquity soon again prevailed, and so widely as to provoke again the divine retribution. Later history is replete with moral and religious agencies. We see them in the history of Abraham, in the miracles of Moses and the divine legislation through his ministry. God was with the prophets, and through his Spirit their words were mighty. Through all those centuries of Jewish history such moral and religious agencies, often in a supernatural mode, were in active operation. With a responsive moral and religious nature in man, a prevailing and permanent obedience to the divine will would have been secured. There was no such result. The frequent revolts and rebellions, sometimes in the very presence of the most imposing forms of the divine manifestation, witness, not only to the absence of such a nature, but also to the presence of a nature actively propense to evil and strongly resistant of all these moral and religious agencies.[1]

With the advent of the Messiah came the fuller light of the Gospel In the life and miracles and lessons of Christ THE GOSPEL OFTEN FRUITLESS. and the ministry of his apostles moral and religious agencies rose to their highest form. Instead of a ready response to such truth and grace, again there is resistance. Like

[1] Exod. xxxii, 0, 33; xxxiii, 3; Isa. xlviii, 3–5; Acts vii, 51–53.

resistance has continued through all the Christian centuries. Nor has this resistance widely taken the form of infidelity, which so bars the soul against the moral forces of the Gospel. The significant fact is its prevalence with so many who accept the deepest verities of Christianity. With the admission of such truths, only a native aversion to a true religious life could in so many instances void their constraining force. In all this resistance to the moral and religious agencies of Providence, and the comparatively small results of good, proof is given of the truth of native depravity.[1]

4. *The Common Spiritual Apathy.*—This apathy is a manifest fact in human life. It is the mental state of the many. Why is this widely prevalent apathy? Men care for secular good. Self-interest is a potent force in human life. Why are its energies given to mere secular good, while spiritual and eternal interests are so much neglected? Why so much earnest service of mammon in preference to the service of God? Men consent to the paramount duties of religion, and to its infinitely momentous interests, and promise them attention, but slumber again, and slumber on, heedless of all the voices of life and death and the entreating appeals of the divine love. Such spiritual apathy cannot be normal to a soul made in the image of God and for a heavenly destiny. It evinces a moral state which has its only account in the truth of native depravity.

[1] Fletcher: Works, vol. iii, pp. 302-305; Edwards: Works, vol. ii, pp. 348-361.

CHAPTER VIII.

ORIGIN OF DEPRAVITY

THE origin of depravity as a fact, and the ground or law of its entailment upon the race, are distinct questions and open to separate answers. There is not unanimity respecting either. Nor does the answer to the first question necessarily determine the answer to the second. It is better, therefore, to treat them separately.

I. ADAMIC ORIGIN.

1. *Limitations of the Question of Origin.*—These limitations arise from certain facts of depravity. One is, that it is native—a moral state in which we are born. Hence it cannot have its origin in any thing subsequent to our birth. We thus see the error of accounting it to any such thing as evil example or education, or to the influence of environment. Such things may act upon our evil nature and quicken its tendencies into earlier and stronger activity, but cannot be the source of our depravity, because, while it is native, they can affect us only in our actual life. Another fact is that depravity is universal. Hence it cannot arise from any local or temporary source. The true source must be common to all men. Finally, depravity itself is intrinsically the same and one in all. Therefore its origin must be one, not many. The present thinking, the best philosophical thinking, forbids an unnecessary multiplication of causes, and for such a uniform and universal fact as native depravity could allow only one source.[1]

2. *Origin in the Adamic Fall.*—The conditions of limitation respecting the origin of depravity are all met in the Adamic relations of the race. This is not the only case in which they are all met, but it is the most reasonable account of the common depravity, and the source to which the Scriptures lead us. They are all equally met in our relation to physical nature as contemporary with our birth, as common to all, and the same for all. The idea of a

NOT IN MAT- physical origin of moral evil, and of the evil tendencies
TER. of human nature, has widely prevailed. It is in the vast system of Brahmanism, and in the Greek philosophy. It flourished in the Gnosticism of the early Christian centuries. Its

[1] Dwight: *Theology*, sermon xxxii.

tendencies are always evil: to sensuality in one direction, and to extreme asceticism in the other. If matter is intrinsically evil and the inevitable source of corruption to the soul, then such was man's state as originally created, and there is for him no deliverance in the present life. Such facts are not reconcilable with any true idea of God. But as a heresy in Christian theology the physical origin of moral evil is only a matter of history, and needs no present refutation. The conditions of limitation respecting the origin of depravity are also met in the relations of God to the soul. It could not be said that doctrinal opinion has never implicated the divine agency in the origin of depravity—not, indeed, by an immediate constitution of a corrupt nature in primitive man, but mediately by a determination of the Adamic fall. Such determination must be an implication of supralapsarian Calvinism. Happily, supralapsarianism is now almost wholly a matter of history. Neither by an original constitution of human nature, nor by any agency which determined the Adamic fall, could God be the author of such an evil as human depravity. His holiness and goodness declare it an absolute impossibility. The Adamic origin of depravity is thus rendered strongly probable. The three relations which we have named as meeting the limitations of the question complete the circle of such relations in even thinkable sources. It follows that, as the origin of depravity cannot be either in physical nature or in God, it must be in the Adamic fall.

NOT IN GOD.

ORIGIN IN ADAM.

3. *Transmissible Effects of Adam's Sin.*—The effect of Adam's sin in himself was the corruption of his own nature. No one can sin without detriment to his subjective moral state. The higher the state of holiness, the deeper the moral deterioration. There was the deeper consequence of evil in the case of Adam, who was created in holiness. Besides this more direct effect of his sin he suffered a deprivation of the Holy Spirit, whose presence gave to his subjective holiness its highest form. As previously shown, the consequence of this deprivation was the deeper depravation of his moral nature. The corruption of nature which Adam thus suffered must have been transmitted to his offspring. This result is determined by a law of nature, and as fixed a law as nature reveals. There is no need to assume that this law of transmission must rule in the case of such slight changes as may occur in the mere accidents of parental character, but it must rule in the case of so profound a change in the subjective moral state. There is no reference to this law in the case of either Cain or Abel, but there is a reference in the instance of Seth in that he was

LAW OF TRANSMISSION.

begotten in the likeness and image of his father.[1] The transmission of the Adamic likeness, even in his fallen state, is thus fully recognized. In this there is reason for us to find the origin of depravity in the Adamic fall.

4. *Secular Consequences of the Adamic Fall.*—In consequence of the Adamic sin and fall the race is involved in physical suffering and death. The record of such results is clearly given in the Scriptures.[2] With this text we may collate others in which the common mortality is more definitely attributed to the Adamic fall.[3] With this great fact so definitely given, we may include with it other forms of physical suffering, as expressed in the divine judgment upon the progenitors of the race. For the present we are concerned only with the facts of such consequences, without any respect to the law of their entailment. Nor is the fact itself in the least affected by any perplexities of interpretation which the texts may present. We may not be able to get the exact sense in which the earth was cursed and man subjected to wearying toil. We may think of great strength in primitive man as at once providentially given and guarded, and also of the garden prepared for him, with such conditions of fruitfulness as to yield an ample living without any requirement of wearying toil. We may also think of greatly changed conditions: a loss of strength in man, and the allotment of new fields, no longer prepared as a garden, but hard and rough in their primitive nature, and from which bread must be forced in the sweat of the face. But whatever the mode of the divine judgment upon man and the earth, it clearly conveys the sense of physical suffering and death in consequence of the Adamic fall.

5. *Deeper Moral Consequence in Depravity.*—The physical evils which the race suffers in consequence of the Adamic fall are connected with a deeper moral consequence. This connection is specially clear in the case of death. " Wherefore, as by one man sin entered into the world, and death by sin; and so death passed upon all men, for that all have sinned."[4] The sense is not merely that Adam was the first that sinned, but that in some deep sense universal sin and death are connected with his sin and fall. We have

RESULTS OF THE ADAMIC CONNECTION. previously shown that universal actual sin has no rational account except through the common depravity of human nature. We may thus find the connection between the universal actual sin and the sin of Adam. The universal actual sin has its source in the common depravity, and the common

[1] Gen. v, 3.   [2] Gen. iii, 16–19.   [3] Rom. v, 15, 17; 1 Cor. xv, 21, 22.
[4] Rom. v, 12.

depravity has its source in the sin of Adam. There is no other way of accounting for the universality of actual sin through his sin. Thus the corruption of Adam's own nature through sin becomes the source of the common depravity. There is a like connection of the common mortality which is also traced to the Adamic sin and fall. If human nature is not corrupted through the sin of Adam we should be born in the same state in which he was created, with equal fitness for a probationary economy and the opportunity of immortality. Thus the universality of death in consequence of the sin of Adam is mediated by the corruption of human nature through his sin. In the physical suffering and death entailed upon the race through the sin of Adam we thus see the deeper moral consequence in depravity.

II. LAW OF ADAMIC ORIGIN.

With agreement respecting the Adamic origin of depravity, there are different theories respecting its ground or law. For the present we are concerned with the statement and discrimination of these theories. They are so fundamental in doctrinal anthropology as to require separate treatment.

1. *Theory of Penal Retribution.*—In this theory depravity is a punishment, judicially inflicted upon mankind. It is maintained that under the providence of God so great an evil could not befall the race except as a punishment. Advocates of the theory may often use the term original sin instead of depravity, meaning by it not only the corruption of human nature but also its sinfulness or demerit. However, as sinfulness is held to be intrinsic to the depravity, just as it is intrinsic to an actual sin, we need not be careful further to notice any difference of the terms in the present connection. If depravity is in itself sin, then the penal infliction of depravity is the penal infliction of original sin. Nor can this form of sin be inflicted without the infliction of depravity. The theory will more fully appear under the next head.

2. *On the Ground of Adamic Sin.*—If depravity is a punishment it must have its ground in guilt. The most rigid Calvinism holds this principle firmly. Any punishment without a ground in guilt must be an injustice. The alleged guilt in this case is held to arise from a participation in the sin of Adam, as the only precedent sin, and to an intimate connection with which the common depravity is traced.

This is the Calvinistic theory. It is such at least in the general sense. On many questions there are divergences in Calvinistic minds. There may be dissent from the present theory, but there

31

is not enough to disturb its Calvinistic position. On this ques-
THE CALVIN- tion, Cunningham, after noting some Calvinistic dis-
ISTIC THEORY. sent or reserve, proceeds to say: "A second class, comprehending the great body of Calvinistic divines, have regarded it
(the common depravity) as, in some measure and to some extent,
explained by the principle of its being *a penal infliction* upon men,
resulting from the imputation to them of the guilt of Adam's
first sin." And further: "There is no view of God's actings in
this whole matter which at all accords with the actual, proved realities of the case, except that which represents him in the light of
a just judge punishing sin—a view which implies that men's want
of original righteousness and the corruption of their whole nature
have a penal character, are punishments righteously inflicted on
GROUND OF account of sin. . . . And the only explanation which
THE PENAL IN- Scripture affords of this mysterious constitution of
FLICTION   things is, that men have the guilt of Adam's first sin
imputed to them or charged against them, so as to be legally exposed to the penalties which he incurred." [1] On the same question Dr. Shedd quotes with approval from the *Formula Consensus
Helvetica:* "But it does not appear how hereditary corruption,
as spiritual death, could fall upon the entire human race by the
just judgment of God, unless some fault of this same human race
bringing in the penalty of that death had preceded. For the most
just God, the Judge of all the earth, punishes none but the
guilty." [2] While depravity is thus clearly set forth as a punishment on the ground of guilt, it is also declared in the same
Formula that the guilt which justifies the penal infliction arises
from a common participation in the sin of Adam. Dr. Shedd not
only fully indorses this view, but places this *Formula* at the head
of all Calvinistic symbols of the sixteenth and seventeenth centuries as the clearest and most scientific statement of the doctrine of
original sin in its Adamic connection. [3] Here, then, in addition to
the authority of this *Formula*, we have the testimony of two eminent Calvinistic authors, Cunningham and Shedd, who have made
the history of doctrines a special study, who are in opposition respecting the mode of the common participation in the guilt of
Adam's sin, who yet fully agree that Calvinism holds depravity to
be a penal retribution on the ground of such guilt.

3. *Realistic and Representative Modes of Adamic Sin.*—With the
association of a common participation in the sin of Adam, and such
a participation as justly subjects all men to the penal infliction of

[1] *Historical Theology*, vol. i, pp. 511, 526.
[2] *History of Christian Doctrine*, vol. ii, p. 160.   [3] *Ibid.*, p. 157.

depravity, the question must arise as to the ground or mode of such participation. Some answer must be given. No theory could consent to a purely arbitrary implication of the race in the Adamic sin. There are two alleged modes, the realistic and the representative. The former alleges a real oneness of the race with Adam, in some higher or lower form of realism ; the latter, a legal oneness under a law of representation. For the present we simply state the views. Full explication will be given with their discussion. Each is held by its advocates to be valid in principle, and sufficient for the common guilt and punishment.

Calvinists divide on these modes, though the representative is for the present the more prevalent view. The issue really involves two questions: Which is the Calvinistic theory? and, Which is the true theory ? Many of the older Calvinistic divines alleged both modes of Adamic guilt, which fact naturally gives rise to the first question. In the contention both parties quote the same authors, as well they may, since said authors are on both sides. But it is unscientific, mere jumbling, indeed, to hold both modes, for they are in opposition and reciprocally exclusive. If both were valid, each mode must convey to every soul of the race the whole guilt of Adam's sin. This would make each twice as guilty as Adam himself. It is surely enough to be thus made equally guilty. Calvinistic divines are very properly coming to hold more exclusively to the one or the other mode.[1]

4. *Theory of the Genetic Transmission of Depravity.*—This theory is based on the law of " like producing like "—the uniform law of propagated life. It holds sway over the most prolonged succession of generations, and is as fixed and permanent in the human species as in any other. Under this law man is now what he was in the earliest offspring of Adam, and what he has been through all the intermediate generations. As in physiological constitution and mental endowment he is thus the same, so is he the same in his moral state. This is a state of depravity genetically transmitted from the fallen and depraved progenitors of the race. Such is the account of the Adamic origin of the common depravity on the theory of genetic transmission.

5. *Doctrinal Distinction of the Two Theories.*—It should be remembered here that the theory of penal retribution, which accounts the common depravity a punishment on the ground of a common

---

[1] On the realistic side, Shedd *History of Christian Doctrine*, vol. ii, pp. 76–92 ; *Dogmatic Theology*, vol ii, pp 42–48, 181–192 ; Baird: *Elohim Revealed*, chap. xi. On the representative side, *Princeton Essays*, First Series, pp. 114–167 ; Wallace: *Representative Responsibility*.

participation in the sin of Adam, is but one theory, though its advocates divide into two classes respecting the mode of that participation. It will thus be clearly seen that we have in this section presented but two theories respecting the law of the Adamic origin of depravity. Their doctrinal distinction is easily stated, though for greater clearness we should keep entirely separate all questions respecting the intrinsic evil of depravity, or whether in itself it is truly sinful and deserving of the divine wrath. Both theories hold, and equally, the Adamic origin of depravity. Both hold its connection with the sin of Adam through which he fell under the divine retribution and suffered the corruption of his own nature. So far the two theories are the same. Beyond this they differ widely. The one denies a responsible participation in the sin of Adam and the penal infliction of depravity on the race; the other affirms both.

These are fundamental theories, and must be separately treated
TWO FUNDA-
MENTAL THEO-
RIES.
—the Calvinistic in its two modes of accounting for the common Adamic sin which it alleges. They are the only fundamental theories. There is no place for a third, however many speculative or mixed theories may be devised. Whichever is the true one must contain the whole truth of the question.

III. SPECULATIVE OR MIXED THEORIES.

The Calvinistic anthropology involves serious perplexities, particularly in the tenets of a common participation in the sin of Adam and the penal infliction of depravity on that ground. The intrinsic sinfulness of depravity itself, as deserving in all an eternal penal retribution, deepens these perplexities. The division into the two modes of accounting for the common participation in the sin of Adam has a sufficient occasion in these perplexities. Some have thought the facts concerned more manageable or less perplexing on the realistic mode, while others for a like reason have favored the representative mode. Neither party pretends to a solution of the difficulties. In the view of some minds they are too great for the acceptance of either mode. Hence, with professed adherence to the Augustinian anthropology, other theories have been devised, but without any improvement of doctrine, while mostly definite tenets are replaced with speculations or mere assumptions. No light is given.

1. *Mediate Imputation of Adamic Sin.*—It has been attempted to replace the theory of immediate with that of mediate imputation. The former goes properly, in a strictly scientific sense exclusively, with the representative mode of the common Adamic sin. In all forms of the realistic mode every soul is held to be a respon-

sible sharer in the sinning of Adam, and the imputation of the sin is mediated by that responsible participation. In the representative mode the race has no part in the sinning of Adam which mediates the imputation of his sin. Without any fault of the race, and before its corruption through the sin of Adam, the guilt of his sin is imputed, and thus immediately, to every soul.

It is not strange that some Calvinistic minds recoil from such a view In such a recoil, Placæus, an eminent Reformed theologian of Saumur, France, propounded, in the seventeenth century, the theory of mediate imputation. He began with an open denial of immediate imputation as a violation of justice. As such imputation in the very nature of it disclaims all participation of the race in the sinning of Adam, the immediate imputation of his sin to his offspring in a measure to constitute every soul as guilty as himself could not, in the view of Placæus, be other than an injustice. His doctrine was widely assailed. There was more than individual hostility. The doctrine was soon condemned by the National Synod of France, and also by the Churches of Switzerland in the Formula Consensus Helvetici. Under this severe pressure, Placæus propounded a doctrine of mediate or consequent imputation in place of the standard immediate or antecedent imputation.[1] There is a wide difference between the two theories. In the latter the imputation of sin precedes the common depravity and is the ground of its penal infliction ; while in the former the imputation of sin is subsequent to the common depravity, and on that ground. With such a widely different theory Placæus still professed adherence to the doctrine of imputation. Some received his doctrine with favor. Nor has it been without friends even to the present time. Some have claimed for its support the weighty authority of Edwards, though others dispute the claim. There is nothing in his discussion sufficiently definite to determine the question. Edwards was predominantly a realist on the Adamic connection of the race, and so far immediate imputation could have no consistent place in his doctrine.[2] Henry Rogers is one of the later advocates of the doctrine.[3]

THEORY OF PLACÆUS

The doctrine of Placæus as stated by himself is not thoroughly clear. Nor have his critics brought it into clearness. There is no obscurity in the denial of immediate imputation, for that imputation has a well-defined sense in the Calvinistic anthropology. The lack of clearness comes with

OBSCURITIES OF THE THEORY

[1] De Statu Hominis Lapsi ante Gratiam ; De Imputatione Primi Peccati Adami.

[2] Works, pp. 481-495.   [3] Genius and Writings of Jonathan Edwards.

the assertion of mediate in place of immediate imputation. The latter means the imputation of Adam's sin antecedently to any fault or corruption of the race. Seemingly, therefore, mediate imputation, while in the order of thought subsequent to the common depravity and conditioned on it, should still include the accounting of the sin of Adam to the race. Such a view, however, would be utterly inconsistent with the denial of immediate imputation as a violation of justice. The inheritance of the common depravity under a law of propagation could not constitute any ground of responsibility for the sin of Adam; and its imputation simply as mediated by that depravity would as fully violate justice as immediate imputation. What remains of the theory of Placæus? Two things: the common depravity of the race as a genetic transmission, not as a punishment; the sinfulness and demerit of the inherited depravity. The first fact is the same as our second fundamental theory in accounting for the depravity of the race. The second fact is the common Calvinistic doctrine of the sinfulness and demerit of native depravity—a question quite apart from all questions respecting the ground of depravity. It thus appears that the theory of Placæus differs from the Calvinistic anthropology only in the denial of the immediate imputation of Adam's sin; which, however, carries with it the denial that the common depravity is a penal infliction.[1]

2. *Hypothetic Ground of the Imputation of Sin* —The theory thus expressed is technically styled Scientia Media Dei. It is this: God in his absolute prescience knew that any and every soul of the race, if placed in the state of Adam, would sin just as he did; therefore he might justly and did actually impute the sin of Adam to every soul. This hypothetic sin is the ground on which the common, sinful depravity is judicially inflicted upon the race. Strange as the theory is, it has not been without favor. Its acceptance by any one presupposes two things: an unyielding adherence to the common guiltiness of Adam's sin, and a sense of intolerable difficulties in both the realistic and representative modes of accounting CRITICISM OF for such guiltiness. Surely its own difficulties are no THE THEORY. less, while the hypothetic ground on which the sin of Adam is held to be imputed is the merest assumption. Who knows the alleged fact of the divine cognizance, that every soul of the race, if placed in the state of Adam, would sin just as he did? Even if a fact, it could not justify the universal, or even the most

[1] Cunningham· *Reformers and the Theology of the Reformation*, pp. 379–391; Shedd: *History of Doctrines*, vol. ii, pp. 158–163; *Princeton Essays*, First Series, essay viii

limited, imputation of his sin. Otherwise, we might all be held responsible for any and every sin which in any condition we might possibly commit. "But it is a new sort of justice, which would allow us to be punished for sins which we never committed, or never intended to commit, but only might possibly have committed under certain circumstances."[1] "If it were allowable to refer to some intermediate knowledge on God's part as a basis of imputing the guilt and condemnation of original sin to all men, we might with equal propriety argue that God could justly have introduced mankind at once into a state of misery or bliss, upon the ground of his foreknowledge that certain of them would voluntarily make themselves liable to the one or the other destiny."[2]

This theory gives no distinct law of the Adamic origin of depravity. Depravity itself is still a punishment, judicially inflicted on the ground of a common participation in the sin of Adam. The participation is in the mode NO DISTINCT LAW OF DEPRAVITY of imputation, with a valueless, or even worse than valueless, change of its ground. The economy of representation is replaced with the purely hypothetic assumption respecting the cognizance of the divine prescience. If this assumption could be true, or even were true, a more baseless ground of imputation could not be imagined. It is worse than baseless; it would subvert the most sacred principles of moral government. So far from any relief from the perplexities of immediate imputation, it brings in far deeper perplexities.

3. *Origin of Sin in a Pre-existent Life.*—With the tenets of native depravity as a judicial infliction, and the sinfulness of depravity in a sense to deserve eternal punishment, the problem is to account for them. Confessedly, they are not explained to rational thought in any mode previously considered. In the view of some minds the only valid ground of guilt and punishment, in any strict judicial sense, must lie in a free, personal OCCASION OF THE THEORY. violation of duty. The realistic mode of accounting for the penal infliction of depravity might claim to justify itself on this principle, but could hardly pretend to such a claim respecting the alleged demerit of native depravity. Some, however, find no place for this principle in any form of realism; indeed, reject the whole theory. If such must still hold the native sinfulness of all men, there is for them no better resource than the theory of free, personal sinning in a previous state of existence. They would thus avoid the perplexities of the immediate imputation of Adam's sin, and

[1] Knapp. *Christian Theology*, p. 277.
[2] Muller. *Christian Doctrine of Sin*, vol. ii, p. 338.

theoretically secure the only principle which, in their view, can justify the common native sinfulness.

Some have adopted this view. The notion of a pre-existence of human souls has been far more extensive than its acceptance in order to avoid peculiar difficulties of the Augustinian anthropology. It holds a wide place in heathen religions, and appears in Grecian philosophy. It found a place in Jewish thought, as clearly implied in the question of our Lord's disciples: "Master, who did sin, this man, or his parents, that he was born blind?"[1] Origen, of the third century, taught the doctrine. It is the theory of Edward Beecher's *Conflict of Ages*, and is maintained with special reference to the Augustinian anthropology. The eminent Julius Muller maintains it, and for the reason above stated, that only free, personal sinning can justify the sinful state in which he believed all men to be born. He could find no place for such sinning except in a conscious pre-existence of all human souls, and, therefore, accepted this view, that he might justify his theory of native sinfulness.[2]

NOTION OF PRE-EXIST-ENCE

The theory is a purely speculative one. Müller himself so styles it, and freely concedes the absence of all direct proof in both Scripture and consciousness.[3] In his view, as appears in his elaborate discussion, the whole proof lies in its necessity to a vindication of the divine justice in a common native sinfulness. There is native sinfulness. There cannot be sinfulness without free, personal violation of duty. Such action, as an account of native sinfulness, was possible to us only in a pre-existent state. Therefore we must have personally existed and freely sinned in such a state. This is the argument.

A PURELY SPECULATIVE THEORY

Native sinfulness, as maintained in the Augustinian anthropology, is not a problem to be solved in this purely speculative mode. Logical requirements are valid for truth only with validity in the premises. Very few accept both premises in this case. Many deny the native sinfulness in the sense assumed, and many deny the necessity of free, personal agency to such sinfulness. The former have no need of the interpretation which the theory offers, and therefore see no proof in its logical requirements; the latter would rather face the perplexities of the immediate imputation of sin than accept relief in this purely speculative mode. Very serious difficulties beset the theory in its relation to the Scriptures. It implies, and must admit, that our progenitors, just as their offspring, freely sinned in the

DIFFICULTIES OF THE THE-ORY.

---

[1] John ix, 2.   [2] *Christian Doctrine of Sin*, book iv, chap. iv.
[3] *Ibid.*, vol. ii, pp. 36, 396.

/pre-existence assumed, and therefore began their Edenic life in a sinful and fallen state.[1] This is plainly contrary to the Scriptures, in the sense of which, as we have previously shown, the beginning of this life was in innocence and subjective holiness. Again, as the Edenic state was strictly probationary in its moral and religious economy, this theory must assume a possible self-recovery of our progenitors from their fallen state; for such a probation intrinsically requires the possibility of righteousness in the fulfillment of its duties.[2] But it is the clear sense of Scripture that there is no self-recovery of sinners; indeed, that there is no recovery of such except through a redemptive economy. Further, while this theory holds that each soul is born in an evil state in consequence of free, personal sinning in a previous existence, it is the clear sense of Scripture, as previously shown, that this state of evil is the consequence of the Adamic fall in the Edenic probation. Finally, in view of the Adamic connection of the race as set forth in the Scriptures, this theory is constrained to admit a deeper corruption of our nature in consequence of the Adamic fall.[3] But if, as alleged, such corruption is itself sin, then, with the deeper corruption, each without any agency of his own has the deeper sin, and therefore in violation of the fundamental principle of justice which the theory asserts. Thus it falls back into the deepest perplexity of the Augustinian anthropology, from which it has vainly attempted an escape in the mode of pre-temporal sinning.

[1] Muller: *Christian Doctrine of Sin*, vol. ii, p. 380.
[2] *Ibid.*, p. 382.   [3] *Ibid.*, pp. 386, 387.

CHAPTER IX.

REALISTIC MODE OF ADAMIC SIN

WITH a general agreement of Calvinists, that native depravity is a judicial infliction on the ground of a common participation in the sin of Adam, there are, as previously stated, two leading modes of accounting for that participation: the realistic, and the representative. Many authors have appropriated both modes, and seemingly without any notice of their open contrariety. In recent times some have clearly seen their opposition and reciprocal exclusiveness, and more rigidly adhered to the one or the other. We may instance Shedd and Hodge, leading representatives respectively of the two theories.[1] When these theories previously came into notice they were merely stated, and their proper review is still on hand. They are so cardinal in anthropology that such review cannot with any propriety be omitted. We begin with the realistic theory.

I. GENERIC ONENESS OF THE RACE.

1. *A Generic Human Nature.*—The theory, in this view of it, has received no more definite statement than at the hand of Dr. Shedd. After citations from Augustine, as containing his own view, he proceeds: "These passages, which might be multiplied indefinitely, are sufficient to indicate Augustine's theory of generic existence, generic transgression, and generic condemnation. The substance of this theory was afterward expressed in the scholastic dictum, ' natura corrumpit personam '—human *nature* apostatizes— and the consequences appear in human *individuals*. In the order of nature, man*kind* exists before the generations of mankind; the nature is prior to the individuals produced out of it."[2]

The doctrine is constructed upon the principle of the scholastic realism, according to which genera are objective realities, essential existences in distinction from the individuals which represent them. There are two forms of the doctrine respecting the relation of individuals to the generic nature. In the one view, individuals have no separate being in themselves,

PRINCIPLE OF REALISM.

---

[1] Shedd · *Dogmatic Theology*, vol. ii, pp. 15, 16, 38 ; Hodge : *Systematic Theology*, vol ii, p. 164.

[2] *History of Christian Doctrine*, vol. ii, pp. 77, 78.

but are mere modes and manifestations of the generic nature. It is thus one in principle with the pantheism which reduces all things to mere modes of the one being. In the other view each individual has the essence of existence in itself, but that essence was previously in the generic nature, and is derived from it in a process of individuation whereby individuals receive their separate existence. Thus in the instance of any species or genus the total being of all the generations existed in the prior generic nature. The first oak contained the essence of all its generations; the first pair of lions contained the essential being of all their progeny down to the present hour; the first man contained in himself the essence, material and spiritual, of all human generations. Thus the divine creations gave instant existence to genera and species, not in their serial forms, but in the sense of the whole nature out of CREATION OF GENERA. which all individuals are produced. It should be specially noted that the prior existence of individuals in the generic nature is without any individuality even in its most rudimentary form. The generic nature is in itself a single, simple essence. It follows that the production of individuals out of such a nature, with separate and essential existence in themselves, requires in each instance the abscission or outgoing of so much of its substance as will constitute the separate existence. In the case of man, with a dichotomic view of his natures, there must be the separation of so much of the generic essence in the production of each person as will constitute the material and spiritual essence of his being.

This is the doctrine maintained in the higher realism of the Augustinian anthropology. The other form which, as previously stated, reduces all individuals to mere modes of the one substance, and consequently allows them REALISM IN ANTHROPOLOGY only a phenomenal existence, could not be brought into harmony with this anthropology. Its deepest tenets require the deepest reality of individual existence in every human person. Each man as a responsible person must possess in himself the reality of individual existence. Each man's consciousness absolutely affirms such an existence. Therefore the theory of a mere phenomenal existence can have no proper place in Christian anthropology. It allows no distinctively spiritual nature in man. In assuming a merely modal or phenomenal existence of individual men, it must assume a purely unitary substance as the common ground of all human personalities. This is too senseless for any acceptance in rational thought. It is the other form of realism, according to which the generic nature divides itself and distributes a portion to every individual of the race, that is appropriated in the Augus-

tinian anthropology.[1] Thus each individual has his own essential
being, separate and distinct from every other. The theory is constrained to qualify the generic nature, especially on its physical
side. It could not be thought that the substance of all human
bodies in its phenomenal and bulk form existed in the body of
Adam. In this exigency the theory seizes upon the most restricted
sense of substance, dismisses all visible qualities of matter, and
holds as remaining only the invisible and metaphysical essence of
its being.

2. *The Generic Nature Rational and Voluntary.*—The generic
human nature, considered in its purely metaphysical sense, could not
commit the primitive sin. By a process of abstraction we may
separate the substance of matter from its properties, but all that
remains exists only in the abstraction of thought. There is no
such matter in reality. If there were, it could fulfill no function
of matter. This is possible only with its properties. So, for the
agent in the primitive sin we cannot stop with any abstract sense
POSSESSES   of mind. There must be the possession of personal
PERSONAL   faculties, as necessary to any moral action. Accord-
FACULTIES.   ingly, the generic human nature is promptly invested
with such faculties. "But this human nature, it must be carefully noticed, possesses all the attributes of the human individual;
for the individual is only a portion and specimen of the nature.
Considered as an essence, human nature is an intelligent, rational,
and voluntary essence; and accordingly its agency in Adam partakes of the corresponding qualities."[2]

3. *Adam the Generic Nature.*—This higher realism often proceeds in a manner to suggest the existence of the generic human
nature prior to Adam himself. In this view he must be accounted
simply as its first individualized specimen or part in the historic
development of the species. In accordance with this view there is
in the citation given just above a characterization of the agency of
this nature in Adam. The Scriptures, however, so connect the
moral state of the race with the sin of Adam that this realistic
theory cannot dispose of him simply as an individualized form of
the generic nature, with the only distinction from other individualized forms that he was the first. The only alternative is to account Adam the generic human nature, and the race as individualized portions of himself. This is the view taken· "Adam, as the
generic man, was not a mere receptacle containing millions of separate individuals. The genus is not an aggregation, but a single,

[1] Shedd : *Dogmatic Theology*, vol. ii, pp. 63–65, 72–74, 78–80.
[2] Shedd . *History of Christian Doctrine*, vol. ii, p. 78.

simple essence. *As such*, it is not yet characterized by individuality. It, however, *becomes* varied and manifold by being individualized *in its propagation, or development into a series.* . . . The individual, *as such*, is consequently only a subsequent *modus existendi,* the first and antecedent mode being the generic humanity, of which this subsequent serial mode is only another *aspect* or manifestation." [1] In a similar view, Baird holds that the creation of Adam was the creation of the human species. [2] Theoretically, this view most thoroughly identifies the race in a real oneness with Adam.

4. *The Agent in the Primitive Sin.*—The theory is obvious and easily stated at this point. The leading facts are the same, whether the race is located in Adam or in a generic nature back of him. There must in either case be the same endowment of personal qualities. The generic nature, possessing all the necessary faculties of personal agency, was capable of moral action, and in the use of such powers did most responsibly commit the primitive sin. It so committed this sin while yet containing in itself, or, rather, being in itself, the whole substance of the human race. This is the doctrine maintained.

5. *All Men a Part in the Sinning.*—A common participation in the primitive sin is maintained on the ground that all men existed / in Adam when he committed that sin. We have previously seen the mode of that existence, as maintained in this higher realism. It was not in a mere germinal or seminal mode, as embodied in a lower form of realism—a form to be separately considered. A merely germinal or seminal existence in Adam lacks the identity with his very being which is necessary to a responsible part in his sinning. The essential being of the whole race then existed in Adam, and without any individuality even in the most rudimentary sense. Our separate personal existence is by the abscission and individualization of so much of his very being as constitutes the essential existence of each one of the race. As so existing in Adam, we participated in the primitive sin. Indeed, it may as truly be said that we committed that sin as that Adam himself committed it. This is the theory.

This doctrine is maintained with much elaboration and asserted with frequent repetition. A few citations may suffice MAINTENANCE where many are possible. "Adam differed from all OF THE DOC- other human individuals by containing within his per- TRINE. son the entire human nature out of which the millions of generations were to be propagated, and of which they are individual-

[1] Shedd : *Theological Essays*, p. 252.   [2] *The Elohim Revealed*, p. 133.

ized portions. He was to transmit this human nature which was all in himself, exactly as it had been *created* in him; for propagation makes no radical changes, but simply transmits what is given in the nature, be it good or bad." [1] The consequences are then drawn upon the supposition of obedience or sin in Adam. In the former case the result would have been the perfect holiness of every individual of the race. In the actual case of sin there necessarily follows the sinfulness of every man as an individualized portion of the generic nature which sinned in Adam. " The individuals produced out of it must be characterized by a sinful state and condition."

"The aim of the Westminster symbol accordingly, and, it may CLEAR STATE- be added, of all the creeds on the Augustinian side of MENT. the controversy, was to combine two elements, each having truth in it—to teach the fall of the human race as a unity, and, at the same time, recognize the existence, freedom, and guilt of the individual in the fall. Accordingly, they locate the individual in Adam, and make him, in some mysterious but real manner, a responsible partaker in Adam's sin—a guilty sharer, and, in some solid sense of the word, *co-agent* in a common apostasy." [2] Whether the more prevalent Calvinistic view accords with this passage is a question in which Calvinists themselves are far more concerned than others. It forcibly expresses the realistic ground of a common participation in the sin of Adam. " The *total* guilt of the first sin, thus committed by the entire race in Adam, is imputed to each individual of the race, because of the *indivisibility* of guilt. . . . For though the one common nature that committed the 'one offense' is divisible by propagation, the offense itself is not divisible, nor is the guilt of it. Consequently, one man is as guilty as another of the whole first sin—of the original act of falling from God. The individual Adam and Eve were no more guilty of this first act, and of the whole of it, than their descendants are; and their descendants are as guilty as they." [3] We have sufficiently stated the realistic ground of a common participation in the sin of Adam. We have seen in the last citation the measure of the common guilt. Each individual of the race is held to be as guilty as Adam himself. This is one of the leading modes in which the Augustinian anthropology maintains the consistency of a common native sinfulness with the divine justice and goodness.

[1] Shedd: *History of Christian Doctrine*, vol. ii, p. 118.
[2] Shedd: *Theological Essays*, pp. 252, 253.
[3] Shedd: *Dogmatic Theology*, vol. ii, pp. 185, 186.

II. Objections to the Theory.

1. *Groundless Assumption of a Generic Nature.*—Realism itself is a mere assumption, and, as a philosophy, has long been replaced with conceptualism. General terms express general notions or conceptions, but not objective realities. There is no vegetable nature apart from its individual forms of existence, no animal nature apart from individuals. There is no existent human nature apart from individual men. In the organic realm all actual existence is in individual forms. Nominalism is right in such limitation of actual existence, though wrong in the denial of general notions as realities of mental conception. Realism is right in the admission of general notions, but wrong in the assertion of objective existences in accord with these notions. There are no such existences. Hence, there is no generic human nature.

Realism, however, exists in different forms, and is variously appropriated in doctrinal anthropology.[1] This being the DIFFERENCES case, fairness requires that in any criticism respect IN REALISM. should be had to the particular form in which it is maintained. In the present instance the form has been definitely given. The creation of Adam was the creation of the whole human species, not in its individualities, but in its substantive existence. Adam contained in himself this whole substance. In the mode of propagation it is distributed in a manner to constitute the essential existence of each individual. The theory applies to both the physical and mental natures of man. The two are spoken of as a complex, but certainly not with the intention of sinking their distinction or reducing them to unity. Their distinction is fully recognized.

Did the substance of all human bodies exist in that of Adam? Certainly not in the form and bulk of flesh and blood. BODILY SUB-This is not maintained. In place of such a nature STANCE there is posited a form of matter without bodily properties, unphenomenal and metaphysical in its mode. The existence of such a form of matter in Adam is a mere assumption. It certainly does not appear in the account of his creation.[2] His body was formed from the dust of the ground; and there is no suggestion of any other form of matter than science now recognizes in the constitution of the human body. In such a oneness of all human bodies with that of Adam, a portion of his body must exist in every one as its proper substance. Otherwise there is no realistic oneness with him. Any element of the body not originally of the substance of Adam is utterly useless in such a realism. In no reference of

[1] Ueberweg: *History of Philosophy*, vol. i, pp. 358–402. [2] Gen. ii, 7.

Scripture to the constitution of the human body is there any intimation of such a specific substance. Neither physics, nor chemistry, nor physiology knows any thing of it. Its existence in Adam and its individualizations into innumerable parts, so as to constitute the substantive reality of all human bodies, are pure assumptions.

The theory of a generic spiritual nature created in Adam, which MENTAL SUB- served as a personal mind in himself, and by successive STANCE. abscissions furnishes the essence of every personal mind, is equally groundless. No direct proof is offered. Little indirect proof is even attempted. It may attempt a defense of itself by charging other theories of the origin of individual souls with equal mystery and perplexity: as, for instance, the theory of their creation in Adam and propagation from him; or, that of their immediate and successive creations along with the propagations of the race. If all that is thus alleged is true, not an atom of proof is thus gained for this form of realism. After all that may be said either in its support or defense, it must remain a groundless speculation.

2. *Impossible Individuation into the Many.*—Such realism in theological anthropology requires the generic human nature to be invested with personal faculties. It must have originally existed in personality, for else it could not have committed the primitive sin. We have previously seen the full recognition of these facts, and the prompt and unreserved investment of the generic nature PERSONALITY with personal faculties. Its individuation into the INDIVISIBLE. many, into the innumerable personalities of the race, is thus rendered impossible. As personally endowed and capable of free and responsible moral agency, the generic nature, on its mental side, must have existed in simple unity of spiritual essence and personality. Neither is divisible or distributable into the many. It will hardly be pretended that personality can be so treated, though it is claimed that the spiritual essence may be. How can the essence be divided without dividing or destroying the personality? Personality arises with the complex of personal faculties. The faculties are intrinsic to the spiritual essence. All distinction of essence and faculty is purely in thought. No loose connection can be allowed, which might meet the exigency of this form of realism. The whole mental essence is present in every mental faculty and active in every mental action. How then can the essence be divided without dividing or destroying the personality? This very serious difficulty presses the theory not only in respect to generic Adam, but equally in every instance of subdivision of essence in all the individual propagations of the race.

There is no escape from such difficulty through an assumption

that only a small portion of the generic spiritual essence, just enough for the constitution of a single person, belonged   MIND INDI-
to the personality of Adam and was active in his agency.   VISIBLE.
Such an assumption would be openly contradictory to the deepest principles of the theory. It maintains the universal native sinful-ness, in the double sense of corruption and guilt, on the ground that the whole generic spiritual essence was present and active in the sinning of Adam. Hence, as all human souls are individual-ized portions of that generic soul, they had a responsible part in the Adamic sin, are actually guilty of that sin, and justly punish-able on that ground. These are the vital facts of the theory; and with no one of these can it part without self-destruction. It re-mains true that the generic spiritual essence in Adam, as held in this theory, existed and acted in the purest form of personality. Hence the theory cannot void the insuperable difficulties which be-set the notion of its division and distribution into the innumer-able personalities of the race. A statue in metal might be fused and recast into many, but only with the destruction of the original and a diminution of size according to the number of the new; but a spiritual essence existing in the mode of personality cannot be the subject of such treatment.[1]

3. *Equally Sharers in all Ancestral Deeds.*—We put this objection in the broadest application, and maintain that, if on the ground of a real oneness with Adam we are responsible sharers in the primi-tive sin, we must equally share all the sins, and all the good deeds as well, of all our intermediate ancestors.

A like objection, but of narrow application, is put thus: If on the ground of a real oneness with Adam and Eve we   A NARROWER
are responsible sharers in their first sin, so must we   VIEW.
share all their subsequent sins. The objection is logically perti-nent only with respect to such sins as were committed before the division of the generic nature through propagation and the forma-tion of separate parental headships. After such disconnection there could be no responsible sharing in their sins. The objection, however, is thoroughly valid respecting sins previously committed. A refutation of the objection so brought is attempted in this man-ner: "The reply is that the sinful acts of Adam and Eve after the fall differed from the act of eating the forbidden fruit in two respects: 1. They were transgressions of the moral law, not of the probationary statute. 2. They were not committed by the entire race in and with Adam."[2]

[1] Per contra, Shedd : *Dogmatic Theology,* vol. ii, pp. 83–87.
[2] *Ibid.,* p. 88.

The answer in the second point is utterly void within the limita-
THE ANSWER   tion of the objection as above stated.   On the truth of
VOID.   the theory, the whole race must have existed in Adam
and shared in all his acts, prior to the division of the generic nature by propagation, just as completely as in the primitive sin. The
answer in the first point is equally void. There is no difference
between a moral law and a probationary statute, or between the
transgression of the one and the other, which can in the least affect
the ground of a common responsibility, as it is maintained in this
theory.   It is not that the Edenic law was positive in kind and
probationary in economy, that all men are held to be responsible
sharers with Adam in its transgression, but because all then existed in the very essence of his being, and therefore must share in
his sin.   Hence, as the same form of existence in Adam continued
until a division of the generic nature through propagation, all men
must have shared in every previous sin of Adam just as deeply as
in his first sin.   The theory of representation might insist upon
the probationary office of the Edenic law as affecting the question
of our responsibility for any other sins of Adam; but for the realistic theory, such insistence is the surrender of its deepest principle.   A further reply utterly fails.   To the objection that as the
whole human nature remained in Adam and Eve until a division in
the propagation of Cain, therefore all their previous sins as really as
the first must be charged to their posterity, " the reply is that the
imputation, even in this case, would not lie upon any *individual
persons* of the posterity, for there are none, but only upon the
non-individualized nature. These personal transgressions of Adam,
if charged at all, could be charged only upon the species." [1]   True:
there were no individual persons of the posterity in that interval
of time; and no more were there any at the time of the first sin;
and in both cases the relation between Adam and his posterity was
precisely the same; and the first sin, just as the later sins, must be
charged to the generic nature, because as yet no individualized
persons existed.

We have put the same objection more broadly: that, on the truth
THE BROADER   of this realistic theory and the reality of a responsible
OBJECTION   part of each in the primitive sin, we are all responsible
sharers in all the deeds of our ancestors in the long line of descent
from Adam.   This position is maintained on the ground that, according to this realistic theory, we existed in each ancestor in this long
line of descent in precisely the same manner in which we existed
in Adam.   If that manner of existence made us sharers in his sin,

---

[1] Shedd : *Dogmatic Theology*, vol. ii, p. 90.

it must equally make us sharers in the sins, and in the good deeds as well, of all our ancestors. In the division of the generic nature through propagation, in each instance there was communicated, not only enough for the new personality, but enough more for an indefinite number of further individualizations into personalities. This law must rule the whole process of propagation. The theory requires it, and without it would become a nullity. "The specific nature was a deposited invisible substance in the first human pair. . . . As thus deposited by creation in Adam and Eve, it was to be transmitted. In like manner, every individual man along with his individuality receives, not, as Adam did, the *whole* of human nature, but a fraction of it, to transmit and individualize." [1] Thus in the long line of human parentage each one receives from Adam, through his own ancestry, a non-individualized portion of the generic human nature, which he transmits through propagation. Every one possesses the portion transmitted to him in the same manner in which Adam possessed the whole. This is the theory. If it is true, it follows that every man is a sharer in all the moral deeds of his ancestry in the long line of descent from Adam.

No answer voids this consequence. The attempts signally fail. "All individuals excepting the first two include each   FUTILE AN-
but a fractional part of human nature. A sin com-   SWER
mitted by a fraction is not a sin committed by the whole unity. Individual transgression is not the original transgression, or Adam's first sin." [2] In truth, the original unity of the generic nature was severed in the creation of Eve, so that no one sin, not even the first, was committed by that whole nature. Hence this theory must admit that the presence of the whole generic nature in any one sin is not necessary to a responsible sharing therein on the part of the sinner's offspring. Therefore this answer to our objection, which proceeds upon the assumption of a determining distinction between the whole generic nature and only a part of it as it respects the consequence of sin to the offspring of the sinner, is utterly groundless. Further answer must be attempted. That portion of the generic nature which each person receives with his own propagation, "and which he transmits, does not act with him and sin with him in his individual transgressions. It is a latent nature or principle which remains in a quiescent state, in reference to his individuality. It is inactive, as existing in him." [3] All this is easily said; but what is the warrant for saying it? No reason is given for the alleged inactivity of that portion of the generic nature which each one receives for further individualization and trans-

[1] Shedd: *Dogmatic Theology*, vol. ii, p. 90.   [2] *Ibid.*, p. 91.   [3] *Ibid.*, p. 92.

mission. We have previously seen that just as the whole was originally deposited in Adam, so a part is deposited in each individual;
and, also, that the individual possesses the part in the same manner and for the same purpose of transmission that Adam possessed
the whole. As the whole existed in Adam in a simple unity of
spiritual essence, so the portion exists in each individual in the
same unity. If the whole was active in the agency of Adam so as
to constitute all men sharers in his sin, the whole part must be
active in the agency of the individual and constitute his progeny,
even to the latest generation, sharers in his moral deeds.

The results are singular and startling; in some facts, appalling.
SINGULAR   All the descendants of Abraham in the line of Isaac
RESULTS.   shared in the faith which was accounted to him for
righteousness;[1] and were as really as Isaac offered up by faith.[2]
Solomon shared in his own father's adultery, and equally in his profound repentance. These instances are given simply as illustrations of the principle. The principle rules every individual life.
What any one is through his own deeds in the present life is as
nothing compared with what he is through a responsible participation in the deeds of his ancestors. The number of such deeds
is beyond conception. And what a mixture of the good and the
bad, the noble and the vile! deeds of every quality, and running
through every grade of every quality! And how often must every
one have been lost in sharing the sins of some ancestors, and
saved in sharing the repentance and faith of others! As this theory
is usually maintained, the appalling implication is that every one
begins the present life with the accumulation upon his soul of all
the sins of all his ancestors in the long line of his descent from
Adam. There must be error in such a theory.

4. *No Responsible Part in the Primitive Sin.*—The ground on
which this theory maintains a responsible sharing of all men in the
primitive sin should be restated in connection with the present
point. "The first sin of Adam, being a *common*, not an individual sin, is deservedly and justly imputed to the posterity of Adam
upon the same principles upon which all sin is deservedly and
justly imputed; namely, that it was committed by those to whom
it is imputed."[3] The statement proceeds with the assumption of
free agency, "the free agency of all mankind in Adam," as the
ground of their responsible sharing in his sin. "This agency,
though differing in the manner, is yet as real as the subsequent
free agency of each individual." The whole generic human nature

---

[1] Rom. iv, 3; Gal. iii, 6.   [2] Heb. xi, 17.
[3] Shedd: *Dogmatic Theology*, vol. ii, p. 186.

existed in Adam, and was present and active in the commission of his sin.

This generic nature, simply as such, could not sin. Adam could sin only in his own personal agency, and the whole guilt of his sin was his own personal guilt. If it should be said that he was so much the greater in himself, and his guilt so much the greater, because of the presence of the whole generic nature in him, and if all this were true, it could not change the facts as above stated. It is still true, that a nature, simply in itself or without personalization, can exercise no personal agency; still true that the whole agency in the primitive sin was the personal agency of Adam himself, and the whole guilt his own. Hence, when it is said, as it often is, and as the theory requires, that the whole generic nature was present and active in Adam, the meaning must be, if there is any meaning to the purpose, that that whole nature was personalized in him—just as any individualized portion which constitutes the spiritual essence of an individual man must be personalized in him. The theory must accept this view, or else surrender all ground of pretension even, that the whole generic nature was responsibly active in the sinning of Adam. The result gives us a wonderful Adam; an Adam who possessed in his own personality all the spiritual essence out of which, by a ceaseless process of abscission, are produced all individual minds of the race, even to the last man. He should have been far greater than he was; greater even than the infinitely exaggerated Adam of an earlier theology. He appears in no such greatness.

A very serious difficulty again emerges. The theory must answer for the individualization of this Adam into the innumerable personalities of the race. He exists and acts in a simple unity of personality, just as any other individual man. The presence of the whole generic nature in him does not change this fact. To say that it does is to sunder that nature from his personality, and consequently to deny it all and any part in the Adamic sin. The most fundamental principle of the theory would thus be surrendered. The theory must answer for the requisite individualizations of such an Adam. The task is an impossible one. The division and distribution of a spiritual essence, considered simply as an essence, into the innumerable personalities of the race transcends the utmost reach of human philosophy. The notion of such a division and distribution of such an essence, already existing in personality and active in personal agency, is utterly aberrant from all rational thinking upon such a question.

The existence of the generic nature in Adam is held for the sake

of its distribution into all human persons, that they may be accounted responsible sharers in his sin.   The difficulties
of the distribution disprove it, and consequently disprove
the whole theory.   This is not the whole case against the theory.
Neither the existence of the generic nature in Adam, nor its division and personalization in all men, nor both together could make
them guilty sharers in his sin.   The reason is that on neither supposition, nor on both together, was there in them the personal
agency necessary to such participation.   Nor do we here attempt
to force upon the theory any principle not its own.   It affirms the
participation of all men in the guilt of Adam's sin, on the ground
that all participated in its commission, and by the exercise of a
personal agency just as real and free as any which they possess and
exercise in their individual existence.   In previous citations we
have given repeated declarations of this principle.   One appears
under the present head.   It is thus admitted that free personal
agency is necessary to the commission of sin, and that all men can
share the guilt of the first sin only on the ground of sharing its
commission.   This is an accepted principle of this higher realism.
There was no such participation of all men in the primitive sin.
The alleged ground of it is utterly inadequate.   The determining
facts of the question clearly show this.

"For the individuals Adam and Eve were self-conscious.   So
far as they were concerned, the first sin was a very de-
liberate and intensely willful act.   The human species
existing in them at that time *acted* in their act, and *sinned* in their
sin, similarly as the hand or eye acts and sins in the murderous
or lustful act of the individual soul.   The hand or the eye has no
separate self-consciousness of its own, parallel with the soul's self-
consciousness.   Taken by itself, it has no consciousness at all.
But its *union* and *oneness* with the self-conscious soul, in the personal
union of soul and body, affords all the self-consciousness that is possible in the case.   The hand is co-agent with the soul, and hence is
particeps criminis, and has a common guilt with the soul.   In like
manner the psychico-physical human nature existing in Adam
and Eve had no separate self-consciousness parallel with that of
Adam and Eve.   Unlike the visible hand or eye, it was an invisible
substance or nature capable of being transformed into myriads of
self-conscious individuals; but while in Adam, and not yet distributed and individualized, it had no distinct self-consciousness of its
own, any more than the hand or eye in the supposed case.   But
existing and *acting* in and with these self-conscious individuals, it
participated in their self-determination, and is chargeable with

NO GROUND OF THE GUILT

A FRUITLESS REPLY

their sin, as the hand, and eye, and whole body is chargeable with the sin of the individual man. As in the instance of the individual unity, every thing that constitutes it, body as well as soul, is active and responsible for all that is done by this unity, so in the instance of the specific unity, every thing that constitutes it, namely, Adam and the human nature in him, is active and responsible for all that is done by this unity." [1] We have given this passage at such length that the determining facts of the question might stand in the clearest light.

The illustrations of the realistic position are first in place for criticism. Neither the hand nor the eye is a guilty sharer in any sin because a bodily member of the person sinning. Neither is capable of guilt or of any moral act. The hand, for instance: what part has it in the murderous deed supposed? The murder is wholly the deed of the personal agent, and his hand is as purely instrumental to his agency as the knife with which he makes the deadly thrust. Let the hand be amputated and cast away: could it still be guilty? As well count the dagger guilty. Yet, on the principles and requirements of this theory, it ought still to be guilty. The fallacy begins with the assumption of a union and oneness of the hand with the self-conscious soul. There is no such union and oneness of the two. Nor can the hand be a co-agent with the soul, and for the reason that it is capable of no such agency. Nor can it be a *particeps criminis* in any sin of the soul. A *particeps criminis* is an actual sinner, and must have in himself the power of sinning. The same facts must be true of the hand if in any instance it is a *particeps criminis*. They cannot be true of the hand. The illustration betrays the weakness of the realistic position.

VAIN ILLUSTRATIONS

We may readily agree that, if the generic nature—that out of which all individual souls are produced—existed in Adam and Eve at the time of the first sin, it "is chargeable with their sin, as the hand, and eye, and whole body is chargeable with the sin of the individual man," for that is not to be chargeable at all. Whatever the theory may assert respecting the presence of the generic nature with the personal Adam, it must ever distinguish the two and hold the separability of the latter from the former. As so separated, it is simply a nature, without personality until distributed and personalized in individual men. It is a fundamental part of this theory that every man, even from the first moment of his individual existence, is sinful. But the individualization of the generic nature into new per-

DISTINCTION OF NATURE AND PERSON

[1] Shedd *Dogmatic Theology*, vol. ii, pp. 191, 192.

tonalities does not change its character. This is explicitly affirmed. Hence, if guilty as soon as individualized, the nature itself, and simply as such, must have been constituted guilty by the sin of Adam. But guilt is a purely personal fact, and has no ground in a mere nature. The guilt of Adam's sin was purely personal to himself, and could no more become the guilt of a generic nature in him than the hand of a murderer could share the guilt of his crime. The theory is that the sin of Adam constituted the whole generic nature guilty, and, further, that, on the division of this nature into the innumerable individuals of the race, every one is as guilty of that sin as Adam himself. Such facts utterly disprove the theory.

III. A Lower Form of Realism.

There is a lower form of realism on which a common participation in the sin of Adam is maintained. While differing in some respects from the higher realism, it is yet so similar in its leading principles and facts that a much briefer discussion will suffice.

1. *Definitive Statement of the Theory.*—It is grounded on the principle of a germinal or seminal existence of the race in Adam. Whether such form of existence included both body and soul is often left without any definite statement. This is specially the case respecting the latter. It may safely be said that the body is always included, but whether the soul is included is often left an open question. In the distinction of theories this theory is popularly called traducian; but it cannot be so called in precisely the same sense as the higher realism. The reason is that it holds a very different mode of existence in Adam. In the higher realism this existence, as we have previously shown, is in the mode of a unitary generic nature, without any individualization even in the most germinal or rudimentary form; so that the propagation of the race is by a ceaseless abscission of portions of that nature. In the lower, the existence of the race in Adam is with such individualizations as always characterize seminal or germinal entities, and the propagation is through their communication and development. Some hold the immediate creation of the soul on occasion of the propagation of the body. In such case the theory is traducian only with respect to the body, and creational with respect to the soul.

The notion of a germinal existence of the race in Adam as the A FAMILIAR ground of a common participation in his sin very often VIEW. appears in the literature of the Augustinian anthropology. The conception finds its most frequent illustration in the relation subsisting between the root and the branches of a tree, and between the head and members of the body. One instance may suffice. "We say that Adam, being the root and head of all human kind, and we all branches from that root, all parts of that body whereof he was the head, *his will may be said to be ours. We were then all that one man*—we were all in him, and had no other will but his; so that though that be extrinsic unto us, considered as particular persons, yet it is intrinsical, as we are all parts of one common nature. As in him we sinned, so in him we had a will of sinning." [1] This citation is, at once, a clear statement of the theory and a justification of our own statement.

2. *Doctrinal Aim of the Theory.*—The aim is the same as in the higher form of realism; namely, so to identify the offspring of Adam in a real oneness with himself in the primitive transgression that they may be justly chargeable with a guilty participation in that sin. This is so clearly the case that no further explication is required.

3. *The Theory Inadequate to the Aim.*—The offspring of Adam cannot in this mode be identified with him in a responsible oneness. A careful inspection of the illustrations readily discovers the inadequacy of the ground for any such identification.

Here is, first, the relation of all men to Adam in the primitive sin as illustrated by the relation of the body and its members to the head. In this illustration the head HEAD AND BODY. represents the personality. The members of the body are subject to the head, but only as instruments of its agency. If the head sins, no member shares the sinning. No one either chooses the evil or executes the choice. The attempt to distribute the responsibility to the members of the body severally, after locating it entirely in the head, is a fruitless endeavor. The primitive sin was an act of free personal agency, and could not else have been a sin. That agency was wholly in Adam. We had no such existence in him as made us sharers in his personal act or in the guilt of his sin. Indeed, we had less identity with him than exists between the members of the body and the head. In this case there is an organic union and a resulting bodily unity. There is no answering identity of mankind with Adam through the mode of their primordial existence in him. Even their bodies were not organically one with his body, just as the acorns which an oak bears were not organically one with itself. Much less could we have been so one with him in personality as to share in his personal agency and in the guilt of his sin.

Equally useless is the figure of the tree for the purpose of show-

[1] Owen : Works (Goold's), vol. x, p. 73.

ing a responsible oneness of the race with Adam in the primitive

ROOT AND TREE

sin. The root is representatively the personal agent. The branches which exist germinally in the root, and because of such an existence, must be so identified with it as to be responsible sharers in its sinful agency. In like manner all men, as branches from the Adamic root, must be so identified with the personal Adam as to be responsible sharers in the primitive sin. No ground is disclosed for such participation. The branches might suffer from the sin of the root, but could not share its sin and guilt. The first sin was from the personal agency of Adam. That agency was his own, and could not be shared by all men through the mode of a mere germinal existence in him. Distinct personal agency conditions sinful action. Indeed, this is conceded in all attempts to identify the race in a real and responsible oneness with Adam. In this all attempts fail. This lower realism signally fails. The assumed germinal entities, if really existent in Adam and subsequently developed into the personalities of the race, had no personal existence in him. Therefore they could not share either the act or the guilt of his sin.

The passage above cited from Owen is constructed as an argu-

FURTHER CRITICISMS.

ment for the theory which is maintained; but close inspection discovers in it serious logical deficiencies, the pointing out of which will further show the groundlessness of the theory. The argument starts with the assumption of a rudimentary existence of all men in Adam, and respecting the soul as well as the body. Whether the soul so existed in Adam is still an open question with theologians. Augustine himself was always in serious doubt of it. Calvin rejected it, and the Reformed theologians mostly agreed with him. It has no place in any church creed.[1]

[1] There are three theories respecting the origin of the soul :

1. The theory of pre-existence. This theory holds the existence of souls in a conscious and responsible mode anterior to their birth into the present life. It has no necessary distinction from other theories respecting the origin of the soul in a divine creation, but differs from them in placing the creation anterior to the present life. This is all that is peculiar to the theory respecting the origin of the soul.

2. Creationism. This theory holds the creation of souls along with the process of propagation. The body is propagated, but the soul is an immediate creation, either at the inception of the body or during its growth.

3. Traducianism. This theory holds the creation of all souls in Adam, and, consequently, the propagation of the soul with the body.

Theologians divide on these theories—mainly on the last two. Nor is there any unanimity of view in any great school of theology. Some Augustinians are creationists; others, traducianists. The same is true of Arminians.

When so doubtful a principle takes the vital place of a logical premise the whole argument must be weak. On the ground of such an assumed existence in Adam the argument proceeds: "*his will may be said to be ours.*" May be said! Many things may be said without proper warrant for the saying. With a doubtful premise and a merely hypothetic inference as the best support that can be given to the theory, its weakness is manifest. There is no ground for even this hypothetic inference. Such an actual existence in Adam could in no sense and requirement of the theory make his will our own. We had no part in his sin which this hypothetic possession of his will is intended to express. Hence the theory, as set forth in this argumentative statement, utterly fails to furnish any adequate ground for a common participation in the sin of Adam. No stronger statement can be made with any logical warrant.

IV. Objections to the Lower Realism.

In addition to the objections presented in the discussion of this theory, a few special objections should be stated.

1. *Implication of Seminal Guilt.*—The theory clearly has this implication. The common guilt is charged to the account of a seminal existence in Adam when he committed the first sin, and solely on that ground. The development of the seminal entities then in him into a personal mode of existence is in no sense the ground or condition of the guilt. This is the theory. It follows that we must have been guilty in our seminal state. The mode of existence on which the guilt is grounded was then complete. If not guilty then, we could not be guilty now. The result utterly discredits the theory. There is no subject of guilt below personality; and the notion that all human souls, existing in Adam in a mere rudimentary mode, could in that state be guilty of his sin, and the subject of the divine wrath, is too preposterous for the utmost credulity.

2. *Guilty of All Ancestral Sins.*—This objection is the same in principle as one urged against the higher realism. It is as thoroughly valid in this case as in that, and equally weighs against the lower realism. In the inevitable logic of facts the theory has this consequence. It cannot be voided by declaring Adam a public person, while the relation of every subsequent father is merely individual. Such a declaration replaces the realistic ground of guilt with the representative—an entirely different ground, as we have previously pointed out. The surrender of a theory is a very poor way of defending it. Nor is there any escape through such a progenitorship of Adam that all souls existed in him, while only a

part existed in any later parentage. It is not the totality of existence in Adam that is the ground of the alleged guilt, but the fact and mode of that existence. The mode is precisely the same in all subsequent parentages as in Adam himself. Benjamin existed in Jacob, and Jacob in Isaac in the very mode in which each existed in Adam. If the principle is valid in the one case, so is it in all others. If guilty of Adam's sin because then seminally in him, we must be guilty of all the sins of our ancestors committed while seminally in them. Augustine saw this consequence, and admitted its probable reality, though with hesitation.[1] Well might he hesitate to accept the result of such an accumulation of sin upon every human soul. The theory which inevitably involves such a consequence must be false.

3. *Repentance and Forgiveness of the Race in Adam.*—If Adam repented, as generally agreed, he was graciously forgiven. Then, if so really one with him as to be sharers in his sin, on the same ground we should equally share his repentance. If we still existed in him in the same manner as when he sinned, no reason can be given why we should not just as fully share his repentance as his sin. It follows that, on such a repentance, our own in the same moral sense in which it was his, we should have been graciously forgiven with him. Why then should native depravity be inflicted as a punishment on the ground of a common participation in the guilt of Adam's sin, when the whole ground of its infliction was removed before the propagation of the race? No reason can be given for such infliction; which, however, the theory fully holds. Indeed, all the reason of the case is against it. It is plain, in the view of such facts, that the implications of the theory cannot be adjusted to its principles. Hence these implications witness against its truth.

The theory of a realistic oneness of the race with Adam in no form of it offers sufficient ground for a common participation in his sin, or for the judicial infliction of native depravity upon the race.

[1] Wiggers. *Augustinism and Pelagianism*, pp. 284, 285.

CHAPTER X.

REPRESENTATIVE MODE OF ADAMIC GUILT

THIS is the second leading mode in which a common participation in the sin of Adam is maintained as the ground of a judicial infliction of depravity upon the race. It is so cardinal in itself, and so different from the realistic theory, as to require separate treatment. It may be observed that in the present formula we place the word guilt where in the previous one we placed the word sin. There is in the difference of the two theories a reason for this change. In the realistic theory all men are held to have participated in the commission of the primitive sin, so that it is their own as really as it was Adam's; while in the representative there was no actual participation in that sin, but only a sharing in its guilt. This distinction will more fully appear in the discussion of the present question.

I. LEGAL ONENESS OF THE RACE.

1. *Federal Headship of Adam* —The theory is that God instituted a covenant with Adam whereby he was constituted federal head and representative of the race in the primitive probation. This federal headship constituted a moral or legal oneness of the race with Adam; so that the legal consequence of his conduct under the law of probation, and whether good or bad, might justly be reckoned to them. His obedience should thus be accounted to them as their obedience, or his transgression as their transgression. In this sense the probation and fall of Adam were the probation and fall of the race. Hence the guilt of his sin could be justly accounted to them.[1]

2. *Immediate Imputation of His Sin.*—After the representative headship of Adam, there is still the question of the manner in which all men share his sin. It is not theirs intrinsically or immediately, as from an actual sharing in the sin, but becomes theirs by a judicial act of divine imputation. This imputation, however, carries over to them neither the act nor the demerit of Adam's sin,

[1] Witsius: *The Covenants*, vol. 1, chap. ii; Wallace: *Representative Responsibility*, discourse 1; Cunningham: *Theology of the Reformation*, essay vii, sec. ii; Hodge: *Systematic Theology*, vol. ii, pp. 121, 197.

but only its guilt as an amenability to punishment. It is proper to justify this statement from Calvinistic authorities. In this manner the doctrine will receive fuller explication.

In the earlier Calvinian anthropology, largely realistic and often

SENSE OF IM-
MEDIATE IM-
PUTATION

jumbling the two modes of Adamic guilt, the immediate imputation of the first sin to the human race was greatly lacking in clearness of treatment. In later times, and with a more thorough distinction of the two modes of guilt, this imputation has received very exact statement at the hand of masters in the representative school. "Adam was constituted by God the representative and federal head of his posterity, so that his trial or probation was virtually and in God's estimation . . . the trial or probation of the human race; and that thus the transgression of Adam became, in a legal and judicial sense, and without any injustice to them, *theirs*, so that they were justly involved in its proper consequences."[1] "In virtue of the union, federal and natural, between Adam and his posterity, his sin, although not their act, is so imputed to them that it is the judicial ground of the penalty threatened against him coming also upon them. This is the doctrine of immediate imputation." "And when it is said that the sin of Adam is imputed to his posterity, it is not meant that they committed his sin, or were the agents of his act, nor is it meant that they are morally criminal for his transgression; but simply that in virtue of the union between him and his descendants his sin is the judicial ground of the condemnation of his race."[2] When Dr. Hodge speaks of the federal and natural union of Adam and his posterity, respecting the natural he must be understood to express the historic view of the question rather than his own personal view. As a rigid representationist, he could not think the natural relation any part of the ground on which the guilt of Adam's sin is imputed to the race. Something might be said for the congruity of appointing the natural head of the race its legal head, but there could be nothing more than such congruity. In this representative theory the federal headship is the sole ground of a responsible oneness of the race with Adam. The economy is purely a legal one; and the sharing in the sin of Adam is according to its legal character. In the above citations we have seen what that sharing is, and in what mode it becomes actual. By a judicial act of immediate imputation God accounts the guilt of Adam's sin to his posterity on the ground of their legal oneness with him.

[1] Cunningham : *Historical Theology*, vol. i, pp. 337, 338.
[2] Hodge : *Systematic Theology*, vol. ii, pp. 192, 193.

3. *No Demerit from the Imputation.*—The theory has this consequence, that no turpitude or demerit of sin is by such imputation carried over to the offspring of Adam. It is not pretended, not admitted even, that any thing more than the guilt of the first sin is imputed to them. The theory sharply discriminates the demerit of sin and the guilt of sin. The first is personal to the actual sinner, and is intrinsic to his own character; the second is simply amenability to punishment, and arises from the judicial treatment of sin. In the above citations it is denied DEMERIT DENIED that we have any part in the criminality of Adam's sin. Such a view belongs to the realistic theory, from which this theory so widely and radically dissents. It is on the ground of this distinction between the personal demerit and the guilt of sin that Dr. Hodge maintains the possibility of such an imputation of sin to Christ as his doctrine of atonement requires. The transference of demerit by imputation is denied and declared impossible. " Moral character cannot be transferred." The same principle is expressed in different places.[1] And the same principle is declared to rule the imputation of Adam's sin to the race. This may be seen in connection with a passage above cited Hence, when we say that there is no demerit of the race from the immediate imputation of Adam's sin, we are thoroughly sustained by a fundamental principle of the representative theory, and also by its very best exposition. In another place we shall have use for the fact thus established.

II. ALLEGED PROOFS OF THE THEORY.

The representative theory, just as every other, is dependent upon its proofs. Hence their importance rises with its prominence in the Augustinian anthropology. Naturally, therefore, all facts and principles which promise any support are called into service and presented with the utmost exegetical and logical skill. We readily concede a strong plausibility to some of the arguments. Some have so much apparent strength that the answer is not always easy. We shall not attempt so elaborate a review as these statements might suggest or seem to require, and yet shall proceed with the confidence of showing that the arguments are inconclusive.

1. *Responsibility on the Ground of Representation.*—This argument requires both the federal headship of Adam and the sufficiency of such representation for the common participation in the guilt of his sin. For the present, we proceed without questioning

[1] *Systematic Theology,* vol. ii, pp. 189, 582.

the federal headship as maintained in this theory, and first consider the principle of representation, with the argument constructed upon it.

The argument proceeds on the principle of responsibility from
ILLUSTRATIONS. representation, and brings illustrations and proofs from various relations of human life. The minister binds the State; the agent, the principal; the child, the parent; the parent, the child. In purely voluntary or conventional associations it is admitted that representation does not impose a common moral responsibility. It is otherwise in such relations as arise in the providential ordering and requirements of human life. Such are the relations above specified. They are inseparable from our present mode of existence, and must be in the order of providence. The principle of responsibility rules in all such instances of representation, and therefore rules in the instance of Adam.[1]

The argument will not sustain the representative place of Adam
NO GROUND OF GUILT as maintained in this theory. On the ground of his federal headship it is maintained that the guilt of his sin is justly imputed to his offspring, and constitutes in them the ground of divine punishment. The instances of representation adduced fall far short of any analogy for the support of any such view. Neither guilt nor penalty is involved. If in the intercourse of nations a minister is invested with plenipotential functions, the State which he represents is bound by his action, and equally when it is unwise and wrong as when it is wise and right; but this obligation involves neither guilt nor punishment. The same is true in all the other instances. The principal is responsible for the action of his agent, so far as empowered to act for him, but can neither be accounted guilty nor suffer punishment for any wrong-doing of the agent. By provisions of law a father may be held responsible for such action of his child as may involve the pecuniary interests of others, but unless in some way a sharer in the wrong-doing his responsibility is not in the nature of either guilt or punishment. In all such instances as we have considered the responsibility is merely political or pecuniary. The law which imposes it is purely one of economical expediency. Interests are thus protected which otherwise might be greatly wronged. To hold either the State, or the principal, or the father guilty and the subject of punishment in such cases is to depart utterly from the plainest principles of justice and common sense. Hence this utter lack of analogy to the representative place of Adam, as main-

[1] Wallace · *Representative Responsibility*, discourses i, ii; Hodge · *Systematic Theology*, vol. ii, pp. 196–201.

tained in this theory, renders all such instances utterly valueless for the argument.

Special account is made of instances of attainder, in which treason or some other high crime is punished with INSTANCES OF confiscation of estates and political disfranchisement, ATTAINDER. and in which, in the terms of the law and the judicial procedure, the children of the criminal, for successive generations, and even forever, are involved in the same consequences. Any justification of such procedure must arise from the exigencies of the government. Such judicial measures are expedients of government, and can have no other defense. The idea is that such an extension of the evil consequences of treason will more effectually restrain others from its commission. Its justification from its end is not the question now in hand. The point we make is this: Such procedure of government neither constitutes the children guilty of the father's treason nor makes the evil visited upon them in any proper sense a punishment. It is admitted that the act of treason cannot be charged to the children, because it is strictly personal to the high offender; but the guilt of the act is as rigidly and exclusively personal to him as the act itself, and no more can it be charged to them. But guilt absolutely conditions punishment. Hence, as the children cannot be constituted guilty of the parental treason, the evil visited upon them cannot in any proper sense of justice be a punishment. There is nothing in such instances which can support the representative theory.

2. *Biblical Instances of Imputation of Sin.*—Reference to a few instances will suffice for the review of this argument. We may name the cases of Achan, Gehazi, Dathan, and Abiram. Hodge brings these, with many others, into the argument.[1] No one makes a stronger use of them. Seemingly, they sustain his argument; but a deeper view discovers their insufficiency.

Under the divine administration suffering is visited upon families in consequence of parental sins. This is not to be THEIR INTER- questioned. Whether they are strictly penal is the real PRETATION. question. The same insuperable difficulties of guilt and punishment are present in these cases as in those under human administrations. The evil consequences, as affecting others than the actually criminal, are administered on a law of governmental expediency, not on a law of retributive justice. There is such a law in the divine administration, as in the human. The policy may be illustrated by legitimate usages of war. Consequences cannot be restricted to personal demerit. When suffering is even purposely

[1] *Systematic Theology,* vol ii, pp. 198–205

33

inflicted upon the innocent they are not accounted guilty, nor is their suffering a punishment to them. The Jewish theocracy was political in its functions as well as moral and religious. Nor can all its measures and ministries be interpreted without a law of economical expediency. Even under a theocracy men were still men, and could be governed only as such. For rectoral ends, and for the great purposes of the theocracy, its judicial inflictions sometimes involved the innocent with the actual offenders, but not as punishments on the ground of imputed guilt. Nor can such exceptional and temporary instances conclude the guilt and punishment of all mankind on account of the sin of Adam as federal head of the race.

3. *More Direct Proof-Texts.*—A chief text of the class is found in God's proclamation of his name to Moses; which proclamation is a lofty characterization of his own majesty and truth, goodness and mercy. To all the expression of his clemency and gracious forgiveness of sin, it is added, that he "will by no means clear the guilty; visiting the iniquity of the fathers upon the children, and upon the children's children, unto the third and to the fourth generation."[1] The text has special application to the sin of idolatry. Mr. Wesley so regarded it. Maimonides is cited for the same view. There was in this case special reason for such visitation. The tendency to idolatry was persistent and strong. Its restraint was necessary to the great purposes of the theocracy. The severity of means answered to this exigency. So we find God ordering the utter destruction of any city whose inhabitants gave themselves to idolatry.[2] Even the cattle were to be put to the sword, and all the property to be destroyed. This judgment transcended the possibility of guilt in the subjects of its infliction, and therefore could not be to them a punishment. The proper interpretation is upon the same principles on which we interpreted the instances of imputation previously considered. Such extreme measures were necessary to the great ends of the theocracy, and permissible on that ground, but could not be punishments to any who were not actual sharers in the sinning. In this manner we interpret the "visiting the iniquities of the fathers upon the children."

The standard text is from Paul.[3] Since the time of Augustine
THE STAND- this has been the great text in doctrinal anthropology.
ARD TEXT.   Whether it is the formally exact expression of doctrine which its dogmatic use assumes, may fairly be questioned. In the Augustinian anthropology it is equally the reliance of both the realistic and representative schools. Each is sure of its full sup-

[1] Exod. xxxiv, 7. [2] Deut. xiii, 12–18. [3] Rom. v, 12–19.

port, and, equally, that it gives no support to the other; indeed, that it refutes the other. But, with their profound difference, it cannot be the doctrinal ground of both. We may reasonably infer that it supports neither. Arminianism can fairly interpret the text consistently with its own anthropology, though in some facts it differs profoundly from the Augustinian.[1] Respecting individual expositors of the text, we rarely find any two in full agreement.[2] This is the case with expositors of the same school of anthropology. A text so open to diverse and opposing interpretations cannot in itself be the determining ground of any particular doctrine. Such facts strongly suggest the prudence of less dogmatism in its doctrinal use. If the passage is taken as formally exact and scientific in doctrinal statement, no proper consistency of its several parts can be attained; nor can it as a whole be brought into harmony with any system of theology. While seemingly exact and definite in doctrinal expression, it should rather be taken in a popular sense. This is the view of Knapp.[3] His view is appropriated by McClintock and Strong.[4] The passage is a popular statement of great facts for the expression and illustration of a ruling idea—the abounding fullness of grace and life in the redemptive mediation of Christ.

The diversities of interpretation, and particularly the opposing interpretations of the realistic and representative NO PROOF OF schools, with their reciprocal refutations, deny to this ADAMIC SIN. text any sufficient proof of a common sharing in the guilt of Adam's sin, as held in the Augustinian anthropology. After a searching study we are satisfied that it does not contain the proof of such a doctrine.[5]

4. *Imputation of the Righteousness of Christ.*—From an imputation of the righteousness of Christ it is often attempted to prove the imputation of Adam's sin to the race, as maintained in the representative theory. Theoretically, the two imputations stand together in the Federal theology. This theology requires both, and also the federal headship respectively of Adam and Christ. These federal headships are the ground of the imputation

---

[1] As representatives of interpretation in the realistic, representative, and Arminian schools, we may instance Shedd, Hodge, and Whedon, in their respective Commentaries on Romans

[2] Many instances of opposing views are given in the respective Commentaries of Stewart and Meyer on Romans.

[3] *Christian Theology*, sec. lxxvi, iii.   [4] *Cyclopœdia*, "Imputation."

[5] We think this study important, but the extent of its necessary elaboration renders it inappropriate for a place in the body of our work. It will be given in an appendix to the second volume.

respectively of the sin of Adam and the righteousness of Christ.
In the present argument for the representative theory the imputation of the righteousness of Christ is assumed as a fact, and from
this fact is inferred the imputation of Adam's sin to all men.   It
may further be said that the argument also intends the vindication
of this imputation.   Two questions are thus raised: Is the assumed
imputation of the righteousness of Christ a fact? and, if a fact,
would it warrant the inference respecting the imputation of
Adam's sin?   In considering these questions we may change their
order.

There is a profound difference between the immediate imputation of sin as a ground of punishment and the imme-
NO VINDICA-   diate imputation of righteousness as the ground of
TION OF THE   reward.   The representative theory can say much for
THEORY
the latter as the outflowing of the divine grace and love; but what
can it say for the former?   Here no appeal can be made to the
divine love.   Nor can there be any appeal to the divine justice.
The theory denies all actual sharing in the sin of Adam as a ground
of demerit.   This is one of its strong points against the realistic
theory.   The idea of such desert is excluded by the nature of the
imputation as immediate.   The imputed sin is the very first ground
of punitive desert   Hence the theory means a purely gratuitous imposition of guilt upon all men.   Such an imputation could have no
warrant or vindication in the imputation of the righteousness of
Christ.   The profound difference of the two precludes both the
warrant and the vindication.   The words of Shedd are forceful and
to the point: " The doctrine of a gratuitous justification is intelligible and rational; but the doctrine of a gratuitous damnation is
unintelligible and absurd." [1]

It is thus manifest that the imputation of the righteousness of
Christ, even if a truth of the Scriptures, could neither
NO SUCH IM-   support nor vindicate a purely gratuitous imputation
PUTATION OF   of Adam's sin to the race as the judicial ground of de-
RIGHTEOUS-
NESS.   pravity and death.   There is, in truth, no such imputa-
tion of the righteousness of Christ as this theory maintains, and
hence the argument attempted upon its assumption is utterly
groundless.   However, the proper place for this question of impu-
tation is in connection with the doctrine of justification.

III. OBJECTIONS TO THE THEORY.

So far we have considered the arguments which the representative theory brings in proof of the immediate imputation of Adam's

[1] *History of Christian Doctrine*, vol. ii, p. 163.

sin as the judicial or penal ground of the common depravity of human nature. Beyond our answer to these arguments there are a few objections to the theory which must not be omitted.

1. *No Such Headship of Adam.*—It is not the natural headship which is here questioned; it is the federal or forensic headship, as maintained in the representative theory. The deeper SENSE OF THE idea is that of a covenant between God and Adam, with HEADSHIP mutual stipulations of duty and promise—duty on the human side and promise on the divine side. In the obligation of duty Adam should not only answer for himself, but also represent his offspring, so that they should fully share in the righteousness and reward of his obedience, or equally in the guilt and punishment of his disobedience. So, on his side God should reward or punish Adam personally, and equally his offspring as represented by him, just as he might fulfill or violate the obligation of duty as stipulated in the covenant. The implied and the frequently expressed part of Adam in such a covenant would clearly have been a usurpation. Nor is it to be thought that God could have recognized in him any such right, or have entered into any such stipulations with him on its unwarranted assumption. All that can reasonably be meant is, that in the primitive probation God, solely in his own agency, instituted a federal economy, so that the trial of Adam should, on the principle of representation, be the decisive trial of the race. The irrational idea of Adam's part in the covenant is thus excluded, but the fundamental principle remains, and the consequences to the race are the very same. On his obedience, all would have shared with him in the reward of immortality, confirmed holiness, and eternal blessedness. As he sinned, all share with him the full measure of guilt and loss, and the same desert of an eternal penal doom. " Every thing promised to him was promised to them. And every thing threatened against him, in case of transgression, was threatened against them." [1] This is but the repetition, in substance, of what many others have said. As Adam sinned, very naturally the penal consequences of his headship have come into great doctrinal prominence, and received almost exclusive attention; but the principle of reward, which, on his obedience, would have secured to the race all the blessings promised him, is just as central to this federal economy as the principle of penal retribution. Thus the trial of the race was in Adam, with the judicial consequence of an eternal blessedness or an eternal penal doom.

There is little foundation for so great a structure. Appeal is made to the Mosaic narrative of the Adamic probation. Many

[1] Hodge. *Systematic Theology*, vol. ii, p. 121.

things said to Adam and Eve must have had respect to their off-
NO GROUND IN spring, and the race is involved in many and great evils
SCRIPTURE through their sin and fall.[1] This is admitted. We have
previously maintained the same. But the real question is whether
such consequences are punishments, with their judicial ground in the
sin of Adam as representative of the race. To assume that they are is
to assume the full doctrinal content of the federal headship. This,
however, is the question in issue, and its assumption will not answer
the demand for proof. The proof of such a federal headship is not in
the Mosaic narrative. Proof is attempted from the words of Hosea
by rendering the text, "But they like Adam have transgressed the
covenant."[2] There is really no proof, because "like men," as given
in the Authorized Version, may be the true rendering. Even the
rendering, "like Adam," must utterly fail to carry with it the full
sense of the Adamic covenant in the representative theory. Much
use is here made of the two great texts of Paul,[3] which we have
previously considered. But as we found in them no proof of a
common participation in the sin of Adam through imputation, so
they can give no proof of an Adamic covenant which is maintained
as the essential ground of such imputation.

There is no federal headship of Adam on which all men equally
SCRIPTURE with himself share the guilt of his sin. On the Cal-
AGAINST IT. vinistic views of this question Pope says: "But such
speculations as these stand or fall with the general principle of a
specific covenant with Adam as representing his posterity, a covenant of which the Scripture does not speak."[4] The vital connection of personal agency and moral responsibility is too thoroughly
pervasive of the Scriptures to allow any place therein for a federal
headship which sunders that connection and makes all men sharers
in the sin of Adam. "This is so little agreeable to that distinct
agency which enters into the very notion of an accountable being,
that it cannot be maintained, and it destroys the sound distinction
between original and actual sin. It asserts, indeed, the imputation
of the actual commission of Adam's sin to his descendants, which
is false in fact ; makes us stand chargeable with the full latitude of
his transgression, and all its attendant circumstances; and constitutes us, separate from all actual voluntary offense, equally guilty
with him, all which are repugnant equally to our consciousness and
to the equity of the case."[5] The force of this argument is not in
the least weakened by the failure of Mr. Watson to anticipate the

[1] Gen. i, 26-28 ; iii, 16-19.   [2] Hos. vi, 7.
[3] Rom. v, 12-19 ; 1 Cor. xv, 21, 22.   [4] *Christian Theology*, vol. ii, p. 78.
[5] Watson . *Theological Institutes*, vol. ii, p 53.

more recent Calvinistic distinction between the guilt and the act of Adam's sin in the imputation. It is the ethical element involved in the imputation that gives the chief weight to his objection.

2. *Supersedure of a Common Probation.*—In such a covenant as the representative theory maintains the obedience of Adam would have secured to the race severally, and without any personal trial, eternal holiness and blessedness. "The first covenant made with man was a covenant of works, wherein life was promised to Adam and in him to his posterity, upon condition of perfect and personal obedience."[1] Of course, in such a covenant the contingency of universal righteousness and blessedness must answer to the contingency of universal guilt and perdition. We have previously shown how fully the latter is set forth in the maintenance of the representative theory. The former is just as really and fully a part of the theory, and is the part specially set forth in the above citation. Adam represented all men in his own probation. "They stood their probation in him, and do not stand each man for himself."[2]

The theory thus places the probation of the race in Adam, with the contingency of a universal and eternal blessedness or misery, just as he might fulfill or transgress the divine command. There is no ground in either reason, PROBATION OF THE RACE IN ADAM. analogy, or Scripture for such a position. It assumes that all men would have been constituted personally righteous by the imputation of the personal righteousness of Adam, and so have been rewarded with eternal blessedness. This is a most exaggerated account of the temporary obedience of one man, and, in the breadth of its possible blessings, lifts it into rivalry with the redemptive mediation of Christ.

3. *Guilt and Punishment of the Innocent.*—This theory denies all direct sharing of the race in either the act or the demerit of Adam's sin. This is its distinction from the realistic theory, which, in its higher form, asserts both. As the race had no part in the agency of Adam, his sinning could have no immediate consequence of demerit and guilt upon them as upon himself. Hence, until the judicial act of immediate imputation, all must have been innocent in fact, and must have so appeared even in the view of the divine justice as it proceeded to cover them with the guilt of an alien sin, a sin in no sense their own, and then on the ground of such gratuitous guilt to inflict upon them the penalty of moral depravity and death. Thus

---

[1] The Westminster Confession, chap. vii, sec 11.

[2] Hodge · *Systematic Theology*, vol. ii, p. 122. Also Witsius : *The Covenants*, vol. i, p. 36 ; Raymond : *Systematic Theology*, vol ii, pp. 104, 105.

the race, as yet innocent in fact, is made the subject of guilt and punishment.

4. *Factitious Guilt of the Race* —The immediate imputation of sin is by its own definition simply the accounting to all men the guilt of a sin which is confessedly not their own. They had no part in the commission of that sin. The imputed guilt has no ground of demerit in them. In a merely putative mode, and without any desert in themselves, all men are accounted amenable to the divine punishment. This utter separation of the guilt from demerit, this absolute sundering of the *reatus pœnæ* from the *reatus culpæ*, must reduce the guilt of the race to a merely factitious character. The word factitious is here used in no light sense. On the supposition of such imputed guilt, we have simply pointed out its unavoidable character. Further, it is only by an artificial measure of law that the one sin of one man could be made to render equally guilty with himself all the millions of the race. The theory must here keep within its own limit, and assume nothing from the realistic theory. There was the one representative and the one sin, with its own intrinsic demerit. The intrinsic guilt was in just the measure of this demerit. Who shall say that it was sufficient for an eternal penal doom of the race in the retribution of the divine justice? How, then, could it be made to cover every soul of the race with a guilt equal to that of the sinning representative, except by an artificial measure of law?

5. *A Darker Problem of Evil.*—We have previously shown that this theory assumes to vindicate the divine providence in the existence of so great an evil as the common native depravity by accounting it a punishment justly inflicted upon the race. We are born in a state of moral ruin, and the evil is very great. Hence it must be a punishment; for, otherwise, it could not be reconciled with the justice and goodness of God. But if a punishment, it must have its ground in guilt. The principle is accepted, at least by implication, that "no just constitution will punish the innocent." We have seen how it is attempted to secure the principle in this case. The penal infliction of depravity is anticipated by the imputation of the guilt of an alien sin to the race. But no such putative ground could justify the penal infliction. Nor is the native evil any less by calling it a punishment. There is no relief in accounting the innocent guilty in anticipation of such a penal infliction. There is a double and deeper wrong. Verily, there is no theodicy in this doctrine, but only a darker problem of evil.

CHAPTER XI.

GENETIC LAW OF NATIVE DEPRAVITY.

WE have sufficiently reviewed the theory of native depravity which accounts it a penal retribution on the ground of a common participation in the sin of Adam, and have found it unsustained in either the realistic or representative mode of such participation. The disproof of this theory does not affect the reality of native depravity, but leaves it to be accounted for in some other mode. \There is an entirely sufficient account in the law of genetic transmission. The corruption of the progenitors of the race is thus transmitted to their offspring. The uniformity with which this law is accepted in doctrinal anthropology greatly favors the theory, which makes it the account of the common native depravity.

I. GENESIS OF PARENTAL QUALITY.

1. *Reality of the Law.*—It is a law of organic life that every thing produces its own kind. This law was divinely instituted at the very beginning of life.[1] It has determined the results of propagation through all the geological ages and in all organic orders. It is the determining law of species, and gives us the LAW OF ALL orderly forms of life. If it were made known simply LIFE. that life is propagated in other worlds, sober science would promptly affirm the reigning of the same law. The offspring are a reproduction of the parentage, not only in anatomical structure and physiological constitution, but also in the qualities of instinct and disposition. This is clearly seen in the higher animal orders. The lion of the present is the lion of all previous generations. The ferocity of the tiger is a derivation from its earliest parentage. The meekness and gentleness of the lamb of to-day were in the blood of the paschal lamb many ages ago. Man himself is the most striking exemplification of this law. Historically, the diversities of human condition are very great. There is a vast scale from the lowest barbarism up to the highest civilization. The habits of life engendered by location and the modes of subsistence widely differ. Governments, customs, religions, all things which strike the deepest into the nature of man, equally differ. Yet in all the

[1] Gen. i, 11, 12.

constitutive qualities of humanity man is always and every-where the same. This universal and abiding identity is a genetic transmission from the progenitors of the race down through all its generations.

2. *Respecting the Transmission of Adamic Holiness.*—On the obedience of Adam and the maintenance of his own holiness of nature, his offspring would have received their life and begun their probation in the same primitive holiness. There would still have been the possible lapse of individuals, with the corruption of their own nature and the consequent depravity of their offspring ; but apart from this contingency, or so far as the Adamic connection is concerned, all would have been born in the primitive holiness. Under what law would such have been the consequence? Unquestionably, the law of genetic transmission. Any notion of an immediate imputation of Adam's personal righteousness to his offspring as the judicial ground of their birth in subjective holiness is utterly groundless. It must assume that without such imputation all must have been born in depravity, which at once contradicts the determining law of propagation and the holiness and goodness of God. There is no requirement for any other law than that of genetic transmission. There is no place for any other.

3. *Sufficient Account of Native Depravity.*—As the law of genetic transmission rules in all the forms of propagated life and determines the likeness of the offspring to the parentage, and as it was sufficient for the transmission of the primitive holiness to all the race, it must be a sufficient account of the common native depravity. To deny this sufficiency is to assume that simply under the law of nature the moral corruption of Adam would not have been transmitted to his offspring, and consequently that they must have been born in holiness. To assume an intervention of retributive justice, on the ground of a common participation in the sin of Adam, as the only sufficient account of the universal native depravity, is to imply the same results. The implication is utterly in error. Simply under the law of nature the corruption of Adam must have been transmitted to his offspring, and consequently they could not have been born in the primitive holiness. All this is really conceded by such as hold the common depravity to be a punishment. We have previously seen that this view of punishment is maintained in order to vindicate the divine providence in the existence of so great an evil. But except for the efficiency of the law of nature which determines the likeness of the offspring to the parentage there would have been no common evil of depravity requiring the divine vindication. Why account the corruption of human nature a pun-

SUFFICIENCY CONCEDED

ishment when it exists in the fullest accord with all the analogies of propagation ? Punishment is not thought of in any other instance of likeness in the offspring to the parentage. The sufficient account is in the law of genetic transmission. There is no requirement in either nature or Scripture or reason for any other.

Seemingly, this law of genetic transmission should rule in the instance of regenerate or sanctified parents, and determine the subjective holiness of their offspring. Yet the truth of a common native depravity, as previously maintained, forbids this inference. Why should the REGENERATE LIFE NOT TRANSMISSIBLE Adamic connection rule in such instances instead of the immediate connection ? This question naturally arises ; nor is it without perplexity. It might be answered, that in the present life the sanctification is not complete ; that a measure of depravity remains in the regenerate. This doctrine is formulated in most orthodox creeds, and hence furnishes the ground for such an answer as we here suggest. However, it is one which cannot be given by such as hold the doctrine of entire sanctification, and maintain that there are actual instances of such sanctification. There is a further answer, which fully accords with the former doctrine, and is seemingly the only one in accord with the latter. The regenerate or sanctified state is specially a gracious state, and not of the original constitution of man. It is provided for in the economy of redemption. and achieved through the supernatural agency of the Holy Spirit, and therefore is not transmissible through natural generation. The limitations of such a law are as real in the completely sanctified as in the regenerate in whom the rudiments of depravity may still remain. There is such a law in nature The fruit of the graft produces, not its own special quality, but that of the natural stock.

II. The True Law of Depravity.

If this is not the true law of native depravity, the Scripture proofs of depravity itself must be at fault, and the Catholic doctrine of its transmission must be in error. It will be easy to justify these statements.

1. *The Scripture Doctrine.*—The creeds which formulate a doctrine of native depravity, and the theologians who maintain such a doctrine, both appeal to the Scriptures for its proof. Many of the evidences thus adduced, and especially the more explicit, rest on the ground of a genetic transmission of depravity Reference to a few texts will show this. "Who can bring a clean thing out of an unclean ? not one." [1] An unclean vessel defiles its content. This

[1] Job xiv, 4.

deeper idea of the text illustrates the law of native depravity. The reference in the close connection is to natural generation or birth as the source of depravity. "Behold, I was shapen in iniquity; and in sin did my mother conceive me."[1] There is in this text the sense of native evil, but an evil inherited through natural generation. The same truth is given in the profound words of our Lord on the necessity for spiritual regeneration.[2] The necessity lies in the fact that "that which is born of the flesh is flesh." This means the inheritance of a corrupt nature through natural generation. Thus the leading texts which prove the reality of native depravity equally prove its genetic transmission.

2. *The Catholic Doctrine.*—No element of the Augustinian anthropology has been more fully or uniformly asserted than the genetic transmission of depravity. There is no reserve in Augustine's expression of his own view. In nothing have his followers in doctrine more closely adhered to his teaching. This element is common to the doctrinal formulas of original sin in the creeds of the Churches: the Eastern or Greek Church;[3] the Roman Catholic Church;[4] Protestant Churches.[5] The eminent theologians of the Churches follow in the maintenance of this doctrine. There is no need of a law of penal retribution to account for a result which is thus accounted for simply on a law of nature.

If it should be said that the genetic transmission of Adamic depravity is simply the mode in which the divine judgment is executed, the answer is at hand. The position, by inevitable implication, denies that the law of propagation which determines the likeness of the offspring to the parentage was original to the constitution of man, while confessedly original with all other living orders, and assumes that it was subsequently ordained for man simply as the means of a judicial infliction of depravity upon all. Such implications contradict all relative facts, and utterly discredit the principle which involves them.

TRANSMISSION NOT A MODE OF PENALTY

3. *The Arminian Doctrine.*—Arminianism has not the exact and comprehensive formulations of doctrine which we find in some other systems, as, for instance, the Lutheran and the Reformed or Calvinistic. No general synod or council has ever taken this work in hand; yet in other modes the leading doctrines of the system

[1] Psa. li, 5.   [2] John iii, 3–7.
[3] The Orthodox Confession, Q. 24; Larger Catechism, Q. 168.
[4] Decree of the Council of Trent concerning Original Sin.
[5] The Augsburg Confession, article ii, The Belgic Confession, article xv, The Thirty-nine Articles of the Church of England, article ix, The Synod of Dort, *De Hominis Corruptione*, sec. ii; The Westminster Confession, chap. vi, sec iii

are set forth with satisfactory clearness and fullness. Respecting the genetic transmission of depravity there is full accordance with other systems of theology. Expressions are frequently met, particularly in the older Arminianism, and in the Wesleyan, which, at least, imply a judicial ground of the common depravity, but never in contradiction to its genetic mode. The tendency is toward the recognition of this law as the sufficient and whole account of it.[1] This is definitely and explicitly the view of Dr. Whedon.[2]

THE COMMON VIEW.

On the present question our own article is very definite. Original or birth sin "is the corruption of the nature of every man, that naturally is engendered of the offspring of Adam."[3] There is neither suggestion nor implication of any judicial ground of the common depravity. The emphasis placed upon the law of propagation from Adam down through the whole race excludes the sense of a penal infliction on the ground of a common Adamic sin. This sense would require us to hold the propagation simply as the mode of the penal infliction; but, as previously pointed out, such propagation is determined by a law of nature which is common to all orders of propagated life, and therefore cannot be the mere mode of a punishment in any specific case. On any consistent interpretation, the article accounts the common native depravity simply a genetic transmission. This is the specific doctrinal formula of the Methodist Episcopal Church on this question. The same article is held by the other Methodist Churches. We know not any exception.

OUR SEVENTH ARTICLE.

4. *Unaffected Reality of Native Depravity.*—The reality of native depravity is not involved in the question of its penal infliction. Those who hold this view equally hold its genetic transmission; and both its reality and character are determined by the law of propagation. As the offspring of Adam, we all inherit the depravity of nature into which he fell through transgression. It is no less a reality than if a judicial infliction. The noxious quality of a poisonous tree is just as real, and the very same, under the law of propagation as if the immediate product of a divine malediction. The same is true of the ferocity of a tiger propagated from a parentage synchronical with Adam. So the common depravity genetically transmitted is just as real, and the very same in its own nature, as if a penal retribution. Its reality is not placed in any doubt by the disproof of its judicial ground.

[1] Arminius: Writings, vol. i, p. 486; Hill: *Divinity*, pp. 398–400; Shedd: *History of Christian Doctrine*, vol. ii, pp. 178–186.

[2] *Methodist Quarterly Review*, 1861, pp. 649–651. Also Raymond: *Systematic Theology*, vol. ii, pp. 109–336; Summers: *Systematic Theology*, vol. ii, p. 46.

[3] Article vii.

CHAPTER XII.

DOCTRINE OF NATIVE DEMERIT.

In a previous analysis of original sin, as the formula is maintained in the Augustinian anthropology, we found three distinct elements· a common guilt of Adam's sin, the corruption of human nature as a judicial infliction on the ground of that sin, and the intrinsic sinfulness and demerit of the common native depravity. We have disposed of the former two questions, but the third is still on hand. Nor can it be regarded as merely incidental in its relation to systematic theology, but, when properly apprehended, must be viewed as central and determining. Infralapsarian Calvinism, now the prevalent form, can have no standing without it; Arminianism, no consistent and sure ground with it. It conditions the decree of election and reprobation in the former system, and contradicts the fundamental principles of the latter. Such doctrinal consequences of the question will fully appear in its discussion, and therefore require no further statement here.

The doctrine is, that native depravity, in its own intrinsic nature, and wholly irrespective of any personal moral action, is truly sin, or so sin as to have in itself the desert of punishment. On the ground of inherited depravity every soul is amenable to the divine retribution, just as for any free sinful deed. This statement of the doctrine will be fully justified under the next head.

THE DOCTRINE

The strength of Augustine's own view of the common native sinfulness, in the sense of punitive desert, is quite familiar to students of theology. He has left no room for any uncertainty. On no question was he more earnest or intense He pronounced the whole human race, in their natural state, as consequent upon the sin of Adam, one mass of perdition (massa perditionis).[1] The creeds and confessions, whose anthropology is constructed upon Augustinian ground, contain the same doctrine. Some of the stronger terms may be avoided, but the doctrine of a native sinfulness and damnableness is equally present. " This disease, or original fault, is truly sin, condemning and bringing eternal death."[2] Original sin, the corruption of our nat-

AUGUSTINIAN

---

[1] Works (Migne's) vol x, p 403
[2] The Augsburg Confession, article ii.

ure and a hereditary disease, "is sufficient to condemn all mankind."[1] Original sin, the fault and corruption of the nature of every one, naturally engendered of the offspring of Adam, "in every person born into the world it deserveth God's wrath and damnation."[2] Our native corruption, as really as our actual sin, "doth, in its own nature, bring guilt upon the sinner, whereby he is bound over to the wrath of God and curse of the law, and so made subject to death, with all miseries spiritual, temporal, and eternal."[3] Many authorities, both confessional and individual, might easily be added.

I. Alleged Proofs of the Doctrine.

Very naturally, a doctrine so central to the Calvinistic system, and at once so necessary to the infralapsarian decree of election and reprobation, and so entirely sufficient for such decree, has been most vigorously maintained. No resource of proof has been omitted. The arguments adduced must now be questioned.

1. *More Direct Scripture Proofs* —Native depravity is called sin. This is not disputed. The instances given are clear and decisive.[4] The fact, however, is inconclusive of the position. It could be conclusive only on the ground that sin—ἁμαρτία—always contains the sense of demerit. This is not the case; and, as in other applications it is used without this sense, so may it be in these instances There are many instances of a metonymic use, of which a very few will suffice. The golden calf worshiped in the idolatry of Israel is called sin.[5] It cannot mean that this calf was itself the subject of guilt or demerit, but simply the object of a sinful worship. Also the sin-offering is frequently called sin.[6] Such offerings are called sin, not on the ground of any demerit in themselves, but simply from their relation to the forgiveness of sin In a like metonymy our native depravity may properly be called sin for the reason of its tendency to actual sin, but without demerit simply as a subjective state Such a sense will give the meaning of Paul in many instances of its use.[7] That depravity as a native state is called sin is, therefore, inconclusive of its intrinsic demerit.

The great passage of Paul, which we found in such full use on the part of both realists and representationists for the proof of a

DEPRAVITY
CALLED SIN.

---

[1] The Belgic Confession, article xv.
[2] Articles of the Church of England, article ix.
[3] The Westminster Confession, chap. vi
[4] Psa li, 5; Rom vii, 8, 17   [5] Deut. ix, 21.
[6] Exod. xxix, 14; Lev. iv, 24; 2 Cor. v, 21.
[7] Rom. vi, 2, 6, 12, 14; vii, 8–17.

common participation in the sin of Adam, is equally in use here.[1]
GREAT TEXT　The discussion of its doctrinal sense in the former place
OF PAUL.　leaves little requirement for additional treatment.　We
there found it insufficient for the proof of a common guilt of
Adam's sin in either the realistic or representative mode.　Much
more must it fail to prove the intrinsic demerit of the common
native depravity.　Really, the text has no bearing, certainly no
direct bearing, on this question.　It fairly raises the question
of a common participation in the guilt of Adam's sin, but only
remotely can it even suggest the question of demerit in the common depravity inherited from him.　It furnishes no proof of such
demerit.

A text of chief reliance is found in the words of Paul: "and
CHILDREN OF　were by nature the children of wrath, even as others."[2]
WRATH.　This was the state of the Jew, as of the Gentile.　All
alike were by nature the children of wrath.　Being children of
wrath clearly conveys the sense of guilt and condemnation, amenability to the divine punishment.　Hence the ground of this exposure is the real question.　It lies in the sense of the term nature:
"and were by nature—φύσει—the children of wrath."　Does the
term here mean the corruption of nature with which we are born,
or the habit of life formed through the indulgence of its impulses?
The former is the view of such as find in it the proof of native demerit.　Their argument must limit itself to the nature with which
we are born, and may not include "our conversation in times past
in the lusts of our flesh, fulfilling the desires of the flesh and the
mind;" for all this belongs to the actual sinful life.　Is it true,
then, that the nature in which we are born, and before any evil act
through its impulse, or any spontaneous activity, has in itself the
desert of an eternal penal wrath?　The proof is not in this text.　Even
admitting that φύσις might mean our native depravity, it is yet no
necessary sense; indeed, would be a very rare sense.　Further,
after such a portrayal of the actual sinful life in the preceding
connection, it would be very singular for Paul, without any intimation, or even the transition into a new sentence, wholly to
restrict his thought to native depravity as the ground of a common
judicial wrath.　It is far more consistent with the whole passage[3]
to give to φύσις the sense of a second nature or habit of life formed
through the indulgence of our native tendencies to evil.　This accords with the interpretation of Dr. Clarke, who holds the doctrine of original sin, but denies both the sense and the proof of it
in this term.[4]　Our actual sins, as portrayed by Paul, and which

[1] Rom. v, 12–19.　　[2] Eph. ii, 3.　　[3] Eph. ii, 1–3.　　[4] Commentary, in loc.

fulfill the tendencies of our corrupt nature, are the real ground of the divine wrath.[1]

Proof is attempted from the sense of ἀνομία in distinction from ἁμαρτία: "for sin is the transgression of the law "— καὶ ἡ ἁμαρτία ἐστὶν ἡ ἀνομία.[2] By rendering the latter term into lawlessness, it is assumed to be applicable to our nature in its native depravity, and to declare it sinful in the sense of demerit, just as in the case of a sinful act. "When John says, 'Sin is the transgression of the law' ('and sin is lawlessness'), the Catechism cannot be far wrong in understanding him thus· 'Sin is any want of comformity to, or transgression of, the law of God.' Thus the principle out of which the action springs is sinful, as well as the action itself."[3] This is given as a specimen of the argument. It is in the following of many Calvinistic examples. Native depravity is sin in the sense of demerit because it is not in conformity with the divine law. The argument is without any valid ground. The definitions and uses of ἁμαρτία and ἀνομία neither warrant nor allow the assumed specific sense of the latter. It as fully expresses actual sin as the former, and has no more applicability to a mere nature.[4] In this particular instance the one term defines the other, and the two are identical in sense.[5] Each expresses sinful doing—ποιῶν with the former term, ποιεῖ with the latter. Such sin is restrictedly personal ethical doing, and cannot be the sin of a mere nature. It follows that the present argument for native demerit is utterly groundless and void. Thus all the more direct Scripture proofs fail.

2. *A Metaphysical Argument.*—Dr. Shedd maintains the doctrine of a metaphysical sin, a sin of our nature below all actual sin, before the actual and the only sufficient cause of it. This doctrine he supports with the great names of Augustine, Calvin, Turrettin, Owen, Edwards.[6] It is readily conceded that this form of sin lies below consciousness. The argument, therefore, must proceed upon some fundamental principle. It really proceeds upon the principle of causation: every phenomenon or event must have a sufficient cause. Properties of bodies must have a ground in material substance, facts of psychology, a

ANOMIA AND HAMARTIA.

A METAPHYSICAL SIN.

---

[1] Whedon : *Commentary*, in loc   [2] 1 John iii, 4.

[3] Summers : *Systematic Theology*, vol. ii, p. 53.

[4] Cremer : *Lexicon of New Testament Greek ;* Thayer : *Greek-English Lexicon of the New Testament*

[5] Ebrard : *Commentary on St. John's Epistles*, p. 228; Haupt: *The First Epistle of John*, p 171 ; Meyer · *Commentary*, in loc.

[6] *Theological Essays*, pp. 212–215.

34

source or cause in mind. The same law of thought requires a sinful nature as the only sufficient cause of sinful action.[1]

The principle of causation in which the argument is grounded is
CAUSE OF thoroughly valid; but the minor premise, that only a
ACTUAL SIN sinful nature is sufficient cause to sinful action, is a material fallacy. The fallacy is the more manifest as the sinfulness of the nature is interpreted in the sense of punitive demerit. If valid in this sense, there must have been, not only a corrupt nature, but also a guilty nature before there could have been any actual sin. This inevitable implication utterly disproves the doctrine which involves it. It is not in any case the previous merit or demerit of an agent that determines the ethical character of a present deed. Such deed is good or bad from its own relation to the divine law. Native depravity is necessary to account for the universality of actual sin, as we have previously maintained; but the demerit of this depravity is not so necessary. Its incitements to sinful action are precisely the same without this ethical quality that they would be with it; therefore this quality can have no part in any account of actual sin which the common native depravity must render.

3. *Argument from Christian Consciousness.*—In the usual form of this argument it is maintained that Christians, and deeply awakened persons as well, are profoundly conscious of a sinful nature, and therefore have such a nature. There is an invalidating error respecting the alleged consciousness. We are conscious of spontaneous incitements to evil, but not of the nature out of which they spring. Hence consciousness itself can allege no ethical quality of this nature. In order to avoid this fallacy Dr. Shedd has recast the argument and presented it in a new form. The mind reaches the nature through the facts of consciousness, and as the necessary account of them. The mode is valid in both science and philosophy, and equally valid in doctrinal anthropology. When we take into rational thought the many facts of evil which reveal themselves in our consciousness, "that we may look at them, and find the origin and first cause of them, then we are obliged to *assume* a principle below them all, to *infer* a nature back of them all. Thus, this sinful nature is an *inference*, an *assumption*, or, to use a word borrowed from geometry, a *postulate*, which the mind is obliged to grant, in order to find a key that will unlock and explain its own experience."[2] In reply to any objection against the truth or certainty of such inference, the answer proceeds upon the same principle which underlies the above reasoning. When the result of

[1] *Theological Essays*, pp. 221–229.   [2] *Ibid.*, p. 226.

such a rational inquiry forces itself upon the acceptance of the mind, it must be the truth in the case. "If it is not so, then a lie has been built into the very structure of the mind, and it is not to be trusted in regard to any *a priori* truth."[1]

The argument is based on the assumed truthfulness of our cognitions when reached according to the laws of thought. Our faculties were divinely given for the purpose of knowledge, and, when properly used, do not deceive us. Things are as we cognize them. The doctrine is thoroughly valid within the limit of primary or axiomatic truths, but not beyond them. The present argument for native sinfulness goes beyond the sphere of primary truths into the inductive. The corruption of human nature, as the necessary account of the universal tendency to evil, is a very sure inductive truth; but the intrinsic sinfulness or demerit of that nature is not such a truth. The guilt of the nature has nothing to do with its tendency to evil, and therefore is wholly without inductive warrant from this tendency. Much less is its reality warranted by any axiomatic principle. It is not a truth which the mind must accept. Many reject it, however clearly set before them. Many, after the profoundest study and with an intense Christian consciousness, reject it.

GROUND OF THE ARGUMENT.

Nothing is gained for the argument by an appeal to the affirmations of conscience. These affirmations have no more uniformity than the results of induction. Many, with a profound moral consciousness and a painful sense of evil tendencies, have no sense of native demerit. The conscience of some has no infallibility for others; has no infallibility for the truth.

There is no principle which validates all the deliverances of conscience, as facts most fully prove. Through deficient analysis the facts of consciousness may be mistaken. One is the subject of spontaneous impulses and appetences which persistently act as incitements to evil conduct, and he has a sense of condemnation, even though no evil conduct follows. Why? Not simply because he has such impulses and appetences, but because of a sense of responsibility for them. This is necessary to the self-condemnation. Why this sense of responsibility? Because of an underlying conviction that by the help of grace he might have promptly repressed or wholly prevented these feelings, and that he ought to have so done. This deeper insight discovers in his self-condemnation the sense of violated obligation. Conscience condemns him, not for the sin of a nature with which he was born, but for his own actual sin. There is nothing in such an experience

THE CONCLUSION INVALID.

---

[1] *Theological Essays*, p. 228.

which points to a sin of his nature. A sense of native demerit is possible, but possible only with the previous belief of such demerit. Thus one's doctrine must precede one's self-condemnation, and, instead of being an induction reached and verified through experience, actually conditions and determines the experience. When native demerit is an article of one's creed, self-condemnation is in the orderly working of conscience. It is the normal function of conscience thus to affirm the moral judgment which the creed expresses. But surely the creed which conditions and determines one's experience, and must determine it just the same if false as if true, can receive no verification or proof from such experience.

4. *Argument from Primitive Holiness.*—The argument is this: Adam was holy in his primitive nature; therefore we may be sinful in our fallen nature, and sinful in the sense of demerit. If the argument were valid it could prove only the possibility, not the actuality of native sinfulness. It is not valid, because there is far more in the conclusion than the premise warrants. It is proper to place in comparison the primitive state of Adam and the fallen state of the race. What he was in respect to holiness we may be in respect to sinfulness. What was the holiness of Adam? Simply a subjective state, free from evil tendencies, and with spontaneous inclination to the good. It possessed no strictly ethical character, such as arises, and can arise only, from holy obedience to the divine will. There is blessedness in this state, but no rewardable merit, no worthiness in any proper sense rewardable. Compare with this the fallen state of man. What is it in the comparison? A state of depravity, with spontaneous aversion to the good and inclination to the evil. There is moral ruin in this state, but no demerit or damnable sin. This is all the comparison will allow. The holiness of Adam affords no proof of demerit in the common native depravity.

II. DIFFICULTIES OF THE DOCTRINE.

We have found the arguments for native sinfulness in the sense of demerit entirely insufficient for its proof. With this result the question might be dismissed; but there are difficulties of the doctrine which should be adduced in its more direct refutation.

1. *Demerit of a Mere Nature.*—The native demerit is affirmed of the nature itself. The judicial ground of the divine judgment and penal wrath is placed in its own intrinsic sinfulness. The demerit is the sin of the nature with which we are born, and therefore must precede its development into personality. But a mere nature cannot be the subject of demerit; and guilt could as well be

affirmed of a mere animal nature as of the human. Demerit must always be a personal fact. If it be said that the ground of the demerit lies in the impersonal nature, but that the amenability to punishment arises with the development of the nature into personality, then let the doctrine explain and justify the responsibility of the person for the nature with which he was born.

2. *Demerit without Personal Agency.*—This is the implication of the doctrine, and the principle is openly avowed and maintained. The higher realism, as previously reviewed, has the logical right of a denial—that is, consistently with itself it may deny the implication of demerit without personal agency. Indeed, the theory is openly pronounced against the possibility of such demerit. But the mode of securing the personal agency and responsibility for the alleged native sinfulness we have previously shown to be utterly insufficient; so that, while this realistic theory may consistently with itself deny the implication of demerit without personal agency, it is as really involved in this implication as the representative theory. Native demerit, or the demerit of the nature with which one is born, is and must be wholly apart from one's own agency. The only escape from this fact must be sought in the theory of the personal sinning of each soul in a pre-temporal existence. This theory was previously considered and needs no further attention here. The alleged demerit is the fifth link in a chain of five: 1. the sinning of Adam; 2. the immediate imputation of the {A CHAIN OF FIVE LINKS.} guilt of his sin to the race; 3. the divine punishment of the race on the ground of this imputation; 4. the common native depravity as the consequence of that penal infliction; 5. the intrinsic sinfulness and demerit of the common native depravity.

We are all absolutely without any personal agency in a single link of this chain. It is not even pretended that we {NO AGENCY IN ANY ONE.} have any. The doctrine is, that the universal amenability to an eternal penal doom arises from the common native depravity passively inherited from Adam. If consistently with the divine justice there can be such native sinfulness, such penal desert of a mere nature passively received, then the absolute infliction of the deserved punishment upon all the race, and in an eternal penal doom, would be equally consistent with that justice. There can be no injustice in the infliction of deserved penalty. If such are the possibilities respecting the human race, there must be possible modes wherein the guilt of sin could be spread over the moral universe, and all intelligences without any agency of their own be justly whelmed in an eternal penal doom. There must be error in a doctrine which clearly points to such possibilities.

3. *Demerit of Childhood.*—This goes with the doctrine of an intrinsic sinfulness and demerit of the nature with which we are born. The doctrine has the fullest avowal. Hence, if it be true, the infant just born, yea, and before it is born, deserves an eternal penal doom, and might be justly so punished.

4. *Demerit from Punishment.*—This is not only an inevitable implication of the doctrine, but is openly avowed. Sin is punished with sin—the punishment of sin is sin. Native depravity is a judicial infliction on the ground of Adamic sin; and native depravity is the very seat and substance of native sin and demerit. But punishment, however just, cannot deserve further punishment. Penalty carries over no sin to the subject of its infliction. If punishment created the desert of further punishment there could be no arrest of the ever deepening doom. There is no such law of justice either human or divine.

5. *An Unintelligible Sin.*—What is the sin of a nature considered as demerit and amenability to punishment? Native depravity is the corruption of the moral nature, with its characteristic tendency to evil, and the source of actual sin. When we say the source of actual sin we cannot mean the agent in the actual sinning. All that we can mean is that it acts as an incitement of the personal agent toward sinning. The corrupt nature cannot itself sin; and the doctrine is, not that it sins and has demerit on that account, but that it is sin, and in a sense to have penal desert.

What is this intrinsic sin of our common native depravity? Is it definable as sin? Is its demerit a fixed quantity as INDEFINABLE the guilt of one sin, or an increasing quantity as the guilt of repeated sins? This subjective state is in itself ever the same irrespective of our personal agency; the same in our sleeping as in our waking hours. Does the demerit increase as one's life lengthens, and in its unconscious hours just as in the conscious? Dr. Summers, himself an Arminian, after maintaining the doctrine of native sinfulness, says: "Thus the principle out of which the action springs is sinful, as well as the action itself. The unregenerate man is a sinner all the time; that is his character when asleep or at work, as well as when he is in the very act of transgressing. All jurisprudence is based on this." [1] The citation might be accepted as a statement of the sin of our nature, if this could be viewed as one sin, with a definite amount of guilt; but there is no light in the view as stated, and hence no explication of the real perplexities of the question.

This sin is intrinsic to the native corruption of our nature. It

[1] *Systematic Theology*, vol. ii, pp. 53, 54.

does not lie in the inheritance of this corrupt nature, nor in its incitements to evil-doing, nor in the actual sin which it may prompt, which is purely a personal sin com- ONLY OF THE NATURE mitted in the exercise of a responsible personal agency.   To locate this sin in any of these specified facts is to deny it to the corrupt nature, and thus to contradict the deepest principle of the doctrine.   To locate it in the incitements of the corrupt nature to evil-doing is to deny its intrinsicalness to the nature.   If the demerit of the nature is still maintained on the ground of these incitements they must be regarded as actual sins, for otherwise no demerit of the nature could arise from them.   This requires that the nature be invested with the powers of a responsible personality, for only a person responsibly constituted can commit an actual sin. Thus we should be led away from a sinful nature to a sinning nature, and from a nature in itself to a nature invested with personality, and the doctrine of native demerit and damnableness would be wholly lost.   An actual sin, with the desert of punishment in the sinner, is clearly open to the cognizance of the average mind, but the sinfulness of a mere nature, with the desert of punishment, is hidden in obscurity.   Its utter unintelligibility disproves its reality.

6. *The Ground of Election and Reprobation.*—That native sinfulness furnishes the ground of election and reprobation is a perplexity for such Arminians as hold the doctrine rather than for Calvinism.   Indeed, as previously shown, it is not only in full accord with this system, but is a vital principle of the system in its prevalent infralapsarian form.   Of course no Arminian can hold the special election and reprobation so fully wrought into Calvinism   No more can he consistently admit any sufficient ground for them.   Such, therefore, as hold the doctrine of native sinfulness must either deny that it furnishes real and sufficient ground for election and reprobation, or attempt a modification of the doctrine in a manner to avoid this consequence.   The latter is the course uniformly taken.   The question is specially concerned with the decree of reprobation or preterition.

If our native depravity is of the nature of sin, and of sin in a sense to deserve an eternal penal doom, there could be THE GROUND VALID. no injustice in the infliction of the penalty.   Penalty is never unjust, and never can be unjust, while within the limit of sinful demerit.   Hence, out of this world of sinners, if it so please God, he might elect a part unto salvation and leave the rest to the just punishment of their sin.   We might assume that his mercy was partial, but could not say that his justice was cruel or even partial.   It does not appear in the doctrine, that justice asserted any unyielding claim for the punishment of a part, but only that it pleased the divine goodness to save a part, and to leave the rest to the just punishment of their sin. Such would have been the righteous doom of all, had it not pleased the divine love savingly to interpose in behalf of a part. This is the doctrine, and one that has received frequent expression in confessional symbols and individual utterance. If the doctrine of native sinfulness, with the desert of an eternal penal doom, be true, sublapsarian Calvinism is thereby furnished with real and sufficient ground for the doctrine of election and reprobation which it maintains. It is well for Arminians to see this, and to see it clearly. Some do thus see it. "Methodism clearly perceives that to admit that mankind are actually born into the world justly under condemnation is to grant the foundation of the whole Calvinistic scheme. Granted natal desert of damnation, there can be no valid objection to the sovereign election of a few out of the reprobate mass, or to limited atonement, irresistible grace, and final perseverance to secure the present and eternal salvation of the sovereignly predestinated number."[1]

In the way of seemingly, but only seemingly, adverse criticism, INVALID CRITICISM. Mr. Watson says: "It is an easy and plausible thing to say, in the usual loose and general manner of stating the sublapsarian doctrine, that the whole race having fallen in Adam, and become justly liable to eternal death, God might, without any impeachment of his justice, in the exercise of his sovereign grace, appoint some to life and salvation by Christ, and leave the others to their deserved punishment."[2] If the native sinfulness be accepted as a truth, the statement of the sublapsarian doctrine is surely easy enough because of its thorough ground in such sinfulness. Nor is such statement merely plausible or loose and general, but definite, consistent, and well grounded. In these words there is not the slightest dissent from Mr. Watson, and for the reason that in the citation he neither denies nor even questions the sufficiency of such native sinfulness as the ground of election and reprobation. It was in view of this fact that we qualified his statement as only a seemingly adverse criticism of this position.

In accordance with all this, Mr. Watson proceeds at once to dispute the Calvinistic position by an open denial of the THE GROUND CONCEDED assumed native sinfulness. "But this is a false view of the case, built upon the false assumption that the whole race were personally and individually, in consequence of Adam's fall, absolutely liable to eternal death. That very fact which is the

---

[1] Summers: *Systematic Theology*, vol. ii, p. 38. By the editor.
[2] *Theological Institutes*, vol. ii, p. 394.

foundation of the whole scheme, is easy to be refuted on the clearest authority of Scripture; while not a passage can be adduced, we may boldly affirm, which sanctions any such doctrine. ' The wages of sin is death.' That the death which is the wages or penalty of sin extends to eternal death, we have before proved. But ' sin is the transgression of the law;' and in no other light is it represented in Scripture, when eternal death is threatened as its penalty, than as the act of a rational being sinning against a law known or knowable, and as an act avoidable, and not forced or necessary." [1] As only such sin can be justly liable to eternal punishment, and as the human race, descended from Adam, had no part in the commission of any such sin previous to birth, therefore they could not be born with any sin amenable to an eternal penal doom. This is good and wholesome doctrine, and withal truly Arminian. It would be well for Arminians rigidly to adhere to it, and never to hold or maintain the contrary or any thing which implies the contrary. Their fundamental principles would thus be secure, and no open place would be yielded to the doctrine of election and reprobation.

III. The True Arminian Doctrine.

1. *Native Depravity without Native Demerit.*—We have previously shown that native depravity as a fact, and its sinfulness in a sense to deserve divine punishment, are distinct questions, and open to separate answers. The truth of the latter is no consequence of the truth of the former. We have maintained the reality of native depravity, but controverted the doctrine of its intrinsic demerit, and have no occasion to renew the discussion. The present aim is to point out the true position of Arminianism on the question of native sinfulness in the sense of penal desert, whether assumed to be grounded in a participation in the sin of Adam or in the corruption of nature inherited from him. That position, as we view it, is accurately expressed in the above heading: native depravity without native demerit. Native depravity is a part of the Arminian system, and entirely consistent with its principles; native demerit is discordant and contradictory. [2]

[1] *Theological Institutes*, vol. ii, pp. 394, 395.

[2] Much of the Arminian treatment of original sin is unsatisfactory   Native desert of penal retribution cannot be reconciled with the determining principles of the Arminian system. Hence Arminians who accept such a doctrine of original sin, as not a few have done, are involved in confusion and contradiction in attempting its reconciliation with their own system. These facts call for a thorough review of the Arminian treatment of original sin. Such a review will be given in an appendix to our second volume.

The question may be tested by the principle of freedom in Arminianism. There is no more fundamental principle. It occupies much the same position in this system that the divine sovereignty occupies in Calvinism. As this sovereignty underlies the predestination, the monergism, the irresistibility of grace, and the final perseverance in the one, so freedom underlies the synergism, the real conditionality of salvation, and the possibility of apostasy in the other. In Arminianism freedom must include the power of choosing the good, as the necessary ground of a responsible probation. Repentance and faith as requisite to salvation must be possible; punishable deeds must be avoidable; responsible duties must be practicable. This is the meaning of Arminianism in the maintenance of a universal grace through a universal atonement; a grace which lifts up mankind into freedom, with power to choose the good. Such freedom is the condition of moral responsibility; and without it we could be neither sinful nor punishable, because our moral life could not proceed from our own personal agency. This is the doctrine of Arminianism, always and every-where firmly maintained. But if we could not be sinful and punishable in our actual life without free personal agency, or through morally necessitated evil deeds, how can we be sinful and punishable through the sin of Adam, or on the ground of an inherited corruption of nature? Nothing could be more utterly apart from our own agency than the one or the other. Nothing could be imposed by a more absolute necessitation. Native sinfulness in the sense of punitive desert is, therefore, openly contradictory to the deepest and most determining principle of the Arminian system.

With the doctrine of native demerit there is confusion and contradiction in the Arminian treatment of original sin. This result is not from any unskillful handling of that doctrine, but from its intrinsic opposition to the ruling principles of this system. The attempted adjustment to these principles finds no resting-place until it reaches a free cancellation of that form of sin through the grace of a universal atonement. But this outcome is doctrinally much the same as the denial of original sin in the sense of demerit. It may remain in the theory, but must not be allowed to come into actuality. This is the usual outcome with Arminians who start with the doctrine of original sin in the sense of demerit. It is far better to start with the true Arminian doctrine than to reach it through so much doctrinal confusion and contradiction.

2. *The Doctrine of our Seventh Article.*—Articles of faith,

DECISIVE PRINCIPLE OF FREEDOM.

THE FREE JUSTIFICATION.

whether formulated or appropriated by any particular Church, constitute the most definitive and authoritative expression of her doctrines. No exception can be admitted in the case of any doctrine so established. Peculiar doctrines, omitted in such articles, but grounded in approved teaching or in a common consensus, could be no exception. No diversities of interpretation can affect the principle; no improved formulation on the part of individuals can replace any established article. This principle is thoroughly valid for our seventh article, which defines our doctrine "of original or birth sin," and will be of service in its interpretation. We must view it first in its terms, and then in its history.

"Original sin standeth not in the following of Adam, (as the Pelagians do vainly talk,) but it is the corruption of ORIGINAL OR the nature of every man, that naturally is engendered BIRTH SIN. of the offspring of Adam, whereby man is very far gone from original righteousness, and of his own nature inclined to evil, and that continually."

Pelagianism went to the opposite extreme from the Augustinian anthropology, and not only denied all responsible participation of the race in the sin of Adam, but equally the corruption of human nature in consequence of his fall. We enter into life in the same moral state in which Adam began his. The consequence of his sin to the race is limited to the moral force of an evil example. First of all, the article repudiates this view. Its falsity we have previously shown.

Affirmatively defined, original sin "is the corruption of the nature of every man, that naturally is engendered of the AFFIRMA-offspring of Adam, whereby man is very far gone from TIVELY DE-original righteousness, and of his own nature inclined FINED. to evil, and that continually." The doctrine we have maintained is in full accord with these definitive facts. We have fully asserted the loss of original righteousness, and the corruption of human nature, as consequences of the Adamic fall. We have maintained the common inclination to evil as the characteristic fact and the proof of native depravity. In maintaining the genetic transmission of this corruption of nature from Adam down through the race we are thoroughly at one with the article, which declares it to be "naturally engendered of the offspring of Adam."

The omissions of this article, as compared with other formulations of a doctrine of original sin, are worthy of special notice. There is not one word about a sharing of the race in the sin of Adam, or about the corruption of human nature as a judicial infliction on the ground of a common Adamic guilt. Nor is there one word which expresses or even implies an intrinsic sinfulness and damnableness of this inherited corruption of nature. Therefore we could controvert these special elements of the Augustinian doctrine, as we have done, without the slightest departure from our own doctrine as formulated in this article.

The history of the article as a part of our own creed gives special HISTORY OF doctrinal significance to this total absence of any sense THE ARTICLE. of an intrinsic sinfulness of our native depravity. It is the ninth article of the Church of England, but greatly changed, especially by elimination. The change was made by Mr. Wesley, who, in 1784, prepared, and sent over by Bishop Coke, a set of articles for the American Methodists, then to be organized into a Church. These articles came before the notable Christmas Conference of 1784, which organized the Church. Nor were they passively accepted from Mr. Wesley, but were formally adopted by the Conference. So have they stood in our creed from the beginning. What is thus true of all the articles is true of the seventh. The doctrinal meaning of the change made in the original article appears in the light of these facts.[1] If the article, just as it stands, had been an original formulation by Mr. Wesley or the Christmas Conference, the sense of an intrinsic penal desert of an inherited corruption of our nature could not be read into it. Much more is such a sense excluded by the formal elimination of every word which expressed it in the appropriated article. Every such word was so eliminated; not only the strong words, "it deserveth God's wrath and damnation," but the far softer word "fault," as applied to this nature. It follows that native depravity without demerit or penal desert is the doctrine of our seventh article.[2]

It follows, further, that such is the doctrine of the Methodist DOCTRINAL DE- Episcopal Church. There has been much questioning TERMINATION. among divines of the Church of England respecting the terms of penal desert in their own article.[3] Not a few have

[1] We here give so much of the original article as concerns the present question, and italicize the eliminations, that the change may be clearly seen : Original sin standeth not in the following of Adam (as the Pelagians do vainly talk), but it is the *fault and* corruption of the nature of every man, that naturally is engendered of the offspring of Adam, whereby man is very far gone from original righteousness, and is of his own nature inclined to evil, *so that the flesh lusteth always contrary to the spirit, and therefore in every person born into this world, it deserveth God's wrath and damnation*

[2] Such is our article "of original or birth sin ; " and, so far as we know, it is the article of all the Methodist Churches of America. Hence, when Dr. Pope said, as we previously noted, that Methodism accepts the ninth article of the Church of England on original sin, clearly he was historically inaccurate.

[3] Burnet, Lawrence, and Forbes severally on the Thirty-nine Articles, article ix.

recoiled from their more obvious sense, and tried to soften their severer import. The complete elimination of these terms not only frees us from all such questioning, but wholly excludes from our doctrine the sense of demerit in native depravity. On a principle previously stated, our seventh article so determines our doctrine of original sin, that nothing contrary to it can have any authority on this question. For instance, in our second article the words still remain which set forth Christ as a sacrifice "for original guilt" as well as for "actual sins." This recognition of native guilt should have been eliminated from the second article in order to bring it into harmony with the seventh. The simplest explanation of its remaining is through mere oversight in the revision of the articles.

Whatever the explanation, on this question of original sin the words can have no doctrinal weight against the specific seventh article. Any utterances in the writings of NO CONTRARY AUTHORITY. Wesley himself contrary to this article must yield to its doctrinal authority. "Wesley rejects the doctrine of our personal desert of damnation here affirmed, for the very good reason that it contradicts our intuitive sense of right and justice. That rejection removes a contradiction to the moral sense and to common sense from theology. Great were Wesley's logical powers; greater his administrative powers; but greatest of all his intuitive powers. His primitive intuitive perceptions might for the time being be overborne by hereditary prejudices, or clamor of dogmas, or the temporary exigencies of argument; but when he hushed all these hinderances down, his intuitive faculties spoke with an almost infallible clearness. And undoubtedly the moment when he prepared these twenty-four articles was, if any moment of his life, the crisis when he looked at pure, absolute truth. Those articles were to be for all Methodism *standard;* and if ever, in sermon, essay, treatise, or commentary, he has expressed a different view, that different view is canceled before this one monumental work. Wesley himself would have to be over-ruled by his own twenty-four articles by us accepted 'of faith.'"[1] What is thus true of all the articles is specially true of the seventh,—specially, because of the profound doctrinal change made in it by elimination.[2]

Our theologians, who in the treatment of anthropology asserted

[1] Whedon : *Methodist Quarterly Review*, 1882, p. 365.

[2] In the earlier writings of Wesley there are utterances doctrinally contrary to this article, and which therefore must be canceled by its supreme authority. In his *Southern Review*, 1876, Dr. Bledsoe ably discussed the doctrinal significance of the change in this article, and maintained, as a sure implication, that in his later years Wesley repudiated his earlier views of original sin.

a strong doctrine of native demerit, yet in the fuller discussion of the Arminian system, particularly in its issues with Calvinism, practically came into full harmony with the doctrine of our seventh article. Others, however, have denied the native demerit and from the beginning maintained the doctrine of the article. Respecting inherited depravity, Dr. Fisk says. "The guilt of depravity is not imputed to the subject of it until by intelligent volition he makes the guilt his own by resisting and rejecting the grace of the Gospel." [1] It has already appeared that such is the view of Dr. Whedon. Against the doctrine of reprobation, which grounds itself in the assumption that all men deserve an eternal penal doom simply on account of original sin, he says: "We hold, on the contrary, that though sinward tendencies exist in germ in the infant, yet there is no responsibility, and no damnability, until these tendencies are deliberately and knowingly acted in real life, and by that action appropriated and sanctioned." [2] The decisive doctrinal point in both citations is that, with the reality of native depravity, guilt can arise only on the ground of responsible personal volition.

PRACTICAL UNITY OF DOCTRINE.

There is a special Arminian view of original sin which should not be passed without notice. While denying all sharing of the race in the guilt of Adam's sin, it asserts a common guilt on the ground of inherited depravity, and then covers this guilt with the canceling grace of justification. [3] This view is specially open to criticism, and for any consistency of doctrine should maintain a common infant regeneration as well as justification. If inherited depravity is intrinsically sinful, so as to involve us in guilt and condemnation, justification is impossible so long as it remains. It is the doctrine of some creeds that a portion of original sin remains in the regenerate, but that the guilt thereof is not imputed to believers. [4] There is great perplexity even in this view. It is not claimed that this remnant of original sin is different in moral character from the prior whole; rather it is declared to be of the nature of sin, just as the prior whole. How then can we be justified from the guilt of a nature, though but a modicum of the original whole, but which is intrinsically sinful and still remains within us? Let any one analyze this question and set it in the light of clear thought, and he will find the answer very perplexing. How then shall we explain the justification of

A SPECIAL ARMINIAN VIEW.

---

[1] *Calvinistic Controversy*, p. 183   [2] *Commentary*, Eph. ii, 3
[3] Summers *Systematic Theology*, vol. ii, pp. 36–89. By the editor
[4] Articles of the Church of England, article ix ; Westminster Confession, chap. vi, sec v.

infants who are born with the totality of this corrupt and sinful nature? There is no possible explanation. With such a doctrine of original sin infant regeneration must go with infant justification, for otherwise the latter is impossible. Further, if infants are born in a regenerate state, the ground of native guilt has disappeared, and there is no need of the justification. And, finally, with the disappearance of native depravity, the doctrinal outcome stands rather with Pelagius and Socinus than with Arminius and Wesley.

3. *The Requirement of a True Definition of Sin* —There can be no true definition of sin which includes the guilt of an inherited nature. A mere nature cannot be the subject of guilt. No more can it be sinful in the sense of penal desert. Only a person can be the subject of guilt; and a person can be a responsible sinner only through his own agency. There can be no true definition of sin which omits a responsible personal agency. Arminianism can admit no definition which omits such agency or includes the guilt of an inherited corruption of nature.

A prominent definition is given in these words: "Sin is any want of conformity unto, or transgression of, the law of INSTANCES OF God."[1] There is no objection to this formula, as it DEFINITION may be fairly interpreted consistently with a true definition. It does not exclude personal agency from any form of responsible sin. Yet it is often so interpreted and applied to the common inherited depravity. The meaning is, that this nature is out of conformity with the law of God, and therefore it is sin. This sense contradicts the imperative principles above stated, and means that simply on the ground of an inherited corruption of nature every infant is a responsible sinner and deserves an eternal penal doom. Any sinful non-conformity to the law of God must have respect to the law's demands. It, however, lays no demands upon human nature, simply as such, and without personality. Hence there can be no sinful disconformity of an inherited nature to the law of God. The divine law lays its demands upon persons, and only upon persons. If these demands have respect to our inner nature, and even to our inherited depravity, still they are laid upon us in our personality, and with the recognition of our personal responsibility for our present moral state. While not responsible for the corruption of our nature by genetic transmission, yet, with the grace of purification freely offered and at hand, we are justly responsible for its continuance. Still, the law makes its demands of us in our personality, and any sinful disconformity to these de-

[1] Westminster Confession. Shorter Catechism, Q. 14.

mands involves our personal agency. Another definition of the Westminster Confession gives the true principle, which really excludes such an erroneous interpretation: "Sin is any want of conformity unto, or transgression of any law of God, given as a rule to the reasonable creature."[1] The ruling principle of this definition is, that sin is some form of disobedience to a divine law imposed upon a rational subject. Such a subject must be a person, with the power of personal agency; and only through his own agency can he become a responsible sinner according to the terms of this definition.

FURTHER DEF-INITIONS. Arminius gives, by appropriation, a good definition of sin: "Something thought, spoken, or done against the law of God; or the omission of something which has been commanded by that law to be thought, spoken, or done."[2] The sin so defined he calls, by general characterization, actual sin. In the details all the forms of actual sin may be included; and equally all the forms of responsible sin which an Arminian definition can consistently include. In replying to an objection assumed to contradict the possibility of salvation from all sin in the present life, Mr. Wesley gives a definition of sin: "I answer, it will perfectly well consist with salvation from sin, according to that definition of sin (which I apprehend to be the scriptural definition of it), *a voluntary transgression of a known law*."[3] It is entirely consistent with this definition so to broaden the sense of transgression as to include all forms of disobedience to the divine law, and even all the details given in the definition of Arminius. The voluntary element goes with all. In close connection with the definition the same sense of sin is asserted, and a contrary sense discarded. Both the definitions in this paragraph are in full accord with Arminian doctrine.

DEFINITION OF SIN. We add our own definition. *Sin is disobedience to a law of God, conditioned on free moral agency and opportunity of knowing the law.* In this view, law is the expression of the divine will respecting human duty, and the mode of the expression is indifferent to the principles of the definition. The disobedience may be either a transgression or an omission; in either thought or feeling, word or deed. It must be some doing or omission of doing; therefore, really some doing. An omission of duty is as really voluntary as any act of transgression. The specified free agency and opportunity of knowing the law are necessary conditions of moral responsibility, and therefore the necessary condi-

[1] The Larger Catechism, Q. 24.   [2] Writings, vol. i, p. 486.
[3] Sermons, vol. ii, p. 172.

tions of sin. Such disobedience, and only such, is sin in the sense of penal desert. Omit any specified element, or admit any contrary element, and there can be no true definition of sin. Native demerit excludes every element of the true definition. Therefore native depravity cannot be sin in the sense of penal desert.

4. *Native Depravity a Reality and a Moral Ruin.*—We previously pointed out that native depravity, as a subjective moral state, is the very same under a law of genetic transmission that it would be if a judicial infliction on the ground of a common Adamic guilt. So, we here point out that, as such a state, it is the very same without the demerit of sin that it would be with such demerit. It follows that the reality of native depravity is not affected by the disproof of its intrinsic sinfulness. The argument previously maintained in proof of native depravity fully remains in its conclusiveness.

Nor is the common native depravity any less really a state of moral ruin. The evils attributed to it in our own articles are intrinsic to its nature. "It is the corruption STATE OF MORAL RUIN. of the nature of every man, that naturally is engendered of the offspring of Adam, whereby man is very far gone from original righteousness, and of his own nature inclined to evil, and that continually." This is a state of alienage from the true spiritual life, and utterly without fitness for a state of holy blessedness. Nor have we any power of self-redemption. "The condition of man after the fall of Adam is such that he cannot turn and prepare himself, by his own natural strength and works, to faith, and calling upon God; wherefore we have no power to do good works, pleasant, and acceptable to God, without the grace of God by Christ preventing us, that we may have a good will, and working with us, when we have that good will."[1] Such is the doctrine of native depravity which we have maintained, while controverting the assumption of its intrinsic sinfulness.

How then is Christ the Saviour of infants, particularly of such as die in infancy? This question will not fail to be SALVATION OF asked. "But if the infant is irresponsible, how can INFANTS. Christ be to him a pardoner of sin and a Saviour? We might reply, that it does not make Christ any pardoner of sin to imagine a factitious sin, or a guilt which has no foundation in the nature of things. The pardon will remain just as factitious, just as merely verbal, as the guilt to be pardoned. But Christ still stands a Saviour to the infant, as we hold, in the following respects: 1. We have elsewhere shown that had Christ not been given the race

[1] Articles vii, viii.

85

would, in all probability, not have been permitted to be propagated after the fall. . . . So the grace of Christ underlies the very existence of every human being that is born. 2. Between the infant descendant of fallen Adam and God there is a contrariety of moral nature, by which the former is irresponsibly, and in undeveloped condition, averse to the latter, and so displacent to him. By Christ, the Mediator, that averseness is regeneratively removed, and the divine complacency restored: so that the race is enabled to persist under the divine grace. 3. Christ, in case of infant death, entirely removes this sinward nature, so as to harmonize the being with the holiness of heaven. 4. Christ is the infant's justifier against every accuser . . . whether devils, evil men, or mistaken theologians; asserting their claim through his merits, in spite of their fallen lineage, to redemption and heaven. Being thus purified, justified, and glorified by Christ, none are more truly qualified to join in the song of Moses and the Lamb." [1]

Careful and candid students of historical theology, on the question of anthropology assign to Arminianism the doctrinal position which we have maintained—native depravity without native demerit. [2]

5. *Question of Practical Results.*—The doctrine of native demerit is often commended on an assumption of practical value. The view is this: the deeper the sense of sin, the more thorough is the moral recovery and the intenser the spiritual life; the deepest sense of sin is possible only with the doctrine of native demerit; hence the practical value of the doctrine. The major premise is not questioned; but the minor is disputed. Besides, with the admission of practical benefit, the doctrine may have evil consequences which more than balance the good.

The deepest sense of sin is possible only with the sense of personal culpability. No form of original sin can furnish this element. Even the higher realism does not assume that we can have any personal consciousness of a responsible sharing in the sin of Adam. The alleged ground of such sharing is purely speculative, and too shadowy for any real sense of culpability for that sin. The representative theory is quite as impotent. Indeed, in its own definitions it denies the culpability of the race for the sin of Adam. The demerit of that sin was personal to himself and untransferable to his offspring. So the doctrine asserts.

THE SENSE OF SIN.

---

[1] Whedon Commentary, Eph. ii, 3.

[2] Hill. *Divinity*, pp 398–400, Cunningham: *Historical Theology*, vol ii, p. 388; Muller. *Christian Doctrine of Sin*, vol. ii, p. 320; Shedd. *History of Doctrines*, vol. ii, pp 178–186; Schaff. *Creeds of Christendom*, vol. i, p. 897.

Here is the difference between *reatus culpæ* and *reatus pœnæ*. We are amenable to the· punishment of Adam's sin, but not guilty of the sin itself—do not share its culpability or turpitude. The difference is profound, and must be profound for our moral consciousness. A mere guilt judicially imposed, and without any ground in personal desert, never can bring the soul into that deep sense of sin which is of special value in its moral recovery. There can be no true sense of responsibility for the derivation of a depraved nature from Adam. If on reaching a responsible age the stirrings of this nature trouble the conscience, let the experience be analyzed, and there will be found underlying the sense of responsibility the deeper sense of power in hand, or power at hand, to restrain these impulses and to prevent their ruling power in the life. It is only at the point where personal agency meets the activities of this inherited nature that the true sense of responsibility can arise. We do not find in the doctrine of native guilt the element of practical value assumed in its commendation.

The doctrine tends to excess, and in its earlier history soon ran into great exaggeration; so much so as to absorb atten- EVIL TENDEN-tion and quite dismiss the infinitely deeper turpitude CIES OF THE of actual sin as a matter of comparatively little con- DOCTRINE-cern. Since the time of Augustine, and in the line of his following, native sinfulness in the sense of penal desert has been the great theme of doctrinal anthropology. It has dominated the view of the atonement and the interpretation of Scripture. The atonement meets its profoundest necessity in the enormity of native guilt. The question has even been raised whether Christ atoned for any other form of sin. After Paul proves by a great argument the universality of actual sin, and in that truth grounds the necessity for the atonement and justification by faith, his doctrine of sin is interpreted as having almost exclusive reference to original sin—that form of guilt and damnableness in which all are held to be born. The world of actual sinners is thus dismissed from the view of Paul, and the world of infants is put in their place as though the very worst of sinners. This appears in the interpretation of a popular statement of Paul (Rom. v, 12–19) respecting the relation of the Adamic fall to the universal sinfulness, and the relation of the atonement in Christ to our justification and salvation. This exaggeration of native sinfulness, with the consequence of pushing men's actual and personally responsible sins so much out of view, cannot be a practical good; indeed, must be a practical evil.

The early history of the doctrine discloses very serious consequences of evil to the true Christian life. These evils appeared in

baptismal regeneration and sacerdotalism. It is not meant that
SPIRITUAL DET- either had its inception with Augustine. Both appear
RIMENT   in the high ecclesiasticism of which Cyprian was a chief
representative. But there was already a strong doctrine of native
guilt, as may be seen specially in Tertullian; and from their inception both baptismal regeneration and sacerdotalism will be found in
close connection with this doctrine. The doctrine of Augustine
fell in with these evil tendencies, and so was received with the
greater favor.[1] His doctrine of native sin not only fell in with these
evils, but by its own exaggerated form greatly intensified them.
The law of this consequence is easily disclosed.

The doctrine of Augustine carried with it the damnation of infants. This consequence was felt to be horrible. Augustine himself was appalled. No wonder that he cried to Jerome for help in
this awful perplexity. There could be no rest. All the better
feelings of pious souls cried out for relief. There were no eyes to
see the assured blessedness of dying infants in the free grace of a
universal atonement. Relief was sought in the sacrament of baptism. Baptism must have power to wash away sin—must have,
because of the exigency of infant salvation. Baptism thus became
a saving ordinance; and, naturally enough, very soon for adult sinners as well as for dying infants. Here was the source of infinite
detriment to the spiritual life of the Church. But if the sacraments are saving we must have a priesthood for their proper administration. Sacerdotalism is the result. Sacerdotalism, like
baptismal regeneration, has been a calamity to the Christian life.
By legitimate consequence, Augustine's exaggerated doctrine of native sin greatly strengthened and intensified both, and sent them
down the centuries as a fearful heritage of evil. Moral paralysis
and despair were in his doctrine. Within the moral and religious
sphere, man was absolutely helpless; a mass of sin and perdition,
with power only to sin, and under the absolute necessity of sinning.
In the utter blackness and darkness of the doctrine no eyes could
see the universal grace of a universal atonement. We are pleased
to note that many who have inherited the substance of this doctrine
have freed themselves from its more serious consequences. Yet it
still widely nourishes and supports the deadly evils of baptismal
regeneration and sacerdotalism.

The doctrine we maintain is free from all such evil results, and
HIGHEST PRAC- yet carries with it the very best practical forces. It is
TICAL VALUE. well known that the Methodist doctrine of sin is greatly
modified by her doctrine of the atonement and the universality of

[1] Milman : *Latin Christianity*, vol. i, p. 172.

its grace. We have ever held the doctrine of a common native depravity; that this depravity is in itself a moral ruin; and that there is no power in us by nature unto a good life. But through a universal atonement there is a universal grace—the light and help of the Holy Spirit in every soul. If we are born with a corrupt nature in descent from Adam, we receive our existence under an economy of redemption, with a measure of the grace of Christ. With such grace, which shall receive increase on its proper use, we may turn unto the Lord and be saved. With these doctrines of native depravity and universal grace there is for every soul the profoundest lesson of personal responsibility for sin, and of the need of Christ in order to salvation and a good life.

General reference.—Augustine: *On Original Sin*, Works, vol. xii, Edinburgh, 1874; Calvin: *Institutes*, book ii, chaps. i-iii; Witsius: *The Covenants*, book i; Edwards: *Original Sin*, Works, vol. ii, part iv; Wesley: *The Doctrine of Original Sin*, Works, vol. v, pp. 492–609; Wiggers: *Augustinism and Pelagianism;* Hopkins: *Doctrine of the Two Covenants*, Straffen: *Sin as Set Forth in the Scriptures*, Hulsean Lectures, 1874; Persier: *Oneness of the Race in its Fall and its Future*, translated from the French; Wallace: *Representative Responsibility*, Dwight: *Theology*, sermons xxvi-xxxiii; Band: *The Elohim Revealed*, chaps. vii-xviii; Fitch: *The Nature of Sin; Princeton Essays, Original Sin*, v; *Doctrine of Imputation*, vi-viii, Taylor: *The Scripture Doctrine of Original Sin;* Pond: *Christian Theology*, lects xxix-xxxv; Shedd: *The Doctrine of Original Sin, Theological Essays*, pp. 211–264; *Dogmatic Theology*, Anthropology; Hodge: *Systematic Theology*, Anthropology; Laidlaw: *The Bible Doctrine of Man;* Tulloch: *The Christian Doctrine of Sin;* Boardman: *The Scripture Doctrine of Original Sin;* Flower: *Adam's Disobedience and its Results;* Burgess: *Original Sin;* Landis: *Original Sin, and Gratuitous Imputation;* Glover: *A Short Treatise on Original Sin;* Muller: *The Christian Doctrine of Sin;* Fisher: *Discussions in History and Theology*, Augustinian and Federal Theories; Payne: *The Doctrine of Original Sin*, Congregational Lectures, 1845; Curry: *Fragments, Religious and Theological*, i-iii; Raymond: *Systematic Theology*, Anthropology.

Ingram Content Group UK Ltd.
Milton Keynes UK
UKHW020623080623
423095UK00006B/280